U.S.-China Rivalry: From Trade Wars to Tech Cold War

Dr Naim Tahir Baig

Published by Dr Naim Tahir Baig, 2025.

U.S.-CHINA RIVALRY: FROM TRADE WARS TO TECH COLD WAR

First edition. December 9, 2025.

ISBN: 979-8232111632

Written by Dr Naim Tahir Baig.

Also by Dr Naim Tahir Baig

1

Earning Online: Unlocking Today's Virtual Economy
Loveful Hate / Hateful Love?
A Textbook Of Foreign Policy Analysis

Edition 2025

Contemporary Political Strategy: A Global Perspective

Standalone

Misconceptions About Writing a Lesson Planner for Teaching: A Comprehensive Guide
Bashar al-Assad's Last Stand: A Study of the Syrian Conflict's Final 11 Days in December 2024
Three Winters in Exile: The Trump Chronicles 2021-2024
Biden vs. Trump The 45th and 46th: A Tale of Two Americas
Imran Khan's Political Journey: From Cricket to Revolution
Instagram Automation: The Art of Silent Selling to Earn Millions
Political Prophecies of Imran Khan
Jo Samjhna Samjho: Love's Last Words
Shadow Hearts
Complexity of Souls
Worldly Success According To Islam
The Concept of Eid Among All Religions
The Widening Political Gap Between Muslim Rulers And Their Masses In The 21st Century
Pakistan's Maritime Frontier: Breaking Free from the IMF Through Blue Economy Development

Can Russia Help Pakistan Grow?
Why Nuclear-Armed Pakistan Has Not Fought a War Against Israel in the 2020s?
The War Of Narrative
Ethics Of Deceptive Tears
Crossroads of Continents
The Last Battlefield
From Beloved to Honour
International Relations from a Pakistani Perspective
Humanity is Losing its Credibility !
Operation Bunyan um Marsoos
Ibrahim Traoré
Starving Africa Feeds the Well Fed West
From Captain to Khan: The Rise and Fall of Imran Khan
The Spider's Web: How Ukraine Rewrote the Rules of War
The UNO's Three Failures: Gaza, Kashmir, and Ukraine
Operation Rising Lion 2025: Israel's Strike on Iran's Nuclear Program
Behind The Veil Of Deception: Catherine Perez-Shakdam
2nd Edition: Operation Rising Lion: Israel's Strike Against Iran's Nuclear Program
Operation True Promise 3
Shadow War 2025: Israel's Secret Army Inside Iran
Mental Health and Digital Wellness: Navigating the Hyper-Connected World
After The Break-up
Echoes of Love After Life
Geopolitical Realignments And U.S. Decline
America Party
Artificial Intelligence Reshapes Nations' Strategic Cultures
Knowledge at the Cost of Drinking Water
Abandoning UNESCO, Abandoning America's Global Leadership
Why Pakistan Can't Be Ignored ?
Love Seized
Tarifaço: Trump's Tariff Assault on Brazil and the Battle for Hemispheric Power
GAZA: The word 'ETHICS' is at stake
Kiss Cam Crisis
The Boomer Blockade: How an Aging Generation is Reshaping Global Power and Economics at Younger Generations' Expense
Fractured Faith: The Ken Paxton Divorce Scandal and the Crisis of Conservative Authenticity

The New American Empire In 2025
The Last Rock's Secret War: Okinotorishima and Japan's Fight for Tomorrow's Ocean
The Great Realignment
Trump's Siege on the Fed: Politics, Power, and the Fracturing of Global Finance
Nuclear Weapons in Space
Trump vs. Putin: The Secrets Of Alaska Summit 2025
Nuclear Orbits: From Soviet Satellites to Russian Space Power
Learn AI Fast: A Practical Guide for Busy Professionals
Rare Earth Metals in Pakistan: Geopolitics in the New Great Game
The Kulbhushan Affair: Espionage, Diplomacy, and Justice in the Shadow of South Asian Rivalry
Collision Over the Capital: The Untold Story of the 2025 Potomac River Mid-Air Disaster and the Fight for Safer Skies
The Holy Qur'an, Political Fire: The Extremism of Valentina Gomez
World War I of Climate Change: Geopolitical Parallels and Emerging Battles
International Relations: Theoretical Frameworks in the Pakistani Context
Equal and Orderly Multipolarization of the World: The Shanghai Cooperation Organization as a Catalyst
Selbstgehostete E-Mail-Server: Praxisanleitung für Datenschutz und Unabhängigkeit in Deutschland
From Gaza's Siege to Pakistan's Floods 2025: An Islamic Perspective on Collective Accountability and Calamities
Hero's Wings Over the 1965 War: Air Commodore Haider's Story
Zero-Knowledge Machine Learning (zkML): Revolutionizing Privacy in AI Applications
TikTok Bans: Navigating the Social and Political Labyrinth in a Digital Age
Nepal in Turmoil: The 2025 Gen Z Uprising Against Corruption and Censorship
Biography of a Politician
Youth Awakening in South Asia 2024-2025: Gen Z-Led Movements and the Struggle for Democracy in SAARC Countries
Stolen Fortunes: Unraveling Corruption, Economic Communalism, and the Hidden Wealth of Bangladesh's Hasina Era
International Relations in the Qur'anic Perspective
The History of Pakistan-Saudi Arabian Defence Treaties: From Friendship to Mutual Security
NATO-like Alliance Among Muslim Nations: Possibilities and Hurdles
Is Artificial Intelligence a Tool of Dajjal?
Nobels of 2025
The Solution of Gaza by Trump 2025

Storm in the Mountains
Quantum Ancestors
Ghosts in the Machine
The Echo Chamber Escape: Finding Empathy and Growth Through Conversations That Challenge Us
دل کی دھڑکنوں کا سرِ سپُردِگی
خاکسارِ محبت
Code and Cradle: AI's Silent War on Women's Economic Survival
Shadow Scores
India-US 10-Year Defence Pact: A Critical Global Perspective
Sudan in Flames
Are We The Last Generation On The Earth?
China as the Most Brutal Killer of the Muslims?
U.S.-Asia Relations: The Japan Pivot
Two Wars, Two Centuries: A Comparative History of the 1857 Rebellion and the 1971 Bangladesh War
Culture Wars in 2025
Global Conflicts in a Trump World
Civilizational Pragmatism Theory : A Comprehensive Framework for Understanding Chinese International Relations
The Fall Line: America and the Historical Pattern of Superpower Decline
Machiavelli in Practice: Modern Leaders and the Enduring Legacy of The Prince
Saddam's Execution to Trump's 20 Points
Will Palestine Go Extinct?
Evidence Architecture: Bridging Global Policy Gaps in a Post-Truth Multilateral System
Personalist Diplomacy
The Logic of Giants: Understanding the Mindsets of America, China, and Russia
U.S.-China Rivalry: From Trade Wars to Tech Cold War

Watch for more at https://www.naimtahirbaig.com.

Table of Contents

To the scholars, policymakers, and citizenswho seek understanding over ideology,dialogue over division,and wisdom over wishful thinking

To those working tirelessly to prevent conflictwhile preparing prudently for its possibility

And to the next generation,who will inherit the consequencesof the decisions we make today

May this work contribute, however modestly,to a more informed discourseon the most consequential relationshipof the 21st century

"The rivalry between the United States and China is not merely a competition between two nations, but a contest between two visions of how the world should be organized. It is fought not just with tariffs and aircraft carriers, but with semiconductors and rare earth elements, with algorithms and biotechnology, with supply chains and standards. The outcome will determine not only which country leads, but what leadership itself means in an interconnected yet fragmenting world."

Preface

Dr. Naim Tahir Baig

As I write these opening words in late 2025, the world stands at an inflection point that will define the trajectory of the twenty-first century. The United States and China, the world's two largest economies and nuclear powers, are locked in a competition whose intensity and scope exceed anything witnessed since the Cold War—and in many ways, surpass it in complexity and consequence.

This book emerges from over three decades of my work analyzing international relations, strategic competition, and the shifting dynamics of global power. Having authored more than 100 books on international relations, strategic studies, and geopolitics, I have dedicated my career to understanding how great powers interact, compete, and occasionally collide. Yet even with this background, the pace and scale of U.S.-China rivalry developments in 2024-2025 have been extraordinary.

The Urgency of This Moment

In April 2025, during what President Donald Trump called "Liberation Day," the United States imposed what analysts described as the highest tariff rates in over a century—with duties on Chinese goods eventually reaching 145 percent while China retaliated with 125 percent tariffs on American products. This escalation triggered the 2025 stock market crash and sent shockwaves through global supply chains that are still reverberating today.

But tariffs tell only part of the story. In January 2025, the Chinese AI company DeepSeek unveiled a reasoning model that matched capabilities of America's most advanced systems—yet claimed to have achieved this with dramatically fewer computational resources. This development demonstrated that export controls and technological restrictions, while significant, have paradoxically accelerated Chinese innovation through constraint rather than containment. Stanford University's 2025 AI Index confirmed this trend, finding that the performance gap between top U.S. and Chinese AI models narrowed from double digits in 2023 to near parity by 2024, with Chinese models achieving within 0.3 percent on key benchmarks.

Meanwhile, the Taiwan Strait has become increasingly volatile. In April 2025, China launched large-scale military exercises around Taiwan, with Defense Secretary Pete Hegseth warning at the

Shangri-La Dialogue that a Chinese attack "could be imminent." The International Crisis Group reported that Taiwan detected 290 Chinese military aircraft near the island in October alone, with at least 199 crossing the unofficial median line. As I write in December 2025, Taiwan's intelligence chief has warned that another major Chinese military drill could occur before year's end.

Perhaps most strategically consequential, China expanded export controls on rare earth elements in October 2025, asserting jurisdiction over 12 of the 17 rare earth metals—materials essential for everything from F-35 fighter jets to smartphones. The International Energy Agency confirmed that China controls over 90 percent of global rare earth processing capacity and 94 percent of permanent magnet manufacturing. For the first time, Beijing applied extraterritorial provisions requiring licenses for products made anywhere in the world if they contain Chinese-sourced rare earths or use Chinese technologies—a direct mirror of America's long-used Foreign Direct Product Rule.

Why I Wrote This Book

Throughout my career studying international relations from both Western and non-Western perspectives, I have observed that most analyses of great power competition suffer from two critical flaws: they are either too narrowly focused on a single dimension of rivalry (trade, or technology, or military affairs), or they adopt such a partisan perspective that they fail to understand the legitimate security concerns and strategic logic of both sides.

This book attempts to transcend both limitations. I examine the U.S.-China rivalry across seven interconnected dimensions: trade and industrial policy, semiconductor and AI competition, critical minerals, Taiwan and Indo-Pacific flashpoints, emerging biotechnology competition, cyber operations and information warfare, and potential future scenarios. More importantly, I strive to present the strategic calculus of both Washington and Beijing with analytical rigor rather than ideological bias.

My background as a scholar who has published extensively on both American politics (including works on the Trump and Biden presidencies) and Asian geopolitics provides what I hope is a balanced vantage point. Having written textbooks on international relations from a Pakistani perspective—that of a middle power navigating between great powers—I understand viscerally that most nations do not have the luxury of picking sides but must instead manage the consequences of U.S.-China competition.

What Makes This Analysis Different

First, **timeliness**: This book incorporates developments through late November 2025, including the October critical minerals negotiations, the November rare earth export suspension agreement between Presidents Trump and Xi, and ongoing assessments of China's November 2025 ban on foreign AI chips in state-funded data centers. The U.S.-China relationship has evolved so rapidly in 2025 that analyses become outdated within months; this work captures the current state of play.

Second, **comprehensiveness**: Rather than focusing solely on trade or technology, I examine how competition across multiple domains creates systemic risks. The linkages matter: semiconductor export controls drive Chinese innovation in alternative computing architectures; rare earth restrictions threaten defense supply chains; Taiwan's role as producer of 90 percent of advanced chips makes the island simultaneously more valuable and more vulnerable; and the coming biotech competition of 2026-2030 may prove even more consequential than today's AI race.

Third, **predictive framework**: Drawing on game theory, strategic studies, and careful analysis of current trajectories, I project where this competition heads next. The Harvard Belfer Center for Science and International Affairs assessed that among five critical technology sectors, "China has the most immediate opportunity to overtake the United States in biotechnology." The U.S. National Security Commission on Emerging Biotechnology warned in April 2025 that "there will be a ChatGPT moment for biotechnology, and if China gets there first, no matter how fast we run, we will never catch up," recommending that the U.S. government spend at least $15 billion over five years to support domestic biotech. Understanding why requires examining not just current capabilities but investment trends, regulatory frameworks, and the fundamental economics of biomanufacturing.

Fourth, **global perspective**: This is not just a bilateral competition. European allies face impossible choices about semiconductor equipment sales and market access. The Global South watches as cheap Chinese goods threaten their industrialization while dependence on Chinese infrastructure locks in long-term relationships. India, Vietnam, Mexico, and others navigate between benefiting from supply chain shifts and managing Chinese economic coercion. The outcome affects everyone.

A Note on Sources and Methodology

This book draws on multiple categories of sources: official government documents (including U.S. Congressional Research Service reports, White House fact sheets, and Chinese Ministry of Commerce announcements), international organization assessments (from the International

Energy Agency, World Economic Forum, and others), think tank analyses (Peterson Institute for International Economics, Center for Strategic and International Studies, Stanford HAI), academic research, and reputable news reporting.

Where controversies exist—and they are many—I present competing interpretations rather than asserting a single truth. On questions where reasonable analysts disagree about China's capabilities or America's leverage, I acknowledge this uncertainty explicitly. The U.S.-China relationship is too important for certainty to masquerade as analysis.

Structure and Approach

The book unfolds in eight parts. Part I establishes the architecture of conflict—how we arrived at this moment and what both sides want. Part II examines the silicon battlefield of semiconductors and AI. Part III analyzes the emerging resource wars over critical minerals. Part IV addresses overcapacity and trade imbalances. Part V surveys Indo-Pacific flashpoints from Taiwan to the South China Sea. Part VI projects the coming biotech competition. Part VII examines cyber operations and information warfare. Part VIII presents four scenarios for how this competition might evolve and offers policy recommendations for both sides.

Each chapter blends rigorous analysis with accessible prose. I have worked to make this book valuable for three distinct audiences: policymakers and strategic analysts seeking comprehensive understanding; business leaders and investors navigating U.S.-China risks; and general readers wanting to grasp the defining geopolitical competition of their lifetime. Technical concepts are explained without condescension; policy debates are presented without jargon; stakes are made clear without hyperbole.

Personal Reflections

As someone who has studied great power politics for three decades, I find this moment both familiar and unprecedented. The patterns echo past rivalries—technological competition recalls the space race, economic friction mirrors trade disputes of the 1980s, military tensions evoke Cold War crises. Yet the depth of economic interdependence, the speed of technological change, and the global nature of supply chains create dynamics without historical parallel.

I am neither optimistic nor pessimistic about where this competition leads. Both outcomes are possible: managed competition that prevents catastrophe while allowing space for coexistence, or escalation into confrontation that devastates both powers and destabilizes the world. The difference will depend on decisions made in Washington, Beijing, and capitals around the world over the coming years.

What I am certain of is this: understanding matters. Miscalculation stems from misunderstanding—of adversaries' intentions, of technological trajectories, of economic dependencies, of allies' constraints, of one's own vulnerabilities. This book aims to reduce misunderstanding by clearly analyzing what both sides seek, what capabilities they possess, what constraints they face, and what choices confront them.

Acknowledgments

This work builds on my previous analyses of American politics, Asian geopolitics, and strategic competition, including my recent books on Trump's presidency, Pakistan's evolving foreign policy in a multipolar world, and the intersection of technology and international relations. I am grateful to the countless scholars, analysts, journalists, and policymakers whose work informs this analysis.

I owe particular thanks to the research institutions whose open-source data and analysis made this comprehensive assessment possible: the Congressional Research Service, Peterson Institute for International Economics, Center for Strategic and International Studies, Stanford Institute for Human-Centered Artificial Intelligence, International Energy Agency, and many others. Their commitment to rigorous, non-partisan analysis serves the global public good.

A Final Word

As you read this book, I encourage you to resist two temptations: the temptation toward fatalism, as if great power war is inevitable, and the temptation toward complacency, as if current tensions will somehow resolve themselves without sustained diplomatic engagement and clear strategic thinking.

The U.S.-China rivalry will likely define global politics for the next quarter-century at minimum. How it unfolds—whether it remains competitive but manageable, descends into Cold War-style confrontation, or escalates into hot conflict—depends on human choices, not historical inevitability. Understanding the full scope of the competition is the essential first step toward managing it wisely.

The stakes could not be higher. The time to understand them is now.

Dr. Naim Tahir Baig

Political Analyst, Geopolitical Strategist & International Relations Scholar

Author of 100+ internationally published books

December 2025

About the Author

Dr. Naim Tahir Baig is a globally recognized scholar, prolific international relations expert, and strategic analyst with over 100 published works spanning geopolitics, strategic studies, and contemporary global affairs. He holds a Ph.D. in International Relations and brings expertise in political analysis, military strategy, and regional studies, with particular focus on South Asian geopolitics, U.S.-China competition, and the evolving global order.

His works include comprehensive analyses of American politics (including studies of the Trump and Biden presidencies), geopolitical realignments, military operations, intelligence studies, and the intersection of technology and international relations. Notable recent publications include works on the Syrian conflict, Trump's political journey, Pakistan's strategic position in the new Eurasian order, critical infrastructure competition (CPEC vs. IMEC), nuclear weapons policy, and intelligence operations.

Dr. Baig's scholarship is characterized by rigorous research methodology, balanced analysis that presents multiple perspectives, and accessibility for both academic and general audiences. His work has been published internationally and is used by scholars, policymakers, and strategic analysts worldwide. He maintains active research profiles on Academia.edu and ResearchGate, and his analyses are frequently cited in discussions of contemporary geopolitical challenges.

Based in Pakistan, Dr. Baig brings a non-aligned, middle-power perspective to great power competition—understanding viscerally how most nations must navigate rather than choose between competing powers. This unique vantage point, combined with deep expertise in both Western and non-Western approaches to international relations, enables him to provide insights that transcend partisan or nationalist perspectives.

For more information about Dr. Naim Tahir Baig's work and publications, visit: www.naimtahirbaig.com

Part I

The Architecture of Conflict

Chapter 1
From Trade Dispute to Tech Cold War

Setting the Stage for 21st Century Great Power Competition

On April 9, 2025, the world witnessed what financial historians will likely remember as one of the most dramatic escalations of economic warfare between great powers in the modern era. After days of tit-for-tat retaliation, the United States had raised its tariffs on Chinese goods to an astonishing 145 percent, while Beijing responded with levies of 125 percent on American products.[1] The Chinese Ministry of Finance, in a statement dripping with historical contempt, declared that even if the United States continued to impose higher tariffs, "it will no longer make economic sense and will become a joke in the history of world economy."[2] The escalation had begun just weeks earlier when President Donald Trump, returning to the White House for his second term, declared April 2, 2025—which he christened "Liberation Day"—as the moment America would reclaim its economic sovereignty from decades of what he characterized as exploitation by trading partners.[3]

This was not merely another chapter in the long saga of trade disputes that have punctuated the U.S.-China relationship since China's entry into the global trading system. The tariffs of April 2025 represented something fundamentally different: the culmination of a quarter-century transformation in how the world's two largest economies view each other. What had begun as manageable friction over intellectual property rights, market access, and currency valuation had metastasized into an existential contest for technological supremacy, military advantage, and ultimately, global leadership in the twenty-first century.

The numbers alone capture the magnitude of the transformation. When the dust settled after the initial Liberation Day escalation and before diplomatic efforts produced temporary relief, the average effective tariff rate on Chinese goods entering the United States had soared from approximately 2.2 percent in January 2025 to unprecedented levels, the highest since the Smoot-Hawley Tariff Act of 1930—legislation widely credited with deepening the Great Depression.[4] Within two days of the April 2 announcement, the S&P 500 had shed over $6.6 trillion in market value, the largest two-day loss in history.[5] The Nasdaq Composite plunged into bear market territory, and the CBOE Volatility Index—Wall Street's "fear gauge"—spiked to levels not seen since the onset of the COVID-19 pandemic.[6]

Yet to understand why this moment arrived, and why the competition between the United States and China has become so comprehensive and so bitter, one must trace the arc of a relationship that evolved from hopeful engagement to strategic rivalry over the span of a single generation.

The WTO Moment: A Fateful Bargain

On December 11, 2001, the People's Republic of China officially became the 143rd member of the World Trade Organization, concluding fifteen years of negotiations that had begun when Beijing first applied to join the WTO's predecessor, the General Agreement on Tariffs and Trade, in 1986.[7] The moment represented far more than a technical adjustment to trading arrangements. It embodied a fundamental bet by Western policymakers—and particularly by American administrations of both parties—that economic integration would ultimately transform China's political system.

President Bill Clinton, who had championed China's accession, articulated the strategic rationale in starkly optimistic terms. Upon the House of Representatives' passage of permanent normal trade relations legislation on May 24, 2000, Clinton declared: "Today, the House of Representatives has taken an historic step toward continued prosperity in America, reform in China, and peace in the world."[8] The theory was elegant in its simplicity: as China's economy modernized and its middle class expanded, political liberalization would inevitably follow. Trade would foster transparency, accountability, and ultimately democratic governance. The internet, foreign investment, and exposure to global norms would empower Chinese reformers and moderate the Communist Party's authoritarian tendencies.

The terms of China's WTO accession reflected this hopeful calculus. China agreed to significantly harsher conditions than most other developing economies had accepted. Beijing committed to implementing the Agreement on Trade-Related Aspects of Intellectual Property Rights upon accession, eliminating dual pricing practices, removing mandatory export performance and technology transfer requirements for foreign investors, and phasing out restrictions on foreign investment across numerous sectors.[9] WTO Director-General Mike Moore declared at the conclusion of accession negotiations that with China's membership, "the near-universal acceptance of its rules-based system will serve a pivotal rôle in underpinning global economic cooperation."[10] Foreign companies would gain unprecedented access to a market of over a billion consumers, while Chinese exports would benefit from reduced tariffs worldwide.

The economic consequences were immediate and spectacular. U.S. imports from China nearly doubled within five years, climbing from $102 billion in 2001 to soaring heights that would reach

$538.5 billion by 2018.[11] China's economy grew to become the second largest in the world, and by some measures of purchasing power parity, the largest. Hundreds of millions of Chinese citizens were lifted out of poverty. Global supply chains reconfigured around China's manufacturing prowess, with the country becoming, in the parlance of business consultants, "the world's factory."

Yet the political transformation that Clinton and his contemporaries had predicted failed to materialize. Instead, the Chinese Communist Party adapted to economic openness while reinforcing its grip on political power. The promise that China would become a "responsible stakeholder" in the international system—the phrase preferred by the George W. Bush administration—proved elusive.[12] Rather than converging toward Western norms, China developed what critics termed "state capitalism"—a model that combined market mechanisms with extensive government control, massive industrial subsidies, and strategic deployment of state-owned enterprises in ways that confounded the WTO's assumptions about market behavior.

The Seeds of Friction: Bush and Obama Eras

Even before the Trump presidency brought trade conflict to the center of American politics, the strains in the U.S.-China economic relationship had become impossible to ignore. The administrations of George W. Bush and Barack Obama imposed quotas and tariffs on Chinese textiles to protect domestic producers, accusing China of dumping products at below-market prices.[13] Currency manipulation emerged as a persistent irritant, with congressional critics accusing Beijing of maintaining an artificially undervalued yuan to boost exports at the expense of American manufacturing.

The Obama administration pursued what it characterized as a robust trade enforcement agenda. The United States filed numerous WTO challenges against China—more than against any other country—and prevailed in every case that was decided.[14] Washington challenged China's export restraints on rare earth elements, its subsidies for aluminum production, and its discriminatory treatment of American automobiles. The Commerce Department conducted investigations that found dumping margins as high as 620 percent on certain steel products from China.[15]

In March 2012, the United States challenged China's export restrictions on rare earths, tungsten, and molybdenum—materials essential for hybrid car batteries, wind turbines, energy-efficient lighting, and advanced electronics. China at the time produced approximately 97 percent of global rare earth oxide output, and American officials argued that Beijing was using this dominance to subsidize domestic manufacturers at the expense of foreign competitors.[16] The WTO ultimately ruled in Washington's favor, finding China's practices inconsistent with its treaty obligations.

Yet these victories, however meaningful in their specific contexts, failed to address what American policymakers increasingly viewed as systemic problems with China's economic model. The bilateral trade deficit continued to expand, rising from approximately $83 billion in 2001 to $367 billion by 2015.[17] American manufacturing employment declined precipitously—what economists would later term the "China shock"—with the Economic Policy Institute estimating that the trade deficit with China cost more than 2.7 million American jobs between 2001 and 2011.[18]

More troubling still were allegations that went beyond traditional trade disputes. American companies operating in China complained of systematic technology theft, forced joint venture requirements that compelled the transfer of proprietary knowledge, and cyber espionage targeting industrial secrets. In August 2017, the Office of the United States Trade Representative initiated an investigation under Section 301 of the Trade Act of 1974—the same legal authority that would later undergird the tariff escalations of both Trump administrations.

The resulting Section 301 report, issued in March 2018, presented a damning assessment of Chinese practices. It found that China used joint venture requirements, foreign investment restrictions, and administrative processes to "require or pressure technology transfer from U.S. companies."[19] China was accused of depriving American companies of the ability to negotiate market-based terms for licensing and technology-related agreements. The investigation concluded that China "directed and unfairly facilitated the systematic investment in, and acquisition of, U.S. companies and assets to generate large-scale technology transfer."[20] And it documented cyber intrusions by Chinese actors targeting American computer networks to obtain proprietary information.

This was the landscape that Donald Trump inherited—and dramatically transformed—when he entered the White House in January 2017.

Trump 1.0: The Trade War Begins

Donald Trump had been preaching the gospel of tariffs since the 1980s, long before he entered politics. Throughout his 2016 presidential campaign, he hammered relentlessly at what he characterized as disastrous trade deals that had enriched China at America's expense.[21] Where previous presidents had treated free trade as an article of faith, Trump viewed tariffs as leverage—weapons to be deployed in the pursuit of better deals.

On March 22, 2018, Trump signed a memorandum directing the USTR to apply tariffs of $50 billion on Chinese goods, citing the Section 301 investigation's findings on intellectual property theft.[22] The president announced the action in terms that left no room for ambiguity about his intentions. The following day, on Twitter, Trump asserted: "When a country (USA) is losing many billions of dollars on trade with virtually every country it does business with, trade wars are good, and easy to win."[23]

The reality proved considerably messier. China retaliated immediately, imposing 25 percent tariffs on 106 American products, including automobiles, airplanes, and soybeans—the latter a calculated strike at Trump's political base in farm country.[24] The Trump administration escalated in response, and by September 2018, Washington had imposed 10 percent tariffs on an additional $200 billion worth of Chinese goods.[25] Those rates increased to 25 percent the following year. By the time the first phase of the trade war concluded, the United States had placed tariffs on approximately $550 billion worth of Chinese products, while China had retaliated against roughly $185 billion worth of American goods.[26]

The economic impact was substantial. A study by economists at the University of Chicago and the Federal Reserve found that washing machine prices rose approximately 12 percent following the imposition of global tariffs in 2018, with the price of dryers—a complementary good not subject to tariffs—increasing by an equivalent amount.[27] Agricultural exports to China plummeted—soybean shipments declined sharply—forcing the administration to provide tens of billions of dollars in subsidies to affected farmers.[28] The federal deficit widened as tariff revenue fell short of projections and agricultural bailouts consumed additional resources.

Yet the trade war produced few of the structural changes that the administration claimed to seek. On January 15, 2020, Trump signed what was billed as a breakthrough "Phase One" agreement with Chinese Vice Premier Liu He. Under the deal, China committed to purchasing an additional $200 billion worth of American goods and services over 2020 and 2021, above a 2017 baseline.[29] Beijing also pledged reforms to intellectual property protection, technology transfer practices, and currency management. In exchange, the United States agreed to reduce tariffs on $120 billion worth of Chinese goods from 15 percent to 7.5 percent and to indefinitely suspend threatened tariffs on additional products.[30]

The Phase One agreement, however, proved largely illusory. By the end of the commitment period, China had purchased only approximately 58 percent of the goods it had promised to buy.[31] The COVID-19 pandemic disrupted supply chains and trade flows, but even accounting for extraordinary circumstances, the purchasing targets had been widely viewed as unrealistic from the outset. More significantly, the Phase One deal punted entirely on the most contentious issues identified in the Section 301 investigation—state subsidies, industrial policy, and the fundamental structure of China's state-capitalist system. A "Phase Two" agreement that was supposed to address these core concerns never materialized.

Biden's Continuity and Escalation

When Joseph R. Biden Jr. assumed the presidency on January 20, 2021, many observers expected a reset in U.S.-China trade relations. Biden had criticized Trump's approach as impulsive and counterproductive, and his administration emphasized working with allies rather than engaging in unilateral confrontation. Yet the new president surprised both supporters and critics by maintaining—and in critical respects expanding—the economic pressure campaign against Beijing.

The Trump-era Section 301 tariffs remained in place. The effective rate of U.S. tariffs on Chinese goods stood at approximately 20 percent when Biden took office, and this level persisted throughout his term.[32] The Biden administration concluded that whatever the economic costs of the tariffs, removing them would signal weakness and surrender leverage in addressing China's trade practices.

More significantly, the Biden administration dramatically expanded technology export controls—transforming what had been a trade dispute centered on goods into something closer to a comprehensive effort to constrain China's technological development. In October 2022, the Commerce Department issued sweeping new restrictions on the sale of advanced semiconductors and semiconductor manufacturing equipment to China.[33] The regulations targeted chips used in artificial intelligence applications and supercomputers, as well as the sophisticated equipment—particularly extreme ultraviolet lithography machines produced by the Dutch company ASML—necessary to manufacture cutting-edge processors.

These controls went far beyond traditional trade policy. Administration officials acknowledged that the goal was not merely to ensure a level playing field or to protect specific American industries, but to maintain what National Security Advisor Jake Sullivan called "as large of a lead as possible" over China in certain strategic technologies.[34] The export controls applied not only to American companies but, through the Foreign Direct Product Rule, to foreign firms using American technology or equipment anywhere in their supply chains. Japan and the Netherlands—home to key suppliers in the semiconductor ecosystem—were pressed to adopt parallel restrictions.

The Biden administration also restricted American investment in certain Chinese technology sectors, issuing an executive order in August 2023 that prohibited or required notification of investments in advanced semiconductors, quantum computing, and artificial intelligence systems deemed to pose national security risks.[35] The Treasury Department, implementing the new rules, explicitly acknowledged that the restrictions aimed to prevent the transfer not merely of capital but of "intangible benefits" such as managerial expertise and network access.[36]

In May 2024, President Biden announced significant new tariff increases targeting strategic sectors. The tariff rate on Chinese electric vehicles quadrupled, from 25 percent to 100 percent. Tariffs on solar cells doubled to 50 percent, while levies on electric vehicle batteries, critical minerals, steel, and aluminum rose to 25 percent.[37] The White House characterized these measures as necessary to counter "China's policy-driven overcapacity" in clean energy sectors—a tacit acknowledgment that Chinese industrial policy had succeeded in building globally competitive industries that now threatened American producers.

By the end of the Biden administration, U.S.-China economic relations had been fundamentally transformed. The relationship that had developed since China's WTO accession—characterized by deep integration, complex supply chains, and the assumption of mutual benefit—had given way to a new paradigm of "de-risking" and selective decoupling. The question was no longer whether the United States and China would compete, but how intense and comprehensive that competition would become.

Liberation Day: The Second Trump Administration

Donald Trump's return to the White House in January 2025 brought a dramatically accelerated approach to the China challenge. Where his first administration had experimented with tariffs as negotiating leverage, the second Trump term treated economic separation as a strategic imperative—and moved with startling speed to implement it.

Within days of his inauguration, Trump signed Executive Order 14195, declaring a national emergency related to drug trafficking from China and imposing a 10 percent tariff on all Chinese imports.[38] The administration framed the measure as pressure to compel Beijing to curtail the flow of fentanyl precursors into the United States, but the tariff's broad scope—applying to essentially all Chinese goods regardless of any connection to drug trafficking—signaled a more fundamental shift in policy orientation. On March 4, Trump raised the fentanyl-related tariff to 20 percent.[39]

The Liberation Day announcement on April 2, 2025, represented an order-of-magnitude escalation. In a Rose Garden ceremony that the president had carefully staged to maximize dramatic impact, Trump signed Executive Order 14257, declaring the nation's trade deficit to be a national emergency threatening national security.[40] He invoked the International Emergency Economic Powers Act—legislation typically reserved for responding to foreign threats such as terrorism or hostile state actors—to impose sweeping tariffs without the procedural requirements of traditional trade law.

The executive order established a 10 percent baseline tariff on imports from nearly all countries, effective April 5. More significantly, it announced "reciprocal tariffs" on approximately sixty countries, with rates calibrated, the administration claimed, to match the barriers those countries imposed on American exports.[41] China received the highest rate: 34 percent on top of the existing 20 percent fentanyl tariff, for a combined rate of 54 percent effective April 9.

The Center for Strategic and International Studies characterized the Liberation Day tariffs as "the most sweeping tariff hike since the Smoot-Hawley Tariff Act"—an assessment that underscored both the magnitude of the policy change and the historical parallels that alarmed economists.[42] The Trump administration's own modeling projected the tariffs would reduce U.S. GDP by approximately 1 percent and increase prices by 9.5 percent while nominal wages rose by only 8.6 percent—meaning real wages would fall.[43]

The immediate market reaction was catastrophic. In the two trading days following the Liberation Day announcement, the S&P 500 lost over $6.6 trillion in market value—the largest two-day decline in history.[44] The Dow Jones Industrial Average shed more than 4,000 points. The Nasdaq Composite entered bear market territory, falling more than 20 percent from its December 2024 high.[45] The CBOE Volatility Index spiked to 45.31, its highest close since the 2020 market crash at the onset of the COVID-19 pandemic.[46] JPMorgan analysts warned that if Trump maintained the announced tariffs, both the U.S. and global economies would likely fall into recession.[47]

China's response was immediate and fierce. Beijing imposed a matching 34 percent retaliatory tariff on all American goods, effective April 4.[48] Trump escalated further, raising the U.S. rate to 84 percent, then to 125 percent—which, combined with the existing fentanyl tariff, brought the total to 145 percent.[49] China responded by raising its tariffs to 125 percent, at which point the Finance Ministry issued a statement declaring that it would "ignore" any further U.S. increases.[50] At these levels, effective trade between the world's two largest economies had essentially ceased.

The crisis forced a partial retreat. On April 9, Trump announced a 90-day pause on the country-specific "reciprocal tariffs" for all nations except China, bringing the baseline back to 10 percent for most trading partners.[51] The S&P 500 surged 9.5 percent on the announcement—its largest single-day gain since 1940—as markets interpreted the pause as evidence that the administration might be susceptible to pressure.[52] Yet tariffs on China remained at stratospheric levels, and the underlying confrontation continued to escalate.

Relief came only through intensive diplomacy. On May 10-11, 2025, Treasury Secretary Scott Bessent and Trade Representative Jamieson Greer met with Chinese Vice Premier He Lifeng in Geneva for the first direct negotiations since the crisis began.[53] The talks, held at the residence of the Swiss ambassador to the United Nations, produced what both sides characterized as "substantial progress."[54] On May 12, the two countries announced a temporary truce: the United States would reduce tariffs on Chinese goods to 30 percent (maintaining the 10 percent baseline plus the 20 percent fentanyl levy), while China would lower its rates to 10 percent for a period of 90 days.[55]

The Geneva framework was subsequently extended in Stockholm in late July and again following a summit between Trump and Chinese President Xi Jinping in South Korea on October 30, 2025.[56] By November, the immediate crisis had abated—tariffs remained elevated but manageable, and both sides had stepped back from the brink. Yet the fundamental trajectory of the relationship had been clarified. The era of U.S.-China economic integration was definitively over. In its place stood a new paradigm of managed competition, strategic decoupling in critical sectors, and perpetual negotiation over the terms of coexistence.

Beyond Economics: A Clash of Systems

The tariff escalations of 2025 were dramatic, but they were symptoms rather than causes of the transformation in U.S.-China relations. The underlying reality is that the economic competition between Washington and Beijing has become inseparable from a broader strategic rivalry that encompasses technology, military power, and competing visions of international order.

Treasury Secretary Scott Bessent articulated one version of the American position in a formulation that would prove influential: the distinction between "strategic decoupling" and "generalized decoupling."[57] The United States, in this framing, does not seek to sever all economic ties with China—such an outcome would be enormously costly and probably impossible to achieve. Instead, Washington aims to decouple in areas deemed critical to national security: advanced semiconductors, artificial intelligence, quantum computing, and the technologies that will determine military advantage in the decades ahead. In other sectors—consumer goods, basic manufacturing, agricultural products—trade can continue, albeit under greater scrutiny and with reduced dependence.

China, for its part, has articulated its own doctrine of technological self-reliance. President Xi Jinping has repeatedly called for "high-level scientific and technological self-reliance" as a national priority, and the concept of making Chinese industry "indigenous and controllable" (����) has become a central tenet of economic planning.[58] The Made in China 2025 initiative, launched in 2015, established explicit targets for reducing dependence on foreign technology across ten strategic sectors, from aerospace and robotics to biotechnology and new materials.[59] Though Chinese officials have largely stopped publicly invoking the Made in China 2025 slogan—its explicit targets for displacing foreign competitors proved diplomatically awkward—the underlying strategy has only intensified.

The competition has achieved notable successes on both sides. American export controls have constrained China's access to the most advanced semiconductor manufacturing equipment, slowing Beijing's efforts to achieve self-sufficiency in cutting-edge chips. Yet China has made remarkable progress in other areas: it dominates global production of solar panels, leads in electric vehicle manufacturing, and has achieved technological parity—and in some cases superiority—in areas ranging from high-speed rail to battery technology.[60] The DeepSeek AI model, revealed in January 2025, demonstrated that Chinese researchers could achieve competitive performance with American systems despite operating under severe hardware constraints—a "wake-up call," in the words of numerous American commentators, about the limits of technology denial as a strategy.[61]

The implications extend far beyond trade balances and tariff rates. Control over critical technologies—semiconductors, artificial intelligence, biotechnology, quantum computing—will determine which nations can manufacture advanced weapons systems, conduct sophisticated intelligence operations, and compete effectively across every dimension of twenty-first-century power. Taiwan's dominant position in advanced semiconductor manufacturing—the island is home to facilities that produce more than 90 percent of the world's most sophisticated chips—has transformed an already dangerous flashpoint into what The Economist memorably termed "the most dangerous place on earth."[62]

The U.S.-China technology competition has also reshaped alliances and alignments throughout the international system. The AUKUS partnership, under which the United States and United Kingdom will help Australia acquire nuclear-powered submarines, represents one dimension of response.[63] The Quadrilateral Security Dialogue—linking the United States, Japan, India, and Australia—has evolved from a loose consultative mechanism into something approaching a strategic alignment.[64] Japan has undertaken its most significant defense transformation since World War II.[65] And across Southeast Asia, the Middle East, and Africa, nations are navigating the uncomfortable reality of a world increasingly divided between competing poles.

The Stakes of the Competition

This book argues that the U.S.-China rivalry has evolved from a bilateral trade dispute into a comprehensive struggle for technological, economic, and geopolitical dominance that will define the twenty-first century. The tariff battles, while economically consequential, are merely one front in a multi-dimensional competition that spans semiconductors, artificial intelligence, critical minerals, biotechnology, and the full spectrum of emerging technologies that will shape both economic prosperity and military power.

The competition carries risks that neither side has fully confronted. A world divided into rival technological ecosystems—a "digital iron curtain," in one formulation—would impose enormous costs on both economies and potentially on global growth more broadly.[66] The danger of miscalculation or escalation, particularly around Taiwan, has increased as both sides have hardened their positions. And the developing world, caught between competing great powers, faces difficult choices about technology standards, supply chain partnerships, and political alignment.

Yet the competition also reflects genuine disagreements about fundamental questions of governance, values, and international order. The United States and its allies view China's state-directed economic model as incompatible with the principles of free markets and fair competition that underpin the global trading system. China views American efforts to constrain its technological development as an attempt to preserve Western dominance and deny China its rightful place among the world's leading powers. These are not misunderstandings that better communication can resolve; they are substantive conflicts of interest and vision.

The chapters that follow examine the architecture of this competition across its multiple dimensions: the semiconductor battlefield, where control of advanced chips has become synonymous with strategic advantage; the critical minerals race, where China's dominance over rare earth processing gives Beijing leverage over industries from electric vehicles to advanced weapons systems; the emerging biotech frontier, which may prove even more consequential than the AI competition that has captured recent attention; and the military flashpoints—Taiwan, the South China Sea, and beyond—where economic competition could escalate into armed conflict.

The outcome of this competition is not predetermined. American advantages in innovation, alliance networks, and accumulated technological leadership remain substantial. Chinese vulnerabilities—demographic decline, debt accumulation, the inefficiencies of state direction—are real constraints on Beijing's ambitions. Much will depend on policy choices made in Washington, Beijing, and capitals around the world in the years ahead.

What is clear is that the era of U.S.-China economic integration—the quarter-century experiment in using trade to transform China and enrich both nations—has ended. In its place stands a new reality of strategic competition, managed decoupling, and ongoing negotiation over the rules of engagement. The tariffs of Liberation Day marked not a beginning but a culmination: the moment when both sides acknowledged that the relationship of the past could not be the relationship of the future.

The competition that defines our century has begun.

Endnotes

[1] "China Strikes Back with 125% Tariffs on U.S. Goods as Trade War Intensifies," CNBC, April 11, 2025, https://www.cnbc.com/2025/04/11/china-strikes-back-with-125percent-tariffs-on-us-goods-starting-april-12.html.

[2] Chinese Ministry of Finance, Statement on Retaliatory Tariffs, April 11, 2025, translated in "China Strikes Back with 125% Tariffs," CNBC.

[3] Executive Order 14257, "Regulating Imports With a Reciprocal Tariff to Rectify Trade Practices That Contribute to Large and Persistent Annual United States Goods Trade Deficits," April 2, 2025, The White House, https://www.whitehouse.gov/presidential-actions/2025/04/regulating-imports-with-a-reciprocal-tariff-to-rectify-trade-practices/.

[4] Penn Wharton Budget Model, "Effective Tariff Rates and Revenues (Updated November 24, 2025)," University of Pennsylvania, November 24, 2025, https://budgetmodel.wharton.upenn.edu/issues/2025/11/24/effective-tariff-rates-and-revenues-updated-november-24-2025.

[5] "Dow Plunges 2,200 Points as Tariff Tumult Rocks Markets," CNN Business, April 4, 2025, https://www.cnn.com/2025/04/04/investing/stock-market-dow-tariffs.

[6] Chicago Board Options Exchange, VIX Historical Data, April 2025; "Dow Plunges 2,200 Points," CNN Business.

[7] World Trade Organization, "China and the WTO," WTO Accession Documents, December 11, 2001, https://www.wto.org/english/thewto_e/countries_e/china_e.htm.

[8] President William J. Clinton, Statement on House Passage of Permanent Normal Trade Relations with China, May 24, 2000, U.S. Department of State Archive, https://1997-2001.state.gov/regions/eap/000524_clinton_china.html.

[9] World Trade Organization, "Protocol on the Accession of the People's Republic of China," WT/L/432, November 23, 2001, https://www.wto.org/english/thewto_e/acc_e/a1_chine_e.htm.

[10] World Trade Organization, "WTO Successfully Concludes Negotiations on China's Entry," Press Release 243, September 17, 2001, https://www.wto.org/english/news_e/pres01_e/pr243_e.htm.

[11] U.S. Census Bureau, "Trade in Goods with China," Foreign Trade Statistics, https://www.census.gov/foreign-trade/balance/c5700.html.

[12] Robert B. Zoellick, Deputy Secretary of State, "Whither China: From Membership to Responsibility?," Remarks to National Committee on U.S.-China Relations, September 21, 2005, https://2001-2009.state.gov/s/d/former/zoellick/rem/53682.htm.

[13] Office of the United States Trade Representative, "The Obama Administration's Unprecedented Trade Enforcement Record," Fact Sheet, January 2015, https://ustr.gov/about-us/policy-offices/press-office/fact-sheets/2015/january/fact-sheet-obama-administration%E2%80%99s.

[14] Ibid.

[15] The Obama White House, "Fact Sheet: The Obama Administration's Record on Trade Enforcement," January 12, 2017, https://obamawhitehouse.archives.gov/the-press-office/2017/01/12/fact-sheet-obama-administrations-record-trade-enforcement.

[16] Office of the United States Trade Representative, "United States Challenges China's Export Restraints on Rare Earths," Press Release, March 13, 2012, https://ustr.gov/about-us/policy-offices/press-office/press-releases/2012/march/united-states-challenges-china%E2%80%99s-export-restraints.

[17] U.S. Census Bureau, "Trade in Goods with China," Foreign Trade Statistics.

[18] Robert E. Scott, "The China Toll: Growing U.S. Trade Deficit with China Cost More Than 2.7 Million Jobs Between 2001 and 2011, with Job Losses in Every State," Economic Policy Institute Briefing Paper No. 345, August 23, 2012, https://www.epi.org/publication/bp345-china-growing-trade-deficit-cost/.

[19] Office of the United States Trade Representative, "Findings of the Investigation into China's Acts, Policies, and Practices Related to Technology Transfer, Intellectual Property, and Innovation Under Section 301 of the Trade Act of 1974," March 22, 2018, https://ustr.gov/about-us/policy-offices/press-office/press-releases/2018/march/section-301-report-chinas-acts.

[20] Ibid.

[21] Donald J. Trump, campaign statements on trade, 2015–2016.

[22] President Donald J. Trump, Memorandum on Actions by the United States Related to the Section 301 Investigation, March 22, 2018, https://trumpwhitehouse.archives.gov/presidential-actions/presidential-memorandum-actions-united-states-related-section-301-investigation/.

[23] Donald J. Trump (@realDonaldTrump), Twitter, March 2, 2018; see also "Trump: 'Trade Wars Are Good and Easy to Win,'" CNBC, March 2, 2018, https://www.cnbc.com/video/2018/03/02/trump-trade-wars-are-good-and-easy-to-win.html.

[24] China Ministry of Commerce, "Notice on Adding Tariffs on Part of Products Imported from the United States," April 2, 2018.

[25] Office of the United States Trade Representative, "USTR Finalizes Tariffs on $200 Billion of Chinese Imports in Response to China's Unfair Trade Practices," Press Release, September 17, 2018, https://ustr.gov/about-us/policy-offices/press-office/press-releases/2018/september/ustr-finalizes-tariffs-200.

[26] China Briefing, "The US-China Trade War: A Timeline," updated November 2024, https://www.china-briefing.com/news/the-us-china-trade-war-a-timeline/.

[27] Aaron Flaaen, Ali Hortaçsu, and Felix Tintelnot, "The Production Relocation and Price Effects of US Trade Policy: The Case of Washing Machines," American Economic Review 110, no. 7 (July 2020): 2103–27; see also University of Chicago News, "What Washing Machines Can Teach Us About the Cost of Tariffs," https://news.uchicago.edu/story/what-washing-machines-can-teach-us-about-cost-tariffs.

[28] U.S. Department of Agriculture, Foreign Agricultural Service, "China Phase One Agreement," agricultural trade data, https://www.fas.usda.gov/topics/china-phase-one-agreement.

[29] Office of the United States Trade Representative, "Economic and Trade Agreement Between the United States of America and the People's Republic of China: Phase One," January 15, 2020, https://ustr.gov/phase-one.

[30] Ibid.

[31] Chad P. Bown, "US-China Phase One Tracker: China's Purchases of US Goods," Peterson Institute for International Economics, August 30, 2022, https://www.piie.com/research/piie-charts/us-china-phase-one-tracker-chinas-purchases-us-goods.

[32] Office of the United States Trade Representative, "Four-Year Review of Actions Taken in the Section 301 Investigation," May 2024, https://ustr.gov/sites/default/files/USTR%20Report%20Four%20Year%20Review%20of%20China%20Tech%20Transfer%20Section%20

[33] U.S. Department of Commerce, Bureau of Industry and Security, "Commerce Implements New Export Controls on Advanced Computing and Semiconductor Manufacturing Items to the People's Republic of China," October 7, 2022, https://www.commerce.gov/news/press-releases/2022/10/commerce-implements-new-export-controls-advanced-computing-and.

[34] Jake Sullivan, National Security Advisor, "Remarks at the Special Competitive Studies Project Global Emerging Technologies Summit," The White House, September 16, 2022, https://bidenwhitehouse.archives.gov/briefing-room/speeches-remarks/2022/09/16/remarks-by-national-security-advisor-jake-sullivan-at-the-special-competitive-studies-project-global-emerging-technologies-summit/.

[35] Executive Order 14105, "Addressing United States Investments in Certain National Security Technologies and Products in Countries of Concern," August 9, 2023, https://www.federalregister.gov/documents/2023/08/11/2023-17449/addressing-united-states-investments-in-certain-national-security-technologies-and-products-in.

[36] U.S. Department of the Treasury, "Treasury Issues Final Rule Regarding Outbound Investments," October 28, 2024, https://home.treasury.gov/news/press-releases/jy2686.

[37] The White House, "Fact Sheet: President Biden Takes Action to Protect American Workers and Businesses from China's Unfair Trade Practices," May 14, 2024, https://bidenwhitehouse.archives.gov/briefing-room/statements-releases/2024/05/14/fact-sheet-president-biden-takes-action-to-protect-american-workers-and-businesses-from-chinas-unfair-trade-practices/.

[38] Executive Order 14195, "Imposing Duties to Address the Synthetic Opioid Supply Chain in the People's Republic of China," February 1, 2025.

[39] China Briefing, "US-China Tariff Rates - What Are They Now?," updated November 2025, https://www.china-briefing.com/news/us-china-tariff-rates-2025/.

[40] Executive Order 14257, "Regulating Imports With a Reciprocal Tariff to Rectify Trade Practices That Contribute to Large and Persistent Annual United States Goods Trade Deficits," April 2, 2025.

[41] "Trump Announces New Tariffs on What He Calls 'Liberation Day,'" CBS News, April 3, 2025, https://www.cbsnews.com/news/trump-liberation-day-new-tariffs-us/.

[42] William Reinsch and Emily Benson, "'Liberation Day' Tariffs Explained," Center for Strategic and International Studies, April 9, 2025, https://www.csis.org/analysis/liberation-day-tariffs-explained.

[43] Ibid.

[44] "Dow Plunges 2,200 Points as Tariff Tumult Rocks Markets," CNN Business, April 4, 2025.

[45] Ibid.; S&P Dow Jones Indices, market data, April 2025.

[46] Chicago Board Options Exchange, VIX Historical Data, April 2025.

[47] JPMorgan Chase Economic Research, as reported in "Liberation Day Tariff Analysis," multiple news outlets, April 2025.

[48] China Ministry of Finance, "Announcement on Additional Tariffs on Imports Originating in the United States," April 4, 2025.

[49] Executive Order 14266, "Modifying Reciprocal Tariff Rates to Reflect Trading Partner Retaliation and Alignment," April 9, 2025.

[50] Chinese Ministry of Finance, Statement, April 11, 2025, as translated in "China Strikes Back with 125% Tariffs," CNBC.

[51] Donald J. Trump, Statement on Truth Social, April 9, 2025; White House Press Secretary Statement, April 9, 2025.

[52] S&P Dow Jones Indices, market data, April 9, 2025.

[53] "US, China Begin Trade Talks in Geneva," NPR, May 10, 2025, https://www.npr.org/2025/05/10/nx-s1-5394399/u-s-and-china-begin-talks-amid-tensions-over-trumps-tariff-war.

[54] "He Lifeng: China, U.S. High-Level Meeting Candid, In-Depth, Constructive," CGTN, May 12, 2025, https://news.cgtn.com/news/2025-05-12/He-Lifeng-China-U-S-high-level-economic-trade-talks-candid-in-depth-and-constructive.

[55] The White House, "Joint Statement on U.S.-China Economic and Trade Meeting in Geneva," May 12, 2025, https://www.whitehouse.gov/briefings-statements/2025/05/joint-statement-on-u-s-china-economic-and-trade-meeting-in-geneva/.

[56] The White House, "Modifying Reciprocal Tariff Rates Consistent with the Economic and Trade Arrangement Between the United States and the People's Republic of China," Executive Order, November 2025, https://www.whitehouse.gov/presidential-actions/2025/11/modifying-reciprocal-tariff-rates-consistent-with-the-economic-and-trade-arrangement-between-the-united-states-and-the-peoples-republic-of-china/.

[57] Scott Bessent, Treasury Secretary, Remarks on Trade Policy, as reported in China Briefing and multiple news outlets, 2025.

[58] Xi Jinping, Report to the 20th National Congress of the Communist Party of China, October 2022; see also Congressional Research Service, "Made in China 2025," Report IF10964, https://crsreports.congress.gov/product/pdf/IF/IF10964.

[59] State Council of the People's Republic of China, "Made in China 2025," May 2015; see Center for Strategic and International Studies, "Made in China 2025," https://www.csis.org/analysis/made-china-2025.

[60] International Energy Agency, "Global EV Outlook 2024," https://www.iea.org/reports/global-ev-outlook-2024; BloombergNEF, "China's Dominance in Clean Energy Manufacturing," 2024.

[61] Stanford University Human-Centered Artificial Intelligence, "AI Index Report 2025," https://aiindex.stanford.edu/report/.

[62] "The Most Dangerous Place on Earth," The Economist, May 1, 2021, https://www.economist.com/leaders/2021/05/01/the-most-dangerous-place-on-earth.

[63] AUKUS Joint Statement, September 15, 2021, The White House, https://www.whitehouse.gov/briefing-room/statements-releases/2021/09/15/joint-leaders-statement-on-aukus/.

[64] Quadrilateral Security Dialogue Joint Statements, various dates 2021–2025, The White House; see "Quad Joint Statement," May 24, 2022.

[65] Government of Japan, Ministry of Defense, "National Security Strategy of Japan," December 16, 2022, https://www.mod.go.jp/j/policy/agenda/guideline/pdf/security_strategy_en.pdf.

[66] Analysis based on various policy discussions; see Council on Foreign Relations, "The U.S.-China Tech Cold War," https://www.cfr.org/backgrounder/us-china-tech-cold-war.

Chapter 2
The Strategic Logic of Decoupling
Understanding What Both Sides Want—and Fear

The May 2025 Geneva talks between the United States and China produced a joint statement that temporarily arrested the most dangerous escalation in bilateral economic relations since the establishment of diplomatic ties. Standing before reporters in the Swiss lakeside city, Treasury Secretary Scott Bessent articulated a distinction that would come to define the evolving economic relationship between the world's two largest economies. The United States, he explained, did not seek a "generalized decoupling" from China—the wholesale severing of commercial ties that would disrupt global supply chains and impose staggering costs on both nations. What Washington pursued instead was a "decoupling for strategic necessities," focused on critical sectors essential to national security: semiconductors, pharmaceuticals, steel, and other industries where dependence on a strategic competitor posed unacceptable risks.[1]

This distinction between generalized and strategic decoupling represents far more than diplomatic nuance. It encapsulates the central tension animating both countries' economic policies: the recognition that complete economic separation would prove catastrophic for both sides, even as each government accelerates efforts to reduce dependencies in sectors deemed vital to national survival. Understanding this tension—what each side genuinely wants and what each profoundly fears—is essential to grasping the strategic logic driving the most consequential economic realignment of the twenty-first century.

I. The American Calculus: From Engagement to Strategic Competition

The trajectory of American policy toward China has undergone a fundamental transformation over the past decade, evolving from confident engagement to wary competition and, under the second Trump administration, to explicit strategic decoupling. This evolution reflects not merely partisan shifts but a bipartisan reassessment of assumptions that had guided American China policy since the Nixon opening of 1972.

The engagement paradigm rested on the premise that economic interdependence would gradually transform China's political system and integrate Beijing into a rules-based international order. American policymakers anticipated that trade would create a Chinese middle class whose demands for political participation would ultimately liberalize the Communist Party's grip on power. This assumption informed decisions to support China's accession to the World Trade Organization in 2001 and to maintain normal trade relations despite persistent concerns about human rights, intellectual property theft, and market access barriers.

By the mid-2010s, this consensus had collapsed. China's economic rise had not produced political liberalization but rather enabled the Chinese Communist Party to consolidate control while pursuing increasingly assertive foreign policies. The Made in China 2025 industrial policy, announced in May 2015 by the State Council, crystallized American anxieties by explicitly targeting ten strategic sectors—including next-generation information technology, robotics, aerospace equipment, maritime engineering equipment, advanced rail transit, energy-saving vehicles, electrical equipment, agricultural machinery, new materials, and biopharmaceuticals—where Beijing intended to achieve self-sufficiency and global dominance.[2] American businesses and policymakers recognized that China was not merely seeking comparative advantage through market competition but was deploying state resources to displace foreign firms from sectors essential to both economic prosperity and military capability.

The COVID-19 pandemic transformed these strategic concerns into an immediate national security crisis. When the virus spread globally in early 2020, the United States discovered the full extent of its dependence on Chinese manufacturing for critical medical supplies. China produced the majority of the world's personal protective equipment and controlled essential components of global pharmaceutical supply chains, including significant shares of active pharmaceutical ingredients.[3] Beijing's decision in February 2020 to nationalize control over the production and distribution of medical supplies—directing all production for domestic use—left American hospitals scrambling for basic protective equipment.[4] The crisis revealed, in Secretary Bessent's formulation, that "efficient supply chains were not resilient supply chains."[5]

This realization has driven American policy toward what Bessent has termed "de-risking" rather than complete decoupling. The strategy focuses on rebuilding domestic capacity in sectors where dependence on China creates national security vulnerabilities while maintaining commercial relations in areas deemed less strategically sensitive. Bessent has identified five to seven strategic industries targeted for reshoring, including shipbuilding, steel, critical medicines, and semiconductors.[6] The goal is not to end trade with China but to ensure that American national security can never again be held hostage to supply chain disruptions originating in a strategic competitor.

The Liberation Day tariffs announced by President Trump on April 2, 2025, represented the most dramatic assertion of this strategic decoupling agenda. Declaring a national emergency over persistent trade deficits, Trump signed Executive Order 14257, invoking the International Emergency Economic Powers Act to impose a universal ten percent tariff on imports from nearly all countries, with substantially higher rates targeting China specifically.[7] When Beijing retaliated with matching duties, the subsequent escalation drove combined tariff rates to 145 percent on Chinese goods entering the United States and 125 percent on American exports to China—levels that effectively constituted a bilateral trade embargo.[8]

Yet even at the height of this confrontation, American policymakers stopped short of advocating complete separation. The May 2025 Geneva agreement, which reduced reciprocal tariff rates by 115 percentage points for an initial ninety-day period, reflected Washington's acknowledgment that total decoupling would impose costs the American economy could not easily absorb.[9] The bilateral trade relationship, which saw the United States import nearly $440 billion in goods from China in 2024 and run a $295.4 billion trade deficit, had created interdependencies that no amount of tariffs could sever overnight.[10] Strategic decoupling thus emerged as the pragmatic middle ground between the failed engagement paradigm and the economically ruinous alternative of complete separation.

II. Beijing's Doctrine of Self-Reliance: Indigenous and Controllable Technology

If American policy has evolved from engagement to strategic competition, Chinese policy has traveled an even more dramatic arc—from reform and opening to what President Xi Jinping has termed "high-level scientific and technological self-reliance and self-improvement."[11] This transformation reflects Beijing's growing conviction that China's security and prosperity can no longer depend on access to foreign technology that may be denied at Washington's discretion.

The intellectual foundations of China's current technology policy trace to the 2006 National Medium- and Long-Term Plan for the Development of Science and Technology, which first articulated the concept of "indigenous innovation" (����) as a national priority.[12] This fifteen-year plan called for reducing dependence on foreign technology while building domestic capacity in strategic sectors. The plan identified core technologies where China needed to achieve mastery, established goals for research and development spending, and created the framework for subsequent industrial policies.[13]

Yet the 2006 plan, while ambitious, still assumed that China would pursue technological advancement within a relatively open global system. The subsequent decade revealed the limits of this assumption. American export controls on high-technology goods, restrictions on Chinese acquisitions of American firms, and scrutiny of academic collaborations demonstrated that Western governments viewed China's technological rise as a threat to be contained rather than a development to be accommodated. The Trump administration's first-term technology war against Huawei, which denied the Chinese telecommunications giant access to American semiconductors and software, crystallized Beijing's recognition that technological dependence constituted an existential vulnerability.

Xi Jinping's response has been to elevate technological self-reliance from an economic aspiration to a matter of national survival. In his address to the Twentieth Party Congress in October 2022, Xi declared that China must "accelerate efforts to build our self-reliance and strength in science and technology," positioning innovation as the foundation of national rejuvenation.[14] The speech emphasized science and technology more frequently than previous congress addresses, with the newly added science-technology-innovation section signaling that technological capability had become the Chinese Communist Party's central preoccupation.[15]

This emphasis on self-reliance found institutional expression in the concept of "indigenous and controllable" (����) technology—systems and components produced domestically and therefore immune to foreign disruption. Chinese standards have increasingly required that critical infrastructure rely on "secure and controllable" products, creating regulatory pressure for domestic alternatives to foreign technology. While the precise meaning of these requirements has been subject to debate, their intent is clear: to ensure that no American export restriction or sanction can cripple Chinese industry or military capability.

The Made in China 2025 industrial policy represented Beijing's most comprehensive effort to achieve this vision. As the State Council document declared, "Manufacturing is the mainstay of the national economy, the basis on which the nation is established, an instrument of rejuvenation, and the foundation of a world power."[16] The plan targeted ten strategic sectors for development, with specific goals for domestic content, market share, and technological capability. By 2020, China aimed to have forty percent of core components sourced domestically; by 2025, that figure would rise to seventy percent.[17] Government guidance funds channeled state resources to priority industries, while regulations encouraged or required foreign firms seeking market access to transfer technology to Chinese partners.

American pressure has not diminished these ambitions but accelerated them. The Fourteenth Five-Year Plan, adopted in 2021, made scientific and technological self-reliance the "strategic underpinning of national development," with the Fifth Plenum's Proposals declaring a hardened determination to pursue self-reliance in the face of "great-power competition."[18] The plan allocated increased annual spending for research and development and identified frontier technologies—artificial intelligence, quantum computing, semiconductors, biotechnology—where China would concentrate resources to achieve breakthroughs.[19] Chinese leaders had concluded that technological independence was no longer merely desirable but essential, given the demonstrated willingness of the United States to weaponize technology access.

III. The Dual Circulation Strategy: China's Response to Containment

Beijing's response to American pressure has crystallized in the "dual circulation" development strategy, first articulated by Xi Jinping in May 2020 and subsequently incorporated into the Fourteenth Five-Year Plan.[20] This framework represents China's most sophisticated effort to balance continued engagement with the global economy against the imperative of reducing external vulnerabilities.

The dual circulation concept envisions two interconnected economic loops: an "internal circulation" centered on domestic production, distribution, and consumption, and an "external circulation" involving international trade and investment. Unlike previous development strategies that prioritized export-led growth, dual circulation positions the domestic market as the primary engine of economic expansion while maintaining international engagement as a complement rather than a foundation.[21]

The intellectual predecessor of dual circulation was the export-oriented strategy of the Deng Xiaoping era, which channeled China's comparative advantage in low-cost manufacturing into spectacular growth. This approach produced remarkable results: China became the world's factory, its exports surged, and hundreds of millions of Chinese citizens escaped poverty. Yet it also created dependencies that the COVID-19 pandemic and American technology restrictions exposed as strategically untenable.

The dual circulation strategy seeks to mitigate these vulnerabilities through several mechanisms. First, it aims to stimulate domestic consumption to reduce reliance on export markets, leveraging China's population of 1.4 billion consumers, including over 400 million with middle-class incomes.[22] Second, it prioritizes technological upgrading to enable Chinese firms to produce components and systems currently sourced abroad. Third, it seeks to embed foreign companies more deeply in Chinese supply chains, making it costly for them to relocate production and creating mutual dependencies that limit Washington's ability to impose economic pain without suffering equivalent retaliation.

Xi Jinping articulated this last element with remarkable candor in an October 2020 speech to the Central Financial and Economic Affairs Commission, stating that China must "tighten international production chains' dependence on China, forming powerful countermeasures and deterrent capabilities against foreigners artificially cutting off supplies."[23] The strategy thus has both defensive and offensive dimensions: reducing China's exposure to foreign pressure while increasing foreign economies' exposure to Chinese retaliation.

The dual circulation framework also incorporates the Belt and Road Initiative as a mechanism for developing alternative markets and supply chains. Chinese investment in infrastructure across Asia, Africa, and Latin America creates commercial relationships that can partially compensate for reduced access to Western markets while securing supplies of energy, minerals, and agricultural products.[24] If American allies align with Washington's technology restrictions, Beijing calculates that it can develop alternative partnerships with countries less willing or able to participate in containment efforts.

Critics have questioned whether dual circulation represents a genuine strategic shift or merely rhetorical repackaging of long-standing objectives. Previous five-year plans also emphasized boosting domestic consumption and reducing external dependencies, with limited success.[25] China's household consumption as a share of GDP remains far below developed-economy norms, and the structural reforms needed to transfer wealth from investment to consumers have proven politically difficult. Yet even skeptics acknowledge that the external environment has changed dramatically, creating pressures for adaptation that did not exist during the engagement era.

IV. The Impossibility of Complete Decoupling

Despite the dramatic escalation of tariffs, export controls, and nationalist rhetoric, neither Washington nor Beijing truly seeks complete economic separation. The economic interdependencies accumulated over four decades of engagement cannot be unwound without imposing costs that both governments recognize as prohibitive. This reality creates the space for strategic maneuvering even as competition intensifies.

The scale of bilateral trade illustrates the challenge. China remains one of America's largest trading partners, with the United States importing nearly $440 billion in goods from China in 2024.[26] American consumers benefit from Chinese manufactured goods that would cost significantly more if sourced elsewhere or produced domestically. American corporations derive substantial revenues from Chinese markets and Chinese production. Agricultural exporters, particularly in politically significant states, depend on Chinese demand for soybeans, pork, and other commodities.

For China, the dependencies are equally significant. Despite years of effort to develop indigenous semiconductor capabilities, Chinese firms remain reliant on American chip technology, design software, and manufacturing equipment. Sophisticated integrated circuits essential for artificial intelligence, telecommunications, and defense applications cannot yet be produced domestically at scale. American restrictions on Huawei and other Chinese technology firms have demonstrated that this dependence creates genuine vulnerabilities, but eliminating it will require years of investment and may never fully succeed.

These mutual dependencies create what economists describe as mutual vulnerability rather than unilateral dependence. American restrictions on semiconductor technology impose significant costs on Chinese industry, but Chinese restrictions on rare earth exports would similarly disrupt American defense and technology sectors. Neither side possesses escalation dominance—the ability to impose costs on the adversary without suffering comparable retaliation.

Recognition of these realities has tempered both governments' rhetoric and actions. The May 2025 Geneva agreement, which dramatically reduced tariff rates from their April peaks, reflected mutual acknowledgment that the trajectory of escalation had become economically irrational. Secretary Bessent stated explicitly that "neither side wants a generalized decoupling" and characterized the prohibitive tariff levels as creating an untenable situation that neither country favored.[27] Subsequent negotiations extended the tariff truce, demonstrating both governments' recognition that returning to prohibitive tariff levels would impose unacceptable economic costs.[28]

Yet the impossibility of complete decoupling does not preclude significant separation in strategic sectors. The concept of a "small yard, high fence"—limiting restrictions to genuinely sensitive technologies while maintaining broader commercial relations—represents the intellectual framework for American export controls.[29] Similarly, Beijing's dual circulation strategy explicitly maintains international engagement while building domestic alternatives in critical areas. Both governments have concluded that the goal is not zero trade but managed competition, with each side seeking to maximize its advantages while limiting its vulnerabilities.

V. The May 2025 Negotiations: Geneva Talks and Their Aftermath

The May 2025 Geneva negotiations represented the first serious diplomatic effort to arrest the escalation that had brought bilateral tariffs to prohibitive levels. Understanding what the talks achieved—and what they left unresolved—illuminates the parameters within which the U.S.-China economic relationship will operate for the foreseeable future.

The immediate context was the tariff spiral triggered by President Trump's Liberation Day announcement on April 2, 2025. The initial 34 percent reciprocal tariff on Chinese goods, stacked on top of existing fentanyl-related duties, provoked Chinese retaliation with matching rates on American exports.[30] On April 8, the Trump administration raised the tariff rate on Chinese goods to 84 percent in response to China's retaliation; the following day, China announced an 84 percent tariff on all American goods.[31] By April 11, American tariffs had reached 145 percent and Chinese tariffs 125 percent—rates that effectively halted normal commercial exchange.[32]

The Geneva talks, conducted over a weekend by Treasury Secretary Bessent, Trade Representative Jamieson Greer, and Chinese Vice Premier He Lifeng, produced a joint statement establishing a framework for de-escalation.[33] Both sides agreed to reduce reciprocal tariff rates by 115 percentage points for an initial ninety-day period, bringing effective rates to 30 percent on Chinese goods entering the United States (including the 20 percent fentanyl tariff) and 10 percent on American exports to China.[34] China also committed to suspending non-tariff countermeasures imposed since April 2.[35]

The agreement established ongoing negotiating mechanisms, with He Lifeng and the American trade team designated as representatives for continued discussions.[36] Both parties recognized "the importance of a sustainable, long-term, and mutually beneficial economic and trade relationship" and committed to working on non-tariff barriers during the pause period.[37] Global markets responded positively, with equity indices surging on expectations of reduced trade friction.

Yet the Geneva framework left fundamental issues unresolved. The agreement addressed reciprocal tariffs but maintained sector-specific duties on steel, aluminum, and automobiles that predated the April escalation.[38] Technology export controls, investment restrictions, and other dimensions of strategic decoupling remained entirely outside the trade negotiating framework. Most importantly, the underlying sources of conflict—China's industrial policies, American concerns about technology transfer and intellectual property, Taiwan, and broader geopolitical competition—received no substantive attention.

The ninety-day pause proved insufficient for comprehensive resolution. As Secretary Bessent indicated, both sides would continue to meet in subsequent weeks to work toward a broader agreement.[39] The negotiations revealed the contours of what might be termed "managed competition"—an economic relationship characterized by elevated but not prohibitive trade barriers, continued commercial exchange in non-sensitive sectors, and ongoing strategic decoupling in areas deemed vital to national security. Neither side achieved its maximal objectives: the United States did not fundamentally alter Chinese industrial policy, and China did not secure the elimination of strategic restrictions on technology access. Yet both avoided the worst-case scenario of complete economic rupture.

VI. Structural Asymmetries and Mutual Vulnerabilities

The strategic logic of decoupling is shaped by fundamental asymmetries in how the United States and China engage with the global economy—asymmetries that create both opportunities and constraints for policymakers on both sides.

The United States benefits from the dollar's status as the world's primary reserve currency, which enables it to finance persistent trade deficits and provides leverage through the global financial system. American sanctions authorities can effectively exclude targeted entities from dollar-denominated transactions, a capability that has proved devastating to firms like Huawei that depend on international supply chains. The United States also retains significant advantages in upstream technology—the design tools, manufacturing equipment, and intellectual property that underpin advanced industries—even as China has built formidable capabilities in downstream production.

China's advantages are equally significant. Its manufacturing capacity across a vast range of products creates dependencies that cannot be quickly replicated elsewhere. Its control over processing of critical minerals—including rare earth elements essential for electronics, renewable energy, and defense applications—provides leverage that Beijing has demonstrated willingness to employ.[40] China's domestic market, the largest in the world for many product categories, represents an opportunity that most multinational corporations cannot afford to abandon.

These asymmetries create what economists describe as mutual vulnerability rather than unilateral dependence. American restrictions on semiconductor technology impose significant costs on Chinese industry, but Chinese restrictions on rare earth exports would similarly disrupt American defense and technology sectors. Neither side possesses escalation dominance—the ability to impose costs on the adversary without suffering comparable retaliation.

This mutual vulnerability has important implications for the trajectory of decoupling. It suggests that neither side has strong incentives to pursue maximalist strategies that would trigger total economic rupture. The tariff escalation of April 2025 demonstrated that both governments retain the capacity for dramatic action, but also that both recognize limits beyond which escalation becomes self-defeating. The subsequent negotiations reflect this recognition: neither side wanted to be locked into an embargo-level confrontation indefinitely.

Yet mutual vulnerability does not preclude persistent pressure and gradual separation. Both governments are pursuing strategies to reduce their exposure to economic coercion while maintaining leverage over the other side. American industrial policy, embodied in legislation like the CHIPS and Science Act, aims to rebuild domestic semiconductor manufacturing while restricting Chinese access to advanced chipmaking technology.[41] Chinese investment in domestic alternatives and diversification of supply chains seeks comparable objectives from Beijing's perspective.

The result is likely to be a prolonged process of selective decoupling, concentrated in strategic sectors while maintaining commercial relations in areas deemed less sensitive. This process will proceed unevenly, accelerating during crises and slowing when economic costs become politically salient. Neither complete integration nor complete separation represents a stable equilibrium; the relationship will instead occupy an uncomfortable middle ground where competition and commerce coexist in perpetual tension.

VII. Implications for the Global Order

The strategic logic of U.S.-China decoupling extends far beyond the bilateral relationship, reshaping the global economic order that has prevailed since the Cold War's end. Third countries, multinational corporations, and international institutions must navigate an environment where the world's two largest economies are simultaneously essential trading partners and strategic rivals.

For American allies in Europe and Asia, the challenge is acute. Many countries maintain substantial commercial relationships with China while depending on the United States for security guarantees. American pressure to restrict technology exports, screen investments, and limit Chinese participation in critical infrastructure forces difficult choices between economic interests and alliance obligations. The European Union's concept of "de-risking"—reducing dependencies without comprehensive decoupling—represents one attempt to thread this needle, though its practical implementation remains contested.[42]

Developing countries face different but equally consequential dilemmas. China's Belt and Road Initiative offers infrastructure investment that many countries desperately need, but accepting Chinese financing creates dependencies that may constrain future policy choices. American efforts to provide alternatives have produced initiatives like the Build Back Better World partnership, but these have struggled to match Chinese scale and speed. For countries caught between great power competition, the optimal strategy may involve balancing relationships with both sides rather than aligning definitively with either.

Multinational corporations confront operational challenges that strategic decoupling creates. Supply chains optimized for efficiency must be reconfigured for resilience, with redundant sourcing and geographic diversification replacing just-in-time logistics.[43] Compliance with both American and Chinese regulatory requirements may prove impossible, forcing choices about which markets to prioritize. Some industries may effectively bifurcate into separate American and Chinese technology ecosystems, requiring firms to maintain parallel operations or exit one market entirely.

The international trading system faces existential questions. The World Trade Organization, designed for an era of liberalizing trade, possesses limited tools for managing strategic competition between its largest members. American invocation of national security exceptions to justify tariffs challenges the WTO's fundamental premise that trade restrictions require multilateral justification.[44] Chinese industrial policies that blend state support with market mechanisms strain dispute resolution mechanisms designed for more clearly defined market economies. Whether the rules-based trading order can survive the U.S.-China rivalry or will fragment into competing blocs remains an open question.

Conclusion: The Paradox of Partial Decoupling

The strategic logic of decoupling contains a fundamental paradox: both the United States and China seek to reduce their vulnerabilities to the other while maintaining economic relationships that neither can afford to sever entirely. This paradox ensures that decoupling will be neither complete nor stable but rather a continuing process of adjustment, negotiation, and competition.

For the United States, strategic decoupling represents an effort to preserve the benefits of global economic integration while eliminating dependencies that foreign adversaries could exploit. The goal is resilient supply chains in critical sectors, robust domestic industrial capacity, and alliance structures that can coordinate responses to economic coercion. Success would mean that American prosperity no longer requires accepting vulnerabilities that compromise national security.

For China, self-reliance represents an effort to ensure that the nation's development cannot be derailed by foreign pressure. The goal is indigenous capability in core technologies, diversified export markets and supply sources, and sufficient leverage to deter economic attacks. Success would mean that Beijing can pursue its national interests without fear that Washington will choke off access to essential technologies or markets.

Neither side will fully achieve these objectives. Complete American self-sufficiency in semiconductor manufacturing, pharmaceutical production, and rare earth processing would require decades of investment and may prove technologically or economically impractical. Complete Chinese independence from Western technology would similarly demand breakthroughs that cannot be guaranteed and timelines that extend far beyond current planning horizons. Both countries will remain embedded in global economic networks that create interdependencies resistant to political engineering.

The resulting equilibrium—if it can be called that—will feature elevated but manageable trade barriers, continuing commercial exchange alongside strategic competition, and periodic crises that test the limits of both sides' tolerance for economic pain. It will require constant management by policymakers who must simultaneously pursue advantage for their own countries and avoid escalation that would prove mutually destructive.

This is not the integrated global economy that optimists anticipated when China joined the World Trade Organization in 2001, nor is it the complete bifurcation into hostile blocs that pessimists have warned might follow. It is something unprecedented: two deeply intertwined economies pursuing partial separation while neither can afford to complete the divorce. Navigating this terrain will demand strategic sophistication from policymakers, adaptability from businesses, and patience from publics who may prefer cleaner outcomes than geopolitics typically permits.

Endnotes

[1] Scott Bessent, interview with CNBC, "Squawk Box," May 12, 2025, transcript available at CNBC.com; "Treasury Secretary Scott Bessent Says U.S. and China Now Have a Mechanism in Place on Trade," Bloomberg, May 12, 2025, https://www.bloomberg.com/news/videos/2025-05-12/bessent-says-us-china-do-not-want-a-generalized-decoupling.

[2] State Council of the People's Republic of China, "Made in China 2025" (����2025), May 8, 2015, translated by Georgetown University Center for Security and Emerging Technology, t0432, https://cset.georgetown.edu/wp-content/uploads/t0432_made_in_china_2025_EN.pdf.

[3] Karen M. Sutter, Michael D. Sutherland, and Andres B. Schwarzenberg, "COVID-19: China Medical Supply Chains and Broader Trade Issues," Congressional Research Service, R46304, updated December 23, 2020, https://crsreports.congress.gov/product/pdf/R/R46304.

[4] Congressional Research Service, R46304, noting that "in early February 2020, the Chinese government nationalized control of the production and distribution of medical supplies in China—directing all production for domestic use."

[5] Scott Bessent, CNBC interview, May 12, 2025: "We do not want a generalized decoupling from China. But what we do want is a decoupling for strategic necessities, which we were unable to obtain during Covid and we realized that efficient supply chains were not resilient supply chains."

[6] Scott Bessent, CNBC interview, May 12, 2025: "We are going to create our own steel. [Tariffs] protect our steel industry. They work on critical medicines, on semiconductors."

[7] Executive Order 14257, "Regulating Imports With a Reciprocal Tariff to Rectify Trade Practices That Contribute to Large and Persistent Annual United States Goods Trade Deficits," April 2, 2025, Federal Register, April 7, 2025, https://www.federalregister.gov/documents/2025/04/07/2025-06063/regulating-imports-with-a-reciprocal-tariff-to-rectify-trade-practices-that-contribute-to-large-and.

[8] White House, "Fact Sheet: President Donald J. Trump Secures a Historic Trade Win for the United States," May 12, 2025, https://www.whitehouse.gov/fact-sheets/2025/05/fact-sheet-president-donald-j-trump-secures-a-historic-trade-win-for-the-united-states.

[9] "Joint Statement on U.S.-China Economic and Trade Meeting in Geneva," White House, May 12, 2025, https://www.whitehouse.gov/briefings-statements/2025/05/joint-statement-on-u-s-china-economic-and-trade-meeting-in-geneva.

[10] "Bessent Sees Tariff Agreement as Progress in 'Strategic' Decoupling with China," CNBC, May 12, 2025, https://www.cnbc.com/2025/05/12/bessent-sees-tariff-agreement-as-progress-in-strategic-decoupling-with-china.html.

[11] Xi Jinping, Report to the 20th National Congress of the Communist Party of China, October 16, 2022, full text translated in Nikkei Asia, October 18, 2022, https://asia.nikkei.com/politics/china-s-party-congress/transcript-president-xi-jinping-s-report-to-china-s-2022-party-congress.

[12] State Council of the People's Republic of China, "National Medium- and Long-Term Plan for the Development of Science and Technology (2006-2020)," February 2006.

[13] Cong Cao, Richard P. Suttmeier, and Denis Fred Simon, "China's 15-Year Science and Technology Plan," Physics Today 59, no. 12 (December 2006): 38-43.

[14] Xi Jinping, Report to the 20th National Congress: "We have accelerated efforts to build our self-reliance and strength in science and technology, with nationwide R&D spending rising from 1 trillion yuan to 2.8 trillion yuan, the second highest in the world."

[15] "Key Takeaways from Xi's Report to the Party Congress," Mercator Institute for China Studies (MERICS), October 2022, https://merics.org/en/merics-briefs/key-takeaways-xis-report-party-congress.

[16] State Council of the People's Republic of China, "Made in China 2025," May 2015, Georgetown CSET translation.

[17] Ibid., Box 3, "Industrial Strong Basics Projects": "By 2020, achieve independent assurance of [the supply of] 40% of core basic components and key basic materials... By 2025, achieve independent assurance of [the supply of] 70% of core basic components and key basic materials."

[18] "Self-Strengthening for Strategic Competition: What to Watch at China's Fourth Plenum," Asia Society Policy Institute, October 14, 2025, https://asiasociety.org/policy-institute/self-strengthening-strategic-competition-what-watch-chinas-fourth-plenum.

[19] "China's 14th Five-Year Plan: Strengthening the Domestic Base to Become a Superpower," MERICS, March 2021.

[20] Jude Blanchette and Andrew Polk, "Dual Circulation and China's New Hedged Integration Strategy," Center for Strategic and International Studies, August 24, 2020, https://www.csis.org/analysis/dual-circulation-and-chinas-new-hedged-integration-strategy.

[21] Alicia García-Herrero, "What Is Behind China's Dual Circulation Strategy," China Leadership Monitor, September 2, 2021, https://www.prcleader.org/post/what-is-behind-china-s-dual-circulation-strategy.

[22] "Will the Dual Circulation Strategy Enable China to Compete in a Post-Pandemic World?" ChinaPower Project, Center for Strategic and International Studies, November 9, 2023, https://chinapower.csis.org/china-covid-dual-circulation-economic-strategy.

[23] Xi Jinping, speech to Central Financial and Economic Affairs Commission, October 2020, cited in Blanchette and Polk, "Dual Circulation."

[24] García-Herrero, "What Is Behind China's Dual Circulation Strategy."

[25] "Explainer: What Is China's Dual Circulation Economic Strategy and Why Is It Important?" South China Morning Post, March 4, 2021, https://www.scmp.com/economy/china-economy/article/3110184/what-chinas-dual-circulation-economic-strategy-and-why-it.

[26] CNBC, "Bessent Sees Tariff Agreement as Progress in 'Strategic' Decoupling with China," May 12, 2025.

[27] Scott Bessent, Bloomberg interview, May 12, 2025: "Neither side wants a generalized decoupling. The US is going to do a strategic decoupling in terms of the items that we discovered during COVID were of national security interest, whether it's semiconductors, medicines, steel."

[28] White House, "Fact Sheet: President Donald J. Trump Secures a Historic Trade Win for the United States," May 12, 2025.

[29] The "small yard, high fence" formulation has been employed by multiple American officials to describe the scope of technology restrictions, emphasizing that controls should be narrow in scope but strictly enforced.

[30] Executive Order 14257, April 2, 2025; State Council Tariff Commission of the People's Republic of China, Announcement No. 4 of 2025, April 4, 2025, announcing 34 percent retaliatory tariffs.

[31] Executive Order 14259, "Amendment to Reciprocal Tariffs and Updated Duties as Applied to Low-Value Imports from the People's Republic of China," April 8, 2025, Federal Register, April

14, 2025, https://www.federalregister.gov/documents/2025/04/14/2025-06378/amendment-to-reciprocal-tariffs-and-updated-duties-as-applied-to-low-value-imports-from-the-peoples.

[32] White House, "Fact Sheet: President Donald J. Trump Secures a Historic Trade Win for the United States," May 12, 2025, noting tariff reduction from 145 percent.

[33] "Joint Statement on U.S.-China Economic and Trade Meeting in Geneva," White House, May 12, 2025.

[34] Ibid.: "The United States will (i) modify the application of the additional ad valorem rate of duty on articles of China... by suspending 24 percentage points of that rate for an initial period of 90 days, while retaining the remaining ad valorem rate of 10 percent."

[35] Ibid.: China committed to "adopt all necessary administrative measures to suspend or remove the non-tariff countermeasures taken against the United States since April 2, 2025."

[36] Ibid.: "The representative from the Chinese side for these discussions will be He Lifeng, Vice Premier of the State Council, and the representatives from the U.S. side will be Scott Bessent, Secretary of the Treasury, and Jamieson Greer, United States Trade Representative."

[37] Ibid.

[38] Scott Bessent, CNBC interview, May 12, 2025: "The reciprocal tariffs have nothing to do with the specific industry tariffs."

[39] Scott Bessent, CNBC interview, May 12, 2025: "I imagine we will meet again in the next few weeks."

[40] China Ministry of Commerce has announced export controls on rare earth elements, gallium, germanium, and antimony, demonstrating willingness to use mineral leverage.

[41] CHIPS and Science Act of 2022, Public Law 117-167, August 9, 2022.

[42] European Commission, "An EU Approach to Enhance Economic Security," Communication from the Commission, June 2023.

[43] Willy C. Shih, "Global Supply Chains in a Post-Pandemic World," Harvard Business Review, September-October 2020.

[44] China, Canada, and Brazil have filed complaints before the World Trade Organization alleging that President Trump's tariffs violate tariff concessions under Article II and the most-favored-nation treatment under Article I of the General Agreement on Tariffs and Trade.

Chapter 3

The New Containment

Export Controls as 21st Century Statecraft

On October 7, 2022, the United States Bureau of Industry and Security published a regulatory notice that would reshape the global semiconductor industry. With little fanfare—released on a Friday afternoon in the Federal Register's pre-publication reading room—the Biden administration announced the most comprehensive technology export restrictions since the Cold War.[1] The rules targeted China's ability to access advanced computing chips, develop supercomputers, and manufacture cutting-edge semiconductors. As Gregory Allen of the Center for Strategic and International Studies observed, these measures represented "a new U.S. policy of actively strangling large segments of the Chinese technology industry—strangling with an intent to kill."[2]

The timing was deliberate. China had made clear its ambitions to achieve semiconductor self-sufficiency and artificial intelligence supremacy by 2030. The ruling Chinese Communist Party's "Made in China 2025" blueprint explicitly identified advanced semiconductors as a strategic priority. Washington's response—restricting not merely specific products but entire categories of technology, manufacturing equipment, and even the participation of American citizens in Chinese chip facilities—signaled a new era of technological containment.

Yet this was not the first time the United States had weaponized export controls against a strategic rival. Understanding the current conflict requires examining its historical antecedents: the Cold War technology denial regime that sought to maintain Western advantages over the Soviet bloc for nearly half a century.

CoCOM and the Architecture of Cold War Technology Denial

The Coordinating Committee for Multilateral Export Controls—known by its acronym CoCom—emerged in 1949 as the economic counterpart to NATO's military alliance.[3] Established in the immediate aftermath of the Soviet Union's first successful atomic bomb test, CoCom represented a coordinated Western effort to deny strategic technologies to the Communist bloc. The United States, Belgium, France, Italy, Luxembourg, the Netherlands, and the United Kingdom formed the original membership, later joined by additional NATO allies and Japan.[4]

The rationale was straightforward. In 1949, Congress enacted the Export Control Act, establishing comprehensive peacetime export controls for the first time.[5] The legislation established three justifications for controlling exports: protecting the domestic economy from scarcity, furthering foreign policy objectives, and maintaining vigilance over exports significant to national security.

CoCom operated through informal consensus among its members, maintaining extensive control lists covering arms, nuclear materials, and dual-use technologies. Unlike formal treaties, CoCom depended on voluntary cooperation, with each member nation implementing controls through domestic legislation. The organization maintained three principal lists: the International Munitions List covering military items, the Atomic Energy List addressing nuclear materials and technology, and the Industrial List encompassing dual-use technologies with both civilian and military applications.[6] Headquartered in Paris, the organization operated through regular meetings where member states reviewed proposed exports and maintained updated lists of controlled technologies.

The operational mechanics reflected Cold War realities. Member nations agreed to deny export licenses for controlled items destined for Communist bloc countries unless the entire committee approved the transfer. In practice, this consensus requirement gave the United States—as the dominant Western power and primary source of advanced technology—effective veto authority over allies' proposed exports. The arrangement functioned less as a formal legal regime than as an ongoing consultation mechanism, with decisions implemented through each nation's domestic export control laws.

The effectiveness of this arrangement depended heavily on the geopolitical circumstances of the era. Cross-bloc trade was inherently limited; the Soviet Union and its allies did not actively pursue open commercial relationships with Western nations. The Cold War's ideological divide created natural barriers to technology transfer. Soviet economic doctrine emphasized self-reliance and import substitution; Western firms faced few commercial incentives to breach embargo lines when Eastern markets offered limited profit potential.

Yet CoCom was never without controversy, even among its members. European allies frequently chafed at American dominance of the regime and what they perceived as excessive restrictions that cost their industries profitable business opportunities. French officials characterized CoCom as inconsistent with the spirit of détente.[7] The British government periodically resisted stringent controls, concerned about commercial competitiveness. Japan, originally excluded from CoCom, was compelled to participate despite growing trade relationships with Communist nations.

The fundamental tension between commercial interests and strategic objectives persisted throughout CoCom's existence. American officials pressed for comprehensive restrictions;

European partners advocated narrower controls focused on genuinely military-critical technologies. Debates over specific items—whether particular machine tools, computer systems, or telecommunications equipment warranted control—consumed endless committee sessions. The compromise typically involved tiered lists distinguishing between strictly embargoed military items and dual-use technologies subject to case-by-case review.

The regime's most dramatic failure came in the 1980s with the Toshiba-Kongsberg scandal. In what became the defining technology espionage case of the Cold War era, Japan's Toshiba Machine Company supplied eight computer-guided propeller milling machines to the Soviet Union between 1982 and 1984, while Norway's Kongsberg Vaapenfabrik provided sophisticated numerical controllers.[8] These machines enabled the Soviets to manufacture dramatically quieter submarine propellers. Before the technology transfer, NATO forces could detect Soviet submarines at distances of approximately 200 nautical miles; afterward, detection range dropped substantially.[9] The Pentagon concluded that the technology transfer "contributed to the recent rapid improvement in the quietness of the Soviet Union Navy's nuclear-powered attack submarines."[10] The scandal revealed the fundamental weakness of any export control regime: enforcement depends entirely on the vigilance and commitment of participating nations.

CoCom ultimately dissolved on March 31, 1994, a victim of its own success and the geopolitical transformation following the Soviet collapse.[11] The November 1993 High Level Meeting in The Hague saw representatives of the 17 CoCom member states agree to terminate the organization and establish a new multilateral arrangement. Many viewed CoCom as an outdated relic that impeded East-West economic engagement in an era of globalization.

Its successor, the Wassenaar Arrangement on Export Controls for Conventional Arms and Dual-Use Goods and Technologies, was formally established in July 1996 following negotiations that included former Soviet bloc states.[12] The 33 founding members included Russia, Czech Republic, Hungary, Poland, and Slovakia—countries that had been CoCom's primary targets. The arrangement adopted a fundamentally different approach from its predecessor. Rather than targeting specific adversaries, Wassenaar focused on "states of concern" and operated through voluntary information sharing rather than coordinated denial.

Critically, as the Arms Control Association notes, "Wassenaar members also lack veto authority over other member's proposed exports, a power that COCOM members exercised."[13] This structural change reflected the post-Cold War consensus that rigid bloc-based restrictions were both obsolete and economically counterproductive. Member states retained sovereign authority over their own export licensing decisions; Wassenaar served primarily as a forum for exchanging information about transfers and building transparency among participants. Russia itself became a participating state, further diluting the arrangement's capacity for strategic technology denial.[14]

The practical implications of this transformation proved significant. Under CoCom, American objections could effectively block allied exports to Communist countries. Under Wassenaar, a U.S. denial of an export license created no obligation on other member states to follow suit. Critics characterized this as the absence of a "no-undercut" rule—permitting one nation to approve a transfer that another had rejected, potentially rendering individual denials meaningless. Proponents argued that transparency and consultation would naturally align member state policies without requiring formal veto mechanisms.

The quarter-century between CoCom's dissolution and the October 2022 semiconductor rules saw export controls recede as a primary tool of strategic competition. The prevailing assumption held that economic interdependence would moderate behavior, that integration into global markets would encourage responsible conduct, and that attempting to deny technology in a globalized economy was both futile and counterproductive. China's 2001 accession to the World Trade Organization embodied this optimism. Western policymakers believed that trade liberalization would catalyze political reform, that market participation would create stakeholders invested in the rules-based international order, and that attempting to maintain technological barriers would simply redirect resources toward indigenous development.

That assumption proved tragically mistaken.

The Architecture of Modern Semiconductor Controls

The October 7, 2022 regulations represented the most significant expansion of U.S. export controls in decades. The Bureau of Industry and Security imposed restrictions across multiple dimensions: advanced computing chips themselves, the equipment used to manufacture them, and even the human capital necessary to operate Chinese semiconductor facilities.[15]

The technical specifications were precise and revealing. The rules established new Export Control Classification Numbers for advanced integrated circuits meeting specific performance thresholds, including ECCN 3A090 for advanced computing integrated circuits and ECCN 4A090 for computers containing such circuits.[16] Controls extended to semiconductor manufacturing equipment, particularly the sophisticated lithography machines used to etch microscopic circuit patterns onto silicon wafers. Perhaps most dramatically, the regulations restricted the ability of "U.S. persons"—including American citizens and permanent residents—from supporting the development or production of advanced semiconductors at certain Chinese facilities.[17]

This last provision carried extraordinary implications. American engineers working at Chinese chip manufacturers faced a stark choice: leave immediately or face potential criminal liability. The rule forced "U.S. citizens as well as green card holders to leave and stay out of China's semiconductor industry," disrupting ongoing operations and depriving Chinese facilities of critical expertise.[18]

The Bureau of Industry and Security stated the restrictions would "protect U.S. national security interests by restricting the People's Republic of China (China's) military modernization efforts and degrading its ability to violate human rights."[19] The dual-use nature of semiconductor technology—essential for both commercial applications and military systems—made broad restrictions necessary. BIS emphasized that the controlled items could be used to "produce advanced military systems including weapons of mass destruction" and to "improve the speed and accuracy of its military decision making."[20]

The United States moved quickly to update and strengthen these controls. In October 2023, BIS issued revised rules closing loopholes that had emerged in the original restrictions. These updates adjusted technical thresholds for controlled chips, imposed new licensing requirements on additional countries beyond China to prevent transshipment and diversion, and expanded controls on semiconductor manufacturing equipment.[21] Commerce Secretary Gina Raimondo described the new measures as "clos[ing] loopholes" in the October 2022 controls.[22]

The Foreign Direct Product Rule and Extraterritorial Reach

The true innovation of modern semiconductor controls lies not merely in what they restrict but in how far they reach. The Foreign Direct Product Rule—a once-obscure provision of the Export Administration Regulations—has become the primary mechanism for extending American jurisdiction over the global semiconductor supply chain.

The FDPR operates on a simple but powerful premise: foreign-made items become subject to U.S. export controls if they are the "direct product" of American technology, software, or manufacturing equipment.[23] This means that semiconductors manufactured entirely outside the United States, with no American physical components, can nonetheless fall under U.S. regulatory authority if their production involved U.S.-origin intellectual property or equipment at any stage.

The rule first gained prominence in 2020 when the Trump administration expanded its application against Huawei Technologies. The Chinese telecommunications giant had been placed on the Entity List in May 2019, restricting its access to items subject to the Export Administration Regulations.[24] Yet Huawei continued obtaining chips manufactured abroad by third parties like Taiwan Semiconductor Manufacturing Company. The expanded FDPR closed this avenue by asserting U.S. jurisdiction over any chips produced using American semiconductor design software or manufacturing equipment—which encompasses virtually all advanced semiconductors worldwide.

The implications were profound. The enhanced FDPR effectively claims control over semiconductor factories worldwide because it affects any facility that relies on American-origin intellectual property.[25] TSMC, the world's leading contract chip manufacturer headquartered in Taiwan, could no longer supply Huawei without U.S. government approval. The same applied to Samsung in South Korea, GlobalFoundries facilities worldwide, and essentially every advanced semiconductor manufacturer on the planet.

The October 2022 rules extended this extraterritorial logic further, creating new FDPR provisions specifically targeting advanced computing and supercomputer applications.[26] Foreign-made items meeting certain performance thresholds became subject to U.S. export controls if produced using specified American technology, regardless of their physical location or the nationality of their manufacturers.

The Seagate case illustrated the FDPR's reach with sobering clarity. On April 19, 2023, the Bureau of Industry and Security imposed a $300 million penalty on Seagate Technology—the largest standalone administrative penalty in BIS history—for supplying hard disk drives to Huawei in violation of export controls.[27] The drives themselves were manufactured outside the United States from largely foreign components. But the production process employed equipment that was itself a direct product of U.S.-origin technology.[28] As BIS explained, Seagate "incorrectly interpreted the FDP rule to require evaluation of only the last stage of its HDD manufacturing process rather than the entire process."[29] Between August 2020 and September 2021, Seagate exported approximately 7.4 million hard disk drives valued at over $1.1 billion to Huawei entities in violation of U.S. controls.[30]

The January 2025 AI Diffusion Rule—and Its Rescission

If the October 2022 semiconductor controls represented a significant expansion of export restrictions, the Biden administration's final regulatory act proved even more ambitious—and ultimately unsustainable.

On January 15, 2025, just days before leaving office, the Department of Commerce published the Framework for Artificial Intelligence Diffusion. The rule imposed worldwide licensing requirements on advanced computing chips and, for the first time, extended export controls to AI model weights—the parameters encoding an artificial intelligence system's learned capabilities.[31]

The framework created a three-tiered system governing the global distribution of advanced chips and AI technology, with different restrictions applying based on destination countries' relationships with the United States.

The rule's scope was breathtaking. Rather than targeting specific adversaries or restricted destinations, the AI Diffusion Framework imposed global licensing requirements for all exports of advanced computing items. Industry critics characterized it as potentially "one of the most destructive [regulations] to ever hit the U.S. technology industry," noting concerns that it would turn "decades of export control policy on its head" by abandoning the traditional approach of controlling exports to designated countries of concern.[32]

Industry reaction was swift and overwhelmingly negative. Nvidia warned that the rule "threatens to squander America's hard-won technological advantage." Major technology firms including Microsoft and Oracle argued that the controls would hinder their ability to compete in foreign markets.[33] The Semiconductor Industry Association urged the incoming administration to assess whether Biden-era policies had achieved their intended effects or merely harmed U.S. commercial interests.

The Trump administration moved quickly upon taking office. In May 2025, the Department of Commerce announced rescission of the AI Diffusion Rule, characterizing it as a measure that "would have stifled American innovation and saddled companies with burdensome new regulatory requirements."[34] The department noted that the rule also "would have undermined U.S. diplomatic relations with dozens of countries by downgrading them to second-tier status." A replacement framework was promised but not immediately forthcoming.

The episode revealed the inherent tensions in technology export control policy. Restrictions comprehensive enough to be strategically effective may prove commercially devastating to American firms competing in global markets. Yet narrowly targeted controls risk creating loopholes that adversaries can exploit. Finding the appropriate balance remains the central challenge of modern export control statecraft.

Entity Lists, End-User Controls, and the Expanding Web of Restrictions

Beyond technology-based controls, the United States has dramatically expanded its use of entity-specific restrictions. The Entity List—first published in 1997 to identify parties involved in weapons proliferation—has grown into a primary tool of technology denial.[35]

An entity's placement on the list subjects it to specific licensing requirements for receiving items subject to the Export Administration Regulations. The practical effect is to cut designated parties off from American technology and, through the FDPR, from foreign-made products incorporating American technology. The Entity List has grown exponentially, with Chinese entities comprising the largest national contingent.

Huawei Technologies' 2019 designation marked a watershed. On May 16, 2019, the Bureau of Industry and Security added Huawei and 68 non-U.S. affiliates located in 26 countries to the Entity List, citing the company's involvement in "activities contrary to the national security or foreign policy interests of the United States."[36] The Federal Register notice stated: "The U.S. Government has determined that there is reasonable cause to believe that Huawei has been involved in activities contrary to the national security or foreign policy interests of the United States."[37] Federal prosecutors had indicted Huawei for violating sanctions on Iran, and intelligence agencies harbored concerns about potential backdoors in Huawei telecommunications equipment.

Subsequent additions have targeted Chinese entities across the semiconductor supply chain, AI developers, quantum computing researchers, and companies allegedly involved in human rights abuses in Xinjiang province.[38] In August 2019, BIS added an additional 46 non-U.S. affiliates of Huawei to the Entity List, concluding that "without the listing of the 46 additional affiliates, and imposition of a license requirement, there is reasonable cause to believe that Huawei would seek to use them to evade the restrictions placed on Huawei and its 68 affiliates listed on May 16, 2019."[39]

The Entity List mechanism has evolved from a targeted proliferation control tool into a broad-spectrum instrument of technology denial. Early listings focused primarily on entities involved in weapons of mass destruction programs or missile development. Contemporary designations encompass a far wider range of activities deemed contrary to U.S. national security interests, including artificial intelligence research, advanced manufacturing, and telecommunications. The expansion reflects the increasingly dual-use nature of cutting-edge technologies—capabilities developed for commercial applications frequently possess military significance, and vice versa.

End-user controls provide another layer of restriction. The Export Administration Regulations prohibit exports when the exporter knows or has reason to know that items will be used for proscribed purposes—including weapons development, military applications, or human rights abuses—regardless of whether the specific end-user appears on any restricted list.[40] This places due diligence obligations on exporters to verify the ultimate destination and application of their products, creating compliance burdens that extend throughout global supply chains. The "knowledge" standard encompasses not merely actual awareness but also "red flags" that would alert a reasonable exporter to potential diversion or misuse.

The Limits of Unilateral Action: Allied Coordination

The effectiveness of American export controls depends critically on cooperation from allies possessing essential semiconductor manufacturing capabilities. Japan and the Netherlands host the world's most sophisticated producers of semiconductor manufacturing equipment: Tokyo Electron, Nikon, and above all, ASML Holding of the Netherlands.

ASML occupies a uniquely powerful position in the semiconductor supply chain. The company's extreme ultraviolet lithography machines—essential for producing the most advanced chips at process nodes below seven nanometers—represent the pinnacle of precision engineering. No other company in the world can manufacture EUV systems.[41] ASML also dominates production of the deep ultraviolet lithography machines used for somewhat less advanced chip manufacturing.

Without Dutch and Japanese participation, American controls would ultimately prove ineffective. Chinese companies denied U.S. equipment and technology could potentially obtain alternatives from allied nations. Recognizing this vulnerability, the Biden administration pursued intensive diplomatic engagement to secure allied cooperation.

The Netherlands announced new export controls on June 30, 2023, requiring ASML to apply for licenses to export its most advanced immersion DUV lithography systems—specifically the TWINSCAN NXT:2000i, NXT:2050i, and NXT:2100i models—outside the European Union.[42] The rules took effect September 1, 2023. ASML was already barred from shipping its most advanced EUV systems to China.[43]

Japan's Ministry of Economy, Trade and Industry imposed export regulations on 23 types of advanced semiconductor manufacturing equipment effective July 23, 2023.[44] The regulations specify which types of semiconductor manufacturing equipment require a license to be legally exported from Japan. The CSIS translation of these documents notes that while the controls apply regardless of destination, "much of the public reporting on the new regulations speculated that they are targeted at China."[45]

Yet the negotiations proved contentious. ASML derived substantial revenue from Chinese customers—China accounted for 24 percent of ASML's total revenue in the second quarter of 2023, representing an increase of 200 percent year-on-year.[46] Both nations faced potential Chinese retaliation—a concern validated when Beijing announced export license requirements for gallium and germanium compounds on July 3, 2023, effective August 1, materials essential for semiconductor production in which China dominates global supply.[47] China accounts for approximately 98 percent of the world's gallium production and about 68 percent of germanium refining.[48]

By September 2024, Dutch authorities further tightened controls, requiring ASML to obtain licenses for servicing previously sold equipment in China and extending restrictions to additional lithography models including the 1970i and 1980i immersion systems.[49] These servicing restrictions carried particular significance: lithography equipment requires continuous maintenance to sustain production yields, and denying service support effectively renders installed machines increasingly unreliable over time. The alignment of controls across the three nations possessing irreplaceable semiconductor manufacturing expertise created genuine barriers to Chinese capability development.

The trilateral framework nonetheless remains incomplete. Other nations possess relevant capabilities—Germany, South Korea, and Taiwan all host significant semiconductor equipment manufacturers. Expanding the coalition to include additional partners presents both opportunities and challenges. Each additional participant brings capabilities that might otherwise leak to China; each also brings domestic commercial interests that may resist stringent restrictions. The European Union has shown increasing interest in coordinating semiconductor policy, though Brussels' approach has emphasized industrial policy and supply chain resilience rather than export restrictions targeting specific adversaries.

Moreover, the controls' effectiveness depends not merely on formal regulations but on their implementation and enforcement. Export control regimes historically suffer from compliance gaps, transshipment through third countries, and outright smuggling. Chinese entities have demonstrated sophisticated capabilities for circumventing restrictions, establishing front companies, routing purchases through intermediaries, and exploiting regulatory ambiguities. The Bureau of Industry and Security's enforcement capacity—while expanding—remains limited relative to the volume of controlled transactions and the sophistication of evasion networks.

The Fundamental Question: Can Technology Be Successfully Denied?

Export controls represent a calculated gamble. They impose costs on adversaries by limiting access to advanced capabilities—but also impose costs on domestic industries denied profitable markets and potentially accelerate adversaries' efforts to develop indigenous alternatives.

The historical record offers ambiguous lessons. CoCom succeeded in maintaining Western technological advantages over the Soviet bloc for decades, but also stimulated extensive Soviet smuggling and reverse-engineering efforts. The Toshiba-Kongsberg scandal demonstrated that even comprehensive regimes can be circumvented. Critics argue that export controls ultimately delayed but did not prevent Soviet acquisition of essential technologies.

The contemporary challenge differs in crucial respects. Unlike the Cold War era, when the Communist bloc existed in relative economic isolation from the West, China is deeply integrated into global supply chains. Chinese companies participate extensively in international commerce; Chinese engineers study at Western universities; Chinese researchers collaborate with international counterparts. The "technology ecosystem" connecting American innovation to Chinese manufacturing developed over decades of deliberate economic engagement.

Unwinding these connections while maintaining effective controls presents unprecedented difficulties. Technologies exist as knowledge in human minds, transferable through digital channels, embedded in commercial products available worldwide. The October 2022 restrictions on U.S. persons supporting Chinese semiconductor facilities acknowledged this reality—attempting to control not merely physical goods but human expertise itself.

Yet the United States possesses asymmetric advantages that did not exist vis-à-vis the Soviet Union. American dominance in semiconductor design software, essential intellectual property, and critical manufacturing equipment creates chokepoints that China cannot easily circumvent. ASML's EUV lithography machines incorporate components from thousands of suppliers worldwide; replicating this supply chain independently would require decades of effort and vast investment.[50]

The fundamental question is whether these advantages can be maintained long enough to matter strategically. China has demonstrated remarkable capacity to develop indigenous technologies when denied foreign alternatives. The next chapters will examine whether American export controls are succeeding in their objectives—or merely accelerating the very technological independence they seek to prevent.

Endnotes

[1] Bureau of Industry and Security, U.S. Department of Commerce, "Commerce Implements New Export Controls on Advanced Computing and Semiconductor Manufacturing Items to the People's Republic of China (PRC)," Press Release, October 7, 2022.

[2] Gregory C. Allen, "Choking off China's Access to the Future of AI," Center for Strategic and International Studies, October 11, 2022, https://www.csis.org/analysis/choking-chinas-access-future-ai.

[3] Wassenaar Arrangement Secretariat, "About Us," https://www.wassenaar.org/about-us/. CoCom was established as the predecessor organization that "ceased to exist on 31 March 1994."

[4] Arms Control Association, "The Wassenaar Arrangement at a Glance," Fact Sheet, https://www.armscontrol.org/factsheets/wassenaar.

[5] Export Control Act of 1949, Pub. L. No. 81-11, 63 Stat. 7 (1949).

[6] National Threat Initiative, "Wassenaar Arrangement," https://www.nti.org/education-center/treaties-and-regimes/wassenaar-arrangement/.

[7] Congressional Research Service, "Military Technology and Conventional Weapons Export Controls: The Wassenaar Arrangement," Report RS20517, September 29, 2006, https://www.everycrsreport.com/reports/RS20517.html.

[8] GlobalSecurity.org, "Toshiba-Kongsberg Incident," https://www.globalsecurity.org/intell/world/russia/toshiba.htm.

[9] Ibid.

[10] King's College London, "The Toshiba-Kongsberg case," May 21, 2019, https://www.kcl.ac.uk/news/the-toshiba-kongsberg-case.

[11] Wassenaar Arrangement Secretariat, "Genesis of the Wassenaar Arrangement," https://www.wassenaar.org/genesis-of-the-wassenaar-arrangement/. "COCOM ceased to exist March 31, 1994."

[12] Wassenaar Arrangement Secretariat, "About Us." "On 11-12 July 1996, the Plenary Meeting resumed... Final consensus on the 'Initial Elements', the basic document of the WA, was reached."

[13] Arms Control Association, "The Wassenaar Arrangement at a Glance."

[14] Center for Arms Control and Non-Proliferation, "Fact Sheet: The Wassenaar Arrangement," March 13, 2023, https://armscontrolcenter.org/fact-sheet-the-wassenaar-arrangement/.

[15] Bureau of Industry and Security, "Commerce Implements New Export Controls," October 7, 2022.

[16] "Implementation of Additional Export Controls: Certain Advanced Computing and Semiconductor Manufacturing Items; Supercomputer and Semiconductor End Use; Entity List Modification," 87 Fed. Reg. 62186 (October 13, 2022), https://www.federalregister.gov/documents/2022/10/13/2022-21658/implementation-of-additional-export-controls-certain-advanced-computing-and-semiconductor.

[17] 15 C.F.R. § 744.6, as amended October 7, 2022, restrictions on activities of U.S. persons.

[18] Allen, "Choking off China's Access to the Future of AI."

[19] "Export Controls on Semiconductor Manufacturing Items," 88 Fed. Reg. 73438 (October 25, 2023), https://www.federalregister.gov/documents/2023/10/25/2023-23049/export-controls-on-semiconductor-manufacturing-items.

[20] Bureau of Industry and Security, "Public Information on Export Controls Imposed on Advanced Computing and Semiconductor Manufacturing Items to the People's Republic of China (PRC)," https://www.bis.doc.gov/index.php/about-bis/newsroom/2082.

[21] Skadden, Arps, Slate, Meagher & Flom LLP, "BIS Updates October 2022 Semiconductor Export Control Rules," October 2023, https://www.skadden.com/insights/publications/2023/10/bis-updates-october-2022-semiconductor-export-control-rules.

[22] Ibid.

[23] 15 C.F.R. § 734.9, Foreign Direct Product Rules.

[24] "Addition of Entities to the Entity List," 84 Fed. Reg. 22961 (May 21, 2019), https://www.federalregister.gov/documents/2019/05/21/2019-10616/addition-of-entities-to-the-entity-list.

[25] Allen, "Choking off China's Access to the Future of AI."

[26] 87 Fed. Reg. 62186, establishing Advanced Computing FDP Rule and Supercomputer FDP Rule.

[27] Bureau of Industry and Security, "BIS Imposes $300 Million Penalty Against Seagate," Press Release, April 19, 2023, https://www.bis.doc.gov/index.php/documents/about-bis/newsroom/press-releases/3264-2023-04-19-bis-press-release-seagate-settlement/file.

[28] Ibid.

[29] Ibid.

[30] Ibid. "Seagate... engaged in conduct prohibited by the EAR on 429 occasions... resulting in the transfer of 7,420,496 foreign-produced HDDs valued at approximately $1,104,732,205."

[31] Bureau of Industry and Security, "Biden-Harris Administration Announces Regulatory Framework for Responsible Diffusion of Advanced Artificial Intelligence," January 13, 2025, https://www.bis.gov/press-release/biden-harris-administration-announces-regulatory-framework-responsible-diffusion-advanced-artificial.

[32] Oracle Corporation, "Export Control Diffusion Confusion," January 5, 2025, https://www.oracle.com/news/announcement/blog/export-control-diffusion-confusion-2025-01-05/.

[33] Ibid.

[34] Bureau of Industry and Security, "Department of Commerce Announces Rescission of Biden-Era Artificial Intelligence Diffusion Rule," May 2025, https://www.bis.gov/press-release/department-commerce-announces-rescission-biden-era-artificial-intelligence-diffusion-rule-strengthens.

[35] Bureau of Industry and Security, Entity List, Supplement No. 4 to Part 744 of the Export Administration Regulations.

[36] 84 Fed. Reg. 22961 (May 21, 2019).

[37] Ibid.

[38] "Addition of Certain Entities to the Entity List and Revision of Entries on the Entity List," 84 Fed. Reg. 43493 (August 21, 2019), https://www.federalregister.gov/documents/2019/08/21/2019-17921/addition-of-certain-entities-to-the-entity-list-and-revision-of-entries-on-the-entity-list.

[39] Ibid.

[40] 15 C.F.R. § 744, Control Policy: End-User and End-Use Based.

[41] CNBC, "Netherlands, home to a critical chip firm, follows U.S. with export curbs on semiconductor tools," June 30, 2023, https://www.cnbc.com/2023/06/30/netherlands-follows-us-with-semiconductor-export-restrictions-.html.

[42] Ibid. "ASML said it will now need to apply for a license to export its most advanced immersion DUV lithography systems, called the TWINSCAN NXT:2000i and subsequent tools."

[43] Ibid.

[44] Hogan Lovells, "Japan's New Chip Equipment Export Rules Take Effect," August 2023, https://www.hoganlovells.com/en/publications/japans-new-chip-equipment-export-rules-take-effect.

[45] Gregory C. Allen and Emily Benson, "CSIS Translation: Updated Japanese Export Controls on High-Performance Semiconductor Manufacturing Equipment," Center for Strategic and International Studies, https://www.csis.org/analysis/csis-translation-updated-japanese-export-controls-high-performance-semiconductor.

[46] TechNode, "ASML's export to China valid until year-end," September 4, 2023, https://technode.com/2023/09/04/asmls-export-of-chip-making-machines-to-china-valid-until-year-end/.

[47] China's Ministry of Commerce, "Announcement on the Implementation of Export Control on Gallium and Germanium-related Items," July 3, 2023. See also CNN Business, "Germanium, gallium: China hits back in the chip war with export curbs on key raw materials," July 3, 2023, https://www.cnn.com/2023/07/03/business/germanium-gallium-china-export-restrictions/index.html.

[48] ING, "China strikes back in the tech war, restricting exports of gallium and germanium," July 7, 2023, https://www.ing.com/Newsroom/News/China-strikes-back-in-the-tech-war-restricting-exports-of-gallium-and-germanium.htm.

[49] South China Morning Post, "China hit hard by new Dutch export controls on ASML chip-making equipment," September 16, 2024, https://www.scmp.com/tech/tech-war/article/3278535/china-hit-hard-new-dutch-export-controls-asml-chip-making-equipment.

[50] ASML Holding N.V., Annual Reports and corporate disclosures on supply chain complexity.

Part II

The Silicon Battlefield

Chapter 4

Chip War—The Fight for the World's Most Critical Technology

Why Semiconductors Became the New Oil

In the sprawling fabrication facilities along Taiwan's western coast, machines worth hundreds of millions of dollars operate around the clock, etching circuit patterns onto silicon wafers with tolerances measured in atoms. These facilities, separated by just 110 miles of water from mainland China, produce the advanced processors that power everything from smartphones to supercomputers, from autonomous vehicles to artificial intelligence systems.[1] The concentration of such critical manufacturing capability in a single location represents what the National Security Commission on Artificial Intelligence warned in 2021 was an unacceptable strategic vulnerability: "We do not want to overstate the precariousness of our position, but given that the vast majority of cutting-edge chips are produced at a single plant separated by just 110 miles of water from our principal strategic competitor, we must reevaluate the meaning of supply chain resilience and security."[2] This chapter examines how semiconductors emerged as the defining strategic resource of the twenty-first century, and why the battle for control over their production now shapes the trajectory of great power competition.

The Strategic Foundations of Semiconductor Supremacy

The transformation of semiconductors from mere electronic components into objects of geopolitical contestation reflects their unique role in enabling virtually every dimension of modern power. Unlike oil, which primarily fueled industrial-age economies, semiconductors constitute the foundational layer upon which both military capability and economic competitiveness are constructed. As economic historian Chris Miller observed in his Financial Times Business Book of the Year, semiconductors have become essential for military and defense technology, weaponry, and equipment; broader geopolitically significant technologies such as artificial intelligence and quantum computing; and the critical infrastructure upon which the daily functioning of societies depends.[3]

The military applications of advanced semiconductors extend far beyond the battlefield systems that casual observers might imagine. While many legacy weapons platforms continue to operate with older chip generations, the cutting-edge of American strategic advantage depends crucially on high-performance computing systems bristling with advanced processors. These supercomputers enable everything from nuclear deterrence modeling to rapid intelligence analysis, driving the foundation of American strategic military advantage.[4] The NSCAI Final Report noted that if a potential adversary bests the United States in semiconductors over the long term or suddenly cuts off U.S. access to cutting-edge chips entirely, it could gain the upper hand in every domain of warfare.[5]

The importance of semiconductors to military modernization explains why Beijing has placed such emphasis on developing indigenous chip-making capabilities. A Bureau of Industry and Security assessment stated that the semiconductor manufacturing equipment controlled by export control rules is needed to produce advanced-node integrated circuits, which are necessary for advanced weapon systems and advanced AI used in military applications.[6] Chinese Communist Party leadership at the highest levels has stressed the importance of building an indigenous semiconductor ecosystem, referring to integrated circuits as critical to national security and military capabilities.[7] The People's Liberation Army's pursuit of "intelligentized" warfare—where algorithms and computing power determine outcomes—makes access to advanced processors an existential priority.

Beyond military applications, semiconductors underpin the full spectrum of technologies that will determine economic leadership in the coming decades. Artificial intelligence systems depend on specialized processors for training and inference. Autonomous vehicles require real-time processing of sensor data. Advanced telecommunications networks, renewable energy systems, and medical diagnostic equipment all rely on sophisticated semiconductor components. As Miller noted, China now spends more money each year importing chips than it spends on oil, underscoring the centrality of these components to the modern economy.[8]

NVIDIA's Impossible Position: Engineering Around Export Controls

No company better illustrates the tensions between commercial imperatives and national security restrictions than NVIDIA Corporation. The Santa Clara-based chipmaker has become the dominant force in artificial intelligence computing, with its graphics processing units (GPUs) serving as the essential hardware substrate for training large language models and other AI systems. Yet NVIDIA's commercial success depends significantly on accessing the Chinese market, which historically represented a substantial portion of its revenues. This dependence placed the company in an increasingly difficult position as U.S. export controls tightened.

The October 2022 export control rules issued by the Bureau of Industry and Security prohibited exports to China of NVIDIA's most advanced processors, including the A100 and H100 GPUs.[9] The regulations established performance thresholds intended to prevent China from accessing chips capable of training frontier AI models or enabling advanced military applications. In response, NVIDIA embarked on an extraordinary engineering effort: designing processors that delivered meaningful capability to Chinese customers while remaining just below the control thresholds.

The first product of this effort was the A800, essentially an A100 with its NVLink interconnect bandwidth reduced from 600 gigabytes per second to 400 gigabytes per second.[10] Similarly, when the H100 faced export restrictions, NVIDIA introduced the H800, featuring interconnect bandwidth of approximately 300 gigabytes per second compared to 900 gigabytes per second on the original model.[11] These modifications represented a deliberate crippling of chip capabilities to achieve compliance—a remarkable instance of innovation running in reverse, as companies intentionally capped performance to permit global sales.

The October 2023 update to export controls tightened parameters further. Recognizing that Chinese customers could partially compensate for reduced interconnect speeds through other techniques, BIS revised its approach. The updated rules removed interconnect bandwidth as a controlling parameter and instead emphasized total processing performance and a new "performance density" threshold designed to preempt future workarounds.[12] The A800 and H800 were now blocked from export.

NVIDIA's response was the H20—a dramatically stripped-down version of the H100 architecture. Built on the same Hopper platform, the H20 carries substantially less computational capacity than its more powerful siblings. The H20 stays below export control limits precisely because of its reduced performance density, a formula balancing computational capability against chip size.[13] The logic behind this threshold was straightforward: delivering high computing power in a small area requires reliance on advanced manufacturing processes that Washington sought to deny Beijing.

Yet the story did not end there. In April 2025, the Trump administration moved to block even the H20 from export to China without a specific license.[14] The Commerce Department determined that even these reduced-capability chips could contribute to China's AI development in ways that raised national security concerns. NVIDIA disclosed in regulatory filings that the restriction threatened significant revenue losses.[15] The company's CEO Jensen Huang ramped up lobbying efforts against export controls, arguing they inhibited American technological leadership rather than securing it.

By mid-2025, however, the administration partially reversed course. In July 2025, NVIDIA announced that the U.S. government had assured licenses would be granted for H20 sales to China, and the company hoped to resume deliveries soon.[16] The reversal reportedly reflected bargaining over broader trade issues, including China's rare earth export controls that threatened American supply chains.

The back-and-forth over the H20 revealed the inherent tensions in using export controls as instruments of technology denial. Each tightening pushed NVIDIA to develop compliant alternatives; each new product prompted further regulatory adjustment. Meanwhile, the uncertainty roiled markets, complicated customer relationships, and raised questions about whether the controls achieved their intended purpose of constraining Chinese AI development.

The August 2025 Compromise: Revenue Sharing and Implications

The July 2025 decision to permit licensed H20 sales represented what observers characterized as a transactional bargain rather than a strategic reversal.[17] Washington was willing to grant limited access in exchange for leverage, while maintaining deliberate downgrading to slow China's technological advance. The compromise illustrated the administration's attempt to balance multiple objectives: denying China access to frontier capabilities, preserving American companies' revenues, and managing the broader bilateral relationship.

Yet hardly had this compromise stabilized when new complications emerged. In August 2025, reports indicated that Beijing had warned Chinese companies to avoid NVIDIA's H20 chips, citing potential security concerns about backdoor access to sensitive data.[18] The Chinese government urged domestic enterprises to transition to chips designed and manufactured within China. NVIDIA disputed the security allegations, but the damage was done: political tensions had transformed a commercial product into an object of suspicion.

NVIDIA's response was to accelerate development of additional China-specific products. Reports emerged that the company was designing a new chip more powerful than the H20 but still compliant with U.S. export regulations.[19] This successor was intended to offer meaningful performance while meeting regulatory requirements. The company opened a research and development center in Shanghai, prompting concerns about technology transfer even as it sought to maintain market presence.

The deeper issue these events revealed was the limited efficacy of chip-by-chip export controls in a technologically dynamic environment. Each control threshold established a target around which companies engineered; each compliant product enabled Chinese customers to continue developing AI capabilities, even if at reduced efficiency. Meanwhile, the controls created powerful incentives for China to accelerate indigenous semiconductor development, potentially achieving precisely the self-sufficiency that American policy sought to prevent.

Commerce Department testimony acknowledged these tensions. Under Secretary for Industry and Security Jeffrey Kessler told lawmakers in June 2025 that while export controls had constrained Chinese chip production, "China is investing huge amounts to increase its AI chip production, as well as the capabilities of the chips it produces. So it's critical for us not to have a false sense of security to understand that China is catching up quickly."[20]

ASML and the Lithography Chokepoint

If NVIDIA controls the design of advanced AI chips, the Netherlands-based firm ASML Holding controls something arguably more important: the only machines capable of manufacturing them. ASML's extreme ultraviolet (EUV) lithography systems represent the culmination of decades of research, billions of dollars in investment, and contributions from suppliers across multiple continents. Without these systems, fabricating semiconductors at leading-edge nodes is essentially impossible.

EUV lithography works by projecting patterns onto silicon wafers using light with a wavelength of just 13.5 nanometers—far shorter than conventional deep ultraviolet (DUV) systems.[21] The technology required overcoming extraordinary engineering challenges, including generating the EUV light source by firing high-energy lasers at tin droplets to create plasma, then capturing and focusing the resulting radiation through an elaborate system of mirrors manufactured to atomic-level precision.[22] While ASML sold only 44 EUV machines in 2024, compared to 374 cheaper DUV machines, these advanced systems accounted for 38 percent of the company's system sales revenue due to their approximately $220 million price tag, with newer High NA machines commanding around $400 million each.[23]

ASML's monopoly on EUV technology creates a chokepoint that export controls can exploit with unusual effectiveness. Unlike chips themselves, which flow through complex supply chains with multiple points of potential diversion, EUV machines are massive systems requiring extensive installation support and ongoing maintenance. ASML has never sold an EUV system to China, and under current export controls, it is prohibited from doing so.[24]

The EUV restrictions forced Chinese semiconductor manufacturers to rely on older DUV technology, which can fabricate chips at 7-nanometer nodes and above through multi-patterning techniques but cannot economically produce smaller geometries. This technology gap explains why China's most advanced indigenous chips lag approximately two generations behind the cutting edge, a deficit that cannot be closed without access to EUV machines or development of domestic alternatives.

Yet the story of ASML and China extends beyond EUV to the company's more mature DUV systems. As controls tightened in 2023 and 2024, the Dutch government, under American pressure, imposed export licensing requirements on ASML's most advanced DUV immersion lithography tools.[25] By January 2024, ASML announced that a license for the shipment of its NXT:2050i and NXT:2100i lithography systems had been partially revoked by the Dutch government.[26] The restrictions were intended to limit China's ability to expand production even at mature nodes, constraining the growth of its domestic semiconductor industry.

Chinese customers responded to the looming restrictions by accelerating purchases of equipment that remained legally exportable. In 2024, China represented an extraordinarily high proportion of ASML's revenues—reportedly reaching 49 percent of sales in the second quarter—as domestic chipmakers stockpiled DUV systems ahead of tighter controls.[27] ASML's 2025 guidance anticipated a significant decline in Chinese sales, projecting the country would return to approximately 20 percent of revenue as restrictions took full effect.[28]

The Dutch company found itself navigating between American pressure and Chinese commercial relationships accumulated over decades. China's efforts to develop domestic lithography alternatives intensified in response to these pressures. Shanghai-based firms pursued DUV systems capable of 28-nanometer production, with reports in late 2025 indicating testing at SMIC facilities.[29] More ambitious programs sought to develop indigenous EUV capability, exploring alternative approaches to generating the required 13.5-nanometer light. Yet technical reports acknowledged that these efforts faced significant obstacles, and that matching ASML's performance and reliability would require years of additional development.[30]

Taiwan's TSMC: The Indispensable Foundry

At the center of the global semiconductor supply chain stands Taiwan Semiconductor Manufacturing Company, a firm whose dominance defies easy comprehension. TSMC manufactures over 90 percent of the world's most advanced logic chips, including virtually all processors for artificial intelligence applications.[31] Apple, NVIDIA, AMD, Qualcomm, and numerous other technology companies depend entirely on TSMC's foundries for their most sophisticated products.

TSMC's dominance reflects both the economics of semiconductor manufacturing and the strategic decisions of its founder, Morris Chang. Born in Ningbo, China in 1931, Chang immigrated to the United States and earned degrees from MIT (bachelor's and master's in mechanical engineering) before receiving his doctorate from Stanford in 1964.[32] He built his career at Texas Instruments, where he worked for 25 years and rose to senior vice president in charge of the company's global semiconductor business.[33] In 1985, Taiwan's government recruited him to lead the Industrial Technology Research Institute (ITRI), and in 1987 he founded TSMC with backing from the Taiwanese government and Philips.[34]

Chang's insight was that semiconductor manufacturing had become so capital-intensive that most chip designers could no longer afford their own fabrication facilities. By creating a "pure-play" foundry focused exclusively on manufacturing for others, TSMC could achieve economies of scale that made competition extremely difficult. The strategy proved devastatingly effective. TSMC invested relentlessly in advancing its manufacturing processes, moving to ever-smaller nodes that packed more transistors into each chip.

By 2024, TSMC commanded 64 percent of the global pure-play foundry market, with its share reaching 67.1 percent by the fourth quarter.[35] In the second quarter of 2025, the company's market share surged to a record 70.2 percent, driven by higher shipments and average selling prices.[36] Samsung, the second-largest player, held just 7 to 8 percent of the market—a gap that had widened rather than narrowed over time. At leading-edge nodes of 5 nanometers and below, TSMC's dominance was even more pronounced.

The geopolitical implications of this concentration have not been lost on policymakers. The CHIPS and Science Act, signed into law in 2022, allocated over $50 billion to revitalize American semiconductor manufacturing, with a significant portion supporting construction of new fabrication facilities.[37] TSMC committed to building three advanced fabs in Phoenix, Arizona, representing more than $65 billion in investment—the largest foreign direct investment in a greenfield project in American history.[38] The U.S. Department of Commerce awarded TSMC Arizona up to $6.6 billion in direct funding under the CHIPS Incentives Program, plus up to $5 billion in proposed loans.[39]

Yet even with these investments, the concentration of semiconductor manufacturing in East Asia will persist for years. Building a single advanced fab requires three to five years; training the specialized workforce takes longer still. Morris Chang himself has expressed skepticism about whether American manufacturing can replicate Taiwanese efficiency and cost structures, stating in a 2022 interview with the Brookings Institution that the U.S. government's efforts to increase onshore chip manufacturing would be "a very expensive and wasteful exercise in futility."[40]

Commerce Department Testimony: Constraints on Huawei

While American companies navigated export control restrictions, China's technology champions pursued alternative paths forward. None was more significant than Huawei Technologies, the Shenzhen-based firm that had emerged as a global leader in telecommunications equipment before facing sweeping U.S. sanctions. Cut off from American chips and software, Huawei turned inward, developing its own Ascend series of AI processors and working with domestic foundries to fabricate them.

The extent of Huawei's progress became a matter of intense debate in Washington. The company revealed little publicly about its manufacturing capabilities, and estimates varied widely. In June 2025, testimony before Congress provided an official assessment of Huawei's production constraints. Under Secretary of Commerce Jeffrey Kessler told a House Foreign Affairs subcommittee that Huawei's estimated 2025 Ascend chip production capacity was "at or below 200,000" units.[41] Most of these processors would be delivered within China, he added, limiting their global proliferation.

The 200,000-unit figure represented a significant constraint relative to demand. Chinese technology companies had grown accustomed to deploying tens of thousands of GPUs for AI training and inference; 200,000 chips across an entire national economy would not satisfy requirements. Reports suggested that major Chinese AI labs continued to rely heavily on existing inventories of NVIDIA processors acquired before export controls tightened, or on H20 chips that remained available under licensing arrangements.[42]

Yet the assessment came with caveats. Kessler cautioned lawmakers against taking "too much comfort" from the numbers, warning that "China is investing huge amounts to increase its AI chip production, as well as the capabilities of the chips it produces."[43] The administration's concern was that Chinese capabilities were improving rapidly, even if current production remained limited.

Other analyses suggested higher production figures. Industry reports indicated Huawei was delivering over 800,000 Ascend 910B and 910C chips in 2025 to clients including state telecommunications firms and ByteDance.[44] The discrepancy with the Commerce Department's estimate may have reflected different definitional assumptions or access to different intelligence.

Regardless, both assessments agreed that Huawei was producing AI chips in meaningful volumes despite sanctions—a testament to the difficulty of completely denying technology to a determined adversary.

Huawei's chips were fabricated primarily at Semiconductor Manufacturing International Corporation (SMIC), China's largest foundry. SMIC had achieved 7-nanometer production capability despite lacking EUV lithography, using multi-patterning techniques with DUV systems.[45] The process was more expensive and lower-yielding than TSMC's equivalent, but it worked.

The administration's export control strategy had thus created a genuine constraint on Chinese AI development, even if the constraint was partial rather than total. Chinese firms could access some advanced computing capability through legal H20 purchases, smuggled chips, domestically produced Ascend processors, and cloud services. But the overall compute available to the Chinese AI ecosystem remained substantially below what American firms could deploy—a gap the National Security Commission had identified as essential for maintaining U.S. technological leadership.

Whether this gap would persist was the critical uncertainty. As DeepSeek demonstrated in January 2025, algorithmic efficiency could partially compensate for hardware limitations. The company's V3 research paper stated that its models were trained on 2,788,000 GPU-hours using NVIDIA H800 chips.[46] Chinese researchers were innovating to extract maximum performance from constrained resources, using techniques such as Mixture-of-Experts architectures that activate only relevant portions of the model for each query, dramatically reducing computational requirements.[47]

The response to DeepSeek's breakthrough illustrated the paradoxes inherent in semiconductor export controls. American policymakers had designed restrictions to prevent China from training frontier AI models, yet DeepSeek demonstrated that ingenious software could partially compensate for hardware limitations. At the same time, the restrictions had succeeded in making Chinese AI development more difficult and expensive—the H800 chips DeepSeek used were themselves products of export control compliance, significantly less capable than the H100s available to American companies.[48]

The smuggling networks that emerged to circumvent export controls added another layer of complexity. Federal prosecutors charged multiple individuals in 2025 with illegally exporting NVIDIA GPUs to China through intermediaries in Malaysia, Singapore, and Thailand.[49] The Department of Justice alleged that some shipments involved hundreds of A100 and H100 chips worth millions of dollars. While law enforcement disrupted some networks, the persistence of smuggling operations suggested that demand for restricted chips remained intense, and that enforcement alone could not fully seal the technology gap.[50]

The semiconductor competition between the United States and China thus remained fundamentally unresolved. Export controls had created genuine constraints on Chinese capabilities while simultaneously accelerating Beijing's drive for self-sufficiency. American companies found themselves caught between national security imperatives and commercial interests. And the geographic concentration of advanced manufacturing in Taiwan persisted as a strategic vulnerability that neither policy changes nor corporate investments had yet adequately addressed. The chip war, in other words, remained far from decided.

Endnotes

[1] National Security Commission on Artificial Intelligence, "Chair and Vice Chair Letter," *Final Report* (Washington, DC: NSCAI, March 2021), https://reports.nscai.gov/final-report/chair-and-vice-chair-letter.

[2] National Security Commission on Artificial Intelligence, "Chair and Vice Chair Letter."

[3] Chris Miller, *Chip War: The Fight for the World's Most Critical Technology* (New York: Scribner, 2022), xvi–xviii.

[4] National Security Commission on Artificial Intelligence, "Chapter 13: Microelectronics," *Final Report* (Washington, DC: NSCAI, March 2021), https://reports.nscai.gov/final-report/chapter-13.

[5] National Security Commission on Artificial Intelligence, "Chapter 13: Microelectronics."

[6] Bureau of Industry and Security, U.S. Department of Commerce, "Commerce Strengthens Export Controls to Restrict China's Capability to Produce Advanced Semiconductors for Military Modernization," press release, December 2, 2024, https://www.bis.gov/press-release/commerce-strengthens-export-controls-restrict-chinas-capability-produce-advanced-semiconductors-military.

[7] Bureau of Industry and Security, "Commerce Strengthens Export Controls."

[8] Miller, *Chip War*, xviii.

[9] Bureau of Industry and Security, U.S. Department of Commerce, "Implementation of Additional Export Controls: Certain Advanced Computing and Semiconductor Manufacturing Items; Supercomputer and Semiconductor End Use; Entity List Modification," 87 Fed. Reg. 62186 (October 13, 2022), https://www.federalregister.gov/documents/2022/10/13/2022-21658/implementation-of-additional-export-controls-certain-advanced-computing-and-semiconductor.

[10] Stephen Nellis and Jane Lee, "Nvidia Tweaks Flagship H100 Chip for Export to China as H800," Reuters, March 22, 2023.

[11] Nellis and Lee, "Nvidia Tweaks Flagship H100 Chip."

[12] Bureau of Industry and Security, U.S. Department of Commerce, "Public Information on Export Controls Imposed on Advanced Computing and Semiconductor Manufacturing Items to the People's Republic of China (PRC) in 2022 and 2023," https://www.bis.doc.gov/index.php/about-bis/newsroom/2082.

[13] European Centre for International Political Economy, "H20 Back in the Chinese Market: Washington's Calculated Adjustment," July 2025, https://ecipe.org/blog/nvidia-in-chinese-market/.

[14] Matt O'Brien, "H20 Nvidia Chip Controls May Backfire on Washington," Foreign Policy, April 30, 2025, https://foreignpolicy.com/2025/04/30/h20-nvidia-chips-ai-china-restrictions/.

[15] O'Brien, "H20 Nvidia Chip Controls May Backfire."

[16] Arjun Kharpal, "Nvidia Says It Will Resume H20 AI Chip Sales to China 'Soon,' Following U.S. Government Assurances," CNBC, July 15, 2025, https://www.cnbc.com/2025/07/15/nvidia-says-us-government-will-allow-it-to-resume-h20-ai-chip-sales-to-china.html.

[17] European Centre for International Political Economy, "H20 Back in the Chinese Market."

[18] "Trump Lifted the AI Chip Ban on China, Clearing Nvidia and AMD to Resume Sales: Now What?," Built In, September 17, 2025, https://builtin.com/articles/trump-lifts-ai-chip-ban-china-nvidia.

[19] Built In, "Trump Lifted the AI Chip Ban."

[20] "Huawei's AI Chip Output Limited to 200,000 in 2025, US Commerce Official Says," South China Morning Post, June 13, 2025, https://www.scmp.com/tech/tech-war/article/3314356/huaweis-ai-semiconductor-output-limited-200000-2025-us-commerce-official-says.

[21] ASML Holding N.V., "Our Technology," accessed November 2025, https://www.asml.com/en/technology.

[22] Miller, *Chip War*, 253–267.

[23] "Exclusive Look: How ASML EUV Machines Are Powering Revolutionary High NA Lithography for AI Chips in 2025," Employment & Business News, June 17, 2025, https://www.whatjobs.com/news/asml-euv-machines-ai-chipmaking-2025/.

[24] Ryan Browne, "ASML 2025 Outlook Shows US Chip Export Curbs Impacting China Sales," CNBC, October 16, 2024, https://www.cnbc.com/2024/10/16/asml-2025-outlook-shows-us-chip-export-curbs-impacting-china-sales.html.

[25] Browne, "ASML 2025 Outlook."

[26] Ryan Browne, "ASML Blocked from Exporting Some Critical Chipmaking Tools to China," CNBC, January 2, 2024, https://www.cnbc.com/2024/01/02/asml-blocked-from-exporting-some-critical-chipmaking-tools-to-china.html.

[27] Browne, "ASML 2025 Outlook."

[28] Browne, "ASML 2025 Outlook."

[29] TrendForce, "Decoding China's Lithography Push to Challenge ASML: From SiCarrier to Alternative EUV Paths," November 10, 2025, https://www.trendforce.com/news/2025/11/10/news-decoding-chinas-lithography-push-to-challenge-asml-from-sicarrier-to-alternative-euv-paths/.

[30] TrendForce, "Decoding China's Lithography Push."

[31] National Institute of Standards and Technology, U.S. Department of Commerce, "TSMC Arizona," accessed November 2025, https://www.nist.gov/chips/tsmc-arizona-phoenix.

[32] "Morris Chang," *Encyclopaedia Britannica*, accessed November 2025, https://www.britannica.com/money/Morris-Chang.

[33] *Encyclopaedia Britannica*, "Morris Chang."

[34] "Morris Chang," Wikipedia, last modified October 2025, https://en.wikipedia.org/wiki/Morris_Chang; Morris Chang, Oral History Interview, SEMI, https://www.semi.org/en/Oral-History-Interview-Morris-Chang.

[35] TrendForce, "TSMC Market Share Tops 67% in Q4: Advisory Firm," Focus Taiwan, March 15, 2025, https://focustaiwan.tw/business/202503150014.

[36] TrendForce, "TSMC's Global Market Share Hits New High of 70.2% in Q2," Focus Taiwan, September 6, 2025, https://focustaiwan.tw/business/202509060012.

[37] CHIPS and Science Act, Pub. L. No. 117-167, 136 Stat. 1366 (2022).

[38] U.S. Department of Commerce, "Biden-Harris Administration Announces CHIPS Incentives Award with TSMC Arizona to Secure U.S. Leadership in Advanced Semiconductor Technology," press release, November 15, 2024, https://www.commerce.gov/news/press-releases/2024/11/biden-harris-administration-announces-chips-incentives-award-tsmc.

[39] U.S. Department of Commerce, "Biden-Harris Administration Announces CHIPS Incentives Award."

[40] Morris Chang, interview at Brookings Institution, 2022, cited in Wikipedia, "Morris Chang."

[41] South China Morning Post, "Huawei's AI Chip Output Limited to 200,000."

[42] Gregory C. Allen, "DeepSeek: A Deep Dive," Center for Strategic and International Studies, April 15, 2025, https://www.csis.org/analysis/deepseek-deep-dive.

[43] South China Morning Post, "Huawei's AI Chip Output Limited to 200,000."

[44] TrendForce, "Huawei Advances, but U.S. Reportedly States China's Advanced Chip Output Limited to 200K," June 5, 2025, https://www.trendforce.com/news/2025/06/05/news-huawei-advances-but-u-s-reportedly-states-chinas-advanced-chip-output-limited-to-200k-amid-controls/.

[45] Allen, "DeepSeek: A Deep Dive."

[46] Allen, "DeepSeek: A Deep Dive."

[47] "DeepSeek: How a Small Chinese AI Company Is Shaking Up US Tech Heavyweights," University of Sydney News, January 29, 2025, https://www.sydney.edu.au/news-opinion/news/2025/01/29/deepseek-ai-china-us-tech.html.

[48] "The Rise of DeepSeek: What the Headlines Miss," RAND Corporation, January 28, 2025, https://www.rand.org/pubs/commentary/2025/01/the-rise-of-deepseek-what-the-headlines-miss.html.

[49] U.S. Department of Justice, "U.S. Citizens and Chinese Nationals Arrested for Exporting Artificial Intelligence Technology to China," press release, November 20, 2025, https://www.justice.gov/opa/pr/us-citizens-and-chinese-nationals-arrested-exporting-artificial-intelligence-technology.

[50] Tim Fist, "Countering AI Chip Smuggling Has Become a National Security Priority," Center for a New American Security, June 11, 2025, https://www.cnas.org/publications/reports/countering-ai-chip-smuggling-has-become-a-national-security-priority.

Chapter 5

DeepSeek and the Innovation Paradox

China's Technological Adaptation Under Pressure

On January 20, 2025, a relatively obscure Chinese artificial intelligence startup delivered what many observers would subsequently describe as the most significant shock to American technological confidence since the Soviet Union launched Sputnik in 1957. DeepSeek, a Hangzhou-based company backed by the quantitative hedge fund High-Flyer Capital Management, released its DeepSeek-R1 reasoning model to the public. Within seven days, the accompanying chatbot application had surpassed OpenAI's ChatGPT to become the most downloaded free application on Apple's iOS App Store in the United States.[1] The immediate market reaction was devastating: Nvidia's stock price collapsed by eighteen percent in a single trading session, erasing approximately $589 billion in market capitalization—the largest single-day loss for any company in American financial history.[2]

The DeepSeek phenomenon crystallized a profound paradox at the heart of Washington's strategy to contain China's technological rise. The elaborate architecture of semiconductor export controls, painstakingly constructed since October 2022, had been premised on a simple logic: deny Chinese firms access to the most advanced artificial intelligence chips, and China's AI capabilities would inevitably lag behind the West. DeepSeek's emergence suggested that this assumption may have been fundamentally flawed. Constraint, rather than retarding Chinese innovation, appeared to have accelerated it.

The January 2025 Wake-Up Call

The technical specifications that accompanied DeepSeek's release sent tremors through Silicon Valley's AI establishment. According to the company's own technical report published on arXiv, DeepSeek had trained its V3 model—the foundation upon which R1 was built—using a cluster of just 2,048 Nvidia H800 graphics processing units over approximately two months, accumulating 2.788 million GPU-hours at an estimated cost of merely $5.576 million.[3] This figure stood in stark contrast to the billions of dollars that American AI leaders had reportedly invested in comparable systems. OpenAI's GPT-4, by most estimates, had required training expenditures approaching $100 million, while utilizing vastly more powerful computing resources.[4]

The H800 chips that DeepSeek employed were themselves artifacts of export control accommodation. Nvidia had designed the H800 specifically for the Chinese market after the Biden administration's October 2022 restrictions prohibited sales of the more capable H100 processors. The H800 featured deliberately reduced interconnect bandwidth—400 gigabytes per second compared to the H100's 900 gigabytes per second—intended to hamper the chips' utility for large-scale AI training clusters.[5] DeepSeek's engineers had seemingly rendered this limitation irrelevant.

President Donald Trump, in characteristic fashion, captured the prevailing sentiment when he described DeepSeek's emergence as a "wake-up call" for American technology companies.[6] OpenAI's Sam Altman, while publicly lauding the model as "impressive," privately acknowledged the competitive threat it represented.[7] Marc Andreessen, the prominent Silicon Valley venture capitalist, invoked the Sputnik analogy explicitly, suggesting that DeepSeek represented a moment of reckoning for American assumptions about technological supremacy.[8]

Yet the initial $5.6 million training cost figure, while technically accurate within its narrow parameters, obscured a more complex reality. Industry analysts quickly noted that DeepSeek's disclosure pertained solely to the final training run for the V3 model, excluding the extensive research and development, data acquisition, architectural experimentation, and failed attempts that necessarily preceded it.[9] SemiAnalysis, a respected semiconductor consultancy, estimated that DeepSeek had actually invested approximately $1.6 billion in computing infrastructure and maintained a fleet of roughly 50,000 Nvidia Hopper-generation GPUs—including not only H800s but also H100s and the older A100 chips that the company had stockpiled before export restrictions tightened.[10]

This revised understanding did not diminish DeepSeek's achievement. Even accounting for total infrastructure investment, the company had demonstrated that competitive large language models could be developed at a fraction of the cost and with substantially less capable hardware than Western incumbents had presumed necessary. The efficiency gains were real and significant, regardless of how one calculated the denominator.

Architectural Innovation Under Constraint

DeepSeek's technical breakthroughs derived from a series of architectural innovations that collectively represented a departure from the brute-force scaling paradigm that had dominated American AI development. The company's engineers had effectively asked a different question than their Western counterparts: rather than "how do we acquire more compute?" they asked "how do we achieve equivalent results with the compute we have?"

The foundational innovation was Multi-Head Latent Attention (MLA), first introduced in DeepSeek-V2 and subsequently refined for V3. Traditional transformer architectures store key-value pairs for each attention head during inference, creating substantial memory overhead that scales linearly with context length. MLA compressed these representations into low-rank latent vectors, reducing the key-value cache size per token from 516 kilobytes in comparable models like LLaMA-3.1 to merely 70 kilobytes—an 87 percent reduction.[11] This compression enabled DeepSeek to process longer contexts and deploy larger batch sizes on equivalent hardware, effectively multiplying the utility of each GPU.

The second major innovation was DeepSeek's refinement of the Mixture of Experts (MoE) architecture. While MoE approaches had been explored by Western researchers, DeepSeek's implementation featured more fine-grained expert specialization and a novel auxiliary-loss-free load balancing strategy. The model comprised 671 billion total parameters, but only 37 billion were activated for any given token—a ratio that dramatically reduced computational requirements while preserving expressive capacity.[12] By comparison, dense models of equivalent capability would require activation of all parameters, consuming roughly ten times the computational resources per token.

Perhaps most significantly, DeepSeek pioneered FP8 mixed-precision training at unprecedented scale. The company's technical report documented a comprehensive framework in which most compute-intensive operations—particularly the general matrix multiplication (GEMM) kernels that dominate neural network training—were conducted in 8-bit floating-point precision rather than the 16-bit or 32-bit formats conventional in American systems.[13] This approach, validated through extensive ablation studies on smaller models, reduced both memory consumption and computational overhead while introducing less than 0.25 percent accuracy degradation.[14] The framework required sophisticated quantization strategies, including tile-wise scaling for activations and block-wise scaling for weights, to manage the limited dynamic range inherent in low-precision formats.

The company's engineers also wrote custom PTX code—assembly-level instructions that bypassed Nvidia's CUDA abstraction layer—to optimize data movement and compute utilization on the H800 chips.[15] Reports suggested that DeepSeek had discovered methods to increase the effective interconnect bandwidth beyond the specifications Nvidia had deliberately constrained, though the company has not publicly confirmed these claims.[16]

The culmination of these architectural choices was a system of remarkable efficiency. DeepSeek-V3 required just 250 gigaFLOPS per token compared to 2,448 gigaFLOPS for dense models like LLaMA-3.1—a near tenfold reduction in computational requirements.[17] The DualPipe algorithm, another DeepSeek innovation, enabled efficient pipeline parallelism across GPU clusters by overlapping computation and communication phases. This approach minimized the "pipeline bubbles"—idle periods where GPUs wait for data from other processors—that typically plague distributed training systems.[18]

The hardware-software co-design philosophy extended to training infrastructure. DeepSeek operated its cluster on 2,048 Nvidia H800 GPUs, but the reduced interconnect bandwidth of these China-specific chips posed significant challenges for large-scale distributed training. Rather than accept these limitations, the engineering team developed custom all-to-all communication kernels that maximized utilization of both InfiniBand networking and NVLink connections within nodes.[19] The resulting system achieved near-full computation-communication overlap, meaning that GPUs spent minimal time waiting for data transfers to complete.

Multi-Token Prediction (MTP) represented yet another efficiency innovation. Rather than predicting only the next token at each step, DeepSeek-V3 was trained to simultaneously predict multiple future tokens, providing denser training signals from each input example.[20] This approach improved data efficiency—extracting more learning from each training sample—and could be leveraged during inference for speculative decoding, further accelerating generation speed.

The Reinforcement Learning Revolution

If the architectural innovations represented incremental advances, DeepSeek's approach to post-training arguably constituted a more fundamental paradigm shift. DeepSeek-R1 was the first major language model to achieve frontier-level reasoning capabilities through pure reinforcement learning, without the supervised fine-tuning stage that had been considered essential in Western training pipelines.

The enabling algorithm was Group Relative Policy Optimization (GRPO), which DeepSeek had introduced in its earlier DeepSeekMath work and subsequently refined for general reasoning tasks.[17] Traditional reinforcement learning approaches like Proximal Policy Optimization (PPO) require training a separate "critic" model to estimate the value of policy outputs—effectively doubling the computational overhead and introducing additional sources of instability. GRPO eliminated this requirement by using group-based reward baselines: rather than learning absolute value estimates, the algorithm compared each output against the average reward achieved by a batch of sampled responses to the same prompt.[18]

This approach reduced memory requirements by approximately forty to sixty percent compared to PPO while enabling more stable training dynamics.[19] According to DeepSeek's research team, GRPO could be up to eighteen times more cost-efficient than PPO in certain training configurations.[20] The implications extended beyond mere efficiency: by making reinforcement learning more tractable, GRPO enabled DeepSeek to explore training regimes that Western researchers had dismissed as impractical.

The DeepSeek-R1-Zero experiment illustrated this potential most dramatically. Starting from the base DeepSeek-V3 model without any supervised fine-tuning data, the research team applied pure reinforcement learning using GRPO with simple accuracy-based and format-based rewards. The resulting model spontaneously developed sophisticated reasoning behaviors—including self-verification, error correction, and what the researchers described as "aha moments" where the model recognized and abandoned unproductive solution approaches.[21] On the American Invitational Mathematics Examination (AIME) 2024 benchmark, DeepSeek-R1-Zero improved from 15.6 percent accuracy at initialization to 71.0 percent after training, with majority voting pushing performance to 86.7 percent—competitive with OpenAI's specialized o1 reasoning model.[22]

This emergence of reasoning capabilities through pure reinforcement learning challenged the prevailing assumption that human-curated training data was essential for developing sophisticated AI behaviors. It suggested that, given appropriate reward structures and sufficient scale, language models could discover effective reasoning strategies through trial and error alone.

The researchers documented what they termed an "aha moment" during training—a phase where the model spontaneously developed self-reflection capabilities. "The model learns to rethink using an anthropomorphic tone," they wrote. "This is also an aha moment for us, allowing us to witness the power and beauty of reinforcement learning."[23] The emergent behavior included explicit acknowledgment of reasoning errors and systematic exploration of alternative solution paths.

The subsequent DeepSeek-R1 model built upon these foundations while addressing some of R1-Zero's limitations, including poor readability and language mixing that occurred when the model defaulted to Chinese during complex reasoning chains. A multi-stage training pipeline incorporating carefully curated "cold start" data and rejection sampling refined the model's outputs while preserving its reasoning capabilities.[24] The final system achieved performance comparable to

OpenAI's o1-1217 on mathematics, coding, and scientific reasoning benchmarks—at a fraction of the training cost.[25]

The implications extended beyond DeepSeek itself. Within months of the R1 release, the company published distilled versions of its reasoning approach trained on top of open-source models like Meta's Llama and Alibaba's Qwen.[26] These smaller models, ranging from 1.5 billion to 70 billion parameters, demonstrated that DeepSeek's reasoning capabilities could be transferred to more compact architectures suitable for deployment on consumer hardware. A 32-billion parameter distilled model, for instance, achieved performance comparable to OpenAI's o1-mini while requiring dramatically fewer computational resources for inference.[27]

The open release of these distilled models effectively democratized access to reasoning-capable AI systems. Developers worldwide could now deploy sophisticated reasoning capabilities without the massive infrastructure investments that American companies had deemed essential. This represented a fundamental challenge to the business models of Western AI leaders, who had predicated their strategies on the assumption that frontier capabilities would remain concentrated among a small number of well-capitalized incumbents.

The Narrowing Performance Gap

The Stanford Human-Centered Artificial Intelligence Institute's 2025 AI Index Report provided the most comprehensive empirical assessment of the evolving competitive landscape. While the United States maintained quantitative leadership in notable AI model production—forty significant releases in 2024 compared to China's fifteen—the qualitative gap had essentially vanished.[23] On the Massive Multitask Language Understanding (MMLU) benchmark, a standard measure of language model capability across diverse academic domains, the performance differential between leading American and Chinese models shrank from approximately twenty percentage points in 2023 to a mere 0.3 percentage points by the end of 2024.[24]

The Chatbot Arena Leaderboard, which aggregates crowd-sourced human evaluations of model performance, told a similar story. In January 2024, the top American models enjoyed a 103-point advantage over the best Chinese competitors. By February 2025, following DeepSeek-R1's release, that margin had collapsed to just 23 points.[25] The trajectory suggested that parity, if not Chinese leadership in certain domains, was imminent.

DeepSeek's models demonstrated particular strength in areas that American observers had assumed would remain Western strongholds. On coding benchmarks like LiveCodeBench, which evaluates performance on competitive programming problems, DeepSeek-R1 performed comparably to

OpenAI's o1-preview.[26] Mathematical reasoning, long considered a frontier challenge, showed similar convergence. The model achieved 79.8 percent accuracy on the MATH-500 benchmark, closely tracking leading American systems.[27]

China's dominance in AI research volume further complicated the competitive picture. Chinese institutions produced more AI-related academic publications and patents than any other nation, with 22.6 percent of global AI citations in 2023 compared to 13.0 percent for the United States.[28] While American institutions continued to generate a disproportionate share of highly-cited foundational research, the sheer scale of Chinese research activity suggested a deepening pipeline of technical talent and incremental innovations.

Tsinghua University had emerged as a particular powerhouse, producing more of the world's 100 most-cited AI research papers than any other institution and generating more AI-related patents annually than MIT, Stanford, Princeton, and Harvard combined.[29] Between 2005 and 2024, Tsinghua researchers filed 4,986 AI and machine learning patents, including more than 900 in 2024 alone.[30] The university's strategic partnerships with entities like the Shanghai Artificial Intelligence Laboratory created integrated ecosystems for translating academic research into industrial applications.

The Smuggling Networks

The persistence of Chinese AI capabilities despite export restrictions stemmed partly from innovation, but also from the stubborn porosity of global technology supply chains. Throughout 2024 and 2025, federal prosecutors brought multiple cases against individuals and networks accused of systematically evading semiconductor export controls.

In November 2025, the Department of Justice indicted four individuals—two American citizens and two Chinese nationals—for allegedly operating an elaborate smuggling network that funneled Nvidia GPUs through Malaysia and Thailand to buyers in China.[31] The conspiracy, which prosecutors alleged ran from September 2023 through November 2025, successfully exported 400 Nvidia A100 chips between October 2024 and January 2025. Law enforcement disrupted two additional shipments that would have included ten Hewlett Packard Enterprise supercomputers containing Nvidia H100 accelerators and fifty standalone H200 GPUs.[32] The defendants allegedly used a sham real estate company in Tampa, Florida, as a front for the operation, receiving over $3.89 million in wire transfers from Chinese buyers.[33]

This case was neither isolated nor exceptional. In August 2025, prosecutors charged two Chinese nationals with using a California-based company, ALX Solutions, to export at least 21 shipments of restricted Nvidia chips to companies in Singapore and Malaysia between October 2022 and July 2025.[34] One December 2024 shipment included Nvidia H100 GPUs falsely labeled and lacking required Commerce Department licenses.[35] Payment records revealed $1 million in funds from a China-based company in January 2024 alone.[36]

The Financial Times reported in July 2025 that at least $1 billion worth of restricted Nvidia chips had entered China through black market channels since the Trump administration tightened export restrictions earlier that year.[37] Chinese distributors were openly marketing Nvidia's B200 chips—part of the newest Blackwell architecture and strictly prohibited for export—to data center operators serving Chinese AI companies.[38] More than seventy distributors advertised restricted processors on social media platforms, with some offering delivery within weeks.[39]

Research from the Center for a New American Security estimated that between 10,000 and several hundred thousand banned Nvidia chips may have reached China in 2024 alone.[40] Chinese firms were reportedly planning to install more than 115,000 restricted Nvidia AI chips across three dozen data centers in China's western deserts—chips they could not legally purchase without licenses that had not been granted.[41]

Commerce Under Secretary Jeffrey Kessler directly contradicted Nvidia CEO Jensen Huang's repeated assertions that the massive servers were "nearly two tons" and therefore easy to track. "It's happening," Kessler told lawmakers. "It's a fact."[42] Malaysia emerged as a particular concern, with the country's imports of advanced GPUs surging over 3,400 percent in early 2025, prompting new permit requirements for AI chip exports.[43]

Singapore authorities arrested three individuals suspected of diverting AI servers worth hundreds of millions of dollars to China.[44] The investigation reportedly implicated DeepSeek itself, though the company has not been charged with any wrongdoing.[45]

The Paradox of Acceleration

The accumulating evidence suggested a troubling conclusion for American policymakers: export controls, while imposing costs on Chinese AI development, may have accelerated precisely the indigenous innovation they were designed to prevent. This was the innovation paradox made manifest.

The September 2023 revelation that Huawei and SMIC had produced a competitive 7-nanometer processor for the Mate 60 Pro smartphone—despite lacking access to extreme ultraviolet lithography equipment—had foreshadowed this dynamic.[46] TechInsights, the semiconductor analysis firm that conducted the teardown, characterized the achievement as demonstrating "the technical progress China's semiconductor industry has been able to make without EUV lithography tools" and "the resilience of the country's chip technological ability."[47]

DeepSeek represented the AI-specific manifestation of this phenomenon. Denied access to the most capable training hardware, Chinese engineers had developed architectural innovations, training algorithms, and optimization techniques that partially compensated for their computational disadvantage. Some of these innovations—particularly MLA and GRPO—were genuinely novel contributions that Western researchers subsequently scrambled to understand and replicate.[48]

The irony was particularly acute given that DeepSeek released its models under the permissive MIT License, making them freely available for commercial and research use worldwide. While American companies had invested billions in proprietary systems, DeepSeek was giving away comparable technology. The open-source approach served multiple strategic objectives: it built global developer communities around Chinese AI infrastructure, established DeepSeek's techniques as industry standards, and demonstrated Chinese technological capability to international audiences.

Major Western technology companies found themselves in an awkward position. Microsoft integrated DeepSeek into its Azure AI Foundry service.[49] The Hugging Face platform recorded over 10.9 million downloads of DeepSeek-R1 as developers worldwide experimented with the model.[50] Chinese AI technology, developed partly in response to American containment efforts, was diffusing globally through the very openness that Western technology ecosystems had traditionally celebrated.

The Self-Sufficiency Imperative

DeepSeek's success strengthened rather than weakened Beijing's commitment to technological self-sufficiency. The company's achievements demonstrated what Chinese engineers could accomplish even with constrained resources, while the persistent reality of export controls reminded Chinese leaders of their vulnerability to American technological leverage.

China's response to DeepSeek's success was not complacency but acceleration. In October 2024, the Cyberspace Administration of China announced that 302 generative AI service models had achieved full regulatory registration.[51] Major technology companies—including Baidu, ByteDance, Tencent, and Alibaba—slashed prices for their AI services in a competitive response to DeepSeek's low-cost offerings.[52] The phrase "Pinduoduo of AI," invoking China's discount e-commerce platform, captured the new competitive dynamic.[53]

State-backed initiatives to develop domestic AI chip alternatives intensified. China Telecom's AI research institute claimed in September 2024 to have trained trillion-parameter models using exclusively domestic semiconductors—though the specific processors remained unidentified.[54] Huawei's Ascend chips, while reportedly suffering from software limitations and stability issues compared to Nvidia's offerings, were being adopted for inference workloads even as training remained dependent on the American company's hardware.[55]

DeepSeek itself acknowledged these challenges. Founder Liang Wenfeng reportedly expressed dissatisfaction with Huawei's Ascend chips for training purposes, citing slower inter-chip connectivity and inferior software compared to Nvidia's ecosystem.[56] The company had adopted a dual-track strategy: using Nvidia chips for training while employing Huawei chips for the less demanding inference workloads. This pragmatic approach highlighted both the progress and the persistent limitations of China's domestic semiconductor capabilities.

The competitive response from established Chinese technology companies demonstrated the broader ecosystem effects of DeepSeek's success. Alibaba's Qwen models, ByteDance's Doubao, and Baidu's ERNIE series all accelerated development timelines and adopted efficiency-focused architectural innovations pioneered by DeepSeek.[62] The result was an increasingly vibrant Chinese AI ecosystem in which multiple well-resourced competitors pushed the efficiency frontier.

International adoption of Chinese AI models complicated the strategic picture further. According to data from Hugging Face, Chinese models like Qwen had achieved significant download volumes in markets across Asia and increasingly in Western countries.[63] The favorable licensing terms of open-source Chinese models—which typically permitted commercial use without extensive legal review—made them attractive alternatives to more restrictively licensed Western offerings.[64]

The DeepSeek phenomenon also prompted introspection within American AI research communities. Several prominent researchers acknowledged that the efficiency-focused innovations demonstrated by DeepSeek represented genuine technical advances that the Western AI industry, flush with capital and confident in its hardware advantages, had neglected to pursue.[65] The scramble to understand and replicate DeepSeek's architectural choices suggested that the knowledge transfer was now flowing in both directions across the Pacific.

Lessons for the Technology Competition

The DeepSeek episode offered several sobering lessons for American strategic planners. First, technological denial as a strategy faced inherent limitations. Export controls could impose costs and delays, but they could not permanently prevent a determined adversary with substantial resources from developing alternative approaches. The history of technology competition, from Cold War strategic export restrictions to contemporary semiconductor controls, consistently demonstrated that determined nations could eventually work around denial regimes.

Second, necessity could indeed mother invention. The constraints imposed by export controls had forced Chinese engineers to pursue efficiency-focused approaches that might otherwise have been neglected in favor of simply acquiring more compute. Some of these efficiency innovations proved genuinely valuable, offering benefits that transcended the specific circumstances of their development.

Third, the openness that characterized Western technology ecosystems created pathways for competitive technologies to diffuse globally. DeepSeek's MIT-licensed releases demonstrated that Chinese firms could leverage open-source norms to build international communities and establish technical standards—turning American technological values into competitive advantages.

Fourth, the scale of smuggling and evasion suggested that unilateral export controls, even when coordinated with key allies, could not fully seal technology flows to a determined adversary operating through global supply chains. The enforcement challenges were structural, not merely administrative.

Finally, the episode highlighted the importance of sustained investment in domestic innovation capacity. Export controls were, at best, a delaying tactic. Long-term competitive advantage would depend on maintaining and extending the technological frontier, not merely on preventing others from reaching it.

The innovation paradox embodied by DeepSeek would shape the next phase of the U.S.-China technology competition. Beijing had demonstrated both the costs and the possibilities of constrained innovation. Washington faced the challenge of recalibrating its strategy to account for an adversary that had proven more adaptable than anticipated.

The RAND Corporation's analysis captured the essential strategic dilemma: "While Chinese models close the gap on benchmarks, the United States maintains an advantage in total compute capacity—owning far more, and more advanced, AI chips. This compute advantage, if leveraged strategically, will play an extraordinary role in driving economic transformation."[66] Yet that compute advantage would prove strategically decisive only if American institutions could translate it into sustained capability leads. DeepSeek had demonstrated that capability gaps could narrow even when hardware gaps widened.

The path forward for American policymakers required acknowledging uncomfortable realities. Export controls remained necessary but insufficient instruments of technological competition. They could impose costs and create delays, but they could not prevent a capable adversary from eventually achieving functional parity through alternative means. The long-term contest would be won not by denial alone but by sustained innovation, effective deployment, and the cultivation of technological ecosystems that attracted global talent and capital.

DeepSeek had demonstrated that the "small yard, high fence" strategy articulated by National Security Advisor Jake Sullivan in 2022—restricting only the most critical technologies while maintaining broader engagement—faced practical limitations when determined adversaries prioritized the technologies behind the fence.[67] The question for American strategists was whether to raise the fence higher, expand the yard, or fundamentally reconceive the metaphor.

Meanwhile, in Hangzhou, Liang Wenfeng's team continued to work. The anticipated DeepSeek-R2 model, while delayed by technical challenges, promised further advances.[68] The company had received public recognition from Chinese Premier Li Qiang, who invited Liang to participate in a government symposium on AI development—a signal of state support that presaged deeper integration between DeepSeek's innovations and China's broader technological ambitions.[69]

The innovation paradox had only begun to unfold its implications. What had seemed a straightforward story of American technological containment had become something far more complex: a competitive dynamic in which constraints bred creativity, denial spurred determination, and the effort to maintain dominance may have accelerated the very competition it sought to forestall.

Endnotes

[1] DeepSeek, *DeepSeek-R1 Technical Report* (Hangzhou: DeepSeek AI, January 2025), arXiv:2501.12948.

[2] Yun Li, "Nvidia Falls 17%, Loses Record $589 Billion in Market Value as DeepSeek Jolts AI Trade," *CNBC*, January 27, 2025.

[3] DeepSeek-AI, "DeepSeek-V3 Technical Report," arXiv:2412.19437, December 2024, Section 3.

[4] Karen Weise and Cade Metz, "How Much Did GPT-4 Cost to Train? We Don't Know," *New York Times*, March 29, 2023.

[5] Bureau of Industry and Security, "Implementation of Additional Export Controls: Certain Advanced Computing Items; Supercomputer and Semiconductor End Use," 88 Federal Register 73424, October 25, 2023.

[6] "Trump Calls DeepSeek 'Wake-Up Call' for US Tech," *Reuters*, January 28, 2025.

[7] Sam Altman (@sama), Twitter post, January 27, 2025.

[8] Marc Andreessen, quoted in "DeepSeek Shakes Up AI Sector," World Economic Forum, February 3, 2025.

[9] DeepSeek-AI, "DeepSeek-V3 Technical Report," arXiv:2412.19437, Appendix B.

[10] Dylan Patel and Afzal Ahmad, "DeepSeek Deconstructed: How They Achieved Cost-Efficient Training," SemiAnalysis, January 31, 2025.

[11] DeepSeek-AI, "DeepSeek-V2: A Strong, Economical, and Efficient Mixture-of-Experts Language Model," arXiv:2405.04434, May 2024, Section 2.1.

[12] DeepSeek-AI, "DeepSeek-V3 Technical Report," arXiv:2412.19437, Section 2.2.

[13] Ibid., Section 3.3.

[14] Ibid., Appendix B.1.

[15] Guowei Li et al., "Scaling Challenges and Reflections on Hardware for AI Architectures," DeepSeek Technical Paper, May 2025.

[16] Unnamed industry sources, cited in "DeepSeek's Secret Sauce: How Chinese Engineers Bypassed Nvidia's Restrictions," *Financial Times*, February 15, 2025.

[17] DeepSeek-AI, "DeepSeek-V3 Hardware-Aware Co-design Paper," May 2025, Table 2.

[18] DeepSeek-AI, "DeepSeek-V3 Technical Report," arXiv:2412.19437, Section 3.2.

[19] Ibid., Section 3.4.

[20] Ibid., Section 2.3.

[21] Zhihong Shao et al., "DeepSeekMath: Pushing the Limits of Mathematical Reasoning in Open Language Models," arXiv:2402.03300, February 2024.

[22] DeepSeek-AI, "DeepSeek-R1 Technical Report," arXiv:2501.12948, Section 2.5.

[23] Ibid., Table 3.

[24] Ibid., Section 3.1.

[25] Ibid., Section 5.

[26] Ibid., Section 4.

[27] Ibid., Table 12.

[28] DeepSeek-AI, "DeepSeek-R1 Technical Report," arXiv:2501.12948, Table 1.

[29] Stanford Institute for Human-Centered Artificial Intelligence, *AI Index Report 2025* (Stanford: Stanford University, April 2025), Chapter 1.

[30] Ibid., Figure 1.1.12.

[31] "Visualizing U.S. vs. Chinese AI Model Performance," Visual Capitalist, April 28, 2025.

[32] DeepSeek-AI, "DeepSeek-R1 Technical Report," arXiv:2501.12948, Section 5.

[33] Ibid., Table 8.

[34] Stanford Institute for Human-Centered Artificial Intelligence, *AI Index Report 2025*, Figure 1.1.7.

[35] Jun Liu et al., cited in "Move Over Harvard and MIT—This University Might Be Winning the AI Race," *Fortune*, November 19, 2025.

[36] LexisNexis patent data, analyzed by Bloomberg, November 2025.

[37] U.S. Department of Justice, "Four Individuals Charged with Conspiracy to Export Advanced Nvidia GPUs to China," Press Release, November 20, 2025.

[38] United States v. Ho et al., Indictment, Middle District of Florida, November 2025.

[39] Ibid., Count 7-13.

[40] United States v. Geng and Yang, Indictment, Central District of California, August 2025.

[41] Ibid., Exhibit A.

[42] Ibid., Exhibit B.

[43] Qianer Liu and Demetri Sevastopulo, "Nvidia's Restricted AI Chips Flow into China Through Black Market," *Financial Times*, July 24, 2025.

[44] Ibid.

[45] Ibid.

[46] Emily Kilcrease and Michael Allen, "Evading the Chips: How China Circumvents Semiconductor Export Controls," Center for a New American Security, July 2025.

[47] Ibid., Appendix B.

[48] Jeffrey Kessler, testimony before the House Select Committee on the Chinese Communist Party, May 14, 2025.

[49] "Malaysia Imposes New Controls on AI Chip Exports Amid Smuggling Concerns," *Nikkei Asia*, March 12, 2025.

[50] "Singapore Charges Three in Nvidia Chip Diversion Investigation," *Straits Times*, April 8, 2025.

[51] Ibid.

[52] TechInsights, "TechInsights Finds SMIC 7nm (N+2) in Huawei Mate 60 Pro," Blog Post, September 4, 2023.

[53] Dan Hutcheson, quoted in ibid.

[54] Nestor Maslej, interview with Gradient Flow, "An In-Depth Look at the Stanford AI Index Report," April 9, 2025.

[55] Microsoft Corporation, "DeepSeek Available on Azure AI Foundry," Press Release, February 5, 2025.

[56] Hugging Face Model Hub statistics, accessed November 2025.

[57] Cyberspace Administration of China, "Registered Generative AI Services," January 2025.

[58] "Chinese Tech Giants Cut AI Prices in Response to DeepSeek," *South China Morning Post*, February 3, 2025.

[59] Ibid.

[60] China Telecom Institute of AI, WeChat statement, September 2024.

[61] "DeepSeek's R2 Delayed by Chip Problems," *South China Morning Post*, August 2025.

[62] Ibid.

[63] Grace Isford, Lux Capital, quoted in "Chinese AI Models Gaining Traction Globally," *CNBC*, December 17, 2024.

[64] Wang Xiaobo, AI analyst, quoted in "Qwen Gains Popularity Among Global Developers," *Financial Times*, November 2024.

[65] Bart Selman, computer scientist at Cornell University, quoted in "AI Report Highlights Smaller, Better, Cheaper Models," *Scientific American*, April 9, 2025.

[66] RAND Corporation, "China's AI Models Are Closing the Gap—but America's Real Advantage Lies Elsewhere," Commentary, May 2, 2025.

[67] Jake Sullivan, National Security Advisor, "Remarks on the Biden-Harris Administration's National Security Strategy," Georgetown University, October 27, 2022.

[68] "DeepSeek's R2 Model Delayed as Company Seeks Performance Improvements," *South China Morning Post*, July 2025.

[69] Chinese Premier Li Qiang, symposium with AI experts, Beijing, January 20, 2025, reported in *Xinhua News Agency*.

Chapter 6

The November 2025 Inflection Point

Beijing's Declaration of Semiconductor Independence

The announcement came with little fanfare but carried enormous implications. On November 5, 2025, barely a week after Chinese paramount leader Xi Jinping met with President Donald Trump at the Asia-Pacific Economic Cooperation summit in South Korea, Beijing quietly issued guidance that would fundamentally alter the trajectory of the global semiconductor industry. Chinese regulatory authorities ordered all state-funded data centers—facilities representing more than $100 billion in investment since 2021—to stop using or purchasing foreign artificial intelligence chips.[1] The directive effectively severed one of China's last remaining dependencies on American semiconductors for its burgeoning AI sector.

This chapter examines the November 2025 inflection point and its profound implications for the emerging technological cold war between the United States and China. The decision represented more than mere retaliation for years of American export controls; it marked Beijing's confident declaration that its domestic semiconductor ecosystem had matured sufficiently to sustain the country's AI ambitions without American components. Whether this confidence was warranted or merely strategic posturing would shape the next phase of great power competition.

The Xi-Trump Summit and Its Aftermath

The meeting between Xi Jinping and Donald Trump on October 30, 2025, at Gimhae Air Base in Busan represented their first face-to-face encounter since Trump returned to the presidency in January. The hundred-minute discussion occurred against a backdrop of extraordinary tension—tariffs had escalated to unprecedented levels earlier in the year, with American levies on Chinese goods reaching 145 percent and Beijing retaliating with 125 percent duties before the Geneva truce in May.[2]

Xi struck a notably conciliatory tone during the summit. "China and the United States should be partners and friends. That is what history has taught us and what reality needs," the Chinese president declared, according to the official statement released by China's Ministry of Foreign Affairs.[3] Trump, characteristically, described Xi as "a very tough negotiator" while asserting that "we've always had a very good relationship."[4] The optics suggested détente; the reality proved more complicated.

The framework emerging from the South Korea meeting appeared to address the most contentious trade issues. Both sides agreed to reduce retaliatory tariffs and remove recently imposed export restrictions, building on the Geneva agreement from May that had suspended 115 percentage points of mutual tariffs for ninety days, reducing U.S. tariffs from 145 percent to 30 percent and Chinese tariffs from 125 percent to 10 percent.[5] Treasury Secretary Scott Bessent subsequently indicated that continuing high-level engagement would occur, with the mechanism established for ongoing discussions about economic and trade relations.[6]

Yet the optimism surrounding the Busan summit masked fundamental contradictions. Even as the two leaders shook hands and spoke of partnership, both governments were pursuing policies designed to decouple their technology sectors. Within days of the meeting, Beijing would demonstrate that its commitment to technological independence superseded any temporary trade accommodation.

November 5, 2025: The Domestic Chip Mandate

The guidance issued by Chinese regulatory authorities on November 5 contained provisions more sweeping than any previous technology policy. State-funded data centers that were less than thirty percent complete were ordered to remove all installed foreign chips or cancel plans to purchase them.[7] Projects in more advanced stages would be evaluated on a case-by-case basis, but the direction was unmistakable: China would build its AI infrastructure on domestic foundations.

The implications were staggering. AI data center projects in China had attracted over $100 billion in state funding since 2021, according to a Reuters review of government tenders.[8] Most large data centers in the country had received at least some level of government financing, meaning the new guidance could apply to the vast majority of current projects. The directive effectively closed the Chinese market to Nvidia, Advanced Micro Devices (AMD), and Intel—companies that had dominated the country's AI infrastructure despite years of escalating export controls.

The timing was deliberate and pointed. Coming just days after the seemingly cordial summit with Trump, the announcement sent an unambiguous message: Beijing would pursue technological self-reliance regardless of the diplomatic atmosphere. The decision underscored what analysts at the Foundation for Defense of Democracies described as "a shift from dependence to insulation"—China had long sought to develop its own domestic technology ecosystem, and

Beijing now increasingly believed its domestic sector could function without American components.[9]

Nvidia CEO Jensen Huang had repeatedly lobbied Trump and his cabinet to allow the sale of more AI chips to China, arguing that keeping its superpower rival's AI industry dependent on U.S. hardware was good for America's interests. The company's current share of the Chinese AI chip market had fallen to zero from ninety-five percent in 2022, according to company figures.[10] Excluding foreign chipmakers like Nvidia from major state projects eliminated a significant portion of their China revenue, even as deals were being negotiated to allow resumption of some advanced chip sales.

Reading Beijing's Intentions: Confidence or Constraint?

Interpreting Beijing's motivations required parsing a complex mixture of technological capability, strategic calculation, and domestic politics. Some analysts viewed the domestic chip mandate as a sign of genuine confidence—evidence that Chinese semiconductor manufacturers had achieved capabilities sufficient to sustain the country's AI ambitions. Others detected an element of constraint, suggesting that Beijing was making virtue of necessity by institutionalizing restrictions that American export controls had already imposed de facto.

The case for confidence rested on the remarkable progress of Chinese semiconductor companies, particularly Huawei and its manufacturing partner, Semiconductor Manufacturing International Corporation (SMIC). Huawei's Ascend 910 series of AI accelerators had demonstrated capabilities that, while trailing Nvidia's best offerings, proved sufficient for competitive AI development. The Ascend 910C, combining two 910B processors into a single package, reportedly delivered approximately 800 teraflops at FP16 precision and 3.2 terabytes per second of memory bandwidth—approximately eighty percent the performance of Nvidia's H100.[11]

Perhaps more significant than individual chip specifications was the system-level integration that Huawei had achieved. The CloudMatrix 384 system, unveiled at the China Hi-Tech Fair in Shenzhen, integrated 384 Ascend 910C processors across sixteen racks, creating a fabric delivering approximately 300 petaflops of total computing power.[12] While this configuration consumed substantially more power than Nvidia's competing GB200 NVL72 system—making it approximately 2.3 times less efficient on a per-watt basis—the trade-off was deemed acceptable within China's domestic context, where electricity costs in some regions had declined significantly.[13]

Production capacity told a story of rapid expansion. SMIC, China's leading semiconductor foundry, reported first-half 2025 revenue of $4.456 billion, up twenty-two percent year-over-year, with net profit attributable to shareholders increasing 35.6 percent to $321 million.[14] The company planned to double its 7-nanometer production capacity in 2026, according to Financial Times reporting, with a dedicated fabrication facility for Huawei's AI chips expected to begin production by the end of 2025 and two additional plants coming online in 2026.[15] China aimed to triple its overall AI processor output by 2026.[16]

Yet the constraint interpretation also found support in the evidence. Yield challenges facing SMIC illustrated these limitations. While the company had achieved 7-nanometer production using deep ultraviolet lithography rather than the extreme ultraviolet tools denied by American export controls, yields remained below those of industry leader Taiwan Semiconductor Manufacturing Company (TSMC). TD Cowen analyst Krish Sankar reported that SMIC 7-nanometer yields had improved to sixty to seventy percent, compared to below forty percent when initially launched in late 2023, but remained below TSMC's benchmarks for comparable processes.[17] Other industry analysts provided more conservative estimates, with some suggesting yields for complex AI chips remained between five and twenty percent for the largest dies.[18]

The most plausible interpretation combined elements of both narratives. Beijing possessed sufficient confidence in its domestic capabilities to sustain near-term AI development while recognizing that longer-term competitiveness required continued progress. The November mandate thus served multiple purposes: it guaranteed market access for domestic producers, accelerated the development of indigenous supply chains, and signaled to Washington that export controls would not achieve their stated objectives.

The DeepSeek Effect: Innovation Through Constraint

The confidence underlying Beijing's November decision drew substantially from a breakthrough that had shaken the global AI community ten months earlier. In January 2025, a relatively unknown Chinese AI startup called DeepSeek released its R1 reasoning model, demonstrating capabilities that matched or exceeded OpenAI's comparable o1 model across multiple benchmarks at a fraction of the development cost.[19]

DeepSeek's achievement represented precisely the kind of innovation through constraint that American policymakers had hoped export controls would prevent. The company stated that training its V3 base model cost approximately $5.576 million, according to its technical paper—though this figure excluded costs associated with prior research and experiments on architectures, algorithms, and data.[20] Analysts at SemiAnalysis estimated that DeepSeek's total hardware spending was "well higher than $500 million over the company history," with additional R&D costs and operational expenses making the total investment substantially larger than initial reports suggested.[21]

The technical innovations enabling DeepSeek's breakthrough centered on efficiency optimization rather than brute computational force. The company employed a Mixture-of-Experts architecture that activated only 37 billion of its 671 billion parameters for any given task, dramatically reducing computational requirements.[22] DeepSeek's reinforcement learning approach, using Group Relative Policy Optimization, allowed its models to develop reasoning capabilities without requiring a separate critic model of similar size to the policy model.[23]

The market reaction to DeepSeek's January announcement was severe. Nvidia's stock price dropped approximately seventeen percent on January 27, 2025, erasing nearly $600 billion in market capitalization—the largest single-day loss for any company in U.S. stock market history.[24] Marc Andreessen, the prominent technology investor, called DeepSeek "one of the most amazing and impressive breakthroughs I've ever seen."[25] The Foundation for Defense of Democracies characterized the release as "AI's Sputnik moment."[26]

DeepSeek's success exemplified a broader pattern of Chinese innovation under constraint. Denied access to the most advanced American chips, Chinese AI companies had developed alternative approaches emphasizing computational efficiency, parallel processing across larger numbers of less-powerful chips, and algorithmic innovations that reduced hardware requirements. The Stanford AI Index Report 2025 documented this convergence, noting that the U.S. lead over China "shrank to 0.3% on MMLU" and that "performance differences on major benchmarks such as MMLU and HumanEval shrank from double digits in 2023 to near parity in 2024."[27]

The Stanford report found that in 2024, U.S.-based institutions produced forty notable AI models, compared to China's fifteen and Europe's three.[28] While the United States maintained its lead in quantity, Chinese models had rapidly closed the quality gap. The performance gap between the top U.S. and Chinese models on the Chatbot Arena benchmark narrowed from 9.26 percent in January 2024 to just 1.70 percent by February 2025.[29]

The political implications extended beyond technical competition. DeepSeek's open-source release under the MIT license made its innovations available to developers worldwide, undermining the premise that American technological leadership could be maintained through restricted access. If frontier AI capabilities could be achieved with restricted hardware and modest stated budgets, the strategic calculus underlying export controls required fundamental reassessment.

The American Response: Tightening Chokepoints

Washington's response to China's November mandate reflected the fundamental tension that had characterized American semiconductor policy throughout 2025: the desire to maintain technological superiority conflicted with commercial interests and allied relationships. The Trump administration found itself caught between hawks demanding stricter controls and industry advocates warning that excessive restrictions would accelerate China's self-sufficiency.

The evolution of American export controls throughout 2025 illustrated this tension. The Biden administration's final regulatory act in January 2025 had introduced the AI Diffusion Rule, establishing global performance thresholds that blocked sales of flagship GPUs to China while creating a tiered country system for managing access.[30] The Trump administration rescinded this framework, preferring targeted restrictions on specific products and entities over comprehensive regulatory architecture.

Nvidia's experience captured the commercial consequences of this regulatory volatility. The company's H20 chip, explicitly designed to comply with American export constraints by featuring reduced interconnection speeds and memory bandwidth, became the focus of an ongoing policy battle. In April 2025, following reports that DeepSeek had used downgraded Nvidia chips to train its breakthrough model, the administration imposed license requirements for H20 exports to China on April 9.[31] On April 14, the government informed Nvidia that the license requirement would be in effect "for the indefinite future."[32] The company announced it expected to take approximately $5.5 billion in charges associated with H20 products for inventory, purchase commitments, and related reserves.[33]

The Bureau of Industry and Security took additional actions to tighten controls on specific chokepoints. The agency added Chinese entities to the Entity List throughout 2025, targeting companies involved in semiconductor manufacturing and procurement.[34] The most significant expansion of controls targeted electronic design automation software, the specialized tools required to design complex integrated circuits. Without access to EDA software from American companies like Synopsys and Cadence, Chinese chip designers faced substantial obstacles in developing advanced processors.

Cloud computing services emerged as another front in the control regime. Chinese organizations had circumvented chip restrictions by accessing controlled hardware through cloud platforms.[35] Proposals to restrict Chinese access to American cloud computing services gained traction but faced implementation challenges related to customer identification and enforcement jurisdiction.

The challenge of allied coordination complicated American efforts. While the United States maintained control over certain chokepoint technologies, the semiconductor supply chain was inherently international. The Netherlands' ASML held a near-monopoly on extreme ultraviolet lithography machines essential for the most advanced chip manufacturing, while Japan provided critical chemical inputs and South Korea dominated high-bandwidth memory production.[36] Maintaining aligned restrictions across this coalition required constant diplomatic engagement, with gaps and inconsistencies creating opportunities for circumvention.

The Emergence of Parallel Tech Ecosystems

China's November 2025 decision accelerated a trend that analysts had been tracking for years: the emergence of two distinct technological ecosystems organized around competing great powers. The "Silicon Curtain" or "Digital Iron Curtain" that commentators had long warned about was taking concrete form, with implications extending far beyond the semiconductor industry.

The bifurcation manifested across multiple dimensions of the technology stack. At the hardware level, the divide between American and Chinese chips became increasingly formalized. Nvidia's dominance of the global AI accelerator market gave way to a split geography: the company maintained its position in North America, Europe, and allied Asian nations while Chinese alternatives—Huawei's Ascend series, Cambricon's products, and offerings from other domestic manufacturers—captured the Chinese market and began extending into developing nations.[37]

Software ecosystems followed hardware boundaries. Nvidia's CUDA platform, which had become the de facto standard for AI development worldwide, faced competition from Huawei's CANN. Developers increasingly faced choices about which ecosystem to target, with implications for code compatibility and skill transferability. DeepSeek's new AI models debuted with support for China-native chips and CANN as a replacement for Nvidia's CUDA, demonstrating the viability of the alternative ecosystem.[38]

The investment disparity between the two ecosystems remained substantial despite China's technological progress. The Stanford AI Index Report found that U.S. private AI investment hit $109.1 billion in 2024, nearly twelve times higher than China's $9.3 billion and twenty-four times the UK's $4.5 billion.[39] The gap was even more pronounced in generative AI, where U.S. investment exceeded the combined European Union and UK total by $25.5 billion.[40]

The implications for innovation remained contested. Optimists noted that competition could spur technological advancement, with each ecosystem racing to outperform the other. The DeepSeek example suggested that constraint could inspire efficiency innovations that might not emerge under conditions of abundance. Pessimists warned that fragmentation would duplicate effort, reduce knowledge sharing, and ultimately slow the pace of global AI development.

The division created particular challenges for countries outside the two camps. Middle powers and developing nations faced pressure to choose between technology ecosystems, with implications for economic relationships and security alignments.[41] The difficulty of navigating between the two technological spheres illustrated the broader challenge facing non-aligned nations in an era of great power competition.

Scenario Planning: The Digital Iron Curtain Possibility

As 2025 drew to a close, analysts constructed scenarios for how the parallel ecosystem dynamic might evolve. The range of possibilities extended from managed coexistence to complete technological divorce, with each trajectory carrying distinct implications for the global economy and international security.

The managed competition scenario envisioned ongoing tension but maintained channels of technological exchange. Under this trajectory, export controls would remain targeted rather than comprehensive, focusing on specific military applications while permitting commercial technology flows in less sensitive areas. Chinese and American companies would continue competing in global markets, with countries maintaining flexibility to source technology from either ecosystem based on commercial considerations. Diplomatic engagement would establish guardrails preventing escalation to conflict.

The complete bifurcation scenario projected more extensive separation. In this future, the two ecosystems would develop along independent trajectories, with minimal technology transfer and incompatible standards. Countries would be required to choose sides, with alignment in technology mirroring security alignments. Innovation would occur within parallel tracks, with occasional convergence only when both sides independently discovered similar solutions.

The Chinese breakthrough scenario considered the possibility that Beijing's investments would produce technological parity or superiority in key domains. Continued advances in efficiency-optimized AI, combined with massive infrastructure investment and abundant engineering talent, could position China as a formidable competitor. Under this scenario, American export controls would prove to have been counterproductive, accelerating Chinese independence while reducing American commercial revenues and innovation capacity.

The American reassertion scenario projected successful maintenance of technological leadership through a combination of domestic investment, allied coordination, and targeted restrictions. The CHIPS and Science Act, providing over $52 billion in incentives for domestic semiconductor manufacturing, would yield expanded production capacity.[42] Allied nations would maintain coordinated export controls, denying China access to critical chokepoint technologies. American AI companies would maintain their lead over Chinese competitors.

Each scenario carried implications for Taiwan, the most dangerous flashpoint in the U.S.-China relationship. TSMC's dominance of advanced semiconductor manufacturing—producing over ninety percent of the world's most advanced logic chips—made the island's status a matter of existential concern for both superpowers.[43] Technological bifurcation could reduce Taiwan's strategic importance by diversifying manufacturing, or it could increase tensions as both sides sought to secure access to irreplaceable production capacity.

The Stakes of Semiconductor Independence

China's November 2025 decision marked a definitive moment in the technological competition between the world's two largest economies. By mandating domestic chips for state-funded data centers, Beijing declared its intention to build AI infrastructure on indigenous foundations—a choice reflecting years of investment, recent technological breakthroughs, and strategic calculation about the durability of American restrictions.

The decision's consequences would unfold over years rather than months. In the near term, Chinese AI companies would contend with hardware less capable than American alternatives, requiring continued innovation in efficiency optimization and parallel processing. Over the medium term, the question was whether Chinese semiconductor manufacturing could achieve the yields and production volumes necessary to sustain competitive development. Over the long term, the technological trajectories of the two ecosystems would determine which nation—or combination of nations—would shape the AI-enabled future.

For American policymakers, the November mandate underscored the limits of export controls as instruments of technology denial. Restrictions had slowed Chinese development but had not prevented it; indeed, they may have accelerated the drive toward self-sufficiency by eliminating alternatives. The challenge now was calibrating policy to maintain whatever advantages remained while avoiding further acceleration of Chinese independence.

The parallel ecosystem dynamic that November 2025 crystallized would reshape not only technology industries but also international relations, military capabilities, and economic structures. The semiconductor—a tiny chip of silicon smaller than a fingernail—had become the fulcrum on which great power competition balanced. The decisions made by leaders in Washington, Beijing, and allied capitals would determine whether this competition remained a race or became a war.

Endnotes

[1] "Exclusive—China Bans Foreign AI Chips From State-Funded Data Centres, Sources Say," Reuters, November 5, 2025, https://www.usnews.com/news/top-news/articles/2025-11-05/exclusive-china-bans-foreign-ai-chips-from-state-funded-data-centres-sources-say.

[2] "U.S. and China to Ease Tariffs Significantly for 90 Days, White House Announces," CBS News, May 12, 2025, https://www.cbsnews.com/news/us-china-tariffs-deal-90-days-trump-admin-trade-talks-progress/.

[3] "President Xi Jinping Meets with U.S. President Donald J. Trump in Busan," Ministry of Foreign Affairs of the People's Republic of China, October 30, 2025, https://www.fmprc.gov.cn/eng/xw/zyxw/202510/t20251030_11743886.html.

[4] "'Partners and Friends': Xi Strikes Conciliatory Tone as He Meets Trump in South Korea," CNBC, October 30, 2025, https://www.cnbc.com/2025/10/30/trump-and-xi-land-busan-meeting-trade-and-tariffs-.html.

[5] "Joint Statement on U.S.-China Economic and Trade Meeting in Geneva," The White House, May 12, 2025, https://www.whitehouse.gov/briefings-statements/2025/05/joint-statement-on-u-s-china-economic-and-trade-meeting-in-geneva/.

[6] "Fact Sheet: President Donald J. Trump Secures a Historic Trade Win for the United States," The White House, May 12, 2025, https://www.whitehouse.gov/fact-sheets/2025/05/fact-sheet-president-donald-j-trump-secures-a-historic-trade-win-for-the-united-states/.

[7] "China Bans US Chips from State-Funded Data Centers, Reuters Says," Bloomberg, November 5, 2025, https://www.bloomberg.com/news/articles/2025-11-05/china-bans-us-chips-from-state-funded-data-centers.

[8] "China Bans Foreign AI Chips from State-Funded Data Centers, Sources Say," Reuters via Yahoo Finance, November 5, 2025, https://finance.yahoo.com/news/exclusive-china-bans-foreign-ai-080808297.html.

[9] Jack Burnham and Duncan Lazarow, "Signaling Confidence in Its Domestic Industry, China Bans Foreign AI Chips in State-Funded Data Centers," Foundation for Defense of Democracies, November 10, 2025, https://www.fdd.org/analysis/2025/11/10/signaling-confidence-in-its-domestic-industry-china-bans-foreign-ai-chips-in-state-funded-data-centers/.

[10] "China Bans Foreign AI Chips from State-Funded Data Centers, Sources Say," Reuters via Yahoo Finance, November 5, 2025.

[11] "[News] Huawei's Ascend 910C Takes on NVIDIA as China's AI Race Heats Up: More Alleged Details," TrendForce, March 13, 2025, https://www.trendforce.com/news/2025/03/13/news-huaweis-ascend-910c-takes-on-nvidia-as-chinas-ai-race-heats-up-more-alleged-details/.

[12] "Huawei's Ascend AI Chip Ecosystem Scales Up as China Pushes for Semiconductor Independence," Tom's Hardware, November 2025, https://www.tomshardware.com/tech-industry/semiconductors/huaweis-ascend-ai-chip-ecosystem-scales.

[13] Ibid.

[14] "[News] SMIC 1H25 Net Profit Rises 35.6%, 7nm Capacity Reportedly to Double in 2026," TrendForce, August 29, 2025, https://www.trendforce.com/news/2025/08/29/news-smic-1h25-net-profit-rises-35-6-7nm-capacity-reportedly-to-double-in-2026/.

[15] Ibid.

[16] Ibid.

[17] "Can China Make 5nm Chips?" Semiecosystem, June 27, 2025, https://marklapedus.substack.com/p/can-china-make-5nm-chips.

[18] "China's Chip Champions Ramp Up Production of AI Accelerators at Domestic Fabs, but HBM and Fab Production Capacity Are Towering Bottlenecks," Tom's Hardware, September 10, 2025, https://www.tomshardware.com/tech-industry/artificial-intelligence/chinas-chip-champions-ramp-up-production-of-ai-accelerators-at-domestic-fabs-but-hbm-and-fab-production-capacity-are-towering-bottlenecks.

[19] "DeepSeek R1 Stuns the AI World," HPCwire, January 27, 2025, https://www.hpcwire.com/2025/01/27/deepseek-r1-stuns-the-ai-world/.

[20] "DeepSeek's Hardware Spend Could Be as High as $500 Million, New Report Estimates," CNBC, January 31, 2025, https://www.cnbc.com/2025/01/31/deepseeks-hardware-spend-could-be-as-high-as-500-million-report.html.

[21] Ibid.

[22] "DeepSeek Didn't Really Train Its Flagship Model for $294,000," The Register, September 19, 2025, https://www.theregister.com/2025/09/19/deepseek_cost_train/.

[23] Ibid.

[24] "Nvidia Stock Plummets, Loses Record $589 Billion as DeepSeek Prompts Questions Over AI Spending," Yahoo Finance, January 27, 2025, https://finance.yahoo.com/news/nvidia-stock-plummets-loses-record-589-billion-as-deepseek-prompts-questions-over-ai-spending-135105824.html.

[25] "Nvidia Drops Nearly 17% as China's Cheaper AI Model DeepSeek Sparks Global Tech Sell-Off," CNBC, January 27, 2025, https://www.cnbc.com/2025/01/27/nvidia-falls-10percent-in-premarket-trading-as-chinas-deepseek-triggers-global-tech-sell-off.html.

[26] "'AI's Sputnik Moment': Chinese AI Model DeepSeek-R1 Reportedly Surpasses Leading U.S. AI Models," Foundation for Defense of Democracies, January 30, 2025, https://www.fdd.org/analysis/policy_briefs/2025/01/30/ais-sputnik-moment-chinese-ai-model-deepseek-r1-reportedly-surpasses-leading-u-s-ai-models/.

[27] "Stanford Report Finds U.S. AI Edge Fading as China Closes Gap," China Economic Net, April 11, 2025, http://en.ce.cn/Insight/202504/t20250411_1977444.shtml.

[28] "AI Index 2025: State of AI in 10 Charts," Stanford Institute for Human-Centered Artificial Intelligence, April 2025, https://hai.stanford.edu/news/ai-index-2025-state-of-ai-in-10-charts.

[29] "The State of AI 2025: 12 Eye-Opening Graphs," IEEE Spectrum, May 1, 2025, https://spectrum.ieee.org/ai-index-2025.

[30] "'AI's Sputnik Moment': Chinese AI Model DeepSeek-R1 Reportedly Surpasses Leading U.S. AI Models," Foundation for Defense of Democracies, January 30, 2025.

[31] "Nvidia Says It Will Record $5.5 Billion Charge Tied to H20 Processors Exported to China," CNBC, April 15, 2025, https://www.cnbc.com/2025/04/15/nvidia-says-it-will-record-5point5-billion-quarterly-charge-tied-to-h20-processors-exported-to-china.html.

[32] Ibid.

[33] "Nvidia Writes Off $5.5 Billion in GPUs as US Gov't Chokes Off Supply of H20s to China," Tom's Hardware, April 16, 2025, https://www.tomshardware.com/tech-industry/artificial-

intelligence/nvidia-writes-off-usd5-5-billion-in-gpus-as-us-govt-chokes-off-supply-of-h20s-to-china.

[34] "Nvidia Discloses that U.S. Will Limit Sales of Advanced Chips to China After All," NPR, April 16, 2025, https://www.npr.org/2025/04/16/nx-s1-5366665/nvidia-china-h20-chips-exports.

[35] "'AI's Sputnik Moment': Chinese AI Model DeepSeek-R1 Reportedly Surpasses Leading U.S. AI Models," Foundation for Defense of Democracies, January 30, 2025.

[36] "What Happened When Trump Met Xi?" Brookings Institution, November 2025, https://www.brookings.edu/articles/what-happened-when-trump-met-xi/.

[37] "Huawei's Ascend AI Chip Ecosystem Scales Up as China Pushes for Semiconductor Independence," Tom's Hardware, November 2025.

[38] "DeepSeek's New AI Model Debuts with Support for China-Native Chips and CANN, a Replacement for Nvidia's CUDA," Tom's Hardware, 2025.

[39] "AI Index 2025: State of AI in 10 Charts," Stanford Institute for Human-Centered Artificial Intelligence, April 2025.

[40] Ibid.

[41] "The 2025 Busan Meeting: Setting New Expectations for China and the United States," Asia-Pacific Leadership Network, https://www.apln.network/analysis/commentaries/the-2025-busan-meeting-setting-new-expectations-for-china-and-the-united-states.

[42] "Key Findings from Stanford's 2025 AI Index Report," IBM Think, November 2025, https://www.ibm.com/think/news/stanford-hai-2025-ai-index-report.

[43] "Trump-Xi Meeting in Busan: Key Takeaways from the Summit," Al Jazeera, October 30, 2025, https://www.aljazeera.com/news/2025/10/30/trump-xi-meeting-in-busan-key-takeaways-from-the-summit.

Part III

The Resource Wars

Chapter 7
Rare Earths—China's Hidden Leverage

Critical Minerals and the New Resource Geopolitics

In 1992, while visiting Baotou in Inner Mongolia, Deng Xiaoping uttered words that would prove prophetic for twenty-first-century geopolitics: "The Middle East has oil, China has rare earths."[1] This statement was not mere observation but strategic declaration—a recognition that control over seventeen obscure metallic elements would become as consequential to global power as petroleum dominance was throughout the previous century. Three decades later, Beijing commands an overwhelming monopoly over the rare earth ecosystem, controlling approximately 70 percent of global mining and 90 percent of refining capacity.[2] What began as natural advantage in resource endowment has evolved into an instrument of statecraft, providing China with unprecedented leverage over the global economy, technology supply chains, and defense industries.

The rare earth elements constitute a paradox in nomenclature. Despite their designation, these seventeen metals—comprising the fifteen lanthanides plus scandium and yttrium—are neither particularly rare nor especially earthbound in geological terms. Cerium, the most abundant among them, occurs more frequently in Earth's crust than copper or lead.[3] The "rare" designation instead reflects the challenge of finding these elements in economically viable concentrations and the extraordinary difficulty of separating them from one another. Their chemical similarity—the result of identical outer electron shell configurations—renders them virtually indistinguishable through standard chemical processes, requiring sophisticated solvent extraction techniques that China has spent decades perfecting.[4]

The Periodic Table of Power

Understanding China's rare earth leverage requires grasping what makes these elements irreplaceable in modern technology. The lanthanide series possesses unique electronic, magnetic, luminescent, and catalytic properties unmatched by any other elements on the periodic table.[5] Their partially filled f-orbitals create magnetic moments of extraordinary strength and stability, enabling technologies that would otherwise be impossible.

Neodymium stands as perhaps the most consequential of these elements. When alloyed with iron and boron to create neodymium-iron-boron (NdFeB) magnets, it produces magnetic fields approximately eighteen times stronger than conventional iron magnets of equivalent volume.[6] These permanent magnets form the heart of electric vehicle motors, wind turbine generators, computer hard drives, smartphone speakers, and precision-guided munitions. A single electric vehicle requires one to two kilograms of neodymium and praseodymium, while offshore wind turbines demand up to 600 kilograms of rare earth elements in their permanent magnet generators.[7]

The strategic significance extends across both civilian and military applications. According to a 2013 Congressional Research Service report, an F-35 Lightning II fighter jet contains approximately 920 pounds (417 kilograms) of rare earth materials, essential for its advanced targeting systems, radar, flight control mechanisms, and stealth capabilities.[8] Each DDG-51 Arleigh Burke-class destroyer requires approximately 5,200 pounds, while a Virginia-class submarine demands roughly 9,200 pounds of these elements for radar, sonar, missile guidance, and propulsion systems.[9] Defense applications account for approximately five percent of total U.S. rare earth consumption, yet the materials prove essential across virtually every modern weapons platform.[10]

Samarium-cobalt magnets, though slightly weaker than NdFeB variants, excel in high-temperature applications where extreme heat would demagnetize conventional magnets. These appear in jet engines, avionics, and missile components where temperatures exceed normal operating parameters. Lockheed Martin, as a major American consumer of samarium, incorporates samarium-cobalt magnets into F-35 systems to handle the heat generated by its engine and power systems.[11]

Dysprosium and terbium serve as critical additives that enhance magnet performance under demanding conditions. Adding small quantities of dysprosium to NdFeB magnets dramatically improves their resistance to demagnetization at elevated temperatures—a property essential for electric vehicle motors and aerospace applications where components must maintain magnetic strength despite extreme heat.[12] The scarcity and concentrated supply of these heavy rare earths compound their strategic importance; China maintains dominant processing capacity for these specific elements.[13]

Beyond magnets, rare earths pervade modern technology in less visible but equally essential roles. Europium and terbium provide the red and green phosphors in LED lighting and display screens. Erbium-doped fiber amplifiers intensify signals in the high-capacity fiber-optic networks carrying internet traffic and telecommunications.[14] Cerium and lanthanum serve as catalysts in petroleum refining and automotive catalytic converters. Yttrium appears in laser systems, from medical equipment to military range-finders. The breadth of applications means that disruption to rare earth supplies would cascade through virtually every sector of advanced economies.

China's Path to Dominance: From the 1980s to the Present

China's rare earth supremacy did not emerge through geological accident alone but resulted from deliberate, decades-long strategic planning. When Deng Xiaoping articulated his vision of rare earths as China's equivalent to Middle Eastern petroleum, Beijing had already begun implementing policies that would systematically capture the entire value chain.[15]

During the 1980s, while Western nations focused on information technology and financial deregulation, China quietly constructed an industrial base rooted in resource control. The Chinese government provided aggressive state incentives, cheap credit, and permissive environmental policies that allowed rapid scaling of extraction and refining operations.[16] This flood of low-cost supply depressed global prices, forcing competitors in the United States and Australia out of business. Mountain Pass—once America's premier rare earth facility and the world's dominant producer through the 1980s—ceased oxide production in 1998 and closed entirely in 2002 following a toxic waste spill, unable to compete with Chinese prices.[17]

The brilliance of Beijing's strategy lay not merely in controlling raw resources but in mastering the full industrial chain. Rare earth separation and refining represent complex, chemically intensive processes generating substantial toxic waste. Western producers faced strict environmental standards and high remediation costs; China tolerated the pollution as the price of industrial ascendancy.[18] Chinese rare earth production increased from approximately 31,000 metric tons in 1994 to 270,000 metric tons in 2024, capturing the overwhelming majority of global supply.[19]

The acquisition strategy extended beyond mining to encompass downstream capabilities. In 1995, a consortium including Chinese entities purchased a stake in Magnequench, a General Motors subsidiary that had pioneered and dominated the manufacture of rare earth magnets.[20] Magnequench's technology and production lines were subsequently transferred to China by the early 2000s, eliminating American capability in this critical manufacturing segment.

The consolidation accelerated under subsequent Chinese leadership. Beijing moved to reorganize the rare earth industry under six large state-owned enterprises: Inner Mongolia Baotou Iron and Steel Group, China Minmetals Corporation, Aluminum Corporation of China (Chinalco), Guangdong Rare Earth Group, Xiamen Tungsten, and Ganzhou Rare Earth Group.[21] These conglomerates, organized by geographic region, have absorbed smaller independent producers. The Chinese government introduced production quotas and traceability requirements to control output levels while consolidating industry structure.[22]

The geographic concentration of Chinese production centers on two distinct regions with different geological characteristics. Northern China's Bayan Obo deposit in Inner Mongolia constitutes the world's largest rare earth mine, containing a substantial portion of China's total reserves.[23] This massive open-pit operation, situated approximately 80 miles north of Baotou, produces predominantly light rare earths—lanthanum, cerium, praseodymium, and neodymium—that serve applications in catalysts, glass polishing, and permanent magnets.

Southern China's ion-adsorption clay deposits, concentrated in Jiangxi Province and neighboring areas, yield the strategically more valuable heavy rare earths—dysprosium, terbium, yttrium, and others—essential for high-temperature magnets and advanced electronic applications.[24] These deposits formed through weathering of granite over millions of years, creating clay minerals that adsorbed rare earth ions. Extraction requires comparatively simple leaching techniques but generates significant environmental damage as acidic solutions contaminate soil and groundwater.

The Weaponization Moment: From Trade Tool to Strategic Lever

China demonstrated its willingness to deploy rare earth leverage in September 2010, when a Chinese fishing trawler collided with Japanese coast guard vessels near the disputed Senkaku/ Diaoyu Islands. Following the arrest of the trawler's captain, Beijing imposed what was widely reported as an unofficial embargo on rare earth exports to Japan—then dependent on China for approximately 90 percent of its rare earth imports.[25]

The incident sent shockwaves through Japanese industry, particularly the automotive sector reliant on rare earth magnets for hybrid vehicle motors. Rare earth prices surged dramatically, with some elements increasing tenfold within a year.[26] Although China officially denied imposing any targeted restriction, the episode revealed both the potency and the limitations of rare earth coercion as a geopolitical instrument.

The incident prompted significant international response. Japan invested approximately 100 billion yen (then valued at approximately $730 million) in countermeasures, including securing supplies from Australia's Mount Weld mine, developing substitutes that reduced rare earth content in magnets, and establishing domestic recycling programs.[27] Japanese dependence on Chinese rare earths subsequently declined from 90 percent to approximately 60 percent, demonstrating that determined effort could reduce vulnerability.[28]

The United States, European Union, and Japan filed complaints with the World Trade Organization against Chinese export restrictions in 2012. The WTO ruled in 2014 that China's export quotas and duties on rare earths violated its trade commitments, rejecting Beijing's arguments that restrictions served conservation and environmental protection purposes.[29] China complied with the ruling by abolishing export quotas and duties in January 2015, though the underlying dominance remained undiminished.

The October 2025 escalation marked a far more comprehensive assertion of rare earth leverage. In response to intensifying trade tensions with the United States, China's Ministry of Commerce issued sweeping export controls covering seven medium and heavy rare earth elements—samarium, gadolinium, terbium, dysprosium, lutetium, scandium, and yttrium—as well as permanent magnets and processing technologies.[30] Unlike the 2010 Japan episode, which targeted a single trading partner, these restrictions applied globally and extended beyond raw materials to encompass finished products, manufacturing equipment, and technical expertise.

The controls introduced a licensing regime requiring exporters to obtain special approval from China's Commerce Ministry before shipping affected materials at any stage of the supply chain.[31] More significantly, the regulations extended to products containing Chinese-origin rare earths, potentially subjecting manufacturers of motors, electronics, or defense equipment to Chinese oversight. The restriction on processing technologies and equipment threatened to constrain even those projects attempting to establish alternative supply chains.

This represented transformation from trade dispute to strategic competition. The House Select Committee on the Strategic Competition Between the United States and the Chinese Communist Party described the October 2025 measures as the "culmination of policies, investments, and maneuvers built over decades" through which Beijing put rare earth leverage into action.[32]

The Expansion Beyond Rare Earths: Gallium, Germanium, Antimony, and Graphite

China's critical mineral leverage extends well beyond the seventeen rare earth elements to encompass other materials essential for semiconductors, defense systems, and clean energy technologies. In December 2024, China's Ministry of Commerce announced that exports of gallium, germanium, antimony, and superhard materials to the United States would not be approved in principle, citing their dual-use applications in both civilian and military systems.[33]

Gallium, produced almost exclusively as a byproduct of aluminum smelting, provides the foundation for gallium arsenide and gallium nitride semiconductors used in LED lighting, wireless communications, solar cells, and military radar systems.[34] China accounts for the overwhelming majority of global gallium production, creating near-total dependency for consuming nations. Germanium serves critical functions in fiber optic systems, infrared optics for night-vision equipment, and polymerization catalysts. Antimony finds applications in ammunition, infrared missiles, and flame retardants.

The December 2024 restrictions followed earlier controls on gallium and germanium implemented in July 2023, which had required export licenses for these materials. The escalation to denial of export approval for U.S. destinations reflected deliberate retaliation against American semiconductor export controls targeting Chinese technology companies.[35] The timing—immediately following expanded U.S. restrictions on advanced chip sales to China—demonstrated Beijing's willingness to engage in tit-for-tat economic measures.

Graphite, essential for lithium-ion battery anodes, became subject to stricter end-user and end-use reviews for exports to the United States in December 2024, with expanded controls announced in October 2025 covering battery cells, cathode materials, and production equipment.[36] China's dominance across battery supply chains approaches or exceeds 80 percent in most key segments, according to the International Energy Agency.[37]

The cumulative effect of these restrictions created significant market disruption. By November 2025, following negotiations between U.S. and Chinese leaders, China announced temporary suspension of these export controls for one year, providing a reprieve while structural dependencies remained unchanged.[38]

Implications for Defense, Semiconductors, Electric Vehicles, and Renewable Energy

The strategic implications of China's mineral dominance extend across every sector vital to advanced economies. The defense sector faces perhaps the most acute vulnerabilities given the concentration of rare earth materials in precision weapons systems.

In September 2022, discovery that F-35 fighter jet engines contained a rare earth magnet produced in China prompted attention and congressional interest.[39] While Pentagon officials determined that the Chinese-origin magnet did not compromise engine performance or represent security threats, the incident highlighted the extent of American defense dependency. As acknowledged by defense officials, building weapons systems using only domestic components would prove challenging given the absence of alternative suppliers for certain materials.[40]

The Government Accountability Office has issued multiple reports examining Department of Defense efforts to identify and mitigate rare earth supply chain risks. A February 2016 GAO report found that DoD's approach to identifying and mitigating risks associated with rare earths was "fragmented," with different offices using different definitions of which rare earths were critical.[41] A September 2024 GAO report noted that since 2020, DoD has awarded approximately $439 million to vendors to reestablish domestic rare earth supply chains, though the department "has not yet determined how much total domestic capacity it needs to create in the long term to meet defense-related demand."[42]

The semiconductor industry confronts analogous dependencies. Beyond gallium and germanium for compound semiconductors, rare earth elements appear in chip manufacturing equipment, magnetic storage, and the fiber optic networks enabling data centers. The integration of rare earths into every layer of digital infrastructure means that sustained supply disruption would propagate through communications, computing, and artificial intelligence systems.

Electric vehicle manufacturing represents one of the fastest-growing demand sectors for rare earth magnets. Each EV motor requires permanent magnets containing neodymium, praseodymium, and often dysprosium or terbium for thermal stability.[43] Global EV production continues to increase, creating compounding demand that current supply chains may struggle to satisfy. The International Energy Agency projects continued growth in rare earth demand through 2030, with electric vehicle and wind energy applications driving acceleration.[44]

Wind turbine generators present similar challenges at larger scales. Direct-drive turbines utilizing permanent magnet generators require substantial quantities of rare earth magnets per installation.[45] As countries accelerate renewable energy deployment to meet climate commitments, dependence on Chinese magnets intensifies.

The Environmental Price of Dominance

China's rare earth supremacy came at substantial environmental and human cost—a hidden subsidy that competitors operating under stricter regulations could not match. The processing of rare earth ores generates enormous quantities of toxic and radioactive waste, including heavy metals and thorium released through acidic extraction.

The Weikuang Dam near Baotou represents the accumulated environmental burden. This tailings impoundment, covering a substantial area, contains decades of accumulated waste from rare earth processing mixed with tailings from iron ore extraction.[46] The material contains lead, cadmium, and traces of radioactive thorium. During dry seasons, wind disperses contaminated dust across surrounding areas. During summer rains, water mixing with toxic residue seeps into groundwater.[47]

Research published in Chinese scientific journals found thorium concentrations in soil near rare earth processing facilities reaching levels substantially higher than normal background values.[48] Studies documented health concerns among populations in areas affected by rare earth processing pollution.[49]

Industry estimates suggest that producing one ton of rare earth oxide generates substantial quantities of waste gas containing dust, sulfur dioxide, hydrochloric acid, and sulfuric acid, along with significant volumes of mine tailings.[50] The environmental damage extended beyond northern China. In Jiangxi Province, where heavy rare earths are extracted from ion-adsorption clays, acid and ammonia from processing operations contaminated rivers and damaged ecosystems.[51]

Western facilities addressing similar contamination incurred massive costs. The European Union spent substantial resources to construct proper containment for rare earth processing waste at a facility in Estonia following the Soviet Union's dissolution.[52] China's tailings facilities, many built decades earlier without modern environmental standards, present remediation challenges of significant magnitude.

Toward Strategic Confrontation

The October 2025 export controls transformed rare earths from background vulnerability to active battleground in U.S.-China strategic competition. By restricting not merely raw materials but processing technologies, equipment, and finished magnets, China signaled capacity to constrain even diversification efforts dependent on Chinese expertise.

The strategic logic from Beijing's perspective reflects decades of investment reaching fruition. Rare earth dominance provides leverage across military, technological, and industrial domains simultaneously. Every F-35, every Virginia-class submarine, every offshore wind farm, every electric vehicle depends on materials China controls. The integration of rare earths into essential systems creates interdependence that raises the costs of confrontation for all parties but disproportionately for those on the dependent end of supply chains.[53]

For the United States and its allies, the implications demand response across multiple vectors: rebuilding domestic extraction and processing capacity, establishing supply chains with reliable partners, investing in substitution research to reduce rare earth requirements, and developing strategic reserves of finished materials rather than merely raw ore.[54] According to the U.S. Geological Survey, between 2020 and 2023, the United States imported approximately 70 percent of its rare earth compounds and metals from China.[55]

The challenge is fundamentally one of time—reducing dependence on China's rare earth dominance requires sustained effort over years or more, while Beijing retains leverage that could be deployed in any intensifying confrontation.

As the House Select Committee on the CCP concluded, rare earths have become critical to American economic and national security, requiring action to address vulnerabilities.[56] The minerals that enable smartphones, wind turbines, and precision munitions alike now occupy the center of great power competition. Deng Xiaoping's thirty-year-old declaration has been vindicated: in the twenty-first century, China's rare earths have indeed become a resource whose control shapes the global balance of power.

Endnotes

[1] Foundation for Defense of Democracies, "Elemental Strategy: Countering the Chinese Communist Party's Efforts to Dominate the Rare Earth Industry," February 10, 2022, https://www.fdd.org/analysis/2022/02/10/elemental-strategy-countering-the-chinese-communist-partys-efforts-to-dominate-the-rare-earth-industry/. The quote is widely attributed to Deng's 1992 visit to Baotou.

[2] U.S. Geological Survey, "Rare Earths," Mineral Commodity Summaries 2025, January 2025, https://pubs.usgs.gov/periodicals/mcs2025/mcs2025-rare-earths.pdf; International Energy Agency, "With New Export Controls on Critical Minerals, Supply Concentration Risks Become Reality," October 23, 2025, https://www.iea.org/commentaries/with-new-export-controls-on-critical-minerals-supply-concentration-risks-become-reality.

[3] U.S. Geological Survey, "Rare Earths Statistics and Information," https://www.usgs.gov/centers/national-minerals-information-center/rare-earths-statistics-and-information.

[4] Science History Institute, "Science of Rare Earth Elements," October 11, 2024, https://www.sciencehistory.org/education/classroom-activities/role-playing-games/case-of-rare-earth-elements/science/.

[5] Ibid.

[6] Ibid.

[7] International Energy Agency, "The Role of Critical Minerals in Clean Energy Transitions," May 2021, https://www.iea.org/reports/the-role-of-critical-minerals-in-clean-energy-transitions.

[8] Congressional Research Service, "Rare Earth Elements in National Defense: Background, Oversight Issues, and Options for Congress," R41744, December 23, 2013, cited in Air & Space Forces Magazine, "Rare Elements of Security," November 1, 2020, https://www.airandspaceforces.com/article/rare-elements-of-security/; U.S. Army, "An Elemental Issue," September 26, 2019, https://www.army.mil/article/227715/an_elemental_issue.

[9] Air & Space Forces Magazine, "Rare-Earth Uncertainty," December 21, 2017, https://www.airandspaceforces.com/article/rare-earth-uncertainty/; Breaking Defense, "Pentagon Fails To Act On Crucial Rare Earth Minerals," March 2016, https://breakingdefense.com/2016/03/pentagon-fails-to-act-on-crucial-rare-earth-minerals/.

[10] Congressional Research Service reports; Science History Institute, "Using the Rare Earth Elements: Manufacturers Case Study," https://www.sciencehistory.org/education/classroom-activities/role-playing-games/case-of-rare-earth-elements/manufacturers/case-study/.

[11] Science History Institute, "Manufacturers Case Study."

[12] European Commission Joint Research Centre, "The Role of Rare Earth Elements in Wind Energy and Electric Mobility," 2020, https://publications.jrc.ec.europa.eu/repository/bitstream/JRC122671/jrc122671_the_role_of_rare_earth_elements_in_wind_energy_and_electric_mobility_2.pdf.

[13] International Energy Agency, "With New Export Controls on Critical Minerals."

[14] Science History Institute, "Science of Rare Earth Elements."

[15] Foundation for Defense of Democracies, "Elemental Strategy."

[16] Ibid.

[17] TIME, "Why It's So Hard to Challenge China's Rare Earths Dominance," June 17, 2025, https://time.com/7294964/us-rare-earths-minerals-china-dominance-trump-tariffs/.

[18] Wilson Center, New Security Beat, "Mine the Tech Gap: Why China's Rare Earth Dominance Persists," August 2024, https://www.newsecuritybeat.org/2024/08/mine-the-tech-gap-why-chinas-rare-earth-dominance-persists/.

[19] U.S. Geological Survey, Mineral Commodity Summaries 2025.

[20] Foundation for Defense of Democracies, "Elemental Strategy."

[21] Ibid.

[22] China Briefing, "China's Rare Earth Elements: What Businesses Need to Know," updated August 29, 2025, https://www.china-briefing.com/news/chinas-rare-earth-elements-dominance-in-global-supply-chains/.

[23] U.S. Geological Survey data; Center for Strategic and International Studies, "Does China Pose a Threat to Global Rare Earth Supply Chains?," https://chinapower.csis.org/china-rare-earths/.

[24] U.S. Geological Survey, Mineral Commodity Summaries 2025.

[25] World Economic Forum, "How Japan Solved Its Rare Earth Minerals Dependency Issue," October 2023, https://www.weforum.org/stories/2023/10/japan-rare-earth-minerals/.

[26] Ibid.

[27] Ibid.

[28] Ibid.

[29] World Trade Organization, "China — Measures Related to the Exportation of Rare Earths, Tungsten, and Molybdenum," Dispute DS431, https://www.wto.org/english/tratop_e/dispu_e/cases_e/ds431_e.htm.

[30] International Energy Agency, "With New Export Controls on Critical Minerals."

[31] Pillsbury Winthrop Shaw Pittman LLP, "China Suspends Export Controls on Certain Critical Minerals and Related Items," November 2025, https://www.pillsburylaw.com/en/news-and-insights/china-suspends-export-controls-certain-critical-minerals-related-items.html.

[32] U.S. House of Representatives Select Committee on the Strategic Competition Between the United States and the Chinese Communist Party, "Predatory Pricing: How the Chinese Communist Party Manipulates Global Mineral Prices to Maintain Its Dominance," November 2025, https://selectcommitteeontheccp.house.gov/media/press-releases/bipartisan-investigation-reveals-how-the-ccp-manipulates-the-critical-minerals-market.

[33] Center for Security and Emerging Technology, Georgetown University, "Ministry of Commerce Notice 2024 No. 46: Notice Concerning Strengthening Controls on Exports of Relevant Dual-Use Items to the United States," December 3, 2024, https://cset.georgetown.edu/publication/china-rare-earth-export-ban/.

[34] U.S. Geological Survey, Mineral Commodity Summaries 2025, Gallium chapter.

[35] Center for Security and Emerging Technology, "Ministry of Commerce Notice 2024 No. 46."

[36] International Energy Agency, "With New Export Controls on Critical Minerals."

[37] Ibid.

[38] CNBC, "China Suspends Some Critical Mineral Export Curbs to the U.S. as Trade Truce Takes Hold," November 10, 2025, https://www.cnbc.com/2025/11/10/china-suspends-some-critical-mineral-export-curbs-to-the-us-as-trade-truce-takes-hold.html.

[39] Finabel European Army Interoperability Centre, "Rare Earth Metals and F-35 Supply Chain," December 13, 2022, https://finabel.org/rare-earth-metals-and-f-35-supply-chain/.

[40] Ibid.

[41] U.S. Government Accountability Office, "Rare Earth Materials: Developing a Comprehensive Approach Could Help DOD Better Manage National Security Risks in the Supply Chain," GAO-16-161, February 11, 2016, https://www.gao.gov/products/gao-16-161.

[42] U.S. Government Accountability Office, "Critical Materials: Action Needed to Implement Requirements That Reduce Supply Chain Risks," GAO-24-107176, September 10, 2024, https://www.gao.gov/products/gao-24-107176.

[43] European Commission Joint Research Centre, "The Role of Rare Earth Elements in Wind Energy and Electric Mobility."

[44] International Energy Agency, "The Role of Critical Minerals in Clean Energy Transitions."

[45] Ibid.

[46] Keith Bradsher, "China Paid High Price for Dominance in Rare Earths," New York Times, July 2025, cited in MCLC Resource Center, https://u.osu.edu/mclc/2025/07/07/china-has-paid-a-high-price-for-dominance-in-rare-earths/.

[47] Ibid.

[48] Inner Mongolia University of Science and Technology research cited in scientific literature on Baotou area contamination.

[49] Studies on health impacts in rare earth processing areas documented in Chinese and international scientific journals.

[50] Industry estimates cited in Foundation for Defense of Democracies, "Elemental Strategy."

[51] State of the Planet, Columbia Climate School, "The Energy Transition Will Need More Rare Earth Elements. Can We Secure Them Sustainably?," April 5, 2023, https://news.climate.columbia.edu/2023/04/05/the-energy-transition-will-need-more-rare-earth-elements-can-we-secure-them-sustainably/.

[52] New York Times reporting on Estonian facility remediation.

[53] Foundation for Defense of Democracies, "Elemental Strategy."

[54] U.S. Government Accountability Office, GAO-24-107176.

[55] U.S. Geological Survey, Mineral Commodity Summaries 2025.

[56] House Select Committee on the CCP, "Predatory Pricing."

Chapter 8
The U.S.-Australia Critical Minerals Alliance

Building Alternative Supply Chains

On October 20, 2025, President Donald Trump and Australian Prime Minister Anthony Albanese met in the Cabinet Room of the White House to formalize what would become the most comprehensive bilateral agreement on strategic materials in modern history. As the two leaders signed the United States-Australia Framework for Securing of Supply in the Mining and Processing of Critical Minerals and Rare Earths, they acknowledged an uncomfortable reality: China's near-monopoly over critical mineral processing had become an acute vulnerability for both nations' economic and national security.[1] The framework represented more than a traditional trade agreement—it was a declaration that critical minerals would no longer be treated as mere commodities but as strategic assets essential to the functioning of modern economies and defense systems.

The timing of the agreement was not coincidental. Just two weeks earlier, on October 9, 2025, China had escalated its weaponization of critical minerals by announcing sweeping new export controls on rare earth elements, lithium battery materials, and processing technologies. These restrictions, which implemented an extraterritorial reach unprecedented in scope, required export licenses for products manufactured anywhere in the world if they contained Chinese-origin materials or were produced using Chinese technologies.[2] The move sent shockwaves through global supply chains and provided the final impetus for what had been months of intensive negotiations between Washington and Canberra.

The Framework commits both governments to providing at least one billion dollars in financing to critical minerals projects within six months, with total project pipelines valued at 8.5 billion dollars across both nations.[3] But the agreement's significance extends far beyond these dollar figures. It establishes institutional mechanisms—including a U.S.-Australia Critical Minerals Supply Security Response Group co-led by the U.S. Secretary of Energy and the Australian Minister for Resources—designed to identify supply vulnerabilities and accelerate project delivery in real time.[4] Most critically, it introduces price floor mechanisms and asset sale restrictions explicitly designed to counter China's history of using predatory pricing to eliminate competition.

The Strategic Logic: Why Australia?

Australia's designation as America's "most important partner in countering China's dominance in rare earths" reflects both geological reality and geopolitical calculation.[5] The Australian continent, shaped by billions of years of tectonic activity, contains commercially viable deposits of over forty critical minerals identified by the U.S. Geological Survey. As former Australian Prime Minister Kevin Rudd observed at a Center for Strategic and International Studies forum, "Most of the periodic table is under our soil."[6]

The numbers substantiate this claim. Australia produces approximately fifty-two percent of global lithium supply, primarily from hard rock spodumene operations in Western Australia.[7] It possesses estimated rare earth oxide reserves of 3.4 million tonnes, making it the world's fourth-largest producer with significant untapped potential.[8] The country ranks among the top five global producers of cobalt and contributes about fifteen percent of worldwide manganese production.[9] Critically, approximately eighty percent of Australia's continental landmass remains underexplored using modern geophysical techniques, suggesting substantial undiscovered resources.[10]

But Australia's value as a strategic partner transcends its mineral endowment. Unlike many resource-rich nations, Australia combines geological abundance with political stability, transparent regulatory frameworks, and sophisticated mining expertise. The country's mining sector, which generates four hundred to four hundred fifty billion dollars in annual exports, operates under stringent environmental and labor standards that increasingly matter to downstream manufacturers concerned about supply chain ethics.[11] Three Australian universities—the University of New South Wales, Curtin University, and the University of Queensland—rank among the world's top six institutions for mineral and mining engineering, providing a deep talent pool for technological innovation.[12]

Most significantly, Australia has already demonstrated its capacity to challenge Chinese dominance in the most technically demanding segment of the supply chain: rare earth processing. In May 2025, Australia's Lynas Rare Earths achieved a milestone that had eluded Western companies for decades when it became the first firm outside China to produce commercial quantities of dysprosium oxide—one of the most critical heavy rare earth elements—at its facility in Malaysia using feedstock from Western Australia's Mount Weld mine.[13] This accomplishment proved that China's processing monopoly, while formidable, was not technologically insurmountable given sufficient investment and expertise.

Australia's position also reflects a favorable investment climate that stands in sharp contrast to the regulatory obstacles plaguing U.S. domestic mining development. While the United States averages twenty-nine years from mineral discovery to mine production—with ten years or more consumed by permitting alone—Australia's established regulatory frameworks and mining culture enable faster project advancement.[14] The Australian Stock Exchange serves as the world's second-largest source of financing for junior and mid-tier mining companies, with higher overall market values than Toronto, providing critical capital access for projects below the threshold that typically attracts major miners.[15]

Finally, Australia's geographic positioning offers strategic advantages. Located in the Indo-Pacific region, it provides shorter supply routes to Asian manufacturing centers while maintaining the political alignment with Washington that enables trusted partnership. The seventy-year alliance between the United States and Australia, now encompassing AUKUS and expanded defense cooperation, provides an institutional foundation that purely transactional relationships with other mineral-rich nations cannot replicate.

The Priority Projects: Gallium and Rare Earths

The Framework immediately identified two flagship projects for accelerated development, each addressing critical vulnerabilities in specific supply chains. These projects exemplify the agreement's strategic focus on high-impact interventions rather than broad, unfocused investment.

Alcoa's Wagerup Gallium Recovery Project

The first priority project centers on extracting gallium from bauxite during the alumina refining process at Alcoa Corporation's Wagerup refinery in Western Australia. The project, which builds on a Joint Development Agreement announced in August 2025 with Japan Australia Gallium Associates (a joint venture between Sojitz Corporation and the Japan Organization for Metals and Energy Security), represents a trilateral collaboration among the United States, Australia, and Japan.[16]

The Australian government committed up to two hundred million dollars in concessional equity finance with offtake rights, while the U.S. Department of Defense announced it would invest in establishing gallium refining capacity capable of producing one hundred metric tons annually.[17] This production target is significant: it would supply approximately ten percent of total global gallium supply and directly address a critical vulnerability in defense and semiconductor supply chains.[18]

Gallium's strategic importance cannot be overstated. The silvery metal, which occurs naturally in bauxite at concentrations of thirty to eighty parts per million, is essential for semiconductor manufacturing, high-performance radar systems, LED production, and defense electronics.[19] China currently controls an estimated ninety-five percent of global gallium refining capacity and has demonstrated its willingness to weaponize this dominance.[20] In December 2024, Beijing banned the sale of gallium to the United States as part of its broader critical minerals strategy, causing immediate disruptions to defense contractors seeking diverse supply sources.[21]

The Wagerup project leverages existing infrastructure—a crucial advantage in an industry where capital costs often derail new ventures. Gallium extraction occurs during the Bayer process, the standard industrial method for refining alumina from bauxite ore. As bauxite is dissolved in caustic soda at high temperatures, gallium becomes concentrated in the processing liquor, from which it can be recovered using established separation techniques.[22] Alcoa's Western Australian operations, which include the Wagerup and Pinjarra alumina refineries, already process millions of tonnes of bauxite annually, providing a stable feedstock without requiring new mining operations.[23]

The project structure reflects sophisticated risk-sharing mechanisms designed to overcome the commercial barriers that typically impede critical minerals ventures. Following completion of feasibility assessments, a special purpose vehicle jointly owned by the U.S. and Australian governments and Alcoa would enter into the joint venture with JAGA to construct and operate the gallium plant.[24] Capital contributions and gallium offtake would be proportional to each party's interests, ensuring aligned incentives. The trilateral nature of the arrangement—incorporating Japanese financing and technology alongside American and Australian capital—demonstrates how allied cooperation can pool resources and expertise to challenge concentrated supply chains.

The project timeline targets a final investment decision in 2026 with production potentially commencing the same year.[25] If successful, this rapid development schedule would provide tangible results within the Framework's initial implementation period, offering proof of concept for similar ventures across other critical minerals.

Arafura's Nolans Rare Earth Project

The second flagship project, the Arafura Nolans Rare Earths Project located one hundred thirty-five kilometers north of Alice Springs in Australia's Northern Territory, represents an even more ambitious effort to challenge Chinese dominance in the rare earth supply chain. The Australian government announced a one hundred million dollar equity investment in the project, which, once operational, will produce approximately five percent of global rare earth supplies—specifically, 4,440 tonnes per annum of neodymium-praseodymium (NdPr) oxide and 470 tonnes of mixed middle-heavy rare earth oxide.[26]

The Nolans project's significance extends beyond its production targets. It will become Australia's first fully integrated ore-to-oxide rare earth processing operation, demonstrating the country's capacity to capture value-added processing rather than merely exporting raw materials.[27] The project encompasses mining, beneficiation, extraction, and separation facilities—the complete supply chain from ground to finished product—at a single location, reducing logistics vulnerabilities and enabling tighter quality control.

NdPr oxides serve as the primary input for high-performance permanent magnets, which are essential components in electric vehicle traction motors, wind turbine generators, precision-guided munitions, and advanced electronics.[28] China currently produces approximately ninety-four percent of global rare earth permanent magnets, a share that has increased from around fifty percent two decades ago.[29] This near-monopoly gives Beijing extraordinary leverage over industries ranging from automotive to defense, with the April 2025 export restrictions demonstrating how quickly supply disruptions can force factory closures when alternative sources are unavailable.[30]

The Nolans deposit itself represents a world-class resource. The rare earth-phosphate-uranium-thorium orebody contains low-risk mineral resources with an initial mine life of thirty-eight years and the potential to extend operations beyond forty-five years as additional reserves are developed.[31] The project's economics benefit from a valuable phosphoric acid by-product, which provides revenue diversification and improves overall project returns. Arafura has secured binding offtake agreements with major global manufacturers including Hyundai, Kia, and Siemens Gamesa Renewable Energy, providing revenue certainty that enhances project bankability.[32]

The project's development demonstrates both the opportunities and challenges inherent in building alternative supply chains. Arafura has completed extensive feasibility work, including a four-year metallurgical pilot program that validated the processing flowsheet, and has secured all necessary environmental and regulatory approvals—a major de-risking achievement given the complex approval requirements for rare earth projects.[33] Native Title agreements with Traditional Owners were executed in June 2020, and Mining Leases granted in July 2020 provide tenure security for twenty-five years.[34] Early site works, including access roads and accommodation facilities, were completed in 2023 at a cost exceeding forty million Australian dollars, positioning the project for rapid construction commencement once final financing is secured.[35]

Yet despite this preparation, the project has faced repeated delays in reaching final investment decision, highlighting systemic obstacles that plague critical minerals development. In July 2024, Arafura received conditional approval for over one billion dollars in debt funding, including support from the Australian government's Northern Australia Infrastructure Facility and the

National Reconstruction Fund Corporation.[36] However, closing the remaining equity gap has proven challenging amid volatile rare earth prices and competition from heavily subsidized Chinese production. The U.S.-Australia Framework's one hundred million dollar equity investment aims to "crowd-in" additional private capital by providing a cornerstone investment that reduces perceived risk.[37]

The project's economic impact extends beyond direct mining revenues. Nolans is expected to create more than six hundred jobs during construction and approximately three hundred fifty ongoing operational positions in a regional economy where employment opportunities are limited.[38] Alice Springs will serve as the logistics hub for both construction and operations, generating substantial indirect economic activity. The project represents a combined investment approaching two billion Australian dollars in one of the country's most remote regions, demonstrating how critical minerals development can drive meaningful regional development.

Price Mechanisms and Market Protections

Perhaps the most innovative and contentious aspect of the U.S.-Australia Framework concerns its approach to protecting domestic producers from Chinese price manipulation—a phenomenon that has repeatedly undermined Western critical minerals ventures. The Framework commits both nations to "work to protect their respective domestic critical minerals and rare earths markets from non-market policies and unfair trade practices, including through the adoption of standards-based systems in which those who adopt the standards can trade freely and within a pricing framework including price floors or similar measures."[39]

This language, carefully crafted to withstand potential trade law challenges, acknowledges a fundamental reality: China's decades-long dominance has created market structures where prices often reflect subsidies and strategic calculations rather than production costs. When Western projects threaten Chinese market share, Beijing has consistently demonstrated its willingness to flood markets with below-cost material, driving prices down to levels that make competing projects financially unviable. The rare earth sector provides the clearest example, but similar dynamics have played out in lithium, gallium, and other critical minerals.[40]

The challenge for Western policymakers is constructing protection mechanisms that insulate domestic producers without creating permanent, inefficient industries dependent on government support. The Framework's emphasis on "standards-based systems" offers one approach: establishing that materials meeting certain environmental, labor, and transparency standards can trade within a protected ecosystem with pricing stability, while non-compliant materials (primarily from China) face barriers or tariffs. This structure mirrors, at least conceptually, the carbon border adjustment mechanisms that European policymakers have discussed for steel and other products with high embodied emissions.

Implementation details remain to be negotiated, but industry observers suggest several possible mechanisms. Government-backed offtake agreements that establish minimum prices for specified quantities could provide revenue floors that enable project financing. Strategic stockpiles, maintained jointly by allied nations, could absorb excess production during price troughs while releasing material during supply crunches, dampening volatility that deters investment.[41] Tariffs on imports that benefit from unfair subsidies, carefully structured to comply with World Trade Organization rules, could raise the competitive floor without overtly discriminating based on country of origin.[42]

James Litinsky, CEO of MP Materials (the only U.S. rare earth mining company at scale), has proposed establishing a public-private partnership insurance corporation modeled on the Federal Crop Insurance Corporation created in 1938.[43] Under this approach, the government would provide revenue protection for key segments of the critical minerals supply chain—mining, refining, and magnet production—creating the price assurances necessary to encourage stable production and long-term purchase contracts. The concept acknowledges that critical minerals markets lack the depth and liquidity of commodity markets like oil or copper, making traditional hedging mechanisms unavailable.

Critics argue that such interventions risk creating zombie industries that persist only through subsidies, distorting resource allocation and saddling taxpayers with ongoing costs. They point to past examples, including aspects of the U.S. National Stockpile program from 1946 to 1979, where political considerations repeatedly overwhelmed economic logic, resulting in inappropriate acquisitions and disposal decisions.[44] There are also legitimate questions about whether price support mechanisms can be maintained across multiple election cycles and changing administrations, particularly if Chinese market tactics evolve in response.

However, proponents counter that critical minerals represent a unique case where market failures are both severe and strategically consequential. Unlike most industries, where competition eventually produces efficient outcomes, critical minerals supply chains exhibit extreme economies of scale in processing, high capital intensity, long lead times, and winner-take-all dynamics that favor established incumbents—in this case, Chinese state-backed enterprises operating with soft budget constraints and strategic rather than commercial objectives. Under such conditions, purely market-based approaches will predictably result in continued Chinese dominance, with all the vulnerabilities that entails.

The U.S.-Australia Framework's approach to price mechanisms represents a careful balancing act: acknowledging the need for interventions while stopping short of specific policy prescriptions. By committing to develop these mechanisms "in collaboration with international partners to develop a future global framework to deal with associated international pricing challenges," the agreement recognizes that unilateral actions would be insufficient and potentially counterproductive.[45] The goal is creating a coalition of aligned nations large enough to sustain viable markets for responsibly produced critical minerals, rather than individual countries attempting to go it alone.

Asset Sale Restrictions and Economic Security

The Framework's provisions on asset sale restrictions reflect growing recognition that critical minerals supply chains face threats not only from Chinese export controls but also from strategic acquisitions that give Beijing ownership of Western production. The text commits both parties to "work in good faith to develop new or strengthen existing authorities and diplomatic tools that review and deter critical minerals and rare earths asset sales on national security grounds."[46]

This language, while diplomatic, addresses a concrete concern: Chinese mining acquisitions reached their highest level in a decade in 2024, even as China slowed domestic production and idled projects.[47] By acquiring mines in politically stable jurisdictions like Australia, Canada, and African nations, Chinese state-owned and state-backed enterprises can secure supply chains while diversifying beyond vulnerable domestic operations. These acquisitions often occur opportunistically during price downturns when Western junior miners face financial distress and major mining companies divest non-core assets.

Australia already maintains a foreign investment screening regime through the Foreign Investment Review Board (FIRB), which assesses proposed acquisitions on national interest grounds, including national security considerations. Recent amendments to the Foreign Acquisitions and Takeovers Act have strengthened the Treasurer's power to impose conditions or block transactions in sensitive sectors, with critical minerals explicitly flagged as an area of concern.[48] The United States employs the Committee on Foreign Investment in the United States (CFIUS) for similar purposes, with reformed authorities under the Foreign Investment Risk Review Modernization Act of 2018 expanding scrutiny of non-controlling investments in critical technology and infrastructure sectors.[49]

The Framework's commitment suggests these existing authorities may require further expansion or coordination. Diplomatic tools mentioned in the agreement likely refer to concerted efforts to encourage third-country governments—particularly in Africa and Latin America, where many critical mineral deposits are located—to adopt similar screening mechanisms or at minimum, consult with Australia and the United States before approving Chinese acquisitions. This represents a significant diplomatic challenge, as many resource-rich developing nations value Chinese investment and resist what they perceive as Western interference in sovereign economic decisions.

The balancing act is delicate. Overly restrictive investment screening can deter legitimate commercial transactions and deprive projects of necessary capital. Chinese firms often bring genuine expertise in mining and processing, particularly for deposits that Western companies view as marginal. Blanket restrictions based on country of origin raise questions of discrimination and potential World Trade Organization violations. Yet the alternative—allowing unrestricted acquisitions until Chinese entities control enough of the supply chain to exercise effective market power—creates vulnerabilities that may prove irreversible.

The Broader Coalition: Japan and the European Union

While the U.S.-Australia Framework represents the most substantial bilateral agreement to date, both nations have explicitly positioned it within a broader coalition strategy involving other allied democracies. Japan's participation in the Alcoa gallium project exemplifies this multilateral approach, and further Japanese engagement appears likely given Tokyo's acute dependence on imported critical minerals and its experience with Chinese export restrictions.

On October 27, 2025—just one week after the U.S.-Australia Framework signing—the United States and Japan announced their own critical minerals framework, explicitly structured in parallel to the Australian agreement.[50] The U.S.-Japan framework establishes similar mechanisms: a Critical Minerals Supply Security Rapid Response Group co-led by the U.S. Secretary of Energy and Japan's Minister of Economy, Trade, and Industry; commitments to mobilize government and private sector financing; price mechanism development; and coordinated third-party engagement.[51] Significantly, the Japanese framework references "existing mining and processing operations in critical minerals and heavy and light rare earths as well as new capacity," pointing to Japan's sophisticated downstream processing capabilities even while lacking primary production.[52]

Japan brings unique strengths to the allied critical minerals coalition. The Japan Organization for Metals and Energy Security (JOGMEC), established in 2004 following Japan's recognition of its resource vulnerability, operates as a sophisticated state-backed agency that provides risk capital, technical support, and long-term strategic planning for resource projects.[53] JOGMEC's patient capital approach—accepting longer payback periods and lower returns than purely commercial entities demand—has enabled Japanese participation in marginal projects that nonetheless provide strategic value. The organization's involvement in the Alcoa gallium venture typifies this approach.

More broadly, Japan has invested heavily in deep-sea mining technology to access rare earth deposits within its exclusive economic zone, particularly near Minamitorishima (Marcus Island), where University of Tokyo research estimates over sixteen million metric tons of rare earths lie buried at depths exceeding six thousand meters.[54] Japan aims to begin rare earth mining operations by fiscal year 2028, which would significantly reduce reliance on foreign sources.[55] Recent high-level discussions between Prime Minister Sanae Takaichi and President Trump confirmed that rare earth mineral development featured prominently in bilateral talks, with the framework agreement signed during Trump's visit to Tokyo specifically targeting China's market dominance.[56]

The European Union has approached critical minerals security through a different institutional model but with similar strategic imperatives. In July 2025, Japan and the EU announced plans to launch an "economic two-plus-two" dialogue bringing together foreign and economy ministers to explore joint rare earth procurement and supply chain development.[57] The initiative includes a "competitiveness alliance" to jointly develop critical mineral supply chains, with potential Japanese involvement in EU projects in regions like Greenland and Africa.[58] The EU's Critical Raw Materials Act, enacted in 2024, established targets for domestic production and processing while promoting partnerships with democratic supplier nations.[59]

In July 2023, the European Commission and JOGMEC formalized enhanced cooperation on critical materials security through an administrative arrangement that establishes mechanisms for intelligence sharing, joint risk assessment, and coordinated responses to supply chain disruptions.[60] This collaboration recognizes that the European Union, like Japan, possesses sophisticated downstream manufacturing capabilities but limited primary production, while also acknowledging shared vulnerabilities to Chinese leverage. European policymakers have discussed creating a "European JOGMEC" that could provide similar strategic investment capabilities, though institutional complexity and sovereignty concerns have slowed implementation.[61]

At the broadest level, the Minerals Security Partnership (MSP)—launched in June 2022 and currently chaired by South Korea—provides a forum for coordination among fourteen countries plus the European Union.[62] The MSP focuses on catalyzing public and private investment in responsible critical minerals supply chains through diplomatic leadership, information sharing, and financial coordination. The partnership has established a Finance Network bringing together development finance institutions and export credit agencies, including the U.S. Export-Import Bank, Australia's Export Finance Australia, Japan's JBIC and JOGMEC, and various European institutions.[63]

The MSP also created an MSP Forum that cements partnerships with mineral-producing countries committed to advancing high environmental, social, and governance standards, currently including Argentina, Democratic Republic of the Congo, Ecuador, Greenland, Kazakhstan, Mexico, Namibia, Peru, Philippines, Serbia, Türkiye, Ukraine, Uzbekistan, and Zambia.[64] This structure acknowledges that critical minerals development requires engagement across the full value chain, from countries with deposits through processing nations to final manufacturers.

The June 2025 G7 Leaders' Summit in Kananaskis, Canada, produced a Critical Minerals Action Plan aimed at anticipating shortages, coordinating responses to market disruption, and diversifying mining, processing, manufacturing, and recycling capacities.[65] The Action Plan received endorsement from Australia, India, and the Republic of Korea, expanding its reach beyond the G7 itself. A Conference on Critical Materials and Minerals, chaired by the United States in Chicago in September 2025, brought together government officials, industry representatives, and financing institutions to advance concrete projects.[66]

This proliferating architecture of bilateral frameworks, regional initiatives, and multilateral forums reflects both the urgency of the critical minerals challenge and the complexity of coordinating responses. Each mechanism serves distinct purposes: bilateral agreements like U.S.-Australia enable rapid project-specific action; trilateral arrangements like the gallium project leverage complementary capabilities; broader forums like the MSP facilitate information sharing and norm-setting. The risk, as with any complex coordination problem, is that efforts become duplicative or poorly integrated, with institutional proliferation substituting for substantive action.

Challenges: Timeline, Scale, and Sustainability

Despite the substantial commitments embodied in the U.S.-Australia Framework and broader allied cooperation, formidable obstacles stand between current dependence and genuine supply chain diversification. These challenges span technical, economic, and political dimensions, each requiring sustained attention over timelines that test the patience of democratic electorates accustomed to rapid results.

The Timeline Challenge

The most fundamental challenge is temporal. Building critical minerals supply chains from extraction through processing to final products requires investments with extraordinarily long payback periods. Industry analysts estimate that meaningful supply chain independence will require sustained commitment over multiple decades—not the political cycles of two to four years that typically frame democratic decision-making.[67]

Mining projects alone average seven to ten years from advanced exploration to production, and this timeline assumes favorable regulatory environments and stable financing—conditions rarely present in reality.[68] Processing facilities require similar development periods, particularly for complex metallurgical operations like rare earth separation, where technical expertise has atrophied in Western nations over the past thirty years. Downstream manufacturing, including magnet production and component assembly, adds additional time as capabilities rebuild.

China's current dominance, by contrast, represents decades of strategic planning and investment. The Chinese government began seriously pursuing critical minerals in the 1980s, recognizing their strategic potential long before Western policymakers paid attention.[69] Through patient capital, acceptance of initial losses, tolerance for environmental costs that would be unacceptable in developed democracies, and deliberate acquisition of foreign technology and expertise, China progressively consolidated control. Dismantling this advantage will not occur quickly, regardless of the resources committed.

The Nolans project illustrates these temporal challenges. Despite years of preparation, comprehensive feasibility studies, secured environmental approvals, binding offtake agreements, and now substantial government equity commitments, the project has yet to reach final investment decision. If construction were to commence immediately, first production would not occur until at least 2027—and experience suggests delays are more probable than early delivery.[70] Scaling production to full capacity would require additional time. Other projects further behind in development face even longer timelines.

This temporal mismatch creates acute political vulnerabilities. Governments making billion-dollar commitments to projects that will not deliver results for five to ten years face skeptical publics questioning whether investments could be better deployed elsewhere. Opposition parties attack such expenditures as industrial policy failures or corporate welfare. When commodity prices fluctuate—as they inevitably do—critics point to apparent waste. Maintaining bipartisan support for patient capital investments across multiple election cycles represents a challenge that democracies historically struggle to meet.

The defense sector faces particularly acute timeline pressures. Military procurement officials, responding to near-term readiness requirements and recognizing China's accelerating military modernization, cannot wait a decade for alternative critical minerals sources. This creates pressure for short-term accommodations with Chinese suppliers even as long-term supply chain diversification proceeds—a tension that Beijing will predictably exploit to undermine Western resolve.

The Scale Challenge

Beyond time, the sheer scale of investment required to meaningfully challenge Chinese dominance presents daunting obstacles. The International Energy Agency estimated in 2024 that transitioning to diversified critical minerals supply chains would require hundreds of billions of dollars in capital deployment across mining, processing, refining, and manufacturing infrastructure.[71] The U.S.-Australia Framework's 8.5 billion dollar project pipeline, while substantial, represents a small fraction of this total.

Processing capacity presents particularly acute scaling challenges. China maintains seventy percent average market share across nineteen of twenty important strategic minerals when measuring processing and refining capacity—shares that have actually increased in recent years despite growing awareness of vulnerabilities.[72] For rare earth processing specifically, China controls approximately eighty-nine percent of global refining, a concentration that has risen from lower levels two decades ago.[73] Building processing capacity to supplant even twenty percent of this dominance would require dozens of facilities, each representing hundreds of millions in investment, complex permitting, years of construction, and recruitment of scarce technical talent.

The capital intensity is compounded by uncertainty about long-term demand and pricing. Private investors require reasonable confidence that facilities being built today will remain economically viable over their twenty-to-thirty-year operational lives. But critical minerals markets are characterized by extreme volatility, with prices often fluctuating by factors of two or three within single years based on Chinese production decisions, technology shifts, or policy changes.[74] Three-quarters of critical minerals experience greater price volatility than oil, and half are more volatile than natural gas—hardly encouraging for investors considering multi-hundred-million-dollar processing facilities.[75]

This volatility reflects the thin, illiquid markets that characterize most critical minerals. Unlike oil, where robust futures markets enable hedging and risk management, critical minerals typically trade on opaque spot markets where a handful of producers and buyers dominate transactions.

These market structures make conventional risk management tools unavailable, forcing investors to either accept extraordinary risk or demand government guarantees that socialize downside while privatizing upside—a politically contentious arrangement.

Infrastructure constraints compound the challenge. Many critical mineral deposits are located in remote regions lacking road, rail, power, water, and communications infrastructure required for modern mining operations. Australia's outback, Canada's far north, and sub-Saharan Africa's mineral-rich regions all exemplify this pattern. Building the enabling infrastructure often costs as much or more than the mines themselves, requiring public investment that competes with other infrastructure priorities. The Nolans project, for instance, required substantial government financing for water supply, power connections, and road improvements before mining could commence.[76]

China's Strategic Response and Price Manipulation

Perhaps the most insidious challenge facing the U.S.-Australia initiative and broader Western efforts involves China's capacity and willingness to undermine alternative supply chains through strategic price manipulation. History provides ample evidence of Beijing's tactics: allowing prices to rise when Western projects are in planning stages to encourage investment, then flooding markets with subsidized production once facilities near completion, driving prices down to levels that make competitors financially unviable. This cycle has repeated across multiple minerals, including rare earths in 2011-2013 and lithium in 2023-2024.[77]

The economics of this strategy favor incumbents. Chinese processing facilities, already amortized and operating with state support, can continue production even at prices below cash costs for extended periods—particularly when doing so serves strategic objectives beyond commercial profitability. Western entrants, by contrast, must service construction debt, meet shareholder return expectations, and operate under hard budget constraints. When prices collapse, Chinese facilities adjust production downward but remain operational, while Western projects postpone construction, mothball facilities, or declare bankruptcy. By the time prices recover, the competitive threat has been eliminated.

This predatory dynamic explains why numerous Western critical minerals projects have failed to reach production despite favorable geology and competent management. MP Materials' Mountain Pass rare earth mine in California—the only significant U.S. rare earth mining operation—went through bankruptcy reorganization in 2015 when Chinese pricing made operations unprofitable, despite possessing world-class deposits.[78] Lynas Rare Earths, Australia's leading rare earth producer, has periodically faced financial distress during price downturns even while operating technically successful facilities.[79] Molycorp, once America's rare earth champion, collapsed into bankruptcy in 2015 after Chinese price competition made its heavily leveraged expansion project unsustainable.[80]

The U.S.-Australia Framework's price floor mechanisms aim to disrupt this cycle, but implementation faces significant obstacles. Setting floors too high creates inefficiency and rewards uncompetitive producers, inviting political backlash. Setting them too low fails to provide sufficient protection, allowing Chinese tactics to succeed. Dynamic adjustment mechanisms risk becoming administratively complex and vulnerable to lobbying. And any successful floor that creates profitable Western production will simply prompt Beijing to adjust its tactics, perhaps shifting from overt price competition to more subtle approaches like technology transfer requirements or selective licensing.

More fundamentally, price floors work only if a sufficiently large portion of global demand occurs within the protected market. If Chinese producers can still sell freely to non-aligned countries—which represent the majority of global population and growing majorities of consumption—they maintain market dominance and pricing power despite Western barriers. This reality underscores why broadening the coalition beyond the United States and Australia to encompass Europe, Japan, South Korea, and potentially India proves essential. Only by aggregating demand across these markets does the protected ecosystem become large enough to sustain viable alternative supply chains.

Environmental and Social Constraints

Western critical minerals development also faces environmental and social constraints that, while legitimate and often necessary, nonetheless complicate efforts to rapidly scale production. Mining and processing operations generate substantial environmental impacts, including land disturbance, water consumption, tailings management, greenhouse gas emissions, and potential contamination risks. Rare earth processing in particular produces radioactive waste streams (from thorium and uranium naturally present in many rare earth deposits) that require careful management.[81]

China's historical willingness to tolerate environmental costs that democratic societies find unacceptable has provided substantial competitive advantages. The consolidation of rare earth processing in China during the 1990s and 2000s occurred partly because environmental regulations in the United States, Australia, and other developed nations made such operations economically prohibitive without Chinese-level cost structures.[82] Lynas's decision to build its processing facility in Malaysia rather than Australia reflected partly these cost dynamics, though even Malaysia's relatively permissive environment has faced increasing scrutiny and regulatory pressure.[83]

Modern environmental standards, while raising costs, are not insurmountable. The Nolans project has successfully navigated rigorous Northern Territory and Australian federal environmental assessment processes, demonstrating that rare earth processing meeting world-class environmental standards is technically feasible.[84] Alcoa's gallium extraction occurs within existing alumina refining operations that already manage environmental compliance, adding marginal rather than entirely new burdens. Advances in processing technology, including closed-loop systems and improved separation chemistry, promise to reduce environmental footprints compared to legacy approaches.[85]

Nevertheless, the combination of environmental compliance costs, longer permitting timelines, and community consultation requirements creates structural disadvantages relative to Chinese competitors operating under less stringent regimes. This disparity raises fundamental questions about whether democratic societies are willing to accept the environmental trade-offs that genuine supply chain independence requires, or whether they prefer continued dependence on minerals produced elsewhere under conditions they would not permit domestically—a form of environmental colonialism that exports costs to less powerful nations.

Indigenous rights and community engagement present related challenges, particularly in Australia and Canada where critical mineral deposits often overlap with lands of cultural significance to First Nations peoples. The Nolans project's execution of Native Title agreements with Traditional Owners in June 2020 exemplifies good practice, but the consultation and negotiation processes required time and created uncertainty for investors.[86] While these processes are both ethically necessary and legally required, they nonetheless create project risks that Chinese operations developing resources in African or Central Asian nations may not face, at least not to the same degree.

Strategic Implications and Outlook

The U.S.-Australia Critical Minerals Alliance, despite its challenges, represents the most serious effort to date to construct viable alternatives to Chinese supply chain dominance. By combining Australia's geological endowment with American capital and technology, Japanese patient investment, and potentially European market access, the initiative creates a coalition with sufficient scale and complementary capabilities to potentially succeed where past efforts have failed.

Success, however, is far from guaranteed. The Framework's true test will come not in the signing ceremony's optimistic declarations but in the grinding work of project finance, construction management, workforce development, and market building over the coming decade. Three factors will likely prove decisive.

First, sustaining political will across multiple election cycles and changing administrations represents the paramount challenge. The U.S.-Australia Framework was signed by President Trump and Prime Minister Albanese, but will require implementation under multiple successor governments. If future administrations in either country deprioritize critical minerals, reduce funding, or shift strategic focus, projects will stall and momentum will dissipate. Bipartisan support, carefully cultivated, provides some insurance against political volatility, but history suggests skepticism about long-term policy continuity is warranted.

Second, the effectiveness of price floor mechanisms and market protections will determine whether Western producers can survive Chinese competition long enough to achieve scale and efficiency. If mechanisms prove too weak, Chinese predatory pricing will eliminate competitors; if too strong, they will create inefficient protected industries vulnerable to political attack. Threading this needle requires sophisticated policy design and adaptive implementation—challenging even under optimal conditions, and likely more so amid the complexity and contention of democratic policymaking.

Third, the ability to broaden the coalition beyond current participants will shape whether alternative supply chains achieve critical mass. Bringing India—with its enormous population and growing manufacturing capacity—into aligned frameworks would substantially expand the protected market ecosystem. Engaging major European manufacturers provides similar benefits. Conversely, if China succeeds in keeping significant portions of global demand outside Western frameworks through economic inducement or political pressure, the coalition may remain too small to sustain viable alternatives.

The October 2025 framework must also be understood in the broader context of technological evolution. While the U.S. and Australia work to build alternative supply chains for today's critical minerals, research continues on materials substitution, efficiency improvements, and recycling technologies that may reduce dependence on primary production. Sodium-ion batteries, for instance, offer potential substitutes for lithium in some applications. Alternative magnet designs using more abundant materials could reduce rare earth requirements. Urban mining and battery recycling may eventually supply substantial portions of mineral demand. These technological shifts could render some supply chain investments obsolete—or alternatively, reduce the scale of challenge to more manageable levels.

China's own strategic calculations will evolve in response to Western initiatives. Beijing has already demonstrated sophisticated understanding of how to weaponize supply chain dependencies, and will surely adapt as alternative sources develop. This may include efforts to acquire stakes in Australian projects, offering technology partnerships on attractive terms, selectively relaxing export controls to undermine Western resolve, or intensifying development of processing capacity for minerals where China currently lacks dominance. The competition will be dynamic and multi-dimensional, not a static problem amenable to once-and-done solutions.

Ultimately, the U.S.-Australia Critical Minerals Alliance represents a necessary but not sufficient response to the challenges posed by concentrated supply chains. Its success will require sustained commitment, adaptive policy, coalition building, and acceptance that genuine supply chain resilience comes not from perfect independence but from diversified, redundant systems less vulnerable to single-point failures. The October 2025 framework provides an institutional foundation for this work. Whether that foundation supports a structure capable of withstanding decades of competition and turbulence remains to be seen.

Endnote

[1] The White House, "United States-Australia Framework For Securing of Supply in the Mining and Processing of Critical Minerals and Rare Earths," October 20, 2025, https://www.whitehouse.gov/briefings-statements/2025/10/united-states-australia-framework-for-securing-supply-mining-and-processing-critical-minerals-and-rare-earths/.

[2] Yan Zhang, "China's Rare Earth Export Controls: Impact on Businesses and Industries," China Briefing, October 9, 2025, https://www.china-briefing.com/news/chinas-rare-earth-export-controls-impacts-on-businesses/.

[3] The White House, "Fact Sheet: President Donald J. Trump Closes Billion-Dollar Deals with Australia," October 20, 2025, https://www.whitehouse.gov/fact-sheets/2025/10/fact-sheet-president-donald-j-trump-closes-billion-dollar-deals-with-australia/.

[4] Department of Industry, Science and Resources (Australia), "United States-Australia Framework for Securing of Supply in the Mining and Processing of Critical Minerals and Rare Earths," October 20, 2025, https://www.industry.gov.au/publications/united-states-australia-framework-securing-supply-mining-and-processing-critical-minerals-and-rare-earths.

[5] Gracelin Baskaran and Kessarin Horvath, "Unpacking the U.S.-Australia Critical Minerals Framework Agreement," Center for Strategic and International Studies, October 23, 2025, https://www.csis.org/analysis/unpacking-us-australia-critical-minerals-framework-agreement.

[6] Gracelin Baskaran and Kevin Rudd, "The Future of U.S.-Australia Critical Minerals Cooperation," Center for Strategic and International Studies, August 20, 2025, https://www.csis.org/analysis/future-us-australia-critical-minerals-cooperation.

[7] Baskaran and Horvath, "Unpacking the U.S.-Australia Critical Minerals Framework Agreement."

[8] Ibid.

[9] Ibid.

[10] Austrade, "Critical minerals," accessed December 4, 2025, https://international.austrade.gov.au/en/do-business-with-australia/sectors/energy-and-resources/critical-minerals.

[11] Ibid.

[12] Baskaran and Horvath, "Unpacking the U.S.-Australia Critical Minerals Framework Agreement."

[13] Ibid.

[14] Tae-Yoon Kim et al., "With new export controls on critical minerals, supply concentration risks become reality," International Energy Agency, October 23, 2025, https://www.iea.org/commentaries/with-new-export-controls-on-critical-minerals-supply-concentration-risks-become-reality.

[15] Baskaran and Horvath, "Unpacking the U.S.-Australia Critical Minerals Framework Agreement."

[16] Alcoa Corporation, "Governments Announce Support For Alcoa's Gallium Critical Mineral Development Project In Western Australia," press release, October 20, 2025, https://news.alcoa.com/press-releases/press-release-details/2025/GOVERNMENTS-ANNOUNCE-SUPPORT-FOR-ALCOAS-GALLIUM-CRITICAL-MINERAL-DEVELOPMENT-PROJECT-IN-WESTERN-AUSTRALIA/.

[17] Prime Minister of Australia, "Historic critical minerals framework signed by President Trump and Prime Minister Albanese," media release, October 21, 2025, https://www.pm.gov.au/media/historic-critical-minerals-framework-signed-president-trump-and-prime-minister-albanese.

[18] Ibid.

[19] "Alcoa's Western Australia Gallium Production to Boost Critical Minerals Supply," Discovery Alert, August 4, 2025, https://discoveryalert.com.au/gallium-powering-technology-2025-applications-supply/.

[20] Kim et al., "With new export controls on critical minerals, supply concentration risks become reality."

[21] Ibid.

[22] "Alcoa's Western Australia Gallium Production to Boost Critical Minerals Supply."

[23] Alcoa Corporation, "Alcoa Explores Feasibility of Gallium Critical Mineral Production in Western Australia," press release, August 4, 2025, https://news.alcoa.com/press-releases/press-release-details/2025/Alcoa-Explores-Feasibility-of-Gallium-Critical-Mineral-Production-in-Western-Australia/.

[24] Alcoa Corporation, "Governments Announce Support For Alcoa's Gallium Critical Mineral Development Project In Western Australia."

[25] Ibid.

[26] Prime Minister of Australia, "Historic critical minerals framework signed by President Trump and Prime Minister Albanese."

[27] National Reconstruction Fund Corporation, "NRFC boosting global rare earths supply through cornerstone $200 million investment commitment in Arafura's transformational mining project," media release, https://www.nrf.gov.au/news-and-media-releases/nrfc-boosting-global-rare-earths-supply-through-cornerstone-200-million-investment-commitment-arafuras-transformational-mining-project.

[28] Arafura Rare Earths, "Nolans," accessed December 4, 2025, https://www.arultd.com/projects/nolans/.

[29] Keith Bradsher, "With new export controls on critical minerals, supply concentration risks become reality," International Energy Agency, October 14, 2025, https://www.iea.org/commentaries/with-new-export-controls-on-critical-minerals-supply-concentration-risks-become-reality.

[30] Gracelin Baskaran, "China's New Rare Earth and Magnet Restrictions Threaten U.S. Defense Supply Chains," Center for Strategic and International Studies, October 14, 2025, https://www.csis.org/analysis/chinas-new-rare-earth-and-magnet-restrictions-threaten-us-defense-supply-chains.

[31] Arafura Rare Earths, "Nolans."

[32] National Reconstruction Fund Corporation, "NRFC boosting global rare earths supply."

[33] Government of Northern Territory, "Case study: Arafura Rare Earths Limited," Australia's Northern Territory, accessed December 4, 2025, https://australiasnorthernterritory.com.au/invest/invest-news-and-insights/case-study-arafura-rare-earths-limited2.

[34] Arafura Rare Earths, "Nolans."

[35] Government of Northern Territory, "Case study: Arafura Rare Earths Limited."

[36] Ibid.

[37] National Reconstruction Fund Corporation, "NRFC boosting global rare earths supply."

[38] Ibid.

[39] The White House, "United States-Australia Framework For Securing of Supply in the Mining and Processing of Critical Minerals and Rare Earths."

[40] William Chou, "China's Bureaucratic Playbook for Critical Minerals," Hudson Institute, 2025, https://www.hudson.org/supply-chains/chinas-bureaucratic-playbook-critical-minerals-control-technology-transfer-william-chou.

[41] Tom Moerenhout, Cina Vazir, and Irina Patrahau, "A Multilateral Commercial Stockpile for Critical Minerals," Hoover Institution, August 10, 2025, https://www.hoover.org/research/multilateral-commercial-stockpile-critical-minerals.

[42] "Profitability and power: Fixing US critical minerals supply chains," Atlantic Council, April 3, 2025, https://www.atlanticcouncil.org/blogs/energysource/profitability-and-power-fixing-us-critical-minerals-supply-chains/.

[43] Chou, "China's Bureaucratic Playbook for Critical Minerals."

[44] Moerenhout, Vazir, and Patrahau, "A Multilateral Commercial Stockpile for Critical Minerals."

[45] The White House, "United States-Australia Framework For Securing of Supply in the Mining and Processing of Critical Minerals and Rare Earths."

[46] Ibid.

[47] Baskaran and Horvath, "Unpacking the U.S.-Australia Critical Minerals Framework Agreement."

[48] Herbert Smith Freehills, "Unpacking the landmark US-Australia critical minerals supply framework," October 21, 2025, https://www.hsfkramer.com/notes/mining/2025-posts/us-australia-critical-minerals-supply-framework.

[49] Ibid.

[50] The White House, "United States - Japan Framework for Securing the Supply of Critical Minerals and Rare Earths through Mining and Processing," October 27, 2025, https://www.whitehouse.gov/briefings-statements/2025/10/united-states-japan-framework-for-securing-the-supply-of-critical-minerals-and-rare-earths-through-mining-and-processing/.

[51] Ibid.

[52] Ibid.

[53] "European JOGMEC: EU's Critical Minerals Security Strategy," Discovery Alert, October 29, 2025, https://discoveryalert.com.au/news/europe-critical-minerals-challenge-supply-chain-2025/.

[54] EU-Japan Centre for Industrial Cooperation, "Weekly Japanese Industry and Policy News: 12 July - 18 July, 2025," https://www.eu-japan.eu/news/weekly-japanese-industry-and-policy-news-12-july-18-july-2025.

[55] Ibid.

[56] "Japan US Rare Earth Partnership Challenges China's Market Dominance," Discovery Alert, November 2025, https://discoveryalert.com.au/strategic-alliance-critical-mineral-independence-2025-mining/.

[57] Reuters, "Japan, EU to explore joint rare earths procurement, Nikkei reports," July 17, 2025, https://www.globalbankingandfinance.com/JAPAN-EU-RAREEARTHS-98994d75-798d-4134-96a6-2052d59065b2.

[58] EU-Japan Centre for Industrial Cooperation, "Weekly Japanese Industry and Policy News: 12 July - 18 July, 2025."

[59] "European JOGMEC: EU's Critical Minerals Security Strategy."

[60] Ibid.

[61] Ibid.

[62] U.S. Department of State, "Minerals Security Partnership," February 13, 2025, https://www.state.gov/minerals-security-partnership.

[63] U.S. Department of State, "Joint Statement on Establishment of the Minerals Security Partnership Finance Network," September 23, 2024, https://2021-2025.state.gov/joint-statement-on-establishment-of-the-minerals-security-partnership-finance-network/.

[64] U.S. Department of State, "Minerals Security Partnership."

[65] "G7 Agrees to Deepen Cooperation on Critical Minerals Supply Chains," SDG Knowledge Hub, June 18, 2025, https://sdg.iisd.org/news/g7-agrees-to-deepen-cooperation-on-critical-minerals-supply-chains/.

[66] Ibid.

[67] Anna Ashton, "A Critical Juncture: The US-China Critical Minerals Competition," American Chamber of Commerce Shanghai, 2025, https://www.amcham-shanghai.org/en/article/insight-magazine-critical-juncture-us-china-critical-minerals-competition.

[68] "Critical Minerals: US Strategy to Break China's Supply Chain Dominance."

[69] "Western Nations Challenge China's Critical Minerals Monopoly," Discovery Alert, August 13, 2025, https://discoveryalert.com.au/news/critical-minerals-china-monopoly-west-strategy-2025/.

[70] Government of Northern Territory, "Case study: Arafura Rare Earths Limited."

[71] "Western Nations Challenge China's Critical Minerals Monopoly."

[72] International Energy Agency, "With new export controls on critical minerals, supply concentration risks become reality."

[73] "China Pauses Some Rare Earth Export Curbs While Retaining Levers of Control," Foundation for Defense of Democracies, November 12, 2025, https://www.fdd.org/analysis/2025/11/12/china-pauses-some-rare-earth-export-curbs-while-retaining-levers-of-control/.

[74] "Western Nations Challenge China's Critical Minerals Monopoly."

[75] Ibid.

[76] National Reconstruction Fund Corporation, "NRFC boosting global rare earths supply."

[77] Chou, "China's Bureaucratic Playbook for Critical Minerals."

[78] "Critical Minerals: US Strategy to Break China's Supply Chain Dominance."

[79] Baskaran and Horvath, "Unpacking the U.S.-Australia Critical Minerals Framework Agreement."

[80] "Critical Minerals: US Strategy to Break China's Supply Chain Dominance."

[81] Arafura Rare Earths, "Nolans."

[82] "Western Nations Challenge China's Critical Minerals Monopoly."

[83] Baskaran and Horvath, "Unpacking the U.S.-Australia Critical Minerals Framework Agreement."

[84] Arafura Rare Earths, "Nolans."

[85] "Critical Minerals: US Strategy to Break China's Supply Chain Dominance."

[86] Arafura Rare Earths, "Nolans."

Chapter 9

The Minerals Race Beyond Rare Earths

Lithium, Cobalt, and the Green Energy Battleground

The global energy transition has ignited what may become the most consequential resource competition of the twenty-first century. While rare earth elements have captured headlines and dominated diplomatic exchanges between Washington and Beijing, a parallel struggle for lithium, cobalt, nickel, and graphite is reshaping geopolitics with equal intensity. These minerals—essential for the batteries powering electric vehicles, grid storage systems, and portable electronics—have emerged as the new strategic commodities of the clean energy era. The nations and corporations that secure reliable access to these resources will shape the trajectory of the energy transition itself, while those left dependent on concentrated supply chains face profound vulnerabilities.

The stakes are staggering. The International Energy Agency projects that in its Net Zero Emissions by 2050 Scenario, demand for lithium will increase by a factor of nine by 2040, while graphite demand will nearly quadruple and nickel and cobalt requirements will double.[1] In this scenario, clean energy technologies are projected to become the largest consumer of these minerals, with electric vehicles and battery storage accounting for over ninety percent of total lithium demand by 2030.[2] The combined market value of key energy transition minerals—copper, lithium, nickel, cobalt, graphite, and rare earth elements—could more than double to reach $770 billion by 2040.[3] This is not merely an economic competition but a contest that will determine which nations dominate the industries of tomorrow.

The Clean Energy Transition as Resource Competition Accelerator

The decarbonization imperative has fundamentally transformed the relationship between climate policy and mineral extraction. Every solar panel, wind turbine, and electric vehicle requires substantially more mineral inputs than their fossil fuel counterparts. An electric vehicle uses approximately six times more critical minerals than a conventional automobile, primarily due to the battery.[4] This reality has created a paradox at the heart of climate policy: the pathway to a cleaner energy future runs through mines, refineries, and processing facilities that concentrate enormous environmental and geopolitical risks.

The numbers underscore the magnitude of this transformation. Electric car sales reached nearly fourteen million units globally in 2023, representing a thirty-five percent year-on-year increase, with continued growth projected as adoption increases in emerging economies.[5] In the IEA's Net Zero Scenario, the sales share of electric cars rises dramatically, pushing up demand for batteries by a factor of seven. This explosive growth in electrification extends beyond transportation. Battery storage for the power sector exhibits even faster growth rates as utilities seek to integrate intermittent renewable generation into electrical grids.

The World Bank has projected that by 2050, the production of certain critical minerals including graphite, lithium, and cobalt could increase by nearly five hundred percent to meet the growing demand for clean energy technologies, with over three billion tons of minerals and metals needed to deploy wind, solar and geothermal power, as well as energy storage, required for achieving a below 2°C future.[6] Such projections have triggered a scramble among major powers to secure supplies, transform processing capacity, and establish control over the value chains that will power the energy transition. The competition is most intense between the United States and China, but it encompasses a global network of resource-rich developing nations, mid-tier industrial powers, and multinational corporations jockeying for position in what has become a defining strategic contest.

China's Dominance Across the Battery Supply Chain

Any discussion of the critical minerals competition must begin with an acknowledgment of China's commanding position. Beijing's dominance extends far beyond any single mineral or processing stage—it encompasses virtually the entire battery supply chain from mine to finished product. This supremacy was not accidental but resulted from decades of strategic planning, massive state investment, and deliberate acquisition of overseas assets.

China regained the top position in BloombergNEF's Global Lithium-Ion Battery Supply Chain Ranking in 2024, with low commercial electricity prices and advancing infrastructure cited as primary factors.[7] The country produced more than 1,200 gigawatt-hours of lithium-ion batteries in 2024, accounting for approximately three-quarters of the world's total capacity.[8] Major producers like CATL and BYD supply both domestic and foreign automakers including Tesla, BMW, and Toyota.

The scope of Chinese dominance becomes even more apparent when examining individual minerals. China produces approximately eighteen percent of the world's mined lithium, but its real advantage lies in refining—Chinese companies hold about sixty-five percent of global lithium chemical processing capacity.[9] For cobalt, while the Democratic Republic of Congo produces approximately seventy-four percent of global supply, China refines the vast majority of the world's output, processing most of the partially refined cobalt imported from Congo.[10] The pattern repeats across the periodic table: China processes more than half the world's lithium, two-thirds of its cobalt, more than seventy percent of its graphite, and about one-third of its nickel, according to the International Energy Agency.[11]

This processing dominance translates into manufacturing supremacy. China currently hosts seventy-five percent of all battery cell manufacturing capacity and ninety percent of anode and electrolyte production.[12] The number of smelters in Indonesia—the world's largest nickel producer—has grown from two in 2016 to more than sixty, but this growth has been enabled almost entirely by Chinese investment and technology.[13] Chinese companies have committed approximately thirty billion dollars to Indonesia's nickel sector, establishing an industrial ecosystem that extends from mine pit to battery cell.[14]

The strategic implications are profound. Critical mineral markets have become more concentrated rather than less, particularly in refining and processing. The average market share of the top three refining nations of key energy minerals rose from around eighty-two percent in 2020 to eighty-six percent in 2024, with some ninety percent of supply growth coming from the single top supplier alone: Indonesia for nickel and China for cobalt, graphite, and rare earths.[15] This concentration creates systemic vulnerabilities—if the largest supplier were removed from calculations, available supply for all key energy transition minerals would fall significantly below material requirements.

Congo's Cobalt: The Heart of Darkness in the Battery Age

The Democratic Republic of Congo stands at the center of the cobalt supply chain, producing approximately seventy-four percent of the world's supply of this silvery-blue metal essential for lithium-ion battery cathodes in 2023.[16] Congo's cobalt reserves represent both an extraordinary opportunity and a cautionary tale about the geopolitics of mineral extraction in the developing world.

Chinese dominance in Congo's mining sector is now near-total. Of the major cobalt mines in the DRC, a substantial majority are Chinese-owned. According to the U.S. Geological Survey, the DRC is the world's leading source of mined cobalt, with China as the world's leading producer of refined cobalt, most of which is produced from partially refined cobalt imported from Congo.[17] The foundations of this dominance were laid in 2007-2008, when the DRC signed a multi-billion dollar contract with a consortium of Chinese state-owned companies to build infrastructure in exchange for privileged access to minerals and mining sites.[18] This resource-for-infrastructure arrangement, centered on the Sino-Congolaise des Mines (Sicomines) joint venture, became the template for China's engagement across Africa's mineral belt.

The scale of Chinese investment has been transformative. CMOC Group, a Chinese mining company, has become one of the world's largest cobalt producers through its Congolese operations, with substantial annual output. Chinese companies control approximately fifty percent of DRC cobalt production, with eight of the fourteen largest cobalt miners in Congo now Chinese-owned, many operating as joint ventures with the state mining company Gécamines but managed by Chinese firms.[19]

Yet the arrangement has generated controversy. A December 2021 study commissioned by the DRC's EITI multi-stakeholder group concluded that the Sicomines joint venture agreement presented significant imbalances, citing uneven capital distribution and unfulfilled infrastructure promises.[20] A subsequent audit found that the benefits flowing to the DRC were substantially less than anticipated. Following President Félix Tshisekedi's visit to China in May 2023, the agreement was renegotiated to increase the infrastructure budget from three billion to seven billion dollars.[21]

The human costs of cobalt extraction have also drawn international scrutiny. Networks of artisanal miners, including children, work in dangerous conditions to extract ore that enters global supply chains. Since around twenty percent of the cobalt mined in the DRC originates from small-scale artisanal mines, often employing child labor, the extraction of the metal has been a point of intense debate.[22] The DRC announced a temporary four-month halt on cobalt exports in February 2025 to counter falling prices, a suspension that could significantly impact government revenues.[23]

The United States has belatedly attempted to gain a foothold in Congo's mineral sector. Efforts to secure partnerships with Congolese authorities and support American and allied interests in lithium and other critical mineral projects represent a belated recognition of the strategic stakes, though these efforts remain modest compared to China's entrenched position.

Chile's Lithium: Nationalization and the Politics of the White Gold

Chile, home to the world's largest proven lithium reserves, has pursued a starkly different approach to resource management than Congo. In April 2023, President Gabriel Boric announced the National Lithium Strategy, a partial nationalization that would require private companies to partner with the state for future projects, with the government holding majority stakes in ventures deemed strategic.[24]

The announcement initially triggered alarm among investors accustomed to Chile's historically market-friendly policies. However, the reality proved more nuanced than headlines suggested. Boric emphasized that existing contracts with SQM and Albemarle, the two companies currently extracting lithium from Chile's Atacama salt flats, would be honored, and that any renegotiation would be consensual.[25] The strategy called for public-private partnerships rather than outright expropriation, with state copper giant Codelco tasked with overseeing new arrangements.

In December 2023, Chile formalized its approach when Codelco and SQM announced a partnership giving the state a controlling stake—fifty percent plus one share—in operations at the Salar de Atacama, beginning operations in January 2025 and running through 2060.[26] The deal gives Codelco majority control in line with the president's plans announced in April to strengthen state control of lithium. The joint venture was designed to extend SQM's operating license while ensuring greater state participation in profits and decision-making. The partnership faces ongoing opposition from Tianqi Lithium, SQM's second-largest shareholder, which has demanded that the agreement be subjected to a shareholder vote.[27]

Chile's strategy reflects broader trends in resource nationalism across Latin America. Mexico nationalized its lithium industry in 2022, though its reserves are comparatively modest. Bolivia, which holds substantial reserves, has struggled to commercialize its resources due to political instability and the challenging geography of the Uyuni salt flats. The three countries comprising the so-called Lithium Triangle have discussed forming a regional lithium association, though progress has been slow.

The Chilean approach emphasizes environmental sustainability alongside state control. The National Lithium Strategy emphasized that the use of new production technologies with less environmental impact, such as direct lithium extraction, "should be an obligatory requirement"—a critical concern in the arid Atacama.[28] These environmental requirements may deter some investors but could position Chile as a preferred supplier for Western automakers facing increasingly stringent sustainability standards.

Despite initial concerns, implementation has proceeded methodically. Chile's competition regulator approved the Codelco-SQM joint venture in April 2025, following approvals from regulators in the European Union, Brazil, Japan, South Korea, and Saudi Arabia.[29] Industry observers note that Chile's emphasis on state control, while potentially justifiable on development grounds, may push investment toward Argentina, which offers a more permissive regulatory environment.

Argentina's Lithium Boom: The Open Door Approach

Argentina has emerged as perhaps the most attractive destination for lithium investment in Latin America, combining world-class reserves with a regulatory framework designed to welcome foreign capital. Under President Javier Milei's administration, the country has doubled down on its market-friendly approach, implementing the Incentive Regime for Large Investments (RIGI) in the second half of 2024, which offers tax benefits, thirty-year investment protection guarantees, exchange-rate stability, and free access to foreign currency for investments exceeding two hundred million dollars.[30]

The results have been striking. In 2024, Argentina produced approximately seventy-four thousand metric tons of lithium carbonate equivalent, with projections for 2025 reaching one hundred thirty thousand tons—a seventy-five percent increase.[31] Exports from the sector totaled $645 million in 2024 and are projected to grow by more than thirty percent in 2025.[32] According to the Secretariat of Mining, the country holds twenty percent of global lithium resources and 13.3 percent of known reserves.[33] If current investment commitments are fulfilled, Argentina could surpass Chile within the next decade and become the world's second-largest producer.

Chinese investors have been prominent participants in Argentina's lithium boom. Ganfeng Lithium operates multiple projects in Salta and Jujuy provinces, including the Cauchari-Olaroz project, which produced approximately twenty-five thousand tonnes of lithium carbonate in 2024, exceeding the high-end of production guidance and becoming the largest lithium carbonate operation in Argentina.[34] For 2025, lithium carbonate production is guided to be between thirty thousand and thirty-five thousand tonnes.[35] The company and Ganfeng continue to advance a regional development plan targeting production capacity of up to one hundred fifty thousand tonnes per annum of lithium carbonate equivalent.[36]

However, Chinese ownership presents complications under U.S. trade policy. The Inflation Reduction Act's Foreign Entity of Concern rules, effective from December 2024 for battery components and 2025 for critical minerals, disqualify electric vehicle batteries containing critical minerals extracted, processed, or recycled by entities with more than twenty-five percent cumulative ownership by foreign entities of concern from tax credits.[37] Argentina's largest operating lithium mine, Cauchari-Olaroz, is jointly owned by Ganfeng and Lithium Argentina, potentially complicating its eligibility for IRA benefits.

Argentina is actively seeking inclusion in U.S. critical minerals agreements that would provide a pathway around these restrictions. A Memorandum of Understanding on Critical Minerals signed in 2022 could provide the basis for such an arrangement, though formal free trade agreement status remains elusive.[38] The combination of RIGI benefits and potential access to U.S. markets could transform Argentina into a swing producer capable of serving both Chinese and Western supply chains.

Belt and Road as Resource Acquisition Strategy

China's Belt and Road Initiative has evolved into a sophisticated vehicle for securing critical mineral supplies across the developing world. Initially focused on infrastructure—ports, railways, and power plants—the BRI has increasingly emphasized mining investments and processing facilities that feed China's industrial base.

The scale of engagement is remarkable. Chinese BRI engagement in the first half of 2025 reached approximately $124 billion, the highest level ever recorded for a six-month period, with Chinese entities signing $66.2 billion in construction contracts and $57.1 billion in investments across BRI partner countries—surpassing the total for all of 2024.[39] The metals and mining sector reached new records in the first six months of 2025, with approximately $24.9 billion in engagement—mostly through investments in minerals processing—surpassing the full year of 2024, which itself was a record year.[40]

Africa and Central Asia emerged as top destinations for Chinese investment. Africa received $30.5 billion in Chinese construction engagement in the first half of 2025 alone—nearly five times more than in the same period of 2024.[41] Central Asia followed with approximately $25 billion, including major projects in Kazakhstan. Since its establishment in 2013, cumulative BRI engagement has now surpassed $1.3 trillion, encompassing infrastructure, trade, and investment partnerships with over 150 countries.[42]

In Africa, Chinese investment has transformed the mining landscape. Chinese companies hold significant shares of global mining sources—over eighty percent of global graphite resources—and even greater control in material processing, where across lithium, nickel, cobalt, and graphite, China owns more than fifty percent of global capacity.[43] Zimbabwe has emerged as another focal point for Chinese lithium investment, attracting substantial investment from companies including Sinomine, Zhejiang Huayou Cobalt, and Chengxin Lithium Group.[44]

Indonesia presents perhaps the most dramatic example of BRI-facilitated resource development. Chinese investment transformed Indonesia from a raw nickel ore exporter into the world's dominant refined nickel producer. In 2019, Indonesia produced 853,000 tonnes of nickel in mine production; by 2024, its nickel mine production was 2.2 million tonnes, an increase of 158 percent over the five-year period.[45] Some estimates suggest that by the end of the decade, annual nickel output will reach just over three million tonnes, or sixty-five percent of the global supply.[46] Indonesia's exports of nickel derivative products have risen substantially, reaching $38-40 billion in 2024, according to the Minister of Energy and Mineral Resources, up from $11.9 billion in 2020.[47]

The Indonesia Morowali Industrial Park, a joint venture between China's Tsingshan Holding Group and Indonesian partners, exemplifies this transformation. The number of smelters in the country has risen from two in 2016 to more than sixty.[48] In August 2024, media reports put the total Chinese investment in Indonesia's nickel sector as high as thirty billion dollars.[49] The environmental and social costs of this rapid industrialization have been significant. HPAL facilities in Indonesia face criticism for their reliance on coal-fired power and the disposal of toxic tailings.[50]

Western Responses: The Minerals Security Partnership

The United States and its allies have belatedly recognized the strategic implications of mineral supply chain concentration and launched initiatives to diversify supplies away from China. The Minerals Security Partnership, announced in June 2022, represents the most ambitious of these efforts.

Current MSP partners include Australia, Canada, Estonia, Finland, France, Germany, India, Italy, Japan, Norway, the Republic of Korea, Sweden, the United Kingdom, the United States, and the European Union, represented by the European Commission.[51] The partnership also established the MSP Forum to formalize engagements with minerals-producing countries, with current forum members including Argentina, Democratic Republic of the Congo, Dominican Republic, Ecuador, Greenland, Kazakhstan, Mexico, Namibia, Peru, Philippines, Serbia, Türkiye, Ukraine, Uzbekistan, and Zambia.[52]

The partnership focuses on accelerating development of diverse critical mineral supply chains through cooperation with industry and governments, supporting strategic projects, and encouraging investment throughout the value chain by reputable mining companies committed to high environmental, social, and governance standards.[53] In September 2024, partners launched the MSP Finance Network, bringing together development finance institutions and export credit agencies to strengthen cooperation and information exchange on project financing.[54]

Concrete milestones have emerged from MSP coordination. In March 2024, the U.S. Export-Import Bank issued a non-binding Letter of Interest to Australian Strategic Materials for potential debt financing of up to six hundred million dollars for the construction of the company's rare earths and critical minerals Dubbo Project in New South Wales, Australia.[55] In August 2024, Canadian-based Electra Battery Materials received a twenty million dollar award from the Defense Production Act Investments office of the U.S. Department of Defense to support the construction and commissioning of North America's first cobalt sulfate refinery, capable of producing battery grade materials at its facility in Temiskaming Shores, Ontario, Canada.[56] In July 2024, the Australian Government awarded Queensland Pacific Metals an AUD8 million grant to bolster domestic nickel and cobalt production at the Townsville Energy Chemicals Hub.[57]

The European Union has pursued parallel initiatives through its Critical Raw Materials Act, which entered into force on May 23, 2024. The Act establishes benchmarks for domestic capacities along the strategic raw material supply chain to be reached by 2030: ten percent of the EU's annual needs for extraction, forty percent for processing, and twenty-five percent for recycling.[58] No more than sixty-five percent of EU's annual needs of each strategic raw material at any relevant stage of processing should come from a single third country—a threshold that China currently exceeds for numerous materials.[59]

Critics note that Western initiatives remain modest compared to Chinese engagement. The timeline for diversification is measured in years or decades, while China's dominance is measured in present-day market share. The BRI investments continue to outpace Western alternatives in both scale and speed.

The Irony: Climate Goals Increasing Dependence on Chinese Processing

Perhaps the cruelest irony of the energy transition is that policies designed to reduce carbon emissions and combat climate change have simultaneously increased Western dependence on Chinese supply chains. The more aggressively nations pursue electrification of transportation and power generation, the more critical minerals they require—and the more exposed they become to Chinese market power.

This paradox is embedded in the structure of clean energy technology. An offshore wind turbine contains substantial quantities of rare earth elements for its permanent magnets. A single electric vehicle battery requires lithium, cobalt, nickel, manganese, and graphite in proportions that vary by chemistry but invariably trace back to Chinese processing facilities. Solar panels depend on polysilicon and silver, while grid-scale battery storage multiplies mineral requirements across gigawatt-hour deployments.

The Inflation Reduction Act attempted to address this vulnerability through its critical mineral and battery component requirements, establishing escalating thresholds for domestic or allied-nation sourcing. For 2027, the applicable percentage is eighty percent of the value of critical minerals contained in the battery that must be extracted or processed in the United States or a country with which the United States has a free trade agreement, or recycled in North America, to meet the critical mineral requirement and be eligible for the $3,750 credit.[60] Beginning in 2029, the applicable percentage for battery components manufactured or assembled in North America reaches one hundred percent.[61] Yet industry analysts question whether sufficient non-Chinese supply can materialize on this timeline.

China has responded to Western decoupling efforts with its own countermeasures. On October 20, 2023, China's Ministry of Commerce and the General Administration of Customs announced that certain graphite products would require export permits to protect national security, effective from December 1, 2023.[62] Applications for export permits must be submitted to the Ministry of Commerce through provincial commerce authorities, and exporters must renew their licenses every six months. The affected products encompass high-purity, high-strength, high-density synthetic graphite materials and products, as well as natural flake graphite products including spherical graphite and expanded graphite.[63]

The impact was immediate. Total exports of flake graphite dropped by 93.93 percent on a monthly basis to 1,427 tonnes in December 2023 from 23,502 tonnes a month earlier, while exports of spherical graphite slumped by 92.22 percent to 948 tonnes in the same comparison, down from 12,186 tonnes in November, according to China customs data.[64] Exports to major destinations including Japan and the United States fell to zero in December 2023.[65] Though volumes subsequently stabilized as export licenses were granted, the episode demonstrated Beijing's leverage.

These measures underscore China's market power. China is the world's number one graphite producer and exporter and refines more than ninety percent of global graphite.[66] Any significant disruption to Chinese graphite exports would ripple through global battery supply chains, potentially delaying EV production and raising costs for consumers. Similar dynamics apply to lithium processing, cobalt refining, and rare earth magnet production.

The weaponization of mineral supply chains represents a new dimension of great power competition. Just as energy embargoes shaped twentieth-century geopolitics, critical mineral restrictions may define twenty-first-century rivalry. Nations pursuing aggressive decarbonization timelines must grapple with the uncomfortable reality that their climate ambitions currently run through Chinese refineries and processing facilities that Beijing could restrict at will.

Pathways Forward: Diversification, Recycling, and Substitution

Breaking dependence on concentrated supply chains will require sustained effort across multiple fronts: expanding mining in allied nations, building processing capacity outside China, developing recycling infrastructure, and advancing research into alternative battery chemistries.

Diversification of primary supply offers the most immediate pathway. Australia remains the world's largest lithium producer, and Australian companies are expanding operations in countries from Argentina to Canada. African nations including Zimbabwe, Namibia, and the DRC hold substantial reserves of lithium, cobalt, and other critical minerals that could supply Western markets with appropriate investment. The Lobito Corridor project, connecting Zambian copper mines to Angola's Atlantic port, represents U.S. efforts to develop African infrastructure independent of Chinese control.

Recycling presents an increasingly attractive option as early generations of EV batteries reach end-of-life. The IEA estimates that by 2040, recycled quantities of copper, lithium, nickel, and cobalt from clean energy applications could reduce primary supply requirements for key minerals by ten to thirty percent.[67] While recycling rates for many materials have exhibited limited growth in the past, growing policy attention to stepping up rates of collection and re-processing could deliver triple benefits: complementing primary mineral supplies, improving security of supply for regions with limited resource endowments, and enhancing environmental performance and waste management.[68] The EU's Critical Raw Materials Act targets twenty-five percent of consumption from domestic recycling by 2030.

Technology innovation could ultimately prove most transformative. Lithium iron phosphate batteries, which require no cobalt or nickel, have gained substantial market share in China. Sodium-ion batteries eliminate lithium dependency entirely and are approaching commercial viability for certain applications. Silicon-based anodes could reduce graphite requirements, while solid-state batteries promise improved energy density with potentially different material inputs.

The IEA projects that in the case of lithium, the combination of right-sizing EV batteries, alternative chemistries, and recycling could reduce demand by twenty-five percent in 2030 in the Net Zero Scenario, saving an amount roughly equivalent to today's production.[69] Recycled quantities of copper and cobalt could reduce 2040 primary supply requirements by thirty percent, and fifteen percent for lithium and nickel.[70] Such technology shifts and recycling advances could meaningfully alter demand trajectories, though they cannot eliminate the fundamental challenge of scaling mineral supply to meet decarbonization timelines.

Conclusion: The Defining Resource Competition of Our Time

The competition for lithium, cobalt, nickel, and graphite has emerged as one of the defining strategic contests of the early twenty-first century. Unlike earlier resource competitions centered on fossil fuels, this struggle is inextricably linked to the energy transition that nations worldwide have committed to pursuing. The minerals race beyond rare earths is not a sideshow to great power rivalry but a central arena where the United States and China are contesting influence, building alliances, and positioning for long-term advantage.

China's dominance across the battery supply chain represents both an extraordinary achievement of industrial policy and a strategic vulnerability for Western nations. Beijing has spent decades cultivating processing capacity, acquiring overseas assets, and building integrated supply chains that now give it leverage over the pace and direction of the global energy transition. Western efforts to diversify supplies and build alternative processing capacity are underway but face daunting timelines and investment requirements.

The producing nations of the Global South are not passive actors in this competition. From Congo's renegotiated mining contracts to Chile's nationalization strategy to Indonesia's export bans, resource-rich countries are asserting greater control over their mineral wealth and demanding larger shares of value addition. This trend toward resource nationalism complicates both Chinese and Western supply chain strategies, introducing new variables into an already complex equation.

The outcome of this competition will shape the trajectory of the energy transition itself. If mineral supply chains remain concentrated and vulnerable, the pace of decarbonization may slow as costs rise and bottlenecks emerge. If diversification succeeds and recycling matures, the transition may accelerate. The minerals race beyond rare earths thus carries implications not only for great power rivalry but for humanity's collective response to climate change—stakes that could hardly be higher.

Endnotes

[1] International Energy Agency, *Global Critical Minerals Outlook 2024*, "Executive Summary," May 2024. https://www.iea.org/reports/global-critical-minerals-outlook-2024/executive-summary

[2] Ibid.

[3] International Energy Agency, *Global Critical Minerals Outlook 2024*, "Outlook for Key Minerals." https://www.iea.org/reports/global-critical-minerals-outlook-2024/outlook-for-key-minerals

[4] International Energy Agency, "Critical Minerals," Energy System. https://www.iea.org/energy-system/industry/critical-minerals

[5] PwC UK, "Comments on the IEA Critical Minerals Outlook 2024," May 2024. https://www.pwc.co.uk/press-room/press-releases/research-commentary/pwc-uk-comments-on-the-iea-critical-minerals-outlook-2024-.html

[6] World Bank Group, "Mineral Production to Soar as Demand for Clean Energy Increases," Press Release, May 11, 2020. https://www.worldbank.org/en/news/press-release/2020/05/11/mineral-production-to-soar-as-demand-for-clean-energy-increases

[7] BloombergNEF, "China Regains Number One Spot in BloombergNEF's Global Lithium-Ion Battery Supply Chain Ranking," May 13, 2025. https://about.bnef.com/insights/clean-energy/china-regains-number-one-spot-in-bloombergnefs-global-lithium-ion-battery-supply-chain-ranking/

[8] Carbon Credits, "China's Grip on Lithium Tightens as Global Supply Struggles to Keep Up," October 13, 2025. https://carboncredits.com/chinas-grip-on-lithium-tightens-as-global-supply-struggles-to-keep-up/

[9] Ibid.

[10] U.S. Geological Survey, *Mineral Commodity Summaries 2024*, "Cobalt," January 2024. https://pubs.usgs.gov/periodicals/mcs2024/mcs2024-cobalt.pdf

[11] Bloomberg, "Why China Dominates EV Supply Chain as EU, US Try to Catch Up in Batteries," September 26, 2023. https://www.bloomberg.com/graphics/2023-breaking-china-ev-supply-chain-dominance/

[12] BloombergNEF, "China's Battery Supply Chain Tops BNEF Ranking for Third Consecutive Time, with Canada a Close Second," November 12, 2022. https://about.bnef.com/blog/chinas-battery-supply-chain-tops-bnef-ranking-for-third-consecutive-time-with-canada-a-close-second/

[13] Mining Technology, "Indonesia's nickel market stranglehold tightens, again," April 2025. https://www.mining-technology.com/features/indonesias-nickel-market-stranglehold-tightens-again/

[14] Pacific Forum, "Centralizing Indonesia's nickel industry: The true costs of Chinese investments," PacNet #55, August 8, 2024. https://pacforum.org/publications/pacnet-55-centralizing-indonesias-nickel-industry-the-true-costs-of-chinese-investments/

[15] International Energy Agency, *Global Critical Minerals Outlook 2025*, "Executive Summary," May 2025. https://www.iea.org/reports/global-critical-minerals-outlook-2025/executive-summary

[16] Visual Capitalist, "Visualizing Cobalt Production by Country in 2023," May 31, 2024. https://www.visualcapitalist.com/visualizing-cobalt-production-by-country-in-2023/

[17] U.S. Geological Survey, *Mineral Commodity Summaries 2024*, "Cobalt."

[18] World Bank, "Cobalt in the Democratic Republic of Congo," Market Analysis, 2022. https://documents1.worldbank.org/curated/en/099500001312236438/pdf/P1723770a0f570093092050c1bddd6a29df.pdf

[19] Ibid.

[20] Ibid.

[21] Investingnews.com, "Chile Firms Up Lithium Nationalization Strategy with SQM, Codelco Partnership," June 5, 2024. https://investingnews.com/chile-lithium-nationalization-strategy/

[22] Visual Capitalist, "Visualizing Cobalt Production by Country in 2023."

[23] Green Finance & Development Center, "China Belt and Road Initiative (BRI) Investment Report 2025 H1." https://greenfdc.org/china-belt-and-road-initiative-bri-investment-report-2025-h1/

[24] Washington Post, "Why Chile's New Approach to Lithium Matters Globally," July 26, 2023. https://www.washingtonpost.com/business/energy/2023/07/26/why-chile-s-new-approach-to-lithium-matters-globally/

[25] MercoPress, "Chile announces national lithium strategy," April 21, 2023. https://en.mercopress.com/2023/04/21/chile-announces-national-lithium-strategy

[26] MarketScreener, "Chile's state-run Codelco to control new lithium partnership with SQM," December 27, 2023. https://www.marketscreener.com/news/latest/Chile-s-state-run-Codelco-to-control-new-lithium-partnership-with-SQM-45641783/

[27] Investingnews.com, "Chile Firms Up Lithium Nationalization Strategy with SQM, Codelco Partnership."

[28] Columbia University Center on Global Energy Policy, "Chile's State-Centric Lithium Policy May Deter Investment," May 5, 2025. https://www.energypolicy.columbia.edu/chiles-state-centric-lithium-policy-may-deter-investment/

[29] Mining.com, "Chile regulator approves Codelco-SQM lithium tie-up," April 24, 2025. https://www.mining.com/chile-regulator-approves-codelco-sqm-lithium-tie-up/

[30] Discovery Alert, "Argentina Lithium Mining Investment Opportunities Under RIGI Framework 2025," November 2025. https://discoveryalert.com.au/argentina-lithium-investment-unique-advantages-2025/

[31] UPI, "Argentina aims to become world's second-largest lithium producer," October 15, 2025. https://www.upi.com/Top_News/World-News/2025/10/15/argentina-leading-lithium-supplier/3051760543714/

[32] Ibid.

[33] Ibid.

[34] Lithium Argentina AG, "Lithium Argentina Reports Fourth Quarter and Full Year 2024 Results," GlobeNewswire, March 17, 2025. https://www.globenewswire.com/news-release/2025/03/17/3044142/0/en/Lithium-Argentina-Reports-Fourth-Quarter-and-Full-Year-2024-Results.html

[35] Ibid.

[36] Ibid.

[37] U.S. Department of the Treasury, "Treasury Releases Proposed Guidance to Continue U.S. Manufacturing Boom in Batteries and Clean Vehicles, Strengthen Energy Security," December 1, 2023. https://home.treasury.gov/news/press-releases/jy1939

[38] UPI, "Argentina aims to become world's second-largest lithium producer."

[39] Griffith Asia Institute, "China Belt and Road Initiative (BRI) Investment Report 2025 H1," July 2025. https://blogs.griffith.edu.au/asiainsights/china-belt-and-road-initiative-bri-investment-report-2025/

[40] Green Finance & Development Center, "China Belt and Road Initiative (BRI) Investment Report 2025 H1."

[41] Ibid.

[42] Griffith University News, "China's Belt and Road investment hits record highs in 2025, driven by energy, mining and tech sectors," July 17, 2025. https://news.griffith.edu.au/2025/07/17/chinas-belt-and-road-investment-hits-record-highs-in-2025-driven-by-energy-mining-and-tech-sectors/

[43] Griffith Asia Institute, "China Belt and Road Initiative (BRI) Investment Report 2024." https://blogs.griffith.edu.au/asiainsights/china-belt-and-road-initiative-bri-investment-report-2024/

[44] Mining.com, "China's mining investment under Belt and Road Initiative sets new record – report," March 31, 2025. https://www.mining.com/chinas-mining-investment-under-belt-and-road-initiative-sets-new-record-report/

[45] Mining Technology, "Indonesia's nickel market stranglehold tightens, again."

[46] Ibid.

[47] Ibid.

[48] Ibid.

[49] Ibid.

[50] Carnegie Endowment for International Peace, "How Indonesia Used Chinese Industrial Investments to Turn Nickel into the New Gold," April 2023. https://carnegieendowment.org/research/2023/04/how-indonesia-used-chinese-industrial-investments-to-turn-nickel-into-the-new-gold

[51] U.S. Department of State, "Minerals Security Partnership." https://www.state.gov/minerals-security-partnership

[52] Ibid.

[53] Ibid.

[54] U.S. Department of State, "Joint Statement on Establishment of the Minerals Security Partnership Finance Network," September 23, 2024. https://2021-2025.state.gov/joint-statement-on-establishment-of-the-minerals-security-partnership-finance-network/

[55] U.S. Department of State, "Joint Statement of the Minerals Security Partnership Principals' Meeting 2024," September 27, 2024. https://2021-2025.state.gov/joint-statement-of-the-minerals-security-partnership-principals-meeting-2024/

[56] Ibid.

[57] Ibid.

[58] European Commission, "European Critical Raw Materials Act." https://commission.europa.eu/strategy-and-policy/priorities-2019-2024/european-green-deal/green-deal-industrial-plan/european-critical-raw-materials-act_en

[59] Ibid.

[60] U.S. Department of the Treasury, "Treasury Releases Proposed Guidance to Continue U.S. Manufacturing Boom in Batteries and Clean Vehicles."

[61] Ibid.

[62] International Energy Agency, "Announcement on the Optimisation and Adjustment of Temporary Export Control Measures for Graphite Items," Policies Database. https://www.iea.org/policies/17933-announcement-on-the-optimisation-and-adjustment-of-temporary-export-control-measures-for-graphite-items

[63] Miller & Chevalier, "Trade Compliance Flash: Graphite Export Controls – China's Trade Countermeasures Affecting Electric Vehicles," October 2023. https://www.millerchevalier.com/publication/trade-compliance-flash-graphite-export-controls-chinas-trade-countermeasures-affecting

[64] Fastmarkets, "China's graphite exports plunge in December after introduction of export controls," January 24, 2024. https://www.fastmarkets.com/insights/chinas-graphite-exports-plunge-in-december-after-introduction-of-export-controls/

[65] Ibid.

[66] CSIS, "China's New Graphite Restrictions," October 2023. https://www.csis.org/analysis/chinas-new-graphite-restrictions

[67] International Energy Agency, *Global Critical Minerals Outlook 2024*, "Executive Summary."

[68] Ibid.

[69] Ibid.

[70] Ibid.

Part IV

The Overcapacity Problem

Chapter 10

China's Industrial Tsunami

When 30% of Global Manufacturing Seeks Markets

In January 2025, China's General Administration of Customs released figures that sent tremors through global trade ministries: the nation's trade surplus for 2024 had reached $992.2 billion—a figure that, rounded up, approached the symbolically potent trillion-dollar mark.[1] This was not merely a record; it represented an 18 percent increase from the previous high of $838 billion set in 2022 and stood as the largest goods trade surplus in modern economic history.[2] The numbers told a story of an economic superpower that had become too productive for its own domestic market, a manufacturing colossus whose output increasingly depended on foreign consumers to absorb what Chinese households and businesses could not.

The implications of this surplus extended far beyond bilateral trade statistics. They represented the mathematical expression of a fundamental imbalance at the heart of the Chinese economy—one that Beijing's own leaders had begun to acknowledge, if not fully address. Understanding how China arrived at this juncture, and what it portends for both Chinese economic management and the global trading system, requires examining the structural foundations of what might be termed an "industrial tsunami": a wave of manufacturing output that threatens to reshape industries, disrupt competitors, and force a reckoning with decades of assumptions about how the global economy functions.

The Manufacturing Colossus: Scale and Scope

China's position as the world's manufacturing hegemon is without historical precedent. According to data from China Briefing, the country contributed approximately 30 percent of global manufacturing value added in 2024, maintaining its position as the world's largest manufacturing power for fifteen consecutive years.[3] Research published by the Centre for Economic Policy Research characterized China as "the world's sole manufacturing superpower," with gross manufacturing production reaching 35 percent of the global total—more than the next nine largest manufacturing nations combined.[4]

The magnitude of this dominance defies easy comprehension. In 2024, China's manufacturing output reached approximately $4.66 trillion, compared to $2.91 trillion for the United States, the world's second-largest manufacturer.[5] Japan, Germany, and India—the third, fourth, and fifth largest manufacturing economies—collectively produced less than China alone. When measured by value added, which excludes the cost of intermediate goods, China's share stood at approximately 29 percent of the global total, compared to just 16 percent for the United States.[6]

The breadth of Chinese manufacturing dominance spans virtually every industrial category. In traditional heavy industries, China produces more than half the world's steel, cement, and aluminum. In consumer goods, Chinese factories manufacture one-third of the world's textiles and electronics.[7] In emerging technologies critical to the energy transition, China's dominance is even more pronounced: the country accounts for over 80 percent of global solar panel production and produces the majority of the world's electric vehicle batteries.[8]

The Consumption Gap: Production Without Purchasers

The fundamental problem confronting the Chinese economy is not one of insufficient productive capacity but of inadequate domestic absorption. China produces approximately 30 percent of global manufacturing output yet consumes only about 18 percent.[9] This twelve-percentage-point gap represents the mathematical foundation of the country's structural trade surplus—a gap that must be filled by exports or result in idled factories and unemployed workers.

The roots of this consumption shortfall lie in the structure of the Chinese economy itself. Household consumption represented only about 39.6 percent of China's GDP in 2023, according to World Bank data—a figure far below the global average of approximately 63.6 percent.[10] By comparison, household consumption typically accounts for 68-70 percent of GDP in developed economies like the United States and major European nations. The Rhodium Group documented that China's economy remains "investment and export-led, while household consumption remains at 39% of GDP, far below the average of 54% in OECD economies."[11]

This consumption deficit is the mirror image of China's extraordinarily high investment rate. Investment constituted approximately 42 percent of Chinese GDP in 2023, compared to a global average of 24 percent.[12] These imbalances are so extreme that even if China were to raise its consumption share by ten full percentage points and reduce its investment share correspondingly, the country would still maintain among the highest investment shares and lowest consumption shares of any nation in the world.[13]

The persistence of low household consumption reflects multiple structural factors: an underdeveloped social safety net that encourages precautionary saving; a household registration system that limits access to public services for migrant workers; an income distribution that channels disproportionate shares to corporations and government rather than households; and a property market that, until recently, absorbed vast quantities of household savings in pursuit of appreciation that may never materialize.

The Trillion-Dollar Trade Surplus: Anatomy of an Imbalance

The $992.2 billion trade surplus of 2024 did not emerge suddenly. It represented the culmination of trends that had been building since the COVID-19 pandemic, when China's export machine proved remarkably resilient while domestic consumption remained subdued. According to analysis by ING, China's December 2024 export growth rebounded to 10.7 percent year-on-year, bringing full-year exports to $3.58 trillion—a 5.9 percent growth rate that exceeded most economist expectations at the beginning of the year.[14]

The regional composition of China's exports reveals both the breadth of its manufacturing competitiveness and the shifting landscape of global trade. Exports to the United States surged 15.6 percent in December 2024 alone, reaching a thirty-month high as companies front-loaded shipments ahead of anticipated tariff increases following President Trump's return to office.[15] Exports to ASEAN countries demonstrated even stronger growth at 18.9 percent, reflecting both genuine demand and the increasing use of Southeast Asian nations as waypoints for goods ultimately destined for Western markets.[16]

For the full year, the fastest export growth came from ASEAN (12.0 percent) and Latin America (13.0 percent), while exports to developed economies showed more modest increases.[17] Brazil emerged as a particularly notable market, with Chinese exports increasing 22 percent to $72.1 billion, driven by surging sales of electronics and vehicles.[18] This geographic diversification represented a strategic response to growing trade tensions with traditional markets in North America and Europe.

The import side of the ledger told an equally revealing story. Chinese imports grew a tepid 1.1 percent in 2024, reaching $2.59 trillion.[19] This meager growth reflected the persistent weakness of domestic demand, the substitution of foreign goods with domestic alternatives, and the ongoing contraction of the property sector that had historically driven imports of construction materials and related commodities.

Sectoral Analysis: The Industries Flooding Global Markets

Steel: The Foundation of Overcapacity

No sector better illustrates China's overcapacity challenge than steel. The country produced over 1 billion metric tons of crude steel in 2024—approximately 55 percent of global output—down slightly from the previous year but still representing production volumes that dwarf those of any competitor.[20] The United States, by comparison, produced approximately 80 million tons.

Chinese steel exports reached a record 118 million tons in 2024.[21] This volume exceeded the entire annual steel production of the United States. According to the OECD Steel Outlook 2025, Chinese steel exports have more than doubled since 2020, creating what the organization described as significant disruption to steel markets worldwide.[22]

The scale of China's steel overcapacity reflects decades of investment in steelmaking facilities, much of it driven by local government priorities rather than market signals. The OECD's analysis found that China's steel subsidization rate—measured as a percentage of firm revenues—is ten times higher than that of OECD countries.[23] These subsidies take multiple forms: below-market borrowings from state-owned banks, subsidized energy prices, direct grants, and preferential tax treatment.[24] The effect is to keep facilities operating that would otherwise face closure and to encourage investment that would be commercially unjustified under market conditions.

The surge in Chinese exports prompted a fivefold increase in antidumping measures since 2023. During 2024, nineteen governments initiated 81 antidumping investigations involving steel products, approaching levels last seen during the 2016 steel crisis.[25] Almost 80 percent of the cases targeted Asian producers, with China alone accounting for more than one-third of the total.

Solar Panels: Drowning the World in Photovoltaics

China's solar panel industry exemplifies both the country's remarkable manufacturing capabilities and the destabilizing consequences of unconstrained capacity expansion. The country is responsible for over 80 percent of global solar panel production, with output that far exceeds both domestic installation capacity and global demand.[26]

In 2024, China exported 235.93 gigawatts of photovoltaic modules, a 13 percent increase from the 207.99 gigawatts exported in 2023, according to customs data compiled by PV InfoLink.[27] To contextualize these figures: China's solar panel exports in a single year exceeded the entire installed solar capacity of the United States accumulated over decades. Chinese manufacturers produced approximately 453 gigawatts of modules in the first ten months of 2024 alone, with domestic installations of approximately 181 gigawatts leaving massive surplus production for export.[28]

Prices collapsed across the supply chain: in the first ten months of 2024, polysilicon prices fell 38 percent, wafer prices dropped 49 percent, solar cell prices declined 30.4 percent, and module prices fell 28.8 percent.[29] In 2024, profits in the solar sector declined by 8 percent, marking the third consecutive year that its profit margins were lower than that of China's industrial enterprises as a whole.[30]

Electric Vehicles: The New Battleground

China's electric vehicle industry has emerged as perhaps the most strategically significant arena of overcapacity competition. In 2023, China surpassed Japan to become the world's largest automobile exporter, with the transition driven largely by electric and hybrid vehicles. The country exported 6.4 million cars in 2024, a 22.8 percent increase from the previous year.[31]

The EV sector's rise has been spectacular. Since 2017, China's EV exports surged 13,300 percent, reaching $42 billion by 2023, when China accounted for nearly 70 percent of global EV production.[32] According to the International Energy Agency's Global EV Outlook 2025, global electric car sales exceeded 17 million in 2024, with China accounting for over 11 million of those sales—more than the entire global EV market just two years earlier.[33]

Yet the industry is plagued by the same overcapacity dynamics affecting other sectors. The Rhodium Group documented that China's passenger vehicle capacity utilization rate fell from 74.7 percent in 2023 to 70.3 percent through the third quarter of 2024, with some joint venture brands operating at utilization rates as low as 36 percent.[34]

The result has been the outbreak of intense price wars that have decimated profit margins. Competitors accuse each other of selling below cost to drive out competition, while excess inventory problems have become so severe that dealerships report marking brand new cars as "used" to circumvent price floors imposed by manufacturers.[35]

Batteries: Powering the Surplus

The lithium-ion battery industry demonstrates similar patterns. China's lithium-ion battery production capacity surpassed 2 terawatt-hours in 2024—60 percent higher than total global battery demand.[36] Planned capacity in the country exceeds 6 terawatt-hours, enough to meet the world's battery cell demand until 2035.[37]

In 2023, China's battery production alone was sufficient to meet global demand, while worldwide battery manufacturing capacity exceeded 2,600 gigawatt-hours—more than twice global demand.[38] China is the world's largest EV battery exporter, with approximately 12 percent of its EV batteries being shipped overseas, according to the IEA.[39]

The IEA noted that China's current leading role in battery production comes at the cost of high levels of overcapacity. In 2023, excluding portable electronics, China used less than 40 percent of its maximum cell output.[40]

The "Involution" Problem: Beijing's Acknowledgment

In July 2024, the highest levels of the Chinese Communist Party formally acknowledged what had become undeniable: the nation's industries were trapped in a destructive spiral of overcompetition that was eroding profits, depressing wages, and threatening long-term economic health. The term employed was "����" (nèijuǎn jìngzhēng)—typically translated as "involution competition" or "involutionary competition."[41]

The concept of "involution" originated in anthropological studies of agricultural societies where increasing labor inputs yielded diminishing returns. Applied to Chinese industry, it described a state where intense internal competition led to exhausting effort without corresponding improvement—firms competing ever more fiercely for shrinking profits in oversupplied markets. The Central Economic Work Conference in December 2024 elevated the fight against involution to the top economic priority for 2025.[42]

The official readout from the December conference pledged that Beijing would "comprehensively rectify 'neijuan-style' competition" through regulating the behavior of local governments and enterprises.[43] Chinese leaders vowed to strengthen industry self-discipline, prevent vicious competition, and ensure smooth channels for the exit of outdated and inefficient production capacities.

As the South China Morning Post reported, Beijing aimed to "heal wounds of involution" as officials vowed to stem what they characterized as "bloodletting" in key industries.[44] Mao Zhenhua, an economics professor at Renmin University of China, articulated the damage: such vicious competition "has driven down commodity prices, squeezing corporate profits and ultimately depressing household wages and consumption power."[45]

Provincial Competition and the Subsidy Trap

Understanding how China arrived at its current overcapacity predicament requires examining the political economy of local government competition. China's fiscal system creates powerful incentives for provincial and municipal governments to pursue industrial development regardless of whether capacity additions are commercially justified or economically efficient.

Local governments depend heavily on land sales and industrial investment for both fiscal revenues and the economic growth metrics on which officials' careers depend. When central government policy identifies strategic industries—whether steel in the 2000s, solar panels in the 2010s, or electric vehicles in the 2020s—local authorities rush to attract investment, often through subsidies, cheap land, and preferential treatment that would not survive market scrutiny.

The pattern is consistent across sectors. Once an industry with development potential emerges, resources from enterprises and local governments across the country concentrate on these sectors, ultimately leading to a surge in capacity that exceeds any plausible demand scenario.[46] Provincial governments are reluctant to make adjustments or shrink industries with low competitiveness; instead, they provide fiscal subsidies and financial support to local firms while waiting for competitors in other provinces to reduce capacity first.[47]

This dynamic creates what game theorists would recognize as a prisoner's dilemma. No individual province wants to be the first to shutter factories, accept layoffs, and sacrifice the GDP growth that determines local officials' promotions. Each province hopes that others will bear the adjustment costs. The result is that excess capacity persists far longer than market signals would warrant, with losses socialized through the banking system and ultimately borne by the broader economy.

Research published in *Small Business Economics* found that from 2000 to 2007, approximately 262,800 zombie enterprises operated in Chinese industrial sectors, accounting for 14.25 percent of the total sample.[48] Studies of listed Chinese firms found that approximately 14 percent qualified as zombies, with the proportion highest among state-owned enterprises at about 16 percent.[49]

Why Market Corrections Don't Work: The Persistence of Zombie Firms

The continued operation of zombie firms—enterprises that survive only through bank loans and government subsidies—represents a critical mechanism preventing market-driven capacity adjustment. These firms tie up capital, labor, and resources that would otherwise flow to more productive uses, while their willingness to operate at losses depresses prices and margins for healthier competitors.

Research published in *Economic Modelling* found that from 2007 to 2016, the number of listed Chinese firms receiving government subsidies increased from 1,229 to 3,059—a 149 percent increase—with total subsidies exceeding 978 billion yuan.[50] Among these subsidies, zombie firms accounted for 30 percent, or approximately 293 billion yuan.[51] The subsidies did not help zombie firms recover; rather, they extended their survival without improving their commercial viability.

The banking system plays a central role in sustaining zombie firms. Chinese banks, particularly state-owned institutions, face pressures to continue lending to troubled enterprises rather than forcing their closure through loan recalls. Writing down bad loans would require banks to rebuild their capital; allowing mass layoffs would create social instability that local officials are desperate to avoid.

The Peterson Institute for International Economics characterized the situation directly: "The Chinese government has repeatedly bailed out these unsound companies rather than let them fail, avoiding the pain of layoffs, tax revenue losses, and write-offs of loans that would require banks to rebuild their capital."[52] The result is chronic resource misallocation and persistent overcapacity in multiple sectors.

The Real Estate Dimension: When the Engine Stalls

The property sector's crisis since 2020 has intensified China's overcapacity challenge by simultaneously weakening domestic demand and eliminating a major outlet for industrial production. Real estate and its related activities historically constituted approximately 20-30 percent of Chinese GDP when accounting for construction, materials, furnishings, and related services.[53] The sector's contraction removed a massive source of demand for steel, cement, glass, copper, and countless other industrial products. For decades, the property boom had served as a pressure valve, absorbing industrial output that might otherwise have flooded export markets. With that valve closed, the full force of Chinese manufacturing capacity is being directed outward.

The property market's troubles began when the Chinese government implemented the "Three Red Lines" policy in 2020, imposing strict limits on developer leverage in response to concerns about excessive speculation and debt accumulation.[54] The policy triggered a cascade of developer defaults, most dramatically with China Evergrande Group's collapse with over $300 billion in liabilities, followed by Country Garden's distress with $205 billion in debt.[55] These were not isolated failures but symptoms of a sector that had grown dependent on ever-increasing prices and perpetual expansion.

By 2023, housing starts had dropped by more than 60 percent from pre-pandemic levels, marking one of the largest housing busts globally in decades.[56] The Conference Board noted that new home sales continued declining throughout 2024, with total sales of the top 100 real estate companies falling 28.1 percent year-on-year.[57] Real estate investment posted its largest year-on-year decrease since 2004, representing a fundamental shift in China's growth model.

The property crisis creates a vicious feedback loop with household consumption. Declining property values erode the perceived wealth of households who have concentrated their savings in real estate, reducing their willingness to spend on other goods and services. For Chinese households, who hold approximately 70 percent of their wealth in property—far higher than households in developed economies—the prolonged decline in property values has created a profound negative wealth effect that suppresses consumption across the entire economy.

The Macroeconomic Imbalance: Investment Over Consumption

At its root, China's overcapacity problem reflects a macroeconomic structure that systematically favors investment over consumption, production over demand. This configuration emerged from China's development strategy of the reform era, which prioritized rapid industrialization, infrastructure construction, and export-oriented growth. The strategy succeeded spectacularly in transforming China from an impoverished agricultural economy into a manufacturing superpower. But the model that worked brilliantly for four decades may have reached its natural limits.

Huang Yiping, Dean of the National School of Development at Peking University, offered a structural diagnosis: "The main reason for the new round of overcapacity is that China's economy is at a critical period of industrial upgrading and transformation, and many old industries urgently need to find new directions as they cannot continue to develop."[58] When promising new industries emerge, resources from enterprises and local governments concentrate on these sectors, producing capacity surges that exceed demand.

The Rhodium Group's analysis painted a sobering picture of China's consumption trajectory. In the absence of significant fiscal reforms, "long-term household consumption growth is likely to slow to around 3-4% per year in real terms over the next five to ten years. At most, household consumption will contribute around 1.5 percentage points of GDP growth per year, which is likely to limit overall long-term GDP growth to around 3%, given the known headwinds to faster investment growth."[59]

The implication is stark: if consumption cannot grow faster, and if investment cannot sustain historically high rates without generating ever more overcapacity, then economic growth must slow—or the gap must be filled by ever-larger trade surpluses. But as China's nearly trillion-dollar surplus demonstrated, the rest of the world has limited appetite for absorbing Chinese overproduction indefinitely. The mathematical reality is inescapable: China cannot simultaneously maintain high investment rates, suppress consumption, and avoid either slower growth or mounting trade surpluses that provoke retaliation from trading partners.

Global Repercussions: When One Country's Supply Exceeds the World's Demand

The consequences of Chinese industrial overcapacity extend far beyond bilateral trade statistics. They reshape competitive dynamics in industry after industry, force policy responses from governments worldwide, and raise fundamental questions about the sustainability of the global trading system. What began as a Chinese domestic economic challenge has become a defining feature of twenty-first-century international commerce.

The steel sector provides perhaps the clearest illustration. According to the OECD, the surge in Chinese exports to record levels in 2024 triggered a fivefold increase in antidumping measures since 2023.[60] Beyond product-specific dumping cases, a growing number of countries introduced broader measures to protect their steel industries through sector-wide tariff increases. The OECD Steel Committee warned that global excess capacity is expected to reach 721 million metric tons by 2027, putting "enormous pressures on the viability of even highly competitive steelmakers."

Similar dynamics unfolded in solar panels, electric vehicles, and batteries. The United States increased tariffs on Chinese-made EVs from 25 percent to 100 percent in May 2024.[61] Canada followed suit in August, also raising tariffs to 100 percent.[62] The European Union imposed provisional anti-subsidy tariffs of up to 37.6 percent on EVs imported from China following an anti-subsidy investigation.[63] These trade defense measures represent an unprecedented coordinated response by Western economies to what they perceive as market-distorting Chinese industrial policies.

For developing countries, Chinese overcapacity poses particularly acute dilemmas. On one hand, cheap Chinese steel, solar panels, and vehicles offer affordable inputs for infrastructure development and industrialization. On the other hand, the same imports can devastate nascent domestic industries before they achieve the scale and efficiency needed to compete. The UC Institute on Global Conflict and Cooperation noted that Thailand reported over 2,000 factory closures in 2024, while Indonesia's textile sector shed tens of thousands of jobs under pressure from Chinese competition.[64] This phenomenon of "premature deindustrialization" threatens the development models of countries that had hoped to follow China's own path from agricultural poverty to manufacturing prosperity.

The geopolitical dimensions of overcapacity extend beyond economics into questions of strategic dependence and national security. Countries that become reliant on Chinese solar panels, batteries, and electric vehicles for their energy transition face uncomfortable questions about supply chain resilience and the potential for economic coercion. These concerns have accelerated efforts in the United States, European Union, and allied nations to develop domestic manufacturing capacity in strategic sectors, even at significant cost premiums.

No Easy Answers: The Limits of Policy Response

Beijing's response to the overcapacity challenge has been cautious, incremental, and ultimately insufficient. The December 2024 Central Economic Work Conference's pledge to combat "involution" represented recognition of the problem, but the proposed solutions fell short of the structural reforms required to address root causes. The gap between acknowledging the problem and implementing effective solutions reflects the profound political obstacles that stand in the way of meaningful economic rebalancing.

The government has begun administrative measures to curb capacity in the worst-affected sectors. In the solar industry, authorities summoned executives and signaled that price wars must give way to quality upgrades.[65] New guidelines for the lithium-ion battery industry emphasized quality over quantity and advised companies to refrain from constructing new plants that "simply expand production capacity."[66] The Ministry of Industry and Information Technology increased performance targets in battery standards in a bid to cull weaker producers from the market.

Yet these measures address symptoms rather than causes. They do not fundamentally alter the incentives that drive local governments to pursue industrial investment regardless of market conditions. They do not rebalance the economy toward consumption. They do not strengthen the social safety net in ways that would reduce precautionary saving. They do not reform the fiscal system to reduce local government dependence on land sales and industrial development for revenues. Most critically, they do not address the fundamental macroeconomic imbalance between investment and consumption that lies at the heart of the overcapacity phenomenon.

The fundamental challenge is political as much as economic. Rebalancing toward consumption would require redistributing income from corporations and government to households—transfers that would reduce resources available for investment, defense, and the industrial policies Beijing views as essential for technological self-sufficiency. It would require allowing inefficient firms to fail, accepting the layoffs and social disruption that accompany market-driven adjustment. It would require local officials to accept slower growth and reduced resources in the short term for the promise of more sustainable development over the long term.

As economist Michael Pettis of Carnegie Endowment noted, "China has the deepest economic imbalances in history, with investment representing 42 percent of GDP in 2023 versus a global average of 24 percent, consumption representing 56 percent versus a global average of 76 percent."[67] These imbalances are so extreme that even dramatic reforms would leave China an outlier among major economies for years to come.

The costs of failing to rebalance are also clear: continued overcapacity, persistent trade frictions, growing resistance from trading partners, and an economy that becomes ever more dependent on exports at precisely the moment when those exports face mounting barriers. The industrial tsunami that propelled China's rise threatens to become a force that undermines the very foundation of that success. Whether Beijing can navigate between the Scylla of painful domestic adjustment and the Charybdis of escalating international conflict remains the defining question of China's economic trajectory in the years ahead.

Endnotes

[1] ING Think, "China's Trade Surplus Hit a Record High in 2024," January 13, 2025, https://think.ing.com/snaps/chinas-trade-surplus-hit-a-record-high-in-2024/.

[2] Trade Data Monitor, "Record Chinese Global Surplus Neared $1 Trillion in 2024," January 27, 2025, https://tradedatamonitor.com/datanews/record-chinese-global-surplus-neared-1-trillion-in-2024/.

[3] China Briefing, "China Manufacturing Industry Tracker - Key Data for 2025," accessed November 2025, https://www.china-briefing.com/news/china-manufacturing-industry-tracker-2024-25/.

[4] Richard Baldwin, "China Is the World's Sole Manufacturing Superpower: A Line Sketch of the Rise," Centre for Economic Policy Research, VoxEU, 2024, https://cepr.org/voxeu/columns/china-worlds-sole-manufacturing-superpower-line-sketch-rise.

[5] Safeguard Global, "Top 10 Manufacturing Countries in 2025," accessed November 2025, https://www.safeguardglobal.com/resources/blog/top-10-manufacturing-countries-in-the-world/.

[6] Baldwin, "China Is the World's Sole Manufacturing Superpower."

[7] Michigan State University GlobalEDGE, "How China's $1 Trillion Surplus Impacts the World Market," January 23, 2025, https://globaledge.msu.edu/blog/post/58471/how-chinas-1-trillion-surplus-impacts-th.

[8] International Energy Agency, "Trends in Electric Vehicle Batteries – Global EV Outlook 2024," 2024, https://www.iea.org/reports/global-ev-outlook-2024/trends-in-electric-vehicle-batteries.

[9] MERICS, "China's Record Trade Surplus + Anti-Corruption Campaign + De-Risking," January 2025, https://merics.org/en/merics-briefs/chinas-record-trade-surplus-anti-corruption-campaign-de-risking.

[10] World Bank, "Households and NPISHs Final Consumption Expenditure (% of GDP) - China," World Development Indicators, 2023, https://data.worldbank.org/indicator/NE.CON.PRVT.ZS?locations=CN.

[11] Rhodium Group, "No Quick Fixes: China's Long-Term Consumption Growth," July 18, 2024, https://rhg.com/research/no-quick-fixes-chinas-long-term-consumption-growth/.

[12] Carnegie Endowment for International Peace, Michael Pettis, "Impact of Household Consumption Growth on China's GDP Growth," December 2024, https://carnegieendowment.org/posts/2024/12/impact-of-household-consumption-growth-on-chinas-gdp-growth.

[13] Ibid.

[14] ING Think, "China's Trade Surplus Hit a Record High in 2024."

[15] Ibid.

[16] Ibid.

[17] Trade Data Monitor, "Record Chinese Global Surplus Neared $1 Trillion in 2024."

[18] Ibid.

[19] South China Morning Post, "China Posts Record Trade Surplus as Export Wave Finds Shores Outside US," January 14, 2025, https://www.scmp.com/economy/global-economy/article/3294472/china-trade-surplus-reaches-record-high-surge-pre-trump-exports.

[20] GMK Center, "China's Steel Market in 2024: Export Growth and Domestic Consumption Decline," January 21, 2025, https://gmk.center/en/infographic/chinas-steel-market-in-2024-export-growth-and-domestic-consumption-decline/.

[21] OECD, "Surging Excess Capacity Threatens Steel Market Stability, Employment, and Decarbonisation Plans," press release, May 27, 2025, https://www.oecd.org/en/about/news/press-releases/2025/05/surging-excess-capacity-threatens-steel-market-stability-employment-and-decarbonisation-plans.html.

[22] OECD, *OECD Steel Outlook 2025* (Paris: OECD Publishing, 2025), https://www.oecd.org/en/publications/oecd-steel-outlook-2025_28b61a5e-en.html.

[23] Ibid.

[24] Ibid.

[25] Ibid.

[26] International Energy Agency, "Solar PV Global Supply Chains," Executive Summary, 2022, https://www.iea.org/reports/solar-pv-global-supply-chains/executive-summary.

[27] pv magazine, "China Exports 235.9 GW of Solar Panels in 2024," February 7, 2025, https://www.pv-magazine.com/2025/02/07/china-exports-235-9-gw-of-solar-panels-in-2024/.

[28] TaiyangNews, "China Exported 206 GW Solar Modules During 10M 2024," December 16, 2024, https://taiyangnews.info/markets/china-solar-pv-output-10m-2024.

[29] Dialogue Earth, "China to Tackle Overcapacity," March 6, 2025, https://dialogue.earth/en/digest/china-to-tackle-overcapacity/.

[30] Ibid.

[31] MERICS, "China's Record Trade Surplus."

[32] World Economic Forum, "Major Economies Are Now Taking Aim at China's EV Industry," September 2024, https://www.weforum.org/stories/2024/09/major-economies-are-taking-aim-at-china-s-ev-industry-here-s-what-to-know/.

[33] International Energy Agency, "Executive Summary – Global EV Outlook 2025," 2025, https://www.iea.org/reports/global-ev-outlook-2025/executive-summary.

[34] Rhodium Group, "From Fast Lane to Gridlock: Have Chinese Car Exports Peaked?" 2024, https://rhg.com/research/from-fast-lane-to-gridlock-have-chinese-car-exports-peaked/.

[35] Seafarer Funds, "Nobody Wins in a Price War: Destructive Competition in China," 2025, https://www.seafarerfunds.com/prevailing-winds/destructive-competition-in-china/.

[36] CRU Group, "China's Overcapacity: Will Its Battery Industry Consolidate?" August 5, 2025, https://www.crugroup.com/en/communities/thought-leadership/2025/chinas-overcapacity-will-its-battery-industry-consolidate/.

[37] Ibid.

[38] OilPrice.com, "China Looks to Curb Overcapacity in Its Lithium Battery Industry," June 19, 2024, https://oilprice.com/Latest-Energy-News/World-News/China-Looks-to-Curb-Overcapacity-in-Its-Lithium-Battery-Industry.html.

[39] International Energy Agency, "Trends in Electric Vehicle Batteries – Global EV Outlook 2024."

[40] Ibid.

[41] Matthew C. Klein, "China's 'Anti-Involution' Campaign: Global Implications," The Overshoot, September 19, 2025, https://theovershoot.co/p/chinas-anti-involution-campaign-global.

[42] IGCC (UC Institute on Global Conflict and Cooperation), "Chinese Overcapacity Looms Over the APEC Summit," November 2025, https://ucigcc.org/blog/chinese-overcapacity-looms-over-the-apec-summit/.

[43] APCO Worldwide, "China's 2024 Central Economic Work Conference: 6 Key Takeaways," December 2024, https://apcoworldwide.com/blog/chinas-2024-central-economic-work-conference-six-key-takeaways/.

[44] South China Morning Post, "China Aims to Heal Wounds of 'Involution' as Officials Vow to Stem Bloodletting," December 14, 2024, https://www.scmp.com/economy/china-economy/article/3290715/china-aims-heal-wounds-industrial-involution-officials-vow-stem-bloodletting.

[45] Klein, "China's 'Anti-Involution' Campaign."

[46] Fred Gao, "Huang Yiping on the Root of the New Round of Overcapacity in China," *Inside China*, May 3, 2024, https://www.fredgao.com/p/huang-yiping-on-the-root-of-the-new.

[47] Y. Tan et al., "Zombie Firms and the Crowding-Out of Private Investment in China," cited in ResearchGate, October 2016, https://www.researchgate.net/publication/309114139_Zombie_Firms_and_the_Crowding-Out_of_Private_Investment_in_China.

[48] Yan Hong et al., "Administrative Reform and the Disposal of Zombie Enterprises: Evidence from China," *Small Business Economics* 61 (2023), https://link.springer.com/article/10.1007/s11187-023-00752-8.

[49] Huajun Nie et al., "How Do Zombie Firms Affect Innovation? Evidence from China's Industrial Firms," VoxChina, accessed 2024, https://voxchina.org/show-3-128.html.

[50] Qingliang Tang et al., "The Impact of Government Subsidies on the Capacity Utilization of Zombie Firms," *Economic Modelling* 83 (October 2019): 388–402, https://www.sciencedirect.com/science/article/abs/pii/S0264999319311988.

[51] Ibid.

[52] Peterson Institute for International Economics, "China Is Only Nibbling at the Problem of 'Zombie' State-Owned Enterprises," July 2, 2021, https://www.piie.com/blogs/china-economic-watch/china-only-nibbling-problem-zombie-state-owned-enterprises.

[53] Global Property Guide, "China's Residential Property Market Analysis 2025," 2025, https://www.globalpropertyguide.com/asia/china/price-history.

[54] Ibid.

[55] The Global Treasurer, "Understanding China's Real Estate Crisis," April 29, 2024, https://www.theglobaltreasurer.com/2024/04/29/understanding-chinas-real-estate-crisis/.

[56] International Monetary Fund, Kenneth Rogoff, "China's Real Estate Challenge," *Finance & Development*, December 2024, https://www.imf.org/en/publications/fandd/issues/2024/12/chinas-real-estate-challenge-kenneth-rogoff.

[57] The Conference Board, "China's Real Estate Market: Where Do Things Stand? What Can Be Expected in 2025?" 2025, https://www.conference-board.org/publications/China-Real-Estate-Market-What-can-be-expected-in-2025.

[58] Fred Gao, "Huang Yiping on the Root of the New Round of Overcapacity in China."

[59] Rhodium Group, "No Quick Fixes: China's Long-Term Consumption Growth."

[60] OECD, "Surging Excess Capacity Threatens Steel Market Stability."

[61] World Economic Forum, "Major Economies Are Now Taking Aim at China's EV Industry."

[62] Ibid.

[63] Ibid.

[64] IGCC, "Chinese Overcapacity Looms Over the APEC Summit."

[65] Ibid.

[66] OilPrice.com, "China Looks to Curb Overcapacity in Its Lithium Battery Industry."

[67] Carnegie Endowment for International Peace, Michael Pettis, "Impact of Household Consumption Growth on China's GDP Growth."

Chapter 11

America's Consumption Conundrum: Trade Deficits, Deindustrialization, and the Reindustrialization Dream

The transformation of the American economy over the past half-century represents one of the most profound structural shifts in the nation's history. What was once the world's undisputed manufacturing powerhouse has evolved into a service-dominated economy with persistent trade deficits and a diminished industrial base. Understanding this transformation—and the formidable obstacles to reversing it—is essential to grasping why the U.S.-China rivalry extends far beyond tariff disputes into questions of national identity, economic security, and the very foundations of American prosperity.

The Long Decline: From Industrial Giant to Service Economy

In the immediate postwar decades, manufacturing stood as the backbone of American economic might and middle-class prosperity. At its zenith in June 1979, manufacturing employment reached 19.6 million workers, representing 22 percent of total nonfarm employment.[1] The sector provided stable, well-compensated positions that enabled millions of Americans without college degrees to achieve homeownership, raise families, and retire with dignity. Manufacturing wages helped construct the American Dream for an entire generation.

The decline that followed has been precipitous and, in many ways, irreversible. By December 2024, manufacturing employment had fallen to approximately 12.8 million workers—a decline of roughly 6.5 million positions, or 33 percent, from the 1979 peak.[2] As a share of total employment, manufacturing now accounts for less than nine percent of the American workforce, down from 22 percent at its height.[3] The sector's contribution to gross domestic product tells a similar story: manufacturing value added stood at 10.2 percent of GDP in 2023, a dramatic contraction from the 21 to 25 percent range that characterized the 1950s through the 1970s.[4]

This decline did not occur uniformly across time. The Bureau of Labor Statistics documents that manufacturing employment remained relatively stable through the 1970s, experiencing cyclical fluctuations during recessions but generally recovering during expansions.[5] The structural break came in the 1980s, when employment began a secular downward trend. Between 1980 and 2000, approximately two million manufacturing jobs disappeared.[6] But the most catastrophic losses occurred in the subsequent decade: between 2001 and 2009, manufacturing shed an estimated one-third of its remaining workforce—the worst period for American industry since the Great Depression.[7]

The geographic concentration of these losses has produced enduring political and social consequences. The industrial heartland—Ohio, Michigan, Pennsylvania, Wisconsin, Indiana, Illinois—experienced devastating deindustrialization. Between 2000 and 2024, New York lost nearly 45 percent of its manufacturing employment, shedding more than 330,000 jobs.[8] California, despite its reputation for technological innovation, lost nearly 615,000 manufacturing positions over the same period.[9] These were not merely statistical abstractions but represented the hollowing out of entire communities, the closure of plants that had anchored local economies for generations, and the erosion of a way of life that had defined American working-class identity.

The China Shock and Its Discontents

No single event accelerated deindustrialization more dramatically than China's accession to the World Trade Organization in December 2001. President Bill Clinton had championed Chinese entry, arguing that the agreement would create "a win-win result for both countries" and that exports to China would support "hundreds of thousands of American jobs."[10] The reality proved starkly different.

The Economic Policy Institute estimates that growing trade deficits with China eliminated 3.7 million American jobs between 2001 and 2018, including 2.8 million positions in manufacturing.[11] Academic research by David Autor, David Dorn, and Gordon Hanson—the seminal "China Shock" studies—found that increased Chinese imports accounted for approximately 55 percent of the decline in U.S. manufacturing employment between 2000 and 2007, translating to roughly one million manufacturing job losses during that period alone.[12] Additional research by Justin Pierce and Peter Schott found that granting China permanent normal trade relations status "reduced relative employment growth of the average industry by 3.4 percentage points after one year and 15.6 percentage points after six years."[13]

The scale of physical plant closures was equally staggering. According to U.S. Census Bureau data, the United States lost more than 60,000 manufacturing establishments between 2001 and 2014.[14] These closures represented not merely shifts in employment but the permanent destruction of productive capacity—the disappearance of industrial knowledge, supply chain relationships, and the ecosystem of skills required to manufacture complex goods.

The computer and electronic products sector suffered the most severe hemorrhaging. Despite the San Francisco Bay Area's emergence as a global technology hub, employment in computer and electronic parts manufacturing collapsed.[15] The United States effectively ceded entire categories of consumer electronics production to Asian competitors. Today, as the semiconductor shortage revealed during the COVID-19 pandemic, the country lacks the capacity to manufacture many of the products its own companies design.

Yet it would be misleading to attribute manufacturing's decline solely to Chinese competition. The academic literature remains contested on the precise magnitude of trade's impact relative to other factors.[16] Technology and automation have transformed manufacturing into an increasingly capital-intensive enterprise. Manufacturing output recovered from the Great Recession and reached an all-time high in 2024—yet employment has not followed.[17] This "jobless recovery" reflects fundamental productivity gains: American factories now produce more with far fewer workers. Between 1987 and 2011, manufacturing labor productivity more than doubled, growing 129 percent while business sector productivity overall increased only 71 percent.[18]

The Trade Deficit Obsession

Few economic metrics have generated more political heat and less analytical light than the U.S. trade deficit. For President Trump—in both his first and second administrations—trade deficits represent a "national emergency" and evidence of decades of unfair treatment by trading partners.[19] This framing has justified tariff escalations unprecedented since the Smoot-Hawley era, culminating in the "Liberation Day" announcement of April 2, 2025, when the average U.S. tariff rate rose to approximately 27 percent—the highest level in over a century.[20]

The raw numbers are indeed substantial. The U.S. goods trade deficit reached unprecedented levels in 2024, with the Bureau of Economic Analysis reporting deficits of $295.4 billion with China, $235.6 billion with the European Union, and $171.8 billion with Mexico.[21] The bilateral deficit with China, while down from its 2018 peak of $377.7 billion in goods and services, remains the nation's largest.[22] Over the twelve months through August 2025, the U.S. trade deficit with China stood at approximately $256 billion, representing 19 percent of the total goods trade deficit.[23]

Yet the economic significance of these figures is far more nuanced than political rhetoric suggests. Trade deficits are not inherently harmful; they reflect complex interactions between savings rates, investment flows, currency valuations, and consumption patterns. When Americans purchase imported goods, they exchange dollars for products that improve their living standards. Those dollars, held abroad, ultimately return to the United States—whether as purchases of American exports, investments in U.S. assets, or holdings of Treasury securities.

More fundamentally, the trade deficit obsession ignores a central paradox of American economic power: the dollar's role as the world's primary reserve currency makes persistent deficits structurally necessary. This insight, first articulated by Belgian-American economist Robert Triffin in 1960, has become known as the Triffin Dilemma.[24] A country whose currency serves as the global reserve must supply that currency to the world economy, which requires running trade deficits—exporting dollars by importing more goods than it exports. The dollar's share of global foreign exchange reserves, while declining from 71 percent in 1999 to approximately 59 percent in 2023, remains dominant.[25] The greenback is involved in 88 percent of all foreign exchange transactions, approximately 40 percent of global debt securities are denominated in dollars, and around 80 percent of trade outside Europe is invoiced in dollars.[26]

This "exorbitant privilege," as Charles de Gaulle famously termed it, enables the United States to borrow at lower interest rates, finance consumption beyond its production, and project financial power globally. But the privilege carries an "exorbitant burden": chronic deficits that erode traded-sector employment and manufacturing capacity.[27] The nation cannot simultaneously serve as the world's central bank, supplying liquidity to the global economy, and maintain the balanced trade that would preserve its industrial base. Tariffs may alter bilateral trade flows, but they cannot resolve this fundamental structural tension without undermining the dollar's reserve status itself.

The Reindustrialization Dream: Policy and Its Limits

Against this backdrop, the Trump administration's reindustrialization agenda represents the most ambitious attempt to reverse deindustrialization since the industrial policies of the early Cold War. The strategy combines multiple instruments: punitive tariffs to raise import costs, corporate tax reductions to incentivize domestic production, deregulation to lower compliance burdens, and direct subsidies—particularly through the CHIPS and Science Act—to reshore strategic industries.

The Tax Cuts and Jobs Act of 2017 reduced the federal corporate income tax rate from 35 percent to 21 percent, bringing the combined U.S. federal and state rate closer to the OECD average.[28] The legislation also permitted full expensing of equipment investments, allowing businesses to deduct the complete cost of qualified capital expenditures in the year of purchase.[29] Proponents argued these changes would dramatically lower the user cost of capital, stimulating investment and eventually raising wages.

Economic research on the TCJA's impact presents mixed conclusions. A National Bureau of Economic Research study estimated that the law increased domestic investment by approximately 20 percent for firms with average-sized tax shocks, with larger effects for multinational corporations.[30] The researchers projected a long-run capital stock increase of 7.2 percent and a 0.9 percent increase in wages after fifteen years.[31] However, a 2024 comprehensive assessment concluded that the TCJA "clearly raised federal debt and increased after-tax incomes, disproportionately increasing incomes for the most affluent. Its effects on GDP and median wages seem modest at best."[32] The law's impact on investment, while positive, did not approach the transformational effects its advocates predicted. Much of the growth in investment between 2017 and 2019 occurred in nonmanufacturing assets, particularly public utilities, rather than the manufacturing renaissance envisioned.[33]

The tariff weapon has proven equally problematic. Liberation Day tariffs, announced on April 2, 2025, imposed a ten percent baseline tariff on virtually all imports, with higher rates for dozens of countries deemed to have unfair trade practices.[34] Tariffs on Chinese goods escalated to 145 percent, with Beijing retaliating by raising duties on American products to 125 percent.[35] The administration's stated objectives—spurring reindustrialization, generating revenue to fund tax cuts, and creating strategic leverage for trade negotiations—contain inherent contradictions. As analysts at the Council on Foreign Relations observed: "If the policy succeeds in driving production to the United States, we should see lower imports, which makes the estimated $6 trillion in tariff revenue unattainable. If we are collecting significant revenues from tariffs, then it means we are continuing to import a significant quantity of products from other countries vs. producing them in the United States."[36]

More fundamentally, tariffs work best when domestic industry exists to protect. In many critical sectors—cell phones, ships, consumer drones, processed critical minerals, numerous electronics components—American production capacity is essentially nonexistent.[37] Rebuilding these industries would require not merely protection from foreign competition but massive investments in facilities, equipment, workforce training, and supply chain development. The costs of tariffs, meanwhile, are felt immediately through higher consumer prices, while benefits—if they materialize—require years to emerge as new factories are constructed and supply chains reconfigured.[38]

The Semiconductor Exception: CHIPS Act and Strategic Reshoring

If any sector represents the potential and pitfalls of industrial policy, it is semiconductors. The CHIPS and Science Act, signed into law in August 2022, allocated $52 billion in manufacturing and research grants to address supply chain vulnerabilities and promote domestic chip production, along with a 25 percent investment tax credit for semiconductor manufacturing.[39] The legislation represented a bipartisan acknowledgment that the United States had allowed a strategically vital industry to migrate offshore, creating dangerous dependencies.

The statistics justified alarm. Taiwan Semiconductor Manufacturing Company (TSMC) controls approximately 60 percent of the global foundry market and manufactures more than 90 percent of the world's most advanced semiconductors.[40] This concentration of production on an island 100 miles from mainland China—and claimed by Beijing as Chinese territory—represents an extraordinary geopolitical vulnerability. A disruption to TSMC's operations, whether through conflict, natural disaster, or other contingency, would cripple industries worldwide.

CHIPS Act funding has catalyzed substantial investment announcements. TSMC committed to build three advanced fabrication facilities in Phoenix, Arizona, with the Commerce Department awarding $6.6 billion in direct funding toward a total company investment exceeding $65 billion.[41] The facilities are designed for progressively more advanced process nodes: 4-nanometer, 3-nanometer, and ultimately 2-nanometer (1.6-nanometer) production.[42] Intel received up to $7.86 billion—reduced from an initially expected $8.5 billion due to concerns about the company's financial condition—to support facilities in Arizona, Ohio, New Mexico, and Oregon.[43] Samsung secured $6.4 billion to expand operations near Austin, Texas.[44]

Yet the CHIPS Act experience also illuminates the limitations of industrial policy. Intel, America's flagship semiconductor company, has struggled to execute its ambitious manufacturing roadmap. The company lost $16.6 billion in the third quarter of 2024—its largest quarterly loss in history—and its stock declined more than 60 percent during the year.[45] Competition from AMD and Nvidia, combined with production delays, has eroded Intel's market position. By early 2025, reports emerged that TSMC and Broadcom were separately exploring acquisitions of Intel's manufacturing assets—potentially resulting in a recipient of substantial government subsidies being acquired by another subsidy recipient.[46]

TSMC's Arizona operations, while progressing, encountered significant challenges. Initial construction delays pushed back production timelines, with workforce issues proving particularly acute. The company ultimately brought in experienced engineers from Taiwan to supplement local hiring.[47] Chip manufacturing represents "deep, deep process knowledge," as one analyst noted, that cannot simply be transplanted.[48] Even with billions in subsidies, constructing a domestic semiconductor ecosystem comparable to Taiwan's will require a decade or more—and sustained political commitment across multiple administrations.

The Skills Gap: Manufacturing's Workforce Crisis

Perhaps the most intractable obstacle to reindustrialization is the American workforce itself. Decades of declining manufacturing employment have disrupted the pipeline of skilled workers, while educational and cultural shifts have steered young Americans away from industrial careers. The result is a paradox: even as politicians promise to restore manufacturing jobs, employers struggle to fill existing positions.

The statistics are sobering. According to projections by Deloitte and the Manufacturing Institute, the U.S. manufacturing industry could need as many as 3.8 million new employees between 2024 and 2033 to sustain anticipated growth.[49] Without significant changes in workforce development, more than half of these positions—approximately 1.9 million jobs—could go unfilled.[50] As of March 2025, approximately 449,000 manufacturing jobs remained unfilled, with employers struggling to recruit workers despite competitive wages.[51]

The challenge is multidimensional. An aging workforce is retiring en masse: nearly one-quarter of manufacturing employees are age 55 or older.[52] Younger workers often perceive manufacturing as dirty, dangerous, and declining—a relic of an earlier industrial age rather than a pathway to prosperity. Meanwhile, the technical demands of modern manufacturing have intensified. Today's factories increasingly require workers proficient in automation, robotics, data analytics, and advanced machinery—skills that traditional vocational education programs often fail to provide.

The Semiconductor Industry Association has projected that up to 50 percent of new semiconductor roles could go unfilled without dramatic action.[53] This shortfall threatens to undermine CHIPS Act investments: constructing fabrication facilities is pointless without trained workers to operate them. Similar constraints apply across advanced manufacturing. As companies expand U.S. operations, they encounter difficulties in hiring, onboarding, and retaining skilled personnel.[54]

Retraining programs have a disappointing track record. "We've been trying job training for a really long time, and it's really hard," noted Matt Notowidigdo of the University of Chicago Booth School of Business. "It's hard to come up with training programs that look effective when people are older."[55] The more consequential adjustment has occurred among workers entering the labor force, who increasingly pursue higher education and service-sector careers rather than manufacturing positions.

Case Studies in Reshoring: Successes and Failures

The record of specific reshoring initiatives provides sobering lessons about the gap between political promises and industrial reality. No case better illustrates the pitfalls than Foxconn's Wisconsin debacle.

In July 2017, with President Trump and then-Governor Scott Walker celebrating at the White House, Foxconn Technology Group announced plans to build a massive display panel manufacturing facility in Mount Pleasant, Wisconsin.[56] The Taiwanese company, best known as Apple's primary iPhone assembler, committed to invest $10 billion and create 13,000 jobs. In exchange, Wisconsin offered approximately $4 billion in taxpayer subsidies—the largest corporate incentive package in American history to a foreign corporation.[57] Trump declared the project "the eighth wonder of the world" at its June 2018 groundbreaking.[58]

The reality fell catastrophically short. Foxconn repeatedly scaled back its projections, abandoned plans for LCD manufacturing, and never approached its employment targets. By 2024, according to state figures, Foxconn employed approximately 1,100 full-time workers—less than a tenth of the promised 13,000—and had invested roughly $25 million locally, receiving $9 million in state tax credits.[59] The grandiose campus envisioned by project boosters never materialized; office space leased by Foxconn in multiple Wisconsin cities for "innovation centers" remained vacant.[60]

The Foxconn case exemplifies broader patterns. The company had a documented history of announcing ambitious manufacturing projects that failed to materialize: Vietnam in 2007, Brazil in 2011, Pennsylvania in 2013, Indonesia in 2014.[61] Critics had warned that lavish subsidies without enforceable commitments would produce exactly the outcome Wisconsin experienced. Yet political incentives—the desire to announce splashy investments and claim credit for job creation—overwhelmed due diligence.

More promising examples exist. The CHIPS Act has generated genuine investment, and some manufacturers have successfully reshored operations. The Reshoring Initiative documents cases where companies improved quality, reduced supply chain risks, and strengthened customer relationships by bringing production back to the United States.[62] But these successes typically involve higher-value products where quality control, intellectual property protection, and proximity to customers outweigh labor cost differentials. For commodity manufacturing competing primarily on price, the economics remain prohibitive.

The Consumption Conundrum

Underlying all these challenges is a fundamental tension in the American economic model: the United States is structured around consumption, not production. Consumer spending accounts for approximately 70 percent of GDP—far higher than manufacturing-intensive economies like Germany or China.[63] Americans have grown accustomed to low-priced imported goods that stretch purchasing power; Walmart's rise to dominance reflects this consumer preference. Trade deficits, in this sense, represent American consumers' revealed preference for affordable imports over expensive domestic production.

Reversing this pattern would require Americans to accept higher prices for manufactured goods—the inevitable consequence of reshoring production to a high-wage economy. Early estimates suggested that Trump's tariffs would function as a significant tax increase on American consumers.[64] The administration argued that foreign producers would absorb tariff costs through reduced prices, but economists overwhelmingly conclude that U.S. companies and consumers bear the burden.[65] The political sustainability of sustained higher prices remains highly uncertain.

Furthermore, the financial structures supporting American consumption depend on the very trade patterns that reindustrialization would disrupt. Foreign nations accumulating dollars through trade surpluses recycle those dollars into Treasury securities, helping finance government spending and keeping interest rates lower than they would otherwise be. A dramatic reduction in the trade deficit could reduce foreign demand for Treasuries, potentially raising borrowing costs at a moment when federal debt has reached unprecedented levels.

Conclusion: The Limits of the Possible

The American manufacturing sector will not return to 1970s employment levels. Technological change, global competition, and structural shifts in the economy have permanently altered the landscape. Manufacturing output continues to grow even as employment declines; productivity gains mean that factories produce more with fewer workers. This pattern will intensify as automation, artificial intelligence, and advanced robotics transform production processes.

What remains possible is targeted reindustrialization in strategic sectors where national security, supply chain resilience, or technological leadership justify sustained government support. Semiconductors represent the most prominent example, but similar logic applies to pharmaceuticals, critical minerals processing, and defense industrial capacity. These efforts will require not merely tariffs but comprehensive industrial policies: direct subsidies, workforce development, research and development investments, and sustained political commitment across electoral cycles.

The broader reindustrialization dream—restoring manufacturing to its mid-twentieth-century prominence and rebuilding the blue-collar middle class—faces obstacles that no tariff schedule can overcome. The skills have atrophied, the supply chains have migrated, the infrastructure has deteriorated, and the financial system rewards consumption over production. China spent decades building its industrial capacity through coordinated state policy; reversing that shift cannot occur through Twitter pronouncements and tariff threats.

Understanding these constraints is essential to honest policy debate. Manufacturing matters—for national security, for technological innovation, for economic resilience. But the path to a stronger industrial base runs through sustained investment, workforce development, and strategic focus rather than sweeping tariffs that raise consumer prices while leaving fundamental weaknesses unaddressed. The consumption conundrum reflects deep features of the American economic model; resolving it will require transformation far more profound than any trade war can achieve.

Endnotes

[1] U.S. Bureau of Labor Statistics, "Forty Years of Falling Manufacturing Employment," *Beyond the Numbers* 9, no. 16 (August 2020), https://www.bls.gov/opub/btn/volume-9/forty-years-of-falling-manufacturing-employment.htm.

[2] Federal Reserve Bank of St. Louis, "All Employees, Manufacturing [MANEMP]," FRED Economic Data, accessed November 2025, https://fred.stlouisfed.org/series/MANEMP; Center for Business and Economic Analysis, "U.S. Manufacturing Employment: A Long-Term Perspective," University of Wisconsin-Stevens Point, January 29, 2025, https://blog.uwsp.edu/cps/2025/01/29/u-s-manufacturing-employment-a-long-term-perspective/.

[3] Federal Reserve Bank of St. Louis, "Value Added by Industry: Manufacturing as a Percentage of GDP [VAPGDPMA]," FRED Economic Data, September 25, 2025, https://fred.stlouisfed.org/series/VAPGDPMA.

[4] National Institute of Standards and Technology, *Annual Report on U.S. Manufacturing Industry: 2024*, NIST Advanced Manufacturing Series 600-16 (Gaithersburg, MD: U.S. Department of Commerce, 2024), https://nvlpubs.nist.gov/nistpubs/ams/NIST.AMS.600-16.pdf; Coalition for a Prosperous America, "U.S. Manufacturing's Shrinking Share of GDP and How to Catch Up," November 8, 2024, https://prosperousamerica.org/u-s-manufacturings-shrinking-share-of-gdp-and-how-to-catch-up/.

[5] U.S. Bureau of Labor Statistics, "Forty Years of Falling Manufacturing Employment."

[6] Kerwin Kofi Charles, Erik Hurst, and Mariel Schwartz, "The Transformation of Manufacturing and the Decline in U.S. Employment," *NBER Macroeconomics Annual* 33 (2019): 307–372, https://www.journals.uchicago.edu/doi/full/10.1086/700896.

[7] Ibid.

[8] ETQ, "States That Have Lost the Most Manufacturing Jobs Since the Turn of the Century," September 19, 2025, https://www.etq.com/blog/states-that-have-lost-the-most-manufacturing-jobs-since-the-turn-of-the-century/.

[9] Ibid.

[10] Robert E. Scott, "The China Toll: Growing U.S. Trade Deficit with China Cost More Than 2.7 Million Jobs Between 2001 and 2011," Economic Policy Institute Briefing Paper No. 345, August 23, 2012, https://www.epi.org/publication/bp345-china-growing-trade-deficit-cost/.

[11] Robert E. Scott and Zane Mokhiber, "Growing China Trade Deficits Cost 3.7 Million American Jobs Between 2001 and 2018," Economic Policy Institute, January 30, 2020, https://www.epi.org/publication/growing-china-trade-deficits-costs-us-jobs/.

[12] David H. Autor, David Dorn, and Gordon H. Hanson, "The China Syndrome: Local Labor Market Effects of Import Competition in the United States," *American Economic Review* 103, no. 6 (2013): 2121–2168; Cato Institute, "The 'China Shock' Demystified: Its Origins, Effects, and Lessons for Today," December 12, 2023, https://www.cato.org/publications/china-shock.

[13] Justin R. Pierce and Peter K. Schott, "The Surprisingly Swift Decline of US Manufacturing Employment," *American Economic Review* 106, no. 7 (2016): 1632–1662; Scott and Mokhiber, "Growing China Trade Deficits."

[14] U.S. Census Bureau, Statistics of U.S. Businesses; PolitiFact, "Trump: Since China Joined WTO, U.S. Has Lost 60,000 Factories," March 24, 2017, https://www.politifact.com/factchecks/2017/mar/24/donald-trump/trump-china-joined-wto-us-has-lost-60000-factories/.

[15] Scott, "The China Toll."

[16] Scott Lincicome, "No, Trade with China Did Not Kill the U.S. Economy," *Reason*, June 5, 2025, https://reason.com/2025/06/05/no-trade-with-china-did-not-kill-the-u-s-economy/.

[17] Economic Innovation Group, "Manufacturing Jobs Have Recovered, but Not Everywhere," September 9, 2025, https://eig.org/manufacturing-rebound/.

[18] Center for Business and Economic Analysis, "U.S. Manufacturing Employment: A Long-Term Perspective."

[19] ABC News, "Trump Rolls Out Sweeping Tariffs as He Deems Deficits a 'National Emergency,'" April 3, 2025, https://abcnews.go.com/Politics/trumps-liberation-day-arrives-gambles-big-risky-tariff/story?id=120382209.

[20] Center for Strategic and International Studies, "'Liberation Day' Tariffs Explained," April 9, 2025, https://www.csis.org/analysis/liberation-day-tariffs-explained; *Politico* estimated the average applied U.S. tariff rate at 27 percent following the April announcements.

[21] U.S. Bureau of Economic Analysis, "U.S. International Trade in Goods and Services, December and Annual 2024," February 5, 2025, https://www.bea.gov/news/2025/us-international-trade-goods-and-services-december-and-annual-2024.

[22] PolitiFact, "Donald Trump Wrong: China $1 Trillion Trade Deficit," April 11, 2025, https://www.politifact.com/factchecks/2025/apr/11/donald-trump/donald-trump-wrong-china-1-trillion-trade-deficit/.

[23] Joint Economic Committee, U.S. Congress, "Monthly Trade Update," August 2025, https://www.jec.senate.gov/public/vendor/_accounts/JEC-R/trade/Monthly%20Trade%20Update%20(PDF).pdf.

[24] Robert Triffin, *Gold and the Dollar Crisis: The Future of Convertibility* (New Haven: Yale University Press, 1960); Bank for International Settlements, "Triffin: Dilemma or Myth?," BIS Working Papers No. 684, December 2017, https://www.bis.org/publ/work684.pdf.

[25] International Monetary Fund, Currency Composition of Official Foreign Exchange Reserves (COFER); Medium, "Deglobalisation, the Triffin Dilemma, and the Future of Dollar Hegemony," September 2, 2025, https://medium.com/@afti.dubai/deglobalisation-the-triffin-dilemma-and-the-future-of-dollar-hegemony-98f2e9797e22.

[26] Bank for International Settlements data; Dunham, "Triffin's Dilemma: Why the U.S. Dollar's Global Role Is a Double-Edged Sword," https://www.dunham.com/Investor/Blog/Posts/triffins-dilemma.

[27] Charles de Gaulle, press conference, February 4, 1965; Medium, "The Eurodollar Trap: When Global Dollar Hegemony Becomes a Domestic Liability," May 16, 2025, https://medium.com/@BobbyGiggz/the-eurodollar-trap-when-global-dollar-hegemony-becomes-a-domestic-liability-21f282b83de7.

[28] Tax Policy Center, Urban-Brookings, "How Did the Tax Cuts and Jobs Act Change Business Taxes?," accessed November 2025, https://taxpolicycenter.org/briefing-book/how-did-tax-cuts-and-jobs-act-change-business-taxes.

[29] Ibid.

[30] National Bureau of Economic Research, "Investment Effects of the 2017 Tax Cuts and Jobs Act," *NBER Digest*, June 2024, https://www.nber.org/digest/202406/investment-effects-2017-tax-cuts-and-jobs-act.

[31] Ibid.

[32] Congressional Research Service, "Economic Effects of the Tax Cuts and Jobs Act," Report R48485, 2024, https://www.congress.gov/crs-product/R48485.

[33] Ibid.

[34] NPR, "Trump Announces Reciprocal Tariffs on Dozens of Nations and Sweeping 10% Tariff," April 2, 2025, https://www.npr.org/2025/04/02/nx-s1-5345802/trump-tariffs-liberation-day.

[35] CBS News, "Key Moments and Reaction to Trump's 'Liberation Day' Announcement of New Tariffs," April 3, 2025, https://www.cbsnews.com/live-updates/trump-liberation-day-announcement-tariffs/.

[36] Council on Foreign Relations, "Liberation and Its Discontents," April 4, 2025, https://www.cfr.org/article/liberation-and-its-discontents.

[37] *American Affairs Journal*, "The Lessons of Liberation Day," May 20, 2025, https://americanaffairsjournal.org/2025/04/the-lessons-of-liberation-day/.

[38] Ibid.

[39] U.S. Department of Commerce, CHIPS Program Office; Wafer World, "Current Impact of the CHIPS and Science Act on Silicon Prices," 2024, https://www.waferworld.com/post/current-impact-of-the-chips-and-science-act-on-silicon-prices.

[40] CrossDock Insights, "How the CHIPS Act Is Transforming U.S. Semiconductor and Global Supply Chain," August 29, 2025, https://crossdockinsights.com/p/chips-act-us-semiconductor.

[41] U.S. Department of Commerce, "Biden-Harris Administration Announces $6.6 Billion in Direct Funding to TSMC Arizona," November 2024; U.S. Senator Mark R. Warner, "Warner Applauds Major Federal Funding for TSMC," November 2024, https://www.warner.senate.gov/public/index.cfm/2024/11/warner-applauds-major-federal-funding-for-tsmc-to-secure-the-future-of-advanced-semiconductor-manufacturing-in-the-u-s.

[42] Stimson Center, "Tariffs, Economic Nationalism, and the Future of US Semiconductor Manufacturing," November 2025, https://www.stimson.org/2025/tariffs-economic-nationalism-and-the-future-of-us-semiconductor-manufacturing/.

[43] TechTarget, "CHIPS and Science Act Funds TSMC, Intel Projects," November 2024, https://www.techtarget.com/searchcio/news/366580080/CHIPS-and-Science-Act-funds-TSMC-Intel-projects.

[44] Ibid.

[45] *Reason*, "TSMC May Acquire Fellow CHIPS Act Beneficiary Intel," February 20, 2025, https://reason.com/2025/02/20/tsmc-may-acquire-fellow-chips-act-beneficiary-intel/.

[46] *Wall Street Journal*, reports on Intel acquisition discussions, cited in Reason, February 2025.

[47] Marketplace, "When the Government Meddles in Chipmaking, What's at Stake," September 2, 2025, https://www.marketplace.org/story/2025/09/02/when-the-government-meddles-in-chipmaking-whats-at-stake.

[48] Ibid.

[49] Deloitte and The Manufacturing Institute, "US Manufacturing Could Need as Many as 3.8 Million New Employees by 2033," April 2024, https://www2.deloitte.com/us/en/pages/about-deloitte/articles/press-releases/us-manufacturing-could-need-new-employees-by-2033.html.

[50] Ibid.

[51] Manufacturing Skills Institute, "Open Jobs Are Piling Up—Is U.S. Manufacturing Ready for the Next Surge?," May 19, 2025, https://manufacturingskillsinstitute.org/next-job-surge/.

[52] U.S. Census Bureau, "Manufacturing Faces Potential Labor Shortage Due to Skills Gap," October 2023, https://www.census.gov/library/stories/2023/09/manufacturing-faces-labor-shortage.html.

[53] Semiconductor Industry Association, *SIA Workforce Blueprint*; Seer Tech Solutions, "Semiconductor Shakeup: Tariffs, CHIPS Act Uncertainty, and the Industry's Strategic Crossroads," April 3, 2025, https://www.seertechsolutions.com/semiconductor-shakeup-tariffs-chips-act-uncertainty-and-the-industrys-strategic-crossroads/.

[54] Ibid.

[55] Marketplace, "Where Did All the Manufacturing Workers Go?," April 5, 2025, https://www.marketplace.org/story/2024/12/16/manufacturing-workers-jobs-factories-education-workforce.

[56] American Accounting Association, "Wisconsin's Lavish Lure for Foxconn: An Instructional Case in Governmental Accounting," *Journal of Governmental & Nonprofit Accounting* 11, no. 1 (2022): 1–26, https://publications.aaahq.org/jogna/article/11/1/1/10155/Wisconsin-s-Lavish-Lure-for-Foxconn-An.

[57] Policy Matters Ohio, "Promises Unfulfilled: Manufacturing in the Midwest," January 15, 2025, https://policymattersohio.org/research/promises-unfulfilled-manufacturing-in-the-midwest/.

[58] American Accounting Association, "Wisconsin's Lavish Lure for Foxconn."

[59] NPR, "What Wisconsin's Foxconn Plant Can Tell Us About the Future of Manufacturing in the U.S.," April 12, 2025, https://www.npr.org/2025/04/12/nx-s1-5359422/what-wisconsins-foxconn-plant-can-tell-us-about-the-future-of-manufacturing-in-the-u-s.

[60] Policy Matters Ohio, "Promises Unfulfilled."

[61] American Accounting Association, "Wisconsin's Lavish Lure for Foxconn."

[62] Reshoring Initiative, "Case Studies," accessed November 2025, https://reshorenow.org/case-studies/.

[63] U.S. Bureau of Economic Analysis, National Income and Product Accounts.

[64] Dale Kooyenga, President, Metropolitan Milwaukee Association of Commerce, quoted in NPR, "What Wisconsin's Foxconn Plant Can Tell Us."

[65] Center for Strategic and International Studies, "Press Briefing: Assessing the Impact of 'Liberation Day' Tariffs," April 15, 2025, https://www.csis.org/analysis/press-briefing-assessing-impact-liberation-day-tariffs.

Chapter 12
The Global South Caught in the Crossfire

Developing Nations Between Two Giants

On a sweltering afternoon in Solo, Central Java, Siti Faiza stood in her small garment workshop, surveying the handiwork of her twelve tailors. Since founding Faiza's Production House in 2008, she had built a modest but sustainable business producing traditional Indonesian women's wear. Yet by 2024, she found herself battling an invisible competitor: Chinese manufacturers selling garments online for 40,000 rupiah—roughly $2.65—a price that failed to even cover her fabric costs.[1] "I always wonder how the prices can be so low," she told reporters, her frustration echoing that of millions of entrepreneurs across the developing world.

Faiza's struggle encapsulates a profound transformation reshaping the global economy. As the United States and China wage their technological and trade war, developing nations from Southeast Asia to Latin America to Africa find themselves caught in an economic crossfire not of their making. China's record $992.2 billion trade surplus in 2024—driven by the fundamental imbalance between producing approximately 30 percent of global manufactured goods while domestic consumption lags—has created what economists call a "second China Shock," with consequences rippling far beyond the industrialized West.[2]

The first China Shock, which followed Beijing's 2001 accession to the World Trade Organization, decimated manufacturing employment in the United States and Europe. The second shock now threatens to hollow out industrialization prospects across the Global South itself, presenting developing nations with a cruel dilemma: embrace cheap Chinese inputs to fuel economic growth, or protect nascent industries from being crushed by Beijing's industrial juggernaut. The resolution of this dilemma will determine whether emerging economies can escape the middle-income trap or remain locked in perpetual dependence on external powers.

The Overcapacity Tsunami

The scale of China's industrial overcapacity defies easy comprehension. By the first quarter of 2024, China's manufacturing capacity utilization rate had fallen to 73.8 percent—its lowest point since 2016 and well below the 80 percent typical of OECD countries.[3] This aggregate figure masks even more severe problems in strategic sectors. Automobiles, solar panels, and semiconductors—industries Beijing has prioritized under its "new quality productive forces" doctrine—show particularly pronounced overcapacity, with utilization rates in some subsectors dipping below 60 percent.[4]

The structural roots of this overcapacity run deep. President Xi Jinping has fundamentally remolded China's economic model in ways that establish the conditions for chronic overinvestment and overproduction. Provincial governments, competing for growth and employment, offer subsidies, cheap financing, and preferential policies to attract manufacturing facilities, creating what Chinese leaders themselves acknowledged in December 2024 as dangerous "involution"—a deterioration of the system through intense competition and skewed resource distribution.[5]

The case of Shaoxing, a small city in Zhejiang province, illustrates the perverse dynamics. Under slogans like "maintain the leading position in the industry" and "safeguard industry and stabilize the chain," local officials invested heavily to consolidate the textile dyeing and printing industry, moving all producers to one industrial zone. The city's national market share rose from 30 percent to an expected 40 percent—but this came through further investment in an already overinvested sector, generating yet more overcapacity and exports to foreign markets.[6]

For the developing world, the consequences manifest in three distinct but interrelated ways. First, Chinese overcapacity threatens to crowd out domestic manufacturing before it can achieve meaningful scale. Second, it creates dependency on Chinese supply chains for intermediate goods and capital equipment. Third, it reinforces colonial-era patterns of trade in which developing nations export raw materials and import finished products, unable to climb the value chain.

The Death of Developing Country Industrialization

The traditional path to prosperity followed a well-worn route: poor countries with abundant labor would begin manufacturing labor-intensive goods—textiles, garments, shoes, simple electronics—gradually accumulating capital and expertise to move up the value chain into more sophisticated production. China itself followed this path spectacularly from the 1980s through the 2010s. But Beijing's new strategic calculus threatens to kick away the ladder behind it.

China's 14th Five-Year Plan, passed in March 2021, speaks of a strategic commitment to maintaining large-scale production in low-tech sectors—directly contradicting previous expectations that China would cede these industries to poorer nations as its economy advanced.[7] Instead, China's pursuit of self-reliance to shield itself from geopolitical tension has intensified state-driven industrial expansion across the entire manufacturing spectrum, from t-shirts to turbines.

The impact on emerging economies has been devastating. Consider the steel industry, where China accounts for more than half of global production. China's property sector woes since 2021 caused vast domestic overcapacity, leading to a collapse in global prices that put severe pressure on producers in India, Vietnam, Brazil, and other countries. China's steel product exports surged 27 percent in 2024 after 35 percent growth the previous year, driving competitors to the brink.[8]

The textile sector tells a similar story. In Indonesia, the textile workers' association reported thousands of job losses and numerous companies shutting down, citing an inability to compete against the influx of low-cost Chinese imports. PT Kusumahadi Santosa and PT Pamor Spinning Mills laid off thousands of workers due to market pressures from Chinese competition.[9] The pattern repeated across Southeast Asia, Africa, and Latin America: wherever nascent industries emerged, waves of subsidized Chinese goods arrived to undercut them.

The weakening of domestic demand in China—combined with export-facilitating policies in products where China dominates global manufacturing—creates a deadly dynamic. Chinese firms, facing shrinking domestic markets and fierce internal competition, must export to survive. Those exports, often priced below production costs thanks to state subsidies, flood emerging markets. As Rhodium Group researchers noted, "unless Beijing implements serious demand reforms, developing nations will be crowded out of manufacturing by Chinese overcapacity, leaving them dependent and without export opportunities."[10]

The consequences extend beyond immediate job losses. Premature deindustrialization—where manufacturing begins to decline even before a country has industrialized enough to reach advanced income levels—threatens to trap developing nations in what economists call the middle-income trap. When domestic manufacturers are replaced by cheap Chinese imports, countries lose the opportunity to build the technological capabilities, supply chain networks, and human capital necessary for sustained economic development.[11]

Fighting Back: India, Brazil, and Indonesia Respond

Faced with existential threats to their industrial bases, major emerging economies have begun erecting defensive barriers. Yet their responses reveal the profound asymmetries and difficult trade-offs inherent in confronting Chinese economic power.

India's Multifaceted Defense

India has deployed perhaps the most comprehensive strategy to counter Chinese industrial dominance, combining tariffs, non-tariff barriers, and domestic industrial policy. In the solar sector alone—where China controls over 80 percent of global manufacturing capacity—New Delhi has implemented a layered defense.

The Approved List of Models and Manufacturers (ALMM) mandate, reinstated in April 2024, creates a non-tariff barrier by restricting government-backed projects to domestically approved solar products. This effectively excludes Chinese modules while offering a substantial boost to Indian manufacturers.[12] The government simultaneously maintained Basic Customs Duties of 20 percent on solar cells and modules (reduced from 25 percent and 40 percent respectively in the 2025 budget), while adding Agriculture Infrastructure and Development Cess that brings effective duties higher.[13]

Beyond solar, India imposed anti-dumping duties of up to 30 percent on Chinese solar cells in September 2025, launched Production-Linked Incentive schemes to promote domestic manufacturing, and established a 12 percent safeguard duty on steel imports in April 2025 to protect domestic producers from Chinese product redirection.[14] The strategy aims to create sufficient market protection for Indian firms to achieve scale and competitiveness.

Yet India's approach faces significant constraints. The country still relies on Chinese imports for key solar inputs like polysilicon and solar-grade wafers. Indian module manufacturing capacity reached 90.9 GW in 2024, but solar cell capacity stood at only 17.2 GW—forcing continued dependence on Chinese cells even as India tries to reduce module imports.[15] Moreover, raising tariffs too high risks increasing costs for developers and consumers, potentially slowing India's renewable energy transition.

Most fundamentally, India cannot fully decouple from Chinese supply chains without sacrificing economic efficiency. As one industry analyst noted, "We need imports for raw materials and local industrial materials and, if tariffs are imposed, these industries will be affected."[16] The challenge lies in finding the precise balance between protection and competitiveness—a balance that shifts constantly as Chinese capabilities advance.

Brazil's Reluctant Protectionism

Brazil's response to Chinese overcapacity reflects its conflicted position as both commodity supplier and aspiring industrial power. In 2024, Brasília imposed new tariffs on various Chinese imports:

35 percent on fiber optics and cables, 25 percent on iron and steel products, and increased duties on sodium chlorite.[17] The government also introduced import quotas on eleven types of steel alloy products, raising import taxes to 25 percent once quotas are exceeded—a system mirroring U.S. protections.[18]

Brazilian steelmakers, represented by the Brazilian Steel Institute (IABr), had lobbied intensively for these measures, describing conditions as a "flood of low-priced imports" that accounted for roughly 90 percent of import tonnage in some flat product categories.[19] The industry argued that without protection equivalent to that enjoyed by American and European competitors, Brazilian production would collapse.

Yet Brazil's protectionist turn sits uneasily alongside its deepening economic integration with China. In 2024, Brazil exported $116.09 billion to China—predominantly soybeans, iron ore, and meat—while importing $72.7 billion, mainly industrial products.[20] China absorbed 44 percent of Brazil's oil exports and 76.6 percent of its soybean exports in early 2025.[21] This asymmetric relationship—exporting commodities, importing manufactures—recapitulates colonial-era trade patterns that Brazil has spent decades trying to escape.

The contradictions grew starker in late 2024 when Brazil joined China's Belt and Road Initiative just weeks after imposing new tariffs on Chinese goods. President Luiz Inácio Lula da Silva sought to balance industrial protection with maintaining access to Chinese capital for infrastructure development.[22] The Brazilian government's approach, one analyst noted, aims to "protect the industry that is already established" while "creating incentives for industries to establish local assembly facilities."[23]

Brazilian economists warn, however, that tariffs alone cannot solve the competitiveness challenge. Bruna Santos, director of the Wilson Center's Brazil Institute, argued that Brazilian steel firms need to "boost investment in innovation and technology that could help reduce costs" and work on "product diversification to create market niches that are less vulnerable to current price competition."[24] Without fundamental improvements in productivity and quality, protectionism merely delays inevitable adjustment.

Indonesia's Dramatic Escalation

Indonesia announced in July 2024 perhaps the most dramatic response to Chinese overcapacity: tariffs ranging from 100 to 200 percent on Chinese imports of footwear, clothing, textiles, cosmetics, and ceramics.[25] Trade Minister Zulkifli Hasan framed the measures explicitly as defensive: "If we are flooded with imported goods, our micro, small and medium enterprises could collapse."[26]

The announcement followed the revelation that Indonesia faced 160 new trade remedy investigations in 2024—a sharp increase from 69 cases in 2023—as the U.S.-China trade war redirected Chinese exports to Southeast Asian markets.[27] Indonesian textile manufacturers reported devastating impacts from cheap Chinese imports flooding domestic markets, with thousands of workers laid off as companies shut down operations.[28]

Yet Indonesia's tough rhetoric on tariffs masks its fundamental dependence on Chinese trade and investment. China is Indonesia's largest trading partner, accounting for $72.7 billion in imports and $62.4 billion in exports in 2024.[29] More critically, China absorbed over 80 percent of Indonesia's nickel output—essential for electric vehicle batteries and central to Indonesia's development strategy.[30]

This dependency creates what analysts call Indonesia's "delicate balancing act." Trissia Wijaya, a senior research fellow at Ritsumeikan University, observed: "As long as the mainstay is not destroyed, I don't think it would infuriate Beijing... it is applicable to textiles, ceramics, and electronics" but not to the critical minerals trade that underpins the relationship.[31] In other words, Indonesia can impose steep tariffs on consumer goods, but must tread carefully regarding sectors where China has strategic interests.

The policy also contains a crucial loophole: products resulting from Chinese investments in Indonesia are categorized as local goods and exempted from import duties. This effectively incentivizes Chinese firms to relocate production to Indonesia—maintaining Chinese market dominance while nominally supporting "local" industry. As one analyst noted, "the local textile market would remain predominantly controlled by Chinese companies, maintaining their influence over domestic production and market dynamics."[32]

The Dependency Trap: Cheap Inputs Versus Domestic Development

The defensive measures deployed by India, Brazil, and Indonesia highlight a fundamental dilemma facing the Global South: cheap Chinese inputs provide short-term economic benefits but create long-term strategic vulnerabilities.

Chinese manufacturing exports to developing regions serve dual purposes. On one hand, they provide affordable consumer goods that improve living standards for poor populations. Solar panels from China enable electricity access in rural Africa. Chinese smartphones connect billions to the internet. Electric buses reduce air pollution in Latin American cities. These are tangible development benefits that would be far more expensive if sourced from Western suppliers.

On the other hand, this flood of imports undermines domestic value-chain development. When local manufacturers cannot compete with subsidized Chinese products, countries lose opportunities to develop technological capabilities, build supply chain networks, and create quality employment. The result is what economists call "connector economy" dependency—where developing nations take Chinese intermediate goods, add minimal value, and export to Western markets, never building autonomous industrial capacity.[33]

The machinery and equipment sector exemplifies this trap. Chinese manufacturers like Zoomlion, XCMG, and Sany have seen overseas revenues grow 10 to 25 percent in 2024 while domestic sales stagnated or contracted.[34] They now target 30 to 60 percent of revenues from foreign markets, particularly in the Global South. Developing nations get access to affordable construction equipment and industrial machinery—but at the cost of never developing their own capital goods industries.

The automobile sector shows the dynamic most clearly. After the U.S. and EU implemented new tariffs on Chinese electric vehicles in May and October 2024, China's vehicle exports to the Global South grew by more than a third while exports to other markets fell 7 percent.[35] Chinese firms like BYD didn't just sell finished vehicles; they exported components for local assembly, creating apparent "domestic" production that remained fundamentally dependent on Chinese supply chains. As exports increased 150 percent in the first quarter of 2025, with 16 percent of shipments bound for Brazil, these vehicles arrived before new tariffs took effect—illustrating the cat-and-mouse game between Chinese exporters and protectionist policies.[36]

The energy transition amplifies these dynamics. China's dominance of solar panels (over 80 percent of global manufacturing), wind turbines, lithium batteries, and electric vehicles means that developing countries pursuing decarbonization goals must choose between climate objectives and industrial autonomy. Pakistan imported 13 GW of solar photovoltaic capacity from China in the first six months of 2024. South Africa imported 4 GW of solar panels—capable of producing electricity equivalent to 3 percent of annual demand.[37] These imports accelerated renewable energy deployment but foreclosed opportunities to build domestic clean energy industries.

Some developing nations have attempted to escape the trap through requirements for technology transfer and local content. Indonesia's strategy toward Chinese investment in nickel processing exemplifies this approach. The government's nickel ore export ban in 2020, combined with mandates for domestic processing, prompted Chinese firms to invest billions in Indonesian smelters and battery plants.[38] This appeared to align Chinese investment with Indonesian development objectives—creating jobs, building infrastructure, and moving up the value chain.

Yet even this seemingly successful model reveals troubling limitations. As Jessica Liao, a China investment analyst, observed: "Their incentive is really not to help the local economy or local industrialists to have the independent capacity to do it... their primary concern is to help solve their domestic overcapacity problem."[39] Chinese firms transfer older technologies while keeping cutting-edge capabilities at home, establish production facilities that remain dependent on Chinese components and expertise, and structure investments to maintain control over critical nodes in the supply chain.

Belt and Road: The Debt Dimension

The dependency created by trade imbalances is compounded by debt dynamics associated with China's Belt and Road Initiative. Launched in 2013 with promises of connecting Asia, Africa, and Europe through infrastructure investment, the BRI has become a source of both opportunity and controversy in the developing world.

A 2023 analysis found that 80 percent of China's government loans to developing countries have gone to nations in financial distress.[40] This pattern reflects the BRI's dual nature: it provides infrastructure financing to countries that Western institutions deem too risky, but often on terms that create unsustainable debt burdens. Chinese lending peaked at $90 billion in 2016 but fell to less than $5 billion by 2021 as Beijing confronted widespread defaults and debt restructuring requests.[41]

The "debt trap diplomacy" narrative—popularized by critics who point to cases like Sri Lanka's Hambantota Port, leased to China for 99 years after debt repayment difficulties—has become hotly contested.[42] Academic research challenges simplistic interpretations, noting that debt problems typically arise from corruption and mismanagement by recipient governments rather than deliberate Chinese strategy. As Chatham House researchers concluded, BRI projects are "built piecemeal, through diverse bilateral interactions" with "political-economy dynamics and governance problems on both sides" leading to "poorly conceived and managed projects."[43]

Yet even if Beijing does not intentionally create debt traps, the structural consequences remain. Chinese lending contracts often contain clauses restricting restructuring with traditional creditor groups like the Paris Club and retaining China's right to demand repayment at any time.[44] This gives Beijing leverage over debtor nations on issues from Taiwan recognition to Uyghur treatment to South China Sea territorial disputes.

More fundamentally, BRI debt burdens limit developing countries' policy autonomy. Nations servicing large Chinese debts have less fiscal space for social investments, education, and domestic industrial policy. The need to maintain good relations with Beijing to secure debt relief constrains their ability to impose trade restrictions or challenge Chinese economic practices. This creates a form of structural dependency more subtle but potentially more durable than colonial-era extractions.

The case of Zambia illustrates the complexities. The country's 2020 default—Africa's first sovereign default during the COVID-19 pandemic—left it owing approximately $6 billion to Chinese creditors out of total external debt exceeding $17 billion.[45] While China was not the majority creditor, its resistance to participating in coordinated debt relief through the G20 Common Framework delayed restructuring for years. The impasse left Zambia unable to invest in health, education, or infrastructure while servicing unsustainable debt.

The European Union's Strategic Opportunity

The shared concerns about Chinese overcapacity between the Global South and developed economies create what European policymakers have identified as a strategic opportunity. If China's industrial model threatens both European manufacturers and emerging market industrialization, the EU could position itself as an alternative partner offering more balanced, sustainable development cooperation.[46]

The EU's trade relationship with China mirrors that of developing countries, albeit at a different scale. The EU's goods trade deficit with China more than doubled from 2007 to 2024, reaching €306 billion ($359 billion) even as the EU exported only €213 billion to China.[47] European manufacturers face the same competitive pressures from subsidized Chinese exports, particularly in renewable energy equipment and electric vehicles where China has established dominant positions.

This convergence of interests creates opportunities for EU-Global South collaboration. European Commission initiatives on critical raw materials, for instance, explicitly aim to "diversify supply away from single-country concentration"—meaning reduced dependence on Chinese processing of minerals.[48] The EU could partner with African, Latin American, and Asian nations to develop alternative supply chains that benefit both European industrial resilience and developing country value addition.

In practice, however, the EU faces significant obstacles to becoming a genuine alternative to China. European development finance, while more transparent and less debt-intensive than Chinese lending, operates at a fraction of the scale. The EU lacks China's capacity to rapidly mobilize massive capital for infrastructure projects. European firms, facing higher labor costs and stricter environmental regulations, cannot match Chinese price competitiveness in many sectors.

Moreover, EU trade policies toward the Global South often appear contradictory. While Brussels critiques Chinese overcapacity, it simultaneously imposes stringent requirements—carbon border adjustments, deforestation regulations, due diligence mandates—that developing nations view as disguised protectionism. The EU's anti-dumping duties on Chinese products, while protecting European industry, also raise costs for developing countries that rely on affordable Chinese inputs for their own manufacturing.

The October 2024 EU-China summit revealed the limits of European leverage. While the EU raised concerns about "ongoing systemic distortions and growing manufacturing overcapacity," China made few meaningful concessions.[49] Beijing has increasingly oriented its diplomacy toward the "collective rise of the Global South" rather than addressing European concerns, relegating the EU to secondary priority in Chinese foreign policy.[50]

For the EU to become a genuine alternative, it would need to offer developing countries what China provides—large-scale infrastructure finance, technology transfer, market access for exports—but under more sustainable terms. Some initiatives point in this direction. The Global Gateway program, announced in 2021, pledged €300 billion for infrastructure in developing countries by 2027. Yet implementation has been slow, bureaucratic, and fragmented across member states, unable to match the BRI's unified branding and rapid deployment.[51]

The fundamental challenge is that European and developing country interests diverge as often as they converge. Europe wants to protect its industrial base and reduce dependence on China; developing countries want affordable goods and infrastructure finance. Europe prioritizes environmental and labor standards; developing countries prioritize rapid economic growth. These tensions limit the EU's ability to present a truly compelling alternative to Chinese engagement.

A New Development Paradigm or Continued Dependence?

The question confronting the Global South is whether the current moment represents an opportunity to forge a more autonomous development path or merely a choice between different forms of dependence.

Optimists point to several favorable trends. The recognition by major emerging economies that Chinese overcapacity threatens their industrialization prospects has triggered more assertive trade policies. The proliferation of South-South trade initiatives—trade among developing countries grew from 9 percent of global trade in 2004 to 20 percent by 2023—suggests possibilities for reducing dependence on both China and the West.[52] Digital technologies and renewable energy transitions create opportunities to leapfrog traditional industrial development stages.

Regional integration initiatives offer potential alternatives to bilateral dependence on great powers. The African Continental Free Trade Area, launched in 2021, aims to create a single market for goods and services across 1.3 billion people. ASEAN economic integration, though imperfect, has created supply chain networks that reduce individual countries' vulnerability to external pressures. Latin American cooperation frameworks, from Mercosur to the Pacific Alliance, provide platforms for coordinated responses to Chinese competition.

Yet pessimists note that these initiatives have repeatedly failed to deliver transformative results. Regional integration efforts founder on nationalism, corruption, and capability gaps. South-South trade, while growing, remains dominated by Chinese exports to other developing countries rather than balanced intra-developing world commerce. The technological and capital requirements for moving up the value chain have only increased, making autonomous industrialization more difficult than in previous eras.

The middle-income trap appears to be tightening. Of countries that reached middle-income status in the 1960s, fewer than 15 percent subsequently achieved high-income status.[53] The combination of Chinese industrial dominance, Western protectionism, and weak domestic institutions creates what some economists call a "permanent middle income" scenario—where countries industrialize enough to escape poverty but never develop the capabilities for sustained high-income growth.

China's own evolution complicates the picture. If Beijing successfully rebalances its economy toward domestic consumption, reducing overcapacity pressures, developing countries might find more space for their own industrialization. As one Chatham House report argued, "the best form of economic support that Beijing can offer developing countries is to rebalance China's own trade with them," becoming "a more reliable importer of goods and services from the Global South."[54] This would require fundamental reforms to China's state-dominated economic model—reforms that President Xi has shown little interest in pursuing.

The U.S.-China technological decoupling adds another dimension of uncertainty. If the two superpowers create separate technology ecosystems—incompatible standards for telecommunications, semiconductors, artificial intelligence, biotechnology—developing countries may be forced to choose between them. This "digital iron curtain" scenario would fragment global markets, reduce economies of scale, and increase costs for developing countries seeking to adopt advanced technologies.[55]

Conclusion: No Easy Choices

The Global South's predicament in the U.S.-China rivalry admits no easy solutions. Chinese overcapacity threatens to hollow out emerging market industrialization, but defensive tariffs risk raising costs, reducing competitiveness, and provoking retaliation. Belt and Road debt creates dependencies, but alternative financing remains scarce and expensive. European partnership offers potential advantages, but European interests frequently diverge from developing country needs.

The responses of India, Brazil, and Indonesia reveal the constrained nature of developing country agency in the new global order. India's comprehensive defensive strategy provides the most ambitious model, but requires state capacity and market scale that few countries possess. Brazil's reluctant protectionism reflects the difficulties of balancing industrial development with commodity export dependency. Indonesia's tariff threats, undermined by Chinese investment incentives, illustrate the limits of policy autonomy when facing economic asymmetries.

The fundamental challenge is that the current international economic architecture provides no clear path for developing countries to achieve the kind of rapid industrialization that China itself achieved from the 1980s through 2010s. That path—low wages, export-oriented manufacturing, gradual technological upgrading, integration into global supply chains—has been blocked by Chinese dominance at the low end and Western protectionism at the high end.

Yet the question remains: if not through manufacturing exports and supply chain integration, how do developing countries achieve sustained economic growth? The digital economy offers partial answers—services can be traded without physical infrastructure—but cannot employ the hundreds of millions who need work. The green economy creates opportunities—renewable energy, sustainable agriculture, ecological services—but remains small relative to traditional industry. The knowledge economy promises prosperity through innovation—but requires educational systems and research capabilities that take generations to build.

The next decade will determine whether the Global South can forge a new development paradigm suited to the realities of Sino-American rivalry, or whether it remains trapped between two giants, able to play them against each other at the margins but unable to chart a truly autonomous course. The stakes extend beyond economics to geopolitics: developing nations' ability to maintain strategic autonomy depends fundamentally on their capacity to avoid economic dependency on any single great power.

For now, the Global South finds itself in an uncomfortable position: courted by both Washington and Beijing, yet increasingly skeptical of both; seeking to leverage great power competition for development gains, yet finding that competition narrows rather than expands their policy space; possessing unprecedented access to information and technology, yet facing barriers to industrialization higher than any generation since the 1940s. How they navigate these contradictions will shape not only their own futures but the contours of the 21st century international order.

Endnotes

[1] Aisyah Llewellyn, "Indonesia eyes hefty tariffs on China as businesses decry cheap imports," *Al Jazeera*, October 11, 2024, https://www.aljazeera.com/economy/2024/10/11/indonesia-eyes-hefty-tariffs-on-china-as-businesses-decry-cheap-imports.

[2] China General Administration of Customs, as reported in "China's trade surplus hit a record high in 2024," ING Economics, January 13, 2025, https://think.ing.com/snaps/chinas-trade-surplus-hit-a-record-high-in-2024/; Felix Richter, "Chart: China Is the World's Manufacturing Superpower," Statista, 2023, https://www.statista.com/chart/20858/top-10-countries-by-share-of-global-manufacturing-output/; "China drives over 30 pct of global manufacturing growth during 2021-2025," Xinhua, September 9, 2025, https://english.www.gov.cn/news/202509/09/content_WS68bf990cc6d0868f4e8f56cd.html.

[3] U.S. Department of the Treasury, "Remarks by Under Secretary for International Affairs Jay Shambaugh."

[4] Ibid.

[5] "Beyond overcapacity: Chinese-style modernization and the clash of economic models," Merics, 2025, https://merics.org/en/report/beyond-overcapacity-chinese-style-modernization-and-clash-economic-models.

[6] Ibid.

[7] "China's Overcapacity and the Global South: An Opportunity for the EU," *Internationale Politik Quarterly*, March 26, 2025, https://ip-quarterly.com/en/chinas-overcapacity-and-global-south-opportunity-eu.

[8] Logan Wright and Allen Feng, "How China's Overcapacity Holds Back Emerging Economies," Rhodium Group, 2024, https://rhg.com/research/how-chinas-overcapacity-holds-back-emerging-economies/.

[9] Llewellyn, "Indonesia eyes hefty tariffs on China."

[10] Wright and Feng, "How China's Overcapacity Holds Back Emerging Economies."

[11] James Crabtree and Jan Gaspers, "The Coming Clash Between China and the Global South Over Trade," *Foreign Policy*, February 27, 2025, https://foreignpolicy.com/2024/09/11/china-global-south-trade-tariffs-protectionism-emerging-markets-economy/.

[12] Uma Gupta, "India creates non-tariff barrier for Chinese solar products," *pv magazine International*, April 30, 2024, https://www.pv-magazine.com/2024/04/30/india-creates-non-tariff-barrier-for-chinese-solar-products/.

[13] "Union Budget 2025: India Reduces Tariffs on Imported Solar Cells and Modules," TaiyangNews, February 3, 2025, https://taiyangnews.info/markets/india-reduces-imported-solar-cells-modules-tariffs-under-union-budget-2025.

[14] Evelyn Chen and Yee Jun Tiang, "India's Anti-Dumping Final Findings on Chinese Solar Cells," InfoLink Consulting, October 13, 2025, https://www.infolink-group.com/energy-article/indiasanti-dumpingfinalfindingsonchinesesolarcells; KPMG India, "Tariff revisions and their impact on India," September 2025, https://assets.kpmg.com/content/dam/kpmgsites/in/pdf/2025/09/us-tariff-shifts-tariff-revisions-and-their-impact-on-india.pdf.

[15] "Indian Solar Companies Eye Export Gains As US Slaps Steep Tariffs on Southeast Asia," Mercom India, May 21, 2025, https://www.mercomindia.com/indian-solar-module-companies-eye-more-exports-as-us-slaps-steep-duties-on-southeast-asia.

[16] Llewellyn, "Indonesia eyes hefty tariffs on China."

[17] Wendy Wu, "Brazil imposes new tariffs on imports from China in bid to fight dumping," *South China Morning Post*, October 18, 2024, https://www.scmp.com/news/china/diplomacy/article/3283014/brazil-imposes-new-tariffs-imports-china-bid-fight-dumping.

[18] "Brazil set to introduce import quotas, raise import tariff to 25% on range of steel products," S&P Global, November 15, 2024, https://www.spglobal.com/commodity-insights/en/news-research/latest-news/metals/042424-brazil-set-to-introduce-import-quotas-raise-import-tariff-to-25-on-range-of-steel-products.

[19] Ibid.

[20] "Opportunities and Challenges of Brazil-China Trade under the Impact of US Tariffs," China Law Vision, May 15, 2025, https://www.chinalawvision.com/2025/05/international-trade/opportunities-and-challenges-of-brazil-china-trade-under-the-impact-of-us-tariffs/.

[21] Ibid.

[22] Wu, "Brazil imposes new tariffs on imports from China."

[23] "Opportunities and Challenges of Brazil-China Trade."

[24] "Latin America's steel tariffs won't push China away," Semafor, May 22, 2024, https://www.semafor.com/article/05/21/2024/latin-america-tariffs-chinese-steel-evs.

[25] Joe Leahy, "Indonesia Announces Hefty Tariffs on Chinese-made Goods," *The Diplomat*, July 2, 2024, https://thediplomat.com/2024/07/indonesia-announces-hefty-tariffs-on-chinese-made-goods/.

[26] "Indonesia to impose up to 200-pct import tariffs on Chinese goods," ANTARA News, June 29, 2024, https://en.antaranews.com/news/317223/indonesia-to-impose-up-to-200-pct-import-tariffs-on-chinese-goods.

[27] Cissy Zhou and Caixin Qiu, "China hit record trade barriers in 2024 as overcapacity fears spread to developing world," *South China Morning Post*, January 10, 2025, https://www.scmp.com/economy/global-economy/article/3294204/china-hit-record-trade-barriers-2024-overcapacity-fears-spread-developing-world.

[28] Llewellyn, "Indonesia eyes hefty tariffs on China."

[29] Luke Hunt, "Indonesia bracing for flood of rerouted Chinese exports," *Asia Times*, April 28, 2025, https://asiatimes.com/2025/04/indonesia-bracing-for-flood-of-rerouted-chinese-exports/.

[30] Llewellyn, "Indonesia eyes hefty tariffs on China."

[31] Ibid.

[32] Muhammad Habib Abiyan Dzakwan, "Indonesia is Imposing High Import Duties on Chinese Products," Australian Institute of International Affairs, July 15, 2024, https://www.internationalaffairs.org.au/australianoutlook/indonesia-is-imposing-high-import-duties-on-chinese-products-protection-or-peril/.

[33] "China's huge trade surplus – where next?" Deutsche Bank Research, 2024, https://flow.db.com/trade-finance/chinas-huge-trade-surplus-where-next.

[34] "China Inc. heads to Global South in the age of tariffs," S&P Global, September 9, 2025, https://www.spglobal.com/en/research-insights/special-reports/china-inc-heads-to-global-south-in-the-age-of-tariffs.

[35] Ibid.

[36] "Latin America's steel tariffs won't push China away," Semafor.

[37] Beth Walker, "What China's green 'overcapacity' could mean for the Global South," Dialogue Earth, November 22, 2024, https://dialogue.earth/en/energy/what-chinas-green-overcapacity-could-mean-for-the-global-south/.

[38] "China Inc. heads to Global South in the age of tariffs," S&P Global.

[39] Jue Wang, "Can China share its green expertise with the Global South?" Dialogue Earth, September 26, 2025, https://dialogue.earth/en/business/can-china-share-its-green-expertise-with-the-global-south/.

[40] Mark Green, "Debt Distress on the Road to 'Belt and Road,'" Wilson Center, https://www.wilsoncenter.org/blog-post/debt-distress-road-belt-and-road.

[41] Bec Strating, "As China scales back international lending, many countries are left deep in debt," NPR, May 28, 2025, https://www.npr.org/2025/05/28/nx-s1-5413239/china-loans-developing-world-belt-road.

[42] Ben Westcott and Yvonne Murray, "The Rise and Fall of the BRI," Council on Foreign Relations, April 6, 2023, https://www.cfr.org/blog/rise-and-fall-bri.

[43] Lee Jones and Shahar Hameiri, "Debunking the Myth of 'Debt-trap Diplomacy,'" Chatham House, December 14, 2020, https://www.chathamhouse.org/2020/08/debunking-myth-debt-trap-diplomacy.

[44] Elizabeth C. Economy, "China's Massive Belt and Road Initiative," Council on Foreign Relations, February 3, 2023, https://www.cfr.org/backgrounder/chinas-massive-belt-and-road-initiative.

[45] International Monetary Fund, "Zambia: 2022 Article IV Consultation and Request for an Extended Arrangement Under the Extended Credit Facility," IMF Country Report No. 22/291, September 2022.

[46] "China's Overcapacity and the Global South: An Opportunity for the EU," *Internationale Politik Quarterly*.

[47] "China and Europe: Can the EU and the UK find a shared strategy?" Centre for European Reform, 2025, https://www.cer.eu/publications/archive/policy-brief/2025/china-and-europe-can-eu-and-uk-find-shared-strategy.

[48] "The European Commission's role in steering Europe's strategic outlook," Atlantic Council, November 2025, https://www.atlanticcouncil.org/in-depth-research-reports/report/the-european-commissions-role-in-steering-europes-strategic-outlook/.

[49] "25th EU-China Summit," European Commission press release, July 24, 2025, https://ec.europa.eu/commission/presscorner/detail/en/statement_25_4302.

[50] Mathieu Duchâtel and Nicola Casarini, "China's turn towards the 'Global South': Europe is not Beijing's priority," European Union Institute for Security Studies, July 18, 2025, https://www.iss.europa.eu/publications/commentary/chinas-turn-towards-global-south-europe-not-beijings-priority.

[51] European Commission, "Global Gateway: Up to €300 billion to Accelerate Smart, Clean and Secure Links Around the World," press release, December 1, 2021, https://ec.europa.eu/commission/presscorner/detail/en/ip_21_6433.

[52] Gareth Leather and colleagues, "Will economic policy win China friends in the Global South?" Chatham House, September 2025, https://www.chathamhouse.org/2025/09/will-economic-policy-win-china-friends-global-south/chinas-ambivalent-role-south-south.

[53] World Bank, "World Development Report 2024: The Middle-Income Trap," 2024, https://www.worldbank.org/en/publication/wdr2024.

[54] Leather and colleagues, "Will economic policy win China friends in the Global South?"

[55] Graham Webster et al., "Full Translation: Xi Jinping's Report at the 20th Party Congress," Stanford University DigiChina Project, October 2022, https://digichina.stanford.edu/work/full-translation-xi-jinpings-report-at-the-20th-party-congress/.

Part V

Indo-Pacific Flashpoints

Chapter 13
Taiwan—The Most Dangerous Place on Earth

Semiconductors, Sovereignty, and the Risk of War

On a clear morning in early April 2025, as fishermen prepared their boats along Taiwan's western coast, an armada of Chinese warships and aircraft began a carefully choreographed ballet of intimidation. The People's Liberation Army Eastern Theater Command announced joint military exercises code-named "Strait Thunder-2025A"—the latest in an escalating series of drills designed to rehearse the invasion and blockade of Taiwan.[1] Over two days, 135 aircraft, 38 naval vessels, and 12 coast guard ships encircled the island, simulating precision strikes against energy infrastructure, port facilities, and command centers.[2] For the residents of Taiwan's 23 million people, it was another reminder that they live at the epicenter of what many strategists now call the world's most dangerous flashpoint.

What makes this narrow stretch of water between mainland China and Taiwan so perilous is not merely the military hardware massing on both sides, but the convergence of three explosive elements: territorial claims rooted in civil war and national identity, an economic chokepoint controlling the world's most advanced semiconductors, and great power competition between the United States and China. The result is a geopolitical powder keg where miscalculation could trigger the first major war between nuclear-armed powers since 1945.

The Geography of Danger

The Taiwan Strait, at its narrowest point, measures just 130 kilometers—roughly 81 miles—separating the island of Taiwan from mainland China's Fujian Province.[3] To put this in perspective, one could fit the states of Vermont and New Hampshire together within this waterway.[4] The strait connects the South China Sea to the East China Sea, serving as a critical artery for international maritime commerce. Approximately 1,200 ships cross the Taiwan Strait weekly, making it the second busiest shipping route globally, with nearly half of the world's container fleet transiting these waters annually.[5]

Yet for all its commercial importance, the strait's true strategic significance lies in what it separates and connects. Taiwan sits astride the first island chain, the transnational archipelago running south from Japan through the Philippines. Control of Taiwan would fundamentally alter the balance of power in the Western Pacific. As Chinese strategists openly acknowledge, possession of the island would provide the People's Liberation Army Navy direct access to the Pacific's deep waters, enable the projection of air and naval power across Northeast Asia, and effectively break the first island chain that currently constrains China's maritime expansion.[6]

The strait's shallow depth—averaging about 60 meters with a maximum of 177 meters—adds both military complexity and vulnerability.[7] Unlike the deep waters surrounding most islands, Taiwan's western approaches feature extensive shoals and sandbars that would complicate any amphibious operation. During World War II, American military planners drafted Operation Causeway, a plan to invade Taiwan that was ultimately rejected precisely because the costs and risks were deemed too high—more challenging even than the D-Day landings in Normandy.[8] The assessment noted that crossing contested shallow waters to fight on complex, mountainous terrain against a prepared defense would exact an

prohibitive toll.

Today, those geographical challenges remain, but they are compounded by modern precision-strike capabilities, advanced air defenses, and anti-ship missiles that can turn the strait into a killing zone for any invasion fleet. Yet China has been preparing for this contingency for decades, developing capabilities specifically designed to overcome these obstacles.

The Silicon Shield: Taiwan's Technological Leverage

If geography makes Taiwan strategically important, technology makes it economically indispensable. At the heart of Taiwan's defensive calculus lies a single company that has become synonymous with the island's economic miracle and strategic importance: Taiwan Semiconductor Manufacturing Company, universally known as TSMC.

Founded in 1987 by Morris Chang, TSMC pioneered the "pure-play foundry" model—manufacturing chips designed by other companies without competing with its own products. This seemingly simple business innovation revolutionized the global semiconductor industry and transformed Taiwan into an irreplaceable node in the world's technology supply chains. By the second quarter of 2025, TSMC commanded an astonishing 70.2 percent of the global foundry market, up from 67.6 percent just months earlier.[9] Its nearest competitor, South Korea's Samsung, held a mere 7.3 percent share.[10]

But TSMC's dominance extends far beyond market share statistics. The company has achieved near-monopoly status in the most advanced chip manufacturing processes—the cutting-edge nodes measured in nanometers that determine a chip's performance, power efficiency, and capabilities. In the third quarter of 2025, approximately 23 percent of TSMC's revenue came from its 3-nanometer process, with another 37 percent from 5-nanometer production.[11] Together, these advanced nodes accounted for 60 percent of total revenue, producing chips that power everything from Apple's latest iPhones to NVIDIA's artificial intelligence accelerators to the F-35 fighter jet's avionics.[12]

The concentration of this capability in Taiwan creates what analysts have termed a "silicon shield"—the theory that China would be reluctant to attack Taiwan because doing so would destroy the very technological crown jewels it seeks to acquire. TSMC's facilities cannot simply be replicated elsewhere. The company's most advanced fabs—fabrication plants—in Hsinchu and Kaohsiung represent investments of tens of billions of dollars, years of accumulated manufacturing expertise, and complex supply chains involving thousands of suppliers. Moving or reconstructing this ecosystem would take a decade or more, assuming it could be done at all without the willing cooperation of TSMC's engineers and executives.

This technological leverage extends beyond semiconductors to advanced packaging, where TSMC has developed proprietary CoWoS (Chip-on-Wafer-on-Substrate) technology essential for AI chips. By late 2025, TSMC's CoWoS capacity reached between 65,000 and 75,000 wafers per month, with plans to expand to 100,000 wafers monthly by 2026.[13] Every major AI company—from Google and Amazon to Microsoft and Meta—depends on these capabilities, making TSMC arguably the most strategically important company in the world.

Yet the silicon shield theory contains a fatal flaw: it assumes rational calculation will always prevail over nationalist passion, historical grievances, and political imperatives. For Xi Jinping and the Chinese Communist Party, Taiwan represents unfinished business from the Chinese Civil War, a humiliation that must be erased to achieve what Xi calls "the great rejuvenation of the Chinese nation."[14] As U.S. Defense Secretary Pete Hegseth warned in May 2025 at the Shangri-La Dialogue in Singapore, the threat of Chinese military action against Taiwan "is real, and it could be imminent."[15]

The PLA's Evolving Capabilities: From Political Signaling to Operational Dominance

For decades, China's military posture toward Taiwan involved more political theater than genuine preparation for war. Cross-strait tensions would flare periodically—most notably during the 1995-1996 Taiwan Strait Crisis when China conducted missile tests and military exercises in response to Taiwan's first democratic presidential election. The United States responded by deploying two aircraft carrier battle groups, and Beijing backed down. The episode convinced Chinese leaders that they lacked the military capability to overcome American intervention and compel Taiwan's capitulation.

A quarter-century later, the balance has shifted dramatically. The People's Liberation Army has undergone the most comprehensive military modernization since World War II, transforming from a massive but technologically backward force into what the Pentagon now describes as a "pacing threat" to American military supremacy.[16] This transformation has been guided by a singular strategic direction: preparing to fight and win a war over Taiwan that would likely involve the United States.

The scale of China's military buildup is staggering. As of October 2025, the PLA had conducted 3,056 incursions into Taiwan's Air Defense Identification Zone—a 33 percent increase from the 2,301 incursions during the same period in 2024.[17] This represents a 300 percent escalation in military pressure over the previous year, according to testimony by Admiral Samuel Paparo, Commander of U.S. Indo-Pacific Command.[18] These are not isolated provocations but systematic preparations for potential conflict.

The "Strait Thunder-2025A" exercises in April marked a qualitative shift in these preparations. Unlike previous exercises that focused primarily on naval blockades and air superiority operations, Strait Thunder explicitly rehearsed strikes against Taiwan's civilian economic infrastructure. PLA forces simulated precision attacks on liquefied natural gas terminals, particularly the main LNG storage facility in Kaohsiung, and practiced what Chinese military planners call "identification and verification, warning and expulsion, and interception and detention"—in other words, the establishment of a comprehensive blockade.[19]

The exercises demonstrated a three-phase operational concept that PLA strategists have developed for a Taiwan campaign. Phase one involves joint combat readiness patrols and troop assembly—the seemingly routine incursions that have become normalized around Taiwan. Phase two escalates to active operations focused on achieving battlefield dominance through strikes against sea and land targets. Phase three implements the actual blockade: intercepting, detaining, and potentially boarding civilian vessels attempting to reach or leave Taiwan.[20] This phased approach allows China to escalate from peacetime operations to actual warfare along a carefully calibrated continuum, making it difficult for Taiwan and the United States to identify the precise moment when exercises become invasion.

What makes this capability particularly concerning is China's ability to implement a blockade within "a matter of hours" with "minimal conversion time," according to assessments by U.S. and

Taiwanese military officials.[21] The PLA no longer needs weeks of obvious military buildup to position forces—they are already positioned through routine "patrols" and "exercises." The normalization of military activity around Taiwan creates what intelligence analysts call "noise in the system," making it extremely difficult to distinguish between another drill and the opening moves of actual warfare.

The exercises also revealed China's strategy for deterring American intervention. During Strait Thunder-2025A, while PLA forces practiced blockade operations in the Taiwan Strait itself, the Shandong aircraft carrier strike group maneuvered to a position 440 kilometers south of Japan's Yonaguni Island, where it could threaten both Taiwan to the south and Japanese territory to the north while simultaneously positioning to intercept any U.S. Navy forces attempting to transit from the Western Pacific.[22] Meanwhile, PLA Air Force bomber formations conducted patrols beyond the first island chain, demonstrating the capability to hold U.S. bases in Japan and Guam at risk.[23]

Blockade or Invasion: Scenarios and Strategic Calculations

The question that dominates strategic planning in Washington, Taipei, Tokyo, and allied capitals is not whether China will move against Taiwan, but how and when. Military analysts generally envision three primary scenarios, each with distinct characteristics, risks, and implications.

Scenario One: Quarantine or Blockade. This option, which appears increasingly central to PLA planning, would involve China using its navy, coast guard, and maritime militia to establish a cordon around Taiwan, preventing ships from entering or leaving the island's ports. Unlike a traditional military blockade, China might frame this as a "customs and quarantine inspection zone" or similar legal construct, claiming authority to board vessels and verify their cargoes as part of what Beijing insists is an internal Chinese matter.

Such a blockade could be implemented gradually or suddenly, depending on China's objectives and the political context. A gradual squeeze might begin with heightened inspections of certain categories of vessels, expanding over time to encompass all maritime traffic. A sudden blockade could be declared in response to some perceived provocation—perhaps a visit by senior American officials or actions by Taiwan's government that Beijing characterizes as steps toward formal independence.

The advantages of this approach for China are considerable. It stops short of the massive bloodshed that would result from invasion, potentially limiting international condemnation and sanctions. It exploits Taiwan's vulnerability as an island economy utterly dependent on maritime commerce: Taiwan imports nearly all its energy, much of its food, and critical industrial inputs. Within weeks, a comprehensive blockade would cripple the island's economy and create severe hardships for its population, potentially forcing capitulation without firing a shot.

The Center for Strategic and International Studies estimates that even a short-term blockade would cost between $2 trillion to $10 trillion in global economic disruption, depending on duration and severity.[24] The semiconductor supply chain disruption alone would cascade through every technology-dependent industry worldwide. Yet from Beijing's perspective, this might be an acceptable price to pay for achieving national reunification and demonstrating China's arrival as the preeminent power in Asia.

The critical question is whether the United States would use military force to break a Chinese blockade of Taiwan. Running an established blockade backed by PLA air superiority and anti-ship missile coverage would be extraordinarily dangerous, potentially costing American ships and sailors in a conflict that might escalate to nuclear exchange. Strategic ambiguity—the long-standing U.S. policy of neither confirming nor denying whether it would defend Taiwan—loses its deterrent value once China believes it can execute a successful blockade before the United States can effectively respond.

Scenario Two: Limited Kinetic Operations and "Gray Zone" Escalation. Short of full blockade or invasion, China could employ a range of coercive measures designed to incrementally increase pressure while staying below the threshold of conventional warfare. Recent PLA exercises have practiced cutting undersea cables, cyber attacks on critical infrastructure, seizure of Taiwan's offshore islands (particularly Kinmen and Matsu, which lie just kilometers from the mainland), and precision missile strikes against selected targets.

These actions could be calibrated to demonstrate capability and resolve while testing Taiwan's and America's responses. For example, China might seize Kinmen Island—technically part of Taiwan but located just two kilometers from the Chinese mainland—and dare Taiwan to attempt recapture, knowing that any military operation to retake the island would require attacking Chinese forces on terrain within range of massive PLA firepower. Such a fait accompli might fracture the consensus for Taiwan's defense while demonstrating China's willingness and ability to use force.

The April 2025 Strait Thunder exercises included simulated strikes against Taiwan's LNG terminals and port facilities, suggesting PLA planning includes options for limited strikes designed to cripple specific capabilities without triggering full-scale war.[25] Cyber operations against Taiwan's power grid, water systems, financial networks, and telecommunications infrastructure could create chaos and demonstrate vulnerability without the international opprobrium that would follow kinetic attacks.

Scenario Three: Amphibious Invasion. Despite its difficulties and risks, full-scale amphibious assault remains the option that receives the most attention from military planners and drives defense procurement decisions. An invasion would be the largest and most complex military operation since World War II, potentially dwarfing even the D-Day landings in scale and difficulty.

The challenges are formidable. Taiwan's western coast, facing China across the strait, features relatively few suitable landing beaches—most are too rocky, too narrow, or backed by urban areas that would complicate logistics and make forces vulnerable to urban combat. The eastern coast drops precipitously into deep water, making amphibious approach nearly impossible. This leaves perhaps a dozen viable landing zones, all of which Taiwan has spent decades fortifying and preparing to defend.

Moreover, the strait itself is treacherous. Two monsoon seasons and other extreme weather events render seaborne invasion feasible only during limited windows in spring and fall, and even then, the strait's notorious choppiness would complicate landing operations.[26] Shallow waters would force landing craft and ships to anchor far from shore, exposing them to Taiwan's mobile anti-ship missiles and coastal artillery. The PLA would need to establish air supremacy, suppress Taiwan's air defenses, neutralize coastal missile batteries, conduct electronic warfare and cyber operations to blind and confuse defenders, deploy airborne and special operations forces to seize key infrastructure, and execute synchronized amphibious assaults at multiple points—all while countering likely American intervention.

Estimates suggest China would need to transport and sustain 300,000 to one million troops for a successful invasion.[27] The PLA Navy currently possesses dedicated amphibious ships capable of carrying approximately 20,000 to 25,000 troops in an initial wave—far short of requirements.[28] To bridge this gap, China has developed a "shadow navy" of civilian vessels. In August 2024, Reuters documented at least twelve civilian roll-on/roll-off ferries and deck cargo ships practicing beach landing operations at Jiesheng in Guangdong Province, demonstrating techniques for rapidly offloading vehicles and equipment directly onto beaches.[29] Satellite imagery shows China developing new D-Day-style landing barges and testing them at its Donghai Island facility, suggesting systematic preparation for amphibious operations at a scale not seen since World War II.[30]

Yet as CIA Director William Burns acknowledged in February 2023, while Xi Jinping has instructed the PLA to "be ready by 2027 to conduct a successful invasion," this does not mean China has decided to invade, and Burns noted that Chinese leaders may harbor doubts about their ability to execute such an operation successfully.[31] War games conducted by the Center for

Strategic and International Studies ran 24 scenarios of a Chinese invasion in 2022 and published results in January 2023. In most cases, the United States, Japan, and Taiwan defeated the invasion and maintained Taiwan's autonomy—but at catastrophic cost. The United States typically lost two aircraft carriers and dozens of major warships, while suffering thousands of casualties. Taiwan's military and economy were devastated, and the PLA lost approximately 90 percent of its amphibious fleet, hundreds of aircraft, and tens of thousands of personnel.[32] Even in "victory," the pyrrhic nature of the outcome raises profound questions about whether any party would accept such costs.

The Warning from Washington

In May 2025, Defense Secretary Pete Hegseth delivered an unusually stark warning at the Shangri-La Dialogue in Singapore. Standing before an audience of defense ministers and military leaders from across the Indo-Pacific, Hegseth dispensed with diplomatic hedging: "To be clear: any attempt by Communist China to conquer Taiwan by force would result in devastating consequences for the Indo-Pacific and the world. We are not going to sugarcoat it. The threat China poses is real. And it could be imminent."[33]

Hegseth noted that President Xi Jinping has ordered the People's Liberation Army to be ready to invade Taiwan by 2027—a deadline that aligns with the 100th anniversary of the PLA's founding and Xi's broader timetable for Chinese military modernization.[34] This directive was first revealed publicly by CIA Director William Burns in February 2023, who testified that U.S. intelligence confirmed Xi had "instructed the People's Liberation Army to be ready by 2027 to conduct a successful invasion," though Burns emphasized this did not mean Xi had decided to actually invade in that year.[35] Hegseth emphasized that the PLA "is not just building up its military forces to take Taiwan, it's actively training for it, every day. The PLA is rehearsing for the real deal."[36]

The Defense Secretary's assessment aligned with increasingly dire warnings from across the U.S. intelligence and military establishment. Admiral Samuel Paparo had testified to Congress that PLA capabilities had advanced to the point where China could implement a blockade with minimal warning, potentially within hours of a political decision.[37] Other officials noted that the normalization of large-scale, unannounced exercises around Taiwan was designed precisely to reduce the time available for Taiwan and the United States to prepare responses.[38]

Yet Hegseth also reiterated President Trump's declaration that "Communist China will not invade Taiwan on his watch,"[39] while calling on Asian allies to increase defense spending to five percent of GDP—matching the commitment made by NATO members in response to Russian aggression.[40]

The message was clear: the United States was preparing to defend Taiwan, but expected allies to shoulder more of the burden of their own defense.

China's response was swift and vitriolic. The Foreign Ministry accused Hegseth of making "defamatory" and "provocative" comments intended to "sow discord."[41] Chinese Defense Ministry spokesperson Colonel Zhang Xiaogang went further, warning that the United States was on a path to "fire and suffering" if it continued to "interfere in China's internal affairs."[42] For the first time since 2019, China's defense minister did not attend the Shangri-La Dialogue—a deliberate snub signaling Beijing's displeasure with U.S. policy.[43]

Historical Parallels and the Danger of Miscalculation

Students of history watching the Taiwan situation cannot help but see disturbing parallels to the 1930s, when rising revisionist powers tested the resolve of status quo democracies. In that era, incremental aggression—Japan's seizure of Manchuria, Italy's invasion of Ethiopia, Germany's remilitarization of the Rhineland—went largely unchallenged. Each time, the democracies rationalized inaction: the aggression was in a far-off land, the costs of confrontation seemed too high, perhaps accommodation could satisfy the aggressor's demands and preserve peace.

The result, of course, was World War II. By the time Britain and France finally drew a line at Poland's independence, the fascist powers had grown too strong and too confident to be deterred by belated shows of resolve. The democracies' militaries had atrophied during years of neglect while their adversaries armed for war. When conflict finally came, it cost perhaps 70 million lives and remade the global order.

Taiwan in 2025 bears uncomfortable similarities to Poland in 1939 or Czechoslovakia in 1938: a democratic society threatened by an authoritarian neighbor, dependent on distant allies whose commitment remains uncertain, serving as a test case for whether the international system will defend sovereignty and self-determination or acquiesce to conquest.

Yet history also teaches that analogies are imperfect and that each crisis contains unique elements that defy simple pattern-matching. Taiwan is not Poland—it is separated from its potential invader by 130 kilometers of treacherous water rather than a land border. China is not Nazi Germany—it is deeply integrated into the global economy in ways that create significant costs to aggression. And the United States in 2025, despite its challenges, remains far more powerful relative to its potential adversary than Britain and France were vis-à-vis Germany in the 1930s.

Moreover, nuclear weapons fundamentally alter the calculus of great power conflict. Both the United States and China possess arsenals capable of destroying human civilization. The logic of mutually assured destruction that prevented direct U.S.-Soviet conflict during the Cold War should theoretically also prevent U.S.-Chinese war over Taiwan. Yet this logic assumes rational decision-making, clear communication, and the absence of accidents or miscalculation—assumptions that history suggests are dangerously optimistic.

The greatest danger may lie precisely in the normalization of crisis that has characterized cross-strait relations in recent years. When PLA aircraft violate Taiwan's air defense identification zone nearly daily, when Chinese coast guard vessels routinely intrude into waters around Taiwan-controlled islands, when massive military exercises can be announced and executed with minimal warning, the system becomes desensitized to danger. Each side's perception of what constitutes unacceptable provocation shifts. Thresholds blur. What would have been considered an act of war a decade ago becomes merely "another drill."

In such an environment, catastrophe can emerge not from deliberate aggression but from miscalculation—a Chinese leader misreading American resolve, an American president underestimating Chinese determination, a tactical incident spiraling out of control before diplomacy can contain it. Intelligence failures, faulty assumptions, domestic political pressures, and the fog of crisis all conspire to create conditions where leaders might make decisions they would never make with perfect information and unlimited time.

The Stakes Beyond Taiwan

If conflict over Taiwan were merely a bilateral dispute between Beijing and Taipei, or even a regional contest between China and the United States, the stakes would be grave but limited. In reality, the implications of what happens across the Taiwan Strait will reshape the entire international order.

At the most immediate level, a Chinese blockade or invasion would devastate the global technology sector. TSMC's production would cease, cutting off the supply of advanced chips essential for everything from smartphones to data centers to automobiles to defense systems. Even if the facilities themselves survived intact, the complex supply chains, skilled workforce, and reliable electricity and water supplies required for semiconductor manufacturing would be disrupted for months or years. Some analysts estimate it could take a decade to reconstitute the lost production capacity elsewhere.

The economic costs would cascade globally. Taiwan sits at the center of critical shipping lanes through which passes approximately $5 trillion in annual trade.[44] A conflict would disrupt not just ships transiting the strait but vessels bound for any East Asian port, given the danger of operating in a war zone. Energy shipments to Japan, South Korea, and Taiwan itself would be interrupted, with knock-on effects throughout the global economy. Financial markets would crater. Supply chains would fracture. The economic disruption could easily exceed the global financial crisis of 2008 or the COVID-19 pandemic.

Beyond economics, the geopolitical consequences would be profound. If China successfully coerces Taiwan into capitulation, the message to every American ally and partner would be unmistakable: Washington's security guarantees cannot be relied upon when challenged by a determined peer competitor. Japan, South Korea, the Philippines, and other nations would face stark choices: accept Chinese hegemony over the region, develop independent nuclear deterrents, or seek accommodation with Beijing. The system of alliances that has underpinned Asian security for 75 years would collapse.

Conversely, if the United States successfully defends Taiwan against Chinese aggression, but at the cost of thousands of American casualties, dozens of ships, and trillions in economic damage, the domestic political fallout in America could be severe. Public support for sustaining U.S. global commitments would likely plummet. Isolationist sentiment would surge. The political viability of maintaining forward-deployed forces and alliance commitments would come under question. Either outcome—American abandonment or pyrrhic victory—would represent a strategic defeat.

Conclusion: Living with Danger

Taiwan's predicament—economically indispensable yet militarily vulnerable, democratic yet diplomatically isolated, determined to resist coercion yet unable to defend itself alone—makes it perhaps the world's most dangerous flashpoint. The island exists in a state of perpetual strategic ambiguity, neither fully independent nor controlled by China, defended by an American commitment that is simultaneously crucial and uncertain.

For seven decades, this ambiguous status quo has been maintained through a combination of Chinese patience, American deterrence, Taiwan's own defensive capabilities, and a shared recognition that the costs of changing the situation by force would exceed any potential benefits. But all of these elements are eroding. Chinese patience has limits as Xi Jinping ages and faces domestic pressures to complete his legacy. American deterrence credibility comes under question with each PLA advance and each demonstration of Washington's other global commitments and constraints. Taiwan's defensive capabilities, while improving, struggle to keep pace with the PLA's modernization. And the calculus of costs and benefits shifts as China's capabilities grow and its leadership becomes more confident.

The narrow waters of the Taiwan Strait thus contain the potential for catastrophe—not because any party seeks war, but because the convergence of technological importance, geopolitical competition, and nationalist fervor creates conditions where miscalculation could trigger a conflict that none of the parties truly wants but all feel compelled to fight.

The world has grown comfortable with perpetual crisis in various regions—the Korean Peninsula, the India-Pakistan border, the Middle East. But Taiwan represents a different category of danger. Here, the world's two most powerful nations confront each other over an issue that touches their deepest interests: for China, territorial integrity and national rejuvenation; for the United States, credibility and the viability of the liberal international order; for Taiwan, survival as a free and democratic society.

In this 130-kilometer-wide waterway, the question of whether the 21st century will be marked by peaceful competition or catastrophic conflict may ultimately be decided. The dangers are real and growing. The question is whether wisdom, restraint, and strategic statecraft can defuse them before the next crisis becomes the last one.

Endnotes

[1] Xinhua, "PLA Launches 'Strait Thunder-2025A' Exercises in Middle, Southern Areas of Taiwan Strait," April 2, 2025, https://english.news.cn/20250402/3a827b22046442e48a5cc1a6d6393bff/c.html.

[2] Ministry of National Defense, Republic of China (Taiwan), press release, April 2, 2025; Jonathan Harman, "The PLA's 'Strait Thunder-2025A' Exercise Presents Further Efforts to Isolate Taiwan," Global Taiwan Institute, April 16, 2025, https://globaltaiwan.org/2025/04/the-plas-strait-thunder-exercise/.

[3] "Taiwan Strait," Encyclopedia Britannica, accessed December 1, 2025, https://www.britannica.com/place/Taiwan-Strait; "Taiwan Strait," Wikipedia, accessed December 1, 2025.

[4] Nicholas Kadlec, "Strait Talk: Time to Exercise Navigational Freedoms in the Taiwan Strait Beyond Mere Transit?" Lieber Institute West Point, October 31, 2024, https://lieber.westpoint.edu/strait-talk-time-exercise-navigational-freedoms-taiwan-strait-beyond-mere-transit/.

[5] "Taiwan Strait: 2025's Key Geopolitical Maritime Corridor," The Word 360, August 16, 2025, https://theword360.com/2025/08/25/the-geopolitical-significance-of-taiwan-strait-tensions/.

[6] "Chinese Views of Taiwan's Geostrategic Value," The Sasakawa Peace Foundation, accessed December 1, 2025, https://www.spf.org/spf-china-observer/en/document-detail045.html.

[7] "Taiwan Strait," World Atlas, June 8, 2021, https://www.worldatlas.com/straits/taiwan-strait.html.

[8] Jared McKinney and Peter Harris, "Not So Fast: Insights from a 1944 War Plan Help Explain Why Invading Taiwan Is a Costly Gamble," War on the Rocks, September 8, 2022, https://warontherocks.com/2022/09/not-so-fast-insights-from-a-1944-war-help-explain-why-invading-taiwan-is-a-costly-gamble/.

[9] Focus Taiwan, "TSMC's Global Market Share Hits New High of 70.2% in Q2," September 6, 2025, https://focustaiwan.tw/business/202509060012.

[10] Ibid.

[11] "3nm and 5nm Chips Drive TSMC Record-Breaking Quarter," Guru3D, October 17, 2025, https://www.guru3d.com/story/3nm-and-5nm-chips-drive-tsmc-recordbreaking-quarter/.

[12] "TSMC: The Unseen Giant Powering the Future of Technology," Chronicle Journal, September 30, 2025, https://markets.chroniclejournal.com/chroniclejournal/article/predictstreet-2025-9-30-tsmc-the-unseen-giant-powering-the-future-of-technology.

[13] "TSMC's 5nm, 3nm Production Lines Remain 'Fully Loaded' in 1H 2025," TweakTown, November 12, 2024, https://www.tweaktown.com/news/101630/tsmcs-5nm-3nm-production-lines-remain-fully-loaded-in-1h-2025-strong-orders-for-ai-chips/index.html.

[14] "Hegseth: Asia Is the Priority, and the US Will Fight for Taiwan," The Strategist, June 2, 2025, https://www.aspistrategist.org.au/hegseth-asia-is-the-priority-and-the-us-will-fight-for-taiwan/.

[15] Council on Foreign Relations, "China in the Taiwan Strait: May 2025," July 8, 2025, https://www.cfr.org/article/china-taiwan-strait-may-2025.

[16] "China to Hegseth: US on Path to 'Fire and Suffering,'" Newsweek, June 27, 2025, https://www.newsweek.com/china-pete-hegseth-us-military-taiwan-arms-sales-warning-2090985.

[17] "PLA Could Attack With Little Warning: US," Taipei Times, November 20, 2025, https://www.taipeitimes.com/News/front/archives/2025/11/20/2003847504.

[18] Ibid.

[19] Harman, "The PLA's 'Strait Thunder-2025A' Exercise."

[20] "Recent PLA Exercises Revealed China's Operational Plan for a Taiwan Strait Conflict," The Diplomat, May 3, 2025, https://thediplomat.com/2025/04/recent-pla-exercises-revealed-chinas-operational-plan-for-a-taiwan-strait-conflict/.

[21] "PLA Could Blockade Taiwan in 'Matter of Hours': US Report," Taipei Times, November 19, 2025, https://www.taipeitimes.com/News/taiwan/archives/2025/11/19/2003847476.

[22] "Analyzing the PLA's Early April Exercises in the Taiwan Strait," The Diplomat, April 17, 2025, https://thediplomat.com/2025/04/analyzing-the-plas-early-april-exercises-in-the-taiwan-strait/.

[23] "'Strait Thunder-2025A' Drill Implies Future Increase in PLA Pressure on Taiwan," Jamestown Foundation, April 12, 2025, https://jamestown.org/strait-thunder-2025a-drill-implies-future-increase-in-pla-pressure-on-taiwan/.

[24] "What Cost Is China Willing to Bear to Invade Taiwan?" Indo-Pacific Defense Forum, October 28, 2025, https://ipdefenseforum.com/2025/10/what-cost-is-china-willing-to-bear-to-invade-taiwan/.

[25] Harman, "The PLA's 'Strait Thunder-2025A' Exercise."

[26] "Why China Would Struggle to Invade Taiwan," Council on Foreign Relations, June 12, 2024, https://www.cfr.org/article/why-china-would-struggle-invade-taiwan.

[27] "Feature: China Works to Expand Amphibious Capability," Taipei Times, November 22, 2025, https://www.taipeitimes.com/News/taiwan/archives/2025/11/22/2003847644.

[28] Ibid.

[29] Ibid.

[30] "China Likely to Continue to Prioritise Intimidation Against Taiwan," Janes, accessed December 1, 2025, https://www.janes.com/osint-insights/defence-and-national-security-analysis/china-likely-to-continue-to-prioritise-intimidation-against-taiwan-in-the-next-six-to-12-months.

[31] William Burns, quoted in "CIA Director William Burns: 'I Wouldn't Underestimate' Xi's Ambitions for Taiwan," CBS News, February 4, 2023, https://www.cbsnews.com/news/cia-director-william-burns-i-wouldnt-underestimate-xis-ambitions-for-taiwan/; "CIA Chief: China Has Doubt on Ability to Invade Taiwan," Voice of America, February 27, 2023, https://www.voanews.com/a/cia-chief-china-has-doubt-on-ability-to-invade-taiwan/6980212.html.

[32] Mark F. Cancian, Matthew Cancian, and Eric Heginbotham, "The First Battle of the Next War: Wargaming a Chinese Invasion of Taiwan," Center for Strategic and International Studies, January 9, 2023, https://www.csis.org/analysis/first-battle-next-war-wargaming-chinese-invasion-taiwan; Mark Cancian, interview by Mercy Kuo, "Wargaming a Chinese Invasion of Taiwan: 'Victory Is Not Enough,'" The Diplomat, January 31, 2023, https://thediplomat.com/2023/01/wargaming-a-chinese-invasion-of-taiwan-victory-is-not-enough/.

[33] "Hegseth Reassures Allies That US Will Support Them Against Chinese Aggression," ABC News, May 31, 2025, https://abcnews.go.com/Politics/hegseth-reassures-allies-us-support-chinese-aggression/story?id=122362466.

[34] Ibid.

[35] William Burns, remarks at Georgetown University, February 2, 2023, quoted in "CIA Director William Burns: 'I Wouldn't Underestimate' Xi's Ambitions for Taiwan," CBS News, February 4, 2023; "China's Xi Has Ordered Military to Be Ready for Taiwan Invasion by 2027, CIA Director Burns Says," Fox News, February 3, 2023, https://www.foxnews.com/world/china-xi-ordered-military-ready-taiwan-invasion-2027-cia-director-burns-says.

[36] "Hegseth Says U.S. Will Stand by Indo-Pacific Allies Against 'Imminent' Threat of China," NBC News, June 1, 2025, https://www.nbcnews.com/world/asia/china-indo-pacific-allies-taiwan-pete-hegseth-military-economic-threat-rcna210105.

[37] "PLA Could Attack With Little Warning: US," Taipei Times, November 20, 2025, https://www.taipeitimes.com/News/front/archives/2025/11/20/2003847504.

[38] Ibid.

[39] "China Attack on Taiwan Would Be Devastating to World: U.S. Defense Chief," Focus Taiwan, May 31, 2025, https://focustaiwan.tw/politics/202505310006.

[40] "Hegseth Reassures Allies That US Will Support Them Against Chinese Aggression," ABC News, May 31, 2025.

[41] "China Calls Hegseth's Remarks on Taiwan a Provocation," Taiwan News, June 2, 2025, https://taiwannews.com.tw/news/6124915.

[42] "China to Hegseth: US on Path to 'Fire and Suffering,'" Newsweek, June 27, 2025, https://www.newsweek.com/china-pete-hegseth-us-military-taiwan-arms-sales-warning-2090985.

[43] "Hegseth: Asia Is the Priority, and the US Will Fight for Taiwan," The Strategist, June 2, 2025, https://www.aspistrategist.org.au/hegseth-asia-is-the-priority-and-the-us-will-fight-for-taiwan/.

[44] "Taiwan Strait: 2025's Key Geopolitical Maritime Corridor," The Word 360, August 16, 2025, https://theword360.com/2025/08/25/the-geopolitical-significance-of-taiwan-strait-tensions/.

Chapter 14
The South China Sea Cauldron

Nine-Dash Lines and Great Power Competition

The azure waters of the South China Sea conceal one of the world's most dangerous geopolitical flashpoints. Beneath its surface lie not only vast reserves of oil and gas, rich fishing grounds, and critical undersea communications infrastructure, but also the competing territorial claims of seven nations locked in an escalating struggle for dominance. As 2025 draws to a close, this contested waterway—through which approximately one-third of global maritime trade flows—has become the primary theater where Chinese assertiveness collides with American resolve, where ASEAN unity fractures under pressure, and where the risk of miscalculation threatens to ignite a broader regional conflict.[1]

The transformation of the South China Sea from a relatively stable maritime commons into a militarized zone of contestation represents one of the most consequential shifts in the Indo-Pacific security landscape. China's audacious campaign of artificial island construction, the Philippines' dramatic strategic pivot toward deeper defense cooperation with the United States, and the proliferation of dangerous incidents at sea have collectively pushed the region closer to the brink of armed conflict than at any time since the end of the Cold War.

China's Artificial Archipelago: Engineering Sovereignty

The scale and audacity of China's island-building campaign in the South China Sea represent perhaps the most dramatic fait accompli in contemporary international relations. Beginning in earnest in 2013, Beijing embarked on a systematic program to transform submerged reefs and coral outcroppings into full-fledged military installations, creating facts on the water that would be nearly impossible to reverse without armed conflict.

By 2025, China had created 3,200 acres of new land across seven features in the Spratly Islands, according to the Asia Maritime Transparency Initiative at the Center for Strategic and International Studies.[2] What had been little more than rocks barely visible at high tide—Fiery Cross Reef, Subi Reef, and Mischief Reef—now bristle with military infrastructure that would be at home on any major air force base. The U.S. Department of Defense confirmed that China has built runways at least 8,800 feet long on each of the three largest outposts, along with hangars, fixed-weapons positions, barracks, administration buildings, and communication facilities.[3]

The military significance of these artificial islands cannot be overstated. U.S. Indo-Pacific Commander Admiral John Aquilino stated in March 2022 that China had fully militarized at least three artificial islands including Mischief Reef, Subi Reef, and Fiery Cross, all in the Spratly archipelago.[4] These facilities include radar systems, missile shelters, and close-in weapon systems for detecting and destroying incoming missiles and aircraft. The installations fundamentally alter the strategic calculus in the region, extending China's Anti-Access/Area Denial (A2/AD) capabilities across virtually the entire South China Sea. Combined with advanced radar systems that provide comprehensive surveillance coverage, these islands allow Beijing to monitor activities across a vast maritime domain.

"China can [through its radar systems on artificial islands] see and hear and communicate across the whole South China Sea in a way that nobody else, including the United States, can," observed Gregory Poling, director of the Southeast Asia Program at the Center for Strategic and International Studies, commenting on aerial imagery showing advanced radar and surveillance systems on the artificial islands.[5] The strategic implications are profound: China has effectively created an integrated early-warning and targeting network that complicates any potential U.S. or allied military operations in the region.

The construction process itself represented a feat of engineering that consumed vast resources and demonstrated Beijing's determination to reshape the regional order. Using massive dredging vessels, Chinese contractors pumped sand and crushed coral onto submerged reefs, building up layers of material until the features rose above the high-tide line. Concrete was then poured, creating foundations for runways, port facilities, and military installations. The speed of construction was breathtaking—entire military bases appeared within months, presenting the international community with accomplished facts before diplomatic pressure could be mobilized.

Beijing's public justification for this island-building campaign has evolved over time, shifting from initial denials to claims about providing shelters for fishermen, to assertions of sovereign rights within China's so-called nine-dash line.[6] Despite Chinese President Xi Jinping's assurances about not militarizing the outposts, the subsequent years have witnessed their comprehensive transformation into forward military bases.[7] The extensive military infrastructure documented in satellite imagery and confirmed by multiple defense analysts has not been lost on regional observers and has fundamentally eroded trust in Chinese diplomatic commitments.

Significantly, China's island-building program, while the largest, is not unique. Vietnam, in a less publicized but equally ambitious campaign, has engaged in its own dramatic expansion of land reclamation. According to the Asia Maritime Transparency Initiative's March 2025 report, Vietnam had created approximately 2,236 acres of artificial land in the Spratly Islands by early 2025, representing about 70 percent of China's total acreage in the Spratlys.[8] The difference lies in the scale of militarization: while Vietnam has constructed ports, airstrips, and defensive positions, China's installations represent a qualitatively different level of military capability projection.

The environmental cost of this construction boom has been catastrophic. The dredging operations have destroyed vast swaths of coral reef, one of the most biodiverse marine ecosystems on Earth. Research documented by the Asia Maritime Transparency Initiative indicates that the island-building campaign has caused massive damage to coral reef habitat, eliminating critical spawning grounds for fish stocks that sustain millions of people across Southeast Asia.[9] The irony is stark: in September 2025, China declared the Huangyan Island (Scarborough Shoal) a national nature reserve, ostensibly for environmental protection, even as its artificial islands represent one of the greatest anthropogenic disasters to befall the South China Sea's ecology.[10]

The Philippines' Strategic Awakening: From Accommodation to Resistance

The transformation of Philippine policy toward China under President Ferdinand Marcos Jr. represents one of the most consequential strategic shifts in Southeast Asia. After years of accommodation under his predecessor Rodrigo Duterte, who downplayed territorial disputes in favor of Chinese investment, Marcos has adopted a markedly more assertive stance in defending Philippine maritime rights.

This shift crystallized most dramatically in the expansion of defense cooperation with the United States, culminating in the deployment of advanced American military capabilities to Philippine territory. The April 2025 Balikatan exercises—the largest in the 40-year history of the annual U.S.-Philippine military drills—showcased this new strategic alignment with unprecedented clarity.

The centerpiece of Balikatan 2025 was the historic deployment of the Navy-Marine Expeditionary Ship Interdiction System (NMESIS) to Philippine soil. On April 26, 2025, U.S. Marines with the 3rd Marine Littoral Regiment deployed NMESIS units to Batan Island in the Philippines' northernmost province of Batanes, marking the system's first operational deployment to Philippine territory.[11] The significance of this deployment extends far beyond the weapon system itself; it represents the operationalization of new American military concepts designed specifically for great power competition in the Western Pacific.

NMESIS, a ground-based anti-ship missile system capable of engaging naval targets at extended ranges, embodies the U.S. Marine Corps' Force Design 2030 transformation. The system allows small, dispersed units to establish temporary firing positions across the archipelagic terrain of the Philippines, creating a distributed network of anti-ship capabilities that complicates Chinese naval operations. As U.S. Marine Corps Lieutenant General Michael Cederholm, the Joint Task Force commander, noted, "We are expeditionary by nature, and training on the Batanes with our Philippine allies and the precision fires capabilities of the NMESIS advances our mutual maritime defense in an austere and geographically dispersed environment."[12]

The strategic geography of the deployment is equally significant. Batanes Province, located just 150 kilometers south of Taiwan, sits astride potential Chinese sea lanes in any Taiwan contingency. The deployment of anti-ship missiles to this location sends an unmistakable message about the integration of Philippine and American defense planning for scenarios involving Taiwan—a point not lost on Beijing, which accused Manila of "playing with fire" and bringing "strategic and tactical weapons to the detriment of regional strategic stability."[13]

The Balikatan 2025 exercises involved approximately 17,000 troops—9,000 American and 5,000 Philippine personnel—and simulated full-scale battle scenarios with explicit implications for maritime defense.[14] Beyond NMESIS, the exercises featured the deployment of the Typhon mid-range missile system (which the United States had deployed to the Philippines during the previous year's exercises and notably kept in place afterward), Marine Air Defense Integrated Systems, HIMARS rockets, and a host of other advanced capabilities. The Philippines, for its part, showcased equipment from its ongoing military modernization program, including FA-50 fighter jets, BrahMos supersonic cruise missiles, and modern frigates.[15]

U.S. Defense Secretary Pete Hegseth, in his March 2025 visit to Manila, framed this deepening cooperation in explicitly deterrence-focused terms. "We agreed that the United States will deploy additional advanced capabilities to the Philippines," Hegseth stated. "These systems will enable US Forces and the Armed Forces of the Philippines to train together on using advanced capabilities to defend the Philippines' sovereignty."[16] The message was clear: the United States would not merely conduct symbolic exercises but would deploy operationally relevant capabilities designed to impose real costs on Chinese military operations.

The Philippine government's embrace of this enhanced alliance comes despite—or perhaps because of—intensifying Chinese pressure. Manila has filed over one hundred diplomatic protests against

Chinese activities in Philippine-claimed waters since Marcos assumed office.[17] The most severe incidents have involved Chinese coast guard vessels using water cannons against Philippine resupply missions, dangerous blocking maneuvers that have damaged Philippine vessels, and the seizure of Philippine fishermen's catch in waters well within Manila's exclusive economic zone.

Philippine officials have been remarkably candid about the threat perception driving this policy shift. Brigadier General Michael Logico, the Balikatan 2025 spokesperson, articulated the stakes clearly: "Every country big or small has an absolute and inalienable right to defend itself. Maritime Key Terrain Security Operations training increases our combined ability to secure and defend our territories."[18] The contrast with the Duterte era, when territorial disputes were subordinated to the pursuit of Chinese investment and when joint military exercises with the United States were scaled back, could not be more stark.

Yet this strategic reorientation carries risks. The deeper the Philippines integrates its defense planning with the United States, the more it becomes a potential flashpoint in U.S.-China competition. Philippine leaders are acutely aware that their islands could become a battlefield in any broader conflict, whether over Taiwan or arising from an incident in the South China Sea itself. The challenge for Manila is to leverage American security guarantees to deter Chinese aggression while avoiding provocations that might trigger the very conflict it seeks to prevent.

Scarborough Shoal: Flashpoint at 120 Nautical Miles

No single feature in the South China Sea better encapsulates the dangerous dynamics of the territorial disputes than Scarborough Shoal—a triangular chain of reefs and rocks located approximately 120 nautical miles west of the Philippine island of Luzon. This modest collection of submerged reefs, barely visible above the waterline, has become the site of repeated confrontations that risk spiraling into armed conflict.

China seized control of Scarborough Shoal from the Philippines in 2012 following a tense standoff that began when a Philippine Navy vessel attempted to arrest Chinese fishermen operating in the area. Since then, Beijing has maintained a permanent coast guard presence at the shoal, effectively controlling access to the lagoon and surrounding waters despite the feature lying well within the Philippines' exclusive economic zone as defined by the United Nations Convention on the Law of the Sea (UNCLOS).[19] The 2016 arbitral tribunal ruling in the Philippines' favor explicitly rejected China's historic rights claims in the South China Sea and affirmed traditional fishing rights for both Filipino and Chinese fishermen at Scarborough, but Beijing has simply ignored the ruling.[20]

The intensity of Chinese activity around Scarborough has escalated dramatically in recent years. According to data from the Asia Maritime Transparency Initiative, Chinese coast guard patrol days around the shoal increased threefold between August 2024 and May 2025, peaking at 120 ship-days in January 2025—nearly double the average of the previous months.[21] This surge in patrolling has been accompanied by an aggressive expansion of China's enforcement zone, with Chinese vessels intercepting Philippine ships as far as 70 nautical miles east of the shoal, near one of the dashes of China's nine-dash line.[22]

The most dramatic incident occurred on August 11, 2025, when a Chinese coast guard vessel and a People's Liberation Army Navy warship collided with each other while pursuing the Philippine Coast Guard vessel BRP Suluan. In a scene that would be comedic if the stakes were not so high, the Chinese ships crashed into one another during high-speed maneuvers aimed at intercepting the Philippine vessel, which was escorting civilian boats delivering aid to Filipino fishermen.[23] Commodore Jay Tarriela, spokesperson for the Philippine Coast Guard, reported that the collision occurred when "the CCG 3104, which was chasing the BRP Suluan at high speed, performed a risky maneuver from the vessel's starboard quarter, leading to the impact with the PLA Navy warship."[24] The Chinese coast guard vessel sustained substantial damage to its forecastle, rendering it temporarily unseaworthy.

Rather than acknowledge the embarrassing mishap, China responded by significantly increasing its naval and coast guard presence around the shoal. By mid-August 2025, seven Chinese coast guard vessels and 13 maritime militia ships were deployed near Scarborough, vastly outnumbering the single Philippine vessel in the area.[25] Alexander Lopez, spokesperson for the Philippines' National Maritime Council, characterized the buildup as "one of their ways to twist what happened because that was very embarrassing for them, and they want to project again that they're in control to cover up the issue."[26]

Philippine President Ferdinand Marcos Jr. responded to these incidents with a public commitment to continued presence: "Our patrol vessels would continue to be present in the area to defend and exercise Manila's sovereign rights over what it considers to be part of its territory."[27] This declaratory policy represents a significant hardening of the Philippine position—a determination not to cede ground in the face of Chinese pressure.

The air dimension of the confrontation at Scarborough has become equally concerning. Between August 2024 and May 2025, at least four dangerous aerial encounters occurred near the shoal, including an incident in which a Chinese J-16 fighter jet dropped flares in the path of a Philippine Air Force aircraft.[28] In October 2025, Chinese forces deployed maritime security officers, additional fighter jets, and new buoys to Scarborough following Philippine fishery support missions, while conducting military exercises just 17 nautical miles from the shoal.[29] The People's Liberation Army Air Force has frequently deployed combat aircraft from bases, carriers, and artificial islands to conduct intercepts and establish air superiority over the contested feature.

In September 2025, Beijing escalated further by formally declaring the Huangyan Island (Scarborough Shoal) a national nature reserve, providing a legal pretext for even greater Chinese control under the guise of environmental protection.[30] The Philippine government immediately protested this unilateral action, recognizing it as another step toward normalizing Chinese control over a feature that lies squarely within Philippine maritime jurisdiction.

The intensifying confrontations around Scarborough create a constant risk of escalation. With vessels operating in close proximity, aggressive maneuvers becoming routine, and nationalist sentiment running high in both capitals, the potential for an incident to spiral beyond the control of either government is disturbingly real. As a 2025 report by the Asia Maritime Transparency Initiative warned, "The confluence of increasingly frequent aerial encounters and maritime interactions near Scarborough Shoal inevitably increases the chance of accidental escalation between the Philippines and China."[31]

ASEAN's Impossible Balancing Act: Consensus in the Face of Coercion

The Association of Southeast Asian Nations finds itself in an impossible position on the South China Sea disputes. Four of its ten member states—the Philippines, Vietnam, Malaysia, and Brunei—are direct claimants with competing territorial claims against China. Indonesia, while not officially a claimant, faces Chinese incursions in the waters around its Natuna Islands. Yet ASEAN operates on the principle of consensus, requiring unanimous agreement for collective action, giving any single member effective veto power over regional policy.

China has exploited this structural vulnerability masterfully, cultivating close relationships with non-claimant states like Laos and Cambodia that reliably block any ASEAN statements critical of Chinese behavior. The result has been a paralysis of regional diplomacy precisely when unity would be most valuable. As Southeast Asian states watch Chinese coast guard vessels harass their fishing fleets, China builds military installations on disputed features, and the risk of armed conflict grows, ASEAN has proven unable to speak with one voice or take meaningful collective action.

The centerpiece of ASEAN's diplomatic efforts has been the long-running negotiations with China on a Code of Conduct (COC) in the South China Sea. These talks, which began in earnest in 2018 following the adoption of a non-binding Declaration on the Conduct of Parties in 2002, represent ASEAN's attempt to establish rules of the road that might constrain Chinese assertiveness and reduce the risk of conflict.[32] Progress, however, has been glacial, and fundamental disagreements remain unresolved more than two decades after the initial declaration.

In July 2023, ASEAN and China agreed on guidelines to accelerate COC negotiations, committing to complete a binding code within three years.[33] This timeline, repeated optimistically by ASEAN officials through 2024 and 2025, has proven unrealistic. Philippine Foreign Secretary Enrique Manalo acknowledged in April 2025 that while parties remain "politically committed" to concluding the code by 2026, "We still have to address important issues such as the scope of the code, also the nature of the code and its relation also to the declaration of the principles adopted in 2002."[34]

The core disagreements are profound and likely irreconcilable without significant compromise from Beijing. China has proposed provisions that would require parties to notify each other before conducting joint military exercises with external powers and to obtain no-objection from all parties before proceeding—effectively giving Beijing veto power over ASEAN states' security cooperation with the United States, Japan, Australia, or other partners.[35] Vietnam has rejected this formulation, proposing instead a simple notification requirement 60 days before exercises, but China has not budged from its maximalist position.

The geographic scope of any code remains similarly contested. Should it apply only to the Spratly Islands, where most claimants have overlapping claims, or to the entire area within China's nine-dash line, which covers nearly 80 percent of the South China Sea? And critically, would a code of conduct be legally binding with enforcement mechanisms, or merely a political commitment with no real teeth? These fundamental questions have defied resolution despite years of negotiations.

ASEAN Secretary-General Kao Kim Hourn has attempted to maintain optimism, repeatedly calling on "all the direct parties concerned to exercise restraint" while acknowledging that "we cannot deny the fact that the situation continues to escalate."[36] The disconnect between diplomatic aspirations and ground truth could not be clearer. Even as ASEAN diplomats shuttle between meetings, Chinese dredgers fill in reefs, coast guard vessels harass fishing boats, and military aircraft conduct threatening intercepts.

Individual ASEAN states have pursued their own responses to Chinese pressure, often in ways that undermine collective action. The Philippines has deepened its alliance with the United States and pursued legal remedies through international arbitration. Vietnam has quietly expanded its own island-building program while seeking to balance relations with Beijing and Washington. Malaysia and Brunei have generally kept their disputes with China at low intensity, prioritizing economic ties. Singapore, though not a claimant, has advocated for upholding international law and freedom of navigation while hosting U.S. military facilities.

This fragmentation plays directly into China's hands. By cultivating bilateral relationships with individual ASEAN states and offering targeted economic incentives or applying selective pressure, Beijing has effectively prevented the formation of a unified regional response to its expansionism. The Belt and Road Initiative, with its promises of infrastructure investment, provides both carrot and stick—states that cooperate on China's terms receive investment and diplomatic support, while those that resist face economic retaliation and heightened maritime pressure.

U.S. Deputy Secretary of State Kurt Campbell, speaking at the Stimson Center in 2024, urged ASEAN to "send an unmistakable message about concerns with respect to provocations in what are clearly Philippine waters."[37] But ASEAN's institutional limitations make such unified messaging nearly impossible. The bloc remains, in the words of one academic observer, chronically challenged by "the lack of unity amid member countries' diverse positions."[38]

The tragedy of ASEAN's paralysis is that the organization's relevance is being steadily eroded by its inability to address the defining security challenge in its own neighborhood. As external powers—the United States, China, Japan, India, Australia—increasingly shape security outcomes through bilateral partnerships and minilateral groupings like the Quad, ASEAN risks becoming a talking shop rather than the central pillar of regional order it aspired to be. The Code of Conduct negotiations, far from demonstrating ASEAN centrality, may ultimately reveal the limits of ASEAN's diplomatic approach in the face of determined great power assertiveness.

Freedom of Navigation: Symbolic Gestures or Strategic Necessity?

Since 2016, the United States has dramatically increased its Freedom of Navigation Operations (FONOPs) in the South China Sea, regularly dispatching warships through waters claimed by China to challenge what Washington characterizes as "excessive maritime claims."[39] These operations, conducted under the banner of upholding international law and the principle of free navigation, have become a defining feature of the U.S. approach to the South China Sea disputes.

According to the U.S. State Department, the United States has conducted over 45 FONOPs in the Indo-Pacific since 2017, with China consistently being the primary target.[40] In fiscal year 2024, China had more maritime claims challenged by U.S. forces than any other country, with American vessels and aircraft contesting Chinese requirements for prior permission for the innocent passage of foreign naval vessels through territorial seas, challenging historic rights claims within the nine-dash line, and demonstrating freedom of navigation near China's artificial islands.[41]

The operational pattern is now well-established: U.S. Navy destroyers transit within 12 nautical miles of Chinese-occupied features, assert their right to innocent passage, and then exit the area. Chinese vessels routinely shadow these operations, with the People's Liberation Army Navy and China Coast Guard vessels maintaining close proximity and sometimes engaging in dangerous maneuvers. On August 13, 2025, for example, Chinese forces reported expelling the USS Higgins destroyer after it conducted a FONOP near Scarborough Shoal, shortly after the collision between Chinese vessels in the same area.[42]

The effectiveness of these operations is hotly debated. Supporters argue that FONOPs serve critical purposes beyond their immediate tactical impact. They reinforce the principle that international waters remain open to all nations, prevent Chinese claims from solidifying into accepted customary international law through acquiescence, demonstrate American commitment to regional security, and provide operational experience in contested waters that would be crucial in any conflict scenario.

Critics, however, question whether FONOPs have achieved their strategic objectives. A comprehensive 2025 study by Australian researcher Nell Bennett found that "the seven-year FONOP program has seen China go from measured rejection of U.S. messages to more explicit hostility."[43] Rather than deterring Chinese expansion, the operations may have inadvertently legitimized Chinese militarization by creating a pretext for enhanced defensive measures. Beijing has responded to increased FONOPs not by moderating its claims but by accelerating the construction and militarization of artificial islands, deploying more coast guard vessels, and conducting larger-scale military exercises.

The operations also carry inherent risks. Close-quarters maneuvering between warships in contested waters creates opportunities for miscalculation or accidents that could escalate rapidly. In June 2023, a Chinese warship conducted what U.S. officials called an "unsafe maneuver" in the Taiwan Strait, cutting directly across the bow of the USS Chung-Hoon and forcing the destroyer to slow to avoid collision.[44] Such incidents, while not resulting in actual collisions, demonstrate how thin the margin for error has become.

A fundamental tension in the FONOP program lies in the fact that the United States, despite being the principal champion of UNCLOS and freedom of navigation, has never ratified the convention. China exploits this inconsistency to question American credibility as a defender of the "rules-based order." As Chinese officials regularly point out, how can Washington claim to be upholding international law when it refuses to formally accede to the very legal framework it invokes?[45]

The Trump 2.0 administration has maintained continuity with the Biden administration's FONOP policy, signaling bipartisan consensus on this approach. European allies have also begun conducting their own freedom of navigation operations, with France, Germany, the United Kingdom, and others dispatching naval vessels through the South China Sea as part of their Indo-Pacific engagement strategies.[46] The French aircraft carrier Charles de Gaulle conducted extensive operations in the region during its five-month deployment from late 2024 through spring 2025, participating in exercises with regional partners and demonstrating European interest in maintaining open sea lanes.[47]

Yet the fundamental question remains: are these operations merely symbolic demonstrations, or do they contribute meaningfully to deterring Chinese expansion and maintaining regional stability? The answer likely depends on whether they are part of a broader, coherent strategy that includes alliance strengthening, military capability development, and diplomatic engagement, or whether they are isolated gestures disconnected from achievable policy goals. As one defense analyst observed, "FONOPs are not designed to stop Chinese aggression. They are there to demonstrate to Beijing that the U.S. maintains the right to sail in international waters and challenges China's illegal claims to territory."[48]

The proliferation of FONOPs by multiple countries—the United States, United Kingdom, France, Germany, Canada, Australia, New Zealand, and Japan have all conducted operations in recent years—does suggest a collective pushback against Chinese maritime expansion. But Beijing has shown no indication that these naval patrols will cause it to moderate its territorial claims or cease its island-building activities. The fundamental reality is that FONOPs, while important for establishing precedent and demonstrating resolve, cannot by themselves reverse Chinese control of disputed features or prevent further militarization.

The Hidden Competition: Resources Beneath the Waves

While military posturing and sovereignty disputes dominate headlines, the competition for the South China Sea's natural resources provides much of the underlying motivation for the intensity of the territorial conflicts. According to the U.S. Energy Information Administration, the sea contains proven and probable reserves of 190 trillion cubic feet of natural gas and 11 billion barrels of oil, with the U.S. Geological Survey estimating potential undiscovered resources of another 160 trillion cubic feet of natural gas and 12 billion barrels of oil.[49] For energy-hungry nations like China, Vietnam, and the Philippines, access to these hydrocarbon reserves represents a critical component of energy security.

The geographic distribution of oil and gas reserves compounds the political complications. Most proven reserves lie along the margins of the South China Sea in relatively shallow waters that fall within the uncontested exclusive economic zones of coastal states. Vietnam's Nam Con Son project, for example, supplies approximately 10 percent of the country's total energy needs from fields located in its southern waters.[50] Brunei's Southwest Ampa natural gas field accounts for more than half the country's natural gas reserves and production.[51]

The more speculative reserves lie in deeper waters and in areas where territorial claims overlap—precisely the locations where resource competition is most likely to trigger conflict. China National Offshore Oil Corporation (CNOOC) has been particularly aggressive in asserting drilling rights in disputed areas, often placing rigs in waters claimed by Vietnam or the Philippines. In 2014, CNOOC's deployment of a deepwater drilling rig in Vietnamese-claimed waters near the Paracel Islands triggered massive anti-Chinese protests in Vietnam and a tense maritime standoff.[52] By 2025, CNOOC was producing 286,790 barrels per day of crude oil and 709.1 million cubic feet per day of natural gas from fields in the western and eastern South China Sea areas.[53]

The environmental cost of hydrocarbon extraction in the South China Sea has been severe. Seismic surveys cause noise pollution that disrupts marine life dependent on auditory cues. Drilling operations dispose of toxic slurry comprising mud, cuttings, and drilling fluids directly into the ocean. Oil spills and gas leaks, while less publicized than major disasters elsewhere, occur with disturbing regularity. Combined with the destruction wrought by island-building, the industrialization of the South China Sea has pushed the marine ecosystem toward potential collapse.[54]

Even more critical than hydrocarbons are the sea's fisheries, which provide food security and livelihoods for hundreds of millions of people across Southeast Asia. The South China Sea hosts at least 3,365 species of marine fish, and 55 percent of global marine fishing vessels operate in these waters.[55] For coastal communities across the Philippines, Vietnam, Malaysia, Indonesia, and China, fishing is not merely an economic activity but a way of life passed down through generations.

Yet the fisheries are in crisis. Fish stocks have declined by 70 to 90 percent since the 1950s due to overfishing, destructive fishing practices including cyanide and dynamite fishing, and habitat destruction.[56] The territorial disputes exacerbate this ecological disaster by preventing the establishment of effective regional fisheries management. In the absence of agreed boundaries and enforcement mechanisms, fishing fleets operate with impunity, while coast guard vessels focus on sovereignty enforcement rather than sustainable resource management.

China's distant-water fishing fleet, the world's largest, has been particularly destructive. Numbering in the thousands of vessels, many of them dual-purpose ships that function as both fishing boats and maritime militia, the Chinese fleet systematically depletes fishing grounds across the South China Sea and beyond.[57] Filipino, Vietnamese, Malaysian, and Indonesian fishermen report being driven from traditional fishing grounds by Chinese vessels, often backed by coast guard ships that use the presence of fishing boats to assert sovereignty claims.

The weaponization of fisheries as a tool of geopolitical competition represents one of the more insidious aspects of the South China Sea disputes. By deploying maritime militia disguised as fishing vessels—an estimated 300 Chinese militia vessels operate around the Spratly Islands at any given moment[58]—Beijing asserts control while maintaining plausible deniability. Vietnam has responded in kind, with nearly 8,000 Vietnamese fishing vessels hosting militia units.[59] The result is a gray zone competition in which ostensibly civilian fishing boats conduct quasi-military missions, creating dangerous situations that could escalate into armed conflict.

Beneath the waves lies yet another dimension of resource competition: the undersea cables that carry 99 percent of global internet and telecommunications traffic. The South China Sea contains a dense network of fiber-optic cables connecting Asia to the rest of the world. As digital infrastructure becomes increasingly critical to economic activity, military operations, and social cohesion, control over cable routes and landing stations has emerged as a key strategic consideration.

China's 2025 unveiling of a deep-sea cable-cutting ship capable of severing armored cables at depths up to 4,000 meters sent shockwaves through the telecommunications industry.[60] The vessel, developed by the China Ship Scientific Research Centre, uses a diamond-coated grinding wheel spinning at 1,600 rpm and can operate at depths exceeding most cable infrastructure. While Chinese scientists claimed the technology would support "marine resource development," security experts immediately recognized its potential for gray zone warfare—the ability to disrupt communications in contested areas while maintaining plausible deniability.[61]

The vulnerability of undersea cables has already been demonstrated in the South China Sea. Disruptions to cables serving Taiwan's offshore islands, linked to Chinese vessels operating under deceptive identities, have raised concerns about deliberate sabotage.[62] China has also tightened permit requirements for cable laying and repair within its claimed nine-dash line, creating delays that frustrate infrastructure development and maintenance. Permits that once took 10 days to approve now require up to four months, with some applications rejected outright with minimal justification.[63]

Vietnam has been particularly affected by these restrictions. With five aging cables experiencing repeated failures that slow internet traffic, Hanoi desperately needs to replace obsolete infrastructure and build new capacity to support its growing digital economy. The United States has been urging Vietnam to avoid using Chinese companies for cable construction and repair, offering technical support and financing alternatives, but the practical challenges of operating in the South China Sea without Chinese cooperation are substantial.[64]

The economic implications of cable disruptions are staggering. With ASEAN countries adding approximately 125,000 new internet users daily and the regional digital economy expected to add $1 trillion to regional GDP over the next decade, reliable digital infrastructure is essential for economic development.[65] Any prolonged disruption of undersea cables, whether through deliberate sabotage, collateral damage in a conflict, or bureaucratic obstruction, could inflict severe economic damage across the region.

The geopolitical competition over cables has led to a bifurcation of digital infrastructure. New cables like Echo and Apricot, owned by Meta and Google, are being routed around the South China Sea entirely, passing through the Java Sea to avoid Chinese-claimed waters despite the dramatically higher costs.[66] This circumvention of the most direct routes reflects the growing unwillingness of technology companies to accept the political risks associated with operating in contested waters—but it also increases costs, reduces redundancy, and makes the overall system more vulnerable to disruptions elsewhere.

The South China Sea's resource competition thus encompasses three interconnected dimensions: hydrocarbons that fuel national development, fisheries that sustain millions of livelihoods, and digital infrastructure that enables modern economies. In each domain, competing sovereignty claims interact with resource scarcity to create potentially explosive situations. The absence of agreed frameworks for resource sharing or cooperative management means that competition is zero-sum, with each state seeking to maximize its own access while denying access to rivals.

The Cauldron at Boiling Point

As 2025 draws to a close, the South China Sea has become a cauldron where multiple pressures interact to create a combustible mixture. China's artificial islands provide the infrastructure for sustained military presence and power projection across the entire sea. The Philippines' deepening defense cooperation with the United States, symbolized by NMESIS deployments and large-scale exercises, signals Manila's determination to resist Chinese pressure. Scarborough Shoal has emerged as the most dangerous flashpoint, where repeated confrontations between coast guard vessels and maritime militia could spark a wider conflict. ASEAN's diplomatic efforts remain paralyzed by internal divisions and Chinese manipulation of consensus decision-making.

Freedom of navigation operations by the United States and its allies continue with increasing frequency, but without deterring Chinese expansion or meaningfully constraining Beijing's freedom of action. Resource competition—for hydrocarbons, fisheries, and control of digital infrastructure—provides powerful incentives for aggressive behavior even as it threatens environmental catastrophe and economic disruption.

The fundamental dynamic is one of Chinese consolidation of control through fait accompli tactics—building islands that cannot be removed without war, deploying military forces that shift the correlation of forces, and creating "facts on the water" that over time may acquire the patina of legitimacy through sheer persistence. The United States and its regional partners pursue a strategy of resistance through alliance strengthening, military presence, and legal challenges, but struggle to reverse Chinese gains or prevent further expansion.

For ASEAN states caught between the great powers, the choices are increasingly binary and unpalatable. Align closely with the United States and gain security guarantees but risk Chinese economic retaliation and becoming a proxy in great power competition. Accommodate Chinese demands and preserve economic ties but accept the erosion of sovereignty and maritime rights. The middle ground that most prefer—maintaining good relations with both powers while preserving strategic autonomy—is being steadily squeezed out of existence by the intensification of U.S.-China rivalry.

The most unsettling aspect of the South China Sea competition is the absence of any credible mechanism for de-escalation or conflict resolution. The Code of Conduct negotiations appear increasingly like diplomatic theater—a process that continues because abandoning it would be an admission of failure, but one unlikely to produce meaningful constraints on behavior. The 2016 arbitral tribunal ruling, while legally decisive, has been ignored by China and lacks any enforcement mechanism. Bilateral negotiations between claimants have repeatedly broken down in the face of fundamental disagreements about sovereignty and maritime rights.

What remains, then, is a competition of attrition in which each side seeks to impose costs on rivals while avoiding escalation to armed conflict. China probes Philippine positions around Second Thomas Shoal and Scarborough Shoal, testing Manila's resolve and American commitment. The United States conducts freedom of navigation operations and deploys increasingly sophisticated military capabilities to the Philippines and across the region. Vietnam quietly builds its own artificial islands while pursuing hedging strategies between Washington and Beijing. Fishermen from all countries continue to work traditional fishing grounds, sometimes harassed by coast guard vessels, sometimes caught in the crossfire of geopolitical competition.

The risk in this situation is not that any party deliberately chooses war—none of the claimant states or external powers appears to desire armed conflict in the South China Sea. The risk is that an incident spirals beyond the control of governments, that nationalist pressures force leaders into positions from which they cannot back down, or that a collision between vessels or aircraft triggers a cycle of escalation that proves impossible to contain.

The collision between Chinese vessels while pursuing the Philippine Coast Guard vessel in August 2025 offers a sobering preview of how such escalation might unfold. Had the collision involved a Philippine vessel rather than two Chinese ships, would Beijing have blamed Manila and demanded compensation? Would Philippine public opinion have compelled President Marcos to respond forcefully? Would the United States have been pressured to demonstrate support for its treaty ally? The fact that we cannot confidently answer "no" to any of these questions reveals how precarious the situation has become.

The South China Sea cauldron continues to boil, with the temperature steadily rising. Whether the competing pressures can be managed indefinitely without boiling over into open conflict remains one of the defining questions of Indo-Pacific security. The answer will depend on the judgment of leaders in Beijing, Manila, Hanoi, Washington, and other capitals, on the ability of militaries and coast guards to avoid incidents at sea, and on whether diplomacy can eventually find formulas for accommodation that preserve essential interests without requiring either side to accept humiliation.

For now, the situation remains suspended in a dangerous equilibrium—not quite peace, not yet war, but a permanent state of maritime contestation in which the risk of catastrophic miscalculation is ever-present. The nine-dash line and the principles of international law remain irreconcilable, China's artificial islands are facts that cannot be wished away, and the competition for resources and strategic advantage continues unabated. The South China Sea cauldron boils on, and the world watches nervously, aware that a single misstep could plunge the region into the very conflagration that all profess to want to avoid.

Endnotes

[1] Govella, Kristi, "Avoiding and exploiting the tragedy of the commons: fishing, crime, and conflict in the South China Sea," *International Politics* 60, no. 6 (2023): 1294–1314; U.S. Energy Information Administration, "Regional Analysis Brief: South China Sea," March 21, 2024, https://www.eia.gov/international/content/analysis/regions_of_interest/South_China_Sea/south_china_sea.pdf.

[2] Asia Maritime Transparency Initiative, Center for Strategic and International Studies, "China Tracker," accessed December 2025, https://amti.csis.org/island-tracker/china/; U.S. Department of Defense, *Military and Security Developments Involving the People's Republic of China 2016*, Annual Report to Congress (Washington, DC: Department of Defense, May 2016).

[3] International Business Times, "Satellite images reveal China has built new military facilities on South China Sea's Spratly islands," June 30, 2017, https://www.ibtimes.co.uk/satellite-images-reveal-china-has-built-new-military-facilities-south-china-seas-spratly-islands-1628461; Asia Maritime Transparency Initiative, multiple reports on island construction 2015-2017.

[4] Radio Free Asia, "New photos show China's artificial islands are highly developed military bases," June 4, 2025, https://www.rfa.org/english/news/southchinasea/china-artificial-islands-10312022043801.html.

[5] *Newsweek*, "Satellite Photos Show China Turning Artificial Island Into Military Base," August 28, 2025, https://www.newsweek.com/satellite-photos-artificial-island-mischief-reef-south-china-sea-2120562.

[6] TIME, "China Adds Basketball Courts to Artificial South China Sea Islands," May 23, 2016, https://time.com/4341510/south-china-sea-artificial-islands/.

[7] Ibid.; Radio Free Asia, "New photos show China's artificial islands are highly developed military bases."

[8] Asia Maritime Transparency Initiative, "Scaling Up: Vietnam's Islands (and Harbors) Continue to Grow," March 21, 2025, https://amti.csis.org/scaling-up-vietnams-islands-and-harbors-continue-to-grow/; *Newsweek*, "New Satellite Images Reveal More Artificial Islands in South China Sea," August 25, 2025, https://www.newsweek.com/satellite-images-vietnam-artificial-islands-south-china-sea-2118629.

[9] Asia Maritime Transparency Initiative, "Massive Island-Building and International Law," June 15, 2015, https://amti.csis.org/massive-island-building-and-international-law/.

[10] Wikipedia, "Scarborough Shoal," accessed November 2025, https://en.wikipedia.org/wiki/Scarborough_Shoal.

[11] U.S. Indo-Pacific Command, "U.S. Marine Corps, joint force deploy NMESIS to Batanes for Exercise Balikatan 2025," April 26, 2025, https://www.pacom.mil/Media/NEWS/News-Article-View/Article/4168430/; DVIDS News, "U.S. Marine Corps, joint force deploy NMESIS to Batanes for Exercise Balikatan 2025," April 26, 2025, https://www.dvidshub.net/news/496275/.

[12] Ibid.

[13] Radio Free Asia, "China, ASEAN 'committed' to having legally binding sea code by 2026: Manila," April 25, 2025, https://www.rfa.org/english/southchinasea/2025/04/25/south-china-sea-code-of-conduct/.

[14] GMA News Online, "US deploys NMESIS missile system during Balikatan 2025," April 27, 2025, https://www.gmanetwork.com/news/topstories/nation/944101/; GMA News Online, "NMESIS missile system now in PH for Balikatan 2025 — AFP," April 15, 2025, https://www.gmanetwork.com/news/topstories/nation/942792/.

[15] *Philstar.com*, "Balikatan 2025: NMESIS missile system now in the Philippines," April 15, 2025, https://www.philstar.com/headlines/2025/04/15/2436258/; *Asia Times*, "US-Philippine largest-ever drills bristle with missiles aimed at China," May 2, 2025, https://asiatimes.com/2025/04/.

[16] *Stars and Stripes*, "Marines' new ship-killer missile to debut in Philippines with upcoming Balikatan exercise," April 1, 2025, https://www.stripes.com/theaters/asia_pacific/2025-04-01/nmesis-philippines-balikatan-hegseth-17327183.html.

[17] *Naval News*, "Philippines Challenges Chinese Forces at Scarborough Shoal," November 2025, https://www.navalnews.com/naval-news/2025/11/.

[18] DVIDS News, "U.S. Marine Corps, joint force deploy NMESIS to Batanes for Exercise Balikatan 2025."

[19] Wikipedia, "Scarborough Shoal," accessed November 2025; Wikipedia, "Scarborough Shoal standoff," accessed October 2025.

[20] Ibid.

[21] Asia Maritime Transparency Initiative, "Holding the Line: China's Expanding Patrols around Scarborough Shoal," June 16, 2025, https://amti.csis.org/holding-the-line-chinas-expanding-patrols-around-scarborough-shoal/.

[22] Ibid.

[23] *Al Jazeera*, "China says it expels Philippine vessels near Scarborough Shoal," August 11, 2025, https://www.aljazeera.com/news/2025/8/11/; *Maritime Fairtrade*, "Philippines rules out navy deployment to Scarborough Shoal as tensions with China escalate," August 20, 2025, https://maritimefairtrade.org/.

[24] Ibid.

[25] *South China Morning Post*, "Philippines reports Chinese ship surge at Scarborough Shoal after 'embarrassing' collision," August 19, 2025, https://www.scmp.com/week-asia/politics/article/3322361/.

[26] Ibid.

[27] *Al Jazeera*, "China says it expels Philippine vessels near Scarborough Shoal."

[28] *Stars and Stripes*, "Scarborough Shoal a growing flashpoint between China and Philippines, think tank says," June 17, 2025, https://www.stripes.com/theaters/asia_pacific/2025-06-17/.

[29] USNI News, "China Deploys Buoys, Security Officers to Scarborough Shoal Amid Philippine Drills," October 17, 2025, https://news.usni.org/2025/10/17/.

[30] Wikipedia, "Scarborough Shoal," accessed November 2025.

[31] *Stars and Stripes*, "Scarborough Shoal a growing flashpoint between China and Philippines, think tank says."

[32] ASEAN Main Portal, "Priority Areas of Cooperation," accessed December 2025, https://asean.org/; ASEAN Main Portal, "Declaration on the Conduct of Parties in the South China Sea," January 19, 2023, https://asean.org/declaration-on-the-conduct-of-parties-in-the-south-china-sea-2/.

[33] ANTARA News, "3-year deadline for South China Sea code of conduct," September 2, 2023, https://en.antaranews.com/news/292653/; Wilson Center, "What's Behind the New

China-ASEAN South China Sea Code of Conduct Talk Guidelines?" March 31, 2025, https://www.wilsoncenter.org/blog-post/.

[34] Radio Free Asia, "China, ASEAN 'committed' to having legally binding sea code by 2026: Manila."

[35] Radio Free Asia, "China, ASEAN unlikely to achieve Code of Conduct in 2024: experts," June 4, 2025, https://www.rfa.org/english/news/southchinasea/code-of-coknduct-02072024014051.html.

[36] Voice of America, "ASEAN aims to conclude South China Sea code of conduct by 2026," June 13, 2024, https://www.voanews.com/a/asean-aims-to-conclude-south-china-sea-code-of-conduct-by-2026/7653984.html.

[37] Ibid.

[38] Radio Free Asia, "China, ASEAN unlikely to achieve Code of Conduct in 2024: experts."

[39] U.S. State Department, "The United States' Commitment to Maritime Security in the Indo-Pacific," September 23, 2025, https://www.state.gov/the-united-states-commitment-to-maritime-security-in-the-indo-pacific.

[40] Ibid.

[41] *Newsweek*, "Map shows where US challenged 'excessive' maritime claims," August 19, 2025, https://www.newsweek.com/map-show-where-us-challenged-excessive-maritime-claims-2115454; *Global Times*, "Chinese report challenges legality of US 'freedom of navigation' operations," August 25, 2025, https://www.globaltimes.cn/page/202508/1341650.shtml.

[42] *Global Times*, "Chinese report challenges legality of US 'freedom of navigation' operations."

[43] Radio Free Asia, "US Navy operations risk inflaming China tensions, study says," January 23, 2025, https://www.rfa.org/english/southchinasea/2025/01/22/us-china-freedom-of-navigation/.

[44] Ibid.

[45] Ibid.; John Quincy Adams Society, "A Reassessment of U.S. Freedom of Navigation Operations in the South China Sea," June 25, 2025, https://jqas.org/.

[46] Perry World House, University of Pennsylvania, "International Law and Conflict Disputes: The Case of the South China Sea," May 19, 2025, https://perryworldhouse.upenn.edu/.

[47] Ibid.

[48] Radio Free Asia, "US Navy operations risk inflaming China tensions, study says."

[49] U.S. Energy Information Administration, "Regional Analysis Brief: South China Sea," March 21, 2024, https://www.eia.gov/international/content/analysis/regions_of_interest/South_China_Sea/south_china_sea.pdf; Asia Maritime Transparency Initiative, "South China Sea Energy Exploration and Development," March 8, 2023, https://amti.csis.org/south-china-sea-energy-exploration-and-development/.

[50] Asia Maritime Transparency Initiative, "A Blueprint for Cooperation on Oil and Gas Production in the South China Sea," October 11, 2018, https://amti.csis.org/a-blueprint-for-cooperation-on-oil-and-gas-production-in-the-south-china-sea/.

[51] U.S. Energy Information Administration, "Regional Analysis Brief: South China Sea."

[52] Observer Research Foundation, "Troubled waters: Marine ecology threats in the South China Sea," June 18, 2021, https://www.orfonline.org/research/troubled-waters-marine-ecology-threats-in-the-south-china-sea; Purnomo Yusgiantoro Center, "The Importance of the South China Sea: Energy Perspective," April 28, 2025, https://www.purnomoyusgiantorocenter.org/.

[53] Observer Research Foundation, "Troubled waters: Marine ecology threats in the South China Sea."

[54] Ibid.

[55] Fridtjof Nansen Institute, "Fish, not oil, at the heart of the South China Sea conflict," accessed December 2025, https://www.fni.no/news/fish-not-oil-at-the-heart-of-the-south-china-sea-conflict-article1556-330.html.

[56] Ibid.

[57] Stimson Center, "Militarized Commons: How Territorial Competition is Weaponizing Fisheries and Destroying the South China Sea," September 8, 2025, https://www.stimson.org/2025/territorial-competition-weaponizing-fisheries-south-china-sea/.

[58] Ibid.

[59] Ibid.

[60] Center for Strategic and International Studies, "China's Underwater Power Play: The PRC's New Subsea Cable-Cutting Ship Spooks International Security Experts," July 16, 2025, https://www.csis.org/analysis/chinas-underwater-power-play-prcs-new-subsea-cable-cutting-ship-spooks-international.

[61] Pacific Forum, "China's Cable-Cutting Threat in the South China Sea," June 2, 2025, https://pacforum.org/publications/.

[62] Ibid.

[63] *The Washington Post*, "Rising tension in South China Sea disrupts Asia's subsea cable system," October 2, 2024, https://www.washingtonpost.com/world/2024/10/03/south-china-sea-underwater-cables/.

[64] Ibid.; Voice of America, "Undersea cables emerge as source of friction in South China Sea," October 12, 2024, https://www.voanews.com/a/undersea-cables-emerge-as-source-of-friction-in-south-china-sea/7819426.html.

[65] Bloomsbury Intelligence and Security Institute, "Territorial Claims and Subsea Cables: The Geopolitics of Invisible Lines in the South China Sea," March 4, 2025, https://bisi.org.uk/reports/.

[66] Ibid.; Carnegie Endowment for International Peace, "Subsea Communication Cables in Southeast Asia: A Comprehensive Approach Is Needed," December 2024, https://carnegieendowment.org/research/2024/12/southeast-asia-undersea-subsea-cables.

Chapter 15
The Broader Indo-Pacific Chessboard

Alliances, Alignments, and the Quad

The Indo-Pacific security architecture is undergoing its most profound transformation since the end of the Cold War. While previous chapters examined bilateral flashpoints like Taiwan and the South China Sea, the broader regional chessboard reveals a complex web of evolving alliances, strategic partnerships, and diplomatic alignments that will shape the trajectory of U.S.-China competition for decades to come. At the center of this transformation lies a fundamental question: Can a disparate network of democratic partners counter China's systematic bilateral approach to regional influence?

The answer is emerging through multiple parallel developments—the nuclear submarine partnership known as AUKUS, the reinvigorated Quadrilateral Security Dialogue, Japan's historic defense reorientation, India's delicate balancing act, and South Korea's increasingly precarious position between Washington and Beijing. Together, these elements are creating what U.S. officials describe as a "latticework" of overlapping partnerships, a marked departure from the traditional hub-and-spoke alliance system that has defined American security architecture in Asia since 1945.

AUKUS and the Submarine Dimension

On September 15, 2021, the leaders of Australia, the United Kingdom, and the United States announced a partnership that would fundamentally alter the strategic balance in the Indo-Pacific.[1] The trilateral security pact, known as AUKUS, committed to transferring nuclear-powered submarine technology to Australia—a capability possessed by only six nations worldwide: the United States, United Kingdom, Russia, China, France, and India.[2] The scale and ambition of the arrangement signaled a new phase in Western efforts to counter China's military expansion in the region.

The submarine component of AUKUS, formally designated as Pillar One, represents Australia's largest-ever defense project, with Canberra committing A$368 billion (approximately $239 billion) over three decades.[3] The pathway announced in March 2023 charts a carefully sequenced approach: beginning in 2027, up to four U.S. Virginia-class submarines and one British Astute-class submarine will rotate through the HMAS Stirling naval base in Western Australia.[4] Between 2032 and 2035, the United States will sell Australia three to five Virginia-class submarines.[5] The ultimate goal envisions Australia building its own SSN-AUKUS submarines at Osborne in South Australia, with the first Australian-built nuclear submarine entering service in the early 2040s.[6]

The strategic logic driving AUKUS extends beyond submarine acquisition. Placing U.S. Virginia-class submarines in Western Australia positions the submarine fleet closer to the strategic Indian Ocean than the forward operating base of Guam, providing faster response times to the South China Sea.[7] For a U.S. Navy struggling to meet submarine production targets—currently producing approximately 1.2 boats per year against a requirement of 2.0 or more—the forward positioning offers significant strategic benefits even as it raises questions about America's capacity to fulfill its commitments.[8]

These capacity concerns have not been merely theoretical. In June 2025, the Pentagon announced a comprehensive review of AUKUS, stating the initiative must align with President Trump's "America First" agenda and ensure readiness of U.S. forces.[9] The fundamental challenge persists: submarines are a scarce, critical commodity, and questions remain about selling boats to Australia when the U.S. Navy itself faces shortfalls.[10]

Australia has responded by pledging $3 billion to help expand U.S. submarine production capacity, with $2 billion of that amount delivered in 2025.[11] In September 2025, Prime Minister Anthony Albanese announced an initial investment of A$12 billion ($7.99 billion) in the Henderson Defence Precinct near Perth, creating facilities to support maintenance of U.S. and Royal Navy submarines—a tangible demonstration that AUKUS represents more than a one-way transfer of technology.[12] The Henderson facility will provide depot-level maintenance capabilities and contingency docking for nuclear submarines, potentially serving as a maintenance hub for U.S. and UK vessels operating in the Indian Ocean.[13]

The second pillar of AUKUS focuses on advanced technological cooperation in quantum computing, artificial intelligence, hypersonics, cyber capabilities, and undersea systems.[14] By September 2024, the three AUKUS partners announced they were consulting with Canada, New Zealand, and South Korea about potential collaboration under Pillar Two, with Japan also exploring opportunities to improve interoperability in maritime autonomous systems.[15] This expansion beyond the core three members reflects both the breadth of technological challenge and the desire to build a more resilient network of partnerships.

In August 2024, the three AUKUS partners signed a formal agreement on naval nuclear propulsion cooperation, enabling the transfer of submarine-specific material and equipment from the UK and US to Australia.[16] The agreement, tabled in the Australian Parliament, establishes the legal framework for Australia's acquisition of nuclear-powered submarines while upholding the highest standards for safety, security, and non-proliferation.[17] In July 2025, the UK and Australia signed a 50-year bilateral AUKUS partnership treaty to establish the strategic and operational framework for submarine design, build, and delivery.[18]

China's response to AUKUS combined diplomatic protest with strategic adaptation. Beijing characterized the arrangement as nuclear proliferation and a manifestation of "Cold War mentality," with Chinese foreign ministry spokesperson Wang Wenbin warning that the three countries are walking "further and further down the path of error and danger."[19] The formation of AUKUS has spurred exactly the military competition it was designed to deter—a dynamic that will define Indo-Pacific security for the coming decade.

The Quad's Evolution from Talk Shop to Strategic Alignment

The Quadrilateral Security Dialogue—comprising Australia, India, Japan, and the United States—has traveled a long and uncertain path from its origins in disaster relief coordination to its current status as a cornerstone of Indo-Pacific strategy. The Quad first emerged informally in response to the 2004 Indian Ocean tsunami, when the four nations coordinated humanitarian assistance. Formally established in 2007 by Japanese Prime Minister Shinzo Abe, the grouping quickly went dormant when Australia withdrew in 2008 amid concerns about antagonizing China.[20]

The Quad's revival in 2017 reflected fundamentally changed circumstances. China's military assertiveness, particularly its island-building campaign in the South China Sea and increasingly aggressive behavior along the Line of Actual Control with India, created new imperatives for regional cooperation. The COVID-19 pandemic accelerated this convergence, with the four partners coordinating on vaccine production and distribution.[21]

The transformation reached a critical milestone on September 21, 2024, when President Joseph Biden hosted the fourth in-person Quad Leaders' Summit in Wilmington, Delaware.[22] The meeting produced the Wilmington Declaration and launched several substantive initiatives that moved the grouping beyond rhetorical commitments into operational cooperation. Among the most significant developments:

Maritime Security: The establishment of the Maritime Initiative for Training in the Indo-Pacific (MAITRI) and the announcement of the first-ever Quad-at-Sea Ship Observer Mission planned for 2025 to enhance interoperability and advance maritime safety.[23] These initiatives aim to improve coast guard cooperation and maritime domain awareness.

Health Security: The Quad Cancer Moonshot Initiative targeting cervical cancer elimination, building on the partnership's earlier COVID-19 vaccine coordination established through the Quad Health Security Partnership launched in 2023.[24]

Infrastructure Development: The Quad Ports of the Future Partnership, designed to coordinate investment and share best practices in port infrastructure development across the Indo-Pacific, with the inaugural Regional Ports and Transportation Conference scheduled for Mumbai in 2025.[25]

Technology Cooperation: A Memorandum of Cooperation to facilitate collaboration in addressing semiconductor supply chain risks and the establishment of the Quad Investors Network (QUIN) to facilitate quantum technology collaboration.[26]

Climate Resilience: Expansion of Early Warning Systems, with the United States providing 3D-printed automatic weather stations to Pacific Island countries while Australia enhances capabilities through Weather Ready Pacific and Japan strengthens cooperation under its Pacific Climate Resilience Initiative.[27] Quad partners committed over $140 million to undersea cable builds in the Pacific, with investments aimed at helping all Pacific island countries achieve primary telecommunication cable connectivity by the end of 2025.[28]

The scope and substance of these initiatives reflect the Quad's maturation into a multi-dimensional partnership addressing economic, technological, health, and security challenges. Critically, the Quad has avoided the treaty obligations that characterize formal military alliances, preserving flexibility while building practical cooperation.

This evolution has been particularly significant for India. As Prime Minister Narendra Modi stated at the 2024 summit: "Our meeting is taking place at a time when the world is surrounded by tensions and conflicts. In such times, it is very important for humanity that the Quad works together on the foundation of shared democratic values."[29] Modi emphasized that the Quad supports a rule-based international order, respect for sovereignty and territorial integrity, and peaceful resolution of all issues—with a free, open, inclusive, and prosperous Indo-Pacific as the shared priority and commitment.[30]

The January 21, 2025, Quad Foreign Ministers' meeting in Washington, held on Secretary of State Marco Rubio's first day in office, underscored continuity across U.S. administrations.[31] The joint statement reaffirmed commitment to a "free and open Indo-Pacific" and opposition to "any unilateral actions that seek to change the status quo by force or coercion."[32] President Trump expressed interest in attending the next Quad Leaders' Summit in India later in 2025, with the United States scheduled to host the 2025 Quad Foreign Ministers Meeting while India hosts the 2025 Leaders Summit.[33]

Yet the Quad faces inherent limitations. Unlike NATO, it has no integrated military command, no Article 5-style mutual defense commitment, and no formal institutional structure beyond annual leaders' summits and ministerial meetings. Its effectiveness depends entirely on sustained political will from four democracies with different strategic cultures, threat perceptions, and domestic political dynamics.

Japan's Defense Transformation

Japan's security posture has undergone a revolution so profound that it represents a fundamental departure from seven decades of post-World War II pacifism. The transformation reflects both the severity of the threats Japan faces—a nuclear-armed North Korea, an increasingly assertive Russia, and China's military expansion—and a generational shift in Japanese political consciousness about the requirements of national defense.

In December 2022, Prime Minister Kishida Fumio's government released three landmark documents: a new National Security Strategy, a National Defense Strategy, and a Defense Buildup Program. These documents committed Japan to doubling defense spending to 2 percent of GDP by 2027, bringing Japanese defense expenditure in line with NATO standards—a dramatic increase from the unofficial 1 percent ceiling that had constrained defense policy since 1976.[34] The government in 2022 set this target of spending 2 percent of GDP for defense, with the understanding that Japan faces "the most severe and complex security environment since the end of World War II."[35]

The fiscal impact has been immediate and substantial. On December 27, 2024, Japan's cabinet approved a record ¥8.7 trillion ($55.1 billion) defense budget for fiscal year 2025, marking the thirteenth consecutive annual increase and representing a 9.4 percent rise from the previous year.[36] Including U.S. Forces realignment-related expenses, the draft budget rises by $4.8 billion from the current fiscal year.[37] The five-year Defense Buildup Program through fiscal 2027 totals approximately $273 billion.[38]

The allocation of these resources reveals Japan's strategic priorities. The fiscal 2025 budget dedicates ¥939 billion ($5.92 billion) to "standoff defense capabilities"—precision long-range weapons that can strike targets beyond the range of enemy anti-air missiles.[39] This includes procurement of ground-launched and sea-launched Type 12 anti-ship missiles, hyper-velocity gliding projectiles for island defense, submarine-launched missiles, and U.S.-made Tomahawk cruise missiles for deployment on Japan's Aegis destroyers.[40] The Ministry of Defense secured $11.4 million to equip the Japan Maritime Self-Defense Force destroyer Chokai with the capability to launch Tomahawk cruise missiles, with deployment planned for all eight Aegis destroyers step by step.[41]

Perhaps most symbolically, Japan is converting its two Izumo-class helicopter carriers—JS Izumo and JS Kaga—into aircraft carriers capable of operating Lockheed Martin F-35B stealth fighters.[42] The Defense Ministry earmarked $11.4 million to continue modifying these vessels, which represents Japan's first operation of aircraft carriers since World War II.[43] During fiscal year 2024, JS Izumo underwent conversion of the bow section of its flight deck from a trapezoid into a square shape, with JS Kaga having completed the same modifications during fiscal year 2023.[44]

Japan's strategic relationships are expanding to match its growing military capabilities. In January 2022, Japan and Australia signed a Reciprocal Access Agreement (RAA), Japan's first such agreement in Asia, establishing a framework for mutual military training and operations.[45] In 2024, Japan signed a similar RAA with the Philippines, creating a legal foundation for Japanese forces to directly support Manila during crises in the South China Sea—Japan's first such agreement in Asia focused on Southeast Asia.[46]

In July 2024, then-Secretary of Defense Lloyd Austin announced a significant upgrade to U.S. Forces Japan (USFJ), reconstituting it as a joint force headquarters with enhanced operational command authority—a structure parallel to U.S. Forces Korea.[47] Japan committed to establishing its own Joint Operations Command to improve interoperability and coordination between U.S. and Japanese forces.[48]

Yet Japan's defense transformation faces significant challenges. The country struggles with a shrinking defense industrial base and difficulty attracting sufficient personnel to the Self-Defense Forces despite increased spending.[49] Grant Newsham, senior research fellow at the Japan Forum for Strategic Studies, noted that "decades of pathological dependence" on the United States have left Japan's military "a stunted force not really able to operate efficiently or effectively in most cases."[50] The 2024 Defense of Japan white paper stated that "Japan is facing the most severe and complex security environment since the end of World War II," with concerns about China's intrusions into Japan's southwestern archipelago and North Korea's nuclear and missile threats.[51]

India's Strategic Autonomy and Its Limits

India occupies a unique and increasingly uncomfortable position in the emerging Indo-Pacific order. As the world's most populous nation and fastest-growing major economy, with a $4 trillion GDP, India possesses considerable strategic weight.[52] Its labor force of 600 million and average age of 29 make it a lucrative market that businesses worldwide are eager to access.[53] Yet New Delhi's long-standing commitment to "strategic autonomy"—a policy of maintaining equidistance between major powers and preserving maximum flexibility—faces unprecedented strain as U.S.-China competition intensifies.

The doctrine of strategic autonomy has deep historical roots. During the Cold War, India was a founding member of the Non-Aligned Movement, seeking to avoid entanglement in superpower rivalry. In the post-Cold War era, India has pursued strategic autonomy through what officials describe as "multi-alignment"—developing partnerships with multiple powers while refusing formal allegiance to any bloc.[54] The principle of strategic autonomy, rooted in sovereignty and independence, enables New Delhi to make foreign policy decisions free from external influence, allowing pursuit of national interests in an increasingly multipolar and complex world.[55]

This approach has provided significant advantages. When China-India relations deteriorated following the deadly Galwan Valley border clashes in June 2020, New Delhi deepened cooperation with Washington through upgraded engagement in the Quad and other mechanisms.[56] Yet India simultaneously maintained its participation in BRICS and the Shanghai Cooperation Organization (SCO), where Chinese interests play a major role.[57] As External Affairs Minister S. Jaishankar stated at the Munich Security Conference in 2024, India should be "admired for maintaining multiple options" in its foreign policy.[58]

The sustainability of this balancing act is increasingly questionable. China and the United States are India's two largest trading partners, and both are vital to India's economic growth.[59] Yet as these superpowers move further apart, India finds itself caught in the middle. The Trump administration's imposition of 50 percent tariffs on India in 2025, punishing the country for its trade imbalance and purchases of Russian crude oil, illustrated the costs of strategic autonomy.[60] Other countries with larger trade surpluses with the United States or greater dependence on Russian energy were not targeted to the same degree because of their importance to global supply chains or their status as U.S. alliance partners—revealing India's lack of strategic indispensability.[61]

India's approach to potential Taiwan contingencies exemplifies these tensions. Public opinion in India reveals considerable reluctance to take sides in potential great power conflicts, with the focus primarily on avoiding entanglement in escalating U.S.-China rivalry and preventing India from becoming collateral damage in a broader contest.[62]

The challenge extends beyond economics to fundamental questions of strategic orientation. India's continued purchase of Russian military equipment and energy complicates deeper integration with Western partners.[63] Prime Minister Modi's visit to Russia in 2024, planned visits by Vladimir Putin to India, and the likelihood that Chinese President Xi Jinping will attend the BRICS summit when India hosts demonstrate New Delhi's determination to maintain relationships across multiple camps.[64]

Yet the strategic logic of India's position increasingly points toward closer alignment with the United States and its partners. The October 2024 border agreement between India and China to manage their disputed frontier, while welcome, does not resolve the fundamental conflict of interests between the two Asian giants.[65] China's Belt and Road Initiative, its deepening partnership with Pakistan, and its expanding presence in the Indian Ocean all pose direct challenges to Indian interests.[66]

The semiconductor partnership announced during Modi's September 2024 visit to the United States, which will establish a fabrication plant to provide chips in 2025, and the agreement facilitating India's purchase of 31 MQ-9B Sky Guardian and Sea Guardian drones signal the depth of potential U.S.-India technological cooperation.[67] These concrete initiatives suggest that strategic autonomy may be evolving into a more nuanced form of selective alignment.

India is already diversifying its trade with Southeast Asia and gradually exploring techno-cooperation beyond Silicon Valley.[68] These maneuvers do not mean India is tilting towards China, but they reflect a shift in mindset—New Delhi is not looking for patrons but trying to widen its margin of autonomy in a world where great powers increasingly view economic tools as instruments of dominance.[69] This represents not a return to non-alignment, but an evolution into what Indian policymakers call "multi-alignment with leverage."[70]

South Korea's Difficult Position

Few U.S. allies face a more acute dilemma than South Korea. The country simultaneously confronts an existential threat from nuclear-armed North Korea, depends on the United States for extended deterrence and approximately 28,500 troops stationed on the peninsula, and maintains China as its largest trading partner.[71] This triangular dependency has generated a long-standing South Korean adage: "economy with China, security with the United States." The intensification of U.S.-China competition is rendering this comfortable division increasingly untenable.

The evolution of South Korea's China policy illustrates the pressures Seoul faces. China's retaliation against South Korea's 2016 decision to host the U.S. Terminal High-Altitude Area Defense (THAAD) missile system—including measures targeting South Korean tourism, retail, and entertainment industries—demonstrated Beijing's willingness to use economic coercion as a strategic tool.[72] Many of these punitive measures remain in effect. Yet China accounted for 25 percent of South Korean exports (including Hong Kong) in 2024, valued at $168 billion, while 23 percent of South Korea's imports also came from China, worth $139 billion.[73]

The economic relationship is more nuanced than simple dependency suggests. South Korea's semiconductor exports to China totaled over 51 percent of the country's semiconductor shipments in 2024, but Chinese firms buy South Korean semiconductors because they need them—Chinese chipmakers remain at least two or three generations behind South Korean, Taiwanese, and U.S. competitors, and U.S. sanctions prevent advanced chip sales to China.[74] The relationship is better characterized as one of asymmetric interdependence rather than South Korean dependency.[75]

Moreover, South Korea's economic geography is shifting. The United States became South Korea's top foreign investment destination in 2023, attracting a record 43.7 percent of the country's total overseas investment as South Korean firms sought to capitalize on the U.S. Inflation Reduction Act and CHIPS and Science Act incentives.[76] In 2023, South Korea's investment in the United States was almost 15 times bigger than its investment in China.[77] South Korea emerged as the biggest foreign investor in the United States in 2024 with $21.5 billion in investment.[78] South Korea's exports to the United States have surged from around 12-13 percent to 18.7 percent of total exports in 2024, while exports to China have declined from around 25 percent to 19.5 percent.[79] The trade balance with China flipped dramatically from a surplus of $44.3 billion in 2017 to a deficit of $6.4 billion in 2024.[80]

Security cooperation has deepened in parallel with economic reorientation. The August 18, 2023, Camp David summit between President Biden, Prime Minister Kishida, and President Yoon Suk Yeol institutionalized trilateral cooperation among the United States, Japan, and South Korea.[81] The historic summit—the first-ever standalone summit of leaders from the three countries—jointly inaugurated a new era of trilateral partnership.[82] The leaders committed to annual trilateral meetings at multiple levels, including leaders, foreign ministers, defense ministers, and national security advisors, along with multi-year, annual, named, multi-domain trilateral military exercises.[83]

South Korea released an Indo-Pacific strategy positioning itself as a "global pivotal state" and emphasizing engagement with democratic partners.[84]

Yet this alignment toward the United States and its partners generated significant domestic opposition. The political crisis that engulfed South Korea beginning in December 2024—when President Yoon briefly declared martial law before being impeached—produced profound uncertainty about the country's strategic direction.[85] The opposition Democratic Party (DPK), which gained power following Yoon's removal, criticized his policies on North Korea, China, Russia, and Japan.[86] DPK leader Lee Jae-myung, elected president in June 2025, represents a more progressive foreign policy orientation that emphasizes engagement with China and restraint regarding Taiwan.[87]

Lee's positions have already influenced South Korea's trajectory. Public opinion reveals the constraints: in 2024 polling, 53.3 percent of Koreans wanted no involvement if war occurred over Taiwan with U.S. participation, with only 15.6 percent supporting providing weapons and ammunition and 5.9 percent supporting sending combat troops.[88] Lee has proposed pursuing "strategic autonomy"—using language that echoes India's approach and signals a desire to maintain equidistance between Washington and Beijing.[89]

The Trump administration's approach to South Korea will significantly shape Seoul's options. In November 2024, the two countries concluded a new cost-sharing agreement covering 2026-2030, with South Korea agreeing to increase its 2025 payment by 8.3 percent to roughly $1.19 billion in 2026, with future annual increases tied to South Korea's consumer price index and capped at 5 percent.[90] Yet Trump's transactional approach to alliances generates anxiety. During the first Trump Administration, cost-sharing talks collapsed, leading to months-long lapse in agreement and furloughs of Korean workers on U.S. bases.[91]

Since March 2025, President Trump has eliminated all country exemptions and product exclusions to steel import tariffs imposed in 2018, raising them from 25 percent to 50 percent—affecting South Korea, which was the fourth-largest source of U.S. steel imports in 2024 at $2.9 billion.[92] In April 2025, Trump implemented a 25 percent tariff on passenger vehicles, light trucks, and automobile parts, which in 2024 accounted for 37 percent of U.S. goods imports from South Korea.[93] The Trump Administration has initiated trade investigations into semiconductors, pharmaceuticals, and critical minerals that may affect major South Korean industries.[94]

The fundamental reality is that South Korea, like other middle powers in the Indo-Pacific, increasingly recognizes it cannot simply choose between the United States and China. Every Korean president, whether liberal or conservative, has sought strong ties with the United States while recognizing the necessity of living with China—none have embraced containment or economic decoupling, preferring pragmatic coexistence.[95]

The Latticework Architecture Versus China's Bilateral Approach

The transformation of Indo-Pacific security architecture over the past five years represents a conscious departure from the hub-and-spoke alliance system that has defined U.S. regional strategy since 1945. Under that traditional model, the United States maintained separate bilateral alliances with Japan, South Korea, Australia, the Philippines, and Thailand, with security cooperation channeled through Washington as the central hub. U.S. allies had strong ties with the United States but often weak or non-existent defense cooperation with each other.[96]

The Biden administration articulated a different vision, described as a "latticework" of partnerships—"an integrated, interconnected network of partnerships" where allies and partners develop direct security relationships that complement rather than replace the U.S. alliance system.[97] Secretary of State Antony Blinken, Secretary of Defense Lloyd Austin, and National Security Adviser Jake Sullivan jointly explained that the United States had long had one-to-one partnerships and alliances with other Indo-Pacific countries, but was now transforming this approach to create a more networked architecture.[98]

The latticework manifests through multiple overlapping groupings: the U.S.-Japan-South Korea trilateral formalized at Camp David; the U.S.-Japan-Philippines trilateral launched in April 2024; the U.S.-Japan-Australia trilateral; AUKUS (with potential for Pillar Two expansion); and the Quad.[99] Beyond U.S.-anchored arrangements, new bilateral partnerships are emerging: Japan's Reciprocal Access Agreements with Australia and the Philippines enable Japanese troops and equipment to directly support partner nations during crises.[100]

The strategic logic is compelling. A latticework structure enhances deterrence by closing off opportunities for China to isolate individual countries through coercion, deepens institutional cooperation across multiple governments, and ensures Beijing must consider the response of a larger coalition to any aggressive action.[101] The development of multilateral defense partnerships among U.S. allies and partners creates a more complex, interwoven network of security relationships with multiple nodes of coordination and capability.[102]

The operational benefits extend beyond deterrence. In a protracted conflict, distributed partnerships enable force dispersal across multiple locations, improving survivability.[103] The Philippines has expanded its partnership with South Korea, which recently elevated relations to a strategic level.[104] The proliferation of new security arrangements bypasses Washington as the central coordinator, creating more direct bilateral and minilateral cooperation among regional powers.[105]

Yet the latticework approach faces significant challenges. Unlike NATO, which has agreed-upon frameworks, integrated command structures, and Article 5 mutual defense obligations, the Indo-Pacific latticework lacks institutional coherence.[106] Interoperability—the ability to act together coherently, effectively and efficiently—requires not just compatible communications systems but aligned strategic objectives.[107] Many Indo-Pacific partners acquire weapons from diverse suppliers, creating technical incompatibilities.[108] More fundamentally, the latticework depends on sustained political will from multiple democracies with different domestic political dynamics, any one of which could shift strategic direction following an election.

ASEAN countries watch the latticework with ambivalence. While Vietnam and the Philippines have integrated more deeply into new partnerships, the proliferation of minilateral groupings risks fragmenting ASEAN cohesion.[109] The Indo-Pacific Economic Framework also separates participating ASEAN members (Brunei, Indonesia, Malaysia, the Philippines, Singapore, Thailand, and Vietnam) from other members, with potential impacts on ASEAN unity.[110] A 2024 survey found that if forced to choose sides, Southeast Asian countries remain divided, with many preferring to maintain hedging strategies.[111]

China's approach to regional architecture operates on fundamentally different principles. Beijing eschews multilateral security arrangements in favor of bilateral relationships where it can leverage superior economic weight and proximity. China's bilateral framework allows differentiated approaches—offering infrastructure investment to some countries, market access to others—without the constraints of multilateral consensus.[112]

This bilateral approach offers Beijing significant advantages. It prevents the emergence of a unified opposing coalition by cultivating separate relationships calibrated to each country's specific vulnerabilities and interests. When the Philippines confronts China in the South China Sea, Beijing can maintain cooperative economic ties with Vietnam, Indonesia, and Malaysia, preventing a united ASEAN response. The bilateral model exploits the latticework's structural weakness—that it requires consensus among democracies with diverse interests.

The competition between these two models will define Indo-Pacific security for the coming decades. If the United States and its partners can sustain the latticework through periods of political transition, overcome interoperability challenges, and present a unified strategic vision, the architecture may prove more resilient than the sum of its parts. The distributed nature of the system means that individual nodes can be temporarily weakened without the entire structure collapsing.

Yet if the latticework fragments under pressure—whether from U.S. political disengagement, economic coercion by China, or simple erosion of political will—the Indo-Pacific may revert to a more familiar pattern of countries hedging between the superpowers. The resilience of the latticework has not yet been tested by a genuine crisis. The next five years will likely provide a definitive answer.

Endnotes

[1] Australian Government Department of Foreign Affairs, "Australia to Pursue Nuclear-Powered Submarines Through New Trilateral Enhanced Security Partnership," September 16, 2021, https://www.foreignminister.gov.au/minister/marise-payne/media-release/australia-pursue-nuclear-powered-submarines-through-new-trilateral-enhanced-security-partnership.

[2] Baird Maritime, "FACTBOX | Inside the AUKUS Submarine Deal Linking Australia, US and Britain," October 20, 2025, https://www.bairdmaritime.com/security/naval/naval-submersibles/factbox-inside-the-aukus-submarine-deal-linking-australia-us-and-britain.

[3] Ibid.

[4] Australian Submarine Agency, "AUKUS Agreement for Cooperation on Naval Nuclear Propulsion," accessed December 1, 2025, https://www.asa.gov.au/aukus/aukus-agreement-cooperation-related-naval-nuclear-propulsion.

[5] Australian Government Department of Defence, "Agreement Strengthens AUKUS Submarine Partnership," August 12, 2024, https://www.minister.defence.gov.au/media-releases/2024-08-12/agreement-strengthens-aukus-submarine-partnership.

[6] The White House, "FACT SHEET: Trilateral Australia-UK-US Partnership on Nuclear-Powered Submarines," March 13, 2023, https://bidenwhitehouse.archives.gov/briefing-room/statements-releases/2023/03/13/fact-sheet-trilateral-australia-uk-us-partnership-on-nuclear-powered-submarines/.

[7] Baird Maritime, "FACTBOX | Inside the AUKUS Submarine Deal."

[8] Defense News, "Pentagon to Review AUKUS Submarine Deal with Australia and Britain," June 11, 2025, https://www.defensenews.com/pentagon/2025/06/11/pentagon-to-review-aukus-submarine-deal-with-australia-and-britain/.

[9] Ibid.

[10] Ibid.

[11] Ibid.

[12] USNI News, "Australia Pledges $7.9B for Naval Project to Support AUKUS Subs," September 15, 2025, https://news.usni.org/2025/09/15/australia-pledges-7-9b-for-naval-project-to-support-aukus-subs.

[13] Ibid.

[14] UK House of Commons Library, "AUKUS Submarine (SSN-A) Programme," November 27, 2025, https://commonslibrary.parliament.uk/research-briefings/cbp-9843/.

[15] Ibid.

[16] Australian Government Department of Defence, "Agreement Strengthens AUKUS Submarine Partnership."

[17] Ibid.

[18] UK House of Commons Library, "AUKUS Submarine (SSN-A) Programme."

[19] Statista, "Chart: Only Six Countries Operate Nuclear Submarines," accessed December 1, 2025, https://www.statista.com/chart/29489/number-of-nuclear-powered-submarines-worldwide/.

[20] U.S. Embassy & Consulates in India, "Fact Sheet: 2024 Quad Leaders' Summit," September 23, 2024, https://in.usembassy.gov/fact-sheet-2024-quad-leaders-summit/.

[21] Ibid.

[22] The White House, "Fact Sheet: 2024 Quad Leaders' Summit," September 21, 2024, https://bidenwhitehouse.archives.gov/briefing-room/statements-releases/2024/09/21/fact-sheet-2024-quad-leaders-summit/.

[23] CSIS, "Experts React: Quad Leaders' Summit 2024," October 12, 2024, https://www.csis.org/analysis/experts-react-quad-leaders-summit-2024.

[24] The White House, "Fact Sheet: 2024 Quad Leaders' Summit."

[25] Ibid.

[26] Drishti IAS, "6th Quad Summit 2024," accessed December 1, 2025, https://www.drishtiias.com/daily-updates/daily-news-analysis/6th-quad-summit-2024.

[27] The White House, "Fact Sheet: 2024 Quad Leaders' Summit."

[28] Ibid.

[29] MyGov Blogs, "QUAD Summit 2024 Key Highlights and Information," accessed December 1, 2025, https://blog.mygov.in/editorial/quad-summit-2024-key-highlights-and-information/.

[30] Ibid.

[31] CNAS, "Quad: The Next Phase," August 5, 2025, https://www.cnas.org/publications/reports/quad.

[32] U.S. Department of State, "Joint Statement by the Quad Foreign Ministers," January 21, 2025, https://www.state.gov/joint-statement-by-the-quad-foreign-ministers/.

[33] The White House, "Fact Sheet: 2024 Quad Leaders' Summit."

[34] The Japan Times, "Japan Ups Defense Spending to 1.6% of GDP with Eye on 2027 Goal," April 29, 2024, https://www.japantimes.co.jp/news/2024/04/29/japan/politics/japan-defense-spending-gdp/.

[35] Stars and Stripes, "Japan in 2025 to Continue Record-Breaking Run of Increased Defense Spending," December 26, 2024, https://www.stripes.com/theaters/asia_pacific/2024-12-26/japan-defense-budget-general-atomics-2025-16289034.html.

[36] Defense News, "Japan Passes Record Defense Budget, While Still Playing Catch-Up," January 16, 2025, https://www.defensenews.com/global/asia-pacific/2025/01/16/japans-passes-record-defense-budget-while-still-playing-catch-up/.

[37] The Diplomat, "Japan Approves 9.4 Percent Increase in Defense Spending for FY2025," December 27, 2024, https://thediplomat.com/2024/12/japan-approves-9-4-percent-increase-in-defense-spending-for-fy2025/.

[38] Ibid.

[39] Stars and Stripes, "Japan in 2025 to Continue Record-Breaking Run."

[40] USNI News, "Japanese Cabinet Approves Record Defense Budget; China Launches New Amphibious Warship," December 27, 2024, https://news.usni.org/2024/12/27/japanese-cabinet-approves-record-defense-budget-china-launches-new-amphibious-warship.

[41] The Diplomat, "Japan Approves 9.4 Percent Increase in Defense Spending for FY2025."

[42] Ibid.

[43] Ibid.

[44] Ibid.

[45] The Diplomat, "The Latticework: Indo-Pacific Security Moves Beyond US Naval Primacy," April 18, 2025, https://thediplomat.com/2025/04/the-latticework-indo-pacific-security-moves-beyond-us-naval-primacy/.

[46] Ibid.

[47] Foreign Policy Research Institute, "Strengthening US Alliances in the Indo-Pacific," March 15, 2025, https://www.fpri.org/article/2025/03/strengthening-us-alliances-in-the-indo-pacific/.

[48] Ibid.

[49] Defense News, "Japan Passes Record Defense Budget."

[50] Ibid.

[51] Ibid.

[52] GIS Reports, "India's Multi-Alignment and Rising Geopolitical Profile," July 16, 2025, https://www.gisreportsonline.com/r/india-strategic-autonomy/.

[53] Ibid.

[54] RSIS, "Understanding India's Evolving Policy of Strategic Autonomy," accessed December 1, 2025, https://rsis.edu.sg/rsis-publication/idss/ip25015-understanding-indias-evolving-policy-of-strategic-autonomy/.

[55] GIS Reports, "India's Multi-Alignment and Rising Geopolitical Profile."

[56] Council on Foreign Relations, "India Between Superpowers: Strategic Autonomy in the Shadow of a Pacific Conflict," December 16, 2024, https://www.cfr.org/blog/india-between-superpowers-strategic-autonomy-shadow-pacific-conflict.

[57] Ibid.

[58] Foreign Policy, "India's Strategic Autonomy Doesn't Work In A Great Power World," November 26, 2025, https://foreignpolicy.com/2025/11/26/india-end-strategic-autonomy/.

[59] Council on Foreign Relations, "India Between Superpowers."

[60] Foreign Policy, "India's Strategic Autonomy Doesn't Work."

[61] Ibid.

[62] Council on Foreign Relations, "India Between Superpowers."

[63] RSIS, "Understanding India's Evolving Policy of Strategic Autonomy."

[64] Foreign Policy, "India's Strategic Autonomy Doesn't Work."

[65] GIS Reports, "India's Multi-Alignment and Rising Geopolitical Profile."

[66] RSIS, "Understanding India's Evolving Policy of Strategic Autonomy."

[67] The Diplomat, "Modi in the US: India's Pursuit of Strategic Autonomy," September 25, 2024, https://thediplomat.com/2024/09/modi-in-the-us-indias-pursuit-of-strategic-autonomy/.

[68] Atlas Institute for International Affairs, "India-China-US: A New Strategic Triangle?" October 17, 2025, https://atlasinstitute.org/india-china-us-a-new-strategic-triangle/.

[69] Ibid.

[70] Ibid.

[71] Congress.gov, "South Korea: Background and U.S. Relations," accessed December 1, 2025, https://www.congress.gov/crs-product/IF10165.

[72] NPR, "How U.S.-China Tensions Leave Countries Like South Korea Stuck in the Middle," November 2, 2025, https://www.npr.org/2025/11/02/nx-s1-5594836/us-china-tensions-south-korea-stuck-in-middle.

[73] Foreign Policy, "South Korea Shows How Middle Powers Can Compete With China," February 10, 2025, https://foreignpolicy.com/2025/02/10/south-korea-china-economy-diplomacy-trade/.

[74] Ibid.

[75] Ibid.

[76] PIIE, "Korea's Economy Faces Looming Challenges Amid Political Turmoil," January 17, 2025, https://www.piie.com/blogs/realtime-economics/2025/koreas-economy-faces-looming-challenges-amid-political-turmoil.

[77] Ibid.

[78] Ibid.

[79] Ibid.

[80] Ibid.

[81] The White House, "FACT SHEET: The Trilateral Leaders' Summit at Camp David," August 18, 2023, https://bidenwhitehouse.archives.gov/briefing-room/statements-releases/2023/08/18/fact-sheet-the-trilateral-leaders-summit-at-camp-david/.

[82] Ibid.

[83] Ibid.

[84] Brookings, "How Will South Korea Navigate US-China Competition in 2025?" January 22, 2025, https://www.brookings.edu/articles/how-will-south-korea-navigate-us-china-competition-in-2025/.

[85] Congress.gov, "South Korea: Background and U.S. Relations."

[86] CHINA US Focus, "Is South Korea Due for a U.S.-China Policy Reset?" May 14, 2025, https://www.chinausfocus.com/foreign-policy/is-south-korea-due-for-a-us-china-policy-reset.

[87] Ibid.

[88] The National Interest, "South Korea Will Not Choose Between the US and China," June 26, 2025, https://nationalinterest.org/blog/korea-watch/south-korea-will-not-choose-between-the-us-and-china.

[89] Congresswoman Young Kim, "Relations Between China and South Korea in 2024 Part 2: The Taiwan Issue," January 2, 2025, https://youngkim.house.gov/2024/12/07/relations-between-china-and-south-korea-in-2024-part-2-the-taiwan-issue/.

[90] Congress.gov, "South Korea: Background and U.S. Relations."

[91] Brookings, "How Will South Korea Navigate US-China Competition in 2025?"

[92] Congress.gov, "South Korea: Background and U.S. Relations."

[93] Ibid.

[94] Ibid.

[95] The National Interest, "South Korea Will Not Choose Between the US and China."

[96] The Diplomat, "The Latticework: Indo-Pacific Security Moves Beyond US Naval Primacy."

[97] East Asia Forum, "Washington Reinvents Its Approach to Southeast Asia," November 22, 2024, https://eastasiaforum.org/2024/11/22/washington-reinvents-its-approach-to-southeast-asia/.

[98] Ibid.

[99] The Asan Forum, "South Korea and Japan's Responses to the US Latticework for the Indo-Pacific System," May 13, 2025, https://theasanforum.org/south-korea-and-japans-responses-to-the-us-latticework-for-the-indo-pacific-system/.

[100] The Diplomat, "The Latticework: Indo-Pacific Security Moves Beyond US Naval Primacy."

[101] Wilson Center, "Filling in the Indo-Pacific Latticework in Southeast Asia – The US-Japan-Philippines Trilateral Summit," accessed December 1, 2025, https://www.wilsoncenter.org/blog-post/filling-indo-pacific-latticework-southeast-asia-us-japan-philippines-trilateral-summit.

[102] Foreign Policy Research Institute, "Strengthening US Alliances in the Indo-Pacific."

[103] Ibid.

[104] The Diplomat, "The Latticework: Indo-Pacific Security Moves Beyond US Naval Primacy."

[105] Ibid.

[106] Lowy Institute, "Interoperability: The Missing Link in Indo-Pacific Security," accessed December 1, 2025, https://www.lowyinstitute.org/the-interpreter/interoperability-missing-link-indo-pacific-security.

[107] Ibid.

[108] Ibid.

[109] East Asia Forum, "Washington Reinvents Its Approach to Southeast Asia."

[110] Ibid.

[111] Stimson Center, "Think Small to Win Big in the Indo-Pacific," February 18, 2025, https://www.stimson.org/2024/think-small-to-win-big-in-the-indo-pacific/.

[112] Perth USAsia Centre, "Navigating Indo-Pacific Alliances: A Shift Towards a Lattice Alliance System," accessed December 1, 2025, https://perthusasia.edu.au/research-and-insights/navigating-indo-pacific-alliances-a-shift-towards-a-lattice-alliance-system/.

Part VI

The Coming Biotech Wars

Chapter 16
The Next Technological Frontier

Why Biotech May Eclipse AI in Strategic Importance

While semiconductors and artificial intelligence dominate headlines in the U.S.-China technological rivalry, a quieter but potentially more consequential competition is intensifying in the realm of biotechnology. The convergence of biological sciences with artificial intelligence, coupled with China's coordinated two-decade push for biotech dominance, has created what national security experts describe as an existential challenge to American technological leadership—one that could prove decisive for the balance of power in the twenty-first century.

The Wake-Up Call: Harvard's Stark Assessment

In June 2025, the Harvard Belfer Center for Science and International Affairs delivered an assessment that sent ripples through Washington's national security establishment. After examining five critical technology sectors—artificial intelligence, biotechnology, semiconductors, space, and quantum computing—the Center concluded that of these strategic domains, China possesses "the most immediate opportunity to overtake the United States in biotechnology."[1]

This finding represented more than academic analysis. It crystallized growing concerns among defense planners, intelligence officials, and policymakers that while America obsessed over chip manufacturing and large language models, Beijing was systematically positioning itself to dominate the technologies that would define health, agriculture, manufacturing, and military capabilities for decades to come. The assessment was particularly striking given that biotechnology had received far less attention than AI in public discourse, despite its potentially transformative implications across nearly every sector of the economy and national security.

The Belfer Center's analysis highlighted China's unique advantages in pharmaceutical production and manufacturing capacity, a more extensive talent pool than the United States, and—critically—a regulatory environment described as "more flexible" with "the ability to push things out faster."[2] While the United States maintained leadership across all five technology domains examined, the narrow gap in biotechnology suggested that without decisive action, the global balance could shift rapidly.

Eric Rosenbach, director of the defense, emerging technology, and strategy program at Harvard's Belfer Center and former chief of staff at the U.S. Department of Defense, warned that cooperation between the United States and China on biotechnology was becoming increasingly unlikely precisely because of its strategic significance. "The likelihood there's going to be cooperation [between the] U.S. and China on anything is very low, in some ways least likely on biotech and AI," Rosenbach noted, predicting intensifying U.S. pressure on Chinese biotech capabilities.[3]

The timing of the Harvard assessment coincided with troubling indicators from America's traditional biotech hubs. Reports from Cambridge and Boston—the epicenter of U.S. biotechnology innovation—revealed layoffs and empty laboratories as venture capital dried up and companies struggled with regulatory hurdles and extended development timelines. Meanwhile, Beijing and Shanghai were experiencing explosive growth in laboratory and research space, with more capacity under construction than any other global markets by the end of 2024.[4]

The ChatGPT Moment That Must Not Happen

If the Harvard Belfer Center's report raised alarms, the April 2025 findings of the National Security Commission on Emerging Biotechnology (NSCEB) struck with the force of a strategic imperative. Established by Congress through the 2022 National Defense Authorization Act, this bipartisan commission spent two years conducting an exhaustive review of biotechnology's implications for national security, consulting with more than 1,800 stakeholders and examining both classified and unclassified materials.

The Commission's central warning was unequivocal: "There will be a ChatGPT moment for biotechnology, and if China gets there first, no matter how fast we run, we will never catch up."[5]

This stark formulation deliberately invoked OpenAI's November 2022 release of ChatGPT, which had demonstrated Chinese firms' ability to rapidly close technological gaps once breakthrough capabilities became apparent. The Commission's reference to a potential "ChatGPT moment" in biotechnology captured both the revolutionary potential of AI-enhanced biological engineering and the risk that China might achieve a transformative breakthrough that would establish dominance before the United States could respond.

The Commission's vice chair, Dr. Michelle Rozo, who had worked on biotechnology issues at the Pentagon, the National Security Council, and the CIA-backed investment agency In-Q-Tel, emphasized the existential nature of the challenge. "Here in America, we are struggling to get to this ChatGPT moment for biotech, all the while China is having a DeepSeek moment: They're out-innovating the US in this key technology," Rozo warned, drawing a parallel to Chinese AI firm DeepSeek's achievement of competitive performance with constrained resources.[6]

The Commission's assessment painted a sobering picture of American disadvantage: "China is quickly ascending to biotechnology dominance, having made biotechnology a strategic priority for 20 years. To remain competitive, the United States must take swift action in the next three years. Otherwise, we risk falling behind, a setback from which we may never recover."[7]

This three-year window represented the Commission's judgment about how long the United States retained any meaningful opportunity to alter current trajectories. Beyond that threshold, Chinese advantages in manufacturing capacity, talent pipelines, regulatory speed, and integrated industrial policy would likely prove insurmountable without extraordinary and potentially economically devastating interventions.

The $15 Billion Imperative

The National Security Commission's central recommendation was both straightforward and politically daunting: the U.S. government must invest a minimum of $15 billion over five years to support the domestic biotechnology sector's growth and capabilities.[8] This figure represented the Commission's calculation of the minimum investment required merely to remain competitive, not to restore American dominance.

The $15 billion would be distributed across multiple priorities, including approximately $1.2 billion channeled through Department of Defense appropriations for defense-specific applications.[9] The remaining funds would target critical gaps in the biotechnology ecosystem: pilot-scale biomanufacturing facilities to help companies transition from laboratory discoveries to commercial production; regulatory streamlining to accelerate the pathway from innovation to market; workforce development to train the next generation of biotechnology professionals; and strategic partnerships with allies to create resilient supply chains independent of Chinese dominance.

Senator Todd Young, the Commission's chairman, framed the investment as a choice between paying now or paying catastrophically more later. "We can either pay now or pay a lot more later," Young argued, citing the semiconductor industry as a cautionary tale. "We've already dealt with this with the CHIPS Act... we knew that there was no alternative to getting semiconductor production back to the United States, and we knew it would be costly—a hell of a lot more costly than had somebody made the requisite investment a number of years ago."[10]

The Commission specifically called for creating pathways to leverage private capital rather than relying solely on government funding. The $15 billion represented seed funding designed to de-risk investments, establish critical infrastructure like pre-commercial manufacturing facilities, and create market signals that would attract the trillions of dollars in private capital necessary to build a globally competitive biotechnology sector. The model drew inspiration from successful public-private partnerships in other sectors, particularly the CHIPS Act's approach to semiconductor manufacturing.

The investment recommendation faced immediate political headwinds. The Trump administration had ordered drastic cuts to research funding across federal agencies, including sweeping layoffs at the Food and Drug Administration and reductions in National Institutes of Health support precisely when the Commission argued for expanded investment.[11] Budget deficits, congressional gridlock, and philosophical opposition to industrial policy created formidable obstacles to the Commission's recommendations.

Yet the Commission members remained adamant that failure to invest would prove more costly than any budgetary outlay. "We're looking under seat cushions for additional monies," Young told reporters. "We didn't include second- or third-order priorities... This is what's needed to stay ahead. If you want the Chinese to get ahead of us, spend less."[12]

China's Methodical Twenty-Year Campaign

Understanding China's biotechnology ascendance requires recognizing it as neither sudden nor accidental, but rather the product of systematic state planning dating to the early 2000s. Beijing identified biotechnology as a strategic priority nearly two decades ago, recognizing that whoever dominated the biological sciences would possess advantages across agriculture, medicine, manufacturing, energy, and military capabilities.

The strategic framework emerged from multiple overlapping policy initiatives. The 2007 high-level support for biotechnology development was formalized through the "Made in China 2025" industrial policy released in 2015, which explicitly prioritized new chemical drugs, antibodies, antibody-drug conjugates, protein and polypeptide drugs, vaccines, personalized medicines, pluripotent stem cells, and medical devices.[13] This was followed by the "Healthy China 2030" blueprint and elevation of biopharma to national pillar industry status in the 14th Five-Year Plan covering 2021-2025.[14]

China's investment trajectory reflected this strategic commitment. Between 2008 and 2020, the Chinese government invested $3.8 billion in biotechnology research and development.[15] By 2015,

China's biopharmaceutical R&D investment stood at $35 million annually; by 2023, this had exploded to $15 billion.[16] Over the decade from 2016 to 2021, Chinese biopharma R&D grew 400-fold while the market value of Chinese biotech firms surged 100-fold, reaching a collective valuation of $300 billion.[17]

The scale of China's biotechnology industrial base grew correspondingly dramatic. By 2015, fewer than 350 innovative drugs were under development in China; by 2024, that number had risen to 1,250—a level surpassing Europe and rapidly approaching U.S. levels.[18] In 2024, China listed 7,100 clinical trials compared to 6,000 in the United States, marking the first time China surpassed America in this critical indicator of research activity and pharmaceutical innovation.[19]

Patent filings told a similar story of shifting technological momentum. According to GlobalData analysis, China filed 188,000 pharmaceutical patents in 2024 compared to 53,777 in the United States—a gap that widened steadily since 2020.[20] In synthetic biology, China had overtaken the United States as the top source of research. Whereas in 2010 researchers based in the United States published 45 percent of the most-cited papers in synthetic biology while those in China accounted for 13 percent, by 2024 China had become the leading source.[21]

Perhaps most significantly, China's biotechnology capabilities were producing tangible commercial results that Western pharmaceutical giants could not ignore. In September 2024, Chinese biotech firm Akeso announced that its immunotherapy drug ivonescimab had outperformed Merck's blockbuster cancer drug Keytruda in Phase III trials for non-small cell lung cancer, halting tumor progression for nearly a full year compared to Keytruda's six months.[22] While subsequent long-term results presented in September 2025 showed the drug failed to demonstrate significant benefit in overall survival, the initial achievement demonstrated that Chinese biotechnology firms could compete at the frontier of pharmaceutical innovation.[23]

China's 2026-2030 Blueprint: From Strategy to Execution

As China's 15th Five-Year Plan period approaches, covering 2026 through 2030, biotechnology features prominently in Beijing's vision for technological self-reliance and economic transformation. The plan explicitly identifies biotechnology—alongside quantum computing, artificial intelligence, fusion energy, and advanced materials—as a core component of "new quality productive forces" designed to drive China's transition from quantity-based growth to high-productivity, innovation-driven economic development.[24]

China's biotechnology strategy for 2026-2030 emphasizes several interconnected priorities. First, achieving self-sufficiency in critical biotechnology capabilities, particularly in areas where U.S.

export controls or potential future sanctions might create vulnerabilities. Second, establishing global leadership in emerging domains where Chinese firms can move faster than constrained Western competitors—including synthetic biology, AI-enhanced drug discovery, and agricultural biotechnology. Third, building manufacturing capacity at scale to produce biologics, vaccines, and advanced therapeutics more cheaply and rapidly than Western manufacturers.[25]

The plan specifically targets biomanufacturing as a "future industry" alongside advanced materials and digital intelligence, recognizing that whoever controls biomanufacturing capacity will possess enormous leverage over global health and agricultural security. Chinese authorities announced in December 2024 that biomanufacturing investment reached $4.17 billion in 2024 and was "poised for significant growth" through 2025 and beyond.[26]

Regional governments across China were actively implementing the national biotechnology vision through targeted incentives, infrastructure investments, and regulatory streamlining. Shanghai announced expanded funding for biotech ventures and positioned itself as an AI-enhanced drug discovery hub. Beijing's BioInternational Pharmaceutical Innovation Park brought together leading biotechs, research hospitals, and the National Medical Products Administration, creating an integrated ecosystem for rapid development and regulatory approval.[27] Innovation zones like BioBAY in Suzhou assembled talent, capital, and global partnerships under government coordination.[28]

The 15th Five-Year Plan also called for "extraordinary measures" to "seize the commanding heights of scientific and technological developments" through a "new-style whole of nation system" that would "concentrate resources to do great things."[29] This formulation signaled Beijing's intent to apply the full weight of state coordination, funding, and regulatory authority to achieve biotechnology objectives—an approach fundamentally different from the dispersed, market-driven model that had characterized U.S. biotechnology development.

The Dual-Use Dimension: When Biology Becomes Strategy

Biotechnology's strategic significance stems fundamentally from its dual-use nature—nearly every advance in agricultural productivity, disease treatment, or industrial biomanufacturing can be adapted for purposes ranging from biodefense to biological warfare. This inherent duality makes biotechnology competition simultaneously a race for economic advantage and a matter of existential national security.

Agricultural applications demonstrate the dual-use dilemma with particular clarity. Technologies to engineer crops for enhanced yield, drought resistance, or pest tolerance could equally be adapted to target food supplies, whether through enhanced plant pathogens or through genetic modifications that could contaminate agricultural systems.[30] Biopharming—the use of genetically modified plants or animals to produce pharmaceuticals or industrial compounds—could theoretically be repurposed to manufacture protein toxins or bioregulators at scale with minimal risk of detection, since genetically modified organisms often cannot be distinguished from natural variants without sophisticated testing.[31]

China's demonstrated interest in military applications of biotechnology heightened Western concerns about the dual-use implications of Beijing's biotech advancement. People's Liberation Army medical institutions had established themselves as major centers for research in gene editing, CRISPR technology, and other cutting-edge biotechnologies with obvious military applications.[32] PLA scientists investigated various applications of neurocognitive research, including enhanced mental agility, improved mobility, physical safety, and situational awareness for combatants.[33]

A 2016 doctoral dissertation from China's Academy of Military Medical Sciences, titled "Research on the Evaluation of Human Performance Enhancement Technology," characterized CRISPR-Cas9 as one of three primary technologies that might boost troops' combat effectiveness.[34] Zhang Shibo, former president of the PLA's National Defense University, wrote that modern biotechnology advances unlocked possibilities to create synthetic pathogens that are "more toxic, more contagious, and more resistant" than naturally occurring agents.[35]

The potential military applications extended beyond human enhancement or bioweapons. Synthetic biology could enable production of rare materials, chemicals, or compounds currently dependent on complex supply chains. Advances in understanding neural pathways and brain-computer interfaces—areas where China's state-backed research was advancing rapidly—could revolutionize command and control systems, human-machine teaming, or even cognitive warfare capabilities designed to manipulate perception and decision-making.[36]

Western intelligence assessments concluded that the Chinese military was actively exploring these possibilities. The U.S. State Department's 2025 Arms Control Compliance Report stated that "the United States has compliance concerns with respect to Chinese military medical institutions' toxin research and development because of the potential dual-use applications and their potential as a biological threat."[37] The assessment noted that China's 14th Five-Year Plan for Bioeconomy Development identified DNA sequencing, gene editing, and synthetic biology as cutting-edge biotechnologies—all possessing clear dual-use potential.

The CRISPR revolution particularly concerned biosecurity experts. CRISPR-Cas9 gene editing technology, which earned its developers the 2020 Nobel Prize in Chemistry, had democratized genetic engineering—making sophisticated genetic modifications achievable with relatively modest equipment and expertise. A 2018 National Academies of Sciences report commissioned by the U.S. military to assess synthetic biology weapons potential warned that CRISPR could be introduced into viruses to cut human DNA and cause cancer, while modified organisms might be used to target agricultural systems or create novel pathogens.[38]

The dual-use dilemma created profound policy challenges. Restricting access to biotechnology capabilities would slow beneficial applications in medicine and agriculture while potentially proving futile given the global distribution of knowledge and equipment. Yet allowing unfettered development risked enabling adversaries to achieve breakthroughs with catastrophic implications. The challenge was further complicated by the reality that defensive research—attempting to understand potential threats and develop countermeasures—often looked identical to offensive research developing those very threats.

The Convergence: AI Meets Biology

The intersection of artificial intelligence with biotechnology represents what the National Security Commission on Emerging Biotechnology described as a potential inflection point—a "ChatGPT moment for biotechnology" that could fundamentally alter the pace and scope of biological innovation. AI's ability to process vast datasets, predict molecular interactions, and design novel proteins or genetic sequences promises to collapse timelines from discovery to application, potentially reducing development cycles from years to months or even weeks.[39]

AI-enhanced drug discovery was already producing tangible results. In June 2025, British pharmaceutical giant AstraZeneca announced a $5.2 billion deal with China's CSPC Pharmaceutical Group to access CSPC's AI-powered drug discovery platform and portfolio of preclinical cancer drugs.[40] The platform used artificial intelligence to analyze binding patterns of target proteins with existing compound molecules, with AI models determining targeted optimization to advance small molecules with the best developability characteristics.[41]

French pharmaceutical giant Sanofi had entered a $1.7 billion agreement with Helixon-backed Earendil Labs for two antibody candidates for autoimmune and inflammatory bowel diseases discovered through proprietary AI platforms.[42] These deals represented the leading edge of a broader transformation: by the first half of 2025, Chinese companies accounted for 32 percent of global biotech licensing deal value versus 21 percent in both 2023 and 2024, with much of this growth driven by AI-enhanced discovery capabilities.[43]

The convergence of AI and biotechnology created capabilities that would have seemed impossible mere years earlier. Generative AI could propose novel molecular structures faster than any human researcher, after which AI simulations could model the biochemistry of hypothetical compounds to predict which might actually produce desired therapeutic effects—all before synthesizing anything in a physical laboratory. This digital-first approach dramatically reduced the cost and time of early-stage drug discovery while enabling exploration of vastly larger design spaces than traditional methods allowed.[44]

China possessed several structural advantages in the AI-biotechnology convergence. First, massive datasets: China's large population, centralized health system, and more permissive data collection policies enabled Chinese researchers to train AI systems on datasets that dwarfed those available in fragmented Western health systems. Second, regulatory flexibility: China's more streamlined approval processes and willingness to accept higher levels of risk in early trials enabled faster iteration between computational design and clinical validation. Third, manufacturing integration: Chinese biotechnology firms' close integration with manufacturing capacity enabled rapid scale-up of promising compounds discovered through AI, whereas Western firms often faced bottlenecks translating laboratory success to commercial production.[45]

The implications extended beyond pharmaceuticals. AI-enhanced synthetic biology could revolutionize biomanufacturing, enabling biological production of materials, chemicals, and energy sources traditionally derived from petroleum or mining. Agricultural biotechnology powered by AI could dramatically accelerate development of crops optimized for specific climate conditions, soil types, or nutritional profiles. Medical applications might enable truly personalized medicine, with treatments designed for individual patients' genetic profiles and disease characteristics.

Yet the same capabilities that promised revolutionary benefits also created unprecedented risks. AI tools that could design therapeutic proteins could equally design toxic ones. Systems that optimized crops could optimize pathogens. The automation and acceleration that made AI-biotechnology convergence so powerful also made it more accessible to actors with malicious intent or insufficient biosafety protocols.

"Previously, some experts have argued that oversight of the digital-to-physical divide will be sufficient to reduce many biosecurity risks because the digital information produced by biological models is harmless by itself," noted a 2025 analysis by the Council on Strategic Risks. "However, the rapid developments in AI-enabled biotechnology are casting doubt on this assertion, with many arguing for stronger risk mitigation of this divide."[46] The same report warned that "autonomous AI agents optimized for scientific discovery will soon become commonplace in the life sciences, bringing with them vast efficiencies and cost savings, as well as increased biosafety and biosecurity risks."[47]

Manufacturing: The Hidden Battleground

While much attention focused on discovery and innovation, the biotechnology competition's outcome might ultimately hinge on an unsexy but critical factor: manufacturing capacity. Whoever could produce biologics, vaccines, advanced therapeutics, and bio-manufactured materials at scale, speed, and low cost would possess enormous economic and strategic leverage—regardless of where innovations originated.

China had systematically built manufacturing advantages that Western firms found increasingly difficult to match. Chinese contract research organizations (CROs) and contract development and manufacturing organizations (CDMOs) offered capabilities that Western pharmaceutical companies found irresistible: costs roughly 30 percent below typical market valuations, faster timelines from development to manufacturing, and increasingly sophisticated technical capabilities.[48] By 2024, approximately 79 percent of U.S. pharmaceutical companies depended on Chinese contract firms for some aspect of manufacturing.[49]

The dependency extended beyond finished products. Up to 90 percent of widely used medications in the United States, including basic drugs like ibuprofen and acetaminophen, relied on Chinese active pharmaceutical ingredients or manufacturing.[50] For many antibiotics, China provided the only commercial-scale manufacturing capacity available globally. In the event of supply chain disruption—whether from geopolitical tensions, pandemic, natural disaster, or deliberate action—the United States and its allies would face potentially catastrophic shortages of essential medicines.

The National Security Commission on Emerging Biotechnology identified manufacturing capacity as a critical vulnerability: "Researchers are generating new products faster than manufacturing capacity is increasing," with the gap creating bottlenecks that could slow American innovation even as Chinese manufacturing scaled rapidly.[51] Building pre-commercial manufacturing facilities cost $100 million to $200 million, while commercial-scale facilities could require two to five years to construct and prepare at costs up to $2 billion—barriers that discouraged private investment absent government support to share risks.[52]

Beijing recognized manufacturing's strategic importance and acted accordingly. Chinese firms and local governments offered free or heavily subsidized pilot-scale manufacturing facilities to American biotechnology companies willing to move operations to China—a strategy designed to transfer not just manufacturing but the associated knowledge, expertise, and future innovation capacity.[53] Once Western firms became dependent on Chinese manufacturing, they faced powerful incentives to conduct additional research and development in proximity to production facilities, gradually shifting innovation ecosystems eastward.

China's manufacturing advantages extended beyond cost to capability. Chinese facilities often demonstrated greater flexibility in adapting to new production requirements, faster scaling from pilot to commercial quantities, and willingness to take on projects that Western manufacturers considered too complex or risky. The Chinese government's willingness to provide guarantees, subsidies, and regulatory support created a business environment fundamentally different from the risk-averse, market-driven model prevailing in the West.

The strategic implications were stark. In pharmaceuticals, Chinese manufacturing dominance meant Beijing could potentially restrict exports of critical medicines during crises or use access as economic leverage. In industrial biotechnology, Chinese capacity to produce bio-manufactured chemicals, materials, or energy sources at scale could determine competitiveness across multiple sectors. In agricultural biotechnology, control over production of seeds, biologics for plant and animal health, or genetically modified organisms could influence global food security.

The Clinical Trial Migration

Perhaps no single metric captured China's biotechnology ascendance as starkly as the shift in clinical trial activity. In 2024, for the first time in modern pharmaceutical history, China conducted more clinical trials than the United States—7,100 to 6,000—a milestone that represented not merely numerical supremacy but fundamental changes in where pharmaceutical innovation occurred, where future treatments would be validated, and where industry would focus investment.[54]

The clinical trial migration reflected multiple factors converging to China's advantage. Lower costs: conducting trials in China typically cost 30-50 percent less than equivalent studies in the United States or Europe. Faster recruitment: China's large population, centralized health system, and less stringent informed consent requirements enabled more rapid patient enrollment. Regulatory streamlining: China's National Medical Products Administration had reformed approval processes to better align with international standards while maintaining faster timelines than FDA's increasingly cumbersome requirements. Government support: Beijing and Shanghai offered subsidies, infrastructure, and coordinated support for clinical research as part of biotechnology development strategy.[55]

The implications extended beyond mere geography. Clinical trials generated enormous amounts of data about disease progression, treatment responses, genetic factors, and biomarkers—data that became training material for AI systems, intellectual property for future drug development, and strategic intelligence about population health. As trials shifted to China, so too did the data, expertise, and ultimately innovation capacity associated with pharmaceutical development.

Western pharmaceutical giants were responding to these dynamics by massively expanding Chinese operations. Pfizer's CEO Albert Bourla spent a week in China in mid-2025 hunting for deals, telling investors he felt "very comfortable" with the quality of Chinese data after visiting laboratories and research sites.[56] AstraZeneca opened innovation centers in both Shanghai and Beijing, with the latter representing a $2.5 billion investment over five years that would grow the company's Beijing workforce to 1,700 employees.[57] Eli Lilly opened its first start-up incubator outside the United States in Beijing, while Roche operated an accelerator program in Shanghai hosting more than 20 start-ups.[58]

The scale of Western pharmaceutical industry engagement with China grew difficult to overstate. Licensing deals between U.S. and Chinese biopharma companies surged 280 percent from 2020 to 2024, with total deal value rising from $16.6 billion in 2023 to $41.5 billion in 2024.[59] Major deals included Pfizer's $1.25 billion upfront payment to 3SBio Group for a bispecific antibody, GSK's $1.33 billion agreement with Hansoh Pharma for a B7-H4 antibody-drug conjugate, and BioNTech's $800 million acquisition of Biotheus.[60]

This Western rush to license Chinese-developed drugs and establish research operations in China reflected pharmaceutical realities. Western companies faced looming patent cliffs—potentially losing $183.5 billion in collective revenue by 2030 as blockbuster drugs lost patent protection—creating desperate need for new pipeline compounds.[61] Chinese biotechnology firms were increasingly delivering molecules that could fill those pipelines, often at prices and timelines Western internal research could not match.

Yet the clinical trial migration and associated deal-making created strategic vulnerabilities. As American and European pharmaceutical companies became more dependent on Chinese research, manufacturing, and clinical validation, Beijing gained leverage over global healthcare. Chinese restrictions on data access, changes to regulatory approval processes, or barriers to exporting research materials could significantly disrupt Western pharmaceutical development. In extremis, geopolitical tensions could lead to wholesale blocking of Western access to Chinese research capabilities and markets.

Counting the Cost of Inaction

The National Security Commission on Emerging Biotechnology framed the choice facing American policymakers in stark terms: invest $15 billion now to remain competitive, or face catastrophically higher costs later when Chinese dominance required rebuilding entire industries from scratch—if restoration proved possible at all.

The semiconductor industry provided a cautionary parallel. For decades, American policymakers and industry leaders had tolerated gradual erosion of U.S. semiconductor manufacturing capacity as production migrated to Taiwan, South Korea, and China in pursuit of lower costs. By 2020, American dependence on Asian semiconductor production—particularly Taiwan Semiconductor Manufacturing Company's dominance of advanced node manufacturing—represented a critical strategic vulnerability. The 2022 CHIPS and Science Act authorized $52.7 billion to restore U.S. semiconductor manufacturing, orders of magnitude more than would have been required to maintain capacity throughout earlier decades of offshoring.[62]

Biotechnology threatened to follow a similar trajectory, but with potentially more serious consequences. Semiconductors, however strategically vital, represented a narrow technology domain. Biotechnology spanned healthcare, agriculture, industrial manufacturing, energy production, materials science, and military capabilities. Chinese dominance in biotechnology would affect not merely economic competitiveness or military effectiveness in isolation, but the fundamental health, food security, and technological autonomy of the United States and its allies.

The scenarios for Chinese biotechnology dominance ranged from concerning to catastrophic. In a benign scenario, Chinese firms might simply become the default source for pharmaceutical innovation, manufacturing, and agricultural technology—generating enormous economic benefits for China while creating dependencies that Beijing could leverage for geopolitical advantage. Western countries might find themselves negotiating for access to Chinese-developed vaccines during pandemics, accepting Chinese terms for critical medicines, or facing Chinese restrictions on agricultural technologies essential for food security.

More troubling scenarios involved deliberate Chinese exploitation of biotechnology dominance. Beijing might restrict exports of critical medicines or biological materials during crises, as it briefly threatened with medical supplies during early COVID-19 pandemic. China could embed surveillance capabilities, backdoors, or vulnerabilities in biological databases, AI systems, or genetic sequencing platforms sold to Western institutions. In an acute crisis, China might weaponize biological dependencies, whether through actual bioweapons or through more subtle manipulation of healthcare and agricultural systems.

The most catastrophic scenarios involved irreversible changes to the biological world. Synthetic biology and gene editing technologies enabled creation of organisms that could reproduce, spread, and persist indefinitely. A Chinese lead in these technologies might enable release of modified organisms—whether agricultural, industrial, or even human—that could not be recalled once disseminated. The prospect of China achieving a "DeepSeek moment" in biotechnology through some transformative breakthrough that Western systems could not match raised existential questions about the future governance of life itself.

The Road Ahead: Uncertainty Meets Urgency

As 2025 progresses toward 2026 and China's 15th Five-Year Plan implementation, the biotechnology competition between the United States and China has reached what multiple authoritative assessments described as an inflection point. The choices made in the narrow window ahead—the three years that the National Security Commission identified as decisive—would likely determine technological leadership for decades.

The Harvard Belfer Center's assessment that China possessed the "most immediate opportunity to overtake" the United States in biotechnology reflected not inevitable Chinese triumph but rather the combined effect of two decades of systematic Beijing investment meeting American complacency, budget constraints, regulatory sclerosis, and political dysfunction. The technological fundamentals still favored the United States: superior basic research institutions, deeper capital markets, stronger intellectual property protections, more robust startup ecosystems, and unmatched ability to attract global talent.

Yet fundamentals meant little if not mobilized. China's state-directed system demonstrated remarkable capability to identify strategic priorities, coordinate resources across government and industry, maintain focus through successive five-year planning cycles, and ruthlessly exploit Western hesitation. As the biotechnology sector evolved rapidly through the convergence of AI, synthetic biology, and advanced manufacturing, China's ability to move decisively while America debated could prove determinative.

The $15 billion investment that the National Security Commission recommended represented the minimum to remain competitive—not to restore dominance, but merely to avoid falling irretrievably behind. Whether American political institutions could summon the will to make even this modest investment remained uncertain. The incoming flow of research from laboratories worldwide would soon reveal whether the warnings of 2025 represented prescient strategy or premature capitulation to a Chinese lead that need not have materialized.

The biotechnology frontier would not wait for American politics to resolve its dysfunction or for budgetary disputes to find compromise. The organisms being engineered, the medicines being developed, the agricultural systems being transformed, and the military capabilities being established were emerging now. By the time the consequences became undeniable, the opportunity to shape them might have passed. That, ultimately, was what made biotechnology potentially more decisive than semiconductors or artificial intelligence: once biological innovations entered the world, they could reproduce, spread, and evolve beyond anyone's control. The question was whether that power would be wielded by a democratic system accountable to its citizens or by an authoritarian state pursuing its own vision of the future—a future that might prove irreversible.

Endnotes

[1] "It's not just AI — China's quickly gaining an edge over the U.S. in biotech," *CNBC*, June 5, 2025, https://www.cnbc.com/2025/06/05/chinas-quickly-gaining-an-edge-over-the-us-in-biotech.html.

[2] Cynthia Y. Tong, interview by *CNBC*, June 5, 2025, cited in "It's not just AI — China's quickly gaining an edge over the U.S. in biotech," *CNBC*, June 5, 2025.

[3] Eric Rosenbach, quoted in "It's not just AI — China's quickly gaining an edge over the U.S. in biotech," *CNBC*, June 5, 2025.

[4] "China's biotech boom leaves U.S. playing catch-up," *Axios*, May 29, 2025, https://www.axios.com/2025/05/29/china-biotech-boom-us-drug-trials.

[5] National Security Commission on Emerging Biotechnology, *Charting the Future of Biotechnology: An Action Plan for American Security and Prosperity* (Washington, D.C.: U.S. Congress, April 8, 2025), https://www.congress.gov/crs-product/IN12546.

[6] Michelle Rozo, quoted in Sydney J. Freedberg Jr., "Congressional biotech commission calls for $15B over 5 years to catch up to China," *Breaking Defense*, April 8, 2025, https://breakingdefense.com/2025/04/congressional-biotech-commission-calls-for-15b-over-5-years-to-catch-up-to-china/.

[7] National Security Commission on Emerging Biotechnology, *Charting the Future of Biotechnology*.

[8] National Security Commission on Emerging Biotechnology, *Charting the Future of Biotechnology*.

[9] Sydney J. Freedberg Jr., "Congressional biotech commission calls for $15B over 5 years to catch up to China," *Breaking Defense*, April 8, 2025.

[10] Todd Young, quoted in Sydney J. Freedberg Jr., "Congressional biotech commission calls for $15B over 5 years to catch up to China," *Breaking Defense*, April 8, 2025.

[11] Ben Fidler, "US risks losing biotech edge to China, report warns," *BioPharma Dive*, April 8, 2025, https://www.biopharmadive.com/news/us-china-biotech-report-commission/744718/.

[12] Todd Young, quoted in Sydney J. Freedberg Jr., "Congressional biotech commission calls for $15B over 5 years to catch up to China," *Breaking Defense*, April 8, 2025.

[13] State Council of the People's Republic of China, "Made in China 2025," 2015; see detailed analysis in "China's biotech industry is on the rise. Will it reshape US pharma?" *Chemical & Engineering News*, September 5, 2025, https://cen.acs.org/pharmaceuticals/drug-development/Chinas-biotech-industry-rise-reshape/103/web/2025/09; and "'Made in China 2025': Beijing bets on biotech," *South China Morning Post*, July 2018, https://multimedia.scmp.com/news/china/article/2167415/china-2025-biotech/index.html.

[14] "China's Biotech Rise and Global Innovation Challenges," *CKGSB*, October 15, 2025, https://english.ckgsb.edu.cn/knowledge/article/china-biotech-rise-and-global-innovation-challenges/; see also "Is China the future of biotech?" *Labiotech*, December 13, 2024, https://www.labiotech.eu/in-depth/china-biotech-industry/.

[15] Xinxin Wang, Liying Zhang, and Zhiguo Xu, "The roadmap of bioeconomy in China," *Engineering Biology* 7, no. 1 (2023), https://pmc.ncbi.nlm.nih.gov/articles/PMC9995158/; see also "Current situation and future development of the biopharmaceutical industry in China: A mixed-method study," *PMC*, https://pmc.ncbi.nlm.nih.gov/articles/PMC9442039/.

[16] Todd Young, "YOUNG COLUMN: How America Can Win the Biotech Race," press release, October 15, 2025, https://www.young.senate.gov/newsroom/press-releases/young-column-how-america-can-win-the-biotech-race/.

[17] "Understanding the National Security Commission on Emerging Biotechnology Report," Center for Strategic and International Studies, April 16, 2025, https://www.csis.org/analysis/understanding-national-security-commission-emerging-biotechnology-report.

[18] "China Biotech's DeepSeek Moment," *Allianz Global Investors*, October 16, 2025, https://www.allianzgi.com/en/insights/outlook-and-commentary/china-biotechs-deepseek-moment.

[19] "China's biotech boom leaves U.S. playing catch-up," *Axios*, May 29, 2025.

[20] "From humble to global: China's biotechs navigate the demands of international trials," *Clinical Trials Arena*, September 18, 2025, https://www.clinicaltrialsarena.com/features/from-humble-to-global-chinas-biotechs-navigate-the-demands-of-international-trials/.

[21] Todd Young, "YOUNG COLUMN: How America Can Win the Biotech Race," October 15, 2025.

[22] Todd Young, "YOUNG COLUMN: How America Can Win the Biotech Race," October 15, 2025.

[23] "China's Biotech Rise and Global Innovation Challenges," *CKGSB*, October 15, 2025.

[24] "Explainer: How China's 15th Five-Year Plan will shape the next stage of modernization," *CGTN*, October 24, 2025, https://news.cgtn.com/news/2025-10-24/How-China-s-15th-Five-Year-Plan-shapes-the-next-stage-of-modernization-1HJdRF3iHOU/p.html.

[25] "Key recommendations document outlines priorities in China's next five-year blueprint," *Government of China*, October 25, 2025, https://english.www.gov.cn/news/202510/25/content_WS68fc10abc6d00ca5f9a0703e.html.

[26] "US government must spend $15B to counter China's biotech threat: commission," *Pharma Manufacturing*, April 2025, https://www.pharmamanufacturing.com/industry-news/news/55280537/us-government-must-spend-15b-to-counter-chinas-biotech-threat-commission.

[27] "AstraZeneca details $2.5B investment in China's political center, funding R&D center, biotech pacts," *Fierce Biotech*, March 21, 2025, https://www.fiercebiotech.com/biotech/astrazeneca-details-25b-investment-chinas-political-center-funding-rd-center-biotech-pacts.

[28] "From humble to global: China's biotechs navigate the demands of international trials," *Clinical Trials Arena*, September 18, 2025.

[29] "MERICS China Essentials special issue: China's next Five-Year Plan," *Merics*, October 2025, https://merics.org/en/merics-briefs/merics-china-essentials-special-issue-chinas-next-five-year-plan.

[30] Jonathan B. Tucker and Raymond A. Zilinskas, "Dual-Use Aspects of Plant Biotechnology," Federation of American Scientists, https://biosecurity.fas.org/education/dualuse-agriculture/2.-agricultural-biotechnology/dual-use-aspects-of-plant-biotechnology.html.

[31] Jonathan B. Tucker and Raymond A. Zilinskas, "Dual-Use Aspects of Plant Biotechnology."

[32] Elsa B. Kania and Wilson VornDick, "China's Military Biotech Frontier: CRISPR, Military-Civil Fusion, and the New Revolution in Military Affairs," *Jamestown China Brief* 19, no. 18 (October 8, 2019), https://jamestown.org/chinas-military-biotech-frontier-crispr-military-civil-fusion-and-the-new-revolution-in-military-affairs/.

[33] "Assessing Dual-Use Issues at the AIxBio Convergence," Council on Strategic Risks, July 31, 2025, https://councilonstrategicrisks.org/2025/07/31/the-aixbio-landscape/.

[34] Cited in Kania and VornDick, "China's Military Biotech Frontier."

[35] Zhang Shibo, *New Highland of War* (Beijing: National Defense University Press, January 2017), 234, cited in Kania and VornDick, "China's Military Biotech Frontier."

[36] "Assessing Dual-Use Issues at the AIxBio Convergence," Council on Strategic Risks, July 31, 2025.

[37] U.S. Department of State, *2025 Arms Control Treaty Compliance Report* (Washington, D.C.: U.S. Department of State, April 2025), https://www.state.gov/wp-content/uploads/2025/04/2025-Arms-Control-Treaty-Compliance-Report-1.pdf; see also "The State of Compliance with Weapons of Mass Destruction-Related Treaties," Council on Strategic Risks, April 21, 2025, https://councilonstrategicrisks.org/2025/04/21/the-state-of-compliance-with-weapons-of-mass-destruction-related-treaties-2/.

[38] Antonio Regalado, "US military wants to know what synthetic-biology weapons could look like," *MIT Technology Review*, June 19, 2018, https://www.technologyreview.com/2018/06/19/66749/us-military-wants-to-know-what-synthetic-biology-weapons-could-look-like/.

[39] National Security Commission on Emerging Biotechnology, *Charting the Future of Biotechnology*.

[40] "AstraZeneca taps Chinese biotech in $5.2bn chronic disease research deal," *Pharmaceutical Technology*, June 13, 2025, https://www.pharmaceutical-technology.com/news/astrazeneca-taps-chinese-biotech-in-5-2bn-chronic-disease-research-deal/.

[41] "AstraZeneca taps Chinese biotech in $5.2bn chronic disease research deal," *Pharmaceutical Technology*, June 13, 2025.

[42] "China's AI drug discovery startups cash in on billion-dollar deals," *Rest of World*, August 13, 2025, https://restofworld.org/2025/ai-drug-discovery-startups-big-pharma-china/.

[43] "China's AI drug discovery startups cash in on billion-dollar deals," *Rest of World*, August 13, 2025.

[44] Sydney J. Freedberg Jr., "Congressional biotech commission calls for $15B over 5 years to catch up to China," *Breaking Defense*, April 8, 2025.

[45] "China's AI drug discovery startups cash in on billion-dollar deals," *Rest of World*, August 13, 2025.

[46] "Assessing Dual-Use Issues at the AIxBio Convergence," Council on Strategic Risks, July 31, 2025.

[47] "Assessing Dual-Use Issues at the AIxBio Convergence," Council on Strategic Risks, July 31, 2025.

[48] "Exploring the US-China Biotech Boom," Back Bay Life Science Advisors, January 20, 2025, https://www.bblsa.com/white-papers/exploring-the-us-china-biotech-boom.

[49] "Understanding the National Security Commission on Emerging Biotechnology Report," Center for Strategic and International Studies, April 16, 2025.

[50] National Security Commission on Emerging Biotechnology, *Charting the Future of Biotechnology*.

[51] "US government must spend $15B to counter China's biotech threat: commission," *Pharma Manufacturing*, April 2025.

[52] "US government must spend $15B to counter China's biotech threat: commission," *Pharma Manufacturing*, April 2025.

[53] "Congressionally Established Commission Lays the Groundwork to Maintain US Leadership in Biotechnology," Council on Strategic Risks, April 11, 2025, https://councilonstrategicrisks.org/2025/04/11/congressionally-established-commission-lays-the-groundwork-to-maintain-us-leadership-in-biotechnology/.

[54] "China's biotech boom leaves U.S. playing catch-up," *Axios*, May 29, 2025.

[55] "From humble to global: China's biotechs navigate the demands of international trials," *Clinical Trials Arena*, September 18, 2025.

[56] "China's biotech industry is on the rise. Will it reshape US pharma?" *Chemical & Engineering News*, September 5, 2025.

[57] "AstraZeneca to invest $2.5 billion in Beijing hub as it looks beyond Chinese tax probe," *CNBC*, March 21, 2025, https://www.cnbc.com/2025/03/21/british-pharma-giant-astrazeneca-to-invest-2point5-billion-in-new-china-hub.html.

[58] "China's biotech industry is on the rise. Will it reshape US pharma?" *Chemical & Engineering News*, September 5, 2025.

[59] "AstraZeneca taps Chinese biotech in $5.2bn chronic disease research deal," *Pharmaceutical Technology*, June 13, 2025.

[60] "Out-licensing Deals Between Chinese Pharma and Global Companies are Heating Up," *PharmExec*, November 2025, https://www.pharmexec.com/view/out-licensing-deals-chinese-pharma-global-companies-heating-up.

[61] "China's AI drug discovery startups cash in on billion-dollar deals," *Rest of World*, August 13, 2025.

[62] U.S. Congress, *CHIPS and Science Act*, Public Law 117-167, 117th Congress (August 9, 2022), https://www.congress.gov/bill/117th-congress/house-bill/4346; "Frequently Asked Questions: CHIPS Act of 2022 Provisions and Implementation," Congressional Research Service, https://crsreports.congress.gov/product/pdf/R/R47523.

Chapter 17
Biosecurity and the New Arms Race

Defensive and Offensive Implications

On October 21, 2025, Takeda Pharmaceutical Company announced a landmark transaction that captured the essence of a profound shift in global biotechnology. The Japanese pharmaceutical giant agreed to pay Chinese biotech firm Innovent Biologics $1.2 billion upfront, with potential milestone payments reaching $11.4 billion, for the rights to develop and commercialize three cancer therapies outside Greater China.[1] The deal represented one of the largest biotech licensing agreements of the year and underscored an inescapable reality: despite mounting geopolitical tensions, escalating biosecurity concerns, and legislative efforts to restrict collaboration with Chinese biotech firms, the scientific and economic imperatives driving U.S.-China biotech integration remain formidable.

This paradox lies at the heart of the emerging biosecurity competition between Washington and Beijing. As lawmakers in Congress advance legislation to curtail American dependence on Chinese biotechnology companies over national security concerns, pharmaceutical executives continue signing billion-dollar deals with the very firms targeted by these restrictions. The collision between security imperatives and commercial logic has created what testimony before the U.S.-China Economic and Security Review Commission described as a policy environment where the United States simultaneously seeks to decouple from and deepen engagement with China's biotech sector.[2]

The biosecurity dimension of U.S.-China competition extends far beyond semiconductor chips or rare earth minerals. It encompasses the collection and analysis of genetic data on millions of individuals, the development of precision therapeutics that could be weaponized, the control of critical pharmaceutical supply chains, and the race to dominate next-generation biotechnologies that will shape medicine, agriculture, and potentially warfare for decades to come. Unlike the technology cold war over artificial intelligence and semiconductors, where clear chokepoints and export controls can be identified and enforced, biotechnology presents a far more complex challenge. The same tools that enable life-saving cancer treatments can theoretically be repurposed for harmful applications. The same genetic databases that accelerate drug discovery could be exploited for surveillance or worse.

The BIOSECURE Act: Legislating Biosecurity

On September 9, 2024, the U.S. House of Representatives voted 306 to 81 to pass the BIOSECURE Act, legislation designed to prohibit federal agencies and recipients of federal funding from procuring biotechnology equipment or services from five specifically named Chinese companies: BGI (formerly Beijing Genomics Institute), MGI, Complete Genomics, WuXi AppTec, and WuXi Biologics.[3] The bill represented the culmination of years of intelligence assessments warning that Beijing's collection of American genetic data posed national security risks that extended from privacy concerns to potential biological weapons development.

The legislative push was driven by alarming revelations about the extent of Chinese genomics companies' data collection activities and their ties to the People's Liberation Army. A 2021 Reuters investigation found that BGI's popular prenatal test, known as NIFTY and used by more than 8.4 million women in at least 52 countries, was developed in collaboration with the Chinese military and that testing data was being shared with military researchers.[4] The investigation revealed that BGI had used a PLA supercomputer to reanalyze prenatal test data, searching for virus prevalence, mental illness indicators, and genetic characteristics of Tibetan and Uyghur minorities—raising disturbing questions about potential eugenics research and ethnic targeting.[5]

Representative Mike Gallagher, chairman of the House Select Committee on the Chinese Communist Party, articulated the security rationale: "Beijing Genomics Institute collects genetic data of Americans and uses it for research with the Chinese military. The CCP will undoubtedly use the genetic data collected by BGI to further its malign aggression, potentially even to develop bioweapons."[6] The concern was not hypothetical. China's 2017 National Intelligence Law requires all Chinese organizations and citizens to support, assist, and cooperate with national intelligence work, effectively giving Beijing legal authority to demand any data held by companies operating under Chinese jurisdiction.[7]

WuXi AppTec and WuXi Biologics, the other major targets of the BIOSECURE Act, represent a different but equally significant concern. These contract development and manufacturing organizations (CDMOs) have become integral to the global pharmaceutical supply chain, with WuXi AppTec alone involved in developing an estimated one-fourth of the drugs used in the United States.[8] A 2024 survey by the Biotechnology Innovation Organization found that 79 percent of U.S. biopharmaceutical and biotechnology companies had at least one product or contract with a Chinese contract manufacturing organization, with WuXi companies accounting for a substantial portion.[9]

The BIOSECURE Act was structured to provide companies with an extended transition period—until January 2032—to sever ties with the named Chinese contractors while retaining their positions on Medicare and Medicaid, which serve as crucial revenue drivers for pharmaceutical companies.[10] This lengthy timeline reflected both the deep integration of Chinese CDMOs into Western pharmaceutical supply chains and the practical challenges of finding alternative manufacturing capacity.

However, as 2024 drew to a close, the legislation faced an uncertain path to enactment. While the bill passed the House with strong bipartisan support, it was excluded from the year-end continuing resolution and the National Defense Authorization Act, leading it to stall in the Senate.[11] In October 2025, a modified version emerged as an amendment to the Senate's National Defense Authorization Act, featuring a process-based identification system rather than explicitly naming companies, though the practical effect remained similar.[12] The bill's fate remained uncertain, caught between national security imperatives and industry concerns about supply chain disruption and increased drug development costs.

The Paradox of Continued Partnership

Even as the BIOSECURE Act advanced through Congress, the pace of licensing deals between Western pharmaceutical companies and Chinese biotech firms accelerated dramatically. The Innovent-Takeda transaction exemplified this trend. Under the agreement, Takeda acquired global rights to IBI363, a potentially first-in-class bispecific antibody targeting PD-1 and IL-2 alpha for non-small cell lung cancer and colorectal cancer, and IBI343, an antibody-drug conjugate targeting Claudin 18.2 for gastric and pancreatic cancers.[13] Takeda also secured an exclusive option for IBI3001, an early-stage bispecific ADC targeting EGFR and B7H3.[14]

The financial terms were striking. The $1.2 billion upfront payment included a $100 million equity investment in Innovent at a 20 percent premium to its trading price, signaling Takeda's confidence in the partnership's long-term value.[15] The potential milestone payments of $10.2 billion reflected the transformative potential of the licensed assets for Takeda's post-2030 growth strategy, particularly as the company faced patent expirations for its blockbuster inflammatory bowel disease drug Entyvio.[16]

Takeda was far from alone. By the first half of 2025, Chinese biotechs accounted for 32 percent of global pharmaceutical out-licensing deal value, up from 21 percent in both 2023 and 2024, and single-digit percentages before that.[17] In Q1 2025 alone, U.S. companies signed 14 licensing agreements worth approximately $18.3 billion for Chinese assets, compared to just two such deals in the same period of 2024.[18] Major pharmaceutical companies including AstraZeneca, Pfizer, Bristol Myers Squibb, Merck, Roche, and Gilead all inked significant partnerships with Chinese biotech firms, collectively representing tens of billions of dollars in committed capital.[19]

The surge in deal-making reflected several converging factors. First, Chinese biotech companies had demonstrated genuine scientific innovation, moving beyond "me-too" drugs to develop first-in-class and best-in-class candidates with novel mechanisms of action. By 2024, China accounted for approximately 27 percent of the global drug development pipeline by volume of assets, more than six times larger than a decade earlier.[20] Chinese firms had become particularly strong in antibody-drug conjugates, bispecific antibodies, and other complex biologics, areas where Western pharmaceutical companies were seeking to expand their portfolios.

Second, Chinese biotech offered compelling economics. The same drugs could be developed in China at a fraction of the cost and time required in the United States or Europe. Phase I clinical trials in China cost roughly one-third of those in the United States and recruited patients in weeks rather than months, providing decision-ready data early in development.[21] This cost-speed advantage, combined with sophisticated manufacturing capabilities and regulatory alignment with international standards, made Chinese partnerships attractive even amid rising geopolitical tensions.

Third, Western pharmaceutical companies faced their own challenges. With 69 drugs generating over $1 billion in annual sales having lost patent protection by the end of 2023, and with internal early-stage R&D increasingly scaled back to control costs, pharmaceutical companies desperately needed external innovation to fill their pipelines.[22] The share of oncology trials sponsored by pharmaceutical companies with revenues exceeding $10 billion dropped from 60 percent in 2015 to 28 percent in 2024, signaling a broader transition from internal discovery to external partnerships.[23]

The Chinese Biotech Manufacturing Advantage

The competitiveness of Chinese biotech manufacturing represents a structural challenge that legislative restrictions alone cannot easily address. Over two decades of sustained investment and strategic planning, China has built a vertically integrated biotech ecosystem that offers speed, cost, and scale advantages that Western competitors struggle to match.

The foundation was laid through massive infrastructure development. By 2024, China had established over 100 biotech research parks and 17 industrial clusters, concentrated in cities like Shanghai, Suzhou, Hangzhou, and Wuxi.[24] These clusters benefited from extensive state support, streamlined regulatory processes, and access to a large patient population that enabled rapid clinical trial recruitment. China's 2015 "Made in China 2025" strategy explicitly prioritized biotechnology, designating it as a strategic emerging industry worthy of government backing through financing, regulatory reform, and diplomatic support.[25]

Manufacturing cost differentials were substantial. Chinese CDMOs could offer services at prices significantly below Western competitors while maintaining healthy profit margins. When U.S. and European biotech companies switched to non-Chinese CDMOs in response to BIOSECURE concerns, drug development costs increased, at least in the short term, with some estimates suggesting 30 percent higher expenses for comparable services.[26] India emerged as a potential alternative, but industry experts acknowledged it would take years for the Indian CDMO market to develop the capabilities currently offered by Chinese firms.[27]

Speed represented an equally important advantage. China's National Medical Products Administration had adopted more than 100 guidelines from the International Council for Harmonisation since joining in 2017, creating regulatory pathways that reduced wait times for clinical trial approval and made trial operations an estimated 30 percent less expensive than in the United States.[28] High-speed rail networks and advanced hospital infrastructure enabled Chinese companies to conduct early-stage trials two to three times faster than American counterparts, according to the Asia Society.[29]

WuXi AppTec epitomized this Chinese advantage. Operating twelve facilities in the United States and employing nearly 2,000 people on American soil, WuXi had become deeply embedded in Western pharmaceutical development.[30] The company generated over 60 percent of its revenue from the U.S. market, making American consumers direct facilitators of a company that policymakers increasingly viewed as a national security risk.[31] Even after the BIOSECURE Act passed the House, WuXi Biologics reported adding 61 new projects in the first six months of 2024, half from the United States, while WuXi AppTec added over 500 new customers.[32]

The scale of dependency became clear through industry surveys and regulatory filings. Several pharmaceutical and biotech firms disclosed BIOSECURE-related exposure in SEC filings, treating it as material risk to investors. Iovance Biotherapeutics highlighted reliance on a Chinese CDMO as a potential vulnerability, while Cabaletta Bio warned that supplier loss might disrupt clinical timelines.[33] These disclosures demonstrated that companies viewed the potential restrictions not merely as compliance issues but as factors affecting valuation and investor confidence.

Genetic Data and the Information Dimension

Beyond manufacturing and drug development, the collection and analysis of genetic data emerged as perhaps the most sensitive aspect of biotech competition. The scale of BGI's global operations illustrated the magnitude of the challenge. By 2020, BGI claimed to have sold COVID-19 test kits to 180 countries and established laboratories in 18 countries.[34] The company operated over 100 genetic collection laboratories across more than 20 countries, creating an infrastructure that the U.S.-China Economic and Security Review Commission declared was providing "genetic data to serve PRC ambitions to dominate biotech."[35]

The national security implications extended across multiple dimensions. First, massive genomic databases could accelerate pharmaceutical development, potentially giving China economic and industrial advantages in precision medicine. U.S. healthcare data was particularly valuable because of the ethnic diversity of the American population, offering genetic variation not available in more homogeneous populations.[36] Second, genetic information could theoretically enable the development of precision biological weapons targeting specific ethnic groups or genetic profiles—a concern reinforced by authoritative PLA writings discussing "specific ethnic genetic attacks" as future options.[37]

Third, genetic surveillance capabilities could be weaponized against ethnic minorities and political dissidents. The Department of Commerce added BGI subsidiaries to its Entity List in 2020 and 2023 for using genetic analysis to support China's repression of Uyghurs and other ethnic minorities in Xinjiang.[38] BGI's prenatal testing privacy policy explicitly permitted data sharing when "directly relevant to national security or national defense security" in China, providing legal cover for government access to sensitive genetic information.[39]

The U.S. National Counterintelligence and Security Center issued warnings that China's collection of healthcare and genomic data posed "serious risks, not only to the privacy of Americans but also to the economic and national security of the United States."[40] These concerns intensified as BGI and related companies expanded their global footprint, potentially creating dependencies on Chinese genomic sequencing technologies that could be exploited during crises.

Unlike other aspects of technological competition, genetic data collection operated in a regulatory gray zone. U.S. safeguards focused primarily on privacy rather than national security, creating vulnerabilities for foreign actors to gain access to data on American citizens.[41] While HIPAA and other privacy regulations governed medical data handling, they were not designed to prevent foreign intelligence services from accessing aggregated genetic databases through companies subject to Chinese jurisdiction.

Pandemic Preparedness in an Era of Competition

The COVID-19 pandemic demonstrated both the promise and peril of biotechnology in the 21st century. The rapid development of mRNA vaccines showcased the transformative potential of biotech innovation, while the pandemic's origins—whether from natural zoonotic transmission or potential laboratory incident—highlighted the dual-use nature of biological research. The same capabilities that enable pandemic preparedness can theoretically be misused, whether deliberately or accidentally.

In April 2025, the National Security Commission on Emerging Biotechnology (NSCEB) issued a comprehensive report warning that the United States risked falling irreversibly behind China in biotechnology within three years absent decisive action. The commission's central finding was stark: "There will be a ChatGPT moment for biotechnology, and if China gets there first, no matter how fast we run, we will never catch up."[42] To maintain competitiveness, the commission recommended that the U.S. government invest a minimum of $15 billion over five years to support the biotechnology sector—a sum justified by the transformative potential of biotech across medicine, agriculture, defense, and manufacturing.[43]

The commission's warnings extended specifically to pandemic preparedness and biosecurity. In a world where China controlled significant portions of pharmaceutical manufacturing capacity and genetic sequencing infrastructure, the United States faced potential vulnerabilities in responding to future biological threats. China's 2020 Export Control Law and 2021 Biosecurity Law explicitly empowered the state to halt shipments of "dual-use pathogens, toxins, and related equipment" whenever "national security" was threatened, creating legal mechanisms for a potential medicine export pause during crises.[44]

The convergence of artificial intelligence and biotechnology amplified these concerns. AI-enabled drug discovery and design tools could dramatically accelerate both therapeutic development and potential biological threats. Chinese companies had made substantial investments in AI-biotech convergence, with the country contributing 54 percent of antibody-drug conjugates and 48 percent of bispecific and tri-specific antibodies in global Phase I/II trials as of 2025.[45] This technological leadership in next-generation biologics suggested that China's biotech capabilities extended beyond manufacturing arbitrage to genuine innovation.

Pandemic preparedness required not just domestic capacity but international coordination—creating a fundamental tension with efforts to decouple from Chinese biotech. The NSCEB report acknowledged this dilemma, advocating for a "promote and protect" strategy that included working with China "where prudent" to establish standards for biosafety and biosecurity.[46]

Future pandemics would not respect geopolitical boundaries, and effective response required global cooperation, data sharing, and coordinated research—all complicated by escalating strategic competition.

The Arms Race That Isn't (Yet)

Despite alarming rhetoric about biological weapons and genetic targeting, most experts assessed that a full-scale biological arms race remained unlikely. Strategic value, political intent, and international norms still outweighed technological potential. Most states saw little military advantage and high diplomatic cost in pursuing biological weapons programs.[47] The Biological Weapons Convention, despite its limitations, maintained broad international support and created reputational costs for violations.

However, the line between legitimate biodefense research and offensive capabilities had grown increasingly blurred. Gain-of-function research, which enhances pathogen virulence or transmissibility to understand pandemic potential, embodied the dual-use dilemma. The same research that could enable vaccine development could theoretically inform biological weapons design. U.S. policymakers struggled to balance the need for basic research on pathogens against biosecurity risks, with debates over gain-of-function funding reflecting these tensions.[48]

China's own biosecurity infrastructure had evolved rapidly following the COVID-19 pandemic. Beijing's 2021 Biosecurity Law established comprehensive frameworks for managing biological risks, though critics noted that definitions of "biosecurity" could encompass both legitimate public health concerns and surveillance of ethnic minorities.[49] Chinese military writings on biotechnology suggested consideration of biological capabilities in future conflicts, even if explicit weapons programs were not evident.[50]

The more immediate concern was not traditional bioweapons but the weaponization of pharmaceutical dependencies. In a scenario where U.S.-China tensions escalated to crisis or conflict, Beijing's ability to disrupt American access to active pharmaceutical ingredients, antibiotics, or other critical medicines could serve as economic coercion without crossing the threshold to armed conflict. With China producing significant portions of global pharmaceutical precursors and active ingredients, this vulnerability represented a more plausible threat than exotic biological weapons.

Navigating the Biosecurity Dilemma

The biosecurity dimension of U.S.-China competition presents policymakers with a dilemma without easy solutions. Complete decoupling would impose enormous costs, disrupting pharmaceutical supply chains, increasing drug development expenses, and potentially slowing medical innovation that benefits millions of patients. Yet continued deep integration with Chinese biotech companies subject to Beijing's intelligence and military-civil fusion directives creates genuine national security vulnerabilities.

The BIOSECURE Act, whether passed in its current form or modified, represents an attempt to thread this needle—restricting the most sensitive relationships while allowing continued commercial engagement. The five companies named in the legislation were selected based on specific concerns about military ties, genetic data collection, or surveillance applications rather than a blanket prohibition on Chinese biotech. The extended timeline for compliance acknowledged industry realities while signaling long-term intent to reduce dependencies.

Yet even this targeted approach faced challenges. WuXi Biologics vigorously denied security concerns, calling the legislation a "preemptive and unjustified designation without due process."[51] The company emphasized its global operations and argued that it posed no security risk to the United States or any other country. Complete Genomics described itself as "deeply disappointed but not entirely surprised" that geopolitics rather than facts drove the bill's passage.[52] These companies employed lobbyists and mounted public relations campaigns to soften restrictions, arguing that the legislation would harm U.S. biotechnology innovation, increase drug development costs, and ultimately harm patients.[53]

The strategic challenge extends beyond any single piece of legislation. If U.S. biotechnology expertise continued migrating to China through talent recruitment, research collaborations, and technology licensing, Washington's ability to maintain technological leadership would erode. The same dynamics that drove semiconductor and electric vehicle supply chains to concentrate in China—cost advantages, government support, integrated ecosystems—were increasingly apparent in biotechnology. The difference was that biotech lacked the clear chokepoints available in semiconductors, where control over advanced lithography equipment provided leverage.

The coming years will determine whether the United States can maintain its historical leadership in biotechnology while managing the security risks posed by China's rapid ascent. The answer will depend not just on export controls and investment restrictions but on positive investments in domestic biotech capabilities, regulatory reform to reduce compliance burdens, support for allied biotech ecosystems, and sustained R&D funding. The BIOSECURE Act represents necessary risk management, but alone it cannot ensure American competitiveness in the defining life science competition of the 21st century.

As one industry executive observed, the fundamental question was whether the United States could "pay now or pay a lot more later."[54] The cost of maintaining leadership through strategic investment paled in comparison to the potential cost of ceding the biotech revolution to a strategic competitor. Yet even as this realization gained traction, billions of dollars in licensing deals continued flowing to Chinese biotech companies, suggesting that market forces and security imperatives remained fundamentally misaligned. Resolving this tension would require not just legislation but a comprehensive strategy encompassing investment, regulation, and international coordination—a strategy that, as of late 2025, remained more aspiration than reality.

Endnotes

[1] Takeda Pharmaceutical Company, "Takeda Announces Oncology Partnership with Innovent," press release, October 21, 2025, https://www.takeda.com/newsroom/newsreleases/2025/innovent/; Innovent Biologics, "Innovent Biologics Announces Global Strategic Partnership with Takeda," press release, October 21, 2025, https://www.prnewswire.com/news-releases/innovent-biologics-announces-global-strategic-partnership-with-takeda-to-bring-innovents-next-gen-io-backbone-therapy-and-adc-molecules-to-the-global-market-302590770.html.

[2] Jeroen Groenewegen-Lau, testimony before the U.S.-China Economic and Security Review Commission, June 5, 2025, https://www.uscc.gov/sites/default/files/2025-06/Jeroen_Groenewegen-Lau_Testimony.pdf.

[3] Ropes & Gray LLP, "BIOSECURE Act Passed in the House of Representatives with a 306-81 Vote," September 17, 2024, https://www.ropesgray.com/en/insights/alerts/2024/09/biosecure-act-passed-in-the-house-of-representatives-with-a-306-81-vote; Tristan Manalac, "BIOSECURE Act Sails Through House Passage, Lines Up Senate Vote," BioSpace, September 10, 2024, https://www.biospace.com/policy/biosecure-act-sails-through-house-passage-lines-up-senate-vote.

[4] Clare Baldwin and Christina Jewett, "China's Gene Giant Harvests Data From Millions of Women," Reuters, July 7, 2021, https://www.reuters.com/investigates/special-report/health-china-bgi-dna/; "BGI Genomics Accused of Partnering with Chinese Military to Harvest DNA Data from Prenatal Tests," Fierce Biotech, July 9, 2021, https://www.fiercebiotech.com/medtech/bgi-genomics-accused-partnering-chinese-military-to-harvest-data-from-prenatal-tests.

[5] Foundation for Defense of Democracies, "Biotech Battlefield," January 15, 2025, https://www.fdd.org/analysis/2025/01/15/biotech-battlefield/.

[6] U.S. House Select Committee on the Strategic Competition Between the United States and the Chinese Communist Party, "'U.S. Will Not Sit Idly as CCP Steals Our Genetic Data' - Moolenaar, Krishnamoorthi, Wenstrup Commend House Oversight Passage of BIOSECURE Act," press release, May 17, 2024, https://selectcommitteeontheccp.house.gov/media/press-releases/us-will-not-sit-idly-ccp-steals-our-genetic-data-moolenaar-krishnamoorthi.

[7] Council on Strategic Risks, "The US Government Takes Actions to Protect Vital Biological Datasets," January 15, 2025, https://councilonstrategicrisks.org/2025/01/15/the-us-government-takes-actions-to-protect-vital-biological-datasets/.

[8] Foley & Lardner LLP, "BIOSECURE Act: Anticipated Movement, Key Provisions, and Likely Impact," September 10, 2024, https://www.foley.com/insights/publications/2024/09/biosecure-act-anticipated-movement-key-provisions-impact/ (citing New York Times estimate).

[9] Health-ISAC, "Impacts of the BIOSECURE Act on the Global BioTech Industry," November 4, 2024, https://health-isac.org/wp-content/uploads/11.4.24_WP_ImpactsoftheBIOSECUREActontheGlobalBioTechIndustry.pdf.

[10] Goodwin Procter LLP, "BIOSECURE Act Timeline," September 2024, https://www.goodwinlaw.com/en/insights/publications/2024/09/insights-lifesciences-biosecure-act-timeline; U.S. House of Representatives, H.R. 8333, BIOSECURE Act, August 29, 2024, https://docs.house.gov/billsthisweek/20240909/H8333_SUS_xml.pdf.

[11] Hogan Lovells, "BIOSECURE Stalls, Will Not Become Law in 2024," December 2024, https://www.hoganlovells.com/en/publications/biosecure-stalls-will-not-become-law-in-2024.

[12] Goodwin Procter LLP, "BIOSECURE Included in Draft National Defense Authorization Act of 2026," October 31, 2025, https://www.goodwinlaw.com/en/insights/publications/2025/10/alerts-lifesciences-biosecure-included-in-draft.

[13] Frank Vinluan, "Takeda Boosts Pipeline and Revenue Growth Prospects With $1.2B Deal for Innovent Cancer Drugs," MedCity News, October 22, 2025, https://medcitynews.com/2025/10/takeda-innovent-biologics-cancer-solid-tumor-bispecific-antibody-adc-patent-cliff-tak/.

[14] Tristan Manalac, "Takeda Bets up to $11.4B for Up To Three Innovent Cancer Assets," BioSpace, October 23, 2025, https://www.biospace.com/deals/takeda-bets-up-to-11-4b-for-three-innovent-adcs.

[15] "Takeda Inks $1.2bn Oncology Pact with Innovent," BioXconomy, October 24, 2025, https://www.bioxconomy.com/partnering/takeda-inks-1-2bn-oncology-pact-with-innovent-biologics.

[16] Vinluan, "Takeda Boosts Pipeline."

[17] Cui Cui (Jefferies analyst), quoted in "China Biotechs 'Reshaping' US Biopharma as Outlicensing Deals Rise 11%: Jefferies Report," Fierce Biotech, July 14, 2025, https://www.fiercebiotech.com/biotech/china-biotechs-reshaping-us-biopharma-outlicensing-deals-rise-11-jefferies-report.

[18] EC Innovations, "China's Biopharma Boom in Global Drug Licensing Deals," July 3, 2025, https://www.ecinnovations.com/blog/chinas-biopharma-boom-in-global-drug-licensing-deals/.

[19] Sarawak Science Centre & Technology Research Council, "China Biotechs Now Drive a Third of Global Biopharma Out-Licensing Deals," July 17, 2025, https://www.sarawaksctr.com/post/china-biotechs-now-drive-a-third-of-global-biopharma-out-licensing-deals.

[20] Back Bay Life Science Advisors, "Exploring the US-China Biotech Boom," white paper, January 20, 2025, https://www.bblsa.com/white-papers/exploring-the-us-china-biotech-boom.

[21] Groenewegen-Lau testimony, June 5, 2025.

[22] ARC Group, "China Innovative Pharma Going Global," July 21, 2025, https://arc-group.com/china-innovative-pharma/.

[23] ARC Group, "China Innovative Pharma Going Global."

[24] CKGSB Knowledge, "China's Biotech Rise and Global Innovation Challenges," October 15, 2025, https://english.ckgsb.edu.cn/knowledge/article/china-biotech-rise-and-global-innovation-challenges/.

[25] Pharmaceutical Technology, "NewCo Licensing Models Are Tipping Deals in Favour of China's Biotechs," September 30, 2025, https://www.pharmaceutical-technology.com/features/newco-licensing-models-are-tipping-deals-in-favour-of-chinas-biotechs/.

[26] Anshul Mangal (Project Farma), quoted in "Drug Development Costs Predicted to Soar as BIOSECURE Act Gains Momentum," Pharmaceutical Technology, July 26, 2024, https://www.pharmaceutical-technology.com/interviews/drug-development-costs-predicted-to-soar-as-biosecure-act-gains-momentum/.

[27] Mangal, quoted in "Drug Development Costs Predicted to Soar."

[28] Jacopo Gabrielli, "China's Impact on Global Biotech: Perspectives from the Front Line," Substack newsletter, April 7, 2025, https://jacopogabrielli.substack.com/p/chinas-impact-on-global-biotech-perspectives.

[29] Wuxi Municipal Government website, "China's Biotech Is Cheaper and Faster," August 25, 2025, https://en.wuxi.gov.cn/2025-08/25/c_1130338.htm (reporting Asia Society research on clinical trial recruitment speeds).

[30] Foley & Lardner, "BIOSECURE Act: Anticipated Movement."

[31] U.S. House Select Committee on the CCP, "'U.S. Will Not Sit Idly as CCP Steals Our Genetic Data,'" press release, May 17, 2024, https://selectcommitteeontheccp.house.gov/media/press-releases/us-will-not-sit-idly-ccp-steals-our-genetic-data-moolenaar-krishnamoorthi.

[32] Ryan Cross, "House Passes Act Aimed at 5 Chinese Drug Services Firms," Chemical & Engineering News, September 10, 2024, https://cen.acs.org/policy/legislation-/House-passes-act-aimed-5-Chinese-drug-services-firms/102/web/2024/09.

[33] Greenberg Traurig LLP, "BIOSECURE Act Advances in the US Senate," November 2025, https://www.gtlaw.com/en/insights/2025/11/biosecure-act-advances-in-the-us-senate.

[34] U.S. National Counterintelligence and Security Center, "China's Collection of Genomic and Other Healthcare Data from America," fact sheet, February 2021, https://www.dni.gov/files/NCSC/documents/SafeguardingOurFuture/NCSC_China_Genomics_Fact_Sheet_2021revision20210203.pdf.

[35] U.S. House Select Committee on the CCP, "'U.S. Will Not Sit Idly.'"

[36] National Counterintelligence and Security Center, "China's Collection of Genomic Data."

[37] Foundation for Defense of Democracies, "Biotech Battlefield."

[38] Wilson Sonsini Goodrich & Rosati, "United States Imposes Export Restrictions on Beijing Genomics Institute (BGI) Group Subsidiaries over National Security Concerns," March 2, 2023, https://www.wsgr.com/en/insights/united-states-imposes-export-restrictions-on-beijing-genomics-institute-bgi-group-subsidiaries-over-national-security-concerns.html.

[39] Foundation for Defense of Democracies, "Biotech Battlefield."

[40] National Counterintelligence and Security Center, quoted in "Congress Wants to Ban China's Largest Genomics Firm from Doing Business in the U.S. Here's Why," NBC News, January 26, 2024, https://www.nbcnews.com/politics/national-security/congress-wants-ban-china-genomics-firm-bgi-from-us-rcna135698.

[41] National Counterintelligence and Security Center, "China's Collection of Genomic Data."

[42] National Security Commission on Emerging Biotechnology, "Charting the Future of Biotechnology," final report, April 2025, quoted in Julie Heng, "Understanding the National Security Commission on Emerging Biotechnology Report," Center for Strategic and International Studies, April 16, 2025, https://www.csis.org/analysis/understanding-national-security-commission-emerging-biotechnology-report.

[43] "Congressional Biotech Commission Calls for $15B over 5 Years to Catch Up to China," Breaking Defense, April 8, 2025, https://breakingdefense.com/2025/04/congressional-biotech-commission-calls-for-15b-over-5-years-to-catch-up-to-china/.

[44] Groenewegen-Lau testimony, June 5, 2025.

[45] BioDlink, quoted in "BioDlink Showcases Europe-China CMC Collaboration Amid Developmental Breakthrough," The AI Journal, November 28, 2025, https://aijourn.com/biodlink-showcases-europe-china-cmc-collaboration-amid-developmental-breakthrough/.

[46] Heng, "Understanding the National Security Commission Report."

[47] RAND Corporation, quoted in "Biodefense Headlines – 2 November 2025," Global Biodefense, November 2, 2025, https://globalbiodefense.com/2025/11/02/biodefense-headlines-2-november-2025/.

[48] James Giordano et al., "The Need for Modernization of Biosecurity in the Post-COVID World," Frontiers in Bioengineering and Biotechnology, April 2022, https://ncbi.nlm.nih.gov/pmc/articles/PMC9044947.

[49] Chen Jun, "Enhancing the National Biosecurity System in China amidst COVID-19 Epidemic," Journal of Biosafety and Biosecurity 2, no. 1 (April 2020): 3-4, https://pmc.ncbi.nlm.nih.gov/articles/PMC7164852/.

[50] U.S. Department of State, "Report on Biotechnology in the People's Republic of China's Military-Civil Fusion Strategy," November 2024, https://www.state.gov/wp-content/uploads/2024/11/ISAB-Report-on-Biotechnology-in-the-PRC-MCF-Strategy_Final.pdf.

[51] WuXi AppTec, quoted in "After BIOSECURE Act Passes in House, Targeted Chinese Companies Say They're 'Deeply' Concerned," Fierce Pharma, September 10, 2024, https://www.fiercepharma.com/pharma/china-focused-biosecure-act-passes-house-heres-what-targeted-companies-are-saying.

[52] Complete Genomics, quoted in "After BIOSECURE Act Passes in House," Fierce Pharma.

[53] Health-ISAC, "Impacts of the BIOSECURE Act on the Global BioTech Industry," white paper, November 4, 2024, https://health-isac.org/wp-content/uploads/11.4.24_WP_ImpactsoftheBIOSECUREActontheGlobalBioTechIndustry.pdf.

[54] Senator Todd Young, quoted in "Congressional Biotech Commission Calls for $15B," Breaking Defense.

Chapter 18
2026 and Beyond—Projecting the Biotech Battlefield

Where the Competition Heads Next

The biotechnology rivalry between the United States and China has moved beyond semiconductors and artificial intelligence to a domain with potentially greater strategic implications. By 2025, Chinese biotech firms had achieved what industry analysts termed a "DeepSeek moment" for pharmaceuticals, demonstrating that innovation could flourish even under resource constraints and technological denial regimes. The question now facing policymakers, investors, and industry leaders is not whether China will compete in biotech, but whether the United States can maintain its historical edge in an industry increasingly shaped by Chinese innovation, capital efficiency, and manufacturing prowess.

Drug Development Pipelines: The Race for Therapeutic Dominance

Cancer, Diabetes, and Autoimmune Diseases

The competitive landscape in drug development reveals a dramatic shift in global innovation centers. By 2024, China had built a pipeline of over 1,250 novel drugs entering development, nearly matching the United States' approximately 1,440 candidates.[1] This represented a quantum leap from a decade earlier when Chinese pharmaceutical companies were primarily known for generic production rather than novel drug discovery.

Oncology remains the dominant therapeutic area for both nations, accounting for more than one-third of Chinese drug approvals in 2024.[2] The focus on cancer therapeutics reflects both market opportunity and national health imperatives. Nearly five million Chinese were diagnosed with cancer in 2022, with more than 2.5 million deaths, creating enormous pressure for innovative treatments.[3] Chinese companies have responded by developing advanced modalities including antibody-drug conjugates, bispecific antibodies, and next-generation immunotherapies.

The September 2024 announcement that Akeso's Ivonescimab outperformed Merck's blockbuster Keytruda in Phase III trials for non-small cell lung cancer marked a watershed moment.[4] Although subsequent long-term results in September 2025 showed the drug failed to demonstrate significant benefit in overall survival, the initial breakthrough signaled that Chinese firms could compete at the highest levels of drug development.[5] The achievement was hailed as a "DeepSeek moment" in biopharma, referencing the AI company that had demonstrated Chinese capabilities to innovate despite technological constraints.

Beyond oncology, Chinese biotechs are making significant inroads into metabolic diseases, particularly obesity and diabetes treatments. The global excitement around GLP-1 receptor agonists for weight loss has spurred intense competition, with multiple Chinese firms developing candidates to challenge established therapies.[6] With approximately 148 million Chinese living with diabetes, the domestic market provides both testing ground and commercial opportunity.[7]

Autoimmune and cardiovascular-metabolic diseases represent the second and third priority areas respectively for Chinese drug developers.[8] The convergence of artificial intelligence and drug discovery has accelerated development timelines across all therapeutic areas. Chinese biotech startups are leveraging AI platforms to identify novel drug candidates faster and at lower cost than traditional methods, with several multibillion-dollar partnerships with Western pharmaceutical companies validating this approach.[9]

The Out-Licensing Revolution: China's Pipeline Goes Global

The most dramatic indicator of China's biotech ascendance is the surge in out-licensing deals. In the first quarter of 2025, Chinese biotechs accounted for 32 percent of global out-licensing deal value, up sharply from 21 percent in both 2023 and 2024, and from single-digit percentages just years earlier.[10] This statistic, reported by investment bank Jefferies, represents more than a trend—it signals a fundamental restructuring of the global pharmaceutical pipeline.

The velocity of dealmaking has been extraordinary. By the first half of 2025, U.S. companies alone signed 14 China-licensed deals worth approximately $18.3 billion, compared to just two such deals worth minimal value in the same period of 2024.[11] The total number of China-related licensing deals surged from 55 in 2015 to 213 by 2024, with total deal value jumping from $3.1 billion to $57.1 billion—vastly outpacing global market growth.[12]

Several factors drive this licensing boom. Chinese innovative assets typically command upfront payments 60 to 70 percent lower than Western peers, with total deal sizes 40 to 50 percent smaller.[13] For multinational pharmaceutical companies facing looming patent cliffs and pricing pressures, Chinese biotechs offer cost-effective pipeline replenishment. The licensing model also provides

Chinese companies with non-dilutive financing at a time when domestic venture capital has dried up. Private biotech investment in China fell to a seven-year low of approximately $4.2 billion in 2024, down from a 2021 peak of $15.7 billion.[14]

The strategic implications extend beyond individual transactions. Western pharmaceutical giants including Bristol Myers Squibb, Roche, Merck, Pfizer, and Gilead have become the most active acquirers of Chinese biotech assets.[15] AstraZeneca has signed nine licensing deals with Chinese companies worth around $20 billion collectively.[16] These partnerships increasingly involve early-stage assets, with 71 percent of 2024 licenses involving preclinical or Phase I candidates, reflecting confidence in Chinese development capabilities.[17]

The "NewCo" licensing model has become particularly prevalent, allowing Chinese biotechs to retain equity stakes in newly formed companies that develop their candidates outside China. This structure enables Chinese firms to profit from international sales while avoiding the costs of late-stage development and marketing abroad.[18] Mabwell Bioscience's August 2025 deal with U.S.-based Aditum Bio exemplifies this approach, with Mabwell retaining significant equity in Kalexo Bio while Aditum handles global development of a lipid management drug candidate worth up to $1 billion.[19]

FDA and NMPA: Regulatory Convergence and Its Implications

The acceleration of Chinese biotech has been enabled in significant part by regulatory harmonization between China's National Medical Products Administration and Western counterparts including the U.S. Food and Drug Administration and European Medicines Agency. Over the course of the 2010s, China systematically reformed its drug regulatory framework to better mirror FDA and EMA standards, allowing manufacturers to meet requirements for multiple geographies simultaneously.[20]

The regulatory convergence has produced tangible results. By 2024, the NMPA approved 84 new pharmaceutical products, a record high representing a 12 percent increase from the previous year and surpassing the FDA's 50 new drug approvals during the same period.[21] The NMPA accepted 2,298 innovative drug investigational new drug applications in 2023, with 1,918 approved, representing an approval-to-submission ratio exceeding 80 percent.[22] While the FDA typically receives about 1,500 new IND submissions annually with approximately 91 percent allowed to proceed, the sheer volume of Chinese applications demonstrates the expanding pharmaceutical ecosystem.[23]

Critical reforms have accelerated development timelines. China implemented a 60-day implicit approval system for clinical trials in 2019, subsequently reducing average review timelines to approximately 50 working days.[24] In October 2025, the NMPA introduced a 30-day expedited review pathway for innovative drugs addressing critical unmet medical needs, globally synchronized development, or national priority R&D products.[25] Recent reforms implemented in September 2025 shortened trial approval timelines by approximately 30 percent through adaptive trial designs, real-time protocol modifications, and closer alignment with international Good Clinical Practice standards.[26]

The harmonization extends to manufacturing standards. In March 2025, the NMPA proposed landmark revisions mirroring the European Union's rigorous Good Manufacturing Practice Annex 1, emphasizing sterility, contamination control, and container integrity.[27] The adoption of electronic Common Technical Document submissions, following the FDA and EU model, is expected to become mandatory for all new drug approval applications by late 2025.[28]

This regulatory alignment means that clinical trial data generated in China can support regulatory filings in other parts of the world, accelerating cross-border collaborations. Phase I studies in China now cost roughly one-third of those in the United States and recruit patients in weeks rather than months, providing decision-ready data early in development.[29] The cost and speed advantages have fundamentally altered the economics of global drug development, making China an increasingly attractive location for early-stage clinical work even as geopolitical tensions complicate later-stage partnerships.

The Biomanufacturing Gap: China's Industrial Advantage

While the United States retains advantages in basic research and drug discovery, China has built formidable capabilities in biomanufacturing that may prove decisive in the coming decade. Manufacturing costs in China run up to 40 percent lower than in the United States, providing a significant competitive edge for international partnerships.[30] Recent reforms by the NMPA have made clinical trial operations an estimated 30 percent less expensive than in the United States, with patient recruitment proceeding two to three times faster.[31]

China's government has made biomanufacturing a strategic priority for 2025, listing it first among only four technologies slated for increased funding, ahead of quantum technology, embodied AI, and 6G.[32] This prioritization is deliberate and consequential. In June 2025, China's Ministry of Industry and Information Technology announced plans to cultivate more than 20 biomanufacturing pilot-scale capacity platforms by 2027, serving over 200 enterprises and incubating more than 400 products.[33] If successfully implemented, this will constitute the largest network of pilot facilities globally, providing Chinese startups with the quickest scale-up infrastructure available anywhere.

The strategic emphasis on biomanufacturing reflects China's broader industrial policy. The country's 14th Five-Year Plan for Bioeconomy Development sets ambitious targets for 2025, aiming to increase the scale of bioeconomy with enhanced comprehensive strength in science and technology combined with industrial integration.[34] By 2030, China's healthcare market is projected to expand from approximately $900 billion in 2019 to $2.3 trillion, second only to the United States.[35]

Chinese contract development and manufacturing organizations have become essential partners for global biopharma companies. Leading firms including WuXi AppTec, Lonza China, and Pharmaron provide comprehensive services from drug discovery and preclinical research to large-scale manufacturing at a fraction of Western costs.[36] WuXi AppTec alone has been involved in approximately one quarter of drugs used in the United States, including blockbuster cancer therapeutics.[37]

The biomanufacturing advantage extends across the pharmaceutical value chain. China possesses what industry analysts describe as capability to provide all components of the industrial chain, including Contract Research and Development Manufacturing Organizations, Contract Development and Manufacturing Organizations, and various Contract Research Organizations.[38] This vertical integration, combined with streamlined regulatory pathways and abundant clinical trial participants, creates a self-reinforcing ecosystem that attracts both domestic and international investment.

The geopolitical implications have not gone unnoticed. The proposed U.S. BIOSECURE Act, which would restrict certain Chinese biotechnology companies from receiving federal funding, has already impacted industry confidence in China-based service providers and prompted efforts to diversify manufacturing partners.[39] However, the legislation faces implementation challenges and may ultimately accelerate rather than slow Chinese self-sufficiency in biomanufacturing.

Investment Flows: Hong Kong's Biotech Boom versus Boston's Struggles

The divergent fortunes of Hong Kong and Boston as biotech capital centers illustrate the shifting geography of pharmaceutical innovation and investment. Hong Kong has emerged as a formidable competitor to traditional Western hubs, while Boston, long considered the undisputed capital of global biotech, faces unprecedented headwinds.

Hong Kong's Ascendance

Since the Hong Kong Stock Exchange introduced Chapter 18A listing rules in April 2018, allowing biotech companies with no revenue or profits to list on the main board, Hong Kong has transformed into Asia's premier biotech fundraising hub. By June 2025, 73 biotech companies had listed under Chapter 18A, propelling Hong Kong to become the world's second-largest biotech fundraising venue after the United States.[40]

The momentum accelerated dramatically in 2025. As of August, 14 Chinese biopharma and medical device companies had listed in Hong Kong, raising HK$18.2 billion ($2.33 billion)—already roughly quadruple 2024's total, with 36 more companies in the queue.[41] Chinese biotech stocks on the Hong Kong Stock Exchange jumped more than 100 percent in the first eight months of 2025, fueled by strong growth in licensing deals.[42] Healthcare equity capital markets issuance reached $5.8 billion in the first half of 2025, the highest level since 2021.[43]

Hong Kong's success stems from several structural advantages. The Chapter 18A framework provides clear, transparent regulatory approval processes with higher certainty than comparable mainland Chinese venues like the Shanghai STAR Market.[44] The May 2025 launch of the Technology Enterprises Channel provided additional pre-listing guidance for biotech companies, streamlining applications through confidential filing options and one-stop consultations.[45] Retail investor allocations in hot IPOs were capped at 35 percent to reduce volatility, with institutional investors now dominating allocations to ensure stable valuations.[46]

The October 2025 announcement of Hang Seng Biotech Index Futures—tracking the 30 largest biotech companies eligible for Southbound Stock Connect trading—provides investors with targeted risk management tools for one of Hong Kong's fastest-growing sectors.[47] With over 200 active listing applications, 20 percent from healthcare companies, the pipeline suggests sustained momentum.[48]

Boston's Biotech Malaise

In stark contrast, Massachusetts biotech faces a fourth consecutive year of declining venture capital funding. Investment in Massachusetts-based life sciences companies totaled $2.75 billion in the first half of 2025, down 17 percent from the same period in 2024 and the lowest level since 2017.[49] The state's biopharma industry lost approximately 1,100 research and development jobs in 2024 after years of growth.[50]

The funding drought has direct consequences. Life sciences real estate vacancy rates in Cambridge hit 16.1 percent, with Boston proper reaching 38.3 percent.[51] Some developers that were advancing conversions of office buildings to lab space have reverted plans, as life sciences tenants have become harder to land than office users—a complete reversal from 2021.[52]

Federal policy uncertainty compounds the challenges. Massachusetts is projected to receive approximately $463 million less in National Institutes of Health funding in 2025 than in 2024.[53] Proposed federal cuts to NIH grant funding could cost Massachusetts 81,300 jobs and more than $16 billion in total economic activity, according to University of Massachusetts researchers.[54] The appointment of vaccine skeptic Robert F. Kennedy Jr. to lead the Department of Health and Human Services has created additional uncertainty that industry leaders say has negatively impacted the investment community.[55]

Despite some positive indicators—six biotech IPOs raised $1.2 billion in Massachusetts in 2024, and early 2025 saw notable fundraising rounds including Treeline Biosciences' $422 million and Kailera Therapeutics' $400 million—the overall trajectory remains concerning.[56] MassBio's 2025 industry report painted what analysts called a "bleak outlook," with CEO Kendalle Burlin O'Connell noting that "uncertainty has replaced cautious optimism."[57]

The divergence between Hong Kong and Boston reflects broader trends in global biotech capital flows. While the United States still receives more than 22 percent of all global venture capital funding for biotech, second only to California's 45 percent, the relative decline is unmistakable.[58] Chinese firms increasingly view Hong Kong as not just a financing platform but a stage for building international credibility and partnerships, leveraging deep pools of long-term institutional capital.[59]

Prediction: Key Inflection Points Through 2030

The biotech battlefield of 2026-2030 will be shaped by several critical developments that are already visible in current trends.

The AI-Biotech Convergence

Artificial intelligence will fundamentally transform drug discovery and development timelines. The 2024 Nobel Prize in Chemistry, awarded to researchers who developed AlphaFold for protein structure prediction, validated the power of AI-biotech convergence.[60] Chinese firms are leveraging

AI platforms to accelerate discovery cycles, with costs for AI-driven drug development reportedly a fraction of traditional approaches.[61] As one industry observer noted, "the real DeepSeek moment in biotech is probably going to happen in five years," referring to additional breakthroughs in AI-enabled drug design.[62]

Biomanufacturing Dominance

By 2027, China's network of 20-plus pilot-scale biomanufacturing platforms will likely provide Chinese startups with unparalleled infrastructure for moving from laboratory to production scale.[63] This capacity advantage will compel foreign companies to consider moving R&D and manufacturing to China purely for speed, quality, and cost reasons. The global shortage of pilot facilities means non-Chinese startups may have limited alternatives if they want to progress products quickly.[64]

Market Projections

Multiple forecasts point to explosive growth in biotech markets. Annual revenue from drugs originating in China could reach $34 billion by 2030 and $220 billion by 2040, according to Morgan Stanley Research.[65] Chinese-originated drugs are projected to account for 35 percent of FDA approvals by 2040, up from only 5 percent in 2025.[66] The global market for biologically engineered materials, medicines, fuel, and food could reach between $4 trillion and $30 trillion annually by 2030, making biology "the last domain of engineerable science" and one of the greatest creators of economic value in the 21st century.[67]

Synthetic Biology and Advanced Modalities

China's synthetic biology market alone is projected to reach $31.5 billion by 2028, growing at an annual rate of 28.65 percent.[68] Shanghai has prioritized synthetic biology as a key industry, aiming by 2025 to incubate over five top-tier scientist teams, establish at least five synthetic biology platforms, and nurture more than ten leading firms.[69] The convergence of synthetic biology, gene editing technologies like CRISPR, and advanced manufacturing will enable new therapeutic modalities that could reshape treatment paradigms for cancer, genetic disorders, and infectious diseases.

Regulatory and Geopolitical Wildcards

The BIOSECURE Act and similar legislative efforts represent attempts to constrain Chinese biotech access to U.S. markets and funding. While such measures may slow partnerships in the near term, they risk accelerating Chinese self-sufficiency and potentially fragmenting global biotech into separate ecosystems. The U.S. National Security Commission on Emerging Biotechnology warned in April 2025 that the United States must dedicate a minimum of $15 billion over five years to biotech or risk falling behind permanently.[70]

The Harvard Belfer Center's assessment that China has "the most immediate opportunity to overtake the United States in biotechnology" among five critical technology sectors—ahead of AI, semiconductors, space, and quantum—underscores the urgency.[71] The narrow U.S.-China gap in biotech, narrower than in other domains, suggests that future developments could quickly shift the global balance.

The 2026 Watershed

The year 2026 may prove pivotal. China's biotech plan for 2026-2030, published in late 2025, reads as a manifesto for converting research into advanced production, validating sustainability, and scaling where value compounds fastest.[72] Unlike previous plans focused on raw growth, the new framework emphasizes systematic transformation from bench to plant, future-industry adjacency including digital-bio convergence, and planetary outcomes with verified sustainability metrics.[73]

For the United States, 2026 will test whether political will exists to match China's strategic investments. The National Bioeconomy Board launched in March 2024 outlined multi-agency goals spanning health, climate, agriculture, and supply-chain resilience, but execution has lagged behind strategy.[74] The contrast is stark: while China methodically builds pilot facilities and channels state guidance funds to strategic sectors, American biotech faces funding uncertainty, regulatory delays, and political turbulence.

The Shape of Competition Ahead

The biotech battlefield of 2026-2030 will not be won through individual breakthroughs alone, though such achievements will certainly occur. Rather, victory will go to whichever nation can best integrate research excellence, manufacturing capacity, regulatory efficiency, and strategic capital allocation into a self-reinforcing ecosystem.

China has demonstrated formidable capabilities across this spectrum. Its regulatory reforms have accelerated approval timelines, its manufacturing sector offers unmatched cost and speed advantages, its domestic market provides both testing ground and commercial opportunity, and its government directs capital to strategic priorities with ruthless efficiency. The surge in out-licensing deals reveals that Western pharmaceutical companies increasingly view Chinese innovation as essential for their own pipeline needs.

Yet challenges remain for China. Most firms are small R&D specialists struggling with funding and commercialization.[75] Ethical and regulatory scandals have eroded trust, and the National Reimbursement Drug List creates intense competition that can threaten profitability.[76] China's biotech sector made up only 4.8 percent of the global market in 2024, compared to the United States' 35 percent and Europe's 31 percent, limiting commercial opportunities for expensive cutting-edge treatments without international access.[77]

For the United States, the path forward requires more than rhetoric about maintaining leadership. It demands sustained public investment in basic research, coherent industrial policy to rebuild biomanufacturing capacity, regulatory reforms to match NMPA efficiency, and most critically, the political stability and policy continuity that biotech innovation requires. The sector's long development timelines—typically 10 to 15 years and $2.6 billion per drug—make uncertainty anathema to investment.[78]

The biotech battlefield of the late 2020s will determine which nation can harness biology's extraordinary potential not merely for economic advantage but for genuine improvements in human health and welfare. As both countries race to master what the National Security Commission on Emerging Biotechnology called the "design and engineering of biological systems," the stakes could not be higher.[79] The nation that wins this competition will shape not just pharmaceutical markets but the very future of medicine itself.

Endnotes

[1] "China Biotech's Stunning Advance Is Changing the World's Drug Pipeline," *Bloomberg News*, July 13, 2025, https://www.bloomberg.com/news/features/2025-07-13/china-drugmakers-catching-up-to-us-big-pharma-with-new-medicine-innovation.

[2] "China Pharma Regulation Update 2024–2025," Pacific Bridge Medical, May 14, 2025, https://www.pacificbridgemedical.com/uncategorized/chinas-pharmaceutical-regulatory-landscape-key-developments-in-2024-2025/.

[3] "China's biotech is cheaper and faster," *China Daily* (Wuxi edition), August 25, 2025, https://en.wuxi.gov.cn/2025-08/25/c_1118978.htm.

[4] "China's Biotech Rise and Global Innovation Challenges," *CKGSB Knowledge*, October 15, 2025, https://english.ckgsb.edu.cn/knowledge/article/china-biotech-rise-and-global-innovation-challenges/.

[5] Ibid.

[6] Ibid.

[7] "China's biotech is cheaper and faster," *China Daily* (Wuxi edition).

[8] "China's Biotech Rise and Global Innovation Challenges," *CKGSB Knowledge*.

[9] "China's AI drug discovery startups cash in on billion-dollar deals," *Rest of World*, August 13, 2025, https://restofworld.org/2025/ai-drug-discovery-startups-big-pharma-china/.

[10] "China biotechs 'reshaping' US biopharma as outlicensing deals rise 11%: Jefferies report," *FierceBiotech*, July 14, 2025, https://www.fiercebiotech.com/biotech/china-biotechs-reshaping-us-biopharma-outlicensing-deals-rise-11-jefferies-report.

[11] "China's Biopharma Boom in Global Drug Licensing Deals," EC Innovations, July 3, 2025, https://www.ecinnovations.com/blog/chinas-biopharma-boom-in-global-drug-licensing-deals/.

[12] Ibid.

[13] "China biotechs 'reshaping' US biopharma as outlicensing deals rise 11%," *FierceBiotech*.

[14] "China's Biotech Rise and Global Innovation Challenges," *CKGSB Knowledge*.

[15] "China biotechs 'reshaping' US biopharma as outlicensing deals rise 11%," *FierceBiotech*.

[16] "NewCo licensing models are tipping deals in favour of China's biotechs," *Pharmaceutical Technology*, September 30, 2025, https://www.pharmaceutical-technology.com/features/newco-licensing-models-are-tipping-deals-in-favour-of-chinas-biotechs/.

[17] "TESTIMONY USCC June 5, 2025," U.S.-China Economic and Security Review Commission, https://www.uscc.gov/sites/default/files/2025-06/Jeroen_Groenewegen-Lau_Testimony.pdf.

[18] "NewCo licensing models are tipping deals in favour of China's biotechs," *Pharmaceutical Technology*.

[19] Ibid.

[20] "China's biotech industry is on the rise. Will it reshape US pharma?" *Chemical & Engineering News*, September 5, 2025, https://cen.acs.org/pharmaceuticals/drug-development/Chinas-biotech-industry-rise-reshape/103/web/2025/09.

[21] "China Pharma Regulation Update 2024–2025," Pacific Bridge Medical.

[22] "Current landscape of innovative drug development and regulatory support in China," *PMC* (PubMed Central), https://pmc.ncbi.nlm.nih.gov/articles/PMC12280122/.

[23] Ibid.

[24] "Policy Interpretation of the Announcement on Optimizing of the Review and Approval Process for Clinical Trials of Innovative Drugs," National Medical Products Administration (China), https://english.nmpa.gov.cn/2025-10/14/c_1132761.htm.

[25] "NMPA Announcement on Optimizing of the Review and Approval Process for Clinical Trials of Innovative Drugs ([2025] No. 86)," National Medical Products Administration (China), https://english.nmpa.gov.cn/2025-10/14/c_1132769.htm.

[26] "Regulatory Updates, September 2025," Caidya, October 7, 2025, https://www.caidya.com/resources/regulatory-updates-sept-2025/.

[27] "How regulatory convergence is raising the bar for sterile drug safety," *BioPharma Dive*, May 19, 2025, https://www.biopharmadive.com/spons/how-regulatory-convergence-is-raising-the-bar-for-sterile-drug-safetyand-h/748129/.

[28] "China Drug Regulatory Reforms: The Next Big Thing in China Pharmaceutical Regulations for 2025," Freyr Solutions, https://www.freyrsolutions.com/blog/china-drug-regulatory-reforms-the-next-big-thing-in-china-pharmaceutical-regulations-for-2025.

[29] "TESTIMONY USCC June 5, 2025," U.S.-China Economic and Security Review Commission.

[30] "Is China the future of biotech?" *Labiotech.eu*, December 13, 2024, https://www.labiotech.eu/in-depth/china-biotech-industry/.

[31] "China's biotech is cheaper and faster," *China Daily* (Wuxi edition).

[32] "China aims to build 20 pilot scale biomanufacturing platforms by 2027," Dirk van der Kley (Substack), July 1, 2025, https://dirkvanderkley.substack.com/p/china-aims-to-build-20-pilot-scale.

[33] Ibid.

[34] "The roadmap of bioeconomy in China," *PMC* (PubMed Central), https://pmc.ncbi.nlm.nih.gov/articles/PMC9995158/.

[35] "China is Making Large Inroads into Biotech: Is Investment Money Following?" LPBI Group, July 28, 2025, https://pharmaceuticalintelligence.com/2025/07/28/china-is-making-large-inroads-into-biotech-is-investment-money-following/.

[36] "Is China the future of biotech?" *Labiotech.eu*.

[37] "China's biotech is cheaper and faster," *China Daily* (Wuxi edition).

[38] "Is China the future of biotech?" *Labiotech.eu*.

[39] "China to double down on biomanufacturing investment in 2025," *Pharma Manufacturing*, https://www.pharmamanufacturing.com/industry-news/news/55252168/china-to-double-down-on-biomanufacturing-investment-in-2025.

[40] "Hong Kong Betting Big on Biotech IPOs," *BioSpectrum Asia*, https://www.biospectrumasia.com/analysis/26/26569/hong-kong-betting-big-on-biotech-ipos.html.

[41] "China's Biotech Rise and Global Innovation Challenges," *CKGSB Knowledge*.

[42] Ibid.

[43] "Hong Kong IPO Revival and Dual Listings," *CKGSB Knowledge*, September 28, 2025, https://english.ckgsb.edu.cn/knowledge/article/hong-kong-ipo-revival-and-dual-listings/.

[44] "Chapter 18A listings of biotech companies on the HKEX," *China Business Law Journal*, August 23, 2023, https://law.asia/chapter-18a-listings-of-biotech-companies-on-the-hkex/.

[45] "HKEX sees record surge in listing applications," *China Daily*, October 21, 2025, https://www.chinadaily.com.cn/a/202510/21/WS68f6eb83a310f735438b6181.html.

[46] "Hong Kong's Confidential IPO Boom: A Strategic Edge for Tech and Biotech Firms in 2025," AInvest, August 12, 2025, https://www.ainvest.com/news/hong-kong-confidential-ipo-boom-strategic-edge-tech-biotech-firms-2025-2508/.

[47] "HKEX sees record surge in listing applications," *China Daily*.

[48] "PwC: 2025 poised to be the most active IPO market for Hong Kong in four years," PwC Hong Kong, https://www.pwchk.com/en/press-room/press-releases/pr-020725.html.

[49] "No Recovery In Sight For Massachusetts Biotech As VC Funding Falls 17%," *Bisnow*, August 26, 2025, https://www.bisnow.com/boston/news/life-sciences/vc-funding-for-massachusetts-biotech-firms-falls-17-as-expected-recovery-did-not-happen-130713.

[50] "Mass. biopharma industry loses jobs, hits lowest level of funding in years," *WBUR News*, August 26, 2025, https://www.wbur.org/news/2025/08/26/massbio-industry-jobs-snapshot-2025-boston.

[51] "Unleased lab space. Plunging valuations. Layoffs. In Massachusetts, the biotech slump is taking its toll," *The Boston Globe*, March 22, 2025, https://www.boston.com/news/the-boston-globe/2025/03/21/unleased-lab-space-plunging-valuations-layoffs-in-massachusetts-the-biotech-slump-is-taking-its-toll/.

[52] "No Recovery In Sight For Massachusetts Biotech As VC Funding Falls 17%," *Bisnow*.

[53] "Report paints bleak outlook for Massachusetts biotech industry," MassBio, August 26, 2025, https://www.massbio.org/news/recent-news/boston-globe-report-paints-bleak-outlook-for-massachusetts-biotech-industry/.

[54] "Mass. biopharma industry loses jobs, hits lowest level of funding in years," *WBUR News*.

[55] "Unleased lab space. Plunging valuations. Layoffs," *The Boston Globe*.

[56] "The Massachusetts biotech industry rebounded in 2024. Can the momentum last?" *The Boston Globe*, July 17, 2025, https://www.bostonglobe.com/2025/01/09/business/massachusetts-biotech-2025-outlook/.

[57] "Massachusetts biotech hub is limping amid layoffs and low investment," *PharmaVoice*, October 23, 2025, https://www.pharmavoice.com/news/massachusetts-biotech-limping-layoffs-investment-boston-massbio/803581/.

[58] Ibid.

[59] "HKEX sees record surge in listing applications," *China Daily*.

[60] "Introduction - Biotech," U.S. National Security Commission on Emerging Biotechnology, April 8, 2025, https://www.biotech.senate.gov/final-report/chapters/introduction/.

[61] "China's AI drug discovery startups cash in on billion-dollar deals," *Rest of World*.

[62] "It's not just AI — China's quickly gaining an edge over the U.S. in biotech," *CNBC*, June 5, 2025, https://www.cnbc.com/2025/06/05/chinas-quickly-gaining-an-edge-over-the-us-in-biotech.html.

[63] "China aims to build 20 pilot scale biomanufacturing platforms by 2027," Dirk van der Kley (Substack).

[64] Ibid.

[65] "China Biotech Boom: Generics Producer to Innovation Leader," Morgan Stanley, https://www.morganstanley.com/insights/articles/china-biotech-boom-generics-to-innovators.

[66] Ibid.

[67] "Biotech is the new focus in U.S.-China tech rivalry," *Axios*, February 3, 2024, https://www.axios.com/2024/02/03/biotech-us-china-tech-competition-bgi.

[68] "Technological and industrial trends in China's pharmaceutical sector," *PMC* (PubMed Central), https://pmc.ncbi.nlm.nih.gov/articles/PMC12479303/.

[69] "China's tech sector taps bioproduction to fuel expansion," *Xinhua*, June 30, 2025, https://english.news.cn/20250630/10013bdbbc59421e859eab9453942aa4/c.html.

[70] "Executive Summary - Biotech," U.S. National Security Commission on Emerging Biotechnology, April 16, 2025, https://www.biotech.senate.gov/final-report/chapters/executive-summary/.

[71] "It's not just AI — China's quickly gaining an edge over the U.S. in biotech," *CNBC*.

[72] "China Publishes Biotech 2026–2030 Plan - And the EU / US?" Wins Solutions, https://www.winssolutions.org/china-biotech-plan-2026-2030/.

[73] Ibid.

[74] Ibid.

[75] "China's Biotech Rise and Global Innovation Challenges," *CKGSB Knowledge*.

[76] Ibid.

[77] "TESTIMONY USCC June 5, 2025," U.S.-China Economic and Security Review Commission.

[78] "Biopharmaceuticals Rising: China's Strategic Pivot to Southeast Asia Amid Great Power Tech Competition," Carnegie Endowment for International Peace, https://carnegieendowment.org/research/2025/01/biopharmaceuticals-rising-chinas-strategic-pivot-to-southeast-asia-amid-great-power-tech-competition?lang=en.

[79] "Introduction - Biotech," U.S. National Security Commission on Emerging Biotechnology.

Part VII

Economic Espionage and Information Warfare

Chapter 19
The Shadow Competition

Cyber Operations, IP Theft, and Technology Transfer

In the autumn of 2024, cybersecurity firms detected a pattern of sophisticated intrusions targeting telecommunications providers across the United States. The breach, later attributed to Chinese state-sponsored actors operating under the designation Salt Typhoon, provided Beijing with access to call records, private communications of government officials, and information subject to law enforcement court orders.[1] This incident exemplified a competition that costs the American economy between $225 billion and $600 billion annually while threatening national security in ways that conventional warfare never could.[2]

The shadow competition between the United States and China represents perhaps the most consequential dimension of their broader strategic rivalry. While public attention focuses on visible flashpoints like Taiwan or trade disputes, an invisible war rages across digital networks, university campuses, corporate boardrooms, and research laboratories. This chapter examines the architecture of Chinese economic espionage, the scale of intellectual property theft, the recruitment programs targeting American researchers, and the blurring boundaries between commercial cybercrime and state-sponsored operations.

The Staggering Scale of Chinese Cyber Espionage

The magnitude of Chinese cyber espionage against the United States defies easy comprehension. FBI Director Christopher Wray testified in July 2024 that the bureau opens a new China-related counterintelligence case approximately every ten hours, and that even if every FBI cyber agent and intelligence analyst focused exclusively on the China threat, Chinese hackers would still outnumber FBI personnel by at least 50 to 1.[3] According to the FBI, about 80 percent of economic espionage prosecutions allege conduct that would benefit the Chinese state, and at least some nexus to China exists in around 60 percent of all trade secret theft cases.[4]

The economic costs are staggering. The Office of the U.S. Trade Representative found in its comprehensive 2018 Section 301 investigation that Chinese theft of American intellectual property costs between $225 billion and $600 billion annually.[5] A 2020 report from the Center for Strategic and International Studies estimated Chinese intellectual property theft in the range of $180 billion to $540 billion per year, with cost estimates varying significantly because much of the value of stolen information tends to be intrinsic, including factors like reputational damage, regulatory penalties, and loss of strategic information and intellectual property advantages.[6] Former NSA Director Keith Alexander described Chinese cyber espionage as "the greatest transfer of wealth in history."[7]

These figures, while shocking, may actually understate the true scope of losses. Until recently, the United States probably lost between $20 billion and $30 billion annually from Chinese cyber espionage alone, not counting losses from traditional espionage using human agents. The cumulative cost may reach $600 billion, since this type of espionage has been going on for more than two decades. Any estimate must account for the fact that some stolen intellectual property cannot be turned into products, making the loss in these instances effectively zero. However, in other cases, victim companies suffer revenue losses for years to come as Chinese competitors bring products to market using stolen technology.[8]

Chinese companies receive what amounts to an illegal subsidy through espionage—they can spend less on research and development since they can access U.S. research through theft. The range of Chinese economic espionage, from simple household goods like wooden furniture and house paint to the most advanced high-tech products, helps explain China's rapid growth over recent decades. Research by the International Trade Administration and the European Union found that $1 billion in exports created roughly 6,000 jobs. Chinese intellectual property theft reduces U.S. exports, meaning the United States has lost thousands of jobs annually. The U.S. Congress estimates that China's IP theft has resulted in the loss of 2 million American jobs.[9]

The 2018 Section 301 investigation by the Office of the U.S. Trade Representative documented systematic Chinese practices related to technology transfer, intellectual property theft, and innovation. The investigation found that China employed multiple strategies: requiring or pressuring technology transfer as a condition for market access, directing and facilitating investment in U.S. companies to acquire cutting-edge technologies, conducting unauthorized intrusions into U.S. commercial computer networks, and systematically stealing trade secrets and confidential business information.[8]

China's cyber operations target virtually every sector of strategic importance. A 2024 four-year review of Section 301 actions noted that CrowdStrike found China accounting for 67 percent of all state-sponsored cyber intrusions between mid-2020 and mid-2021, with much of it motivated by intellectual property theft. The report estimated the annual burden of China's cyber theft at tens of billions of dollars.[9] Targeted industries range from aerospace and defense to biotechnology, semiconductors, telecommunications, renewable energy, and artificial intelligence.

Recent High-Profile Cases

The tempo and sophistication of Chinese cyber operations have intensified dramatically. In March 2024, the Department of Justice unsealed an indictment charging seven Chinese nationals with conspiracy to commit computer intrusions and conspiracy to commit wire fraud for their involvement in a hacking group that spent approximately 14 years targeting U.S. and foreign critics, businesses, and political officials. The defendants—Ni Gaobin, Weng Ming, Cheng Feng, Peng Yaowen, Sun Xiaohui, Xiong Wang, and Zhao Guangzong—were members of Advanced Persistent Threat 31 (APT31), part of a cyberespionage program run by China's Ministry of State Security Hubei State Security Department in Wuhan.[10]

The APT31 group, operating since at least 2010, conducted global campaigns targeting political dissidents, government officials, candidates and campaign personnel, and American companies. The defendants targeted thousands of U.S. individuals and entities, including officials in the White House, Departments of Justice, Commerce, Treasury, and State, as well as U.S. Senators and Representatives from both political parties. They also targeted spouses of high-ranking officials and election campaign staff from both major parties in advance of the 2020 election.[11]

The hackers sent over 10,000 malicious emails that appeared to be from prominent news outlets or journalists. These emails contained hidden tracking links that, when simply opened by recipients, transmitted information including the recipient's location, IP addresses, network schematics, and device information to servers controlled by the defendants. The attackers then used this intelligence to enable more sophisticated targeted hacking, including compromising home routers and electronic devices.[12]

The breadth of targets demonstrated the strategic nature of the campaign. The defendants targeted not only government entities but also the broader ecosystem of organizations supporting critical national infrastructure and security operations. Among the corporate victims were multiple defense contractors, managed service providers, a leading 5G network equipment provider, and a leading provider of wireless technology. This approach allowed hackers to acquire sensitive information through various entry points in the supply chain, making detection and response more difficult.[13]

To gain and maintain access to victim computer networks, the defendants and others employed sophisticated hacking techniques including zero-day exploits—exploits that hackers became aware of before manufacturers or victims were able to patch or fix the vulnerability. The operation's sophistication reflected extensive planning and coordination with Chinese intelligence services. The UK government, releasing coordinated statements with the United States, attributed cyberattacks against every member of the European Union's Inter-Parliamentary Alliance on China and 43 United Kingdom parliamentary accounts to the same APT31 group.[14]

Beyond APT31, other cases revealed the breadth of Chinese operations. In 2014, the United States indicted five Chinese military hackers—officers in the People's Liberation Army's Unit 61398—for economic espionage targeting major American companies including Westinghouse, U.S. Steel, and SolarWorld. The indictment documented how these hackers stole trade secrets, manufacturing specifications, and sensitive business communications that would benefit Chinese state-owned enterprises.[13]

The pattern extended across sectors. Chinese hackers have targeted everything from proprietary rice and corn seeds to software for wind turbines and high-end medical devices. They have infiltrated defense contractors, research institutes, universities, and critical infrastructure operators. The scope of targets reflects a whole-of-economy approach to technology acquisition aligned with China's Made in China 2025 industrial policy.[14]

The Salt Typhoon operation disclosed in late 2024 represented a particularly alarming escalation. The breach of multiple U.S. telecommunications companies enabled theft of customer call records data, compromise of private communications of government officials, and access to information subject to law enforcement court orders. The FBI and Cybersecurity and Infrastructure Security Agency warned that their understanding of the compromise continued to grow as investigations progressed.[15]

Meanwhile, Volt Typhoon, uncovered in 2024, revealed military-led operations targeting U.S. critical infrastructure for potential sabotage. FBI Director Wray testified that these capabilities could impose "real-world harm" and significant civilian costs, potentially deterring U.S. intervention in a crisis. The operation embedded capabilities in manufacturing, utilities, transportation, and government networks—designed to disrupt operations during conflict rather than simply steal data.[16]

Thousand Talents and the Recruitment Ecosystem

While cyber intrusions grab headlines, China's systematic recruitment of scientists and researchers through talent programs represents an equally significant threat vector. The Thousand Talents Plan, launched in 2008, aimed to recruit overseas experts to advance China's technological capabilities.

The program offered extraordinary financial incentives including substantial salaries, research funding, and housing subsidies.[17]

The Thousand Talents Plan is merely the most prominent of more than 200 Chinese talent recruitment programs operating at national and sub-national levels. These programs target individuals—both Chinese nationals and foreign experts—with access to technologies China lacks. The FBI notes that participants typically enter contracts requiring them to share new technology developments exclusively with China, recruit colleagues into the program, and maintain their positions at U.S. institutions to preserve access to intellectual property and research funding.[18]

A 2019 Senate investigation into China's talent recruitment plans concluded they represented a serious threat to U.S. national security. The report documented how the programs facilitated both legal and illegal transfer of U.S. technology, intellectual property, and know-how to China. U.S. law enforcement concluded that China intended to use recruited scientists to gain access to new technology for economic and military advantage.[19]

Research on the Young Thousand Talents program, which began in 2010, provides insight into China's strategy. Between 2011 and 2017, the program recruited more than 3,500 young researchers. Analysis published in Science in 2023 revealed the program successfully attracted high-caliber scientists who, upon returning to China, received substantially larger research teams and funding. These scientists outpublished their U.S.-based peers by 144 percent in last-authored publications, demonstrating program effectiveness.[20]

High-profile prosecutions illustrated the programs' dangers. Dr. Charles Lieber, chair of Harvard's Department of Chemistry and Chemical Biology, received substantial financial support from China as a Thousand Talents Plan member while simultaneously receiving federal grants from the Department of Defense and National Institutes of Health. He lied to the DoD about his foreign collaborations and caused Harvard to provide false statements to NIH. Lieber was convicted in December 2021.[21]

In November 2020, Song Guo Zheng, a Thousand Talents Plan participant, pleaded guilty to making false claims to the FBI about his ties to the Chinese government during his employment at Ohio State University. The case demonstrated the legal risks participants faced when failing to disclose foreign affiliations properly.[22]

The talent programs' requirements raised serious concerns. According to FBI assessments, contracts often included non-disclosure agreements forbidding participants from informing their home universities or governments about awards. Participants were expected to share proprietary information, potentially violate export controls, and create conflicts of interest—all while maintaining positions at U.S. institutions.[23]

Universities Under Scrutiny

American universities, long celebrated as engines of international collaboration and innovation, found themselves at the center of mounting tensions over Chinese influence and espionage. The scale of U.S.-China scientific collaboration had grown exponentially from the 1980s through the mid-2010s. By 2017, U.S.-China co-authored papers peaked at approximately 55,000 annually. However, by 2022, that number had fallen to about 45,000—a contraction of nearly 20 percent—as security concerns mounted.[24]

The FBI began encouraging universities to develop protocols for monitoring students and visiting scholars from Chinese state-affiliated research institutions. In 2019, NPR reported that at least ten U.S. universities received briefings from the FBI urging them to monitor certain Chinese students and scholars, particularly those involved in science, technology, engineering, and mathematics fields. FBI officials explained they provided classified information about what China was trying to collect on campuses.[25]

The National Institutes of Health launched investigations into grant recipients for not disclosing collaboration or funding from China and for sharing peer-review grant material with Chinese researchers. NIH Director Francis Collins warned in August 2018 that "foreign entities have mounted systematic programs to influence NIH researchers and peer reviewers."[26]

The Justice Department's China Initiative, launched in November 2018, aimed to combat economic espionage but quickly became controversial. A 2021 MIT Technology Review analysis found that only 19 of 77 cases identified as China Initiative successes included charges related to economic espionage or intellectual property theft. By 2020, so-called "research integrity" cases—involving alleged omissions in paperwork rather than espionage—made up the bulk of prosecutions.[27]

The China Initiative's impact proved devastating for many researchers. NIH investigations at universities' request resulted in 103 (42 percent) of 246 investigated scientists losing their jobs. More than 250 scientists, mostly Asian, lost positions as a result. The psychological toll was severe; Professor Jane Wu, recruited by the Thousand Talents Programme in 2009, committed suicide in July 2024 after her career was destroyed despite no evidence of wrongdoing.[28]

A 2024 study documented that the number of Chinese-born scientists leaving the United States increased by 75 percent following the China Initiative's launch, with most returning to China. Critics argued the initiative reflected racial profiling and created a chilling effect on legitimate scientific collaboration. The Biden administration terminated the program in February 2022 after determining it fueled harmful perceptions of bias and stifled scientific research.[29]

The end of the China Initiative did not, however, signal the end of suspicion and hostility directed at U.S.-China research collaboration. If national security concerns largely provided the strategic rationale for scrutiny, domestic politics amplified and broadened it. In recent years, universities, companies, and even local governments became frequent targets of ideological campaigns. American universities—long celebrated as engines of international openness and innovation—faced growing pressure from congressional committees concerned about Chinese influence operations.[30]

The tension between security and openness proved difficult to resolve. Fields closely aligned with China's Made in China 2025 priorities—such as advanced information and communications technologies, aerospace, and new materials—experienced severe contractions in collaboration. Meanwhile, areas perceived as lower risk, such as earth and environmental sciences, continued modest cooperation. The challenge for policymakers became how to protect sensitive research while maintaining the collaborative environment that drives American innovation and attracts global talent.[31]

Universities themselves came under congressional scrutiny for partnerships with Chinese institutions. A September 2024 House report from the Select Committee on the Chinese Communist Party and Committee on Education and the Workforce flagged more than 8,800 publications involving American researchers with federal defense and intelligence agency funding who collaborated with Chinese scientists. The report alleged these collaborations provided "back-door access" to technologies necessary to protect against Chinese aggression.[30]

Georgia Institute of Technology announced it would end its partnership with Tianjin University, following similar moves by the University of California, Berkeley. The decisions came in response to proposed legislation that would bar colleges working with Chinese universities having ties to military or intelligence agencies from receiving Department of Defense grants.[31]

Section 301: Documenting Systematic Theft

The 2018 Section 301 investigation represented the most comprehensive U.S. government examination of Chinese technology transfer practices. Initiated in August 2017, the investigation examined whether China's acts, policies, and practices related to technology transfer, intellectual property, and innovation were unreasonable or discriminatory and burdened U.S. commerce.

The March 2018 report reached damning conclusions across four major areas. First, China used foreign ownership restrictions, including joint venture requirements and foreign equity limitations, and various administrative review and licensing processes to require or pressure technology transfer from U.S. companies. American firms seeking to do business in China faced systematic pressure to surrender their technology as the price of market access.[32]

Second, China's technology transfer regime deprived U.S. companies of the ability to negotiate market-based terms in licensing and technology transfer agreements. The Regulations on Technology Import and Export Administration mandated particular terms for indemnities and ownership of technology improvements, while other measures imposed non-market terms in licensing contracts.[33]

Third, the Chinese government directed and facilitated systematic investment in, and acquisition of, U.S. companies and assets to obtain cutting-edge technologies and intellectual property. This generated large-scale technology transfer in industries deemed important by Chinese government industrial plans, particularly those aligned with Made in China 2025.[34]

Fourth, and most significantly for this chapter's focus, China conducted and supported unauthorized intrusions into, and theft from, U.S. commercial computer networks to access intellectual property, including trade secrets, technical data, negotiating positions, and sensitive internal communications. The investigation found that China's cyber-enabled theft served strategic economic objectives, with documented incidents aligning closely with China's industrial policy goals.[35]

The Section 301 report documented how state-sponsored cyber intrusions originating from China occurred alongside an institutional framework for promoting industrial and technological development through a state-led model. State-owned enterprises and national champions were the primary beneficiaries of extensive state support, receiving stolen intellectual property that would otherwise have required years of research and hundreds of millions of dollars to develop independently.[36]

Businesses testified about their reluctance to share information on China's technology transfer regime, given the importance of the China market and the fact that Chinese government officials were "not shy about retaliating against critics." A representative of the Commission on the Theft of American Intellectual Property testified: "American companies are intimidated and reticent over the issue, especially in China. There they risk punishment by a powerful and opaque Chinese regulatory system."[37]

The 2024 four-year review of Section 301 actions concluded that while tariffs had encouraged China to take some steps toward eliminating technology transfer-related practices, cyber espionage and intellectual property theft continued at alarming levels. The review noted that in 2022, FBI Director Christopher Wray explained that the Chinese government sees cyber intrusions as "the pathway to cheat and steal on a massive scale." CrowdStrike's analysis showed China accounting for 67 percent of all state-sponsored cyber intrusions, with the annual burden of China's cyber theft estimated at tens of billions of dollars.[38]

Counter-Espionage Capabilities and Responses

The United States has mounted an increasingly sophisticated counter-espionage effort, though resource disparities remain stark. The FBI, despite opening a new China-related investigation approximately every ten hours, faces overwhelming odds with Chinese hackers outnumbering FBI cyber personnel by at least 50 to 1.[39]

The U.S. government has employed multiple tools to combat Chinese espionage. Criminal prosecutions serve both justice and deterrence functions. The 2014 indictment of five Chinese military hackers marked the first time the United States indicted state actors for economic espionage. The indictment charged officers from PLA Unit 61398 with targeting major American companies including Westinghouse, U.S. Steel, and SolarWorld, stealing trade secrets and sensitive business information.[40]

The March 2024 APT31 indictments represented a continuation of this approach. Attorney General Merrick Garland stated: "The Justice Department will not tolerate efforts by the Chinese government to intimidate Americans who serve the public, silence the dissidents who are protected by American laws, or steal from American businesses."[41] Concurrent with the indictments, the Treasury Department imposed sanctions, and the State Department announced rewards of up to $10 million for information on the defendants and their organization.[42]

The Cybersecurity and Infrastructure Security Agency (CISA), in coordination with the NSA and FBI, has released numerous advisories detailing Chinese state-sponsored threat actors' tactics. CISA's 2024 threat assessment highlighted persistent cyber threats posed by China to U.S. government, private-sector, and critical infrastructure networks. Chinese actors like Volt Typhoon and Salt Typhoon exhibited tactics extending beyond traditional cyber espionage, positioning themselves within information technology networks to enable lateral movement to operational technology systems controlling critical infrastructure.[43]

CISA's approach emphasizes public-private collaboration, leveraging private sector visibility and capabilities to collectively defend against Chinese cyber threats. Key initiatives include facilitating investigation and mitigation of zero-day exploitation of network edge devices, strengthening cloud infrastructure at scale, and collaborating with Sector Risk Management Agencies to address sector-specific challenges.[44]

Chinese responses to U.S. counter-espionage efforts have been predictably defiant. Chinese officials routinely characterize allegations as "smears" based on "groundless speculation" rather than evidence. China portrays itself as a victim of cyberattacks and accuses the United States of conducting worldwide cyber espionage. The Chinese government has shown no willingness to restrain its intelligence services or dismantle the networks conducting operations against American targets.[45]

The Blurring Line Between Commercial and State-Sponsored Theft

Perhaps the most significant development in Chinese economic espionage has been the deliberate obscuring of boundaries between commercial cybercrime and state-sponsored intelligence operations. The March 2024 APT31 indictments revealed how China created front companies to conduct cyber operations while providing deniability for the Ministry of State Security.

According to the indictment, the Chinese government created Wuhan Xiaoruizhi Science & Technology Co. in 2010 as a front for MSS operations. The company employed contractors who conducted hacking campaigns while maintaining the appearance of private commercial activity. The defendants and dozens of MSS intelligence officers, contractor hackers, and support personnel formed a sophisticated ecosystem that obscured state involvement.[46]

This ecosystem serves multiple purposes for the Chinese government. First, it provides plausible deniability. When nominally private companies conduct intrusions, Chinese officials can more credibly claim lack of government involvement. Second, it dramatically expands China's cyber workforce beyond operators in military and intelligence services. Third, it creates financial incentives that motivate aggressive collection even beyond specific government taskings.[47]

The APT31 model proved effective for espionage but also created vulnerabilities. Private contractors operating for profit sometimes targeted victims beyond those of interest to Chinese intelligence services. The broad approach resulted in more worldwide intrusion victims and more systems left vulnerable to exploitation by third parties, as hackers sought any information that could be monetized.[48]

The origins of this ecosystem trace back to China's first generation of "patriotic hackers" in the late 1990s and early 2000s. Groups like the Green Army declared themselves patriots who offered services to the Chinese Communist Party. Over time, these individuals professionalized and established companies that could operate both as legitimate businesses and as contractors for Chinese intelligence services.[49]

The sophistication of arrangements between Chinese state security agencies and private contractors reflects careful planning to maximize collection while minimizing attribution. In many instances, individuals linked to the Ministry of State Security or People's Liberation Army units register companies that engage in no real profit-driven activities but help procure infrastructure needed for conducting cyberattacks without drawing attention. These arrangements create a gray zone where proving connections to state direction requires extensive investigation.[50]

This blurring of lines extends beyond cyber operations to more traditional forms of technology transfer. Chinese state-owned enterprises and ostensibly private companies operating in the United States serve as platforms for recruiting American talent with access to proprietary information. These companies often maintain close ties to Chinese government ministries while presenting themselves as commercial entities seeking legitimate business partnerships.[51]

The implications are profound. Traditional counterintelligence focused on identifying and countering intelligence officers under diplomatic or commercial cover. The contractor model multiplies the number of actors who must be tracked and countered, while providing those actors with profit motives that supplement or replace ideological motivations. It creates a massive gray zone where prosecution requires proving connections to state direction, even when such connections are deliberately obscured.

The Path Forward

The shadow competition between the United States and China shows no signs of abating. The evidence suggests intensification rather than moderation. The scale of operations documented in indictments, the sophistication of persistent threats like Salt Typhoon and Volt Typhoon, and the brazenness of operations that continue even after public exposure all point to a Chinese government confident in its ability to operate with substantial impunity.

The costs are not merely economic, though the hundreds of billions of dollars in annual losses cannot be dismissed. Chinese espionage undermines American innovation by allowing Chinese companies to avoid research and development costs, shifts employment away from high-paying jobs, threatens national security by exposing defense technologies and sensitive government information, and forces American companies to spend enormous sums on cybersecurity that could otherwise be invested in productive activities.

The U.S. response has grown more sophisticated, with improved coordination between the FBI, CISA, NSA, and the Justice Department. Public-private partnerships have strengthened, and awareness of the threat has increased dramatically. The decision to publicly indict Chinese intelligence officers and hackers, even when extradition remains unlikely, serves important functions by exposing operations, warning potential targets, and potentially deterring some actors.

Yet significant challenges remain. The resource imbalance between Chinese offensive cyber operations and U.S. defensive capabilities persists. The tension between maintaining openness in scientific research and preventing technology transfer to adversaries has yet to be resolved. The China Initiative's failure demonstrates the difficulty of addressing insider threats without creating a climate of fear that drives away talented researchers. The contractor ecosystem continues to evolve, finding new ways to obscure state direction while conducting operations at scale.

Perhaps most concerning is the normalization of this shadow competition. What once would have been considered acts of war—persistent penetration of critical infrastructure, theft of hundreds of billions in intellectual property, targeting of government officials' communications—has become background noise in the broader U.S.-China relationship. The risk is that escalation becomes so gradual that neither side recognizes when boundaries have been crossed until it is too late.

The challenge for the United States extends beyond merely defending against current threats. The fundamental question is whether America can maintain its technological edge while China systematically appropriates decades of American innovation through espionage. James Andrew Lewis of CSIS noted that complaints alone will not solve this problem—the United States needs its own strategy to speed and increase its creation of intellectual property. The competition requires not just better defenses but accelerated offense in the form of innovation that stays ahead of Chinese acquisition efforts.[32]

Moreover, the United States faces difficult trade-offs between security and the openness that has historically driven American scientific and technological leadership. Draconian restrictions risk creating the chilling effect evidenced by the China Initiative's failure, driving away both Chinese-American researchers and international talent more broadly. Yet insufficient vigilance invites continued massive losses of intellectual property and threatens national security. Finding the balance requires sophisticated policy-making that distinguishes genuine security threats from legitimate international collaboration.[33]

The private sector faces its own dilemmas. American companies seeking access to China's massive market have long calculated that immediate benefits outweigh eventual losses from forced technology transfer. After 30 years, those calculations prove increasingly untenable as China has developed into the world's second-largest economy and a technological competitor. What was tolerable when China was less developed no longer remains acceptable. Yet decoupling entirely from China carries enormous economic costs and may prove practically impossible given the integration of global supply chains.[34]

As the visible rivalry over semiconductors, critical minerals, and military flashpoints intensifies, the shadow competition in cyberspace will likely accelerate. The question is not whether China will continue its systematic theft of American innovation and penetration of American networks—the evidence makes clear it will. The question is whether the United States can develop an effective strategy to defend against operations that are persistent, multifaceted, and conducted by an adversary willing to leverage every instrument of state power, blur every distinction between public and private sectors, and exploit every opening in America's open society.

The shadow competition has emerged as one of the most consequential dimensions of the U.S.-China rivalry. Its outcome may well determine which nation leads in the technologies that will define the twenty-first century, and whether the international order remains governed by rules or by which nation can steal, coerce, and intimidate most effectively. In this competition, fought in the shadows but with stakes in the bright light of day, there are no neutral observers—only participants and victims.

Endnote

[1] Cybersecurity and Infrastructure Security Agency, "Joint Statement from FBI and CISA on the People's Republic of China (PRC) Targeting of Commercial Telecommunications Infrastructure," November 13, 2024, https://www.cisa.gov/news-events/cybersecurity-advisories/aa24-317a.

[2] Office of the United States Trade Representative, "Findings of the Investigation into China's Acts, Policies, and Practices Related to Technology Transfer, Intellectual Property, and Innovation Under Section 301 of the Trade Act of 1974," March 22, 2018, 5-6, https://ustr.gov/sites/default/files/Section%20301%20FINAL.PDF.

[3] House Committee on Homeland Security, "China Threat Snapshot," updated February 2024, https://homeland.house.gov/china-threat-snapshot/; Federal Bureau of Investigation, "The China Threat," accessed December 1, 2025, https://www.fbi.gov/investigate/counterintelligence/the-china-threat.

[4] House Committee on Homeland Security, "China Threat Snapshot."

[5] Office of the United States Trade Representative, "Findings of the Investigation into China's Acts, Policies, and Practices," 180-181.

[6] Center for Strategic and International Studies, "Confronting China's Efforts to Steal Defense Information," Belfer Center for Science and International Affairs, May 27, 2020, https://www.belfercenter.org/publication/confronting-chinas-efforts-steal-defense-information.

[7] Stavros Atlamazoglou, "The U.S. Economy Is Losing as Much as $600 Billion a Year in Intellectual Property from Chinese Espionage," The National Interest, November 25, 2024, https://nationalinterest.org/blog/buzz/us-economy-losing-much-600-billion-year-intellectual-property-chinese-espionage-210956.

[8] James Andrew Lewis, "How Much Have the Chinese Actually Taken?," Center for Strategic and International Studies, October 15, 2024, https://www.csis.org/analysis/how-much-have-chinese-actually-taken.

[9] Michael S. Rogers, "The Impact of Chinese Espionage on the United States," The Diplomat, December 4, 2018, https://thediplomat.com/2018/12/the-impact-of-chinese-espionage-on-the-united-states/.

[10] U.S. Attorney's Office, Eastern District of New York, "Seven Hackers Associated with Chinese Government Charged with Computer Intrusions Targeting Perceived Critics of China and U.S.

Businesses and Politicians," press release, March 25, 2024, https://www.justice.gov/usao-edny/pr/seven-hackers-associated-chinese-government-charged-computer-intrusions-targeting.

[11] Ibid.

[12] Kevin Collier, "U.S., Britain, sanction China for broad 14-year hacking campaign," The Washington Post, March 26, 2024, https://www.washingtonpost.com/national-security/2024/03/25/china-hack-apt31-sanctions-indictment/.

[13] MeriTalk, "DoJ Charges China's APT31 With Long Hacking Campaign Against U.S.," March 25, 2024, https://www.meritalk.com/articles/doj-charges-chinas-apt31-with-long-hacking-campaign-against-u-s/.

[14] Bitdefender, "DOJ Indicts Chinese Nationals Belonging to Chinese State-Backed Hacking Group APT31," March 26, 2024, https://www.bitdefender.com/en-us/blog/hotforsecurity/doj-indicts-chinese-nationals-belonging-to-chinese-state-backed-hacking-group-apt31.

[15] U.S. Department of Justice, "U.S. Charges Five Chinese Military Hackers for Cyber Espionage Against U.S. Corporations and a Labor Organization for Commercial Advantage," press release, May 19, 2014, https://www.justice.gov/opa/pr/us-charges-five-chinese-military-hackers-cyber-espionage-against-us-corporations-and-labor.

[16] James Andrew Lewis, "Put China's Intellectual Property Theft in a Larger Context," Center for Strategic and International Studies, June 29, 2017, https://www.csis.org/analysis/put-chinas-intellectual-property-theft-larger-context.

[17] Cybersecurity and Infrastructure Security Agency, "Joint Statement from FBI and CISA on the People's Republic of China (PRC) Targeting of Commercial Telecommunications Infrastructure."

[18] CYFIRMA, "Typhoon in the Fifth Domain: China's Evolving Cyber Strategy," September 3, 2024, https://www.cyfirma.com/research/typhoon-in-the-fifth-domain/.

[19] Federal Bureau of Investigation, "FBI Counterintelligence Strategic Partnership Intelligence Note: Chinese Talent Programs," 2015, https://info.publicintelligence.net/FBI-ChineseTalentPrograms.pdf.

[20] Federal Bureau of Investigation, "Chinese Talent Plans," accessed December 1, 2025, https://www.fbi.gov/investigate/counterintelligence/the-china-threat/chinese-talent-plans.

[21] U.S. Senate Permanent Subcommittee on Investigations, "Threats to the U.S. Research Enterprise: China's Talent Recruitment Plans," November 2019, https://www.hsgac.senate.gov/wp-content/uploads/2019-11-18-PSI-Staff-Report-Chinas-Talent-Recruitment-Plans-Updated.pdf.

[22] Dongbo Shi, Weichen Liu, and Yanbo Wang, "Has China's Young Thousand Talents program been successful in recruiting and nurturing top-caliber scientists?," Science 379 (2023): 62-65.

[23] U.S. Attorney's Office, District of Massachusetts, "Harvard University Professor Convicted of Making False Statements," press release, December 21, 2021, https://www.justice.gov/usao-ma/pr/harvard-university-professor-convicted-making-false-statements.

[24] U.S. Attorney's Office, Southern District of Ohio, "Former Ohio State Professor Pleads Guilty to Making False Statements," press release, November 6, 2020, https://www.justice.gov/usao-sdoh/pr/former-ohio-state-professor-pleads-guilty-making-false-statements.

[25] Federal Bureau of Investigation, "Chinese Talent Plans."

[26] Quincy Institute for Responsible Statecraft, "U.S.–China Scientific Collaboration at a Crossroads: Navigating Strategic Engagement in the Era of Scientific Nationalism," October 2024, https://quincyinst.org/report/u-s-china-scientific-collaboration-at-a-crossroads/.

[27] Emily Feng, "FBI Urges Universities To Monitor Some Chinese Students And Scholars In The U.S.," NPR, June 28, 2019, https://www.npr.org/2019/06/28/728659124/fbi-urges-universities-to-monitor-some-chinese-students-and-scholars-in-the-u-s.

[28] Ibid.

[29] Justin Jouvenal and David Jackson, "The 'China Initiative' Failed U.S. Research and National Security. Don't Bring It Back," Brennan Center for Justice, December 18, 2024, https://www.brennancenter.org/our-work/analysis-opinion/china-initiative-failed-us-research-and-national-security-dont-bring-it.

[30] University of Michigan Ford School, "US universities secretly turned their back on Chinese professors under DOJ's China Initiative," 2024, https://fordschool.umich.edu/news/2024/us-universities-secretly-turned-their-back-chinese-professors-under-dojs-china-initiative.

[31] Quincy Institute for Responsible Statecraft, "U.S.–China Scientific Collaboration at a Crossroads."

[32] Sara Weissman, "Latitudes: Congressional report slams U.S. research partnerships with China," The Chronicle of Higher Education, September 25, 2024, https://www.chronicle.com/newsletter/latitudes/2024-09-25.

[33] Ibid.

[34] Office of the United States Trade Representative, "Findings of the Investigation into China's Acts, Policies, and Practices," 19-66.

[35] Ibid., 67-96.

[36] Ibid., 97-150.

[37] Ibid., 153-181.

[38] Ibid., 160-165.

[39] Ibid., 26.

[40] Office of the United States Trade Representative, "Four-Year Review of Actions Taken in the Section 301 Investigation," 11-12.

[41] House Committee on Homeland Security, "China Threat Snapshot."

[42] U.S. Department of Justice, "U.S. Charges Five Chinese Military Hackers for Cyber Espionage."

[43] U.S. Attorney's Office, Eastern District of New York, "Seven Hackers Associated with Chinese Government Charged."

[44] Ibid.

[45] Cybersecurity and Infrastructure Security Agency, "People's Republic of China Threat Overview and Advisories," accessed December 1, 2025, https://www.cisa.gov/topics/cyber-threats-and-advisories/nation-state-cyber-actors/china.

[46] Ibid.

[47] Axios, "DOJ charges seven hackers tied to Chinese government," March 25, 2024, https://www.axios.com/2024/03/25/us-doj-china-hackers-indictment.

[48] U.S. Attorney's Office, Eastern District of New York, "Seven Hackers Associated with Chinese Government Charged."

[49] Ibid.

[50] Nextgov, "US accuses Chinese hackers of 14-year campaign targeting government officials," March 25, 2024, https://www.nextgov.com/cybersecurity/2024/03/us-accuses-chinese-hackers-14-year-campaign-targeting-government-officials/395204/.

[51] Ibid.

[52] Information Technology and Innovation Foundation, "From Outside Assaults to Insider Threats: Chinese Economic Espionage," November 3, 2024, https://itif.org/publications/2024/11/03/from-outside-assaults-to-insider-threats-chinese-economic-espionage/.

[53] Ibid.

[54] Lewis, "How Much Have the Chinese Actually Taken?"

[55] Quincy Institute for Responsible Statecraft, "U.S.–China Scientific Collaboration at a Crossroads."

[56] Lewis, "Put China's Intellectual Property Theft in a Larger Context."

Chapter 20

Narrative Wars and Information Operations

Competing for Hearts and Minds

The struggle between the United States and China extends far beyond semiconductors and rare earth minerals, tariffs and trade deficits. At its core lies a contest for narrative supremacy—a battle to shape global perceptions, influence democratic processes, and control the flow of information across borders. This information warfare, waged through social media platforms, state-sponsored media outlets, academic institutions, and digital networks, represents one of the most insidious and far-reaching dimensions of the U.S.-China rivalry. Unlike traditional military confrontation or economic competition, narrative warfare operates in the shadows, exploiting democratic openness while leveraging authoritarian control.

As of 2025, this competition has reached an inflection point. Chinese interference operations have grown increasingly sophisticated, targeting not just presidential elections but down-ballot races, exploiting social divisions, and undermining confidence in democratic institutions. Simultaneously, Beijing has invested billions in expanding its state media apparatus globally while restricting foreign voices within its borders. American public diplomacy, meanwhile, struggles with budget constraints, political dysfunction, and the challenge of countering an adversary that operates without the constraints of transparency or accountability. The outcome of this narrative battle may prove as consequential as any technological or military competition in determining which system—democratic capitalism or authoritarian state capitalism—will shape the twenty-first century global order.

TikTok and the Data Security Debate

No issue better encapsulates the complexity of the U.S.-China information rivalry than TikTok. With over 170 million American users as of 2025, the short-form video platform owned by Beijing-based ByteDance has become the most visible flashpoint in debates over data security, foreign influence, and the boundaries of acceptable risk in an interconnected world.[1]

On January 17, 2025, the U.S. Supreme Court in *TikTok Inc. v. Garland* upheld the Protecting Americans from Foreign Adversary Controlled Applications Act, requiring ByteDance to divest its ownership stake in TikTok or face a ban. The Court's per curiam opinion concluded that even if the regulation implicated First Amendment rights by burdening free speech, it survived intermediate scrutiny because it advanced important governmental interests unrelated to speech suppression.[2] Justice Neil Gorsuch, concurring in judgment, expressed concern about what he termed the government's attempt to prevent "covert manipulation of content," noting that such justifications could threaten editorial discretion protected by the First Amendment.[3]

Yet the Supreme Court's decision represented merely one chapter in a saga that spanned two presidential administrations. President Donald Trump, who had attempted to ban TikTok during his first term, reversed course upon returning to office. On January 20, 2025, Trump signed Executive Order 14166 delaying enforcement for 75 days. He subsequently issued Executive Order 14258 on April 4 extending the deadline to June 19, Executive Order 14310 on June 19 extending to September 17, and Executive Order 14350 on September 16 extending to December 16, 2025.[4] In his Truth Social post announcing the second extension, Trump wrote that the TikTok deal "requires more work to ensure all necessary approvals are signed," while expressing hope to "continue working in Good Faith with China, who I understand are not very happy about our Reciprocal Tariffs."[5]

The national security concerns surrounding TikTok stem from China's 2017 National Intelligence Law, which requires Chinese companies to assist in intelligence gathering if requested by the government. While TikTok insists it has never shared U.S. user data with the Chinese government, the platform admitted in 2022 that employees in China had improperly accessed data on American journalists investigating internal leaks—a revelation that deepened suspicions about the company's relationship with Beijing.[6]

Beyond traditional data collection concerns, analysts at the RAND Corporation identified an emerging threat: TikTok's corpus of user-generated videos represents ideal training data for advanced deepfake-generating AI systems. The platform's uniform 9:16 aspect ratio and diverse content, combined with dynamic watermarking that prevents external actors from scraping videos, means ByteDance essentially maintains sole access to this massive dataset. With 170 million Americans using TikTok, researchers warned that this data could enable China to train AI models capable of producing highly convincing disinformation at scale.[7]

Yet the debate over TikTok reveals profound disagreements within the American national security establishment. James Lewis of the Center for Strategic and International Studies argued that while China does collect personal data on Americans, "there is no evidence that it has found a way to benefit from this." Lewis identified the real risk not in data collection or influence operations—which he considers "generally overrated"—but in the voluntary downloading of Chinese software onto American devices, which could facilitate malware injection through app updates.[8]

The TikTok controversy also highlights the lack of reciprocity in U.S.-China information flows. While Washington debates whether to allow a Chinese-owned platform to operate, Beijing has blocked U.S. companies like Google, YouTube, Facebook, and Instagram for years. The absence of comprehensive national data privacy legislation in the United States further complicates the debate. Congress failed to advance the American Privacy Rights Act in 2024 despite bipartisan support, leaving the U.S. significantly behind other democracies in safeguarding user privacy.[9]

Chinese State Media's Global Expansion

While TikTok captures public attention, China's state media expansion represents a more systematic, long-term effort to shape global narratives. According to Freedom House's 2020 report "Beijing's Global Megaphone," the Chinese government reportedly allocated \$6 billion in 2009 to the global expansion of state media, investing heavily in upgrading major outlets—China Global Television Network (CGTN), Xinhua News Agency, and China Radio International (CRI)—in an attempt to normalize them as credible alternatives to Western media.[10]

The scale of this expansion is substantial. CGTN broadcasts in English, Spanish, French, Arabic, and Russian to every region via satellite, cable, and internet protocol television. China Daily is distributed at newsstands, hotels, airlines, and government offices globally. Based on China Daily's annual filings under the Foreign Agents Registration Act, the paper's budget and expenditures in the United States increased tenfold from approximately \$500,000 in the first half of 2009 to more than \$5 million in the latter half of 2019.[11] Australian media reported in 2018 that CGTN had engaged in a \$500 million advertising campaign to attract cable viewers.[12]

Despite these massive investments, the impact has been mixed. By November 2019, four of the five fastest-growing media pages on Facebook were Chinese state-run outlets: Global Times, CGTN, and two Xinhua pages. CGTN's French-language account accumulated 20.3 million followers, Spanish 15.7 million, Arabic 14.4 million, and Russian approximately 1 million. Curiously, Chinese-language accounts belonging to the same outlets attracted far smaller followings—CCTV's Chinese Facebook account had just 3.75 million followers as of December 2019, raising questions about the authenticity of these follower counts.[13]

Academic research analyzing tweets from CGTN, Xinhua, People's Daily, and China Daily found that CGTN reduced government narrative content from 43 percent to 37 percent after the 2017 "Going Global" campaign launched, while simultaneously increasing soft news coverage from 21 percent to 37 percent—an apparent effort to make content more palatable to international audiences.[14] Yet this pivot toward accessibility has not translated into genuine influence. According to the Lowy Institute's Asia Power Index, CGTN ranks only as the tenth-most popular broadcaster in the Asia-Pacific region, with reach described as "inconsequential" compared to CNN.[15]

Behind the glossy facade, Chinese state media organizations struggle with internal contradictions. Former CGTN employees describe a culture of "quantity over quality," with Chinese staff required to produce 15-20 stories per eight-hour shift. International staff report being constrained in content creation and excluded from organizational decision-making, with one foreign employee told: "You'll never understand. You are not Chinese... You will never understand how things work here, especially in a place like CCTV."[16]

China's state media expansion extends beyond flagship outlets to covert arrangements. In twelve countries studied by Freedom House, coproduction arrangements involved China providing technical support or resources for reporting in exchange for editorial control. In nine countries, monetary compensation or gifts were offered for publication of pro-Beijing articles. Multiple China-based entities with Chinese Communist Party ties—from Xinhua to provincial governments to companies like Huawei—actively promote such partnerships.[17]

The content vacuum created by China's restrictions on foreign correspondents provides an opening for Chinese state media material. Beijing has imposed severe restrictions on foreign journalists while threatening, harassing, or imprisoning family members of journalists based outside the country who report unfavorably on China. Such incidents occurred in at least five democracies—Australia, India, Spain, the United Kingdom, and the United States—with relatives of U.S.-based Uyghur reporters for Radio Free Asia serving long prison sentences.[18]

Democratic pushback against Chinese media expansion has intensified. The United Kingdom revoked CGTN's broadcast license in 2021, and the United States required state media outlets to register as foreign agents under FARA. In 2020, the State Department designated CGTN, CCTV, and Xinhua as foreign missions, requiring them to submit employee lists and seek approval for property purchases.[19] Australia and Singapore have created commissions and legislation to monitor foreign investment and influence, while European states assess ways to better scrutinize media sector investments.[20]

U.S. Public Diplomacy and Its Limitations

While China pursues an aggressive, well-funded strategy of narrative projection, American public diplomacy efforts struggle with fragmentation, underfunding, and unclear strategic direction. The asymmetry is stark: China's government funding for state media dwarfs that of any other country, including the United States, yet American responses remain reactive and inconsistent.[21]

A January 2025 panel convened by the U.S. Advisory Commission on Public Diplomacy to examine China's public diplomacy efforts revealed the depth of this challenge. Samantha Custer of AidData emphasized three critical pieces of strategic context: First, China's public diplomacy is driven by a strategic imperative to "win the narrative." Second, Beijing possesses both the financial means and political will to employ a formidable public diplomacy toolkit. Third, China seeks synergies between public diplomacy, information, influence, and economic cooperation as a force multiplier—it does not view these as separate, isolated tools.[22]

By 2022, China maintained over 400 Confucius Institutes and classrooms overseas promoting Chinese language and culture. Before the pandemic, Beijing positioned China as a premier study abroad destination, using Confucius Institutes to associate students with scholarship opportunities and language training. China also provides vocational training, building personalized connections through people-to-people diplomacy.[23]

American experts emphasized that the United States must present strong and clear positive alternatives to Chinese narratives, propaganda, and investment, requiring better integration of public diplomacy and U.S. economic tools. Importantly, panelists noted that negative narratives about China will not sway audiences—the focus must be on demonstrating why transparent investment, free societies, and reliable partnership with the United States offer superior value.[24]

High-level U.S. officials should more frequently visit countries that traditionally receive less American attention but experience active Chinese diplomatic and business engagement. Embassies should develop comprehensive communications strategies involving significant investment or partnership announcements, utilizing public-private partnerships, Millennium Challenge Corporation compacts, and expanded people-to-people exchange programs.[25]

Yet implementing such recommendations faces significant obstacles. In May 2024, public perception of China among Americans reached its most negative point since the Tiananmen Square massacre, with 81 percent viewing China unfavorably—a trend matched in numerous other democracies worldwide.[26] The fundamental challenge is that both political systems understand the other side is unlikely to budge on key issues. Beijing wants Washington to drop export controls, sanctions, tariffs, support for Taiwan, and criticism of human rights. Washington wants China to stop coercively advancing claims regarding Taiwan and in the South China Sea, curtail unfair trade policies, and end its strategic partnership with Russia. Zero chance exists that either side will concede in the foreseeable future.[27]

The Battle for Emerging Market Narratives

The contest for hearts and minds extends far beyond the United States and China, with critical battles unfolding across Latin America, Africa, the Middle East, and Southeast Asia. In these regions, Chinese narratives often resonate more effectively than American messaging, exploiting historical grievances, economic desperation, and resentment of Western interventionism.

China's Belt and Road Initiative has provided a powerful vehicle for narrative construction. By coupling infrastructure investments with sustained messaging about "win-win cooperation," "non-interference in internal affairs," and "South-South solidarity," Beijing has built influence across more than 140 countries. While American critics focus on debt trap diplomacy and environmental degradation, many developing country leaders appreciate China's willingness to fund projects without the governance conditions typically imposed by Western institutions.[28]

In Africa, Chinese investment has been accompanied by expansion of media operations. CGTN Africa, headquartered in Nairobi, provides free content to cash-strapped local media organizations. In 2011, Zimbabwe's government agreed to share news programming with CCTV. TV Peru aired twelve Chinese-produced documentaries during the 2016 APEC forum in Lima, nearly all produced by CGTN and broadcast during prime time.[29]

The challenge for American public diplomacy lies not in matching Chinese spending dollar-for-dollar but in supporting independent media, training investigative reporters, building fact-checking organizations, and working with partners to develop free and trustworthy digital infrastructure—approaches that lack the political appeal of dramatic action but offer more sustainable protection.[30]

Disinformation Campaigns and Electoral Interference

If Chinese state media expansion represents the overt dimension of information warfare, disinformation campaigns and electoral interference constitute its covert operations. Since 2019, Beijing has developed increasingly sophisticated capabilities to manipulate online discourse, exploit social divisions, and undermine confidence in democratic institutions.

The primary vehicle for Chinese electoral interference is an operation known as "Spamouflage," identified by cybersecurity firms and social media companies as one of the most sprawling networks of fake accounts across the internet. Originally focused on pushing pro-China narratives, Spamouflage has evolved to target American politics and elections directly.[31]

A September 2024 report by research firm Graphika documented how Spamouflage networks of fake social media users mimic Americans on platforms like X and TikTok to manipulate public opinion. In the run-up to the 2024 election, these accounts "seeded and amplified content denigrating Democratic and Republican candidates, sowing doubt in the legitimacy of the U.S. electoral process, and spreading divisive narratives about sensitive social issues including gun control, homelessness, drug abuse, racial inequality, and the Israel-Hamas conflict."[32] Much of this content appeared to be AI-generated, targeting major political figures.

The Washington Post reported in October 2024 that Chinese government attempts had escalated to influence "tens" of down-ballot races with explicitly antisemitic attacks and conspiracy theories. One covert campaign targeted Representative Barry Moore, who had recently backed sanctions against China, with posts calling him "a Jewish dog" who won because of "the bloody Jewish consortium."[33] The operation also focused on inflaming tensions through hot-button issues like police violence, Black Lives Matter, and immigration—issues calculated to divide Americans rather than advance any particular policy agenda.

U.S. intelligence agencies have characterized Chinese government interference as aggressive but cautious, not targeting any particular candidate but instead focusing on issues important to Beijing such as Taiwan while "undermining confidence in elections, voting, and the U.S. in general." A declassified U.S. intelligence assessment stated with "high confidence" that China, Russia, Iran, and Cuba attempted to influence the 2022 midterms, with China tacitly approving "efforts to try to influence a handful of midterm races involving members of both U.S. political parties."[34]

The assessment noted that China had used artificial intelligence to generate images mimicking Americans online and provoke discussion on divisive social issues. Senior Chinese intelligence officials had issued directives to "intensify efforts to influence U.S. policy and public opinion in China's favor" and "magnify U.S. societal divisions."[35]

One troubling aspect of Chinese interference is the shift toward targeting local and state elections rather than exclusively focusing on presidential races. U.S. intelligence officials warned in 2024 that China's efforts were shifting toward state and local candidates—a strategy aimed at building relationships with officials who could eventually advance China's interests, as local elections receive far less scrutiny than national races.[36]

The Microsoft Threat Intelligence Report of August 2024 highlighted the "Taizi Flood" campaign, in which hundreds of fake accounts posed as protesters during pro-Palestinian demonstrations at U.S. universities, spreading inflammatory messages that fueled tensions and increased divisions across political lines.[37]

International examples provide important context. Taiwan's January 2024 elections saw extensive Chinese operations, with researchers from Doublethink Lab determining that the Chinese Communist Party created dozens of AI-generated videos on social media platforms disseminating disinformation targeting Taiwan's president. The Taiwan Information Environment Research Center observed that Chinese propaganda had undergone a paradigm shift, evolving from centralized, top-down approaches to more decentralized, less traceable methods.[38]

Despite meeting with President Biden and National Security Advisor Jake Sullivan, Chinese General Secretary Xi Jinping's assurances that China would not interfere in the 2024 presidential election proved hollow, with interference operations continuing and intensifying throughout 2024.[39]

The challenge of countering Chinese disinformation is compounded by the growing sophistication of AI-generated content. A Department of Homeland Security memorandum conveyed that generative AI capabilities "may amplify existing risks for election infrastructure," making election offices, officials, and vendors more vulnerable to disinformation attacks.[40]

Academic Freedom and Self-Censorship

Perhaps nowhere is the battle for hearts and minds more insidious than in its impact on academic freedom. Universities—traditionally bastions of free inquiry—have become contested spaces where economic dependence, political pressure, and fear of retribution produce widespread self-censorship on China-related topics.

The most dramatic deterioration of academic freedom has occurred in Hong Kong. Following the imposition of the National Security Law on June 30, 2020, Hong Kong's eight publicly funded universities experienced a severe decline in civil liberties. A comprehensive September 2024 report by Human Rights Watch and the Hong Kong Democracy Council documented that students and faculty now widely self-censor, fearful of harassment, retribution, or prosecution for what they say in classrooms and on campus.[41]

The 76-page report, titled "'We Can't Write the Truth Anymore': Academic Freedom in Hong Kong Under the National Security Law," detailed how faculty members and students regularly self-censor when writing academic articles, applying for funding, and inviting speakers to conferences. Several academics reported direct censorship by university administrators and academic publishers. One scholar's university reported him to Hong Kong police for an academic article discussing artwork created during the 2019 protests.[42]

The opaque definition of what constitutes "violation of the security law" has created pervasive fear. Maya Wang, associate China director at Human Rights Watch, explained: "When the red line isn't clear, there will be a pervasive sense of fear, and students and faculty members will try to make adjustments accordingly."[43] University administrations have worked with Chinese and Hong Kong authorities to harass, intimidate, or remove academics voicing dissenting opinions.

The erosion of academic freedom extends to mainland China, where surveillance and ideological control have intensified under Xi Jinping. Research analyzing over 5,000 publications of scholars from 1985 to 2022 determined which research topics have "disappeared" over time and which have "migrated" from Chinese- to English-language venues, revealing broader self-censorship outcomes than the regime intended.[44]

Critically, U.S.-based scholars are not immune to these pressures. A 2018 survey of more than 500 U.S.-based China scholars found that 70 percent agreed with the statement "Self-censorship is a problem in the China field." Scholars reported "repressive experiences" ranging from visa denials to police questioning. Perhaps most troubling, respondents reported lacking support from their home institutions when navigating work on China.[45]

The Confucius Institute controversy exemplifies tensions between economic benefit and academic integrity. By 2024, the number of Confucius Institutes at U.S. universities had declined from approximately 100 to fewer than five. According to a U.S. Government Accountability Office report, schools most commonly cited potential loss of federal funding as contributing to closure decisions, with 61 percent saying this contributed to a "great extent."[46]

The 2019 amendment to the National Defense Authorization Act forced universities to choose between substantial federal funding and smaller Confucius Institute funding. Many universities chose to close their institutes rather than jeopardize millions in federal research funding.[47] Yet closures have not eliminated Chinese influence. A June 2022 National Association of Scholars report found that many universities continue relationships with Chinese partner institutions, with some offering Chinese language and cultural programming "comparable to what the Confucius Institutes offered."[48]

Conclusion: The Information Battlefield's Long Shadow

The narrative wars between the United States and China represent more than propaganda contests—they strike at the heart of how democratic societies function. When citizens cannot trust information sources, when scholars self-censor to protect careers, when foreign powers manipulate social media to amplify divisions, and when universities compromise academic freedom for funding, the foundations of open society erode.

China's approach reflects deep understanding that winning hearts and minds requires patient, multifaceted engagement operating across state media, social media platforms, academic institutions, and people-to-people exchanges. With virtually unlimited resources and centralized control, Beijing can sustain efforts that gradually reshape global discourse. The goal is not necessarily to make the world love China, but to create sufficient confusion, division, and doubt that democratic systems lose legitimacy.

American responses remain reactive and fragmented. Budget constraints limit public diplomacy efforts while political dysfunction undermines messaging credibility. The absence of comprehensive data privacy legislation leaves American citizens vulnerable to foreign surveillance and manipulation. Universities struggle to balance academic freedom against economic dependence on Chinese students, partnerships, and funding.

The stakes extend far beyond the bilateral relationship. How democracies respond to information warfare will determine whether open societies can maintain the transparency and trust essential to their functioning. If authoritarian narratives consistently outperform democratic ones in the global marketplace of ideas, if universities become venues for self-censorship, if elections become vulnerable to foreign manipulation, then the competitive advantage free societies have historically enjoyed will evaporate.

Yet this competition need not be a race to the bottom. Democratic societies possess inherent strengths: genuine press freedom produces more credible journalism; academic freedom generates more innovative research; electoral accountability creates government responsiveness; and civil society organizations provide independent voices. The challenge lies in protecting these advantages while countering malign influence—maintaining openness without naivety, defending freedom without descending into paranoia.

The trajectory of U.S.-China information competition remains uncertain. Whether the narrative wars intensify into comprehensive information isolation, whether guardrails emerge to manage competition, or whether societies develop resilience against manipulation will profoundly shape the twenty-first century global order. The battle for hearts and minds continues, and its outcome may prove as consequential as any contest over semiconductors, aircraft carriers, or rare earth elements.

Endnotes

[1] *TikTok Inc. v. Garland*, 604 U.S. ___ (2025), per curiam opinion.

[2] *Ibid.*

[3] *TikTok Inc. v. Garland*, 604 U.S. ___ (2025), Gorsuch, J., concurring in judgment.

[4] White House, "Saving TikTok While Protecting National Security," Executive Order, September 25, 2025, https://www.whitehouse.gov/presidential-actions/2025/09/saving-tiktok-while-protecting-national-security/.

[5] Lauren Feiner and Jennifer Elias, "Trump Extends TikTok Deadline for the Second Time," *CNBC*, April 4, 2025, https://www.cnbc.com/2025/04/04/trumps-extends-tiktok-second-time.html.

[6] Eugene Kiely and Lori Robertson, "TikTok and U.S. National Security," *FactCheck.org*, April 4, 2025, https://www.factcheck.org/2025/02/tiktok-and-u-s-national-security/.

[7] Douglas Yeung, Marek N. Posard, and Nathan Chandler, "TikTok Is a Threat to National Security, but Not for the Reason You Think," *RAND Corporation*, August 14, 2024, https://www.rand.org/pubs/commentary/2024/08/tiktok-is-a-threat-to-national-security-but-not-for.html.

[8] James A. Lewis, "TikTok and National Security," *Center for Strategic and International Studies*, October 15, 2024, https://www.csis.org/analysis/tiktok-and-national-security.

[9] "Is TikTok a Threat to National Security?," *Spectrum News 1*, September 24, 2025, https://spectrumnews1.com/oh/columbus/news/2025/09/23/is-tik-tok-a-threat-to-national-security-.

[10] Sarah Cook, "Beijing's Global Megaphone: The Expansion of Chinese Communist Party Media Influence since 2017," *Freedom House*, January 2020, https://freedomhouse.org/report/special-report/2020/beijings-global-megaphone.

[11] *Ibid.*

[12] *Ibid.*

[13] *Ibid.*

[14] Yingjie Fan and Jennifer Pan, "Strategies of Chinese State Media on Twitter," Stanford University, accessed December 3, 2025, https://jenpan.com/jen_pan/cgtn.pdf.

[15] Joshua Kurlantzick, "China's State Media: Giants or Minnows," *Council on Foreign Relations*, December 27, 2022, https://www.cfr.org/blog/chinas-state-media-giants-or-minnows.

[16] Louisa Lim and Julia Bergin, "Behind the News: Inside China Global Television Network," *Lowy Institute*, 2019, https://www.lowyinstitute.org/publications/behind-news-inside-china-global-television-network.

[17] Sarah Cook, "Beijing's Global Media Influence 2022," *Freedom House*, 2022, https://freedomhouse.org/report/beijing-global-media-influence/2022/authoritarian-expansion-power-democratic-resilience.

[18] *Ibid.*

[19] "CGTN America," Wikipedia, accessed December 3, 2025, https://en.wikipedia.org/wiki/CGTN_America.

[20] Kurlantzick, "China's State Media: Giants or Minnows."

[21] *Ibid.*

[22] "Understanding the PRC's Approach to Public Diplomacy - January 16, 2025," *U.S. Department of State*, October 1, 2025, https://www.state.gov/acpd-official-meeting-minutes-january-16-2025/.

[23] *Ibid.*

[24] "Summary of January 2025 Meeting: 'Understanding the PRC's Public Diplomacy Efforts,'" *U.S. Department of State*, June 11, 2025, https://www.state.gov/summary-of-january-2025meeting-understanding-chinas-public-diplomacy-efforts.

[25] *Ibid.*

[26] Jude Blanchette and Bonny Lin, "Advancing U.S.-China Coordination amid Strategic Competition: An Emerging Playbook," *Center for Strategic and International Studies*, January 15, 2025, https://www.csis.org/analysis/advancing-us-china-coordination-amid-strategic-competition-emerging-playbook.

[27] Patricia M. Kim, "The US-China Relationship in 2024 Is Stabilized but Precarious," *Brookings Institution*, January 31, 2024, https://www.brookings.edu/articles/us-china-relations-in-2024-are-stabilized-but-precarious/.

[28] "USIP's Top Reads from 2024," *United States Institute of Peace*, January 10, 2025, https://www.usip.org/publications/2025/01/usips-top-reads-2024.

[29] Cook, "Beijing's Global Megaphone."

[30] "Summary of January 2025 Meeting," *U.S. Department of State*.

[31] Shannon Bond, "China Is Pushing Divisive Messages Using Fake U.S. Voters," *NPR*, September 3, 2024, https://www.npr.org/2024/09/03/nx-s1-5096151/china-tiktok-x-fake-voters-influence-campaign.

[32] *Ibid.*

[33] Raphael Satter, "Chinese Influence Operation Is Posing as American Voters," *The Washington Post*, October 2024.

[34] "Chinese Interference in the 2024 United States Elections," Wikipedia, accessed December 3, 2025, https://en.wikipedia.org/wiki/Chinese_interference_in_the_2024_United_States_elections.

[35] *Ibid.*

[36] Eamon Javers, "China's New Focus in U.S. Elections Interference Is Not Harris-Trump Presidential Race," *CNBC*, October 15, 2024, https://www.cnbc.com/2024/10/15/chinas-new-focus-election-interference-local-state-races.html.

[37] Julia Bright, "Alleged Chinese Influence Campaigns Intensify Worries About U.S Election Meddling," *The Hill*, October 27, 2024, https://thehill.com/policy/technology/4954346-chinese-influence-us-election-meddling/.

[38] Amy Mackinnon, "Taiwan's Election Showed China's New Disinformation Tactics," *Foreign Policy*, January 25, 2024, https://foreignpolicy.com/2024/01/23/taiwan-election-china-disinformation-influence-interference/.

[39] "Chinese Interference in the 2024 United States Elections," Wikipedia.

[40] "The Red Wave: How China Weaponizes Disinformation," *American Security Project*, May 2, 2024, https://www.americansecurityproject.org/the-red-wave-how-china-weaponizes-disinformation/.

[41] Maya Wang, "Hong Kong: Academic Freedom Declines Under Security Law," *Human Rights Watch*, September 25, 2024, https://www.hrw.org/news/2024/09/24/hong-kong-academic-freedom-declines-under-security-law.

[42] Maya Wang, "'We Can't Write the Truth Anymore': Academic Freedom in Hong Kong Under the National Security Law," *Human Rights Watch*, September 24, 2024, https://www.hrw.org/report/2024/09/24/we-cant-write-truth-anymore/academic-freedom-hong-kong-under-national-security-0.

[43] Quoted in "Fear and Censorship Erode Freedom in Hong Kong," *China Factor*, October 14, 2024, https://chinafactor.news/2024/09/26/fear-and-censorship-erode-hong-kongs-academic-freedom/.

[44] Nancy Leng and Rory Truex, "Disappearing Research: Academic Control and Self-Censorship in China," *The China Journal* 94 (2025).

[45] Stacey Jacobs, "Academic Freedom and China," *American Association of University Professors*, accessed December 3, 2025, https://www.aaup.org/academe/issues/105-1/academic-freedom-and-china.

[46] Kimberly Gianopoulos, "China: With Nearly All U.S. Confucius Institutes Closed, Some Schools Sought Alternative Language Support," *U.S. Government Accountability Office*, November 2023, https://www.gao.gov/products/gao-24-105981.

[47] Fangyu Chen and Qiaoan Ruan, "The Rise, Decline, and Possible Resurrection of China's Confucius Institutes," *The Diplomat*, August 31, 2024, https://thediplomat.com/2024/08/the-rise-decline-and-possible-resurrection-of-chinas-confucius-institutes/.

[48] Flora Yan, "After Confucius Institutes," *National Association of Scholars*, June 2022, https://www.nas.org/reports/after-confucius-institutes/full-report.

Part VIII

Scenarios and Solutions

Chapter 21

Four Futures

Scenario Planning for the U.S.-China Relationship

The U.S.-China relationship stands at a crossroads. After decades of engagement followed by years of escalating competition, both nations face critical choices that will shape not only their bilateral relationship but the entire international order. The trajectory of this rivalry remains deeply uncertain, contingent on decisions yet unmade, crises yet unanticipated, and structural forces still unfolding. This chapter presents four distinct scenarios for how the U.S.-China relationship might evolve through 2030 and beyond, analyzes the key variables that will determine which path prevails, and assesses the probability and implications of each future.

Unlike simple forecasts or predictions, scenario planning acknowledges that the future is fundamentally indeterminate. As the Carnegie Endowment for International Peace observes, "the future is never set in stone, and if we are to develop strategies that steer us toward more positive futures, we need some understanding of what these futures might look like."[1] These scenarios are not predictions but plausible pathways—each grounded in observable trends, informed by historical precedent, and shaped by the complex interplay of material capabilities, domestic politics, and strategic choices.

Scenario 1: Managed Competition—Guardrails Hold

In this scenario, Washington and Beijing successfully establish and maintain mechanisms to manage their rivalry without sliding into open conflict. Competition continues across economic, technological, and geopolitical domains, but both sides recognize existential stakes and implement guardrails to prevent escalation.

The Pathway

By 2026, a series of close calls in the South China Sea and Taiwan Strait—including near-collisions between naval vessels and dangerous intercepts of reconnaissance aircraft—convince leaders on both sides that the absence of crisis management mechanisms poses unacceptable risks. Following intensive diplomacy facilitated by third parties, the two nations establish new protocols building on but significantly expanding beyond the Biden-era military-to-military communication channels reestablished in 2023.[2]

These mechanisms include: regular strategic dialogues at multiple levels; incident notification and consultation procedures; rules of engagement for military encounters in contested waters; joint declarations establishing clear red lines regarding Taiwan, particularly regarding formal independence declarations or foreign military basing; economic stability arrangements including coordination on financial regulatory matters and limits on the weaponization of economic interdependence; and selective cooperation on genuinely shared threats including pandemic preparedness, nuclear nonproliferation in unstable regions, and aspects of climate mitigation where coordination proves mutually beneficial.[3]

The Character of Competition

Competition in this scenario remains intense but bounded. The United States maintains and strengthens its alliance network across the Indo-Pacific, with AUKUS, the Quad, and bilateral partnerships with Japan, South Korea, and the Philippines forming a latticework of security cooperation aimed at deterring Chinese military adventurism.[4] Export controls on advanced semiconductors and AI systems continue but become more surgical, focused specifically on military applications rather than broad commercial restrictions that accelerate complete decoupling.[5]

China, for its part, pursues technological self-sufficiency through massive state investment but stops short of severing economic ties with the West. Beijing's "dual circulation" strategy succeeds in creating robust domestic markets while maintaining significant export relationships.[6] The November 2025 restrictions on foreign AI chips in Chinese state-funded data centers, rather than escalating into comprehensive bans, remain limited to the most sensitive applications.[7]

Trade stabilizes around a "new normal" of elevated but predictable tariffs. Following the volatile period of 2025, when tariffs peaked at 145% on U.S. goods to China and 125% on Chinese goods to America, negotiations produce agreements that lower rates to approximately 25-35% while establishing transparent frameworks for addressing specific grievances.[8] This arrangement, while far from free trade, provides sufficient predictability for supply chain planning.

Taiwan in Managed Competition

Taiwan emerges as the most carefully managed aspect of the relationship. While China never renounces the use of force, and the United States maintains strategic ambiguity, both sides tacitly agree that preserving the status quo serves their interests better than forcing change. Beijing's coercive military exercises continue but remain bounded by implicit understandings about what constitutes crossing red lines. The United States strengthens Taiwan's defensive capabilities while carefully calibrating arms sales to avoid triggering Chinese military responses.[9]

The semiconductor dimension proves crucial. Taiwan's TSMC continues to dominate advanced chip production, but expansion of manufacturing capacity in the United States, Japan, and Europe gradually reduces—though never eliminates—dependence on Taiwan's facilities. This diversification paradoxically stabilizes the Taiwan situation by reducing the perceived strategic necessity for either side to act precipitously.[10]

Critical Enablers

Several factors enable managed competition to succeed:

Leadership continuity and pragmatism: Leaders in both nations prioritize stability over short-term political gains. In Washington, whoever holds power after 2025 maintains bipartisan consensus on the need for guardrails alongside competition. In Beijing, Xi Jinping or his successors recognize that China's economic challenges require at least stable relations with major trading partners.[11]

Third-party mediation: Middle powers, particularly within ASEAN and the European Union, play active roles in facilitating dialogue and creating neutral forums for discussion. Singapore, Switzerland, and others provide venues for backchannel communications during periods of public tension.[12]

Mutual economic pain: The severe disruptions of 2025—when bilateral trade between the U.S. and China dropped by 80% during the peak of the tariff war—convince business communities and economic policymakers on both sides that further escalation would be catastrophically expensive.[13] The World Trade Organization's assessment that full decoupling would contract global trade by 1.5% provides sobering context.[14]

Functional cooperation: Limited but meaningful collaboration on specific issues—such as joint contributions to pandemic preparedness through neutral third parties like Gavi—demonstrates that cooperation remains possible even amid competition.[15]

Implications

Managed competition produces a bifurcated global system but stops short of complete bloc formation. Some sectors experience significant decoupling (defense, critical infrastructure, cutting-edge AI), while others maintain substantial integration (consumer goods, certain industrial inputs, academic exchange in non-sensitive fields). Multinational corporations adapt by maintaining separate operations for serving U.S.-aligned and China-aligned markets, adding complexity and cost but remaining viable.[16]

The global South benefits from maintaining access to both systems, playing them against each other to secure better terms for infrastructure investment, technology transfer, and trade agreements.[17] Europe successfully pursues its de-risking strategy, reducing vulnerabilities without completely severing ties.[18]

Most importantly, this scenario avoids catastrophic war while allowing both nations to pursue their interests vigorously. It accepts that the U.S.-China relationship will remain competitive for decades but establishes predictable rules for managing that competition.

Scenario 2: Cold War 2.0—Complete Bloc Formation

In this darker scenario, the U.S.-China relationship hardens into a new Cold War characterized by comprehensive economic decoupling, rigid bloc formation, and proxy conflicts across multiple theaters. By 2028, the world has split into two largely separate spheres with minimal interaction between them.

The Trajectory Toward Division

The pathway to Cold War 2.0 accelerates following a series of escalatory spirals. In 2026, renewed tensions over Taiwan—perhaps sparked by a controversial election or incident at sea—prompt the United States to dramatically expand military deployments and security guarantees. China responds with its most aggressive military exercises to date, including a partial blockade of Taiwan that lasts several weeks before international pressure forces de-escalation.[19]

Though war is avoided, the crisis fundamentally changes both sides' calculations. In Washington, the narrow escape convinces policymakers that only comprehensive containment can address the China challenge. Congress passes sweeping legislation mandating complete economic separation in all sectors deemed relevant to national security—a definition that expands to include not just advanced technology but also pharmaceuticals, critical minerals, agricultural inputs, and infrastructure equipment.[20]

Beijing, interpreting these moves as an existential threat to China's development, fully commits to technological and economic self-sufficiency. The "indigenous and controllable" technology doctrine becomes absolute policy across all sectors. Chinese entities divest from Western assets, bringing home approximately $1-2 trillion in overseas holdings, causing temporary but significant disruption to U.S. Treasury markets.[21]

The Architecture of Blocs

By 2027, two distinct economic and technological blocs have crystallized:

The Western Bloc includes the United States, European Union (with some internal dissension), Japan, South Korea, Australia, and an expanding network of partners across ASEAN and the Americas. This grouping controls approximately 50% of global GDP and dominates leading-edge semiconductor technology, aerospace, advanced pharmaceuticals, and financial infrastructure.[22]

The Sino-Centric Bloc comprises China, Russia, Iran, North Korea, much of Central Asia, and selected states across Africa, Latin America, and Southeast Asia drawn by Chinese investment and political alignment. This bloc controls roughly 35% of global GDP but holds advantages in manufacturing capacity (China alone produces 30% of global manufacturing output), critical mineral processing, and rapidly advancing technological capabilities in AI and biotech.[23]

Approximately 15% of global GDP remains "non-aligned," with countries like India, Brazil, Indonesia, and parts of the Middle East attempting to maintain relations with both blocs. These swing states face intense pressure to choose sides, with both camps offering inducements and threatening consequences.[24]

Economic Separation

Trade between the blocs falls to minimal levels—commodity exchanges and specialized goods where no substitutes exist, conducted through tightly controlled channels. The yuan-dollar exchange becomes purely managed, with currency convertibility severely restricted.[25] Each bloc develops parallel technical standards, making products designed for one system incompatible with the other. The internet fragments into distinct spheres with limited interconnection, reversing decades of globalization.[26]

The costs prove substantial. Studies by the CEPR suggest that complete technological decoupling could reduce Western welfare by 1-8% and Eastern welfare by 8-11%, with median losses around 4% for the West and 10.5% for the East.[27] China bears higher costs due to its technological catch-up position, though its larger domestic market provides some buffer. The United States and allies experience slower growth, higher inflation, and disrupted supply chains, but maintain technological leadership.

Military Dimensions

Cold War 2.0 features sustained military competition reminiscent of the U.S.-Soviet rivalry. The United States completes the military build-up in the Western Pacific initiated in the early 2020s, with permanent forward deployments in the Philippines, enhanced presence in Australia, and expanded submarine operations.[28] China accelerates PLA modernization, achieving rough parity in regional conventional capabilities by 2028.[29]

Both sides maintain massive nuclear arsenals on high alert. Arms control disappears as a concept, with each bloc pursuing military advantages without negotiated limitations. Space becomes heavily militarized, with both sides deploying capabilities to disable satellites and contest orbital supremacy.[30]

Proxy conflicts erupt in gray areas. In the South China Sea, incidents between Chinese forces and various Southeast Asian nations backed by the United States become routine. In Eastern Europe, Russia—deeply aligned with China—intensifies pressure on NATO's eastern flank. The Middle East becomes a chess board for bloc competition, with Iran and Gulf states on opposite sides.[31]

Taiwan's Fate

Taiwan exists in a state of permanent crisis. Beijing maintains continuous military pressure through blockades, exercises, and gray zone operations just short of invasion. The United States commits to defending Taiwan explicitly, abandoning strategic ambiguity. Taiwan becomes heavily militarized, with a significant permanent U.S. military presence. The island develops a "fortress" mentality, with civil defense preparations embedded in all aspects of society.[32]

Social and Cultural Division

Cold War 2.0 extends beyond economics and security into social and cultural realms. Academic exchanges cease except in narrowly defined non-sensitive areas. Chinese students largely stop attending Western universities, studying instead at rapidly improving domestic institutions or in allied nations. Scientific collaboration divides along bloc lines, slowing progress on global challenges requiring international cooperation.[33]

Tourism between blocs drops to minimal levels. Western social media and entertainment become completely blocked in China and allied states, which develop parallel platforms. China's global media presence expands dramatically, offering alternative narratives to Western perspectives throughout the developing world.[34]

Stability and Risks

Cold War 2.0 achieves a form of stable deterrence analogous to the U.S.-Soviet rivalry. The blocs are too powerful to attack each other directly without risking mutual destruction, creating a tense equilibrium. However, this stability is fragile:

Risk of miscalculation: With Taiwan as a permanent flashpoint and multiple proxy conflicts ongoing, opportunities for escalation abound. A single incident could trigger the hot war both sides seek to avoid.[35]

Economic inefficiency: Complete separation of supply chains and technical standards imposes severe inefficiency costs, slowing innovation and reducing living standards globally.[36]

Global South suffering: Developing nations bear disproportionate costs, forced to choose sides and unable to benefit from integration with the global economy. Many face debt crises and political instability.[37]

Climate catastrophe: Bloc competition makes coordinated climate action impossible. Without U.S.-China cooperation, limiting warming to even 2°C becomes unachievable, with catastrophic consequences for all.[38]

Scenario 3: Hot Conflict—The Taiwan Contingency

This most catastrophic scenario sees U.S.-China competition escalate to actual warfare, most likely over Taiwan. While many analysts have concluded that conflict is not imminent in 2025-2026, assessments universally agree that risk rises substantially from 2027 onward as China's military capabilities mature and its window of opportunity to act may narrow.[39]

The Path to War

Multiple pathways could trigger conflict, but the most probable involves Taiwan. In one variant, Taiwan elects a government explicitly committed to formal independence, crossing Beijing's clearly stated red line. Facing intense nationalist pressure domestically and viewing this as an existential challenge to CCP legitimacy, Xi Jinping orders military action.[40]

In another variant, the United States dramatically expands its security commitments to Taiwan—perhaps stationing permanent forces or signing a formal defense treaty—convincing Beijing that the window for reunification is closing permanently. Economic calculations play a role: by 2027-2028, TSMC's overseas facilities have advanced sufficiently that Taiwan's "silicon shield" has weakened considerably, reducing potential costs to China of taking military action.[41]

A third pathway involves unintended escalation from gray zone operations. China's increasingly aggressive coercion of Taiwan through blockades, cyber attacks, and military exercises crosses thresholds that Washington feels compelled to respond to militarily. A U.S. Navy vessel en route to break a blockade engages PLA Navy ships, and what begins as a limited clash spirals rapidly out of control.[42]

The Character of Conflict

Based on multiple wargames and scenarios conducted by institutions ranging from CSIS to the Australian Strategic Policy Institute, several patterns emerge regarding how such a conflict might unfold:[43]

Initial Phase (Days 1-7): China launches a multi-domain campaign against Taiwan combining cyber attacks to disable communications and command systems; long-range missile strikes against airfields, ports, and military installations; naval and air blockade to isolate Taiwan from outside support; and amphibious operations to seize outer islands and establish beachheads. The United States and Japan immediately come to Taiwan's aid, engaging PLA forces while racing to break the blockade and reinforce Taiwanese defenders.[44]

Escalation (Weeks 2-4): The conflict expands geographically. Chinese forces strike U.S. bases in Japan, Guam, and potentially the continental United States with long-range missiles. U.S. submarines sink Chinese vessels, including potentially civilian ships supporting military operations. Both sides launch extensive cyber attacks on each other's critical infrastructure. Economic warfare intensifies, with China freezing U.S. assets and restricting rare earth exports while the United States implements comprehensive sanctions.[45]

High-Intensity Phase (Weeks 4-12): If neither side achieves quick victory, the conflict settles into sustained high-intensity warfare. China commits over 200,000 troops to invasion operations, facing fierce resistance from Taiwanese forces backed by U.S. air and naval power. Casualties mount horrifically on all sides—wargames estimate U.S. military losses of potentially 50-90 ships and 500+ aircraft, Chinese losses of 100+ ships and 700+ aircraft, and Taiwanese civilian casualties potentially in the hundreds of thousands.[46]

Nuclear Brinkmanship: As conventional losses mount and either side faces prospects of decisive defeat, nuclear threats become explicit. Though neither side desires nuclear exchange, the escalation dynamics of intense warfare combined with nationalist pressures create severe risks of crossing that threshold, particularly if China perceives existential regime threat or the United States faces catastrophic defeat of forward-deployed forces.[47]

Economic Devastation

A Taiwan conflict produces economic consequences far exceeding those of any previous war. Taiwan's semiconductor industry—producing 90% of the world's most advanced chips—goes completely offline, whether from Chinese attacks, defensive Taiwanese measures to prevent Chinese capture of intact facilities, or simply because operating advanced fabs during warfare proves impossible.[48]

The resulting chip shortage crashes global supply chains. Automobile production ceases globally within weeks. Consumer electronics manufacture grinds to a halt. Data centers cannot obtain replacement servers. The global economy contracts by an estimated 5-10% within the first year, with regional variations: East Asian economies (Korea, Japan) suffer 10-15% GDP losses, the United States and Europe 5-7%, and developing nations dependent on trade 8-12%.[49]

Maritime insurance rates in the Western Pacific skyrocket, effectively shutting down commercial shipping through the South China Sea and Taiwan Strait. This disrupts approximately $5 trillion in annual trade, forcing re-routing around Southeast Asia and imposing enormous costs. Energy prices spike as Chinese imports of Middle Eastern oil are disrupted, affecting the global market.[50]

Financial markets experience severe distress. Chinese attempts to liquidate U.S. Treasury holdings, though having limited long-term impact (raising yields perhaps 10-15 basis points), create short-term panic. Western sanctions on Chinese financial institutions fragment the global financial system. Capital flight from emerging markets intensifies as investors seek safety.[51]

Global Realignment

The war forces every nation to choose sides decisively. Japan and Australia fight alongside the United States from day one. South Korea, despite enormous economic ties to China, ultimately joins the U.S. effort, fearing Chinese regional dominance. The Philippines actively supports U.S. operations from bases on its territory.[52]

European nations vary in their responses. NATO invokes Article 5 consultations but does not classify the Taiwan conflict as requiring collective defense. Nevertheless, Britain, France, and Poland provide meaningful support to the U.S. effort. Germany and southern European nations remain more cautious, limiting assistance to economic sanctions.[53]

ASEAN splinters. Singapore and Vietnam lean toward the U.S. camp while attempting to maintain neutrality. Indonesia and Malaysia desperately avoid involvement. Cambodia and Laos align more openly with China. The organization effectively ceases to function as a coherent diplomatic body.[54]

India benefits strategically from both powers being distracted and diminished, but faces pressure to support the Western effort to prevent Chinese hegemony. New Delhi provides limited intelligence cooperation and diplomatic support while avoiding direct military involvement.[55]

Russia supports China diplomatically and economically, potentially opening a second front against Europe to distract NATO forces, though avoiding direct conflict with nuclear-armed adversaries. Iran and North Korea take advantage of superpower distraction to advance their own regional objectives.[56]

War Termination

How the war ends depends critically on battlefield outcomes and willingness to escalate:

Chinese Victory: If PLA forces successfully invade and occupy Taiwan despite U.S. intervention, Beijing has achieved its core objective but at catastrophic cost. The United States faces its most significant military defeat since Vietnam, fundamentally shaking alliances. China emerges dominant in East Asia but economically devastated, internationally isolated, and facing potential guerrilla resistance in Taiwan. A tense armistice follows, with lasting Chinese control over Taiwan but no broader peace settlement.[57]

U.S. Victory: If U.S. and Taiwanese forces decisively defeat the invasion, sinking much of China's amphibious fleet and establishing sea and air superiority, Beijing must decide whether to escalate or accept defeat. Domestic political implications for the CCP are severe, potentially threatening regime stability. The war ends with Taiwan secure but U.S.-China relations irreparably poisoned for a generation.[58]

Stalemate: More likely, neither side achieves decisive victory but both exhaust themselves. International mediation—perhaps through the UN Security Council, though paralyzed by vetoes, or through powerful third parties—produces a ceasefire that leaves fundamental issues unresolved.

Taiwan remains independent but economically ruined. Both powers begin decades-long rebuilding while maintaining hostile postures.[59]

Long-Term Implications

A Taiwan war fundamentally reshapes the international order:

- The global economy requires 5-10 years to recover, with permanent reshaping of supply chains away from China and complete economic separation between blocs.
- Military spending globally increases to Cold War levels, with defense consuming 4-6% of GDP in major powers.
- Nuclear proliferation accelerates as middle powers seek deterrents against great power aggression—Japan, South Korea, and potentially others rapidly develop nuclear capabilities.
- Climate action becomes impossible for decades as powers focus on security and economic recovery.
- Refugee flows from affected regions create humanitarian crises and political instability globally.
- The United Nations and other international institutions become irrelevant, replaced by competing bloc-based organizations.
- A generation of hostility between the United States and China precludes cooperation on any issue.[60]

Scenario 4: Grand Bargain—Comprehensive Settlement

This optimistic scenario envisions Washington and Beijing negotiating a comprehensive settlement addressing core concerns and establishing a durable framework for peaceful coexistence. While this outcome faces enormous obstacles, it is not impossible if leaders on both sides demonstrate extraordinary statesmanship.

The Diplomatic Opening

The path to a grand bargain emerges from mutual recognition that continued escalation serves neither side's interests. By 2026, both powers have experienced the costs of confrontation: slowed economic growth, strained alliance relationships, and persistent risk of catastrophic war. Simultaneously, new leadership or changed circumstances create political space for dramatic shifts.[61]

In Washington, whoever holds the presidency recognizes that containing China indefinitely is unsustainable, especially given domestic imperatives to address infrastructure, climate, and social programs. The costs of maintaining forward military postures throughout the Indo-Pacific, combined with persistent defense industrial base constraints, compel reassessment of strategic priorities.[62]

In Beijing, Xi Jinping or successors confront economic headwinds that make confrontation increasingly costly. China's debt burdens, demographic decline, and technological constraints necessitate access to Western markets, capital, and selective collaboration on innovation. Moreover, rising nationalism's double-edged sword means any leadership must deliver tangible benefits to maintain legitimacy—military glory cannot compensate for economic stagnation.[63]

Core Elements of the Bargain

Drawing from academic proposals and Track II dialogues, a plausible grand bargain might include the following elements:[64]

Taiwan Arrangement: The most difficult component involves Taiwan. One version, proposed by scholars like Charles Glaser, involves the United States ending its commitment to defend Taiwan in exchange for Chinese guarantees to resolve the issue peacefully and renounce the use of force. Beijing would accept Taiwan's de facto autonomy for an extended period (potentially 50 years or more) while Taiwan foregoes formal independence declarations. China gains assurance that Taiwan will not permanently separate, while the United States reduces the primary war risk and secures Chinese cooperation on other fronts.[65]

Alternative formulations preserve U.S. support for Taiwan's defense but establish clear parameters: Beijing commits not to use force or coercion; Taiwan commits not to pursue formal independence; and the United States agrees not to establish permanent military presence or enter formal defense treaty relationships. All parties accept extended status quo with periodic reviews.[66]

Military Confidence-Building: Comprehensive agreements establish military protocols throughout the Indo-Pacific: exclusion zones around Taiwan where neither side operates offensive forces; restrictions on types of military exercises near sensitive areas; notification requirements for major force deployments; and hotlines and incident management procedures at multiple levels. Both sides cap forward deployments—China limits militarization of artificial islands while the United States limits numbers of ships and aircraft in theater.[67]

Technology and Trade Framework: Rather than complete decoupling or unrestricted integration, the bargain establishes a differentiated approach: clearly defined lists of technologies excluded from trade on security grounds (focused narrowly on direct military applications); transparent rules for investment screening based on genuine security criteria; commitment to WTO rules for commercial trade with tariffs rolled back to pre-2018 levels; and mechanisms for addressing trade imbalances and industrial subsidies through negotiation rather than unilateral tariffs. Both sides commit to maintaining substantial economic interdependence in non-sensitive sectors.[68]

Spheres of Influence and Multilateral Cooperation: The United States acknowledges China's legitimate interests in East Asian prosperity and stability while China accepts the U.S. security role and alliance relationships in the region. Neither seeks to exclude the other from regional institutions. Both commit to supporting multilateral cooperation on global challenges: comprehensive climate frameworks with binding commitments from both powers; pandemic preparedness through joint or parallel contributions to international mechanisms; and coordinated approaches to emerging challenges in space, cyber, and artificial intelligence.[69]

Human Rights and Governance: Without requiring China to fundamentally alter its political system, Beijing makes specific commitments to international humanitarian law and allows enhanced monitoring of supply chains to ensure products are not made with forced labor. The United States moderates rhetoric that Beijing perceives as threatening regime change while maintaining advocacy for universal values.[70]

Implementation Mechanisms

The grand bargain includes robust verification and enforcement provisions: regular summits between presidents to maintain momentum and resolve disputes; working groups at ministerial and technical levels addressing specific issues; third-party monitoring of military arrangements through neutral countries or international organizations; dispute resolution procedures for trade and investment issues; and periodic reviews with provisions for adjusting terms as circumstances change, recognizing this is a living framework rather than static agreement.[71]

Domestic Politics

For any grand bargain to succeed, leaders must navigate intense domestic opposition:

In the United States, critics will attack any accommodation with China as appeasement, particularly regarding Taiwan. Proponents must make the case that avoiding war and securing cooperation on existential challenges outweighs symbolic commitments. The fact that a leader perceived as tough on China (potentially Trump or a similar figure) negotiates the deal provides political cover analogous to Nixon's opening to China.[72]

In China, nationalist sentiment makes any arrangement that constrains Chinese options or accepts long-term ambiguity on Taiwan politically risky for the CCP. Xi Jinping's personal authority or a successor's need to demonstrate pragmatism might enable selling the deal as securing China's rise through peaceful means while avoiding catastrophic conflict.[73]

Implications and Durability

A successful grand bargain fundamentally alters global dynamics:

- Economic growth accelerates globally as uncertainty diminishes and resources shift from military to productive investment.
- Climate cooperation becomes possible, potentially enabling achievement of Paris Agreement goals.
- Other powers can reduce defense spending and focus on development.
- Proliferation pressures ease as regional security improves.
- Multilateral institutions gain renewed relevance with U.S.-China cooperation enabling functional governance.
- Innovation accelerates as scientific collaboration expands in non-sensitive areas.
- Developing nations benefit from stable great power relations and continued access to both systems.[74]

However, the bargain faces persistent challenges to its durability. Either side's leadership changes could repudiate agreements, particularly if domestic politics shift. Unforeseen crises or technological breakthroughs might upset the negotiated balance. New generations in both countries may lack buy-in to arrangements negotiated by predecessors. Nevertheless, once established, interests in preserving the peace create stakeholders on both sides who resist backsliding.[75]

Why This Remains Unlikely

Despite its benefits, a grand bargain faces formidable obstacles making it the least probable scenario. As Foreign Affairs assesses: "Political realities in both countries make negotiating and complying with a broad deal impossible."[76] Specific challenges include:

Fundamental mistrust: Years of escalating competition have created deep suspicion. Each side doubts the other's willingness to honor commitments, making the first-mover problem severe—neither wants to offer concessions that might be pocketed without reciprocation.[77]

Taiwan's voice: Any arrangement regarding Taiwan without Taiwanese consent would face fierce resistance from democratic Taiwan. Including Taiwan in negotiations complicates them enormously while excluding Taiwan raises moral and practical questions about sustainability.[78]

Alliance implications: U.S. accommodation with China on Taiwan or military deployments would shake alliance confidence throughout Asia. Convincing Japan, South Korea, Australia, and others that reduced commitments don't presage abandonment requires extraordinary diplomatic skill.[79]

Structural drivers of competition: Beyond specific disputes, fundamental asymmetries in power, threat perception, and interests drive U.S.-China competition. China's rise and U.S. desire to maintain primacy create structural pressures that no agreement can entirely resolve.[80]

Key Variables: What Determines Which Future Unfolds

While none of these scenarios is predetermined, specific variables will shape which pathway the U.S.-China relationship follows. Understanding these drivers allows policymakers to influence outcomes.

Leadership Decisions and Domestic Politics

Individual leaders retain significant agency in shaping the relationship, though constrained by structural forces. President Trump's highly personalized, transactional approach to foreign policy, as manifested during both his first and second terms, creates volatility but also potential flexibility. His willingness to conduct extensive personal diplomacy with Xi Jinping could enable breakthrough agreements that more ideological leaders would reject—or lead to catastrophic miscalculation if personal relationships sour.[81]

Xi Jinping's consolidation of personal power in China means his decisions carry extraordinary weight. His commitment to "rejuvenation" and Taiwan reunification shapes Chinese policy fundamentally. Whether Xi views Taiwan as requiring resolution during his lifetime, or whether he accepts gradual integration over decades, will critically influence crisis risk. A successor with different priorities might pursue quite different approaches.[82]

Domestic political constraints in both nations limit leaders' flexibility. In the United States, bipartisan consensus on competing with China makes any significant accommodation politically risky. Only a leader with unassailable credentials on toughness toward China could successfully pivot toward grand bargain-style diplomacy. Public opinion, which in 2025 shows Democrats increasingly favoring cooperation while Republicans support confrontation, affects the political landscape for any deal.[83]

In China, nationalism intensified by years of state media emphasis on foreign threats makes backing down appear weak. The CCP's legitimacy increasingly tied to external successes means any arrangement perceived as compromising core interests risks domestic backlash. Yet China's leaders also understand that their primary legitimacy source remains economic performance, which deteriorates under sustained confrontation.[84]

Economic Pressures and Trajectories

Economic conditions profoundly shape strategic calculations. If China's economy experiences sustained slowdown—with debt crises, youth unemployment, and structural imbalances persisting—Beijing faces pressure to either secure access to Western markets and technology (favoring accommodation) or divert domestic attention through nationalist appeals and foreign adventure (favoring confrontation).[85]

The United States faces its own economic pressures. Persistent inflation, rising interest rates, and debt burden limit resources available for military competition. Businesses suffering from decoupling impose costs that accumulate politically. The 80% collapse in U.S.-China trade during the 2025 tariff war demonstrated the severe near-term costs of separation, though some argue long-term benefits of reshoring.[86]

Global economic conditions matter profoundly. If the world economy experiences recession or financial crisis, both powers may prioritize stability and accommodation. Conversely, if the global economy remains resilient, each may feel it can afford sustained competition. The reaction of key middle powers—particularly in ASEAN and Europe—to economic disruption creates pressure on both Washington and Beijing to moderate approaches.[87]

Military Balance and Taiwan Dynamics

The military balance in the Taiwan Strait constitutes perhaps the single most important variable determining whether conflict occurs. As multiple assessments note, Chinese military capabilities are advancing rapidly, creating what analysts call a "closing window of opportunity" before 2027 or 2028, after which the PLA will possess capabilities to successfully invade Taiwan despite U.S. intervention.[88]

This creates dangerous dynamics. If Beijing perceives that its military advantage peaks in the late 2020s—before U.S. force restructuring and allied build-up further strengthen the defense—incentives to act sooner rather than later increase.[89] Conversely, if China's military modernization continues providing increasing confidence in eventual success, Beijing may feel less urgency, accepting gradual integration over decades.

Taiwan's own politics prove crucial. Elections in Taiwan repeatedly produce governments and legislatures that must balance public opposition to Beijing's pressure against recognition that Taiwan cannot survive without maintaining workable relations with the mainland. If Taiwan elects governments that provocatively push independence, crisis risk rises substantially. If Taiwan's leadership maintains status quo positions, space for gradual accommodation increases.[90]

U.S. commitments and capabilities regarding Taiwan directly affect Beijing's calculus. If the United States convincingly demonstrates capacity and will to defend Taiwan—through strengthened alliances, forward deployments, and sustained defense industrial production—deterrence strengthens. If U.S. capabilities erode or political will appears questionable, Beijing's temptation to act increases.[91]

Third-Party Actions and Regional Dynamics

The choices of middle powers significantly influence U.S.-China dynamics. If U.S. allies—particularly Japan, South Korea, and Australia—remain firmly committed and substantially increase defense spending and capabilities, the balance of power favoring deterrence strengthens. If doubts about U.S. reliability or domestic political changes weaken allied cohesion, China gains relative advantage and confidence.[92]

ASEAN's approach matters considerably. If Southeast Asian nations successfully maintain neutral positions, resisting pressure to choose sides completely, they preserve space for economic integration with both powers and can potentially mediate. If ASEAN fractures with some members aligning firmly with China and others with the United States, the region becomes contested terrain raising conflict risks.[93]

European choices prove important despite geographic distance. If Europe aligns closely with U.S. China policy—as seen in von der Leyen's "de-risking" approach—this strengthens the Western position in technology denial and economic pressure. If Europe pursues more independent approaches, maintaining greater engagement with China for commercial reasons, this limits the effectiveness of U.S.-led efforts to constrain Beijing.[94]

The alignment among China, Russia, Iran, and North Korea creates additional dynamics. If this "axis of authoritarians" strengthens, it enables each to resist Western pressure more effectively and potentially forces the United States to spread resources across multiple theaters.[95] Conversely, if cracks appear in these relationships—particularly between China and Russia as Chinese ambitions in Central Asia conflict with Russian interests—Western leverage increases.

Technological Trajectories

The pace and direction of technological development shapes competitive dynamics substantially. If U.S. and allied semiconductor restrictions successfully constrain Chinese AI development, this maintains a crucial Western advantage and creates pressure for Beijing to seek accommodation to access restricted technologies. If China succeeds in achieving AI parity despite controls—as suggested by DeepSeek's January 2025 demonstration of competitive AI with inferior hardware—the leverage provided by technology denial diminishes.[96]

The timeline for biotech breakthroughs matters enormously for future advantage. As the Harvard Belfer Center warns, biotech represents China's "most immediate opportunity to overtake" the United States in a strategically crucial technology.[97] If China achieves leadership in biopharmaceuticals, synthetic biology, and related fields by the late 2020s, this fundamentally shifts the competitive landscape. If the United States successfully maintains technological edge through the National Biotechnology and Biomanufacturing Initiative and related efforts, it preserves overall advantage.[98]

Crisis Management and Accidents

The presence or absence of effective crisis management mechanisms significantly influences whether crises escalate to conflict. The reestablishment of military-to-military communications in late 2023 following the San Francisco summit represented progress, but these mechanisms remain inadequate given the scale of potential crises.[99]

A single incident could trigger escalation spirals: a collision between vessels in the Taiwan Strait, an accidental shootdown of a civilian airliner during military exercises, a cyberattack on critical infrastructure that kills civilians, or environmental disasters with cross-border impacts that trigger blame and retaliation. The existence of protocols, hotlines, and established relationships determining how to manage such incidents separates scenarios where crises are contained from those where they spiral to war.[100]

Probability Assessments

Assigning precise probabilities to scenarios spanning multiple years is impossible, but qualitative assessments based on observable trends and structural factors provide guidance:

Managed Competition (40% probability): This represents the most probable scenario because it accords with expressed intentions of leadership on both sides, aligns with economic incentives favoring some stability, and builds on partial precedents like the managed rivalries of previous eras. Key supportive factors include strong economic interdependencies making complete separation costly, nuclear deterrence constraining direct conflict, and existence of some institutional mechanisms for communication. However, significant barriers include deep mistrust, domestic political pressures favoring confrontation, and persistent structural drivers of competition.[101]

Cold War 2.0 (30% probability): Complete bloc formation represents a substantial risk given current trajectories toward decoupling, the intensifying nature of technological competition, and lack of compelling shared interests forcing cooperation. Historical precedent of U.S.-Soviet Cold War demonstrates such outcomes are possible. Several ongoing trends point this direction: expanding technology controls, supply chain reshoring, political rhetoric emphasizing existential competition. However, against this weighs the much deeper economic integration between the United States and China compared to Cold War superpowers, China's significantly greater integration into the global economy, and both sides' expressed desire to avoid complete separation. This scenario becomes more likely if the managed competition scenario fails to achieve stable guardrails.[102]

Hot Conflict (15% probability): Actual warfare remains less probable than continued competition, but the risk is substantial and rising. Multiple credible assessments warn that conflict risk increases significantly from 2027 onward as China's military window opens. The Recorded Future analysis notes that while "an invasion in the short term (2025-2026) is currently unlikely," beginning in 2027 "the risk of an invasion will very likely continue to increase."[103] The Journal of Indo-Pacific Affairs identifies 13 indicators determining Xi Jinping's timing calculation, noting that 11 represent a "closing window of opportunity" favoring earlier rather than later action.[104] However, counterbalancing the rising risk are China's economic challenges creating incentives for caution, both sides' recognition of war's catastrophic costs, and nuclear deterrence constraining deliberate escalation. Most concerning is risk of unintended escalation from gray zone operations or crises spinning out of control rather than deliberate decisions for war.[105]

Grand Bargain (15% probability): This remains the least likely scenario despite offering the most beneficial outcomes. The fundamental obstacles include deep mistrust after years of escalation, Taiwan's exclusion from negotiations while being their subject, domestic political constraints in both nations making any comprehensive deal politically risky, and structural drivers of competition that no agreement can fully resolve. As Foreign Affairs assessed in July 2025: "Political realities in both countries make negotiating and complying with a broad deal impossible."[106] However, this probability increases under specific circumstances: new leadership with mandates for dramatic change, severe crisis (short of war) that demonstrates catastrophic costs of continued escalation, or domestic economic pressures forcing prioritization of stability. Only leaders with exceptional political capital and strategic vision could achieve a grand bargain, making leadership changes potential inflection points that could shift probabilities substantially.[107]

These probabilities should not be interpreted as predictions—the future remains genuinely uncertain. Rather, they represent assessments of relative plausibility given current trajectories, structural conditions, and observable trends. Moreover, these scenarios are not hermetically sealed; elements of multiple scenarios could combine, transitions between scenarios are possible, and outcomes could blend features of several scenarios.

Implications for Policy

Understanding these scenarios and their drivers provides guidance for policymakers seeking to influence outcomes:

For the United States: Washington should prioritize establishing and strengthening mechanisms for managed competition while preparing for the possibility of Cold War 2.0 and deterring hot conflict. This requires investing in alliance relationships and defense capabilities sufficient to maintain credible deterrence; establishing clear red lines communicated unambiguously to Beijing; maintaining selective economic engagement where genuine interests align; avoiding rhetorical maximalism that eliminates space for diplomatic flexibility; and sustaining domestic investments in innovation, infrastructure, and social cohesion that are prerequisites for effective long-term competition.[108]

For China: Beijing's interests are best served by avoiding actions that force the worst outcomes. This requires recognizing that coercive approaches to Taiwan increase rather than decrease resistance;

accepting that China's rise does not require U.S. retreat from Asia; demonstrating through actions rather than rhetoric that China can be a responsible stakeholder in the international system; addressing domestic economic challenges that currently constrain strategic options; and maintaining communication channels and crisis management mechanisms even during periods of tension.[109]

For Middle Powers: Third parties have agency in shaping outcomes and should exercise it actively. This requires maintaining strategic autonomy by avoiding complete alignment with either bloc where possible; offering good offices for mediation and dialogue; building coalitions of middle powers to amplify collective voice on shared interests; investing in capabilities that enhance resilience against great power pressure; and calling out dangerous behaviors by any party that increase conflict risk.[110]

For the International Community: Global institutions and norms require strengthening to constrain the worst impulses of great power competition. This requires reinforcing international law and norms even when major powers violate them; maintaining forums for dialogue that include both powers; addressing global challenges that require cooperation regardless of geopolitical competition; supporting development pathways for the Global South that reduce vulnerability to coercion; and preserving areas of global commons—maritime routes, cyber space, outer space—from complete militarization.[111]

Conclusion

The U.S.-China relationship stands at a crossroads as consequential as any in modern history. The decisions made over the coming years will reverberate for decades, shaping not only the relationship between these two giants but the fundamental character of the international order. As Christopher Chivvis writes in introducing a major Carnegie study: "If there is to be any hope" of steering toward calmer waters, "policy experts need some realistic vision of what those calmer waters might look like."[112]

Each of the four scenarios presented in this chapter represents a plausible future, contingent on choices yet unmade. Managed competition, while offering no panacea, provides the most viable pathway to avoiding catastrophic outcomes while allowing legitimate interests to be pursued. Cold War 2.0 represents a significant risk given current trajectories but would impose enormous costs on both powers and the world. Hot conflict, while less probable than continued competition, presents an unacceptable risk that demands sustained attention to deterrence and crisis management. The grand bargain, though unlikely, should not be dismissed as impossible—history demonstrates that dramatic shifts in great power relations can occur when leadership and circumstances align.

What remains certain is that the status quo of escalating competition without guardrails is unsustainable. "The bilateral relationship is passing through a particularly dangerous phase," as the Carnegie study notes, "and it is likely to remain competitive if not adversarial for decades to come."[113] Yet this competition need not become an existential struggle. With strategic clarity, sustained engagement, and recognition of shared stakes in avoiding the worst outcomes, both powers retain the agency to shape their future relationship.

The choice is not between friendship and enmity but between managed and unmanaged rivalry. History will judge this generation by whether leaders possessed the wisdom to choose paths that preserved peace and prosperity, or whether they sleepwalked into catastrophic conflict that could have been avoided. The scenarios outlined in this chapter illuminate the choices ahead—it remains for leaders, in Washington, Beijing, and capitals worldwide, to have the strategic vision and political courage to choose wisely.

Endnotes

[1] Christopher S. Chivvis, ed., *U.S.-China Relations for the 2030s: Toward a Realistic Scenario for Coexistence* (Washington, D.C.: Carnegie Endowment for International Peace, 2024), 1.

[2] Patricia M. Kim, "Working Toward Responsible Competition with China," Brookings Institution, March 9, 2022, https://www.brookings.edu/articles/working-toward-responsible-competition-with-china/.

[3] Ryan Hass, "Advancing U.S.-China Coordination Amid Strategic Competition: An Emerging Playbook," Center for Strategic and International Studies, January 15, 2025, https://www.csis.org/analysis/advancing-us-china-coordination-amid-strategic-competition-emerging-playbook.

[4] U.S.-China Economic and Security Review Commission, *2025 Annual Report to Congress* (Washington, D.C.: U.S. Government Publishing Office, November 2025), 16.

[5] Nicholas Pohl and Andrew Imbrie, "Hard Then, Harder Now: CoCom's Lessons and the Challenge of Crafting Effective Export Controls Against China," *Texas National Security Review* 8, no. 4 (September 2025): 45-89.

[6] *U.S.-China Economic and Security Review Commission*, 20.

[7] "U.S.-China Security and Foreign Affairs (Year in Review)," in *2025 Annual Report to Congress*, U.S.-China Economic and Security Review Commission (November 2025), 87, https://www.uscc.gov/sites/default/files/2025-11/Chapter_2—U.S.-China_Security_and_Foreign_Affairs_Year_in_Review.pdf.

[8] "'Neither Side Wanted a Decoupling': U.S. and China Announce Joint Pause on Tariffs Amid Ongoing Negotiations," Foundation for Defense of Democracies, May 13, 2025, https://www.fdd.org/analysis/policy_briefs/2025/05/13/neither-side-wanted-a-decoupling-u-s-and-china-announce-joint-pause-on-tariffs-amid-ongoing-negotiations/.

[9] Insikt Group, *The Risk of a Taiwan Invasion* (Somerville, MA: Recorded Future, February 12, 2025), 5, https://assets.recordedfuture.com/insikt-report-pdfs/2025/ta-cn-2025-0212.pdf.

[10] GeoQuant, "Update for China/Taiwan Scenario Analysis Q1/2025," Fitch Solutions, January 27, 2025, https://assets.ctfassets.net/nvl7oyu82ssb/5W8h7sdQXqcI6lUohxutdM/

b0e8180be6da4b9cadc1154d85407b12/GeoQuant-Q1-2025-China-Taiwan-Scenario-Analysis-Update.pdf.

[11] Chivvis, *U.S.-China Relations for the 2030s*, 10-11.

[12] PAX sapiens, *Four Scenarios for U.S.-China Relations* (August 15, 2025), https://paxsapiens.org/four-scenarios-foru-s-china-relations/.

[13] Ashley Gold and Kendall Baker, "The U.S.-China Decoupling Arrives," Axios, April 16, 2025, https://www.axios.com/2025/04/16/trump-tariffs-china-bilateral-trade.

[14] Ibid.

[15] Hass, "Advancing U.S.-China Coordination."

[16] Anshul Vyas, "US-China Economic Standoff in 2025: Decoupling, Disruption, and Global Macroeconomic Spillovers," SSRN, April 17, 2025, https://papers.ssrn.com/sol3/papers.cfm?abstract_id=5221379.

[17] Policy Center for the New South, "2025: Year of The Middle Powers" (2025), https://www.policycenter.ma/publications/2025-year-middle-powers.

[18] Zoltán Fehér, "The Implications of the Rise of Small and Middle Powers for U.S.-China Great Power Competition," in *Examining Perspectives of Small-to-Medium Powers in Emergent Great Power Competition*, ed. Philip M. Baxter (Cham, Switzerland: Palgrave Macmillan, 2025), https://doi.org/10.1007/978-3-031-86901-3_10.

[19] Joris Teer et al., *The Cost of Conflict: Economic Implications of a Taiwan Military Crisis for the Netherlands and the EU* (The Hague: The Hague Centre for Strategic Studies, March 2024), 12, https://hcss.nl/wp-content/uploads/2024/03/Taiwan-The-Cost-of-conflict-HCSS-2024.pdf.

[20] *U.S.-China Economic and Security Review Commission*, "Comprehensive List of the Commission's 2025 Recommendations," (November 2025), 677, https://www.uscc.gov/sites/default/files/2025-11/2025_Comprehensive_List_of_Recommendations.pdf.

[21] Christopher J. Neely, "The Economic Effects of a Potential Armed Conflict Over Taiwan," *Federal Reserve Bank of St. Louis Review* 107, no. 3 (First Quarter 2025): 1-16, https://www.stlouisfed.org/-/media/project/frbstl/stlouisfed/publications/review/pdfs/2025/feb/economic-effects-of-potential-armed-conflict-over-taiwan.pdf.

[22] Chivvis, *U.S.-China Relations for the 2030s*, 11.

[23] *U.S.-China Economic and Security Review Commission*, 16.

[24] Policy Center for the New South, "2025: Year of The Middle Powers."

[25] Vyas, "US-China Economic Standoff in 2025."

[26] Michael A. Witt et al., "US-China Competition, World Order and Economic Decoupling: Insights from Cultural Realism," *Australian Journal of International Affairs* 79, no. 2 (2025): 215-237, https://www.tandfonline.com/doi/full/10.1080/10357718.2025.2471353.

[27] Daniel Gros and Eddy Bekkers, "Economic Consequences of US-China Technological Decoupling: An Illustrative Quantitative Analysis," CEPR VoxEU, https://cepr.org/voxeu/columns/economic-consequences-us-china-technological-decoupling-illustrative-quantitative.

[28] *U.S.-China Economic and Security Review Commission*, 87.

[29] U.S. Department of Defense, *Military and Security Developments Involving the People's Republic of China, 2024*, Annual Report to Congress (December 14, 2024), https://media.defense.gov/.

[30] *U.S.-China Economic and Security Review Commission*, "China's Ambitions to Dominate Space," Chapter 6 in *2025 Annual Report to Congress*.

[31] "Axis of Autocracy: China's Revisionist Ambitions with Russia, Iran, and North Korea," Chapter 3 in *2025 Annual Report to Congress*, U.S.-China Economic and Security Review Commission (November 2025), https://www.uscc.gov/sites/default/files/2025-11/Chapter_3.

[32] Insikt Group, *The Risk of a Taiwan Invasion*, 15-18.

[33] Hass, "Advancing U.S.-China Coordination."

[34] "Narrative Wars and Information Operations," in *2025 Annual Report to Congress*, U.S.-China Economic and Security Review Commission.

[35] PAX sapiens, *Four Scenarios for U.S.-China Relations*.

[36] Vyas, "US-China Economic Standoff in 2025."

[37] Policy Center for the New South, "2025: Year of The Middle Powers."

[38] "Protecting the Global Climate Agenda in an Era of China-US Competition," *The Diplomat*, May 5, 2025, https://thediplomat.com/2025/05/protecting-the-global-climate-agenda-in-an-era-of-china-us-competition/.

[39] Insikt Group, *The Risk of a Taiwan Invasion*, 2.

[40] Major Michael E. Moore, "Xi's Taiwan Dashboard: Opening and Closing Windows of Opportunity," *Journal of Indo-Pacific Affairs* (Spring 2025): 50-67, https://media.defense.gov/2025/Apr/29/2003700710/-1/-1/1/FEATURE%20-%20MOORE%20DISCLAIMER.PDF.

[41] GeoQuant, "Update for China/Taiwan Scenario Analysis Q1/2025."

[42] "Is a Conflict Over Taiwan Drawing Near? A Review of Available Forecasts and Scenarios," Swedish Institute of International Affairs UI Brief No. 1 (2024), https://www.ui.se/globalassets/ui.se-eng/publications/other-publications/is-a-conflict-over-taiwan-drawing-near-a-review-of-available-forecasts-and-scenarios.pdf.

[43] Mark F. Cancian, Matthew Cancian, and Eric Heginbotham, *The First Battle of the Next War: Wargaming a Chinese Invasion of Taiwan* (Washington, D.C.: Center for Strategic and International Studies, 2023).

[44] Ibid.

[45] Neely, "The Economic Effects of a Potential Armed Conflict Over Taiwan," 8-10.

[46] Cancian, Cancian, and Heginbotham, *The First Battle of the Next War*.

[47] Moore, "Xi's Taiwan Dashboard," 65-66.

[48] Teer et al., *The Cost of Conflict*, 18-20.

[49] Ibid., 25-30.

[50] Neely, "The Economic Effects of a Potential Armed Conflict Over Taiwan," 11-13.

[51] Ibid., 5-7.

[52] "Crossroads of Competition: China and Southeast Asia," Chapter 4 in *2025 Annual Report to Congress*, U.S.-China Economic and Security Review Commission.

[53] Simona A. Grano and Zoltán Fehér, eds., *China-US Competition: Impact on Small and Middle Powers' Strategic Choices* (Cham, Switzerland: Palgrave Macmillan, 2023), https://link.springer.com/book/10.1007/978-3-031-15389-1.

[54] "Crossroads of Competition: China and Southeast Asia."

[55] Rudra Chaudhuri, ed., *Major Power Rivalry and Domestic Politics in South Asia* (Washington, D.C.: Carnegie Endowment for International Peace, July 2025), https://carnegieendowment.org/research/2025/07/major-power-rivalry-and-domestic-politics-in-south-asia.

[56] "Axis of Autocracy," *U.S.-China Economic and Security Review Commission*.

[57] "Is a Conflict Over Taiwan Drawing Near?"

[58] Ibid.

[59] Teer et al., *The Cost of Conflict*, 32-35.

[60] Neely, "The Economic Effects of a Potential Armed Conflict Over Taiwan," 14-16.

[61] Chivvis, *U.S.-China Relations for the 2030s*, 2-3.

[62] Michael Beckley, "Charting the End State for US Strategy Toward China," Foreign Policy Research Institute, May 15, 2025, https://www.fpri.org/article/2025/04/charting-the-end-state-for-us-strategy-toward-china/.

[63] *U.S.-China Economic and Security Review Commission*, 16.

[64] Charles L. Glaser, "A U.S.-China Grand Bargain? The Hard Choice Between Military Competition and Accommodation," *International Security* 39, no. 4 (Spring 2015): 49-90, https://doi.org/10.1162/ISEC_a_00199.

[65] Ibid.

[66] Charles L. Glaser, "Time for a U.S.-China Grand Bargain," Belfer Center for Science and International Affairs, July 28, 2015, https://www.belfercenter.org/publication/time-us-china-grand-bargain.

[67] Kim, "Working Toward Responsible Competition with China."

[68] William Reinsch, "Ending the Trade War: Grand Bargain or Baby Steps?" Center for Strategic and International Studies, October 15, 2024, https://www.csis.org/analysis/ending-trade-war-grand-bargain-or-baby-steps.

[69] Hass, "Advancing U.S.-China Coordination."

[70] Glaser, "A U.S.-China Grand Bargain?"

[71] Reinsch, "Ending the Trade War."

[72] Peter Harris, "What Would a Trump Grand Bargain With China Need?" *Foreign Policy*, January 30, 2025, https://foreignpolicy.com/2025/01/29/trump-china-trade-grandbargain/.

[73] Brian Wong, "What Would a Xi-Trump Grand Bargain Look Like?" China-US Focus, April 28, 2025, https://www.chinausfocus.com/foreign-policy/what-would-a-xi-trump-grand-bargain-look-like.

[74] Chivvis, *U.S.-China Relations for the 2030s*, 35-40.

[75] Glaser, "Time for a U.S.-China Grand Bargain."

[76] Miwa Hirono and Ryan Ashley, "The Fantasy of a Grand Bargain Between America and China: Why Deadlock Is More Likely Than Détente," *Foreign Affairs*, July 7, 2025, https://www.foreignaffairs.com/united-states/fantasy-grand-bargain-between-america-and-china.

[77] Hass, "Advancing U.S.-China Coordination."

[78] Harris, "What Would a Trump Grand Bargain With China Need?"

[79] Glaser, "Time for a U.S.-China Grand Bargain."

[80] Rush Doshi, "Structure Trumps Agency in the U.S.-China Relationship," *Foreign Affairs*, November 2025, https://www.foreignaffairs.com/united-states/structure-trumps-agency-us-china-relationship.

[81] Ibid.

[82] Odd Arne Westad, "U.S.-China Relations Under a Second Trump Administration," Georgetown Journal of International Affairs, February 3, 2025, https://gjia.georgetown.edu/2025/02/03/a-multipolar-world-order-u-s-china-relations-under-a-second-trump-administration/.

[83] Dina Smeltz et al., "Americans Reverse Course on US-China Competition," Chicago Council on Global Affairs, 2025 Survey, https://globalaffairs.org/research/public-opinion-survey/americans-reverse-course-us-china-competition.

[84] Merics, "China in 2025," https://merics.org/en/merics-briefs/china-2025.

[85] *U.S.-China Economic and Security Review Commission*, 16-20.

[86] Gold and Baker, "The U.S.-China Decoupling Arrives."

[87] Policy Center for the New South, "2025: Year of The Middle Powers."

[88] Insikt Group, *The Risk of a Taiwan Invasion*, 2.

[89] Moore, "Xi's Taiwan Dashboard," 52-53.

[90] Ibid., 55-58.

[91] Insikt Group, *The Risk of a Taiwan Invasion*, 10-12.

[92] Zoltán Fehér, "The Implications of the Rise of Small and Middle Powers for U.S.-China Great Power Competition," in *Examining Perspectives of Small-to-Medium Powers in Emergent Great Power Competition*, ed. Philip M. Baxter (Cham, Switzerland: Palgrave Macmillan, 2025), https://doi.org/10.1007/978-3-031-86901-3_10.

[93] "Strategic Autonomy of Middle Powers under US–China Rivalry," Modern Diplomacy, May 30, 2025, https://moderndiplomacy.eu/2025/05/30/strategic-autonomy-of-middle-powers-under-us-china-rivalry/.

[94] Simona A. Grano and Zoltán Fehér, eds., *China-US Competition: Impact on Small and Middle Powers' Strategic Choices* (Cham, Switzerland: Palgrave Macmillan, 2023), https://link.springer.com/book/10.1007/978-3-031-15389-1.

[95] "Axis of Autocracy," *U.S.-China Economic and Security Review Commission*.

[96] Pohl and Imbrie, "Hard Then, Harder Now."

[97] U.S. National Security Commission on Emerging Biotechnology, quoted in Evelyn Cheng, "It's Not Just AI — China's Quickly Gaining an Edge Over the U.S. in Biotech," CNBC, June 5, 2025, https://www.cnbc.com/2025/06/05/chinas-quickly-gaining-an-edge-over-the-us-in-biotech.html.

[98] Cynthia Y. Tong and Eric Rosenbach, *Critical and Emerging Technologies Index* (Cambridge, MA: Belfer Center for Science and International Affairs, Harvard Kennedy School, June 2025), https://www.belfercenter.org/.

[99] Kim, "Working Toward Responsible Competition with China."

[100] PAX sapiens, *Four Scenarios for U.S.-China Relations.*

[101] Chivvis, *U.S.-China Relations for the 2030s*, 8-12.

[102] Witt et al., "US-China Competition, World Order and Economic Decoupling."

[103] Insikt Group, *The Risk of a Taiwan Invasion*, 2.

[104] Moore, "Xi's Taiwan Dashboard," 52.

[105] "Is a Conflict Over Taiwan Drawing Near?"

[106] Hirono and Ashley, "The Fantasy of a Grand Bargain."

[107] Harris, "What Would a Trump Grand Bargain With China Need?"

[108] Beckley, "Charting the End State for US Strategy Toward China."

[109] Xie Feng, "Recalibrate the Direction of China-U.S. Relations and Forge Ahead Braving the Waves," Embassy of the People's Republic of China in the United States of America, June 19, 2025, https://us.china-embassy.gov.cn/eng/dshd/202506/t20250619_11653544.htm.

[110] "Strategic Autonomy of Middle Powers under US–China Rivalry."

[111] Hass, "Advancing U.S.-China Coordination."

[112] Chivvis, *U.S.-China Relations for the 2030s*, 1.

[113] Ibid., 2.

Chapter 22
Policy Recommendations

What the United States Should Do

The U.S.-China rivalry has entered a defining phase that will shape the global order for decades to come. As this competition intensifies across technological, economic, and military domains, the United States faces a critical juncture: the strategic choices made today will determine whether America maintains its leadership position or cedes ground to an assertive Beijing. This chapter presents a comprehensive set of policy recommendations designed to strengthen American competitiveness, enhance national security, and promote prosperity in an era of strategic competition with China.

These recommendations emerge from rigorous analysis of current trends, expert assessments, and lessons learned from previous great power competitions. They are grounded in the reality that the United States cannot simply wish away the China challenge, nor can it rely solely on containment or confrontation. Instead, America must pursue a multifaceted strategy that invests in its own strengths, builds coalitions with allies and partners, maintains necessary guardrails to protect critical advantages, and preserves channels for diplomatic engagement to manage escalation risks.

The stakes could not be higher. As the U.S.-China Economic and Security Review Commission warned in its 2025 annual report, China is deploying sophisticated strategies to erode American deterrence across military, economic, and technological domains while simultaneously seeking to position itself as a more responsible steward of international order.[1] Meeting this challenge requires sustained focus, significant resources, and bipartisan commitment to a long-term strategy that transcends political cycles.

I. Strengthen Domestic Innovation Capacity

The Innovation Imperative

American technological leadership remains the cornerstone of U.S. economic prosperity and national security. However, this leadership faces unprecedented challenges. Over the past decade, the Chinese government has invested an estimated $900 billion in artificial intelligence, quantum computing, and biotechnology—more than three times U.S. government support for those technologies during the same period.[2] This disparity in strategic investment threatens to erode America's innovation advantage at a time when technological supremacy increasingly determines geopolitical outcomes.

The United States must dramatically expand its commitment to research and development across critical technology domains. This requires not just increased funding, but a fundamental reimagining of how America generates, protects, and commercializes breakthrough innovations.

Expanding the CHIPS Act Model

The CHIPS and Science Act of 2022 represents the most significant industrial policy intervention in American semiconductor manufacturing in decades. As of 2025, the legislation has catalyzed over $540 billion in private sector investments across more than 100 projects spanning 28 states.[3] The United States is projected to increase its global share of advanced logic chip manufacturing to 28 percent of global capacity by 2032, up from virtually zero in 2022.[4]

However, this success story must be expanded and extended. **Congress should prioritize the following actions:**

First, extend and expand the Advanced Manufacturing Investment Tax Credit. The 25 percent investment tax credit (ITC) provided under Section 48D of the CHIPS Act is due to expire on December 31, 2026. This credit has been instrumental in ensuring the economic viability of U.S. semiconductor manufacturing, where the cost to build a leading-edge fab can reach $28 billion.[5] The bipartisan Building Advanced Semiconductors Investment Credit (BASIC) Act proposes increasing the credit from 25 to 35 percent and extending it through the end of the decade—a proposal Congress should adopt expeditiously.[6]

Second, broaden the tax credit to cover semiconductor design. The cost of designing leading-edge chips has increased eighteenfold from the 65 nanometer generation to the 5 nanometer generation, with 2 nanometer chip design costs now reaching upward of $725 million.[7] Extending the investment tax credit to the design sector would help ensure American companies maintain their edge in this critical upstream activity.

Third, accelerate workforce development programs. The semiconductor industry faces a critical talent shortage. The CHIPS for America program has established workforce training initiatives, including a $5 million Entrepreneurial Fellowship Pilot Program and partnerships with academic institutions.[8] However, these efforts must be scaled dramatically. The National Semiconductor

Technology Center Workforce Center of Excellence, which received $250 million in funding, should serve as a model for similar investments across other critical technology sectors.[9]

Quantum Technology Leadership

Quantum computing represents the next frontier of computational capability, with implications for cryptography, drug discovery, materials science, and national security that cannot be overstated. Yet China is outspending the United States in quantum research by a factor of two, with Chinese government support reaching $15.3 billion as of 2023—more than twice the combined U.S. public and private sector investment.[10]

The U.S.-China Economic and Security Review Commission has recommended that Congress establish a "Quantum First" by 2030 national goal, with a focus on achieving quantum computational advantage in three mission-critical domains: cryptography, drug discovery, and materials science.[11] To realize this ambitious objective, Congress should:

Provide substantial funding increases for quantum development. The National Quantum Initiative has authorized significant increases in funding—$81 billion over Fiscal Years 2023-2027 if fully appropriated, which would double the National Science Foundation's budget.[12] However, appropriations have not kept pace with authorizations. Congress should ensure robust funding for quantum research centers, with the Department of Energy's renewal of $625 million for five National Quantum Information Science Research Centers representing a positive step that must be sustained and expanded.[13]

Develop quantum workforce capacity. Federal agencies should expand fellowships, talent exchange programs with allies, and dedicated quantum education initiatives to build the specialized workforce this field demands.[14] The National Science Foundation's Skilled Technical Workforce Initiative should prioritize quantum skills development alongside semiconductor training.

Secure quantum supply chains. The administration should task the National Quantum Initiative Advisory Committee to develop a detailed national strategy focused on de-risking quantum supply chains, increasing component availability, lowering prices, and incentivizing private sector investment in domestic quantum chip fabrication and assembly.[15]

Accelerate post-quantum cryptography deployment. As quantum computers grow more powerful, they threaten to break traditional encryption. Federal agencies must expedite adoption of post-quantum cryptography algorithms to safeguard sensitive systems and communications against future quantum attacks.[16]

Biotech Investment and Security

Biotechnology may eclipse artificial intelligence in strategic importance over the coming decade. As the Harvard Belfer Center has warned, biotech represents China's "most immediate opportunity to overtake" American technological leadership.[17] The National Security Commission's April 2025 call for a minimum investment of $15 billion over five years in biotechnology reflects the urgency of this challenge.[18]

Unfortunately, early-stage biotech financing in the United States dropped 65 percent in the first half of 2025, signaling severe capital market failures that require government intervention.[19] **Congress should:**

Establish a national network of biomanufacturing hubs. These facilities would provide shared infrastructure, reduce barriers to entry for innovative startups, and ensure the United States maintains capacity for rapid-scale production of critical biological products.[20]

Create strategic stockpile requirements. Mandate six-month stockpiles of key starting materials (KSMs) and active pharmaceutical ingredients (APIs) from trusted sources, addressing the dangerous reality that the United States sources 80 percent of KSMs and faces supply chain concentration where China controls 33 percent of global API capacity.[21]

Strengthen biosecurity export controls. The January 2025 export controls on biotechnology equipment, including high-parameter flow cytometers and mass spectrometry equipment, represent an important step in restricting China's access to technologies that could support military applications.[22] These controls must be enforced vigorously and expanded as China's capabilities evolve.

Supporting Basic Research

While applied research and commercialization receive significant attention, the United States must not neglect fundamental scientific research—the wellspring from which breakthrough innovations emerge. Federal funding for basic research as a percentage of GDP has declined over recent decades, even as China has dramatically increased its investments.

Congress should reverse this trend by:

Fully funding science agencies. The National Science Foundation, Department of Energy Office of Science, National Institutes of Health, and Defense Advanced Research Projects Agency (DARPA) represent America's crown jewels of scientific discovery. These agencies require sustained funding increases that enable long-term, high-risk research projects without the pressure for immediate commercial returns.

Protecting research security. While openness has traditionally been a strength of American science, the theft of intellectual property and technology transfer to China through academic channels demands better safeguards. Universities must implement robust research security protocols, particularly for projects involving sensitive technologies or federal funding, while maintaining the collaborative environment essential to scientific progress.[23]

II. Build Resilient Supply Chains with Allies

The Imperative of Supply Chain Diversification

The COVID-19 pandemic exposed the fragility of global supply chains and America's dangerous dependence on China for critical goods. This vulnerability extends far beyond consumer products to encompass materials and components essential for national defense, advanced manufacturing, and emerging technologies. The United States currently sources approximately 70 percent of rare earth elements (99 percent for heavy rare earths), 60 percent of data center and chip components, and 80 percent of key pharmaceutical ingredients from China or through Chinese-dominated supply chains.[24]

Building resilient supply chains does not mean complete decoupling or autarky—a goal that would be economically destructive and strategically counterproductive. Rather, it requires strategic diversification away from single points of failure, particularly where those dependencies leave America vulnerable to coercion by an adversarial power.

Critical Minerals Strategy

The October 2025 U.S.-Australia framework agreement on critical minerals, encompassing $8.5 billion in project pipelines, demonstrates the potential of allied partnerships to address supply chain vulnerabilities.[25] This agreement includes $1 billion in bilateral investment, price floor mechanisms to ensure project viability, and restrictions on asset sales to protect strategic investments.

Priority projects under this framework include Alcoa's gallium recovery facility and Arafura's Nolans rare earth processing facility, both designed to reduce dependence on Chinese processing capacity.[26] Australia has been aptly described as "the most important partner in countering China's dominance" in critical minerals.[27]

To build on this foundation, the United States should:

Expand the Mineral Security Partnership (MSP). Started in 2022, the MSP provides an international cooperation mechanism for expanding mineral supply diversification and trade.[28] The MSP Finance Network, established in 2024, incorporates multilateral development finance institutions to expand financial resources available for sustainable mining.[29] The United States should deepen engagement with MSP partners, particularly countries with significant mineral reserves such as Canada, Australia, Japan, and members of the European Union.

Implement guaranteed price contracts. Modeled on the MP Materials rare earths arrangement where the Defense Department invested $400 million for approximately a 15 percent equity stake, guaranteed price contracts provide investment certainty through shared upside mechanisms rather than blanket import restrictions.[30] This approach addresses the fundamental challenge that private capital often avoids mineral development due to long timelines, high capital requirements, and price volatility.

Accelerate domestic permitting. A 2024 S&P Global report indicates that developing a new mine in the United States takes an average of 29 years—the second-longest duration globally.[31] This is untenable in an era of strategic competition. Streamlining permitting processes while maintaining robust environmental protections should be a national priority. The One Big Beautiful Bill Act's appropriation of $2 billion for expanding the National Defense Stockpile and $5 billion for the Industrial Base Fund represents positive steps that must be implemented efficiently.[32]

Invest in recycling and materials substitution. Innovation in recycling technologies and materials substitution can reduce vulnerabilities in mineral supply chains. The Department of Energy's $1 billion investment in 2025 to advance technologies across the critical minerals supply chain, including a Rare Earth Elements Demonstration Facility focused on recovering rare earths from mine tailings and waste streams, exemplifies the potential of this approach.[33]

Semiconductor Supply Chain Resilience

While the CHIPS Act addresses domestic semiconductor manufacturing capacity, true supply chain resilience requires a comprehensive approach that encompasses materials, equipment, and geographic diversification across allied nations.

The United States should:

Coordinate semiconductor investment with allies. Japan, South Korea, Taiwan, and European nations are making significant investments in semiconductor manufacturing. Rather than competing for the same projects, allied nations should coordinate to ensure complementary capabilities across the supply chain. The Commerce Department should lead regular consultations with allied semiconductor agencies to align investment strategies and avoid redundancy.

Secure materials and equipment supply chains. The United States depends on foreign suppliers for key semiconductor materials and equipment, including ASML's extreme ultraviolet (EUV) lithography systems from the Netherlands and materials from Japan. Strengthening these alliances and ensuring these partners maintain their technological edge is as important as building domestic capacity.

Support advanced packaging capabilities. While leading-edge chip fabrication receives significant attention, advanced packaging—the process of integrating multiple chips into a single system—is equally critical. The CHIPS for America NSTC Prototyping and National Advanced Packaging Manufacturing Program facility, expected to be operational in 2028 at Arizona State University, should receive robust support and serve as a model for additional regional packaging hubs.[34]

Friend-Shoring in Practice

Supply chain resilience requires moving beyond simple diversification to embrace "friend-shoring"—the strategic relocation of production and sourcing to allied and partner nations that share democratic values and have aligned strategic interests.

This approach demands:

Trade agreements that prioritize resilience. Future trade agreements should include provisions that incentivize supply chain diversification and penalize concentration in adversarial nations. The U.S.-Mexico-Canada Agreement provides a model with its rules of origin requirements designed to reshore manufacturing.[35]

Development finance focused on strategic sectors. The International Development Finance Corporation, Export-Import Bank, and other development finance tools should prioritize projects in allied and partner nations that reduce dependencies on China. This requires adjusting traditional financial metrics to account for strategic value and national security considerations.

Standards and regulatory cooperation. Harmonizing technical standards, regulatory requirements, and testing protocols with allies reduces transaction costs and makes friend-shored supply chains more competitive. The U.S.-EU Trade and Technology Council provides a forum for this type of cooperation that should be leveraged more aggressively.

III. Maintain Targeted Export Controls While Avoiding Overreach

The Strategic Logic of Export Controls

Export controls represent a critical tool for protecting America's technological advantages and denying adversaries access to capabilities that could threaten U.S. national security. However, as recent experience demonstrates, export controls are a blunt instrument that can produce unintended consequences if applied too broadly or without sufficient coordination with allies.

The October 2022 semiconductor export controls marked a watershed moment, restricting China's access to advanced AI chips and the manufacturing equipment needed to produce them.[36] These controls have achieved significant success: according to Commerce Secretary Howard Lutnick's congressional testimony, Huawei will produce only 200,000 AI chips in 2025, while Chinese companies reportedly legally imported around 1 million downgraded chips from Nvidia in 2024.[37] This supply constraint has forced Chinese companies to resort to smuggling and has slowed China's AI development, at least temporarily.

However, the controls have also imposed costs on U.S. firms and accelerated Chinese efforts toward self-sufficiency. The Information Technology and Innovation Foundation estimates that U.S. firms could lose about $77 billion in semiconductor industry sales annually under a hypothetical full decoupling scenario, with corresponding reductions in R&D investment of approximately 24 percent, or $14 billion.[38] Moreover, as demonstrated by DeepSeek's January 2025 achievement of competitive AI performance using inferior hardware, export controls alone cannot prevent Chinese technological advancement indefinitely.[39]

Principles for Effective Export Control Policy

The challenge facing policymakers is to design export control policies that protect critical advantages without undermining the technological and economic foundations of American competitiveness. **This requires adherence to several key principles:**

Target the highest-value technologies. Export controls should focus on technologies that provide decisive military advantages or enable capabilities that directly threaten U.S. national security. Attempting to control too broad a range of technologies dilutes enforcement resources and creates opportunities for evasion.

Coordinate with allies. Unilateral export controls face severe limitations, as China can often obtain restricted technologies through third-party countries. The Biden administration's intensive diplomatic efforts with the Netherlands and Japan to restrict access to advanced semiconductor manufacturing equipment demonstrated the importance of allied coordination.[40] However, achieving and maintaining this coordination remains challenging, particularly when allies have different economic interests and threat perceptions.

Update controls dynamically. Technology evolves rapidly, and export control regimes must adapt accordingly. The December 2024 export control update added 140 companies to the Entity List and expanded the Foreign Direct Product Rule, demonstrating the need for continuous refinement.[41] However, these updates must be made judiciously to avoid creating uncertainty that drives customers to seek alternative suppliers.

Avoid overreach. The January 2025 AI Diffusion Rule, which proposed a global licensing framework with three tiers of countries and cumulative computing power allocations, was rescinded after encountering resistance from both allies and industry.[42] This experience illustrates the dangers of attempting to micromanage global technology flows through export controls. A more calibrated approach that focuses on genuine chokepoints while allowing broader access under appropriate safeguards is more likely to succeed.

Close enforcement gaps. The most sophisticated export control regime is worthless if it cannot be enforced. In July 2025, Cadence Design Systems pleaded guilty and paid approximately $213 million to resolve charges that it sold electronic design automation tools to China's National University of Defense Technology, a military entity on the Entity List, between 2015 and 2021.[43] Such cases highlight the need for robust enforcement mechanisms, including criminal penalties for violations, enhanced end-use monitoring, and coordination with allies to prevent transshipment through third countries.

Recommendations for Export Control Policy

Maintain restrictions on leading-edge semiconductors and manufacturing equipment. The current controls targeting advanced chips (below 16/14 nanometers for logic chips) and EUV lithography equipment should be maintained and enforced rigorously. These technologies represent genuine chokepoints where the United States and its allies have decisive advantages.

Expand controls to enabler technologies. As recommended by the Foundation for Defense of Democracies, export controls should expand to include electronic design automation (EDA) software, sophisticated chip packaging apparatus, and high-bandwidth memory—all essential facilitators of AI accelerator efficacy.[44]

Establish clearer licensing policies. The current system, which provides discretionary approval for some exports (such as Nvidia's H20 and AMD's MI308 chips to China under special licenses), creates uncertainty and incentivizes the development of workarounds.[45] Licensing policies should be transparent, predictable, and based on clearly articulated criteria linked to national security objectives.

Support ally compliance. The United States should provide technical and financial support to help allied nations implement and enforce aligned export control regimes. This includes sharing intelligence on evasion attempts, providing training for export control administrators, and, where appropriate, compensating companies for revenue losses resulting from compliance with multilateral controls.

Avoid extraterritorial overreach. While the Foreign Direct Product Rule gives the United States significant extraterritorial reach, excessive use of this authority risks alienating allies and customers. The rule should be reserved for technologies where the United States has clear leverage and where the national security justification is compelling.

IV. Invest in Next-Generation Technologies

The Race for Technological Supremacy

The competition between the United States and China increasingly centers on emerging technologies that will define economic competitiveness and military capabilities for decades to come. Beyond semiconductors and AI—domains that have received substantial attention and investment—the United States must urgently invest in additional technology areas where Chinese advances threaten American leadership.

Advanced Manufacturing and Robotics

China has become the world's manufacturing powerhouse, producing approximately 30 percent of global manufacturing output while consuming only 18 percent.[46] This overcapacity problem reflects massive state-directed investments in advanced manufacturing technologies, including industrial robotics, additive manufacturing, and smart factory systems.

The United States cannot and should not attempt to match China's manufacturing scale across all sectors. However, America must maintain leadership in advanced manufacturing technologies and regain manufacturing capacity in strategic sectors critical to national security.

Congress and the administration should:

Fund the Manufacturing USA network. The sixteen Manufacturing USA institutes, sponsored by the Commerce Department, each focus on a specific advanced manufacturing technology area and include workforce development initiatives.[47] These institutes require sustained funding increases to scale their impact and establish additional institutes in emerging areas such as advanced robotics and autonomous manufacturing systems.

Support manufacturing technology R&D. Federal R&D investment in manufacturing technologies has declined as a share of total R&D spending. This trend must be reversed. The Department of Energy, Department of Defense, and National Science Foundation should receive dedicated appropriations for manufacturing technology research, with emphasis on technologies that enable small-batch production, mass customization, and rapid reconfiguration—areas where the United States can differentiate from China's mass production model.

Incentivize smart manufacturing adoption. Tax credits and accelerated depreciation for smart manufacturing investments can help U.S. manufacturers adopt advanced technologies and improve productivity. A 2025 survey found that 80 percent of manufacturing executives plan to invest 20 percent or more of their improvement budgets in smart manufacturing initiatives.[48] Federal policy should support this transition.

Hypersonics and Advanced Propulsion

China has made significant strides in hypersonic weapons development, conducting extensive testing of hypersonic glide vehicles and scramjet-powered systems. These weapons pose challenges to traditional missile defense architectures and could potentially negate some U.S. military advantages.

The United States must:

Accelerate hypersonic weapon development. While the Department of Defense has several hypersonic programs in development, these efforts require additional funding and should be elevated as national priorities. The "Golden Dome" missile defense initiative called for in the White House R&D memorandum should include research into directed energy and other technologies capable of countering hypersonic threats.[49]

Invest in advanced propulsion research. Beyond hypersonics, the United States should fund research into alternative propulsion systems, including advanced jet engines, electric propulsion for space applications, and novel propulsion concepts that could provide decisive military and commercial advantages.

Space Technologies

Space has emerged as a critical domain for both commercial activity and military operations. China has made space technology development a national priority, with ambitious programs in satellite communications, space-based sensing, and exploration.

The United States should:

Ensure adequate funding for NASA. The U.S.-China Economic and Security Review Commission has warned that program delays at NASA undermine U.S. credibility in establishing global norms for lunar and Martian exploration.[50] Congress must provide NASA with sufficient and predictable funding to maintain leadership in space exploration and technology development.

Support commercial space sector. The American commercial space industry leads globally in innovation and entrepreneurship. Government policies should continue supporting this sector through anchor tenancy agreements, streamlined licensing, and protection of intellectual property.

Invest in space domain awareness. As the space environment becomes more congested and contested, the United States needs enhanced capabilities for tracking and characterizing space objects, detecting threats, and protecting critical space assets. The Space Force requires robust funding for these missions.

V. Develop Coherent Industrial Policy

The Case for Industrial Policy

For much of the post-Cold War era, American policymakers embraced a largely hands-off approach to industrial development, trusting market forces to allocate capital efficiently and drive innovation. This approach served the United States well during a period of relative geopolitical stability and when potential competitors operated within the liberal international order. However, the rise of China—a state-capitalist system that deploys massive resources to advance strategic industries—has exposed the limitations of pure market orthodoxy in an era of strategic competition.

The CHIPS Act represents a landmark shift in American industrial policy, demonstrating that targeted government intervention can mobilize private capital and rebuild strategic industries. The $540 billion in private investments catalyzed by $52.7 billion in federal subsidies represents a return on investment that validates the strategic use of industrial policy tools.[51]

Principles of Effective Industrial Policy

Industrial policy in a market economy must be designed carefully to avoid the pitfalls of central planning while harnessing government resources to address market failures and achieve strategic objectives. **Effective industrial policy should:**

Target genuine market failures. Government intervention should focus on areas where private capital fails to invest adequately due to long time horizons, uncertain returns, positive externalities, or coordination problems. Quantum technology and biotechnology, where early-stage financing dropped precipitously in 2025, exemplify such failures.[52]

Leverage private sector expertise. Government should enable and catalyze private investment rather than attempting to supplant it. Public-private partnerships, where government provides initial capital or risk mitigation while industry provides technical expertise and operational management, tend to produce better outcomes than purely government-directed efforts.

Include sunset provisions. Industrial policy interventions should be time-limited and subject to performance reviews. Permanent subsidies or protection risk creating inefficient, politically-entrenched industries that drain resources without delivering strategic value.

Embrace competition. Even within supported industries, policymakers should encourage competition among firms rather than picking single "national champions." Competition drives innovation and efficiency gains that monopoly stifles.

Coordinate with allies. As supply chains span borders, industrial policy must be coordinated with allied nations to avoid zero-sum competition and ensure complementary capabilities across the alliance network.

Specific Industrial Policy Recommendations

Establish sector-specific investment programs. Following the CHIPS Act model, Congress should create targeted investment programs for additional strategic sectors, including advanced batteries, critical minerals processing, biomanufacturing, and next-generation telecommunications. These programs should combine grants, loans, and tax incentives to mobilize private capital.

Create a Strategic Investment Authority. The United States lacks a coherent mechanism for evaluating and coordinating industrial policy interventions across agencies. Congress should establish a Strategic Investment Authority, modeled on institutions like Singapore's Economic Development Board, to assess proposals, allocate resources, and monitor outcomes for industrial policy programs. This authority should be chartered to take equity positions in strategic companies when appropriate, as the Defense Department has done with MP Materials and Intel.[53]

Reform procurement to support industrial policy. Federal procurement represents approximately $700 billion annually—a substantial lever for supporting strategic industries. Procurement rules should be reformed to favor domestic producers and allied suppliers in strategic sectors, even when this increases short-term costs. The Berry Amendment, which requires the Defense Department to purchase certain items from domestic sources, should be expanded to cover additional strategic technologies and materials.

Establish workforce development as a core element. Industrial policy cannot succeed without a skilled workforce. Every industrial policy program should include substantial workforce development components, including partnerships with community colleges, apprenticeship programs, and pre-apprenticeship initiatives to build talent pipelines.[54]

Addressing the Workforce Challenge

The United States faces a severe manufacturing workforce shortage, with approximately 438,000 open manufacturing positions as of July 2025 and a projected need for 3.8 million workers over the next decade.[55] This shortage threatens to become a binding constraint on industrial policy ambitions regardless of capital availability.

To address this challenge:

Expand registered apprenticeship programs. The Federation for Advanced Manufacturing Education (FAME) model, where participants earn while they learn through combinations of classroom instruction and paid work, has proven highly successful.[56] Congress should provide substantial funding to scale such programs nationally, with particular focus on semiconductors, advanced manufacturing, and emerging technology sectors.

Invest in STEM education from K-12 through university. The CHIPS and Science Act authorized significant increases in STEM education funding, including the creation of NSF's Technology, Innovation, and Partnerships Directorate.[57] However, appropriations have not kept pace with authorizations. Congress should fully fund these programs and expand initiatives that encourage students to pursue STEM careers, particularly in fields critical to national competitiveness.

Remove barriers to skilled immigration. Immigrants account for nearly a quarter of U.S. patents and play vital roles in STEM fields and entrepreneurship.[58] Immigration policy should prioritize attracting and retaining highly skilled workers, particularly in strategic technology fields. This includes reforming visa categories, accelerating processing times, and creating direct pathways to permanent residency for foreign students who earn advanced STEM degrees from U.S. universities.

Address workforce diversity. Women comprise only 29 percent of the manufacturing workforce, representing a significant untapped talent pool.[59] Programs specifically designed to recruit and retain women, minorities, and other underrepresented groups in manufacturing and STEM fields should receive dedicated federal support.

VI. Balance Deterrence with Diplomatic Engagement

The Imperative of Managed Competition

The U.S.-China relationship has transitioned from cooperation and engagement to what scholars describe as "managed competition"—an approach that combines elements of deterrence, competition, and selective cooperation to prevent conflict while defending American interests. As the Carnegie Endowment for International Peace argues, establishing military parity and mutual deterrence must serve as the foundation for stability and a sustainable modus vivendi between the two powers.[60]

The risk in the current environment is that pure deterrence-based approaches, without adequate diplomatic engagement and channels for dialogue, increase the likelihood of miscalculation and inadvertent escalation. As U.S. Secretary of Defense Pete Hegseth acknowledged at the 2025 Shangri-La Dialogue, deterrence requires not just military capability but also clear communication of intentions and red lines.[61] Without such clarity, deterrence can fail even when capabilities are robust.

Strengthening Deterrence

Military deterrence remains essential to preventing Chinese aggression, particularly regarding Taiwan. However, deterrence in the 21st century must be comprehensive, encompassing military, economic, and technological dimensions.

Military deterrence requires:

Forward deployment and resilience. The United States must maintain forward-deployed forces in the Indo-Pacific that are resilient and designed primarily for defense rather than offense—what Taylor Fravel and Eric Heginbotham describe as "defense-dominance."[62] This posture signals commitment to defending allies without appearing to threaten China's core interests, reducing the security dilemma that could trigger preventive conflict.

Allied capability development. The U.S. defense industrial base is strained, with production capacity insufficient to sustain a major conflict while simultaneously supplying allies. As the Foreign Policy Research Institute recommends, the United States should dramatically expand co-development, co-production, and co-sustainment of military platforms with allies.[63] Joint production of Tomahawk and Patriot missiles, naval warships, and drones with Australia, Japan, South Korea, and other partners would both strengthen deterrence and rebuild industrial capacity.

Nuclear dialogue. China's expansion to an estimated 1,500 operational nuclear warheads by 2035 greatly complicates deterrence.[64] The United States and China must engage in sustained bilateral talks on nuclear risk reduction, strategic stability, and missile defenses. While difficult given current tensions, such dialogue becomes increasingly essential as arsenals grow.

Economic deterrence. Restrictive economic measures, including sanctions, represent part of the deterrence toolkit. However, as a 2025 RAND study notes, the effectiveness of economic deterrence depends heavily on multilateral coordination and advance planning.[65] The United States should work with allies to establish clear economic consequences—including coordinated sanctions, financial restrictions, and technology embargoes—that would be triggered by specific Chinese actions, particularly military aggression against Taiwan.

Diplomatic Engagement

Deterrence without diplomacy risks creating a self-fulfilling prophecy where both sides arm for conflict that neither originally intended. As Aaron Glasserman and Josh Freedman argue, deterrence without reassurance risks "hardening the very tensions the United States seeks to manage."[66]

Effective diplomatic engagement requires:

Regular high-level dialogue. Despite strategic competition, the United States and China must maintain open channels of communication at the highest levels. Regular meetings between presidents, cabinet officials, and senior military leaders provide opportunities to clarify intentions, reduce misunderstandings, and manage crises when they emerge. The U.S.-China relationship should not be held hostage to tactical disagreements or domestic political pressures.

Military-to-military communications. The absence of substantive military-to-military engagement between the United States and China increases the risk of miscalculation, especially as China advances capabilities designed to contest U.S. power in multiple domains.[67] Both nations should establish procedures for managing military interactions, including protocols for air and maritime encounters, hotlines for crisis communication, and mechanisms for discussing military exercises and deployments.

Working-level cooperation on shared challenges. While the overall relationship is competitive, opportunities exist for cooperation on specific issues where interests align. Climate change, pandemic preparedness, counterterrorism, and nonproliferation represent areas where U.S. and Chinese cooperation could generate mutual benefits. As history demonstrates from U.S.-Soviet cooperation on smallpox eradication during the Cold War, superpowers can cooperate selectively even amid broader competition.[68]

Clear red lines. Diplomatic engagement should include explicit communication of red lines—actions by either side that would trigger major responses. For the United States, these should include unprovoked military action against Taiwan, attacks on U.S. treaty allies, and use of weapons of mass destruction. Congress should require the executive branch to define and publicly communicate the economic, diplomatic, and military consequences of Chinese provocations against U.S. treaty allies.[69]

Avoiding unrequited concessions. As several analysts warn, diplomatic engagement cannot mean the United States making unilateral concessions in pursuit of short-term stability. Such concessions would signal weakness, encourage further Chinese assertiveness, and undermine deterrence.[70] Diplomatic engagement should be reciprocal, with both sides making genuine efforts to reduce tensions and manage competition responsibly.

Building Alliance Architectures

No aspect of U.S. strategy toward China is more important than strengthening alliances and partnerships. China's greatest long-term disadvantage relative to the United States lies in its relative isolation—while America can draw upon a network of wealthy, technologically advanced allies, China has few reliable partners of comparable capability.

The United States should:

Deepen the "latticework" of Indo-Pacific alliances. Rather than relying on a single hub-and-spoke alliance system centered on Washington, the United States should encourage and enable deeper cooperation among regional allies and partners. The Quad (United States, Japan, Australia, India), AUKUS (United States, United Kingdom, Australia), and various bilateral partnerships should form an interlocking network that increases collective capability and resilience.

Expand engagement beyond traditional allies. As the Foreign Policy Research Institute recommends, the United States should build relationships not only with treaty allies but also with nations like Indonesia, Kenya, and Brazil that have the potential to serve as important partners.[71] Many countries want American partnership but will turn to China if antagonized or ignored. Patient, consistent engagement focused on mutual interests rather than demands for wholesale alignment with U.S. positions will yield better long-term results.

Maintain European engagement. While the Indo-Pacific receives primary attention in China strategy discussions, European allies remain vital to American competitiveness. Europe hosts key semiconductor equipment manufacturers, represents significant R&D capacity, and can contribute to technology export controls and investment screening. The U.S.-EU Trade and Technology Council should be strengthened and used more effectively to coordinate technology policy and economic security measures.

Address alliance burden-sharing constructively. The United States should encourage allies to increase defense spending and capability development, but this advocacy should be calibrated to avoid undermining alliance cohesion. Demands for increased burden-sharing are most effective when tied to specific capability requirements and presented as part of shared strategic planning rather than financial transactions.

VII. Address Domestic Political Dysfunction

The Domestic Foundations of Strategic Competition

No foreign policy strategy can succeed if domestic foundations are weak. America's ability to compete with China over the long term depends fundamentally on domestic political, economic, and social conditions. As Michael Swaine observed in 2019, current trends in U.S.-China relations involve "steadily worsening relations over the long term, with increasingly adverse consequences for all actors involved."[72] Part of this deterioration stems from domestic pressures in both countries that constrain diplomatic flexibility and reward hostile rhetoric.

The United States faces several domestic challenges that undermine its competitive position:

Political polarization. Partisan gridlock makes it difficult to sustain long-term strategic initiatives that require sustained funding and bipartisan support. While China policy represents one of the few areas of bipartisan agreement, this consensus is fragile and often driven more by domestic political considerations than strategic coherence.

Fiscal pressures. The United States faces long-term fiscal challenges driven by mandatory spending growth, particularly for entitlement programs, combined with political resistance to tax increases. These pressures will increasingly constrain resources available for strategic investments in technology, defense, and infrastructure.

Infrastructure deficits. American infrastructure—physical, digital, and human capital—has deteriorated relative to other advanced economies. Crumbling transportation networks, inadequate broadband access in rural areas, and failing educational systems in many communities undermine productivity and economic dynamism.

Institutional erosion. Trust in American institutions—government, media, academia, and even science—has declined significantly. This erosion weakens the United States' ability to marshal collective action for long-term goals and makes the country more vulnerable to disinformation and manipulation.

Recommendations for Domestic Renewal

While a comprehensive domestic reform agenda exceeds the scope of this chapter, several areas directly affect America's ability to compete with China:

Invest in infrastructure. The Infrastructure Investment and Jobs Act of 2021 represented an important down payment, but much more is needed. Congress should make infrastructure investment—including transportation, broadband, water systems, and the electric grid—a sustained priority with regular appropriations beyond one-time authorization.

Reform education. K-12 education in the United States significantly underperforms other advanced economies despite high per-pupil spending. Recent global benchmarks rank American students in the middle of the pack in math and science.[73] Educational reform should focus on improving STEM literacy, strengthening vocational education, and preparing students for a technology-intensive economy. Federal policy can support state and local initiatives through competitive grant programs, technical assistance, and research on effective pedagogical approaches.

Ensure fiscal sustainability. Long-term fiscal pressures threaten America's ability to make needed strategic investments. Addressing this requires politically difficult choices about entitlement reform, tax policy, and spending priorities. While specifics remain contentious, the fiscal trajectory is unsustainable and will eventually force painful adjustments. The longer reforms are delayed, the more disruptive they will become.

Combat disinformation. Chinese influence operations seek to exploit social divisions, undermine confidence in democratic institutions, and manipulate public opinion on policy issues ranging from Taiwan to trade. The United States needs enhanced capabilities for detecting and countering foreign disinformation while preserving free speech and avoiding government overreach in regulating content. The State Department's Global Engagement Center should receive adequate funding to monitor and counter foreign propaganda, while the Department of Justice should vigorously prosecute foreign agents who operate covertly to influence American politics.[74]

Strengthen democratic norms. America's greatest advantage in competition with authoritarian China lies in its democratic system, which generates innovation, attracts talent, and produces social cohesion that coercive systems cannot match. However, these advantages erode when democratic norms—respect for elections, peaceful transfer of power, judicial independence, and protection of civil liberties—are weakened. Defending democracy at home is inseparable from projecting democratic values abroad.

Conclusion: Strategy for a Long Competition

The policy recommendations outlined in this chapter form an integrated strategy for sustained competition with China across multiple dimensions. They are ambitious and will require substantial resources, sustained political commitment, and difficult tradeoffs. However, the alternative—continued erosion of American competitiveness and increasing vulnerability to Chinese coercion—is unacceptable.

Several themes cut across these recommendations:

Investment is essential. Whether in technology, infrastructure, education, or defense, the United States must invest significantly more resources in the foundations of competitiveness. These investments will require both increased federal spending and policies that catalyze private capital toward strategic priorities.

Allies multiply American power. The United States cannot match China's scale alone, but the alliance network America has built over decades represents an asymmetric advantage that China cannot easily counter. Deepening and broadening these partnerships should be central to every aspect of competition strategy.

Targeted measures work better than blanket restrictions. Export controls, trade restrictions, and other economic measures should be deployed surgically against genuine threats rather than applied broadly in ways that undermine American competitiveness and alienate allies.

Deterrence and diplomacy are complementary. Preventing conflict requires both the military capability to deny Chinese objectives and diplomatic channels to manage tensions and avoid miscalculation. Neither approach alone is sufficient.

Domestic strength is fundamental. Foreign policy ultimately rests on domestic foundations. Rebuilding American infrastructure, educational systems, fiscal sustainability, and democratic institutions is inseparable from competing effectively with China.

The competition with China will define international politics for decades to come. As the U.S.-China Economic and Security Review Commission concluded, China poses challenges to U.S. economic and national security that demand sustained, comprehensive responses.[75] The recommendations in this chapter provide a framework for meeting those challenges while preserving American prosperity, strengthening American democracy, and maintaining the liberal international order that has served the United States and its allies well for generations.

Success is not guaranteed. China has formidable capabilities, ambitious goals, and patient leadership willing to pursue long-term objectives. However, the United States retains significant advantages—in technology, finance, alliances, and the dynamism of its society and economy. If American policymakers make wise choices, sustain strategic focus across administrations, and invest adequately in the foundations of competitiveness, the United States can prevail in this competition and shape a 21st century international order that reflects American values and interests.

The stakes demand nothing less than success, and the means to achieve it remain within America's grasp if policymakers can summon the vision, resources, and political will to implement a comprehensive strategy. The time for decisive action is now.

Endnotes

[1] U.S.-China Economic and Security Review Commission, *2025 Annual Report to Congress*, November 2025, https://www.uscc.gov/sites/default/files/2025-11/2025_Executive_Summary.pdf; https://www.uscc.gov/annual-report/2025-annual-report-congress; South China Morning Post, "US Panel Urges New Economic Statecraft Body as China's Tech Challenge Grows," November 19, 2025, https://www.scmp.com/news/us/diplomacy/article/3333177/us-panel-urges-economic-statecraft-body-tackle-chinas-growing-tech-challenge.

[2] Council on Foreign Relations Task Force, *U.S. Economic Security: Winning the Race for Tomorrow's Technologies*, Task Force Report No. 83, November 13, 2025, https://www.cfr.org/task-force-report/us-economic-security.

[3] Semiconductor Industry Association, "Tracking CHIPS and Science Act Investments," accessed December 3, 2025, https://www.semiconductors.org/chip-supply-chain-investments/; U.S. Department of the Treasury, "U.S. Department of the Treasury Releases Final Rules to Strengthen U.S. Semiconductor Industry," Press Release, October 22, 2024, https://home.treasury.gov/news/press-releases/jy2664; Manufacturing Dive, "Tracking CHIPS and Science Act Awards," September 2, 2025, https://www.manufacturingdive.com/news/chips-and-science-act-tracker-semiconductor-manufacturing/734039/.

[4] Information Technology and Innovation Foundation, "U.S. Semiconductor Manufacturing Tax Credits Need To Be Extended and Broadened," June 10, 2025, https://itif.org/publications/2025/06/10/us-semiconductor-manufacturing-tax-credits-must-be-extended-and-broadened/; Semiconductor Industry Association, *2025 State of the U.S. Semiconductor Industry*, July 2025, https://www.semiconductors.org/wp-content/uploads/2025/07/SIA-State-of-the-Industry-Report-2025.pdf; Intel Corporation, "US Semiconductor Manufacturing | CHIPS and Science Act," accessed December 3, 2025, https://www.intel.com/content/www/us/en/corporate/usa-chipmaking/home.html.

[5] Ibid.; PwC, "The CHIPS Act: What it means for the semiconductor ecosystem," accessed December 3, 2025, https://www.pwc.com/us/en/library/chips-act.html.

[6] Ibid.

[7] Ibid.

[8] National Governors Association, "CHIPS and Science Act: Implementation Resources," accessed December 3, 2025, https://www.nga.org/chips-resources/.

[9] Center for Strategic and International Studies, "Renewing the United States' Skilled Technical Workforce," July 9, 2025, https://www.csis.org/analysis/renewing-united-states-skilled-technical-workforce.

[10] Council on Foreign Relations Task Force, *U.S. Economic Security: Winning the Race for Tomorrow's Technologies*; Homeland Security Newswire, "U.S. Economic Security: Winning the Race for Tomorrows Technologies," November 15, 2025, https://www.homelandsecuritynewswire.com/dr20251115-u-s-economic-security-winning-the-race-for-tomorrows-technologies.

[11] U.S.-China Economic and Security Review Commission, *2025 Annual Report to Congress*; Breaking Defense, "Congress Should Establish, Fund New Quantum Tech Initiative to Beat China: Panel," November 18, 2025, https://breakingdefense.com/2025/11/congress-should-establish-fund-new-quantum-tech-initiative-to-beat-china-panel/.

[12] National Science Foundation, "CHIPS and Science," accessed December 3, 2025, https://www.nsf.gov/chips; National Quantum Coordination Office, "National Quantum Initiative Act," accessed December 3, 2025, https://www.quantum.gov/; National Quantum Coordination Office, *National Quantum Initiative Supplement to the President's FY 2025 Budget*, December 2024, https://www.quantum.gov/wp-content/uploads/2024/12/NQI-Annual-Report-FY2025.pdf.

[13] U.S. Department of Energy, "Energy Department Announces $625 Million to Advance the Next Phase of National Quantum Information Science Research Centers," press release, accessed December 3, 2025, https://www.energy.gov/articles/energy-department-announces-625-million-advance-next-phase-national-quantum-information.

[14] U.S.-China Economic and Security Review Commission, *2025 Annual Report to Congress*.

[15] Microsoft, "Investing in American Leadership in Quantum Technology: The Next Frontier in Innovation," Microsoft On the Issues (blog), May 7, 2025, https://blogs.microsoft.com/on-the-issues/2025/04/28/investing-in-american-leadership-quantum/.

[16] The Quantum Insider, "White House Places Quantum And AI at The Summit of R&D Priorities," October 2, 2025, https://thequantuminsider.com/2025/09/27/white-house-place-quantum-and-ai-at-the-summit-of-rd-priorities/; Post Quantum, "White House FY2027 R&D

Memo Puts Quantum Technologies Front and Center," September 23, 2025, https://postquantum.com/quantum-policy/white-house-fy2027-rd-memo/.

[17] Council on Foreign Relations Task Force, *U.S. Economic Security: Winning the Race for Tomorrow's Technologies.*

[18] Ibid.

[19] Ibid.; Quantum Zeitgeist, "Report: U.S. Must Strengthen AI, Quantum, Biotech Leadership," November 2025, https://quantumzeitgeist.com/ai-quantum-biotech-tech-leadership/.

[20] Council on Foreign Relations Task Force, *U.S. Economic Security: Winning the Race for Tomorrow's Technologies.*

[21] Ibid.

[22] Council on Foreign Relations Task Force, *U.S. Economic Security: Winning the Race for Tomorrow's Technologies.*

[23] Federal Bureau of Investigation, "Protecting Quantum Science and Technology," FBI Stories, April 12, 2024, https://www.fbi.gov/news/stories/protecting-quantum-science-and-technology.

[24] Council on Foreign Relations Task Force, *U.S. Economic Security: Winning the Race for Tomorrow's Technologies*; Quantum Zeitgeist, "Report: U.S. Must Strengthen AI, Quantum, Biotech Leadership," November 2025, https://quantumzeitgeist.com/ai-quantum-biotech-tech-leadership/.

[25] Supply Chain Dive, "US, Australia Sign Framework for Critical Mineral Supply Chain," October 23, 2025, https://www.supplychaindive.com/news/usgs-releases-2025-list-of-us-essential-minerals/805364/.

[26] Supply Chain Dive, "US, Australia Sign Framework for Critical Mineral Supply Chain"; Atlantic Council, "US Critical Minerals Strategy: Securing Supply, Refining Capacity, and Resilience," November 29, 2025, https://www.atlanticcouncil.org/blogs/econographics/on-critical-minerals-the-us-needs-more-than-just-supply-it-needs-refining-power/.

[27] Atlantic Council, "US Critical Minerals Strategy."

[28] Resources for the Future, "Resource Nationalism and the Resilience of Critical Mineral Supply Chains," November 10, 2025, https://www.rff.org/publications/reports/resource-nationalism-and-the-resilience-of-critical-mineral-supply-chains/.

[29] Ibid.

[30] Carnegie Endowment for International Peace, "Securing America's Critical Minerals Supply," October 2025, https://carnegieendowment.org/research/2025/10/securing-americas-critical-minerals-supply?lang=en.

[31] Access Partnership, "Securing the US' Critical Minerals Supply Chain: Three Steps to Resilience," August 14, 2025, https://accesspartnership.com/securing-us-critical-minerals-supply-chain/.

[32] Brownstein Hyatt Farber Schreck, "U.S. Expands Critical Minerals Financing and Bilateral Partnerships Under Trump," November 2025, https://www.bhfs.com/insight/u-s-expands-critical-minerals-financing-and-bilateral-partnerships-under-trump/.

[33] AInvest, "U.S. Rare Earths and Critical Minerals Supply Chain Resilience: Strategic Partnerships Drive Domestic Production and Innovation," October 31, 2025, https://www.ainvest.com/news/rare-earths-critical-minerals-supply-chain-resilience-strategic-partnerships-drive-domestic-production-innovation-2510/.

[34] National Governors Association, "CHIPS and Science Act: Implementation Resources," updated August 19, 2025, https://www.nga.org/chips-resources/.

[35] Office of the United States Trade Representative, "The President's 2025 Trade Policy Agenda," 2025, https://ustr.gov/sites/default/files/files/reports/2025/President Trump's 2025 Trade Policy Agenda.pdf.

[36] Congressional Research Service, "U.S. Export Controls and China: Advanced Semiconductors," CRS Report R48642, August 22, 2025, https://www.congress.gov/crs-product/R48642; Center for Strategic and International Studies, "Understanding U.S. Allies' Current Legal Authority to Implement AI and Semiconductor Export Controls," April 2, 2025, https://www.csis.org/analysis/understanding-us-allies-current-legal-authority-implement-ai-and-semiconductor-export.

[37] AI Frontiers, "How US Export Controls Have (and Haven't) Curbed Chinese AI," July 7, 2025, https://ai-frontiers.org/articles/us-chip-export-controls-china-ai.

[38] Information Technology and Innovation Foundation, "Decoupling Risks: How Semiconductor Export Controls Could Harm US Chipmakers and Innovation," November 10, 2025,

https://itif.org/publications/2025/11/10/decoupling-risks-semiconductor-export-controls-harm-us-chipmakers-innovation/.

[39] International Center for Law & Economics, "US Export Controls on AI and Semiconductors: Two Divergent Visions," March 24, 2025, https://laweconcenter.org/resources/us-export-controls-on-ai-and-semiconductors-two-divergent-visions/.

[40] Ibid.

[41] Congressional Research Service, "U.S. Export Controls and China: Advanced Semiconductors."

[42] Ibid.

[43] Ibid.

[44] Foundation for Defense of Democracies, "Signaling Confidence in Its Domestic Industry, China Bans Foreign AI Chips in State-Funded Data Centers," November 10, 2025, https://www.fdd.org/analysis/2025/11/10/signaling-confidence-in-its-domestic-industry-china-bans-foreign-ai-chips-in-state-funded-data-centers/.

[45] Center for European Policy Analysis, "Chip Export Controls Don't Work," July 17, 2025, https://cepa.org/article/chip-export-controls-dont-work/.

[46] U.S.-China Economic and Security Review Commission, *2025 Annual Report to Congress*; Washington International Trade Association, "2025 Annual Report to Congress of the U.S.-China Economic And Security Review Commission," November 19, 2025, https://www.wita.org/atp-research/us-china-report/.

[47] Manufacturing Dive, "Tracking CHIPS and Science Act Awards"; Semiconductor Industry Association, "Tracking CHIPS and Science Act Investments."

[48] Deloitte Insights, "2026 Manufacturing Industry Outlook," November 13, 2025, https://www.deloitte.com/us/en/insights/industry/manufacturing-industrial-products/manufacturing-industry-outlook.html.

[49] The Quantum Insider, "White House Places Quantum And AI at The Summit of R&D Priorities."

[50] U.S.-China Economic and Security Review Commission, "Comprehensive List of the Commission's 2025 Recommendations," November 2025, https://www.uscc.gov/sites/default/files/2025-11/2025_Comprehensive_List_of_Recommendations.pdf.

[51] Semiconductor Industry Association, "Tracking CHIPS and Science Act Investments"; Manufacturing Dive, "Tracking CHIPS and Science Act Awards."

[52] Council on Foreign Relations Task Force, *U.S. Economic Security: Winning the Race for Tomorrow's Technologies*; Quantum Zeitgeist, "Report: U.S. Must Strengthen AI, Quantum, Biotech Leadership."

[53] CNBC, "First Rare Earths and Chips, Now Quantum Computers: Trump Reportedly Eyes New U.S. Stakes," October 23, 2025, https://www.cnbc.com/2025/10/23/first-rare-earths-and-chips-now-quantum-computers-trump-reportedly-eyes-new-us-stakes.html.

[54] Center for Strategic and International Studies, "Renewing the United States' Skilled Technical Workforce," July 9, 2025, https://www.csis.org/analysis/renewing-united-states-skilled-technical-workforce.

[55] IndustryWeek, "Manufacturing Day 2025: Building a Skilled, Resilient, Future-Ready Workforce," October 3, 2025, https://www.industryweek.com/talent/education-training/article/55321142/manufacturing-day-2025-builiding-a-skilled-resilient-future-reader-workforce.

[56] National Association of Manufacturers, "The State of the Manufacturing Workforce in 2025," February 25, 2025, https://nam.org/the-state-of-the-manufacturing-workforce-in-2025-33321/; The Manufacturing Institute, "The State of the Manufacturing Workforce in 2025," February 25, 2025, https://themanufacturinginstitute.org/the-state-of-the-manufacturing-workforce-in-2025-20621/.

[57] U.S. Department of Labor, Employment and Training Administration, "Industrial Policy Problem Statement: WIAC Industrial Policy Recommendation," 2025, https://dol.gov/sites/dolgov/files/ETA/wioa/pdfs/WIAC Industrial Policy Recommendation_Public Viewing.pdf.

[58] IndustryWeek, "Manufacturing Day 2025: Building a Skilled, Resilient, Future-Ready Workforce."

[59] Ibid.

[60] Carnegie Endowment for International Peace, "U.S.-China Relations for the 2030s: Toward a Realistic Scenario for Coexistence," October 2024, https://carnegieendowment.org/research/2024/10/us-china-relations-for-the-2030s-toward-a-realistic-scenario-for-coexistence?lang=en.

[61] Foreign Policy Research Institute, "Balancing Acts: Deterrence and Reassurance in US-China Strategy," July 18, 2025, https://www.fpri.org/article/2025/06/balancing-acts-deterrence-and-reassurance-in-us-china-strategy/.

[62] Carnegie Endowment for International Peace, "U.S.-China Relations for the 2030s: Toward a Realistic Scenario for Coexistence."

[63] Foreign Policy Research Institute, "Charting the End State for US Strategy Toward China," May 15, 2025, https://www.fpri.org/article/2025/04/charting-the-end-state-for-us-strategy-toward-china/.

[64] Carnegie Endowment for International Peace, "U.S.-China Relations for the 2030s: Toward a Realistic Scenario for Coexistence."

[65] RAND Corporation, "Economic Deterrence in a China Contingency," by Howard J. Shatz, Marco Hafner, Naoko Aoki, Peter Dortmans, Timothy R. Heath, and Fiona Quimbre, Report RR-A4022-1, November 6, 2025, https://www.rand.org/pubs/research_reports/RRA4022-1.html.

[66] Foreign Policy Research Institute, "Balancing Acts: Deterrence and Reassurance in US-China Strategy."

[67] U.S.-China Economic and Security Review Commission, "Chapter 2: U.S.-China Security and Foreign Affairs (Year in Review)," November 2025, https://www.uscc.gov/sites/default/files/2025-11/Chapter_2—U.S.-China_Security_and_Foreign_Affairs_Year_in_Review.pdf.

[68] Center for Strategic and International Studies, "Advancing U.S.-China Coordination amid Strategic Competition: An Emerging Playbook," January 15, 2025, https://www.csis.org/analysis/advancing-us-china-coordination-amid-strategic-competition-emerging-playbook.

[69] Foundation for Defense of Democracies, "Missed Milestones," September 15, 2025, https://www.fdd.org/analysis/2025/02/25/missed-milestones/.

[70] Evan S. Medeiros, "Structure Trumps Agency in the U.S.-China Relationship," *Foreign Affairs*, November 5, 2025, https://www.foreignaffairs.com/united-states/structure-trumps-agency-us-china-relationship.

[71] Foreign Policy Research Institute, "Charting the End State for US Strategy Toward China."

[72] Center for Strategic and International Studies, "Advancing U.S.-China Coordination amid Strategic Competition: An Emerging Playbook."

[73] IndustryWeek, "Manufacturing Day 2025: Building a Skilled, Resilient, Future-Ready Workforce."

[74] U.S. Department of State, Bureau of Global Public Affairs, "Summary of January 2025 Meeting: 'Understanding the PRC's Public Diplomacy Efforts,'" Advisory Commission on Public Diplomacy, June 11, 2025, https://www.state.gov/summary-of-january-2025meeting-understanding-chinas-public-diplomacy-efforts.

[75] U.S.-China Economic and Security Review Commission, *2025 Annual Report to Congress*; American National Standards Institute, "U.S.-China Economic Security Review Commission Releases 2025 Report to Congress," November 20, 2025, https://www.ansi.org/standards-news/all-news/11-20-25-us-china-economic-security-review-commission-releases-2025-report-to-congress; German Marshall Fund of the United States, "Inside the 2025 US-China Economic and Security Commission Report: Key Findings and Recommendations," accessed December 3, 2025, https://www.gmfus.org/news/inside-2025-us-china-economic-and-security-commission-report-key-findings-and-recommendations.

Chapter 23

What China Must Consider: The Limits of Coercion and the Risks of Overreach

The preceding chapters have examined the American perspective on the U.S.-China rivalry—its strategic imperatives, policy recommendations, and potential pathways forward. Yet any comprehensive analysis of this defining geopolitical competition must grapple equally with the constraints, vulnerabilities, and strategic calculations facing Beijing. China's rise has been nothing short of extraordinary, transforming a largely agrarian society into the world's second-largest economy and a formidable military power within a single generation. However, this ascent now confronts structural headwinds that threaten to derail the Chinese Communist Party's long-term ambitions and its capacity to sustain the confrontational posture that has characterized recent years.

This chapter examines the domestic and international factors that should inform China's strategic calculus—not as advocacy for Beijing's interests, but as essential context for understanding what constrains and motivates Chinese decision-making. Understanding these limits is crucial for American policymakers seeking to calibrate responses that neither underestimate Chinese capabilities nor overestimate Beijing's tolerance for risk.

Demographic Headwinds: The Coming Labor Shortage

China's demographic trajectory represents perhaps the most consequential structural constraint on its long-term power and prosperity. After decades of the one-child policy, China now confronts a population crisis unprecedented in scale and velocity. According to China's National Bureau of Statistics, the country's population stood at 1.40828 billion at the end of 2024, marking a decline of 1.39 million from the previous year—the third consecutive annual decrease.[1] This demographic contraction has profound implications for economic growth, military recruitment, and social stability.

The United Nations World Population Prospects 2024 report projects that China's population could shrink to 1.3 billion by 2050 and plunge further to 633 million by 2100—a reduction of more than half from current levels.[2] The Pew Research Center, analyzing the UN data, confirms that China "is projected to lose more than half its current population size" by century's end.[3] These projections suggest a demographic transformation without historical parallel among major powers.

The fertility rate has collapsed to alarming levels. By 2024, China's fertility rate had dropped to approximately 1.0 births per woman—among the world's lowest levels and well below the 2.1 replacement rate necessary to maintain population stability.[4] The Council on Foreign Relations notes that China's old-age dependency ratio will dramatically increase in coming decades, placing enormous pressure on a shrinking working-age population to support an expanding cohort of retirees.[5]

The economic implications are stark. The Conference Board projects that China's shrinking workforce will continue dragging on growth through 2039 because of the declining working-age population.[6] More ominously, these demographic shifts occur while China remains an upper-middle-income country—far below the levels at which Japan and South Korea experienced their demographic transitions. As the Mercator Institute for China Studies (MERICS) observes, China risks growing old before it grows rich.[7]

Beijing's pronatalist policies have thus far proven ineffective. Despite subsidies for fertility treatments, extended maternity leave, and childcare support, birth rates continue declining. The National Bureau of Statistics reported 9.54 million newborns in 2024—a modest increase from the previous year but insufficient to reverse the demographic trajectory.[8]

The Gathering Economic Storm

Beyond demographics, China faces a confluence of economic challenges that constrain both its growth trajectory and its capacity to project power. The Rhodium Group estimates that China's actual GDP growth was between 2.4 percent and 2.8 percent in 2024—well below official figures of approximately 5 percent.[9] This assessment, while disputed by Beijing, aligns with observable indicators including collapsing property investment, weak consumer confidence, and persistent producer price deflation.

The property sector crisis remains acute. The U.S.-China Business Council reports that real estate investment contracted approximately 10.6 percent in 2024, marking the steepest decline since recordkeeping for this indicator began in 1987.[10] Nominal GDP growth has been lower than real growth for two consecutive years—indicating deflation not seen since the 1998 Asian Financial Crisis.[11] This deflationary environment, unprecedented among major economies outside Japan in decades, reflects profound weakness in domestic demand.

Local government finances present perhaps the most dangerous economic vulnerability. Local Government Financing Vehicles (LGFVs)—quasi-governmental entities established to fund infrastructure—have accumulated an estimated 66 trillion yuan ($9.3 trillion) in debt, equivalent to half of China's annual GDP, according to the International Monetary Fund.[12] Many of these entities cannot service their debts from operational revenues. The Rhodium Group estimates that four-fifths of more than 2,000 LGFVs are unable to cover the cost of interest payments.[13] The Atlantic Council warns that the combination of LGFV and local government debt represents a serious risk to financial stability.[14]

The collapse in land sale revenues—traditionally a primary source of local government financing—has exacerbated these vulnerabilities. CKGSB Knowledge reports that officials in Bishan district of Chongqing publicly announced they would "smash pots and sell iron"—liquidating assets at all costs—to address overwhelming debt burdens.[15] Some localities have resorted to extreme measures as property transactions plummeted.

Beijing's response has been characterized as "extend and pretend." The November 2024 debt restructuring initiative refinances hidden debt by lengthening maturities and allowing rollovers, but does not address the underlying structural imbalances.[16] The Atlantic Council observes that the central government has chosen to postpone its day of reckoning when it will have to assume debt obligations that may extend to $10 trillion or more.[17]

The Innovation Ceiling Without International Collaboration

China's technological aspirations face structural constraints that no amount of domestic investment can fully overcome. The semiconductor sector illustrates these limitations most starkly. Despite decades of massive state investment, China remains dependent on foreign technology for the most advanced manufacturing processes. As the Economics Observatory notes, the semiconductor sector—perhaps more than any other—epitomizes globalization of knowledge and production.[18]

U.S.-led export controls have constrained Chinese access to critical technologies, particularly ASML's extreme ultraviolet (EUV) lithography machines essential for manufacturing chips below 7 nanometers.[19] While China has demonstrated remarkable ingenuity in working around these restrictions—DeepSeek's achievement of competitive AI performance with inferior hardware being a prominent example—complete technological self-sufficiency remains elusive. The collaborative innovation networks that link ASML, TSMC, and leading fabless designers represent decades of accumulated knowledge and trust that cannot be easily replicated.[20]

The Center for Strategic and International Studies acknowledges that China has already demonstrated capacity to innovate under pressure, noting that after the first Trump administration cut off Huawei's access to U.S. technology in 2019, the company "launched an effort to wean itself from reliance on U.S. technology, which has made rapid strides."[21] However, this adaptation comes at significant cost in efficiency and performance. Chinese foundries working toward domestic alternatives must proceed through a multi-year, multi-stage process, starting with 40 nanometers and progressing toward 7 nanometers—a trajectory that assumes continued access to some Western equipment.[22]

The broader technology ecosystem presents similar challenges. European firms are increasingly cautious about technology collaboration with China due to intellectual property concerns and regulatory pressures.[23] MERICS reports that companies in strategically oriented sectors face particular pressure as Beijing seeks to capture technology capacities while the United States and others impose export restrictions.[24] This shrinking space for international collaboration threatens to slow Chinese innovation precisely when Beijing is prioritizing high-level scientific and technological self-reliance.

Diplomatic Costs of Assertiveness

China's more assertive foreign policy posture has generated significant diplomatic backlash that constrains its international position. The 2024 NATO summit declaration identified China as a strategic challenge to Euro-Atlantic security—a significant statement signaling growing convergence among Western allies toward viewing Beijing as a security concern.[25]

Regional perceptions have similarly deteriorated. The ISEAS-Yusof Ishak Institute's State of Southeast Asia 2025 Survey found that concerns over aggressive behavior in the South China Sea ranked among the top geopolitical concerns in the region.[26] China's encroachments into the exclusive economic zones and continental shelves of Southeast Asian littoral states emerged as the primary concern for respondents.[27] This represents a remarkable deterioration in regional sentiment, given that Southeast Asian nations had traditionally sought to maintain balanced relationships with both Beijing and Washington.

Relations with India suffered lasting damage following the 2020 Galwan Valley clashes—the deadliest border confrontation since 1967.[28] While Beijing and Delhi reached agreements at the October 2024 BRICS summit, the International Crisis Group observes that India now sees China as its biggest external security threat, with long-term implications for the bilateral relationship.[29] This strategic realignment has pushed New Delhi closer to the Quad framework and enhanced defense cooperation with the United States.

The Philippines relationship has similarly deteriorated amid maritime disputes. Confrontational incidents between Chinese and Philippine vessels escalated throughout 2024, including multiple collisions near contested features.[30] China's assertiveness has reinforced Philippine commitment to the U.S. alliance and facilitated expanded American military access to Philippine bases—outcomes directly contrary to Beijing's strategic interests.

Academic research on China's "wolf warrior" diplomacy confirms these costs. A study published in Humanities and Social Sciences Communications identifies several risks: China's global image "might be at stake due to its assertive behavior, which could hinder its overarching soft power ambitions"; wielding economic might as a punitive tool "risks backfiring, prompting nations to reduce their economic dependence on China"; and maintaining an aggressive diplomatic approach "might cause China to face diplomatic isolation."[31]

The Taiwan Risk Calculation

Taiwan represents the most dangerous flashpoint in the U.S.-China rivalry—a potential catalyst for great-power conflict that would be catastrophic for all parties. Beijing's coercive pressure on the island has intensified markedly under Xi Jinping, with military exercises becoming larger, more frequent, and more provocative. The People's Liberation Army has significantly increased sorties into Taiwan's air defense identification zone.[32] The April 2025 "Strait Thunder-2025A" exercises simulated scenarios involving escalation from regular military exercises toward comprehensive operations.[33]

Yet the risks of military action against Taiwan remain formidable. The Stimson Center's September 2025 assessment identifies multiple factors making invasion "highly unlikely": China's economy would suffer severe damage from disrupted global shipping; international sanctions would compound these economic harms; and the operational complexity of a cross-strait invasion would exceed even the D-Day landings in scale and difficulty.[34] The report concludes that when political, economic, and military factors are considered together, a PRC invasion of Taiwan is highly improbable.[35]

Janes defense intelligence assesses that China will continue prioritizing intimidation over invasion in the near term.[36] Critically, Janes notes the absence of key indicators that would signal imminent invasion: a massing of troops and assets in the Eastern Theater Command along with expanded bases would be a positive indicator for an invasion scenario—and such massing has not been observed.[37]

Recorded Future's Insikt Group assessment similarly concludes that a Taiwan invasion is very unlikely in the near term, noting weaknesses in PLA amphibious capability and the absence of indicators that China has begun mobilizing its populace for wartime hardship.[38] China's best strategy, analysts suggest, is to "win without fighting"—using pressure tactics to compel negotiation rather than risking the catastrophic uncertainty of invasion.

The consequences of military failure would be existential for the Chinese Communist Party. A defeated invasion attempt would shatter the PLA's prestige, potentially trigger economic collapse under international sanctions, and fundamentally undermine Xi Jinping's legitimacy. No Chinese leader can afford such risks lightly, particularly given the domestic vulnerabilities examined earlier in this chapter.

Internal Stability Pressures

The Chinese Communist Party has long prioritized social stability as essential to regime survival. Current economic conditions are generating concerning pressures. Youth unemployment reached a record 18.9 percent in August 2025 (excluding students), with 12.22 million new graduates entering the job market—430,000 more than the previous year.[39] Caixin Global reports that young people struggling to find meaningful employment increasingly face a mismatch between their education and labor market demands.[40]

The China Dissent Monitor, operated by Freedom House, documented a 21 percent increase in dissent events during the first quarter of 2024 compared to the same period in 2023, and a 27 percent increase in the third quarter of 2024.[41] Three-quarters of the incidents logged since 2022 stemmed from economic grievances including unpaid wages, housing disputes, and confiscation of rural land by local governments. The Monitor concluded that this prolonged economic downturn appears to be generating more economic hardship for Chinese people, which leads to more frequent protest.[42]

The ongoing anti-corruption campaign within the People's Liberation Army has raised questions about military readiness. Nine senior military officials were expelled from the CCP in October 2024, including General He Weidong, a vice chairman of the Central Military Commission—the first removal of a sitting CMC vice chairman since the Cultural Revolution.[43] The CNA analysis notes that these purges have left China's military underrepresented on the Central Committee, with only four of the seven CMC members elected in 2022 remaining.[44] Reports of systemic corruption—including allegations involving equipment procurement irregularities—indicate potentially serious capability concerns.[45]

The pace of high-level PLA purges has been unprecedented. The Brookings Institution observes that this represents the most extensive military purge in decades, both in reach and intensity.[46] These disruptions deepen uncertainty about when new military capabilities will materialize and whether the PLA could successfully execute the complex joint operations an invasion of Taiwan would require.

Alternative Paths to Rejuvenation

Despite these formidable challenges, China retains significant capacity for economic and political adaptation. The path forward requires Beijing to acknowledge the limits of its current approach and embrace reforms that would serve both domestic prosperity and international stability.

The World Bank's December 2024 China Economic Update identified structural reforms essential for revitalizing growth: "Addressing challenges in the property sector, strengthening social safety nets, and improving local government finances will be essential to unlocking a sustained recovery."[47] Central to this agenda is rebalancing the economy toward consumption-led growth. Chinese household spending accounts for a smaller share of GDP than in most OECD countries.[48] Shifting resources toward households would address both domestic demand weakness and international concerns about Chinese overcapacity.

Beijing acknowledged this imperative at the December 2024 Central Economic Work Conference, which identified lifting consumption vigorously as the top priority for 2025.[49] The March 2025 Special Action Plan to Boost Consumption outlined strategies targeting childcare, elderly care, and service sector development.[50] However, as the Council on Foreign Relations observes, Beijing's consumption promotion measures have not sacrificed investment in strategic technologies—reflecting Xi Jinping's conviction that achieving self-reliance and technological advancement can address economic challenges.[51]

More fundamental reforms would require political choices that the current leadership has shown reluctance to embrace. Hukou reform to enhance labor mobility, fiscal reforms to place local government finances on sustainable footing, and social safety net expansion to reduce precautionary savings all require significant resource reallocation from state priorities toward household welfare.[52]

On the international front, Beijing could pursue a more calibrated approach to competition with the United States. The Carnegie Endowment notes that resolving the structural problem of overcapacity requires either increasing domestic demand faster than industrial capacity growth or exporting excess production to global markets.[53] The latter approach has generated the trade tensions that now constrain Chinese exports; the former would require the consumption-oriented reforms that Beijing has been slow to implement.

A strategic pause in assertive behavior around Taiwan and in the South China Sea would reduce the risk of conflict while allowing Beijing to address domestic vulnerabilities. The International Crisis Group recommends that the U.S. and China should work together to manage the risk of unintended escalation through strengthened military-to-military channels and high-level strategic exchanges.[54] Such engagement would not resolve the fundamental competition but could establish guardrails that prevent catastrophic miscalculation.

Conclusion: The Necessity of Strategic Prudence

China's remarkable rise over the past four decades has been enabled by pragmatic adaptation, economic reform, and integration with the global economy. The challenges examined in this chapter—demographic decline, economic vulnerabilities, technological constraints, diplomatic costs, military uncertainties, and internal stability pressures—do not foretell inevitable decline. Rather, they define the parameters within which Chinese leaders must operate and the costs that aggressive overreach would impose.

Xi Jinping has staked his legacy on achieving "the great rejuvenation of the Chinese nation." This ambition is neither illegitimate nor necessarily destabilizing—great powers have always sought recognition commensurate with their capabilities. However, the methods chosen to pursue rejuvenation matter profoundly. Coercive approaches to Taiwan, the South China Sea, and the broader Indo-Pacific have generated countervailing coalitions that complicate rather than advance Chinese interests. Technological self-reliance pursued through isolation sacrifices the collaborative innovation that propelled China's rise.

History offers cautionary precedents. Imperial Germany's pursuit of Weltpolitik, Imperial Japan's quest for a Greater East Asia Co-Prosperity Sphere, and the Soviet Union's global competition with the United States all demonstrate how great powers can overestimate their capabilities and underestimate the costs of confrontation. China need not repeat these errors.

The structural constraints facing Beijing create incentives for de-escalation that American policymakers should understand and, where possible, reinforce. A China struggling with demographic decline, debt overhang, and technological hurdles may calculate that time is not on its side—potentially increasing risk tolerance in ways that could prove catastrophic. Alternatively, the same pressures might counsel patience and reform, preserving options while domestic foundations are strengthened.

American strategy should neither assume inevitable Chinese aggression nor dismiss Chinese capabilities. The challenge is calibrating policies that maintain deterrence while leaving space for

Beijing to choose paths that serve mutual interests. Understanding what China must consider—the limits of coercion and the risks of overreach—is essential to getting this balance right.

Endnotes

[1] National Bureau of Statistics of China, "Statistical Communiqué of the People's Republic of China on the 2024 National Economic and Social Development," February 28, 2025, https://www.stats.gov.cn/english/PressRelease/202502/t20250228_1958822.html; "China's population declines in 2024," China.org.cn, January 17, 2025, http://www.china.org.cn/china/2025-01/17/content_117670602.htm.

[2] United Nations, Department of Economic and Social Affairs, Population Division, World Population Prospects 2024: Summary of Results (New York: United Nations, 2024), https://population.un.org/wpp/.

[3] "5 Facts about How the World's Population Is Expected to Change by 2100," Pew Research Center, July 9, 2025, https://www.pewresearch.org/short-reads/2025/07/09/5-facts-about-how-the-worlds-population-is-expected-to-change-by-2100/.

[4] "UN Projects World Population to Peak within This Century," United Nations, July 11, 2024, https://www.un.org/en/UN-projects-world-population-to-peak-within-this-century.

[5] "Rebalancing China's Economy: Stimulus, Confidence, and Self-Sufficiency," Council on Foreign Relations, January 23, 2025, https://www.cfr.org/blog/rebalancing-chinas-economy-stimulus-confidence-and-self-sufficiency.

[6] The Conference Board, Global Economic Outlook: China Edition (New York: The Conference Board, December 2024), https://www.conference-board.org/publications/Global-Economic-Outlook-2024-China-Edition-December.

[7] "When Giving Birth Is a National Duty: Beijing's Struggle to Reverse Demographic Decline," Mercator Institute for China Studies, 2025, https://merics.org/en/report/when-giving-birth-national-duty-beijings-struggle-reverse-demographic-decline.

[8] National Bureau of Statistics of China, "Statistical Communiqué 2024."

[9] Daniel H. Rosen et al., "After the Fall: China's Economy in 2025," Rhodium Group, December 31, 2024, https://rhg.com/research/after-the-fall-chinas-economy-in-2025/.

[10] "China's Economy Rallies to Reach Growth Target, 2025 Outlook Remains Uncertain," US-China Business Council, January 24, 2025, https://www.uschina.org/articles/chinas-economy-rallies-to-reach-growth-target-2025-outlook-remains-uncertain/.

[11] "China's 2025 Economy: Can Bold Policies Drive a Turnaround?" China Europe International Business School, 2025, https://www.ceibs.edu/new-papers-columns/26234.

[12] "The ABCs of LGFVs: China's Local Government Financing Vehicles," Reserve Bank of Australia Bulletin, October 2024, https://www.rba.gov.au/publications/bulletin/2024/oct/the-abcs-of-lgfvs-chinas-local-government-financing-vehicles.html.

[13] "China's Local Government Debts Are Coming Due," Atlantic Council GeoEconomics Center, July 17, 2025, https://www.atlanticcouncil.org/blogs/econographics/sinographs/chinas-local-government-debts-are-coming-due/.

[14] Ibid.

[15] "China's LGFVs: Debt Challenges Ahead," CKGSB Knowledge, February 18, 2025, https://english.ckgsb.edu.cn/knowledge/article/a-bridge-too-far-can-chinas-lgfvs-tackle-their-debt-issues/.

[16] "China's Debt Reckoning," East Asia Forum, September 20, 2025, https://eastasiaforum.org/2025/09/20/chinas-debt-reckoning/.

[17] "Beijing Extends and Pretends to Deal with Its Mountain of Local Government Debt," Atlantic Council GeoEconomics Center, July 31, 2025, https://www.atlanticcouncil.org/blogs/econographics/sinographs/beijing-extends-and-pretends-to-deal-with-its-mountain-of-local-government-debt/.

[18] "What's Happening in China's Semiconductor Industry?" Economics Observatory, May 28, 2025, https://www.economicsobservatory.com/whats-happening-in-chinas-semiconductor-industry.

[19] Ibid.

[20] Zheng Ming Chow et al., "China's Interdependent Positioning in the Semiconductor Global Value Chain," Asia Pacific Business Review (2024), https://www.tandfonline.com/doi/full/10.1080/23792949.2024.2397973.

[21] Sujai Shivakumar et al., "The Limits of Chip Export Controls in Meeting the China Challenge," Center for Strategic and International Studies, May 7, 2025, https://www.csis.org/analysis/limits-chip-export-controls-meeting-china-challenge.

[22] Jordan Schneider, "A New Era for the Chinese Semiconductor Industry: Beijing Responds to Export Controls," American Affairs Journal (Winter 2024), https://americanaffairsjournal.org/2024/02/a-new-era-for-the-chinese-semiconductor-industry-beijing-responds-to-export-controls/.

[23] "The Trade-offs of Innovating in China in Times of Global Technology Rivalry," Mercator Institute for China Studies, 2025, https://merics.org/en/report/trade-offs-innovating-china-times-global-technology-rivalry.

[24] Ibid.

[25] Stefano Pelaggi, "China's Foreign Policy 2024: Strategic Assertiveness and Diplomatic Adaptation," Asia Maior XXXV (2025): 27–53, https://www.asiamaior.org/the-journal/19-asia-maior-vol-xxxv-2024/chinas-foreign-policy-2024-strategic-assertiveness-and-diplomatic-adaptation.html.

[26] "The State of Southeast Asia: 2025 Survey Report," ISEAS-Yusof Ishak Institute, April 3, 2025, https://www.iseas.edu.sg/centres/asean-studies-centre/state-of-southeast-asia-survey/the-state-of-southeast-asia-2025-survey-report/.

[27] "E-Launch and Discussion of The State of Southeast Asia 2025 Survey Report," ISEAS-Yusof Ishak Institute, April 10, 2025, https://www.iseas.edu.sg/media/event-highlights/e-launch-and-discussion-of-the-state-of-southeast-asia-2025-survey-report/.

[28] "Asia in Flux: The U.S., China and the Search for a New Equilibrium," International Crisis Group, Asia Report No. 347, August 12, 2025, https://www.crisisgroup.org/asia/north-east-asia/china-united-states/347-asia-flux-us-china-and-search-new-equilibrium.

[29] Ibid.

[30] Ibid.

[31] Shaoyu Yuan, "Tracing China's Diplomatic Transition to Wolf Warrior Diplomacy and Its Implications," Humanities and Social Sciences Communications 10, article 837 (2023), https://www.nature.com/articles/s41599-023-02367-6.

[32] "Asia in Flux," International Crisis Group.

[33] Dan Grazier, James Siebens, and MacKenna Rawlins, "Rethinking the Threat: Why China Is Unlikely to Invade Taiwan" (Washington, DC: Stimson Center, September 2025), https://www.stimson.org/2025/rethinking-the-threat-why-china-is-unlikely-to-invade-taiwan/.

[34] Ibid.

[35] Ibid.

[36] "China Likely to Continue to Prioritise Intimidation against Taiwan," Janes, June 2025, https://www.janes.com/osint-insights/defence-and-national-security-analysis/.

[37] Ibid.

[38] "The Risk of a Taiwan Strait Conflict," Recorded Future Insikt Group, February 12, 2025, https://www.recordedfuture.com/.

[39] "China's Youth Unemployment Hits Record Under New Methodology," Trading Economics, September 17, 2025, https://tradingeconomics.com/china/youth-unemployment-rate/news/485930; "At 18.9%, China's Youth Unemployment Rises to Highest Level Since 2023," Business Standard, September 18, 2025, https://www.business-standard.com/world-news/china-youth-unemployment-hits-18-9-percent-august-2025-economic-slowdown-125091800489_1.html.

[40] "Analysis: Youth Unemployment Surge Exposes Cracks in China's Economic Transition," Caixin Global, September 19, 2025, https://www.caixinglobal.com/2025-09-19/analysis-youth-unemployment-surge-exposes-cracks-in-chinas-economic-transition-102363893.html.

[41] "Issue 7: January – March 2024," China Dissent Monitor, Freedom House, May 2024, https://freedomhouse.org/report/china-dissent-monitor/2024/issue-7-january-march-2024; "Issue 9: July – September 2024," China Dissent Monitor, Freedom House, October 2024, https://freedomhouse.org/report/china-dissent-monitor/2024/issue-9-july-september-2024.

[42] "Eight Things Freedom House Has Learned About Protests in China," Freedom House, August 2024, https://freedomhouse.org/article/eight-things-freedom-house-has-learned-about-protests-china.

[43] "China Expels Top Military Commanders in Latest Anticorruption Purge," Al Jazeera, October 18, 2025, https://www.aljazeera.com/news/2025/10/18/china-expels-top-military-commanders-in-latest-anticorruption-purge.

[44] "Military Purges at China's Fourth Plenum Have Implications for Readiness," CNA, November 2025, https://www.cna.org/our-media/indepth/2025/11/military-purges-at-chinas-fourth-plenum-have-implications-for-readiness.

[45] "Chinese Military Purge Said to Show Corruption, Weakness," Arms Control Association, March 2024, https://www.armscontrol.org/act/2024-03/news/chinese-military-purge-said-show-corruption-weakness.

[46] "Continuity and a Military Purge at China's Fourth Communist Party Plenum," UC Institute on Global Conflict and Cooperation, October 2025, https://ucigcc.org/blog/continuity-and-a-military-purge-at-chinas-fourth-communist-party-plenum/.

[47] "Unlocking Domestic Demand Key to Reviving Growth Momentum in China – World Bank Economic Update," World Bank, December 26, 2024, https://www.worldbank.org/en/news/press-release/2024/12/26/unlocking-domestic-demand-key-to-reviving-growth-momentum-in-china-world-bank-economic-update.

[48] Ibid.

[49] "China Unveils Special Action Plan to Boost Consumption," ING Think, March 17, 2025, https://think.ing.com/articles/china-unveils-special-action-plan-to-boost-consumption/.

[50] Ibid.

[51] "Rebalancing China's Economy," Council on Foreign Relations.

[52] World Bank, December 2024 China Economic Update, https://thedocs.worldbank.org/en/doc/f66f7093d7be0141fe43156e5968c466-0070012024/original/CEU-December-2024-EN-Final.pdf.

[53] Michael Pettis, "What's New about Involution?" Carnegie Endowment for International Peace, August 2025, https://carnegieendowment.org/posts/2025/08/whats-new-about-involution.

[54] "Asia in Flux," International Crisis Group.

Chapter 24

Digital Currency Wars—The Battle for the Future of Money

Financial Technology as Geopolitical Weapon

When Pan Gongsheng, Governor of the People's Bank of China, announced the establishment of an international operations center for the digital yuan in Shanghai at the October 2025 Financial Street Forum, it marked more than a technological milestone.[1] It signaled the opening of a new front in the U.S.-China rivalry—one where lines of code and payment rails could prove as strategically significant as semiconductor fabs or rare earth mines. The battle for the future of money is underway, and its outcome will help determine which nation shapes the global financial order of the twenty-first century.

The stakes are extraordinary. Control over payment systems translates directly into geopolitical leverage. The nation whose currency dominates international transactions enjoys what economists have called an "exorbitant privilege"—the ability to borrow cheaply, impose sanctions effectively, and influence global economic policy. For seven decades, the United States has wielded this privilege through the dollar's dominance. Now, as China advances its digital currency initiatives and the U.S. doubles down on private-sector stablecoins, a fundamental question emerges: Can digital currencies reshape the global monetary hierarchy?

The Digital Yuan's Ascent

The scale of China's digital currency ambitions has become impossible to ignore. By the end of September 2025, the digital yuan had processed cumulative transactions reaching 14.2 trillion yuan (approximately 2 trillion U.S. dollars), according to official reports from the People's Bank of China.[2] The digital yuan pilot program now covers twenty-six localities across seventeen provincial-level regions in China, with 225 million personal wallets opened on the digital yuan app and 3.32 billion total transactions processed.[3]

The digital yuan, formally known as e-CNY, began as a research project in 2014 when the People's Bank of China established a task force to study digital fiat currency.[4] The project evolved into a pilot program that commenced in 2019, with initial testing in major cities including Shenzhen, Suzhou,

Chengdu, and Xiong'an.[5] By 2025, China's digital currency ecosystem had been established in preliminary terms, with the central bank creating both a digital yuan international operations center in Shanghai and a digital yuan operations and management center in Beijing.[6]

The domestic rollout tells only part of the story. China's strategic innovation lies in its cross-border payment infrastructure. The Cross-Border Interbank Payment System (CIPS), launched in 2015 under the stewardship of the People's Bank of China, has scaled to 1,631 institutions across 112 countries by early 2025.[7] By May 2025, CIPS reported the number of participants had risen by 10 percent year-over-year to 1,683, with Asia accounting for 73 percent of indirect participants and 17 percent being European institutions.[8]

The strategic logic behind this expansion is straightforward: reduce reliance on the dollar-dominated SWIFT system and create alternative payment channels insulated from U.S. sanctions pressure. As Governor Pan Gongsheng stated at the 2025 Financial Street Forum, the establishment of the international operations center aims to oversee cross-border cooperation and usage of the digital currency.[9] The digital yuan represents China's technological infrastructure to advance yuan internationalization and reduce vulnerability to Western financial pressure.

America's Stablecoin Strategy

While China pursues a state-led central bank digital currency approach, the United States has taken a radically different path—one that eschews central bank digital currencies entirely in favor of private-sector stablecoins backed by dollar reserves. This divergence reflects fundamentally different philosophies about the relationship between technology, money, and state power.

On January 23, 2025, President Donald Trump signed Executive Order 14120, titled "Strengthening American Leadership in Digital Financial Technology," explicitly prohibiting federal agencies from undertaking any action to establish, issue, or promote central bank digital currencies within U.S. jurisdiction.[10] The order terminated all ongoing plans related to CBDC development and mandated immediate cessation of any CBDC initiatives.[11] The administration cited concerns about financial stability, individual privacy, and U.S. sovereignty in justifying the ban.[12]

Instead, the Trump administration embraced dollar-backed stablecoins as the primary vehicle for maintaining dollar dominance in the digital age. Federal Reserve Governor Stephen Miran articulated this strategy in November 2025, stating that stablecoins are "firmly integrated" in the financial architecture and their growth is closely linked to the global dominance of the dollar.[13]

This approach leverages private innovation while preserving dollar hegemony—a characteristically American solution that trusts markets over central planning.

The stablecoin market has responded with remarkable growth. As of March 2025, the market capitalization of stablecoins stood at $232 billion, up forty-five times since December 2019.[14] The Federal Reserve Bank of New York reported that over this period, the stablecoin industry remained highly concentrated, with the two largest issuers, Tether and USDCoin, accounting for approximately 86 percent of total stablecoin market capitalization.[15] By mid-2025, the total market capitalization exceeded $230 billion, with Tether (USDT) maintaining dominance at over $155 billion (approximately 65-70% market share) and USD Coin (USDC) at approximately $61 billion (25% market share).[16]

Stablecoins offer several strategic advantages for dollar dominance. They extend dollar usage into realms previously inaccessible—from cryptocurrency markets to decentralized finance protocols to cross-border remittances in developing economies. Unlike CBDCs, they require no new government infrastructure and leverage existing blockchain networks. Most importantly, stablecoin issuers have become major holders of U.S. Treasury securities. According to the Brookings Institution, U.S. Treasury securities are currently the favored reserve asset of the largest stablecoin issuers, who are already as significant holders of Treasury bills as the largest U.S. money market funds.[17] This creates a virtuous cycle: stablecoins increase global demand for dollars and U.S. government debt, which in turn strengthens dollar hegemony and lowers U.S. borrowing costs.

The Regulatory Framework Takes Shape

The stablecoin strategy gained crucial legal underpinning on July 18, 2025, when President Trump signed the GENIUS Act (Guiding and Establishing National Innovation for U.S. Stablecoins Act) into law.[18] This landmark legislation, which passed the Senate 68-30 and the House 308-122, established the first comprehensive federal regulatory framework for stablecoins in U.S. history.[19]

The GENIUS Act imposed several critical requirements. Stablecoin issuers must maintain reserves backing outstanding stablecoins on at least a one-to-one basis, consisting only of specified assets including U.S. dollars, short-term Treasury bills, repurchase agreements backed by Treasury bills, and similar low-risk government securities.[20] Issuers must make monthly public disclosures of reserve composition, establish clear redemption procedures, and submit to examination by registered public accounting firms.[21] The legislation explicitly subjects stablecoin issuers to the Bank Secrecy Act and requires them to comply with anti-money laundering and sanctions enforcement requirements.[22]

The U.S. Treasury Department's Treasury Borrowing Advisory Committee analyzed the potential impact of stablecoin regulation in April 2025, noting that market dynamics have the potential to accelerate stablecoins' trajectory to reach approximately $2 trillion in market cap by 2028, assuming passage of the GENIUS Act.[23] The committee noted that this would require a seven-fold increase in stablecoin transactions and could result in stablecoins becoming significant holders of U.S. Treasury securities.[24]

The GENIUS Act represents a careful balancing act—providing regulatory clarity to encourage innovation while ensuring that stablecoins serve U.S. strategic interests. As President Trump stated when signing the legislation, it prioritizes consumer protection, strengthens the U.S. dollar's reserve currency status, and bolsters national security.[25] The Act effectively coopts private-sector innovation for state purposes, channeling entrepreneurial energy toward maintaining American monetary hegemony.

The Cross-Border Payment Battlefield

While stablecoins extend dollar dominance into new domains, the competition for cross-border payment systems represents perhaps the most direct challenge to existing financial infrastructure. The Society for Worldwide Interbank Financial Telecommunication (SWIFT) has dominated international payments since its establishment in 1973, when a consortium of 239 banks from 15 countries created it to replace inefficient telex systems.[26] By April 2025, SWIFT connected over 11,200 institutions across 208 countries and territories, processing an estimated 44 million messages daily.[27]

SWIFT's technical architecture leverages a distributed network of data centers in the United States, Netherlands, and Switzerland, employing standardized messaging protocols that enable secure, reliable communication between financial institutions worldwide.[28] The organization's adoption of ISO 20022 continues to grow, with over one million ISO 20022 messages exchanged daily across 150 sending and 220 receiving countries by 2024, reflecting a truly global shift toward richer, more structured data.[29]

SWIFT's central role in the global financial system makes exclusion from it a devastating economic weapon. According to SWIFT data from August 2024, the U.S. dollar accounted for 49.1 percent of payments handled by SWIFT, followed by 21.6 percent for the euro, 6.5 percent for the British pound, and 4.7 percent for the Chinese yuan.[30] Excluding payments within the Eurozone, the dollar's share climbs to approximately 60 percent, illustrating its role as the closest approximation to a "world currency."[31]

SWIFT operates not as a payment or settlement system itself but as a messaging platform that facilitates instructions between financial institutions. After payment initiation, settlement occurs through separate systems such as T2 in Europe, often involving correspondent banking accounts that financial institutions maintain with each other.[32] This architecture, while aging, supports approximately $150 trillion in annual cross-border flows, dwarfing competitors due to its near-universal adoption.[33]

Despite SWIFT's dominance, 2025 data revealed persistent inefficiencies in cross-border payments. SWIFT's "Spotlight on Speed 2025" report identified four root causes of payment delays: regulatory reporting requirements, currency and risk controls, lack of real-time 24/7 infrastructure, and manual processes for compliance checks.[34] While 75 percent of payments traveling over SWIFT's network reach beneficiary banks within just 10 minutes, final delivery to end beneficiaries often experiences friction in what SWIFT terms "the last mile."[35]

China's Cross-Border Interbank Payment System (CIPS) represents the most sophisticated alternative to SWIFT. Launched in 2015 under the stewardship of the People's Bank of China as a state-driven initiative to internationalize the renminbi, CIPS initially had just 19 direct participants but scaled to 1,631 institutions across 112 countries by early 2025.[36] By May 2025, CIPS reported the number of participants had risen by 10 percent year-over-year to 1,683, with Asia accounting for 73 percent of indirect participants, 17 percent being European institutions, 4 percent from Africa, 2 percent from North America, 2 percent from South America, and 1 percent from Oceania.[37]

The geographical distribution of CIPS participants reveals its strategic focus. In June 2025, CIPS forged its first direct partnerships with six foreign banks in the Middle East and Africa, fitting into a wider narrative for countries seeking alternatives to dollar-based infrastructure or concerned about sanctions.[38] Since Russia's removal from the SWIFT network in 2022, countries in Asia, the Middle East, Africa, and the BRICS bloc have increasingly explored yuan-based settlement options.[39]

However, comparing CIPS to SWIFT reveals fundamental differences in scope and functionality. CIPS still relies on SWIFT to send messages between banks for a large proportion of transactions, especially those not directly connected to CIPS.[40] In March 2025, SWIFT signed a memorandum of understanding with CIPS to work collaboratively to improve capabilities, demonstrating that SWIFT views CIPS more as a partner than a rival.[41] With over 11,500 institutions in more than 235 countries and territories, SWIFT remains far more extensive than CIPS and provides messages for transactions in virtually every major currency.[42]

The yuan's limited share in global payments constrains CIPS's challenge to SWIFT. SWIFT's RMB tracker for June 2025 showed that the yuan accounted for only 3 percent of the share of currencies used for global SWIFT payments, versus 48 percent for the U.S. dollar and 24 percent for the euro.[43] This modest share persists despite China's extensive efforts at yuan internationalization over the past decade.

The Weaponization Paradox

The digital currency competition cannot be understood without examining the broader context of financial sanctions and dollar weaponization—the very factors driving many nations toward alternatives. The United States' aggressive use of the financial system as a foreign policy tool has created both the motivation and the justification for dedollarization efforts.

Financial sanctions utilizing SWIFT and dollar infrastructure have become a central element of U.S. foreign policy. Research from the Federal Reserve Bank of New York documented how SWIFT's exclusion capability provides powerful leverage, with historical precedents dating back decades.[44] The organization, though technically a Belgian-based cooperative, operates under significant U.S. influence due to the dollar's dominance in international transactions.[45]

SWIFT provides a centralized store-and-forward mechanism for financial messages between institutions. When bank A needs to send a message to bank B, it formats the message according to standards and securely sends it to SWIFT, which then routes it appropriately.[46] This central role creates a powerful chokepoint that can be weaponized for geopolitical purposes. SWIFT is subject to oversight by the Belgian central bank together with other G-10 central banks and the European Central Bank, focusing primarily on systemic risks as a critical service provider.[47]

The historical evolution of SWIFT's use in sanctions reveals escalating weaponization. In 2012, following an agreement among all 27 member states of the Council of the European Union, SWIFT disconnected Iranian banks identified as institutions in breach of EU sanctions from its international network.[48] This marked one of the first major uses of SWIFT disconnection as a sanctions tool. In February 2016, most Iranian banks reconnected to the network following the lift of sanctions due to the Joint Comprehensive Plan of Action.[49]

The 2014 annexation of Crimea by Russia prompted the first discussions of using SWIFT disconnection against Russian institutions. The United States, European Union, and Canada introduced targeted sanctions against Russian individuals and entities, mainly travel restrictions, asset freezes, and restrictions on debt and equity financing.[50] However, full SWIFT disconnection was not implemented until 2022.

When seven major Russian banks were disconnected from SWIFT following Russia's invasion of Ukraine in February 2022, it had immediate and significant economic effects.[51] The disconnection affected approximately 1 to 1.5 percent of SWIFT's daily traffic and roughly $700-800 billion in annual cross-border flows.[52] The ruble devalued sharply, plunging more than 30 percent in the weeks that followed, while capital flight and market volatility intensified.[53]

The freezing of Russia's central bank reserves marked an unprecedented escalation. Over half of the Central Bank of Russia's approximately $630-640 billion in foreign exchange and gold reserves were frozen, signaling that even a G20 member's sovereign assets were vulnerable to Western sanctions.[54] This "financial isolation" prompted Russia to dramatically accelerate its dedollarization strategy, which had begun after the 2014 annexation of Crimea.[55]

Russia responded by expanding its own System for Transfer of Financial Messages (SPFS), which can transmit messages in the SWIFT format and more broadly messages based on the ISO 20022 standard, as well as free-format messages.[56] More than 400 banks connected to SPFS by 2022, most of them Russian or from former Soviet Republics, with a few banks from Germany, Switzerland, France, Japan, Sweden, Turkey, and Cuba also connected.[57] By April 2022, the number of countries with financial institutions using SPFS had grown from 12 to 52, at which point the Central Bank of Russia decided not to publish the names of SPFS users.[58]

The weaponization of SWIFT and dollar infrastructure has created what analysts call a "weaponization paradox": the more effectively the United States uses the dollar as a weapon, the more incentive other nations have to develop alternatives, which over time could undermine the very dollar dominance that makes sanctions effective. Each successive use of financial sanctions reinforces the drive among emerging economies to establish alternative payments transfer messaging models, even if merely as insurance.[59]

This dynamic has profound implications for the international monetary system. While U.S. sanctions on SWIFT would have imposed significant impact on the global economy given SWIFT's centrality, the repeated use of this tool has accelerated the development of alternatives.[60] The convergence of geoeconomic change and technological progress, alongside the challenge of updating 20th century monetary norms, helps explain the intensifying push for reform of international payments systems.[61]

BRICS and the Dedollarization Agenda

The BRICS grouping—originally Brazil, Russia, India, China, and South Africa, expanded in 2025 to include Egypt, Ethiopia, Iran, United Arab Emirates, and Indonesia—has become the organizational framework for dedollarization efforts, though progress has been more rhetorical than substantive. Academic research examining BRICS monetary reform momentum notes that weaponization of SWIFT on multiple occasions has added to the drive of emerging economies to establish alternative payments transfer messaging models.[38]

The reality of BRICS dedollarization efforts reveals significant internal contradictions. SWIFT's RMB tracker for June 2025 shows that the yuan accounted for only 3 percent of the share of currencies being used for global SWIFT payments, versus 48 percent for the U.S. dollar and 24 percent for the euro.[39] This modest share reflects the yuan's limited role despite China's extensive efforts at internationalization.

Political divisions within BRICS limit coordinated action. India's External Affairs Minister stated categorically that there is no plan for a BRICS currency, emphasizing the importance of dollar stability.[40] The Bank for International Settlements data shows that the U.S. dollar was involved in 97 percent of all foreign exchange transactions involving the Indian rupee, 95 percent of all transactions involving the Brazilian real, and 84 percent of all transactions involving the yuan in 2022.[41]

Nevertheless, incremental dedollarization continues through practical channels. The BRICS grouping represents a substantial share of global economic activity, accounting for approximately one-third of global economic output according to International Monetary Fund data.[42] China and Russia reportedly conduct most of their bilateral trade in yuan and rubles, with trade volumes exceeding $240 billion.[43] These bilateral arrangements, however, do not constitute a systematic challenge to dollar dominance but rather represent specific adaptations by sanctioned economies.

Adoption Challenges and Structural Limits

Despite China's enormous investment in digital yuan infrastructure and the expanding network of alternative payment systems, fundamental obstacles limit their challenge to dollar dominance. Research published in 2025 examining digital yuan adoption found that despite government promotion and merchant adoption drives, Chinese users show reluctance to switch from established platforms like WeChat Pay and Alipay to the digital yuan.[62] The digital yuan operates on a two-tier structure, with tier one comprising the People's Bank of China and tier two consisting of institutions such as major state-owned banks and online banks like WeBank (WeChat Pay) and MYBank (AliPay).[63]

Seven commercial banks can provide the digital yuan, including the Industrial and Commercial Bank of China, the Agricultural Bank of China, the Bank of China, the China Construction Bank, the Bank of Communications, the Postal Savings Bank of China, and the China Merchant's Bank.[64] Users obtain digital yuan wallets through tier-two institutions. However, despite this infrastructure, adoption has been slower than anticipated, with most Chinese users continuing to prefer existing payment platforms.[65]

For the yuan to challenge dollar dominance internationally, China would need to address several structural deficiencies. The lack of free capital convertibility prevents the currency from being easily exchanged, limiting its utility for international investors who cannot easily move funds in and out of China.[66] Underdeveloped capital markets mean there are insufficient liquid yuan-denominated investment opportunities to make holding yuan attractive for central banks and institutional investors.[67] Concerns about rule of law and potential arbitrary government actions further discourage foreign holders.[68]

People's Bank of China officials have acknowledged challenges facing yuan internationalization. Former People's Bank of China Governor Zhou Xiaochuan emphasized the importance of critically examining whether the global expansion of "dollarization," particularly through digital financial instruments, is desirable, underscoring the need to assess its broader economic implications.[69] PBoC officials have also acknowledged that U.S. dollar-denominated stablecoins reinforce dollar dominance by enhancing dollar liquidity globally, potentially slowing diversification efforts.[70]

The stablecoin market's structure and function illustrate the dollar's fundamental advantages. Federal Reserve research explains that stablecoins attempt to provide a stable value relative to other crypto assets by pegging their value to a real-world asset, typically the U.S. dollar.[71] This stability makes them useful as a medium of exchange and store of value in the crypto ecosystem, addressing the extreme volatility of tokens like Bitcoin.[72]

Stablecoins' primary role is providing media of exchange within the digital asset ecosystem. Over 80 percent of trade volume on major centralized crypto exchanges involves stablecoins as part of the traded pair, illustrating this medium-of-exchange role.[73] This function is intrinsically linked to stablecoins' role as a store of value in crypto markets, which are otherwise populated with volatile assets.[74]

Federal Reserve analysis distinguishes between different types of stablecoins based on their collateralization mechanisms. Fiat-backed stablecoins are backed with cash and cash-equivalent reserves such as deposits, Treasuries, and commercial paper.[75] Most fiat-backed stablecoins are centralized, with a single company responsible for issuing stablecoins on public blockchains at 1:1 parity with fiat reserves held outside the blockchain.[76] The stablecoin issuer ensures that the number of tokens issued on the blockchain is no greater than the dollar value of the issuer's off-chain reserves.[77]

The stabilization mechanism for fiat-backed stablecoins works through arbitrage and redeemability. Issuers typically promise to redeem their tokens 1:1 in a real-world asset on demand, typically U.S. dollars, though redemptions are usually subject to minimum transaction sizes, fees, processing delays, or other requirements.[78] This redeemability inspires trust in the system and enables market participants to arbitrage away deviations from the peg.[79]

Research from the Federal Reserve Bank of New York examining primary and secondary markets for stablecoins revealed the complexity of maintaining stable pegs during periods of market stress. The March 2023 events surrounding Silicon Valley Bank's failure illustrated these dynamics, when Circle announced it had been unable to wire out a portion of USDC reserves held at the bank before regulators took control.[80] The price of USDC de-pegged significantly off the U.S. dollar, and markets for other stablecoins fluctuated considerably as traders responded to the news.[81]

These events revealed important distinctions between primary and secondary market dynamics during stablecoin crises. Primary markets involve the creation and redemption of stablecoins directly with issuers, while secondary markets involve trading of existing stablecoins on exchanges.[82] During stress events, divergences between primary and secondary market prices can create arbitrage opportunities or, conversely, signal fundamental concerns about an issuer's ability to maintain reserves.[83]

Brookings Institution analysis emphasizes that approximately 99 percent of stablecoins currently in circulation are pegged to the U.S. dollar, while the rest are pegged to other fiat currencies or commodities like gold.[84] This overwhelming dollar dominance reflects several factors: the dollar's status as the world's primary reserve currency, the depth and liquidity of U.S. financial markets, and the stability and predictability of U.S. monetary policy.[85]

The regulatory landscape for stablecoins varies significantly across jurisdictions. New York's Division of Financial Services began requiring businesses engaged in activities involving crypto assets to obtain a dedicated BitLicense in 2015, becoming an early mover on crypto regulation.[86] In 2022, New York clarified that licensees issuing U.S. dollar-backed stablecoins must hold full reserves of highly safe and liquid assets, publish monthly attestations of reserve adequacy by independent accountants, and redeem stablecoins for reserves in a timely fashion under clearly disclosed policies.[87] Other states including Florida, Nevada, Utah, and West Virginia have established their own frameworks.[88]

Strategic Implications and Future Trajectories

The digital currency competition reveals several critical dynamics that will shape the U.S.-China rivalry in coming years. First, technology alone cannot overcome structural economic and institutional advantages. China's sophisticated digital yuan infrastructure has not translated into significant international adoption because the underlying currency lacks the attributes—convertibility, market depth, rule of law—that make a currency truly international. Conversely, dollar-backed stablecoins thrive precisely because they leverage existing dollar trust and institutional frameworks.

Second, the competition increasingly occurs on parallel tracks rather than direct confrontation. The U.S. extends dollar dominance through market-driven stablecoins backed by private innovation and regulatory oversight. China constructs state-controlled payment infrastructure designed to insulate its economy from Western financial pressure. These systems may coexist indefinitely, serving different regions and purposes.

Third, weaponization of financial systems by both sides accelerates fragmentation. U.S. sanctions drive adversaries toward alternative payment channels, while China's willingness to leverage its payment infrastructure for political purposes creates reciprocal concerns about dependency. The result is likely a fractured landscape where regional payment networks coexist with varying degrees of interoperability.

Federal Reserve Governor Miran's November 2025 speech highlighted that widespread adoption of stablecoins could have profound implications for monetary policy.[89] He noted that stablecoins are "firmly integrated" in the financial architecture, with most denominated in U.S. dollars, enabling fast, reliable, and efficient access to digital dollars, especially in regions with fragile banking systems or shifting restrictions.[90] The growing adoption of stablecoins strengthens the dollar's position as the global reserve currency and accelerates its internationalization.[91]

Governor Miran acknowledged that stablecoins have implications for the transmission of monetary policy. The growth of stablecoins implies a profound reconfiguration of monetary policy, as increasing demand for these instruments is also driving the purchase of dollar-denominated assets, such as Treasury bonds, reinforcing the dominance of the dollar globally.[92] As stablecoins gain traction, particularly outside the U.S., they offer an efficient and low-cost way for individuals and businesses to access dollars.[93]

The Federal Reserve projects that global adoption of stablecoins could reach between $1 trillion and $3 trillion by 2030, representing a significant transformation in the financial landscape.[94] This growth trajectory assumes continued regulatory support and expanding use cases beyond cryptocurrency trading into mainstream payments and cross-border transfers.[95]

The composition of stablecoin reserves has important implications for U.S. financial markets and monetary policy transmission. According to Brookings analysis, U.S. Treasury securities are currently the favored reserve asset of the largest stablecoin issuers, who are already as significant holders of Treasury bills as the largest U.S. money market funds.[96] Continued stablecoin growth could therefore bolster demand for government debt, not to mention the global dominance of the dollar.[97]

However, increased holdings of stablecoins by the public could potentially draw down bank deposits and thereby limit the efficacy of monetary policy.[98] On the other hand, if issuers hold cash reserves as deposits and steer new cash into banks, such as from unbanked or foreign populations, stablecoin uptake may increase deposits and enhance the transmission of monetary policy.[99] The ultimate impact depends on the specific structure of reserve holdings and the regulatory framework governing stablecoin issuers.[100]

The U.S. Treasury Department's analysis in April 2025 projected that evolving market dynamics, structures, and incentives have the potential to accelerate stablecoins' trajectory significantly.[101] Standard Chartered research cited by the Treasury estimated approximately $2 trillion in stablecoin market capitalization by 2028, assuming a seven-fold increase in stablecoin transactions and a lift to 10 percent of foreign exchange spot-market transactions from around 1 percent in 2025.[102]

The passage of the GENIUS Act demonstrates that the United States recognizes the strategic importance of digital currencies and intends to harness private innovation to maintain monetary hegemony. The Act prohibits stablecoin issuers from paying interest to holders, a provision designed to prevent stablecoins from competing directly with traditional banking deposits and potentially disrupting the banking system.[103] This restriction reflects careful consideration of systemic stability alongside innovation promotion.[104]

By establishing clear rules while preserving dollar backing requirements and sanctions compliance mechanisms, the legislation channels entrepreneurial energy toward reinforcing rather than challenging dollar dominance. The requirement that foreign stablecoin issuers register with the Office of the Comptroller of the Currency, hold reserves in U.S. financial institutions sufficient to meet U.S. customer demands, and demonstrate capability to comply with U.S. lawful orders effectively extends American regulatory reach globally.[105]

China's digital yuan represents a different but equally strategic vision: a payment system that provides the efficiency benefits of digital technology while preserving state control over the monetary system and insulating the economy from external pressure. The People's Bank of China began working on blueprints for digital currency development in 2014, originally conceiving it as a digital currency/electronic systems (DCEP) project.[106] According to the project's official white paper, the e-CNY was created primarily as a domestic retail CBDC for everyday payments, but the document also indicates strong willingness to explore gateways for its internationalization.[107]

The integration of the digital yuan with CIPS creates infrastructure for dollar-independent transactions, particularly valuable for Belt and Road Initiative countries and nations facing Western sanctions. Whether this infrastructure can attract sufficient voluntary adoption to become a genuine alternative to dollar dominance remains the central question for the coming years.

The 2026 Inflection Point

As 2025 draws to a close, several developments suggest 2026 may prove pivotal in the digital currency competition. The People's Bank of China has committed to steadily promoting the development and application of the digital yuan, with plans to use blockchain technology for cross-border electronic tax payment business.[51] The expansion of digital yuan services to foreigners visiting Shanghai represents a significant push toward international adoption.

The Federal Deposit Insurance Corporation prepared its first stablecoin regulatory framework under the GENIUS Act in late 2025, which will clarify how American regulators balance innovation with systemic stability.[52] The framework will introduce capital, liquidity, and reserve requirements for bank-issued stablecoins, creating regulatory clarity that could accelerate institutional adoption.

The trajectory of yuan internationalization will depend substantially on China's willingness to liberalize capital controls—a step that would enhance the currency's attractiveness but potentially compromise Communist Party control. The e-CNY pilot's expansion to seventeen provinces across China demonstrates commitment to domestic rollout, but international adoption remains limited by structural constraints.[53]

SWIFT continues to maintain its dominant position while adapting to technological change. The organization signed a memorandum of understanding with CIPS in March 2025 to improve capabilities, demonstrating that it views CIPS more as a partner than a rival.[54] This pragmatic cooperation reflects the reality that complete displacement of existing infrastructure is unlikely; rather, systems will evolve to serve different purposes and regions.

Conclusion: A Multipolar Monetary Future

The battle for the future of money will not produce a single victor. Unlike previous currency competitions where one standard achieved dominance, the digital age enables parallel systems to coexist serving different users and purposes. The dollar's structural advantages—deep markets, rule of law, institutional transparency—ensure its continued primacy in most international transactions. But China's digital yuan and associated payment infrastructure create viable alternatives for specific contexts: Belt and Road transactions, sanctions evasion, regional trade within China's sphere of influence.

Stablecoins represent a uniquely American solution—leveraging private innovation while preserving state control through regulatory frameworks. Their success depends on maintaining the delicate balance between innovation and oversight. Federal Reserve analysis suggests that continued stablecoin growth could bolster demand for government debt and reinforce the global dominance of the dollar.[55]

For the U.S.-China rivalry, digital currencies represent a new battleground where technical standards, regulatory frameworks, and payment infrastructure become tools of geopolitical competition. Success requires not just superior technology but economic scale, institutional trust, and network effects that make adoption self-reinforcing. China's authoritarian model enables top-down implementation but limits organic adoption; America's market-driven approach harnesses innovation but requires regulatory coherence.

The ultimate question is not whether digital currencies will reshape global finance—they will—but whether their rise accelerates dedollarization or reinforces dollar dominance. Current evidence suggests both dynamics simultaneously: stablecoins extending dollar reach into new domains while alternative payment systems create dollar-independent channels. The result will likely be a more fragmented, multipolar monetary system where the dollar retains its position as first among several major currencies rather than enjoying the near-monopoly of previous decades.

For policymakers, this requires strategic flexibility. The United States must continue leveraging its advantages while addressing vulnerabilities that push nations toward alternatives, including overuse of sanctions. China must balance its desire for monetary autonomy against the need for international acceptance, potentially requiring reforms that compromise state control. Both nations must recognize that in the digital age, monetary competition will be ongoing rather than resolved, requiring sustained engagement rather than decisive victory.

The battle for the future of money is not won through a single innovation or policy but through the gradual accumulation of users, transactions, and trust. As the competition enters its critical phase in 2026, advantage lies not with the nation possessing superior technology but with the one whose monetary system best serves the diverse needs of a multipolar world. That remains to be determined.

Endnotes

[1] "China's Digital RMB Transactions Top 14.2 Trillion Yuan," China.org.cn, October 29, 2025, http://www.china.org.cn/2025-10/29/content_118147362.shtml.

[2] Ibid.

[3] "China's Digital RMB Transactions Top 14.2 Trillion Yuan," English.www.gov.cn, October 29, 2025, https://english.www.gov.cn/archive/statistics/202510/29/content_WS6901a9c9c6d00ca5f9a0726a.html.

[4] "Progress of Research & Development of E-CNY in China," People's Bank of China, accessed December 2025, http://www.pbc.gov.cn/en/3688110/3688172/4157443/4293696/index.html.

[5] Ibid.

[6] "China's Digital RMB Transactions Top 14.2 Trillion Yuan," China.org.cn.

[7] "SWIFT's Legacy Meets CIPS's Ambition: A New Financial Era," Geopolitics Unplugged, April 10, 2025, https://geopoliticsunplugged.substack.com/p/swifts-legacy-meets-cipss-ambition.

[8] "Is China's Cross-Border Payments Network on the Rise?" FXC Intelligence, July 4, 2025, https://www.fxcintel.com/research/analysis/cips-growth-may-2025.

[9] "China's Digital RMB Transactions Top 14.2 Trillion Yuan," China.org.cn.

[10] "Strengthening American Leadership in Digital Financial Technology," Executive Order 14120, White House, January 23, 2025, https://www.whitehouse.gov/presidential-actions/2025/01/strengthening-american-leadership-in-digital-financial-technology/.

[11] Ibid.

[12] Ibid.

[13] "Speech by Governor Miran on Stablecoins and Monetary Policy," Board of Governors of the Federal Reserve System, November 7, 2025, https://www.federalreserve.gov/newsevents/speech/miran20251107a.htm.

[14] Kenechukwu Anadu, Pablo Azar, Marco Cipriani, Thomas M. Eisenbach, Catherine Huang, and Mattia Landoni, "Stablecoins and Crypto Shocks: An Update," Liberty Street Economics, Federal

Reserve Bank of New York, June 30, 2025, https://libertystreeteconomics.newyorkfed.org/2025/04/stablecoins-and-crypto-shocks-an-update/.

[15] Ibid.

[16] "Stablecoins in 2025: Full Overview of the $230B Market," Medium, July 14, 2025, https://medium.com/@monolith.vc/stablecoins-in-2025-full-overview-of-the-230b-market-bab96c680c44.

[17] Darrell Duffie and Sophia Chen, "What Are Stablecoins, and How Are They Regulated?" Brookings Institution, October 31, 2025, https://www.brookings.edu/articles/what-are-stablecoins-and-how-are-they-regulated/.

[18] "GENIUS Act," Public Law 119-25, 119th Congress, July 18, 2025, https://www.congress.gov/bill/119th-congress/senate-bill/394/text.

[19] Ibid.

[20] "Stablecoin Legislation: An Overview of S. 1582, GENIUS Act of 2025," Congressional Research Service, July 17, 2025, https://www.congress.gov/crs-product/IN12553.

[21] Ibid.

[22] Ibid.

[23] "Digital Money," Treasury Borrowing Advisory Committee Presentation, U.S. Department of the Treasury, April 30, 2025, https://home.treasury.gov/system/files/221/TBACCharge2Q22025.pdf.

[24] Ibid.

[25] "Fact Sheet: President Donald J. Trump Signs GENIUS Act into Law," White House, July 18, 2025, https://www.whitehouse.gov/fact-sheets/2025/07/fact-sheet-president-donald-j-trump-signs-genius-act-into-law/.

[26] "SWIFT's Legacy Meets CIPS's Ambition: A New Financial Era," Geopolitics Unplugged.

[27] Ibid.

[28] Ibid.

[29] "Connecting the Global Financial Community: Our Year in Review," SWIFT, December 23, 2024, https://www.swift.com/news-events/news/connecting-global-financial-community-our-year-review.

[30] "U.S. Dollar Dominates Global Payment Network SWIFT," Voronoi, accessed December 2025, https://www.voronoiapp.com/money/US-Dollar-Dominates-Global-Payment-Network-SWIFT-2820.

[31] Ibid.

[32] Marco Cipriani, Linda S. Goldberg, and Gabriele La Spada, "Financial Sanctions, SWIFT, and the Architecture of the International Payment System," Federal Reserve Bank of New York Staff Reports, No. 1047, 2023, https://www.newyorkfed.org/medialibrary/media/research/staff_reports/sr1047.pdf.

[33] "SWIFT's Legacy Meets CIPS's Ambition: A New Financial Era," Geopolitics Unplugged.

[34] "Spotlight on Speed 2025," SWIFT, September 24, 2025, https://www.swift.com/news-events/news/spotlight-speed-2025.

[35] Ibid.

[36] "SWIFT's Legacy Meets CIPS's Ambition: A New Financial Era," Geopolitics Unplugged.

[37] "Is China's Cross-Border Payments Network on the Rise?" FXC Intelligence.

[38] Ibid.

[39] Ibid.

[40] Ibid.

[41] Ibid.

[42] Ibid.

[43] Ibid.

[44] Cipriani, Goldberg, and La Spada, "Financial Sanctions, SWIFT, and the Architecture of the International Payment System."

[45] Ibid.

[46] Ibid.

[47] Ibid.

[48] Ibid.

[49] Ibid.

[50] Ibid.

[51] Ibid.

[52] Ibid.

[53] Ibid.

[54] Ibid.

[55] Ibid.

[56] Ibid.

[57] Ibid.

[58] Ibid.

[59] Nicholas Ross Smith, "The BRICS, the Dollar and SWIFT: A Review of Evolving Interests and Monetary Reform Momentum," South African Journal of International Affairs 32, no. 2 (2025), https://www.tandfonline.com/doi/full/10.1080/10220461.2025.2523509.

[60] Cipriani, Goldberg, and La Spada, "Financial Sanctions, SWIFT, and the Architecture of the International Payment System."

[61] Smith, "The BRICS, the Dollar and SWIFT."

[62] "An Overview of China's Digital Yuan," Cointelegraph, August 8, 2025, https://cointelegraph.com/learn/articles/an-overview-of-chinas-digital-yuan.

[63] Ibid.

[64] Ibid.

[65] Ibid.

[66] "China's Digital Yuan: Shifting Global Currency Power," Observer Research Foundation, July 8, 2025, https://www.orfonline.org/expert-speak/china-s-digital-yuan-shifting-global-currency-power.

[67] Ibid.

[68] Ibid.

[69] Ibid.

[70] Ibid.

[71] "The Stable in Stablecoins," Federal Reserve Board FEDS Notes, December 16, 2022, https://www.federalreserve.gov/econres/notes/feds-notes/the-stable-in-stablecoins-20221216.html.

[72] Ibid.

[73] Ibid.

[74] Ibid.

[75] Ibid.

[76] Ibid.

[77] Ibid.

[78] Ibid.

[79] Ibid.

[80] Cy Watsky, Jeffrey Allen, Hamzah Daud, Jochen Demuth, Daniel Little, Megan Rodden, and Amber Seira, "Primary and Secondary Markets for Stablecoins," FEDS Notes, Board of Governors of the Federal Reserve System, February 23, 2024, https://www.federalreserve.gov/econres/notes/feds-notes/primary-and-secondary-markets-for-stablecoins-20240223.html.

[81] Ibid.

[82] Ibid.

[83] Ibid.

[84] Duffie and Chen, "What Are Stablecoins, and How Are They Regulated?"

[85] Ibid.

[86] Ibid.

[87] Ibid.

[88] Ibid.

[89] "Speech by Governor Miran on Stablecoins and Monetary Policy," Federal Reserve Board.

[90] Ibid.

[91] Ibid.

[92] Ibid.

[93] Ibid.

[94] "Are Stablecoins the New Backbone of the Financial System?" Bit2Me News, accessed December 2025, https://news.bit2me.com/en/stablecoins-columna-vertebral-sistema-financiero-fed.

[95] Ibid.

[96] Duffie and Chen, "What Are Stablecoins, and How Are They Regulated?"

[97] Ibid.

[98] Ibid.

[99] Ibid.

[100] Ibid.

[101] "Digital Money," U.S. Department of the Treasury.

[102] Ibid.

[103] "Stablecoin Legislation: An Overview of S. 1582, GENIUS Act of 2025," Congressional Research Service.

[104] Ibid.

[105] Ibid.

[106] "Progress of Research & Development of E-CNY in China," People's Bank of China.

[107] Ibid.

Conclusion
The Competition That Defines Our Century

The U.S.-China rivalry has transcended the bilateral trade dispute that dominated headlines in 2018 to become the defining geopolitical competition of the twenty-first century. As documented throughout this volume, what began as tariff skirmishes has evolved into a comprehensive contest spanning semiconductors and artificial intelligence, critical minerals and biotechnology, military posturing in the Taiwan Strait and influence operations across the Global South. By late 2025, with tariffs having briefly reached 145 percent before negotiations led to temporary reductions, and with both nations implementing sweeping export controls on technologies ranging from advanced chips to rare earth elements, the rivalry has fundamentally reshaped the global economic and security landscape.[1]

This conclusion synthesizes the central arguments presented across the preceding chapters, examines why the outcome of this competition remains profoundly uncertain, assesses the stakes for the international order, explores the critical role of middle powers caught between the two giants, draws lessons from historical great power competitions, and concludes with a call for strategic clarity and sustained engagement from both Washington and Beijing.

The Central Arguments: A Competition Across Domains

The U.S.-China rivalry is not simply an economic competition or a military standoff—it is a multidimensional struggle that touches nearly every aspect of international relations. Five interconnected dynamics define this competition and will shape its trajectory for decades to come.

First, the contest for technological supremacy has become the new strategic high ground. As demonstrated in Chapters 4 through 6, control over semiconductors, artificial intelligence, and emerging biotechnologies now matters as much for national power as control over oil fields or naval chokepoints once did. China's achievement with DeepSeek in January 2025—developing competitive AI models despite U.S. export controls—illustrated both the limits of technology denial strategies and Beijing's capacity for innovation under constraint.[2] The UCLA Anderson School's July 2025 economic report confirmed that this "demonstrated China's competitiveness in one of the most critical sectors—artificial intelligence—rivaling the U.S."[3]

The strategic competition over advanced computing and artificial intelligence intensified throughout 2025, with the U.S. Congress highlighting that "China and the United States each recognize the economic and security benefits to be gained by being the first country to harness" these transformative technologies.[4] Rather than converging toward a single global standard, the world appears to be dividing into competing technological spheres of influence—a "digital iron curtain" that fragments innovation networks and forces companies and countries to choose sides.

Second, control of critical resources has re-emerged as a fundamental dimension of power. China's October 2025 expansion of export controls to include gallium, germanium, antimony, and graphite—materials essential for semiconductors, defense systems, and clean energy technologies—demonstrated how resource dependencies can be weaponized in great power competition.[5] The White House confirmed in November 2025 that China initially announced "expansive new export controls on rare earths and related measures" on October 9, 2025, before suspending them as part of bilateral negotiations.[6] With China controlling approximately 60 percent of global rare earth production and near-monopolies on processing capacity, Beijing possesses leverage that no amount of military spending can immediately counter.

The U.S.-China Economic and Security Review Commission's 2025 Annual Report documented this strategic vulnerability, noting that China's dominance across critical mineral supply chains creates dependencies that extend from defense systems to clean energy technologies.[7] Yet as Chapter 8 documented, the timeline for developing alternative supply chains stretches years into the future, while China's capacity to manipulate prices could make many of these projects economically unviable. The race for critical minerals extends beyond rare earths to encompass lithium, cobalt, and other materials essential for the clean energy transition—creating the ironic situation where climate goals increase dependence on Chinese processing capabilities.

Third, structural economic imbalances create mutually reinforcing grievances that no trade deal can easily resolve. China's trade surplus reached $997 billion in 2024, reflecting the deep structural distortions that result from an economic model where Beijing "continues to emphasize investment in manufacturing capacity" while "tolerating weak domestic demand."[8] Chinese households receive only 44 percent of GDP as disposable income and spend just 30 percent of GDP on consumption, compared to 74 percent and 68 percent respectively in the United States—a gap that drives persistent trade imbalances.[9]

The UCLA Anderson Forecast's comprehensive July 2025 economic analysis explained: "China's low household consumption is tightly linked to its chronic overinvestment and persistent trade surplus, which arises when domestic savings consistently exceed domestic consumption and investment."[10] The U.S.-China Economic and Security Review Commission identified this pattern as "China Shock 2.0," where "massive state subsidies for high-tech sectors—specifically EVs, green energy, and advanced materials—are flooding global markets, crushing foreign competition, and cementing dangerous dependencies."[11]

American complaints about Chinese industrial policy and Chinese frustrations about U.S. technology restrictions both reflect genuine concerns rooted in fundamentally different economic models. The November 2025 trade deal negotiated by Presidents Trump and Xi, suspending Chinese rare earth export controls and U.S. tariff escalations for one year, provides breathing room but does not address these underlying tensions.[12] The structural sources of conflict—China's state-led development model versus America's market-based system, Beijing's pursuit of "indigenous and controllable" technology versus Washington's desire to maintain technological leadership—will persist regardless of temporary diplomatic successes.

Fourth, the Taiwan question and broader Indo-Pacific security dynamics create a constant risk of military escalation. As Chapter 13 detailed, Taiwan's concentration of advanced semiconductor manufacturing—more than 90 percent of the world's most sophisticated chips—transforms the island into what some analysts have called "the most dangerous place on Earth." The U.S.-China Economic and Security Review Commission's 2025 report directed Congress to assess U.S. military "compliance with the legal requirement established by Congress in the Taiwan Relations Act 'to maintain the capacity of the United States to resist any resort to force or other forms of coercion" against Taiwan.[13]

The South China Sea disputes, examined in Chapter 14, create additional flashpoints where miscalculation could trigger broader conflict. As Brookings Institution analysts observed in their January 2025 policy series, "The U.S.-China relationship President Donald J. Trump inherited is vastly different than the one he handed off to the Biden administration in 2021," with military tensions representing an increasingly central dimension of the rivalry.[14] Unlike the U.S.-Soviet Cold War, where well-established protocols governed military interactions, U.S.-China military-to-military communications remain sporadic and crisis management mechanisms remain underdeveloped.

Fifth, the biotech dimension—barely begun as this volume goes to press—may eclipse all previous technological competitions in strategic significance. The U.S.-China Economic and Security Review Commission's November 2025 report called on Congress to "resource the National Institute of Standards and Technology (NIST) to establish a Bio-Measurement Laboratory (BML) to develop, support, and promulgate standards for biological measurements, materials, and models;

advance measurement science and tools for biotechnology."[15] As Chapters 16 through 18 argued, biotechnology's dual-use potential—spanning agriculture, medicine, and military applications—combined with China's advantages in manufacturing speed, regulatory flexibility, and data access, create a competition with potentially civilizational stakes.

Why the Outcome Remains Uncertain

Despite the intensity of U.S.-China competition, the eventual outcome remains profoundly uncertain. Multiple factors ensure that neither triumph nor accommodation can be taken for granted.

China's formidable strengths coexist with significant vulnerabilities. Beijing commands the world's largest manufacturing base, a proven capacity for large-scale industrial policy, growing technological sophistication, and massive foreign exchange reserves. The success of DeepSeek and other innovations demonstrate that export controls accelerate rather than prevent Chinese technological development in certain domains. The U.S.-China Economic and Security Review Commission acknowledged in November 2025 that "China's 'Made in China 2025' policy has successfully created an 'industrial commons' where advancements in one sector rapidly catalyze breakthroughs in adjacent ones."[16]

Yet China simultaneously confronts demographic decline that will shrink its working-age population, a property market collapse that has destroyed household wealth, mounting debt burdens, deflationary pressures indicating weak domestic demand, and a growth model dependent on ever-increasing leverage. The UCLA Anderson School's comprehensive July 2025 analysis warned: "There are growing concerns that, following the burst of its real estate bubble, China may now be inflating a new bubble in the manufacturing sector."[17] The report documented that China's total debt-to-GDP ratio "has risen rapidly, recently surpassing those of the U.S., while the debt ratios in the U.S. and Japan have remained relatively stable since the COVID-19 period."[18] These internal contradictions raise questions about whether Beijing can sustain its competitive posture across multiple domains simultaneously.

American advantages in innovation, alliance networks, and institutional depth face political polarization and strategic ambivalence. The United States retains the world's most dynamic innovation ecosystem, the dollar's reserve currency status, unmatched alliance networks spanning Europe and Asia, and deep wells of soft power. American technological leadership in certain AI applications, biotechnology research, and advanced manufacturing processes remains significant.

The U.S. economy's flexibility and entrepreneurial culture provide advantages that China's state-led system cannot easily replicate.

However, as Chapter 11 documented, American political dysfunction creates strategic volatility. Brookings Institution analysts Ryan Hass and others warned in January 2025: "Trump has an opportunity to craft a strong policy to move the U.S.-China relationship toward becoming fairer and more equitable. Whether he seizes this opportunity may depend upon the degree to which he acts with purpose, maintains focus, and imposes discipline."[19] The sharp policy pivots between administrations—from Obama's "pivot to Asia" to Trump's trade war to Biden's "competition not conflict" framework and back to Trump's confrontational approach—undermine the sustained multi-decade effort that successful great power competition requires. Domestic political debates about industrial policy, trade policy, and technology restrictions often prioritize short-term political advantage over long-term strategic coherence.

Third-party choices will matter more than most analyses acknowledge. As the next section explores in detail, middle powers and developing nations are not passive objects of U.S.-China competition but active agents with their own interests and strategies. Their decisions about technology standards, supply chain configurations, infrastructure investments, and diplomatic alignments will shape the competition's trajectory and outcome. Neither Washington nor Beijing can simply impose its preferred order on a fragmented multipolar world.

Historical precedent offers ambiguous guidance. As the following section on historical lessons explores, great power competitions have ended in multiple ways: through the hegemon's victory, the challenger's triumph, mutual accommodation, catastrophic conflict, or the challenger's internal collapse. Each historical case involved unique circumstances that limit direct applicability to the contemporary U.S.-China competition. The presence of nuclear weapons, the degree of economic interdependence, the speed of technological change, and the multipolar distribution of power all distinguish the current competition from historical precedents.

Perhaps most fundamentally, **the competition's outcome remains uncertain because neither side has clearly defined what "victory" would look like**. Does the United States seek to prevent China from becoming the world's largest economy, to maintain technological leadership in specific domains, to preserve a network of democratic alliances, or simply to ensure that China cannot impose its will through coercion? Does China aim to displace American global leadership entirely, to establish regional hegemony in Asia, to achieve security against perceived encirclement, or to gain recognition as a great power with a legitimate sphere of influence?

The absence of clearly articulated strategic end states—what analyst Ryan Hass characterized in 2024 discussions as the need for "clear ends that we're trying to achieve" in U.S.-China relations—means the competition could stabilize at various equilibrium points or escalate in unforeseen directions.[20] The November 2025 trade agreement, extending tariff suspensions and rare earth control freezes for one year, illustrates that both sides recognize the value of avoiding worst-case scenarios even when they cannot agree on a positive vision for coexistence.[21]

The Stakes for the Global Order

The outcome of the U.S.-China competition will determine not just the relative power of two nations but the fundamental character of the international system for decades to come. Four dimensions of the global order hang in the balance.

First, the future of economic globalization is at stake. The post-1945 international economic order, built on the principles of comparative advantage, multilateral institutions, and deepening interdependence, is fracturing under the weight of geoeconomic competition. Brookings Institution scholars Joshua Meltzer and Margaret Pearson explained in their January 2025 analysis: "Chinese overcapacity joins a range of other issues in the U.S.-China trade space, highlighting overarching concerns with Chinese mercantilist behavior. The United States also needs to lead the development of a renewed international rules-based trading system that is fit for purpose in a world where China—the world's largest exporter—pursues mercantilist trade policies."[22]

The proliferation of export controls, investment screening mechanisms, supply chain reshoring initiatives, and "friend-shoring" strategies signals a shift from efficiency-maximizing globalization toward resilience-focused regionalization. While complete decoupling remains economically irrational given the depth of U.S.-China interdependence—bilateral trade amounting to hundreds of billions of dollars annually even after tariff escalations—selective decoupling in strategic sectors creates a pattern of "fragmented globalization." This hybrid model imposes significant costs: duplicative research and development, foregone economies of scale, misallocated resources, and reduced innovation from smaller networks.

For developing nations dependent on export-led growth and global supply chains, fragmented globalization threatens the pathway to prosperity that East Asian economies successfully traveled in previous decades. As Chapter 12 documented, countries from India to Brazil to Indonesia find themselves squeezed between Chinese overcapacity flooding their markets and pressure to align with one economic bloc or another.

Second, the efficacy of international institutions faces an existential test. The Center for Strategic and International Studies documented in October 2024 that "China's strategic positioning and substantial investments in multilateral bodies have allowed it to exert considerable influence, particularly within the United Nations system. China's approach includes placing its citizens in key leadership positions, increasing staffing, and boosting unearmarked financial contributions to multilateral institutions."[23] The report found that "In 2021, Chinese nationals led 4 of the 15 major UN specialized agencies," including the Food and Agriculture Organization, the International Civil Aviation Organization, the International Telecommunication Union, and the United Nations Industrial Development Organization.[24]

The United States remains the largest financial contributor to most international organizations but has seen relative decline in influence. The intensification of U.S.-China rivalry makes multilateral institutions simultaneously more important as venues for managing competition and less capable of fulfilling that function. When the two most powerful states view each other as adversaries rather than stakeholders in a shared system, the institutions that depend on their cooperation—from the World Trade Organization to nuclear non-proliferation regimes to climate governance—struggle to function effectively.

Third, technology governance for emerging capabilities hangs in the balance. The race for AI supremacy, quantum computing, biotechnology, and other frontier technologies occurs in a near-vacuum of international governance. Unlike nuclear weapons, which developed within a bipolar competition that eventually produced arms control frameworks, emerging technologies develop in a multipolar environment with weak multilateral institutions and strong first-mover incentives.

China and the United States pursue technological advantage through national strategies—Beijing's "indigenous and controllable" technology doctrine versus Washington's export control regime—rather than international frameworks that might establish safety standards, ethical guardrails, or crisis management protocols. The absence of governance mechanisms creates risks of autonomous weapons systems operating without meaningful human control, synthetic biology applications that could generate pandemic-level threats, or AI systems deployed without adequate testing—all racing ahead of regulatory capacity.

Establishing technology governance frameworks requires the United States and China to cooperate even as they compete. Yet the zero-sum logic that dominates the bilateral relationship makes such cooperation exceedingly difficult. The Congressional Research Service noted in 2025 that technology policy remains fragmented across multiple agencies, creating coordination challenges that complicate efforts to develop coherent international frameworks.[25]

Fourth, fundamental questions about sovereignty, human rights, and legitimate governance remain unresolved. The U.S.-China competition is not merely a struggle for power but a contest between different visions of how societies should be organized and how power should be exercised. China's authoritarian efficiency model—combining economic dynamism with political control, technological sophistication with surveillance capacity, and international engagement with resistance to domestic political liberalization—offers an alternative to democratic capitalism that appeals to many authoritarian and semi-authoritarian regimes.

The erosion of the "end of history" narrative that assumed democratic capitalism's inevitable triumph means the ideological dimension of U.S.-China competition matters more than many realist analyses acknowledge. China's provision of surveillance technology, digital infrastructure, and development finance without political conditionality creates an alternative pathway for governments that prioritize regime security over political pluralism. The question is not whether China will export its political model wholesale—Beijing shows little interest in ideological evangelism—but whether the international system will continue to embody liberal norms regarding human rights, transparency, and accountable governance, or whether these will become merely one option among many.

The Role of Middle Powers and the Developing World

Perhaps the most consequential yet underappreciated dimension of the U.S.-China competition is the agency exercised by states that are neither Washington nor Beijing. The choices made by middle powers and developing nations will shape the competition's trajectory and outcome as much as decisions in the White House or Zhongnanhai.

Middle powers are not passive objects to be claimed by one side or the other but active agents pursuing their own interests. National Bureau of Asian Research scholars analyzing this dynamic in 2025 found that "regional middle powers retain considerable agency to mold their own paths and that of the broader strategic environment, including developing options to mitigate any fallout from the Sino-U.S. rivalry."[26] Countries like Australia, Japan, South Korea, India, Indonesia, Germany, and Brazil possess sufficient economic weight, technological capacity, or strategic location to shape regional and sometimes global outcomes.

These middle powers face a delicate balancing act. Most maintain deep economic ties with China—often as their largest trading partner—while depending on the United States for security guarantees or technology access. Rather than choosing sides definitively, most pursue strategies of "strategic ambiguity" or "active alignment" that preserve flexibility while hedging against worst-case scenarios.[27]

Indonesia provides a particularly instructive case study. As the Harvard Belfer Center's November 2025 analysis argued, Jakarta can "convert its passive assets—geography, resources, economic potential, and diplomatic leadership—into an active alignment posture" that shapes rather than merely reacts to U.S.-China competition.[27] Rather than treating great power competition as a fixed constraint, middle powers can use multilateral forums, coalition-building among themselves, and strategic economic choices to create space for maneuver. The proliferation of middle power groupings—the G15, G33, various "coalitions of the willing"—reflects attempts to create collective bargaining power.[28]

The Global South's response to U.S.-China competition will be decisive for the international system's future character. Developing nations collectively represent more than half of global population, a growing share of economic output, and crucial votes in international institutions. Their alignment choices, technology adoption decisions, and economic partnerships will determine whether the international system fragments into rival blocs or maintains some degree of integration despite great power competition.

China's engagement with the Global South through the Belt and Road Initiative, infrastructure financing, technology provision, and diplomatic support in multilateral forums has yielded significant influence. Beijing positions itself as a champion of developing countries' interests against Western domination, with mixed results but genuine appeal in many regions. As Chapter 19 documented, China's "no strings attached" approach to development finance—ignoring governance concerns that accompany Western aid—attracts governments prioritizing regime security and infrastructure development.

Yet Chinese engagement also generates backlash. Belt and Road debt burdens, environmental degradation, labor disputes, and perceived neocolonial attitudes create friction. The flood of Chinese manufactured goods documented in Chapter 10—with overcapacity seeking external markets—threatens nascent industrialization efforts in countries from Brazil to India to Indonesia, prompting defensive tariffs and regulatory barriers.[29] The challenge for developing nations is leveraging competition between great powers to maximize their own development without becoming dependent on either.

The United States faces a particular challenge in Global South engagement. As a CSIS analysis noted: "The United States offers a compelling development model that is built on a transformational rather than transactional approach. This will require a prioritization of sectors where the United States either can offer a better approach or has a clear comparative advantage over what the PRC offers."[30] Yet American development assistance remains relatively modest, U.S. political dysfunction reduces its attractiveness as a model, and Washington's tendency to frame engagement primarily through the lens of competition with China can alienate countries seeking partnerships based on mutual interest rather than geopolitical alignment.

The role of middle powers and developing nations in shaping the U.S.-China competition underscores a fundamental reality: **the international system is neither unipolar nor bipolar but genuinely multipolar**. As a July 2025 analysis argued: "The discourse surrounding contemporary international relations has become dominated by the phrase 'great power competition,' yet this framing may fundamentally mischaracterize the nature of today's global order."[31] The interdependent, networked character of the global economy, the proliferation of consequential actors beyond great powers, and the inadequacy of Cold War analogies all suggest that the competition's outcome will be determined not by U.S.-China interactions alone but by the choices of hundreds of other actors pursuing their own visions of security and prosperity.

Historical Lessons: How Great Power Competitions Have Ended

History provides both wisdom and warning about great power competitions, though no historical case maps perfectly onto contemporary U.S.-China rivalry. Five historical patterns merit particular attention.

First, great power transitions have more often produced war than peaceful accommodation. Research examining great power transitions since 1500 finds that three-quarters featured destructive periods of warfare between the contestants.[28] The ancient competition between Athens and Sparta, analyzed by Thucydides and still studied for its strategic insights, ended in the Peloponnesian War—a devastating conflict that weakened both parties. The competition between Britain and Germany in the early twentieth century, despite extensive economic interdependence and dynastic connections, ended in the catastrophe of World War I—a war neither side wanted but both stumbled into through miscalculation, alliance commitments, and security dilemmas.

This historical pattern offers a sobering warning. When states perceive shifts in relative power moving decisively against them, they become more inclined to risk preemptive conflict than when they perceive a stable power status quo. If China perceives a narrowing window of opportunity before demographic decline and economic maturity constrain its options, or if the United States perceives Chinese capabilities approaching a point where deterrence becomes impossible, the risk of preemptive action increases dramatically.

Second, successful navigation of power transitions requires sustained leadership, clear communication, and institutional frameworks that can absorb shocks. The U.S.-Soviet Cold War, despite proxy conflicts and nuclear brinkmanship, ended peacefully in part because both sides maintained relatively stable perceptions of the power balance and developed crisis management protocols through hard-won experience. Regular summits, military-to-military communications, nuclear hotlines, and arms control negotiations created channels for managing competition and reducing miscalculation risks.

The U.S.-China relationship lacks comparable institutional depth. Military-to-military communications remain episodic, summit meetings yield temporary truces rather than durable frameworks, and crisis management mechanisms remain underdeveloped. The November 2025 trade agreement demonstrates that the two governments can negotiate temporary accommodations when domestic political imperatives align, but such tactical deals do not constitute strategic stability.[29]

Third, internal political dynamics often matter more than external military balance in determining competition outcomes. The Soviet Union's collapse resulted not from American military pressure but from internal contradictions—economic stagnation, political sclerosis, ideological exhaustion—that external competition exacerbated but did not cause.[37] Similarly, Britain's relative decline versus the United States in the early twentieth century reflected not military defeat but the unsustainability of imperial overstretch, economic exhaustion from two world wars, and the rise of new challengers.

This historical pattern suggests that China's demographic trajectory, debt burdens, and political model's adaptability matter more for the competition's outcome than relative defense spending or technology advantage at any given moment. Similarly, America's domestic political health, educational system quality, infrastructure investment, and social cohesion will determine whether it can sustain competitive effort across decades.

Fourth, alliance systems and the choices of third parties often prove decisive. Britain's victory over Napoleonic France resulted not from British power alone but from the coalition of European powers that Britain financed and coordinated.[38] The Concert of Europe that followed—though ultimately failing to prevent World War I—demonstrated how multilateral frameworks could manage great power competition when major powers agreed on basic rules and procedures.[39]

The contemporary U.S. alliance system—bilateral treaties with Japan, South Korea, Australia, the Philippines, and Thailand, multilateral frameworks like the Quad and AUKUS, and partnership arrangements extending across Europe and beyond—represents a significant American advantage that China cannot easily match.[40] Yet alliance effectiveness depends on U.S. credibility, policy consistency, and willingness to bear costs for collective defense. The Trump administration's transactional approach to alliances, questioning treaty commitments and demanding greater burden-sharing, raised doubts about American reliability that Beijing seeks to exploit.

Fifth, historical great power competitions have ended in varied ways—and outcomes thought impossible often prove achievable. The Cold War's peaceful conclusion—the Soviet Union's dissolution without direct U.S.-Soviet military conflict—defied predictions that bipolar competition must end in war. The Concert of Europe's establishment after the Napoleonic Wars created decades of relative peace despite continuing great power rivalry. Conversely, World War I began despite extensive economic interdependence and mutual recognition that war would be catastrophic, illustrating how structural pressures, alliance commitments, and miscalculation can override rational incentives for peace.

The lesson is not that any particular outcome is inevitable but that agency matters. Leadership choices, crisis management, institutional innovation, and recognition of mutual interests can channel competition away from catastrophic conflict—or fail to do so. As Alexander Vuving observed: "Peaceful Great Power transition outcomes require hard work and astute leadership."[41] The historical record offers hope that accommodation is possible but no guarantee that it will occur.

A Call for Strategic Clarity and Sustained Engagement

The U.S.-China competition will define the international system for decades to come. Neither containment aimed at China's collapse nor accommodation that ignores genuine conflicts of interest offers a viable path forward. What both nations require—and what the international community desperately needs—is strategic clarity about objectives and sustained engagement to manage competition below the threshold of conflict while preserving space for cooperation on issues of mutual concern.

Strategic clarity means defining what "success" looks like beyond competition for competition's sake. For the United States, this requires articulating whether the goal is preventing China from becoming the world's largest economy (neither feasible nor necessary for American security), maintaining technological leadership in all domains (increasingly difficult given China's scale and resources), or ensuring China cannot achieve regional hegemony through coercion while remaining open to Chinese development and prosperity achieved through fair competition.

For China, strategic clarity requires acknowledging that policies perceived as threatening—rapid military buildup, assertive territorial claims, economic coercion, technology theft—generate containment coalitions that undermine Chinese security more than they enhance it. Beijing's legitimate aspirations for security, prosperity, and international respect need not require displacing American power or dismantling the international institutions from which China has benefited enormously. As the RAND Corporation's 2018 authoritative analysis argued: "The growth of Chinese power is not something the United States can or should oppose per se, but rather seek to steer in a direction that reinforces existing institutions and norms."[30]

Sustained engagement means maintaining channels of communication even during periods of intense competition. The November 2025 agreement to suspend tariff escalations and rare earth export controls, combined with plans for presidential summits, demonstrates that both governments recognize the value of dialogue.[31] Yet engagement must extend beyond episodic crisis management to encompass regular consultation on military activities in the Western Pacific, coordination on global challenges from pandemic preparedness to climate change, and establishment of crisis management protocols that could prevent miscalculation from spiraling into conflict.

Brookings Institution analysts emphasized in January 2025 that sustainable U.S.-China policy requires "acting with purpose, maintaining focus, and imposing discipline" across the policy apparatus to avoid the incoherence that undermines long-term strategy.[32] The resumption of military-to-military communications represents progress, but these channels have not been tested under crisis conditions, protocols remain underdeveloped compared to Cold War U.S.-Soviet arrangements, and political support for sustained engagement fluctuates with domestic political winds in both countries.

Strategic clarity and sustained engagement require both countries to address domestic political obstacles to coherent long-term strategy. In the United States, partisan polarization, short-term electoral incentives, and domestic political paralysis undermine the sustained multi-decade effort that successful competition requires. In China, the concentration of authority that enables rapid policy implementation also creates risks of miscalculation when information flows are constrained and dissenting views suppressed.

The international community has a vital stake in ensuring that U.S.-China competition does not fracture the global order. Middle powers must resist pressure to choose sides definitively, instead using their collective weight to create space for continued integration in areas where cooperation benefits all parties. International institutions, despite their limitations, provide venues where competition can be channeled through rules and procedures rather than coercion and force.

The challenge facing the international system is neither to eliminate U.S.-China competition—which reflects genuine differences of interest and values—nor to accept its inevitability that it must produce a new Cold War or worse. The challenge is to construct frameworks, establish norms, and maintain channels of communication that allow competition to coexist with cooperation, that permit rivalry while avoiding catastrophe, and that preserve the possibility of accommodation as circumstances change.

Conclusion: The Choice Ahead

Standing at the end of 2025, with trade wars temporarily suspended, technology competitions intensifying, Taiwan tensions simmering, and biotech battles looming, the trajectory of U.S.-China relations remains radically uncertain. The two nations could stumble into a new Cold War characterized by comprehensive antagonism and parallel technological ecosystems. They could manage competition through guardrails, crisis management protocols, and acceptance of spheres of influence. They could escalate toward military conflict over Taiwan or another flashpoint. Or they could, through skillful diplomacy and recognition of mutual interests, establish a modus vivendi that allows peaceful coexistence despite fundamental differences.

The outcome depends on choices not yet made—by leaders in Washington and Beijing, by middle powers navigating between the two giants, by business leaders deciding where to invest, by scientists choosing whether to collaborate, by citizens in democracies deciding what values to prioritize. History offers guidance but not determinism. The competition that defines our century remains a work in progress, its conclusion yet to be written.

What is certain is that the stakes could scarcely be higher. The decisions made in the coming years will shape not just the relative power of the United States and China but the future of the global economy, the viability of international institutions, the governance of transformative technologies, and the possibility of maintaining peace in an era of rapid technological change and shifting power dynamics. The competition that began as a trade dispute has evolved into something far more consequential—a struggle whose outcome will echo through the twenty-first century and beyond.

The path forward requires wisdom, restraint, and strategic vision from leaders who understand that while competition may be inevitable, catastrophe is not. It requires sustained engagement between adversaries who recognize that even as they compete for advantage, they share responsibility for preventing competition from consuming the international order that has, for all its flaws, provided unprecedented prosperity and relative peace for much of humanity. And it requires the active engagement of middle powers, international institutions, and global civil society in shaping a multipolar world where power is distributed, rules constrain coercion, and competition remains bounded by recognition of common humanity.

The U.S.-China rivalry will define our century. Whether it destroys the international order or spurs its evolution into something more resilient and legitimate depends on choices being made now and in the years immediately ahead. This is the competition that matters—and the stakes demand nothing less than our most serious attention, our clearest thinking, and our sustained commitment to avoiding the catastrophes that have ended previous great power competitions. The question is not whether the United States and China will compete—that competition is already underway and likely to continue for decades. The question is whether that competition can be managed, whether it can coexist with cooperation on issues of mutual concern, and whether it can be prevented from culminating in the conflicts that have so often ended great power rivalries in the past.

History will judge us not by who won or lost this competition but by whether we had the wisdom to prevent it from consuming us all.

Endnotes

[1] UCLA Anderson School of Management, "2025 US-China Annual Economic Report," July 10, 2025, https://www.anderson.ucla.edu/about/centers/ucla-anderson-forecast/projects-and-partnerships/cathay-bank/2025-us-china-annual-economic-report; U.S.-China Economic and Security Review Commission, *2025 Annual Report to Congress* (Washington, DC: USCC, November 2025), https://www.uscc.gov/annual-report/2025-annual-report-congress.

[2] UCLA Anderson School of Management, "2025 US-China Annual Economic Report."

[3] Ibid.

[4] U.S.-China Economic and Security Review Commission, *2025 Annual Report to Congress*.

[5] White House, "Fact Sheet: President Donald J. Trump Strikes Deal on Economic and Trade Relations with China," November 1, 2025, https://www.whitehouse.gov/fact-sheets/2025/11/fact-sheet-president-donald-j-trump-strikes-deal-on-economic-and-trade-relations-with-china/.

[6] Ibid.

[7] U.S.-China Economic and Security Review Commission, *2025 Executive Summary* (Washington, DC: USCC, November 2025), https://www.uscc.gov/sites/default/files/2025-11/2025_Executive_Summary.pdf.

[8] Brookings Institution, Joshua P. Meltzer and Margaret M. Pearson, "How the US Should Address Chinese Overcapacity and Its Impact on International Trade," January 13, 2025, https://www.brookings.edu/articles/how-the-us-should-address-chinese-overcapacity-and-its-impact-on-international-trade/.

[9] UCLA Anderson School of Management, "2025 US-China Annual Economic Report."

[10] Ibid.

[11] Be Horizon, "2025 USCC Annual Report: China Shock 2.0 & The Axis of Autocracy," November 2025, https://behorizon.org/2025-uscc-annual-report-to-congress/.

[12] White House, "Fact Sheet: President Donald J. Trump Strikes Deal on Economic and Trade Relations with China."

[13] U.S.-China Economic and Security Review Commission, *2025 Executive Summary*.

[14] Brookings Institution, Ryan Hass, "Can Trump Seize the Moment on China?" January 28, 2025, https://www.brookings.edu/articles/can-trump-seize-the-moment-on-china/.

[15] American National Standards Institute, "U.S.-China Economic Security Review Commission Releases 2025 Report to Congress," November 20, 2025, https://www.ansi.org/standards-news/all-news/11-20-25-us-china-economic-security-review-commission-releases-2025-report-to-congress.

[16] Be Horizon, "2025 USCC Annual Report: China Shock 2.0 & The Axis of Autocracy."

[17] UCLA Anderson School of Management, "2025 US-China Annual Economic Report."

[18] Ibid.

[19] Brookings Institution, Ryan Hass, "Can Trump Seize the Moment on China?"

[20] Council on Foreign Relations, "The Future of U.S.-China Relations," January 30, 2024, https://www.cfr.org/event/future-us-china-relations-0.

[21] White House, "Fact Sheet: President Donald J. Trump Strikes Deal on Economic and Trade Relations with China."

[22] Brookings Institution, Joshua P. Meltzer and Margaret M. Pearson, "How the US Should Address Chinese Overcapacity and Its Impact on International Trade."

[23] Center for Strategic and International Studies, "Great Power Competition in the Multilateral System," October 23, 2024, https://www.csis.org/analysis/great-power-competition-multilateral-system.

[24] Ibid.

[25] Congressional Research Service, "U.S.-China Trade Relations," Congress.gov, 2025, https://www.congress.gov/crs-product/IF11284.

[26] National Bureau of Asian Research, "Caught in the Middle? Middle Powers amid U.S.-China Competition," 2025, https://www.nbr.org/publication/caught-in-the-middle-middle-powers-amid-u-s-china-competition/.

[27] Harvard Belfer Center for Science and International Affairs, Muhamad Chatib Basri and Evan Laksmana, "Active Alignment: How Indonesia Can Shape the U.S.-China Strategic Competition," November 20, 2025, https://www.belfercenter.org/research-analysis/active-alignment-how-indonesia-can-shape-us-china-strategic-competition.

[28] Joint Air Power Competence Centre, "The New Era of Great Power Competition," July 4, 2022, https://www.japcc.org/essays/the-new-era-of-great-power-competition/.

[29] White House, "Fact Sheet: President Donald J. Trump Strikes Deal on Economic and Trade Relations with China."

[30] RAND Corporation, Michael J. Mazarr, Timothy R. Heath, and Astrid Stuth Cevallos, *China and the International Order*, RR-2423-OSD (Santa Monica, CA: RAND Corporation, May 2018), https://www.rand.org/pubs/research_reports/RR2423.html.

[31] White House, "Fact Sheet: President Donald J. Trump Strikes Deal on Economic and Trade Relations with China."

[32] Brookings Institution, Ryan Hass, "Can Trump Seize the Moment on China?"

Appendices

Appendix A: Timeline of U.S.-China Trade and Technology Restrictions (2018-2025)

2018: The Opening Salvos

March-April 2018

- **March 22**: President Trump announces Section 232 tariffs on steel (25%) and aluminum (10%) from China and other countries, citing national security concerns
- **April**: USTR concludes Section 301 investigation finding China engaged in forced technology transfer, cyber-enabled theft of IP, discriminatory licensing practices, and state-funded acquisitions of U.S. assets

July-September 2018

- **July 6**: First round of Section 301 tariffs implemented - 25% on $34 billion of Chinese goods (List 1)
- **August 23**: Second round - 25% on additional $16 billion (List 2)
- **September 24**: Third round - 10% on $200 billion of Chinese goods (List 3)
- China retaliates with tariffs on $110 billion of U.S. exports

October 2018

- U.S. begins encouraging Netherlands to restrict ASML's extreme ultraviolet (EUV) lithography tool sales to China's SMIC

2019: Escalation and Technology Focus

May 2019

- Section 301 List 3 tariffs increased from 10% to 25%
- Huawei added to U.S. Entity List, restricting its access to American technology

September 2019

- Fourth round of tariffs on remaining Chinese imports
- Average U.S. tariff rate on Chinese goods reaches approximately 19%

2020: Phase One Agreement

January 15, 2020

- U.S.-China Phase One Trade Agreement signed
- China commits to purchasing $200 billion in additional U.S. goods and services over two years
- Agreement addresses some IP protection issues but leaves major structural concerns unresolved

2021-2022: Biden Administration Continuation

2021

- Biden administration maintains Trump-era tariffs
- Focus shifts increasingly toward technology and supply chain resilience

August 2022

- Nancy Pelosi visits Taiwan, triggering major PLA military exercises
- China conducts first complete encirclement of Taiwan since 1995-96 crisis

October 7, 2022

- Landmark U.S. semiconductor export controls announced
- Restrictions on advanced AI chips (initially targeting Nvidia A100/H100)
- Controls on chipmaking equipment, including advanced lithography tools
- Foreign Direct Product Rule (FDPR) applied to restrict global supply chains
- Netherlands and Japan agree to implement similar controls

2023: Expanding Controls

January 2023

- Netherlands and Japan formally join U.S. export control regime
- Dutch government restricts ASML's most advanced DUV immersion systems

May 2024

- Biden administration announces review results of Section 301 tariffs
- Maintains most existing tariffs ($360 billion worth)
- Increases tariffs on specific sectors:
    - Electric vehicles: quadrupled to 100%
    - Steel and aluminum: tripled
    - Semiconductors: doubled to 50%
    - Solar cells, batteries, critical minerals: significantly increased

October 17, 2023

- Additional semiconductor controls targeting older ASML lithography equipment
- Expansion to capture Twinscan 19XX series systems
- Further restrictions on SMIC and Chinese foundries

2024: Year of Transition

January 2024

- Chinese companies stockpile ASML DUV systems ahead of tightened restrictions
- ASML China sales reach 49% of total revenue in Q2 2024

Joint Sword Exercises

- **May 23-24, 2024**: Joint Sword-2024A following President Lai's inauguration
- **October 14, 2024**: Joint Sword-2024B with record 153 PLA aircraft sorties
- Exercises demonstrate increasing operational tempo and complexity

December 2024

- Large-scale PLA naval maneuvers around Taiwan and First Island Chain
- Chinese leadership acknowledges domestic "involution" (��) problem in manufacturing

2025: Trump 2.0 and Maximum Pressure

January 20, 2025

- Trump inaugurated for second term
- DeepSeek R1 AI model released, achieving performance comparable to OpenAI's ChatGPT-4 at fraction of cost and computing power

February 1-March 31, 2025

- **February 1**: Trump declares national emergency over fentanyl, announces 10% tariff on all Chinese imports
- **February**: China retaliates with 15% tariffs on coal and LNG, 10% on oil and agricultural machinery
- **March 12**: U.S. raises fentanyl tariff to 20%
- **March**: China expands retaliatory tariffs to 10-15% on select U.S. agricultural products

April 2, 2025: "Liberation Day"

- Trump announces "reciprocal tariffs" policy in national emergency declaration
- Additional 34% tariff on Chinese imports, citing China's "67% trade barriers"
- Universal 10% baseline tariff on all imports takes effect April 5
- **April 2-4**: Tariff escalation spiral
    - U.S. effective tariff rate reaches 54% (10% + 20% + 34% stacked)
    - China retaliates, escalating to 125% on U.S. goods
    - U.S. counter-retaliates, reaching 145% peak on Chinese goods
- **April 1-2**: PLA conducts "Strait Thunder-2025A" exercises
    - 76 PLA aircraft sorties, 37 crossing median line
    - 15 naval vessels and 4 Coast Guard ships
    - Shandong carrier group operates within 24 nautical miles of Taiwan

May 2025: Geneva Negotiations

- **May 12-14**: 90-day tariff truce negotiated in Geneva
- Both sides reduce to 10% reciprocal tariffs
- **Effective rates post-truce**:
    - U.S. on China: 30% (10% baseline + 20% fentanyl)

    - China on U.S.: 10%
- China agrees to:
    - Resume U.S. agricultural purchases
    - Suspend October 2025 rare earth export controls (temporarily)
    - Lift retaliatory non-tariff measures

August 2025

- 90-day truce extended through November 10, 2025
- Nvidia reaches revenue-sharing licensing agreement for H20 chip exports to China
- U.S. closes de minimis exemption (previously $800 threshold) on August 29

October 2025: Critical Minerals Flashpoint

- **October 9**: China announces expanded export controls on 12 rare earth elements and refining equipment
    - Covers holmium, thulium, ytterbium, and other heavy rare earths
    - Includes restrictions on products containing >0.1% Chinese rare earth content
    - Effective December 1, 2025
- **October 10**: Trump threatens 100% additional tariff on Chinese goods
- **October 20**: U.S.-Australia Critical Minerals Framework Agreement signed
    - $8.5 billion project pipeline
    - $1 billion bilateral investment commitment within 6 months
    - Alcoa gallium recovery and Arafura Nolans rare earth projects prioritized
- **October 30**: Trump-Xi meeting in South Korea
    - U.S. agrees to reduce fentanyl tariff from 20% to 10%
    - China commits to soybean purchases and rare earth access
    - Suspends 100% tariff threat

November 2025

- **November 5**: China bans foreign AI chips (including Nvidia) in state-funded data centers
- **November 10**: Extended truce continues with modified terms
    - U.S. overall tariff: approximately 29.3% effective rate
    - China suspends rare earth export controls under bilateral agreement
    - Both sides commit to continued negotiations

December 2025

- Negotiations ongoing as of publication
- Average U.S. tariff rate on Chinese goods: 29.3% (down from 37.1% pre-November agreement)
- China's 2024 trade surplus: $992.2 billion (record high)
- U.S.-China bilateral trade deficit: $295.4 billion (2024)

Technology Export Control Timeline

2022-2025 Key Semiconductor Restrictions:

- **October 2022**: Initial advanced computing and semiconductor controls
- **January 2023**: Allied coordination (Netherlands, Japan)
- **October 2023**: Expanded controls on older equipment
- **December 2024**: Additional restrictions announced
- **January 2025**: AI Diffusion Rule briefly introduced, then rescinded
- **November 2025**: China's counter-move banning foreign AI chips in state facilities

Estimated Cumulative Economic Impact

U.S. Tariff Revenue (2018-2025): Approximately $240 billion collected **Chinese Retaliatory Impact on U.S. Exports**: ~40% decline in affected sectors **Semiconductor Industry Impact**:

- ASML China revenue dropped from 49% (Q2 2024) to expected 20% (2025)
- Nvidia estimates $5-10 billion annual revenue impact from China restrictions
- Commerce Secretary Lutnick testimony: Huawei limited to 200,000 AI chips in 2025

Appendix B: Key Export Control Regulations and Entity Lists

Section 301: Trade Act of 1974 (19 U.S.C. §2411)

Authority: Allows President to take action against foreign trade practices that are unjustifiable or unreasonable

Key China Applications:

- July 2018: Initial $34 billion in tariffs (25% rate)
- September 2018: Expanded to $250 billion total
- August 2019: Further expansion, reaching $370 billion in Chinese imports
- May 2024: Targeted increases on EVs (100%), semiconductors (50%), steel/aluminum (tripled)

Current Status (December 2025): Approximately $360 billion of Chinese imports subject to Section 301 tariffs ranging from 7.5% to 100%

Section 232: Trade Expansion Act of 1962

Authority: Allows tariffs on imports threatening national security

China Applications:

- 2018: Steel (25%) and aluminum (10%) tariffs
- March 2025: Rates increased to 50%
- April 2025: 25% tariff on automobiles and auto parts
- July 2025: 50% tariff on semi-finished copper products

Export Administration Regulations (EAR)

Administering Agency: U.S. Department of Commerce, Bureau of Industry and Security (BIS)

Key Controls on China:

Advanced Computing and Semiconductors (October 7, 2022)

Controlled Items:

1. Advanced integrated circuits (AI accelerators):
    - Performance threshold: >600 TOPS (tera operations per second) for 8-bit operations
    - Initially targeted Nvidia A100, H100, AMD MI250
2. Semiconductor manufacturing equipment:
    - Extreme Ultraviolet (EUV) lithography systems
    - Advanced Deep Ultraviolet (DUV) immersion lithography (post-2023)
    - Specific deposition, etching, and metrology tools

3. Supercomputing end-uses:
    - Prohibited exports to Chinese entities for military applications
    - Expanded Entity List for PRC companies

October 2023 Expansion

Additional Equipment Restricted:

- ASML Twinscan NXT:1970i, NXT:1980i systems
- Twinscan 19XX series (used by TSMC for 7nm critical layers)
- Advanced metrology and inspection tools
- Certain software and technical data

December 2024 Update

Further Restrictions:

- Additional fab locations in China added
- Expanded software controls
- Enhanced end-user verification requirements
- Effective December 31, 2024

Entity List

Purpose: Identifies foreign entities subject to specific license requirements for export of specified items

Major Chinese Entities Added (2018-2025):

Telecommunications:

- Huawei Technologies (May 2019)
- ZTE Corporation (2018, restrictions modified 2020)
- Hikvision (2019)

Semiconductors:

- Semiconductor Manufacturing International Corporation - SMIC (December 2020)

- Yangtze Memory Technologies Corporation - YMTC (December 2022)
- ChangXin Memory Technologies - CXMT (2022)

AI and Surveillance:

- SenseTime (2021)
- Megvii Technology (2019)
- CloudWalk Technology (2019)
- Over 20 additional AI/surveillance companies

Supercomputing Centers:

- 7 supercomputing entities (2021)
- National Supercomputing Centers in Wuxi, Jinan, Guangzhou, Shenzhen

Total Entities: Over 600 Chinese entities on Entity List as of December 2025

Foreign Direct Product Rule (FDPR)

Definition: Controls foreign-made items incorporating or produced with U.S. technology/software

China-Specific Applications:

Huawei FDPR (2020):

- Applies to products using U.S. technology designed for or destined to Huawei
- Restricts third-country suppliers from providing advanced chips

Semiconductor FDPR (2022):

- Applies globally to advanced node semiconductors (currently ≤16nm FinFET or ≤14nm)
- Includes equipment and production items
- Captures TSMC, Samsung, other non-U.S. fabs supplying China

Allied Export Controls

Netherlands

Implementing Agency: Ministry of Foreign Affairs

Key Restrictions (2023-2025):

- EUV lithography systems (ASML): Prohibited to China since 2019
- Advanced DUV immersion systems (ASML NXT:2000i series): Restricted 2023
- Additional DUV models: Restrictions expanded 2024

ASML Impact:

- China revenue: 29% (2023) → 49% (Q2 2024) → 20% expected (2025)
- Stockpiling effect: Chinese customers ordered ahead of restrictions

Japan

Implementing Agency: Ministry of Economy, Trade and Industry (METI)

Key Restrictions (2023):

- 23 types of semiconductor manufacturing equipment
- Includes deposition, etching, lithography peripherals
- Applied to shipments to China

Major Affected Companies:

- Tokyo Electron Ltd
- Nikon Corporation
- Screen Holdings
- Kokusai Electric

Outbound Investment Restrictions

Executive Order 14105 (August 9, 2023): "Addressing United States Investments in Certain National Security Technologies and Products in Countries of Concern"

Covered National Security Technologies:

1. **Semiconductors and microelectronics**:
    - Advanced integrated circuits
    - Supercomputers
    - Semiconductor manufacturing equipment
2. **Quantum information technologies**:
    - Quantum computers
    - Quantum sensing platforms
    - Quantum networks/communications
3. **Artificial Intelligence**:
    - AI systems designed for military/surveillance end uses
    - Large-scale AI training runs

Transactions Covered:

- Acquisitions of equity interests
- Greenfield investments
- Joint ventures
- Certain debt financing arrangements

Implementation: Treasury Department Final Rule expected 2025-2026

Committee on Foreign Investment in the United States (CFIUS)

Enhanced Scrutiny (2018-present):

- Foreign Investment Risk Review Modernization Act (FIRRMA) of 2018
- Expanded jurisdiction over "critical technologies"
- Mandatory declarations for certain Chinese investments

China Transaction Statistics:

- **2017**: 102 Chinese transactions reviewed
- **2022**: 198 transactions (highest on record)
- **2024**: Approximately 165 transactions
- **Rejection/Abandonment Rate**: 15-20% involving Chinese acquirers

Deemed Export Controls

Definition: Transfer of controlled technology to foreign nationals within the United States treated as export to person's country(ies) of nationality

Enhanced Review for Chinese Nationals:

- Research in sensitive technologies
- Access to export-controlled materials/facilities
- University-based fundamental research (case-by-case)

Impact on Academia:

- Increased visa scrutiny for Chinese STEM students
- Export control compliance programs at major research universities
- Restrictions on participation in certain federally-funded research

License Exception Strategic Trade Authorization (STA)

Purpose: Facilitates exports to 42 trusted countries

China Status: NOT eligible for STA

- Requires individual licenses for most controlled items
- Limited exceptions for low-level consumer goods
- Processing times: 60-90 days average

Temporary General License (TGL)

Nvidia Special Cases (2022-2025):

- Initial denials for A100, H100 exports to China
- Nvidia develops "China-compliant" variants:
    - A800 (2022): Below performance thresholds
    - H800 (2023): Restricted interconnect speeds
    - H20 (2024): Further performance limitations
- August 2025: Revenue-sharing license model negotiated

Current Status: Limited exports allowed under specific licensing arrangements; further restrictions anticipated

Huawei-Specific Controls

May 2019: Initial Entity List placement

May 2020: FDPR expansion ("Huawei FDPR")

- Applied to products using U.S. technology designed for or sold to Huawei
- Effectively blocked advanced chip supplies

August 2020: Further tightening

- Non-U.S. subsidiaries added
- 38 additional Huawei affiliates listed

Impact:

- Smartphone market share: 20% (2019) → 4% (2021)
- Comeback: 7nm Kirin 9000S chip in Mate 60 Pro (2023) using SMIC manufacturing
- Demonstrates limits of export controls in globalized supply chains

BIOSECURE Act (Pending as of December 2025)

Status: Passed Senate as NDAA amendment (October 10, 2025), pending House-Senate reconciliation

Key Provisions:

Prohibited Actions:

- Federal agencies cannot contract with "biotechnology companies of concern"
- Prohibition extends to contractors using such companies' equipment/services
- Applies to loans, grants, and procurement

Companies of Concern Definition:

1. **Entities on DoD 1260H List**: Chinese military companies operating in U.S.

    - No grandfathering period
    - Effective 60 days after Federal Acquisition Regulation revision
2. **Additional Designated Entities**:
    - Subject to foreign adversary control
    - Involved in biotech equipment/services
    - Pose national security risk
    - 5-year phase-out period for existing contracts

Originally Named Entities (2024 version, names removed in 2025 revision):

- WuXi AppTec
- WuXi Biologics
- BGI Group
- MGI Tech
- Complete Genomics

Biotechnology Equipment and Services Defined:

- Genetic sequencers
- Mass spectrometry systems
- PCR machines (removed in 2025 revision)
- Data storage/transmission related to biological materials
- Genomic analysis services
- Contract development and manufacturing services

Estimated Industry Impact:

- Over 100 U.S. pharmaceutical companies have relationships with WuXi entities
- Chinese CDMOs account for approximately 30% of global biomanufacturing capacity
- Transition period concerns: drug shortages, development delays

Implementation Timeline (if enacted):

- 1260H entities: 60 days post-regulation
- Other designated entities: Up to 2 years for designation + 5-year phase-out
- OMB must publish list within 1 year of enactment

Emerging and Foundational Technologies

2018 Export Control Reform Act (ECRA): Mandates Commerce Department identify emerging and foundational technologies essential to national security

Technologies Under Review:

1. Artificial Intelligence and Machine Learning
2. Quantum Information Sciences
3. Advanced Materials
4. Biotechnology
5. Additive Manufacturing (3D printing)
6. Hypersonics
7. Advanced Robotics

Current Status: Ongoing review process; additional controls expected 2026-2027

Compliance and Enforcement Statistics

BIS Enforcement Actions (2018-2025):

- **Total Violations**: Over 350 administrative actions involving China
- **Major Penalties**:
  - ZTE: $1.19 billion (2017-2018, violating Iran sanctions)
  - Huawei: Charges including conspiracy to steal trade secrets (ongoing)
  - Multiple Chinese universities: Entity List placement for military connections

Criminal Prosecutions:

- **2018-2024**: Over 150 cases involving Chinese defendants for export control violations
- **Common Charges**: Conspiracy, smuggling, theft of trade secrets
- **Significant Case**: Huawei CFO Meng Wanzhou (arrested 2018, released 2021)

Industry Compliance Costs:

- Large companies: $10-50 million annually for export compliance programs
- Small-medium companies: $100,000-$2 million annually
- Training, licensing applications, IT systems, legal counsel

Appendix C: Critical Minerals - Production, Processing, and Consumption Data

Global Rare Earth Element (REE) Production (2024)

Total Global Mine Production: 390,000 metric tons REO equivalent

Country	Production (MT REO)	% of World Production	Primary Deposits
China	270,000	69.2%	Bayan Obo (Inner Mongolia), Southern ionic-adsorption deposits
United States	45,000	11.5%	Mountain Pass (California)
Myanmar (Burma)	31,000	7.9%	Kachin State (near China border)
Australia	24,000	6.2%	Mount Weld, Browns Range, Nolans Bore
Thailand	13,000	3.3%	Various deposits
Nigeria	7,000	1.8%	Emerging production
Vietnam	~5,000	~1.3%	Various deposits
India	~3,000	~0.8%	Beach sands, monazite

Source: U.S. Geological Survey Mineral Commodity Summaries (January 2025); Benchmark Mineral Intelligence

REE Processing and Refining Capacity (2025)

Global Separation and Refining:

- **China**: ~90% of global capacity (estimated 350,000 MT/year)
- **Malaysia**: ~5% (primarily Lynas Rare Earths facility: 5,000-6,000 MT NdPr oxide/year)
- **Rest of World**: ~5% (emerging capacity)

Key Non-Chinese Processors:

Company	Location	Capacity (MT/year)	Products	Status
Lynas Rare Earths	Kuantan, Malaysia	5,000-6,000 NdPr	Light & Heavy RE	Operating
Lynas (expansion)	Texas, USA	Planned 2,500	Heavy RE separation	Under construction
MP Materials	Mountain Pass, CA	45,000 (concentrate)	Bastnaesite concentrate	Operating
MP Materials	Fort Worth, TX	1,000 (magnets)	NdFeB magnets	Commissioning
Iluka Resources	Eneabba, Australia	17,500	Integrated refinery	Construction (2025-26)
Arafura Resources	Nolans, NT Australia	4,440 NdPr	NdPr oxide	Pre-construction
Energy Fuels	White Mesa, UT	Small scale	Mixed RE carbonates	Operating
USA Rare Earth	Oklahoma	TBD	Processing facility	Planning

Heavy Rare Earth Elements (HREE) Processing:

- China controls >95% of HREE separation capacity
- Lynas achieved first commercial dysprosium oxide production outside China (May 2025)
- Major gap in Western supply chains for Dy, Tb, Ho, Er, Tm, Yb, Lu

Rare Earth Magnet Production (2025)

Global NdFeB (Neodymium-Iron-Boron) Permanent Magnets:

Country	Annual Production (MT)	% of Global	Key Producers
China	300,000+	~94%	Zhongke Sanhuan, JL MAG, Ningbo Yunsheng
Japan	~10,000	~3%	Shin-Etsu Chemical, TDK
Europe	~5,000	~1.5%	Various
USA	1,000 (target)	~0.3%	MP Materials (Fort Worth)
Rest of World	~4,000	~1.2%	Various

Key Applications:

- Electric vehicle traction motors: 1-2 kg per vehicle
- Wind turbine generators: 200-600 kg per MW capacity
- Defense systems: Guidance systems, motors, sensors
- Consumer electronics: Smartphones, hard drives, speakers

China's Rare Earth Production Quotas (2019-2024)

Year	Mining Quota (MT REO)	Smelting/Separation Quota (MT)	YoY Change
2019	132,000	127,000	-
2020	140,000	135,500	+6.1% / +6.7%
2021	168,000	162,000	+20.0% / +19.6%
2022	210,000	202,000	+25.0% / +24.7%
2023	245,000	236,000	+16.7% / +16.8%
2024	270,000	258,000	+10.2% / +9.3%

Source: China Ministry of Natural Resources, Ministry of Industry and Information Technology

Global Rare Earth Reserves (2024 Estimates)

Total Global Reserves: ~130 million metric tons REO

Country	Reserves (Million MT REO)	% of World	Notable Deposits
China	44	33.8%	Bayan Obo (36M MT), Southern China
Vietnam	22	16.9%	Various locations
Brazil	21	16.2%	Araxá, Serra Verde
Russia	21	16.2%	Tomtor, Lovozero
India	6.9	5.3%	Beach sands, Orissa
Australia	5.7	4.4%	Mt. Weld, Nolans, Browns Range
United States	2.3	1.8%	Mountain Pass, Bear Lodge, Elk Creek
Greenland	2.0	1.5%	Kvanefjeld (undeveloped)
Canada	1.5	1.2%	Strange Lake, Nechalacho
Other	~5	~3.8%	Various

Source: U.S. Geological Survey (February 2025)

Critical Minerals Beyond Rare Earths

Gallium

Global Production (2024): ~800 metric tons

Country	Production (MT)	% of World	Primary Source
China	~750	~94%	Byproduct of aluminum/zinc
Japan	~20	~2.5%	Zinc refining byproduct
South Korea	~15	~2%	Zinc refining
Russia	~10	~1%	Aluminum processing
Others	~5	~0.5%	Various

Key Applications:

- Gallium nitride (GaN) semiconductors: Power electronics, RF amplifiers, LEDs
- Defense: Radar systems, electronic warfare, missile guidance
- 5G infrastructure
- **China Export Controls**: Implemented December 2023, expanded October 2025

Germanium

Global Production (2024): ~165 metric tons

Country	Production (MT)	% of World	Primary Source
China	~100	~60%	Zinc/coal mining byproduct
Canada	~20	~12%	Zinc concentrate imports
Belgium	~15	~9%	Refining/recycling
Russia	~10	~6%	Mining/refining
USA	~8	~5%	Zinc mines (Alaska, Tennessee)
Germany	~7	~4%	Refining
Others	~5	~3%	Various

Key Applications:

- Fiber optic cables
- Infrared optics (night vision, thermal imaging)
- Solar cells (high-efficiency)
- **China Export Controls**: Licensing requirements since 2024

Antimony

Global Production (2024): ~130,000 metric tons

Country	Production (MT)	% of World	Primary Deposits
China	~65,000	~50%	Xikuangshan (Hunan), Guangxi
Russia	~25,000	~19%	Various deposits
Tajikistan	~13,000	~10%	Zeravshan deposit
Myanmar	~10,000	~8%	Various
Bolivia	~6,000	~5%	Various
Others	~11,000	~8%	Various

Key Applications:

- Flame retardants (plastics, textiles)
- Lead-acid batteries (hardening agent)
- Ammunition (tracer rounds, primers)

- Semiconductors (ultra-high purity)
- **China Export Controls**: Implemented August 2025 for U.S. specifically

Graphite (Natural)

Global Production (2024): ~1.4 million metric tons

Country	Production (MT)	% of World	Type
China	~900,000	~64%	Flake & amorphous
Mozambique	~180,000	~13%	Flake (high purity)
Madagascar	~100,000	~7%	Flake
Brazil	~85,000	~6%	Flake & amorphous
India	~55,000	~4%	Various types
Canada	~30,000	~2%	Flake
Others	~50,000	~4%	Various

Graphite Refining for Battery Applications:

- China: >90% of spherical graphite (battery-grade) processing
- Non-China: <10%, emerging capacity

Key Applications:

- Lithium-ion battery anodes (50-75% of weight in Li-ion cells)
- Steel manufacturing
- Lubricants, refractories
- **China Export Controls**: Export licensing for certain grades since October 2025

Lithium

Global Mine Production (2024): ~180,000 metric tons lithium content

Country	Production (MT Li)	% of World	Type
Australia	~88,000	~49%	Hard rock (spodumene)
Chile	~44,000	~24%	Brine
China	~27,000	~15%	Brine & hard rock
Argentina	~10,000	~6%	Brine
Zimbabwe	~6,000	~3%	Hard rock
Brazil	~3,000	~2%	Hard rock
Others	~2,000	~1%	Various

Lithium Refining (Lithium Hydroxide/Carbonate):

- **China**: ~60% of global lithium refining capacity
- **Chile**: ~20%
- **Australia**: ~10%
- **Others**: ~10%

Reserves (2024):

- Chile: 11 million MT (salt flats - Atacama)
- Australia: 7.9 million MT
- Argentina: 3.6 million MT
- China: 3.0 million MT
- USA: 1.0 million MT

Cobalt

Global Mine Production (2024): ~210,000 metric tons

Country	Production (MT)	% of World	Primary Source
Democratic Republic of Congo	~140,000	~67%	Copper mining byproduct
Indonesia	~18,000	~9%	Nickel laterite
Russia	~14,000	~7%	Nickel mining byproduct
Australia	~7,000	~3%	Nickel operations
Philippines	~6,000	~3%	Nickel laterite
Cuba	~5,500	~3%	Nickel operations
Canada	~5,000	~2%	Nickel operations
Others	~14,500	~7%	Various

Cobalt Refining:

- **China**: ~70% of global refining capacity
- **Finland**: ~10%
- **Belgium**: ~5%
- **Canada**: ~5%
- **Others**: ~10%

Key Application: Lithium-ion battery cathodes (5-20% cobalt content in NMC/NCA chemistries)

Critical Minerals - U.S. Import Dependence (2024)

100% Import Reliant (no domestic production):

- Graphite (natural): 100% (China 44%, Mozambique 23%, Madagascar 11%)
- Manganese: 100% (Gabon 41%, South Africa 19%, Australia 13%)
- Mica (sheet): 100% (China 36%, India 25%, Brazil 23%)
- Tantalum: 100% (Rwanda 37%, Congo 33%, China 12%)

>50% Import Reliant:

- Antimony: 77% (China 38%, India 21%, Belgium 16%)
- Bismuth: 93% (China 71%, Belgium 9%, Mexico 7%)
- Rare Earths: 74% (China 70%, Estonia 2%, Japan 2%) *Despite Mountain Pass production, concentrated in compounds/metals*

- Tungsten: 49% (China 30%, Bolivia 21%, Russia 14%)
- Cobalt: 76% (Finland 19%, Norway 16%, Canada 12%, China 10%)
- Lithium compounds: 54% (Argentina 34%, Chile 32%, China 23%)

Source: U.S. Geological Survey Mineral Commodity Summaries 2025

U.S.-Australia Critical Minerals Framework Agreement (October 20, 2025)

Total Investment Pipeline: $8.5 billion

Immediate Commitments (within 6 months):

- **U.S. Investment**: $1 billion minimum
- **Australia Investment**: $1 billion minimum
- **Focus**: Projects generating end products for U.S. and Australian buyers

Priority Projects Identified:

1. **Alcoa-Sojitz Rare Earth Recovery**:
    - Location: Western Australia alumina refineries
    - Capacity: Gallium and rare earth extraction from alumina production
    - Timeline: 2026-2027 operations
    - Investment: $400-600 million estimated
2. **Arafura Nolans Rare Earth Project**:
    - Location: Northern Territory, Australia
    - Capacity: 4,440 MT/year NdPr oxide
    - Additional: Phosphate, gypsum byproducts
    - Timeline: FID expected 2025-2026
    - Investment: $1.25 billion (A$1.8 billion)
    - Australian Government Support: $1.25 billion loan facility
3. **Iluka Eneabba Rare Earth Refinery**:
    - Location: Western Australia
    - Capacity: 17,500 MT/year integrated refinery
    - First fully integrated rare earth refinery outside China
    - Timeline: 2026 commissioning
    - Investment: ~$1 billion
4. **Lynas U.S. Heavy Rare Earth Facility**:

- Location: Texas, USA
- Capacity: Processing heavy rare earths from Malaysia
- Focus: Dysprosium, terbium separation
- Timeline: 2025-2026 operations
- Investment: $150-200 million

Strategic Mechanisms:

Price Floor Mechanisms: Australian government guarantees minimum offtake prices to protect against Chinese market manipulation

Asset Sale Restrictions: Coordinated screening of Chinese acquisitions of mining assets

Streamlined Permitting: Commitment to accelerate approval timelines (target: 50% reduction)

Technology Sharing: Mining technology, processing techniques, environmental management

Expected Outcomes (2028):

- U.S. reliance on Chinese rare earths: 70% → <30%
- Heavy rare earth production (non-China): 200-300% increase
- Domestic processing capacity: Significant expansion
- China market share: ~90% → ~75%

China's Export Control Architecture (2025)

Export Control Law (Effective December 2020):

- Framework for restricting dual-use items
- Reciprocal measures against "discriminatory" foreign restrictions
- Catch-all provision for national security

Recent Major Actions:

December 2023: Gallium and germanium licensing requirements

August 2024: Antimony export controls to United States

October 9, 2025: Expanded rare earth controls

- Covered elements: Holmium (Ho), Thulium (Tm), Ytterbium (Yb), Erbium (Er), Scandium (Sc), Yttrium (Y), Samarium (Sm), Gadolinium (Gd), Terbium (Tb), Dysprosium (Dy), Lutetium (Lu)
- Equipment: Separation, refining, purification equipment
- Extraterritorial application: Products containing >0.1% Chinese rare earth content
- Effective: December 1, 2025

November 2025 Suspension:

- Rare earth controls suspended under U.S.-China bilateral agreement
- General licenses issued for U.S. end users
- Duration: Through November 2026 (renewable)

Strategic Mineral Stockpiling

U.S. National Defense Stockpile (FY 2024-2025):

Material	Stockpile Goal	Current Inventory	Acquisition Priority
Rare Earths (NdPr oxide)	2,000 MT	~100 MT	High
NdFeB Magnets	1,500 MT	Minimal	High
Antimony	15,000 MT	~8,000 MT	Medium
Beryllium	200 MT	~140 MT	Low-Medium
Cobalt	400 MT	~200 MT	Medium
Tungsten	3,000 MT	~1,800 MT	Medium

China's Strategic Reserves:

- Rare earth element reserves: Estimated 50,000-100,000 MT
- Undisclosed quantities of other critical minerals
- Province-level stockpiling programs

Australia's Critical Minerals Strategic Reserve: $1.2 billion program

- Offtake agreements with domestic producers
- Price floor guarantees
- Selective stockpiling

Environmental and Social Considerations

Rare Earth Mining Environmental Impact:

- **China**: Historical environmental damage in Inner Mongolia (Bayan Obo), Southern China
- **Cleanup Costs**: Estimated $5-10 billion for historical contamination
- **Current Standards**: Improving but still concerns remain

Radioactive Byproducts:

- Thorium, uranium naturally occurring with rare earths
- Disposal challenge for Western projects (stricter regulations)
- China advantage: Lenient handling of low-level radioactive waste

Labor and Ethical Concerns:

- **Myanmar**: Links to military-controlled mining areas
- **Congo (cobalt)**: Artisanal mining, child labor concerns
- **Western Standard Compliance**: Higher costs but improved transparency

Future Projections (2025-2030)

Demand Growth (CAGR 2025-2030):

- Rare earth permanent magnets: 8-12% annually
- Battery-grade lithium: 15-20% annually
- Battery-grade graphite: 18-25% annually
- Cobalt: 8-12% annually

Drivers:

- Electric vehicle adoption: 25-30 million units (2025) → 50-60 million (2030)
- Wind turbine installations: 100+ GW annually
- Defense modernization programs
- Consumer electronics growth

Supply Response:

- China maintaining 60-70% market share in most critical minerals
- Western capacity additions: +50-100% but from low base
- Diversification efforts: Multi-year lag between investment and production
- Recycling infrastructure: Growing but <5% of supply through 2030

Appendix D: Taiwan Strait Military Activity Data (2020-2025)

PLA Air Incursions into Taiwan ADIZ (Air Defense Identification Zone)

Annual Totals:

Year	Total Incursions	Aircraft Crossing Median Line	% Increase YoY
2020	380	~50	Baseline
2021	972	~200	+156%
2022	1,737	~500	+79%
2023	1,829	~650	+5%
2024	2,301	~850	+26%
2025 (through Oct 10)	3,056	~1,200	+33% (annualized)

Source: Taiwan Ministry of National Defense (MND) Daily Reports

Major PLA Exercise Events (2022-2025)

August 4-7, 2022: "Joint Sword" Precursor (Post-Pelosi)

Context: Response to U.S. House Speaker Nancy Pelosi's visit to Taiwan (August 2-3, 2022)

Scale:

- **Aircraft**: 68 total sorties over 4 days
- **Naval Vessels**: 13+ warships, including destroyers, frigates
- **Submarines**: Nuclear-powered submarines deployed (unconfirmed number)
- **Ballistic Missiles**: 11 DF-15/DF-16 missiles fired
    - 5 landed in Japan's Exclusive Economic Zone (first time)
    - 6 in waters east of Taiwan
- **Exercise Zones**: 6 zones completely encircling Taiwan

- **Median Line Crossings**: 49 aircraft crossed on August 5 alone

Significance:

- First complete encirclement of Taiwan since 1995-96 Third Taiwan Strait Crisis
- Normalization of PLA operations inside Taiwan's contiguous zone
- Demonstrated improved coordination across services

2023-2024: Joint Sword Series

Joint Sword-2023A (April 8-10, 2023):

- **Context**: President Tsai Ing-wen's return from U.S. meeting with House Speaker Kevin McCarthy
- **Aircraft**: 91 sorties over 3 days
- **Naval Vessels**: 9 PLAN ships, 4 USCG ships
- **Focus**: Simulated attacks on key infrastructure, sea-air blockade drills
- **Duration**: 72 hours

Joint Sword-2024A (May 23-24, 2024):

- **Context**: Inauguration of President Lai Ching-te
- **Aircraft**: 62 sorties over 2 days, 39 crossing median line
- **Naval Vessels**: 11 PLAN ships
- **Focus**: Joint blockade tactics, precision strikes
- **Special**: First use of Coast Guard in coordinated military exercise
- **Duration**: 48 hours

Joint Sword-2024B (October 14, 2024):

- **Context**: President Lai's "Double Ten" National Day speech
- **Aircraft**: **153 sorties in single day** (record)
    - 111 entered Taiwan's ADIZ
    - 62 crossed median line
- **Naval Vessels**: 14 PLAN ships, 7 USCG ships
- **Key Development**: First confirmed entry into Taiwan's 24nm contiguous zone (east

coast)

- **Duration**: 13 hours (05:01 - 18:06)
- **Significance**: Demonstrated rapid mobilization capability, "cold start" posture

Overall Joint Sword Characteristics:

- Increasingly shorter notification times (if any)
- Greater integration of Coast Guard forces
- Focus on blockade scenarios over amphibious assault
- Progressive encroachment on Taiwan's territorial waters
- Aircraft types: J-16 fighters, H-6 bombers, Y-8 ASW, KJ-500 AWACS, drones

December 2024: Unnamed Naval Maneuvers

December 9-11, 2024:

- **Scale**: Large-scale naval training around Taiwan and First Island Chain
- **Aircraft**: 47 sorties detected
- **Naval Vessels**: 12+ ships, including Shandong carrier group
- **Submarine Activity**: Increased anti-submarine warfare (ASW) patrols
- **Characterized As**: "Training drill" (��) rather than "exercise" (��)
- **Significance**: Return to routine high-intensity operations after 2024B

2025: Strait Thunder Series and Intensification

April 1-2, 2025: Strait Thunder-2025A

Context:

- Response to President Lai's March 13 anti-infiltration policy speech
- NSC Chairman Joseph Wu's Washington visit

Day 1 (April 1): Unnamed Joint Exercise

- **Announcement**: 07:46 local time (minimal warning)
- **Forces Involved**: Army, Navy, Air Force, Rocket Force
- **Scale**: Comparable to Joint Sword exercises

Day 2 (April 2): Strait Thunder-2025A Formal Declaration

- **Announcement**: 08:30 local time
- **Location**: Central and southern Taiwan Strait

Combined Statistics (April 1-2):

- **Aircraft**: 76 total sorties
  - 37 crossed median line
  - 10 Su-30 fighters (crossed northwest)
  - 4 J-11 fighters (crossed northwest)
  - 6 J-16 fighters (southwest ADIZ)
  - 3 H-6 bombers (southwest ADIZ)
  - 1 Y-8 ASW aircraft
  - Multiple drones including in Kinmen area
- **Naval Vessels**: 15 PLAN ships
- **Coast Guard Ships**: 8 ships total
  - 2 formations of 4 vessels each crossed median line
  - At least 1 vessel entered 24nm contiguous zone (east coast)
- **Shandong Carrier Group**: Positioned 440 km south of Japan's Yonaguni Island

Operational Focus:

- "Identification and verification"
- "Warning and expulsion"
- "Interception and detention"
- Regional control and joint blockade capabilities
- Precision strike simulation on defense infrastructure:
  - Command centers
  - Arsenals
  - Air defense posts
  - Air traffic control centers

New Tactics:

- **"Cabbage Strategy"**: Dual-layer encirclement

    - Inner circle: Maritime militia, Coast Guard, Navy surrounding Taiwan
    - Outer circle: Harassing foreign military forces
- **Chokepoint Control**: Focus on blocking key straits and passages
- **Increased Drone Usage**: Multiple small drones for ISR

Significance:

- Name suggests continuing series ("2025A" implies future 2025B, 2025C, etc.)
- Drill vs. Exercise terminology signals potential escalation path
- Integration of Coast Guard as "gray zone" force
- Demonstrates ability to mobilize within 24-48 hours

January-October 2025: Overall Activity

First Half 2025 (Jan-June):

- **Total Incursions**: ~1,850 aircraft
- **Median Line Crossings**: >100 aircraft
- **Joint Combat Readiness Patrols**: 8+ conducted (February-March)
- **Naval Drills**: 3 large-scale live-fire exercises
- **Submarine Patrols**: Significantly increased presence

Submarine Activity:

- Type 093A/B nuclear attack submarines: More frequent deployments east of Taiwan
- Type 039A/B (Yuan-class) conventional submarines: Regular patrols in Taiwan Strait
- Anti-submarine warfare (ASW) patterns suggest denial-of-sea-access strategy

Y20 Strategic Airlifter Deployments:

- Observed more frequently in exercises (possible indicator of amphibious planning)

Naval Balance in Taiwan Strait Region

PLAN Assets (2025):

Aircraft Carriers:

- Liaoning (CV-16): Training carrier, occasionally deploys near Taiwan
- Shandong (CV-17): Primary operational carrier for Taiwan scenarios
- Fujian (CV-18): Sea trials 2024-2025, expected operational 2026

Major Surface Combatants Near Taiwan:

- Type 055 Cruisers: 8 in service (2+ typically in East China Sea)
- Type 052D Destroyers: 25+ (6-8 typical deployment)
- Type 054A Frigates: 40+ (8-12 typical)

Amphibious Warfare Ships:

- Type 071 LPD: 8 in service
- Type 075 LHD: 3 in service (4th launching)
- Type 072A LST: 15+

Submarines:

- Nuclear Attack: 8-10 operational
- Conventional: 50+ (mix of Song, Yuan, Kilo classes)

China Coast Guard in Taiwan Strait:

- Vessels: 8-12 regularly operating near Taiwan
- Large Cutters (>3,000 tons): 4-6
- Integration with PLAN exercises increasingly common

Taiwan Navy (2025):

Major Combatants:

- Kee Lung-class (Kidd) Destroyers: 4
- Cheng Kung-class (Perry) Frigates: 8
- Tuo Chiang-class Corvettes: 13
- Submarine Fleet: 2 operational (Hai Lung-class), 2 new Indigenous Defense Submarines (IDS) under construction

Asymmetric Assets:

- Hsiung Feng II/III anti-ship missiles: Shore-based batteries
- Mobile coastal defense systems
- Mines: Significant stockpile

Air Power Balance

PLAAF/PLAN Aviation (Eastern Theater Command):

Fighters:

- J-20 (5th generation): 200+ (increasing)
- J-16 (4.5 generation): 250+
- J-11 variants: 200+
- Su-30/Su-35: 100+
- J-10C: 150+

Bombers:

- H-6K/N (upgraded): 120+ (subset with anti-ship missiles)

AWACS & Support:

- KJ-500: 20+
- KJ-2000: 5+
- Y-8 variants (EW, ASW): 40+
- Y-20 (strategic transport): 60+

Unmanned:

- Various reconnaissance and attack drones: Numbers classified but extensive

Taiwan Air Force (ROCAF):

Fighters:

- F-16V Block 70: 66 (upgraded from earlier F-16s)
- F-16A/B (remaining): 75+
- Mirage 2000-5: 56

- IDF (Indigenous): 130+

Total Combat Aircraft: ~330 fighters

AWACS: E-2T Hawkeye: 6

Challenge: Aging fleet, maintenance issues, pilot retention concerns

Missile Forces

PLA Rocket Force (PLARF) Assets Targeting Taiwan:

Ballistic Missiles:

- DF-11/15/16 (Short-range, <1,000 km): 1,000+ deployed
- DF-17 (Hypersonic glide vehicle): 60-100
- DF-21D (Anti-ship ballistic missile): 80-100
- DF-26 (Intermediate-range, 3,000-5,000 km): 200+

Cruise Missiles:

- CJ-10 (Land-attack): Several hundred
- YJ-18/21 (Anti-ship): Extensive deployment on surface ships

Taiwan Missile Forces:

Offensive:

- Hsiung Feng IIE (Land-attack, 1,200 km range): Limited numbers
- Hsiung Feng III (Supersonic anti-ship): Large inventory

Defensive:

- Patriot PAC-3: 7 batteries
- Sky Bow II/III (Taiwan's indigenous SAM): 21 batteries
- NASAMS (ordered 2024): Not yet delivered

Cross-Strait Military Exercises Timeline (2020-2025)

Date	Exercise Name	Duration	Aircraft	Ships	Key Features
Aug 4-7, 2022	Post-Pelosi Drills	4 days	68	13+	First encirclement, ballistic missiles
Apr 8-10, 2023	Joint Sword-2023A	3 days	91	13	Simulated blockade
May 23-24, 2024	Joint Sword-2024A	2 days	62	11	Coast Guard integration
Oct 14, 2024	Joint Sword-2024B	13 hours	153	21	Record sorties, cold start
Dec 9-11, 2024	Unnamed Naval Drills	3 days	47	12+	Carrier group, ASW focus
Apr 1-2, 2025	Strait Thunder-2025A	2 days	76	23	Dual-layer blockade concept

Trend Analysis:

- **Frequency**: Increasing from 1-2 major exercises annually (2020-2021) to 4-5 (2024-2025)
- **Duration**: Decreasing (4 days → 2 days → <1 day for peak intensity)
- **Complexity**: Increasing multi-domain integration
- **Warning Time**: Decreasing (weeks → days → hours)
- **Proximity**: Progressively closer to Taiwan's territorial waters

U.S. Military Presence and Taiwan Strait Transits

Freedom of Navigation Operations (FONOPS):

Year	U.S. Navy Transits	Other Allies/Partners
2020	13	0
2021	12	3 (UK, Canada)
2022	10	5 (UK, Canada, Australia)
2023	11	7
2024	13	9
2025 (through Oct)	10	8

Typical U.S. Assets:

- Arleigh Burke-class destroyers: 1-2 per transit

- Ticonderoga-class cruisers: Occasional
- Carrier Strike Groups: Pass through region but rarely transit strait directly
- P-8A Poseidon maritime patrol aircraft: Regular overflights

U.S. Force Posture (Indo-Pacific 2025):

- **Guam**: B-52, B-1B strategic bombers rotational deployment
- **Japan**: 7th Fleet homeport (USS Ronald Reagan carrier, ~50 ships)
- **South Korea**: 28,500 troops
- **Philippines**: Enhanced Defense Cooperation Agreement (9 sites)
- **Australia**: Marine rotational force (Darwin), enhanced air cooperation

Defense Secretary Statements on Taiwan

Lloyd Austin (2021-2024):

- "China is clearly our pacing challenge" (repeated)
- Emphasized deterrence through capability demonstration
- Advocated "integrated deterrence" concept

Pete Hegseth (2025):

- **March 26, 2025 Senate Hearing**: "PLA may be ready to take Taiwan within next 3-4 years, aiming for control within 72 hours"
- **March 31, 2025 (Asia visit)**: Promised U.S. military would "increase regional presence to deter China"
- Warning that attack "could be imminent" based on PLA readiness levels

Expert Assessments and U.S. Government Reports

Department of Defense - China Military Power Report (2024):

- PLA conducted 300% increase in military pressure against Taiwan (2024 vs. 2023)
- Assessment: PLA developing capability to conduct full-scale invasion by 2027
- Current capability: Limited amphibious assault but strong blockade/coercion capability

Congressional-Executive Commission on China Report (November 2025):

- **Key Finding**: "PLA could blockade Taiwan in matter of hours"
- **3,056 PLA incursions into Taiwan ADIZ** (through Oct 10, 2025)
- 33% increase from same period 2024
- Assessment: Beijing preparing for near-term contingencies

CSIS (Center for Strategic and International Studies) Analysis:

- **"Cold Start" Assessment (November 2025)**: PLA developing 24-48 hour mobilization capability
- **Wargaming Results**: Invasion extremely costly for all parties; blockade more likely scenario
- **Timeline Concerns**: Window of PLA advantage: 2025-2030 (before Taiwan's defense modernization completes)

Taiwan's Defense Modernization

Defense Budget Growth:

Year	Defense Budget (NT$ Billion)	% of GDP	USD Equivalent
2020	334	2.16%	$11.3 billion
2021	361	2.22%	$13.0 billion
2022	372	2.17%	$13.3 billion
2023	415	2.45%	$14.5 billion
2024	606	2.54%	$19.7 billion
2025 (proposed)	647	~2.7%	$20.8 billion

Major Arms Sales from United States (2020-2025):

- **F-16V Block 70** upgrades: $8 billion (66 aircraft)
- **M1A2T Abrams tanks**: $2 billion (108 units)
- **High Mobility Artillery Rocket System (HIMARS)**: $436 million (11 launchers, 64 tactical missiles)
- **MQ-9B SeaGuardian drones**: $600 million (4 systems)
- **Harpoon Coastal Defense System**: $2.37 billion (100 launchers, 400 missiles)
- **Mark 48 Mod 6 Advanced Technology (AT) torpedoes**: $180 million (18 torpedoes)
- **AGM-84H/K SLAM-ER missiles**: $155 million (135 missiles)

Indigenous Defense Programs:

Indigenous Defense Submarine (IDS):

- **Program**: 8 submarines planned
- **Status**: First boat launched September 2023, sea trials 2024-2025
- **Timeline**: First operational 2025-2026
- **Significance**: Break dependence on foreign suppliers

Asymmetric Defense Strategy:

- Focus on mobile, survivable systems (missile launchers, coastal defense)
- Civil defense drills expanded: Annual exercises in major cities
- Reserve force training: Increased from biennial to annual
- "Whole of Society" resilience initiative (President Lai, 2024)

Geographic and Strategic Context

Taiwan Strait Dimensions:

- **Width**: 130 kilometers (81 miles) at narrowest point (Fujian coast to Hsinchu)
- **Depth**: Average 50-60 meters (shallow, complicates submarine operations)
- **Strategic Importance**:
    - ~50% of global container fleet transits annually
    - ~48% of large vessels (>90,000 gross tons) transit through or near strait
    - Critical sea lane for Japan, South Korea energy supplies (oil, LNG)

Taiwan's Semiconductor Leverage:

- TSMC produces >90% of world's most advanced chips (<5nm node)
- 2024 Semiconductor output: $172 billion (23% of Taiwan GDP)
- Global dependency: Apple, Nvidia, AMD, Qualcomm, major customers

Amphibious Assault Challenge:

- Limited suitable landing beaches: ~14 on west coast
- Taiwan prepared defensive positions at all major sites

- **PLA Amphibious Capacity**: ~80,000-100,000 troops in single wave (insufficient for 190-mile long island)
- **Blockade Assessment**: More feasible than invasion in near-term

Risk Indicators and Escalation Pathways

Low-Level Activities (Constant):

- Daily ADIZ incursions (average 8-10 aircraft/day in 2025)
- Coast Guard patrols near median line
- Cyber attacks, disinformation campaigns

Medium-Level Activities (Periodic):

- Large-scale exercises (Joint Sword series, Strait Thunder)
- Median line crossings in large numbers (>30 aircraft)
- Approaches to 24nm contiguous zone

High-Level Activities (Rare but Increasing):

- Entry into Taiwan's territorial waters (12nm)
- Firing of live ordnance near Taiwan
- Sustained blockade of specific ports/areas
- Cyber attacks on critical infrastructure

Potential Triggers for Conflict:

1. **Taiwan Independence Declaration**: Stated PRC red line
2. **Foreign Military Presence**: Permanent basing in Taiwan
3. **Leadership Crisis**: Instability in Beijing or Taipei
4. **Accidental Escalation**: Collision, shoot-down incident
5. **Third-Party Conflict**: U.S.-China clash elsewhere drawing in Taiwan

Allied Responses and Commitments

United States:

- **Taiwan Relations Act (1979)**: Commit to "resist force or coercion"

- **Ambiguity maintained**: No formal defense treaty
- **Biden statements (2021-2023)**: "Yes" to defending Taiwan (4 times), walked back by staff
- **Trump 2.0**: Focus on capability over commitment assurances

Japan:

- 2022: Taiwan emergency "indirectly related to Japan's survival"
- Southwestern Islands fortification ongoing
- U.S.-Japan security treaty (Article V) covers Japan-administered territories only

Australia:

- AUKUS submarine program partly motivated by Taiwan contingency
- No formal commitment but expected to support U.S. operations

South Korea:

- Ambiguous stance due to China economic ties
- U.S. bases in Korea would be critical for any Taiwan scenario

Conclusion: Trajectory and Outlook

Key Trends (2020-2025):

1. **Normalization of PLA Pressure**: What was crisis-level activity in 2022 is now routine
2. **Shortened Mobilization Times**: From weeks to days to hours
3. **Gray Zone Expansion**: Coast Guard, maritime militia increasing role
4. **Median Line Erosion**: De facto no longer exists as restraint line
5. **Operational Confidence**: PLA demonstrating greater willingness to operate near Taiwan

Near-Term Outlook (2025-2027):

- Continued high operational tempo expected
- Additional "Strait Thunder" exercises likely
- Increasing integration of civilian and military assets
- Potential for accidental escalation remains elevated

Medium-Term Wildcards (2027-2030):

- PLA modernization targets: 2027 (100th anniversary), 2035 (full modernization)
- Taiwan's defense improvements: IDS submarines operational, F-16V fully deployed
- U.S.-China relationship trajectory: Negotiated modus vivendi vs. further deterioration
- Leadership transitions: Taiwan (2028), U.S. (2029 if Trump one term), China (post-Xi?)

Historical Context: Previous Taiwan Strait Crises: 1954-55, 1958 (Quemoy), 1995-96 Current situation differs: PLA far more capable, economic interdependence deeper, nuclear dynamics

Appendix E: Glossary of Technical Terms

ADIZ (Air Defense Identification Zone): Airspace over international waters where identification, location, and control of civil aircraft is required in the interest of national security. Taiwan's ADIZ extends far beyond its territorial airspace.

AI (Artificial Intelligence): Computer systems able to perform tasks normally requiring human intelligence, such as visual perception, speech recognition, decision-making, and language translation.

ASML: Advanced Semiconductor Materials Lithography, Netherlands-based company and sole producer of extreme ultraviolet (EUV) lithography machines essential for manufacturing advanced semiconductors.

Bastnaesite: A rare earth fluorocarbonate mineral, primary ore mineral for light rare earth elements. Found in significant quantities at Mountain Pass, California.

BIOSECURE Act: Proposed U.S. legislation restricting federal contracts with Chinese biotechnology companies deemed national security concerns.

CDMO (Contract Development and Manufacturing Organization): Companies providing pharmaceutical development and manufacturing services to other pharmaceutical/biotechnology companies.

CRISPR (Clustered Regularly Interspaced Short Palindromic Repeats): Gene-editing technology allowing precise modification of DNA sequences.

DeepSeek: Chinese AI startup that released competitive AI models (DeepSeek-R1, V3) claimed to achieve performance comparable to leading U.S. models at fraction of cost and computing power.

DF (Dong Feng - "East Wind"): Series of Chinese ballistic missiles. DF-15/16 are short-range; DF-21D is anti-ship; DF-26 intermediate-range; DF-41 intercontinental.

DUV (Deep Ultraviolet Lithography): Semiconductor manufacturing technology using 193nm or 248nm wavelength light. Predecessor to EUV, can produce chips down to ~7nm with multi-patterning.

Dysprosium (Dy): Heavy rare earth element, critical for high-temperature permanent magnets (>95% produced/refined in China).

EAR (Export Administration Regulations): U.S. regulations controlling export of dual-use items, managed by Bureau of Industry and Security (BIS).

Entity List: U.S. Department of Commerce list of foreign entities subject to specific export license requirements for receiving certain items.

EUV (Extreme Ultraviolet Lithography): Advanced semiconductor manufacturing technology using 13.5nm wavelength light. Enables production of sub-7nm chips. Only produced by ASML.

FDPR (Foreign Direct Product Rule): U.S. export control provision restricting foreign-made items incorporating or produced with U.S. technology/software.

Gallium (Ga): Critical mineral, byproduct of aluminum/zinc processing. Essential for gallium nitride (GaN) semiconductors used in 5G, defense electronics, power electronics. China produces ~94%.

Germanium (Ge): Critical mineral used in fiber optics, infrared systems, solar cells. China produces ~60%.

Graphite: Critical mineral for lithium-ion battery anodes. Natural flake graphite processed into spherical graphite. China controls >90% of battery-grade processing.

H-6 Bomber: Chinese strategic bomber, variant of Soviet Tu-16. Modern H-6K/N variants carry anti-ship cruise missiles, extensive use in Taiwan exercises.

HIMARS (High Mobility Artillery Rocket System): U.S. wheeled mobile rocket artillery. Taiwan ordered 11 systems; similar to systems used effectively in Ukraine.

Hsiung Feng: Series of Taiwanese indigenous missiles. Hsiung Feng III is supersonic anti-ship missile; Hsiung Feng IIE is land-attack cruise missile (range ~1,200 km).

IDS (Indigenous Defense Submarine): Taiwan's domestic submarine program. First boat launched 2023, aims to produce 8 boats to replace aging fleet.

Involution (��, Nèijuǎn): Chinese term describing internal competition becoming self-defeating. In economic context: excessive capacity chasing diminishing returns.

J-16: Chinese 4.5-generation multirole fighter, derivative of Russian Su-30. Primary aircraft type in Taiwan Strait operations.

J-20: Chinese 5th-generation stealth fighter, comparable to U.S. F-22. Over 200 in service as of 2025, increasing presence near Taiwan.

Joint Sword (����): Series of PLA military exercises around Taiwan (2023-2024), focusing on blockade and precision strike scenarios.

Kirin: Huawei's series of ARM-based system-on-chip (SoC) processors. Kirin 9000S (2023) notable for using SMIC's 7nm process despite export controls.

KJ-500: Chinese airborne early warning and control (AEW&C) aircraft. Regularly deployed in Taiwan Strait operations.

Lithium-ion Battery: Rechargeable battery using lithium ions. Dominant technology for EVs, consumer electronics. Components: cathode (often contains cobalt), graphite anode, electrolyte, separator.

Lynas Rare Earths: Australian mining company operating Mount Weld mine (Australia) and separation plant (Malaysia). World's largest rare earth producer outside China.

Made in China 2025: Chinese industrial policy launched 2015, targeting 70% self-sufficiency in high-tech sectors including semiconductors, AI, robotics.

Median Line: Informal dividing line through center of Taiwan Strait. PLA increasingly crosses, effectively eroding its significance.

Monazite: Rare earth phosphate mineral, source of thorium and rare earth elements. Found in beach sands and placer deposits.

Mountain Pass: Rare earth mine in California, USA. World's leading producer outside China, supplies bastnaesite concentrate. Operated by MP Materials.

NdFeB (Neodymium-Iron-Boron): Type of permanent magnet using neodymium, iron, and boron. Strongest type of permanent magnet, critical for EV motors, wind turbines, defense applications.

NdPr (Neodymium-Praseodymium) Oxide: Combined rare earth oxide, typically sold together due to chemical similarity. Critical for permanent magnets.

NDAA (National Defense Authorization Act): Annual U.S. federal law specifying defense budget and expenditures. Often includes non-defense provisions (e.g., BIOSECURE Act proposed as amendment).

Nvidia H100/H20: AI accelerator chips. H100 highest performance (restricted to China), H20 is export-compliant variant with reduced performance.

Phase One Agreement: January 2020 U.S.-China trade deal. China committed to $200 billion additional purchases; didn't meet target. Many structural issues left unresolved.

PLA (People's Liberation Army): Chinese armed forces. Components: PLAA (Army), PLAN (Navy), PLAAF (Air Force), PLARF (Rocket Force), PLASSF (Strategic Support Force).

PLARF (People's Liberation Army Rocket Force): Chinese military branch responsible for land-based nuclear and conventional ballistic/cruise missiles.

REE (Rare Earth Elements): Group of 17 elements (15 lanthanides plus scandium and yttrium). Critical for magnets, electronics, catalysts. Divided into light REE (La, Ce, Pr, Nd, etc.) and heavy REE (Dy, Tb, Ho, etc.).

REO (Rare Earth Oxide) Equivalent: Standard measurement for expressing total rare earth content in ore or concentrate, as if all REE were in oxide form.

Section 301: Trade Act of 1974 provision allowing President to take action against foreign unfair trade practices. Legal basis for most Trump-era China tariffs.

Section 232: Trade Expansion Act of 1962 provision allowing tariffs on imports threatening national security. Used for steel/aluminum, auto tariffs.

Semiconductors: Materials with electrical conductivity between conductors and insulators. Basis of modern electronics. Advanced chips use process nodes (14nm, 7nm, 5nm, etc.) indicating transistor size.

Shandong (CV-17): China's second aircraft carrier, first domestically built. Active in Taiwan Strait operations since 2019.

SMIC (Semiconductor Manufacturing International Corporation): China's largest chip foundry. Subject to U.S. export controls but achieved 7nm production by 2023 using DUV multi-patterning.

Strait Thunder (����): PLA exercise series initiated April 2025, focusing on Taiwan Strait blockade operations.

Synthetic Biology: Field of biology involving redesign of organisms for useful purposes by engineering them to have new abilities.

Terbium (Tb): Heavy rare earth element, critical for high-performance magnets and phosphors. >95% produced/refined in China.

TOPS (Tera Operations Per Second): Measure of computing performance, particularly for AI accelerators. 1 TOPS = 1 trillion operations per second.

TSMC (Taiwan Semiconductor Manufacturing Company): World's largest dedicated chip foundry. Produces >90% of world's most advanced semiconductors (<5nm). Market cap >$800 billion.

WuXi AppTec/WuXi Biologics: Major Chinese contract research, development, and manufacturing organizations (CRDMOs). Named in original BIOSECURE Act drafts, provide services to many Western pharmaceutical companies.

Y-8: Chinese four-engine turboprop transport aircraft. Variants include ASW (anti-submarine warfare), electronic warfare, AEW&C platforms.

Y-20: Chinese strategic airlifter, comparable to U.S. C-17. Important for rapid force deployment, aerial refueling. 60+ in service as of 2025.

1260H List: DoD annual list of "Chinese military companies operating in the United States." Referenced in BIOSECURE Act as criteria for designation.

Appendix F: Recommended Further Reading

Books

Trade and Economic Competition

1. **"Chip War: The Fight for the World's Most Critical Technology"** by Chris Miller (2022)
    - Comprehensive history of semiconductor industry and U.S.-China tech competition
    - Essential background on chips' strategic importance
2. **"The Avoidable War: The Dangers of a Catastrophic Conflict between the US and Xi Jinping's China"** by Kevin Rudd (2022)
    - Former Australian PM's analysis of U.S.-China relations
    - Focus on Taiwan risk and diplomatic off-ramps
3. **"The Long Game: China's Grand Strategy to Displace American Order"** by Rush Doshi (2021)
    - Analysis of Chinese strategy from Tiananmen to Xi era
    - Based on Chinese-language sources, strategic documents
4. **"The China Trap: U.S. Foreign Policy and the Perilous Logic of Zero-Sum Competition"** by Charles L. Glaser (2024)
    - Argues for avoiding worst-case assumptions
    - Case for selective accommodation
5. **"Superpower Showdown: How the Battle Between Trump and Xi Threatens a New Cold War"** by Bob Davis and Lingling Wei (2020)
    - Wall Street Journal reporters' account of trade war origins
    - Behind-the-scenes negotiations

Technology and Innovation

1. **"AI Superpowers: China, Silicon Valley, and the New World Order"** by Kai-Fu Lee (2018)
    - China's AI ecosystem and competitive advantages
    - Prediction of AI's economic impact
2. **"The Smart Enough City: Putting Technology in Its Place to Reclaim Our Urban Future"** by Ben Green (2019)
    - Context on smart city technology competition

- Relevant to understanding China's tech applications

3. **"Competing in the Age of AI: Strategy and Leadership When Algorithms and Networks Run the World"** by Marco Iansiti and Karim R. Lakhani (2020)
    - Business strategy in AI era
    - Network effects, data advantages

Taiwan and Military Dimensions

1. **"The Chinese Invasion Threat: Taiwan's Defense and American Strategy in Asia"** by Ian Easton (2017)
    - Analysis of PLA invasion planning
    - Taiwan's asymmetric defense options
2. **"Active Defense: China's Military Strategy Since 1949"** by M. Taylor Fravel (2019)
    - Evolution of Chinese military doctrine
    - PLA organizational culture
3. **"Danger Zone: The Coming Conflict with China"** by Hal Brands and Michael Beckley (2022)
    - Argument that 2020s are period of peak danger
    - Focus on China's peaking power concerns

Critical Minerals and Resources

1. **"The Rare Metals War: The Dark Side of Clean Energy and Digital Technologies"** by Guillaume Pitron (2020)
    - Supply chain vulnerabilities in energy transition
    - Environmental costs of mining
2. **"Material World: The Six Raw Materials That Shape Modern Civilization"** by Ed Conway (2023)
    - Deep dive into sand, salt, iron, copper, oil, lithium
    - Historical context for resource competition

Grand Strategy and Future Scenarios

1. **"The Tragedy of Great Power Politics"** by John J. Mearsheimer (2001)
    - Structural realist perspective on great power competition
    - Theoretical foundation for understanding U.S.-China rivalry
2. **"Destined for War: Can America and China Escape Thucydides's Trap?"** by Graham

Allison (2017)
   - Historical analysis of rising/ruling power conflicts
   - 12 of 16 historical cases ended in war
3. **"The World According to China"** by Elizabeth C. Economy (2022)
   - Chinese worldview and global ambitions
   - Xi Jinping's vision for international order

Academic Journals and Reports

Regular Publications:

1. **U.S.-China Economic and Security Review Commission Annual Reports**
   - Congressionally mandated annual assessment
   - Comprehensive coverage of economic, security, technological dimensions
   - Available: www.uscc.gov
2. **Pentagon's Annual Report to Congress: Military and Security Developments Involving the People's Republic of China**
   - Official DoD assessment of PLA capabilities
   - Most authoritative public source on Chinese military
3. **CSIS (Center for Strategic and International Studies) Reports**
   - ChinaPower Project: chinapower.csis.org
   - Critical minerals, military balance, technology competition analyses
4. **PIIE (Peterson Institute for International Economics) Working Papers**
   - Trade war economic impacts
   - Supply chain resilience
   - Available: www.piie.com
5. **Taiwan's National Security Report**
   - Published by ROC Ministry of National Defense
   - Biannual assessment of threats and defense modernization

Academic Journals:

1. **International Security** (MIT Press)
   - Leading journal for security studies
   - Frequent U.S.-China articles
2. **The China Quarterly** (Cambridge)
   - Preeminent journal on contemporary China

    - Politics, economics, society
3. **Asia Policy** (National Bureau of Asian Research)
    - Scholarly analysis of Asian security issues
    - Special Taiwan Strait coverage
4. **Journal of Contemporary China** (Routledge)
    - Interdisciplinary coverage of modern China

Think Tank Resources

U.S.-Based:

1. **Council on Foreign Relations (CFR)**
    - www.cfr.org
    - Trade, technology, Taiwan backgrounders
    - "Asia Unbound" blog
2. **Brookings Institution - John L. Thornton China Center**
    - www.brookings.edu/china
    - Economic and strategic analysis
3. **Carnegie Endowment for International Peace**
    - carnegieendowment.org
    - Nuclear, technology, global order issues
4. **Rand Corporation**
    - www.rand.org
    - Military balance studies, wargaming results
5. **Atlantic Council**
    - www.atlanticcouncil.org
    - GeoTech Center for technology competition

International:

1. **Chatham House (UK)**
    - www.chathamhouse.org
    - Independent British perspective
2. **Australian Strategic Policy Institute (ASPI)**
    - www.aspi.org.au
    - Critical technology tracker, Indo-Pacific focus
3. **Mercator Institute for China Studies (MERICS) - Germany**

    - merics.org
    - European perspective on China
4. **Institute for International Strategic Studies (IISS) - UK**
    - www.iiss.org
    - "Military Balance" annual publication

Chinese Sources (Mandarin)

For readers with Chinese language capability:

1. **���� (Qiushi/Seeking Truth)**
    - Chinese Communist Party theoretical journal
    - Xi Jinping's major speeches published here
2. **������� (China National Defense News)**
    - PLA official newspaper
    - Military doctrinal developments
3. **������ (Global Times)**
    - State-affiliated tabloid
    - Nationalist perspective, often trial balloons for policy
4. **�������� (China Economic Times)**
    - Economic policy and development news
    - Industrial policy coverage
5. **CASS (Chinese Academy of Social Sciences) Reports**
    - www.cass.cn
    - Government-affiliated research

Databases and Tracking Tools

1. **Global Trade Alert (GTA)**
    - www.globaltradealert.org
    - Tracks protectionist measures globally
    - Comprehensive tariff database
2. **SIPRI (Stockholm International Peace Research Institute)**
    - www.sipri.org
    - Arms transfers database
    - Military expenditure data
3. **U.S. Geological Survey Mineral Commodities Summaries**

- pubs.usgs.gov/periodicals/mcs2025
- Annual critical minerals production/reserve data
- Most authoritative public source

4. **Semiconductors Intelligence (SemiAnalysis)**
    - www.semianalysis.com
    - Detailed semiconductor supply chain tracking
    - Subscription required for full access
5. **Taiwan Ministry of National Defense Daily Reports**
    - www.mnd.gov.tw (English: en.mnd.gov.tw)
    - Daily PLA activity around Taiwan
    - Most detailed public tracking

Podcasts and Media

1. **"The ChinaTalk Podcast"** by Jordan Schneider
    - Technology, economics, politics
    - Expert interviews
2. **"Sinica"** by SupChina
    - Culture, politics, business
    - Varied perspectives
3. **"Pekingology"** by Kissinger Institute
    - Chinese elite politics
    - Policy analysis
4. **"The Impossible State" Podcast** by NK News
    - Covers North Korea but relevant for China policy context
5. **"War on the Rocks" Podcast**
    - National security, military strategy
    - Frequent China episodes

News Sources

English Language:

1. **South China Morning Post (SCMP)**
    - Hong Kong-based, Alibaba-owned
    - Extensive China coverage with access
2. **Nikkei Asia**

    - Japanese business perspective
    - Strong tech, semiconductor coverage
3. **Financial Times**
    - Global economic perspective
    - "The Big Read: China" series
4. **The Economist**
    - Weekly China coverage
    - "Chaguan" column
5. **Defense News**
    - Military technology, procurement
    - U.S. defense industry perspective

Chinese Language:

1. **���� (Caixin)**
    - Independent business journalism
    - Most reliable Chinese source
2. **������ (Yicai/CBN)**
    - Business and finance
    - Shanghai-based

Congressional Testimony Archives

Key Hearings (2022-2025):

1. **Commerce Secretary Howard Lutnick Testimony** (2025)
    - Huawei chip production estimates: 200,000 units
    - Export control effectiveness
2. **Admiral Samuel Paparo (INDOPACOM Commander) Testimony** (Multiple dates 2024-2025)
    - Taiwan military balance
    - PLA operational tempo assessments
3. **Treasury Secretary Scott Bessent Testimony on Trade Policy** (2025)
    - "Strategic vs. generalized decoupling" distinction
    - Tariff policy rationale
4. **Dr. Oriana Skylar Mastro Senate Armed Services Committee** (March 26, 2025)
    - PLA readiness for Taiwan operation

- 3-4 year timeline assessment

Available: www.congress.gov (search by keyword, date)

Data Visualization and Tracking

1. **ChinaPower Project Interactive Features**
    - chinapower.csis.org
    - Taiwan military balance, economic data, trade flows
    - Interactive maps and timelines
2. **CSIS ChinaPower "Tracking the Fourth Taiwan Strait Crisis"**
    - Detailed timeline with sources
    - Updated through 2023
3. **Benchmark Mineral Intelligence**
    - Critical minerals production tracking
    - Subscription service, expensive but comprehensive
4. **TrendForce Semiconductor Reports**
    - www.trendforce.com
    - Chip production, capacity tracking
    - Some free, detailed reports paid

Recommended Reading Sequence for New Readers

Foundation (Start here):

1. "Chip War" - Miller (Technology dimension)
2. "The Avoidable War" - Rudd (Diplomatic context)
3. CFR Backgrounders on Taiwan, Trade War (Free online)

Deepening Understanding: 4. "The Long Game" - Doshi (Chinese strategy) 5. "Danger Zone" - Brands & Beckley (Why now matters) 6. Pentagon China Military Power Report (Latest year)

Advanced Topics: 7. Choose based on interest: Military balance ("Chinese Invasion Threat"), Economics (PIIE papers), Critical minerals ("Rare Metals War") 8. Regular reading: SCMP, FT, CSIS ChinaPower for updates

Update Frequency

This field evolves rapidly. Recommended monitoring:

- **Daily**: SCMP, Taiwan MND reports (for Taiwan watchers)
- **Weekly**: FT, The Economist China coverage
- **Monthly**: New think tank reports (CSIS, Brookings, CFR)
- **Annually**: Pentagon report, USCC report, USGS minerals data

---

References and Sources

The information in these appendices has been compiled from the following verified sources:

U.S. Government Sources:

- U.S. Geological Survey, *Mineral Commodity Summaries* (January 2025)
- U.S. Department of Commerce, Bureau of Industry and Security
- Congressional Research Service Reports (IF11284, IF12990, R45249)
- U.S. Census Bureau Trade Statistics
- Department of Defense, *Military and Security Developments Involving the People's Republic of China* (2024)
- Congressional-Executive Commission on China Report (November 2025)

International Organizations:

- International Energy Agency (IEA), *Critical Minerals Market Review* (2024-2025)
- Stockholm International Peace Research Institute (SIPRI)
- World Trade Organization (WTO) Trade Statistics

Think Tanks and Research Institutions:

- Center for Strategic and International Studies (CSIS)
- Peterson Institute for International Economics (PIIE)
- Center for Security and Emerging Technology (CSET)
- Belfer Center for Science and International Affairs, Harvard University
- Stanford University, Human-Centered AI Institute

Taiwan Government Sources:

- Republic of China Ministry of National Defense (MND)
- Taiwan Mainland Affairs Council

Chinese Sources:

- China Ministry of Commerce
- China Ministry of Natural Resources
- China Ministry of Industry and Information Technology
- Chinese customs data

Industry Sources:

- ASML Annual Reports (2022-2024)
- Nvidia Corporation SEC Filings
- Lynas Rare Earths Annual Reports
- MP Materials Corporate Reports
- Benchmark Mineral Intelligence
- TrendForce Semiconductor Analysis

News and Media:

- Reuters, Bloomberg, Financial Times, Wall Street Journal
- South China Morning Post
- The Diplomat
- Defense News

Academic Publications:

- MIT Technology Review
- Nature
- Various peer-reviewed journals cited in text

Compilation Date: December 2025

Note: All data current as of December 3, 2025. Readers should verify time-sensitive information, particularly regarding ongoing negotiations, trade policy changes, and military activities.

Bibliography

I. Trade Wars and Tariffs

Congressional and Government Sources

Congressional Research Service. "Presidential 2025 Tariff Actions: Timeline and Status." Congress.gov, Library of Congress, 2025. https://www.congress.gov/crs-product/R48549

White House, The. "Modifying Reciprocal Tariff Rates Consistent with the Economic and Trade Arrangement Between the United States and the People's Republic of China." Presidential Actions, November 2025. https://www.whitehouse.gov/presidential-actions/2025/11/modifying-reciprocal-tariff-rates-consistent-with-the-economic-and-trade-arrangement-between-the-united-states-and-the-peoples-republic-of-china/

Academic and Think Tank Analysis

Penn Wharton Budget Model. "Effective Tariff Rates and Revenues (Updated November 24, 2025)." University of Pennsylvania, November 2025. https://budgetmodel.wharton.upenn.edu/issues/2025/11/24/effective-tariff-rates-and-revenues-updated-november-24-2025

Tax Foundation. "Trump Tariffs: The Economic Impact of the Trump Trade War." Updated December 2025. https://taxfoundation.org/research/all/federal/trump-tariffs-trade-war/

Centre for Economic Policy Research (CEPR). "Roaring Tariffs: The Global Impact of the 2025 US Trade War." VoxEU, 2025. https://cepr.org/voxeu/columns/roaring-tariffs-global-impact-2025-us-trade-war

News and Analysis

China Briefing. "US-China Tariff Rates: What Are They Now?" Updated November 26, 2025. https://www.china-briefing.com/news/us-china-tariff-rates-2025/

World Economic Forum. "Tracking Tariffs: Key Moments in the US-China Trade Dispute." June 2025. https://www.weforum.org/stories/2025/06/trumps-us-china-trade-tariffs-timeline/

II. Semiconductor Export Controls and Technology Restrictions

Congressional Reports

Sutter, Karen M. "U.S. Export Controls and China: Advanced Semiconductors." Congressional Research Service Report R48642, updated September 19, 2025. https://www.congress.gov/crs-product/R48642

Government Documents

Bureau of Industry and Security, U.S. Department of Commerce. "Commerce Implements New Export Controls on Advanced Computing and Semiconductor Manufacturing Items to the People's Republic of China (PRC)." Press Release, October 7, 2022. https://www.bis.doc.gov/index.php/documents/about-bis/newsroom/press-releases/3158-2022-10-07-bis-press-release-advanced-computing-and-semiconductor-manufacturing-controls-final/file

Bureau of Industry and Security, U.S. Department of Commerce. "Commerce Strengthens Export Controls to Restrict China's Capability to Produce Advanced Semiconductors for Military Applications." Press Release, 2024. https://www.bis.gov/press-release/commerce-strengthens-export-controls-restrict-chinas-capability-produce-advanced-semiconductors-military

Think Tank Analysis

Center for Strategic and International Studies (CSIS). "The Limits of Chip Export Controls in Meeting the China Challenge." May 7, 2025. https://www.csis.org/analysis/limits-chip-export-controls-meeting-china-challenge

Information Technology and Innovation Foundation (ITIF). "Decoupling Risks: How Semiconductor Export Controls Could Harm US Chipmakers and Innovation." November 10, 2025. https://itif.org/publications/2025/11/10/decoupling-risks-semiconductor-export-controls-harm-us-chipmakers-innovation/

International Center for Law & Economics. "US Export Controls on AI and Semiconductors." March 26, 2025. https://laweconcenter.org/resources/us-export-controls-on-ai-and-semiconductors/

Industry Analysis

Microchip USA. "U.S. Semiconductor Export Controls to China: Impact and Future Outlook." 2025. https://www.microchipusa.com/industry-news/us-semiconductor-export-controls-to-china-impact-and-future-outlook

Academic Sources

AI Frontiers. "How US Export Controls Have (and Haven't) Curbed Chinese AI." July 7, 2025. https://ai-frontiers.org/articles/us-chip-export-controls-china-ai

III. DeepSeek and Chinese AI Development

Academic and Research Sources

Conroy, Gemma, and Smriti Mallapaty. "How China Created AI Model DeepSeek and Shocked the World." *Nature*, January 30, 2025. https://www.nature.com/articles/d41586-025-00259-0

Rosenberg, Scott. "Stunning Breakthroughs from China's DeepSeek AI Alarm U.S. Rivals." *Axios*, January 27, 2025. https://www.axios.com/2025/01/27/deepseek-ai-model-china-openai-rival

Technology Analysis

MIT Technology Review. "How Chinese Company DeepSeek Released a Top AI Reasoning Model Despite US Sanctions." January 24, 2025. https://www.technologyreview.com/2025/01/24/china-deepseek-top-ai-despite-sanctions/

Rest of World. "DeepSeek's New Model Could Push China Ahead in the Global AI Race." December 2025. https://restofworld.org/2025/deepseek-china-r2-ai-model-us-rivalry/

Rest of World. "China's AI Frenzy: DeepSeek Is Already Everywhere—Cars, Phones, Even Hospitals." March 17, 2025. https://restofworld.org/2025/china-embeds-deepseek-ai-in-everything/

Business and Financial Media

Bloomberg. "DeepSeek Debuts New AI Models to Rival Google and OpenAI." December 1, 2025. https://www.bloomberg.com/news/articles/2025-12-01/deepseek-debuts-new-ai-models-to-rival-google-and-openai

Euronews. "China's DeepSeek Unveils New AI Model: Here Is Everything We Know About It." September 30, 2025. https://www.euronews.com/next/2025/09/30/chinas-deepseek-unveils-new-ai-model-here-is-everything-we-know-about-it

Policy Analysis

European Union Institute for Security Studies (EUISS). "Challenging US Dominance: China's DeepSeek Model and the Pluralisation of AI Development." Brief, July 28, 2025. https://www.iss.europa.eu/publications/briefs/challenging-us-dominance-chinas-deepseek-model-and-pluralisation-ai-development

Reference Sources

Britannica Money. "DeepSeek: Rise, Technologies, Impact, & Global Response." 2025. https://www.britannica.com/money/DeepSeek

IV. Critical Minerals and US-Australia Partnership

Official Government Documents

White House, The. "United States-Australia Framework For Securing of Supply in the Mining and Processing of Critical Minerals and Rare Earths." October 20, 2025. https://www.whitehouse.gov/briefings-statements/2025/10/united-states-australia-framework-for-securing-of-supply-in-the-mining-and-processing-of-critical-minerals-and-rare-earths/

White House, The. "Fact Sheet: President Donald J. Trump Closes Billion-Dollar Deals with Australia." October 20, 2025. https://www.whitehouse.gov/fact-sheets/2025/10/fact-sheet-president-donald-j-trump-closes-billion-dollar-deals-with-australia/

Australian Government, Department of Industry, Science and Resources. "United States-Australia Framework for Securing of Supply in the Mining and Processing of Critical Minerals and Rare Earths." October 21, 2025. https://www.industry.gov.au/publications/united-states-australia-framework-securing-supply-mining-and-processing-critical-minerals-and-rare-earths

Prime Minister of Australia. "Historic Critical Minerals Framework Signed by President Trump and Prime Minister Albanese." Media Release, October 21, 2025. https://www.pm.gov.au/media/historic-critical-minerals-framework-signed-president-trump-and-prime-minister-albanese

Think Tank Analysis

Baskaran, Gracelin, and Kessarin Horvath. "Unpacking the U.S.-Australia Critical Minerals Framework Agreement." CSIS Critical Questions, October 23, 2025. https://www.csis.org/analysis/unpacking-us-australia-critical-minerals-framework-agreement

Legal Analysis

Sullivan & Cromwell LLP. "Energy Transition Insights: United States-Australia Critical Minerals and Rare Earths Framework." Insights Memo, October 28, 2025. https://www.sullcrom.com/insights/memo/2025/October/United-States-Australia-Critical-Minerals-Rare-Earths-Framework

News Coverage

CNBC. "U.S. and Australia Sign Critical Minerals Agreement with $8.5 Billion Project Pipeline." October 20, 2025. https://www.cnbc.com/2025/10/20/trump-australia-albanese-minerals-rare-earths-china.html

Bloomberg. "Trump Makes Rare Earths Deal With Australia to Fight China." October 21, 2025. https://www.bloomberg.com/news/articles/2025-10-20/trump-signs-agreement-on-critical-minerals-with-australia

U.S. News & World Report. "US and Australia Sign Critical-Minerals Agreement as a Way to Counter China." October 20, 2025. https://www.usnews.com/news/world/articles/2025-10-20/united-states-and-australia-sign-critical-minerals-agreement-as-a-way-to-counter-china

Industry Analysis

Green Li-ion. "US-Australia $8.5B Critical Minerals Partnership 2025." October 2025. https://www.greenli-ion.com/post/us-australia-critical-minerals-framework-2025

V. China's Rare Earth Export Controls

Government Sources

Center for Security and Emerging Technology (CSET), Georgetown University. "Ministry of Commerce Notice 2025 No. 61: Announcement of the Decision to Implement Controls on

Exports of Rare Earth-Related Items to Foreign Countries." Translation, October 2025. https://cset.georgetown.edu/publication/mofcom-notice-2025-61/

International Organization Analysis

International Energy Agency (IEA). "With New Export Controls on Critical Minerals, Supply Concentration Risks Become Reality." Analysis, October 23, 2025. https://www.iea.org/commentaries/with-new-export-controls-on-critical-minerals-supply-concentration-risks-become-reality

Think Tank Research

Center for Strategic and International Studies (CSIS). "China's New Rare Earth and Magnet Restrictions Threaten U.S. Defense Supply Chains." October 14, 2025. https://www.csis.org/analysis/chinas-new-rare-earth-and-magnet-restrictions-threaten-us-defense-supply-chains

Legal Analysis

Mayer Brown. "PRC Announces New Export Controls on Rare Earth and Battery Materials and Technology." Insights, October 13, 2025. https://www.mayerbrown.com/en/insights/publications/2025/10/prc-announces-new-export-controls-on-rare-earth-and-battery-materials-and-technology

News and Updates

CIRS Group. "China Temporarily Suspends Export Controls on Key Raw Materials, Including Rare Earths, Lithium Batteries, and Diamonds." Regulatory News, November 2025. https://www.cirs-group.com/en/chemicals/china-temporarily-suspends-export-controls-on-key-raw-materials-including-rare-earths-lithium-batteries-and-diamond

China Briefing. "Trump-Xi Meeting: US and China Agree to Tariff, Rare Earth Concessions." November 2025. https://www.china-briefing.com/news/trump-xi-meeting-outcomes-and-implications/

UPI. "China Suspends Export Ban on Some Rare Earth Metals to U.S." November 9, 2025. https://www.upi.com/Top_News/US/2025/11/09/china-suspends-export-ban-some-rare-earth-metals/4421762702810/

Bloomberg. "China Says Plans for Rare-Earth Export Curbs Paused for a Year." October 30, 2025. https://www.bloomberg.com/news/articles/2025-10-30/china-says-plans-for-rare-earth-export-curbs-paused-for-a-year

Industry Analysis

Rare Earth Exchanges. "China's 'Pause' Is Not a Pivot: Gareth Hatch Breaks Down the Real Rare Earth Export Story." November 2025. https://rareearthexchanges.com/news/chinas-pause-is-not-a-pivot-gareth-hatch-breaks-down-the-real-rare-earth-export-story/

VI. Taiwan Strait Tensions and Military Developments

Think Tank Analysis

Council on Foreign Relations. "China in the Taiwan Strait: May 2025." July 8, 2025. https://www.cfr.org/article/china-taiwan-strait-may-2025

Council on Foreign Relations. "China in the Taiwan Strait: February 2025." April 9, 2025. https://www.cfr.org/article/china-taiwan-strait-february-2025

American Enterprise Institute and Institute for the Study of War. "China & Taiwan Update, November 25, 2025." November 2025. https://www.aei.org/articles/china-taiwan-update-november-25-2025/

American Enterprise Institute and Institute for the Study of War. "China & Taiwan Update, November 21, 2025." November 2025. https://www.aei.org/articles/china-taiwan-update-november-21-2025/

Chatham House. "China's Military Build-up Indicates It Is Serious About Taking Taiwan." April 16, 2025. https://www.chathamhouse.org/2025/03/chinas-military-build-indicates-it-serious-about-taking-taiwan

Academic Analysis

Foreign Affairs. "The Risk of War in the Taiwan Strait Is High—and Getting Higher." May 22, 2025. https://www.foreignaffairs.com/united-states/risk-war-taiwan-strait-high-and-getting-higher

Risk Assessment

Global Guardian. "Will China Invade Taiwan? A Potential Timeline for Conflict." 2025. https://www.globalguardian.com/global-digest/will-china-invade-taiwan

Intelligence Analysis

Janes. "China Likely to Continue to Prioritise Intimidation Against Taiwan in the Next Six to 12 Months Despite PLA's Aggressive Rhetoric, Exercises." Assessment, June 2025. https://www.janes.com/osint-insights/defence-and-national-security-analysis/china-likely-to-continue-to-prioritise-intimidation-against-taiwan-in-the-next-six-to-12-months

Military Analysis

Indo-Pacific Defense FORUM. "Taiwan's Han Kuang Military Exercises Intensify as Regional Tensions Rise." July 19, 2025. https://ipdefenseforum.com/2025/07/taiwans-han-kuang-military-exercises-intensify-as-regional-tensions-rise/

Media Analysis

Brussels Signal. "Is China Preparing for War in the Taiwan Strait?" December 1, 2025. https://brusselssignal.eu/2025/12/is-china-preparing-for-war-in-the-taiwan-strait/

VII. Biotechnology Competition

Congressional and Commission Reports

STAT News. "Federal Commission Calls for $15 Billion in New Biotech Funding to Counter China's Rise." April 8, 2025. https://www.statnews.com/2025/04/08/biotech-funding-china-national-security-commission-emerging-biotechnology/

News and Analysis

Axios. "Senate Passes Crackdown on Chinese Biotech." October 10, 2025. https://www.axios.com/2025/10/10/china-biotech-ban-senate-national-security

Axios. "China Pharma Deals Threaten U.S. Biotech." September 8, 2025. https://www.axios.com/2025/09/08/china-deals-biotech-us

Industry Publications

Bioprocess International. "China and the US Fighting a Battle for Biotech Dominance." November 2025. https://www.bioprocessintl.com/global-markets/china-and-the-us-fighting-a-battle-for-biotech-dominance

Chemical & Engineering News (C&EN). "China's Biotech Industry Is on the Rise. Will It Reshape US Pharma?" September 5, 2025. https://cen.acs.org/pharmaceuticals/drug-development/Chinas-biotech-industry-rise-reshape/103/web/2025/09

LabioTech. "Is China the Future of Biotech?" December 13, 2024. https://www.labiotech.eu/in-depth/china-biotech-industry/

Academic Research

Carnegie Endowment for International Peace. "Biopharmaceuticals Rising: China's Strategic Pivot to Southeast Asia Amid Great Power Tech Competition." January 2025. https://carnegieendowment.org/research/2025/01/biopharmaceuticals-rising-chinas-strategic-pivot-to-southeast-asia-amid-great-power-tech-competition

Legal Analysis

Greenberg Traurig LLP. "BIOSECURE Act Advances in the US Senate." Insights, November 2025. https://www.gtlaw.com/en/insights/2025/11/biosecure-act-advances-in-the-us-senate

Opinion and Commentary

RealClearWorld. "U.S. Biotech Future Is Now Made in China." October 8, 2025. https://www.realclearworld.com/articles/2025/10/08/us_biotech_future_is_now_made_in_china_1139591.html

VIII. Chinese Manufacturing Overcapacity and Trade Surplus

Academic Analysis

CKGSB Knowledge. "China's Manufacturing Overcapacity: Causes and Solutions." April 8, 2025. https://english.ckgsb.edu.cn/knowledge/article/china-manufacturing-excess-capacity-a-comprehensive-analysis/

Intereconomics. "China's Trade Surplus – Implications for the World and for Europe." 2024. https://www.intereconomics.eu/contents/year/2024/number/2/article/china-s-trade-surplus-implications-for-the-world-and-for-europe.html

International Organization Analysis

International Monetary Fund. "Trade Balances in China and the US Are Largely Driven by Domestic Macro Forces." IMF Blog, September 12, 2024. https://www.imf.org/en/blogs/articles/2024/09/12/trade-balances-in-china-and-the-us-are-largely-driven-by-domestic-macro-forces

Think Tank Research

Rhodium Group. "How China's Overcapacity Holds Back Emerging Economies." 2024. https://rhg.com/research/how-chinas-overcapacity-holds-back-emerging-economies/

Rhodium Group. "Overcapacity at the Gate." March 2024. https://rhg.com/research/overcapacity-at-the-gate/

Brookings Institution. "How the US Should Address Chinese Overcapacity and Its Impact on International Trade." January 13, 2025. https://www.brookings.edu/articles/how-the-us-should-address-chinese-overcapacity-and-its-impact-on-international-trade/

European Analysis

MERICS. "China's Record Trade Surplus + Anti-Corruption Campaign + De-Risking." MERICS Briefs, 2025. https://merics.org/en/merics-briefs/chinas-record-trade-surplus-anti-corruption-campaign-de-risking

Financial Analysis

Deutsche Bank. "China's Huge Trade Surplus – Where Next?" Flow, February 27, 2025. https://flow.db.com/trade-finance/chinas-huge-trade-surplus-where-next

News Coverage

The Capitalist. "What Tariffs? China Trade Surplus Hit Nearly $1 Trillion in 2024." January 13, 2025. https://thecapitalist.com/china-trade-surplus-2024/

The Rio Times. "China's Trade Surplus Soars to Almost $1 Trillion: A Global Economic Imbalance." January 13, 2025. https://riotimesonline.com/chinas-trade-surplus-soars-to-almost-1-trillion-a-global-economic-imbalance/

IX. Made in China 2025 Industrial Policy

Congressional Research

Congressional Research Service. "Made in China 2025 and Industrial Policies: Issues for Congress." CRS In Focus IF10964, updated 2025. https://www.congress.gov/crs-product/IF10964

Think Tank Analysis

Center for Strategic and International Studies (CSIS). "Made in China 2025." Updated 2025. https://www.csis.org/analysis/made-china-2025

Council on Foreign Relations. "Is 'Made in China 2025' a Threat to Global Trade?" Backgrounder, May 13, 2019. https://www.cfr.org/backgrounder/made-china-2025-threat-global-trade

Institute for Security & Development Policy (ISDP). "Made in China 2025 - Modernizing China's Industrial Capability." Backgrounder, June 2018. https://www.isdp.eu/publication/made-china-2025/

Official Translation

Center for Security and Emerging Technology (CSET), Georgetown University. "Notice of the State Council on the Publication of 'Made in China 2025.'" Translation, May 2015. https://cset.georgetown.edu/wp-content/uploads/t0432_made_in_china_2025_EN.pdf

Academic Analysis

Centre for Economic Policy Research (CEPR). "The Actual Effect of China's 'Made in China 2025' Initiative May Have Been Overestimated." VoxEU, 2022. https://cepr.org/voxeu/columns/actual-effect-chinas-made-china-2025-initiative-may-have-been-overestimated

Industry Commentary

MERICS. "Made in China 2025 – Successful Enough to Make an Industrial-Policy Sequel Credible." Commentary, August 2025. https://merics.org/en/comment/made-china-2025-successful-enough-make-industrial-policy-sequel-credible

World Economic Forum. "Made in China 2025 Set the Tempo of China's Industrial Ambitions." June 2025. https://www.weforum.org/stories/2025/06/how-china-is-reinventing-the-future-of-global-manufacturing/

X. Taiwan Semiconductor Manufacturing Company (TSMC)

News Coverage

NPR. "As Political Winds Shift, Top Chipmaker TSMC Looks Beyond Taiwan." December 1, 2025. https://www.npr.org/2025/12/01/nx-s1-5620992/tsmc-chipmaker-expands-beyond-taiwan

Georgia Public Broadcasting. "As Political Winds Shift, Top Chipmaker TSMC Looks Beyond Taiwan." December 1, 2025. https://www.gpb.org/news/2025/12/01/political-winds-shift-top-chipmaker-tsmc-looks-beyond-taiwan

Oregon Public Broadcasting. "As Political Winds Shift, Top Chipmaker TSMC Looks Beyond Taiwan." December 1, 2025. https://www.opb.org/article/2025/12/01/as-political-winds-shift-top-chipmaker-tsmc-looks-beyond-taiwan/

Industry Analysis

IEEE Spectrum. "TSMC's Arizona Plant to Start Making Advanced Chips." December 27, 2024. https://spectrum.ieee.org/tsmc-arizona

Nasdaq. "This 1 Number May Ensure TSMC's Market Dominance." 2024. https://www.nasdaq.com/articles/1-number-may-ensure-tsmcs-market-dominance

Semiwiki. "No! TSMC Does Not Make 90% of Advanced Silicon." July 17, 2025. https://semiwiki.com/semiconductor-manufacturers/tsmc/342934-no-tsmc-does-not-make-90-of-advanced-silicon/

Policy Analysis

Council on Foreign Relations. "Onshoring Semiconductor Production: National Security Versus Economic Efficiency." April 17, 2024. https://www.cfr.org/article/onshoring-semiconductor-production-national-security-versus-economic-efficiency

Reference Sources

Britannica Money. "Taiwan Semiconductor Manufacturing Co. (TSMC)." 2025. https://www.britannica.com/money/Taiwan-Semiconductor-Manufacturing-Co

TSMC Corporate Website. "Taiwan Semiconductor Manufacturing Company Limited." https://www.tsmc.com/english

---

Additional Key Themes and Cross-Cutting Issues

U.S.-China Economic Relations

Geopolitical Analysis

International Monetary Fund. "Trade Balances in China and the US Are Largely Driven by Domestic Macro Forces." *IMF Blog*, September 12, 2024.

Security Perspectives

Center for Strategic and International Studies. Multiple reports on technology competition, critical minerals security, and semiconductor supply chains, 2024-2025.

Artificial Intelligence Competition

Technology Policy

European Union Institute for Security Studies. "Challenging US Dominance: China's DeepSeek Model and the Pluralisation of AI Development." Brief, July 2025.

AI Frontiers. "How US Export Controls Have (and Haven't) Curbed Chinese AI." Analysis, July 2025.

Supply Chain Security

Critical Infrastructure

International Energy Agency. "With New Export Controls on Critical Minerals, Supply Concentration Risks Become Reality." Commentary, October 2025.

Bureau of Industry and Security, U.S. Department of Commerce. Multiple press releases on export control implementation, 2022-2025.

Regional Security

Indo-Pacific Studies

Council on Foreign Relations. "China in the Taiwan Strait" series, 2025.

American Enterprise Institute and Institute for the Study of War. "China & Taiwan Update" series, 2025.

Notes on Sources

Verification Status: All sources listed above have been verified as accessible and substantive as of December 2025. URLs have been confirmed as active.

Source Selection Criteria: Sources were selected based on:

- Credibility and authority (government documents, peer-reviewed publications, established think tanks)
- Timeliness (primarily 2024-2025 materials reflecting current developments)
- Relevance to book themes
- Geographic and analytical diversity
- Accessibility for verification and follow-up research

Source Categories:

- **Government Documents**: Official policy statements, congressional reports, agency announcements
- **Think Tank Research**: CSIS, CFR, Brookings, Rhodium Group, CEPR, and others
- **Academic Publications**: Peer-reviewed journals, university research centers

- **Industry Analysis**: Trade publications, professional associations, market research
- **News Organizations**: Major international media with investigative capabilities
- **International Organizations**: IMF, IEA, WEF, and multilateral institutions

Important Note on Wikipedia: Per your instructions, Wikipedia sources were used only as starting points for research and were not included in the final bibliography. Information was cross-referenced with primary sources, government documents, and authoritative publications.

Recommended Additional Research Directions

For comprehensive coverage of topics in the book, consider additional research in:

1. **Historical Context**: Cold War technology competition and CoCOM regime
2. **Economic Theory**: Trade balance dynamics, industrial policy effectiveness
3. **Military Affairs**: Defense transformation, asymmetric capabilities
4. **International Law**: WTO dispute mechanisms, trade remedy procedures
5. **Regional Perspectives**: ASEAN, EU, and Global South responses
6. **Technology Futures**: Quantum computing, next-generation biotechnology
7. **Corporate Strategy**: Multinational responses to US-China competition
8. **Demographic Factors**: Workforce implications, innovation pipelines

Research Methodology Notes

Search Strategy: Systematic searches conducted across multiple dimensions:

- Chronological (recent developments 2024-2025)
- Thematic (trade, technology, security, economics)
- Geographic (bilateral, regional, global)
- Institutional (government, academic, industry perspectives)

Quality Control: All sources:

- Verified for accuracy and accessibility
- Cross-referenced across multiple sources
- Evaluated for bias and perspective
- Checked for currency and relevance

Citation Format: Bibliography uses modified Chicago/Turabian style appropriate for popular nonfiction, with full URLs for digital sources and access dates implied as December 2025.

Bibliography compiled December 2025

For: U.S.-China Rivalry: From Trade Wars to Tech Cold War

By Dr. Naim Tahir Baig

Don't miss out!

Visit the website below and you can sign up to receive emails whenever Dr Naim Tahir Baig publishes a new book. There's no charge and no obligation.

https://books2read.com/r/B-A-DLSVC-XBDOI

BOOKS 2 READ

Connecting independent readers to independent writers.

Did you love *U.S.-China Rivalry: From Trade Wars to Tech Cold War*? Then you should read *2nd Edition: Operation Rising Lion: Israel's Strike Against Iran's Nuclear Program*[1] by Dr Naim Tahir Baig!

[2]

Book Description

Operation Rising Lion 2025: Israel's Strike on Iran's Nuclear Program presents the most comprehensive and authoritative analysis of the June 2025 Israel-Iran military conflict that fundamentally transformed Middle Eastern geopolitics. Dr. Naim Tahir Baig, a distinguished scholar of International Relations, delivers an unprecedented examination of the twelve-day crisis that brought the region to the brink of nuclear war and ultimately reshaped the strategic balance of power in the Middle East.

Drawing from extensive primary sources, classified intelligence assessments, diplomatic communications, and real-time military reporting, this meticulously researched work chronicles the events from Israel's pre-dawn strikes on June 13, 2025—codenamed "Operation Rising Lion"—through the dramatic American intervention with "Operation Midnight Hammer" and the fragile ceasefire that ended hostilities on June 24, 2025. The book reveals the sophisticated intelligence operations, advanced military technologies, and strategic calculations that defined this watershed moment in modern warfare.

1. https://books2read.com/u/38wxa7

2. https://books2read.com/u/38wxa7

Dr. Baig's analysis goes beyond mere military chronology to explore the profound implications of these events for nuclear proliferation, international law, regional stability, and global security architecture. The work examines how Israel's systematic targeting of Iran's nuclear infrastructure and scientific personnel, combined with the first operational use of America's most powerful bunker-buster weapons, established new precedents for preventive warfare against nuclear facilities. The author provides critical insights into the diplomatic failures that preceded the conflict, the constitutional crisis it triggered in the United States, and the long-term consequences for Middle Eastern geopolitics.

This second edition, published just thirteen days after the ceasefire, incorporates the latest intelligence assessments, damage evaluations, and strategic analyses from military experts worldwide. It offers readers an unparalleled understanding of how modern warfare integrates stealth technology, precision munitions, cyber operations, and intelligence penetration to achieve strategic objectives previously thought impossible. The work serves as both a definitive historical record and an essential resource for understanding the future trajectory of nuclear non-proliferation efforts, regional security arrangements, and the evolving nature of international conflict in the 21st century.

Read more at https://www.naimtahirbaig.com.

Also by Dr Naim Tahir Baig

1

Earning Online: Unlocking Today's Virtual Economy
Loveful Hate / Hateful Love?
A Textbook Of Foreign Policy Analysis

Edition 2025

Contemporary Political Strategy: A Global Perspective

Standalone

Misconceptions About Writing a Lesson Planner for Teaching: A Comprehensive Guide
Bashar al-Assad's Last Stand: A Study of the Syrian Conflict's Final 11 Days in December 2024
Three Winters in Exile: The Trump Chronicles 2021-2024
Biden vs. Trump The 45th and 46th: A Tale of Two Americas
Imran Khan's Political Journey: From Cricket to Revolution
Instagram Automation: The Art of Silent Selling to Earn Millions
Political Prophecies of Imran Khan
Jo Samjhna Samjho: Love's Last Words
Shadow Hearts
Complexity of Souls
Worldly Success According To Islam
The Concept of Eid Among All Religions
The Widening Political Gap Between Muslim Rulers And Their Masses In The 21st Century
Pakistan's Maritime Frontier: Breaking Free from the IMF Through Blue Economy Development

Can Russia Help Pakistan Grow?
Why Nuclear-Armed Pakistan Has Not Fought a War Against Israel in the 2020s?
The War Of Narrative
Ethics Of Deceptive Tears
Crossroads of Continents
The Last Battlefield
From Beloved to Honour
International Relations from a Pakistani Perspective
Humanity is Losing its Credibility !
Operation Bunyan um Marsoos
Ibrahim Traoré
Starving Africa Feeds the Well Fed West
From Captain to Khan: The Rise and Fall of Imran Khan
The Spider's Web: How Ukraine Rewrote the Rules of War
The UNO's Three Failures: Gaza, Kashmir, and Ukraine
Operation Rising Lion 2025: Israel's Strike on Iran's Nuclear Program
Behind The Veil Of Deception: Catherine Perez-Shakdam
2nd Edition: Operation Rising Lion: Israel's Strike Against Iran's Nuclear Program
Operation True Promise 3
Shadow War 2025: Israel's Secret Army Inside Iran
Mental Health and Digital Wellness: Navigating the Hyper-Connected World
After The Break-up
Echoes of Love After Life
Geopolitical Realignments And U.S. Decline
America Party
Artificial Intelligence Reshapes Nations' Strategic Cultures
Knowledge at the Cost of Drinking Water
Abandoning UNESCO, Abandoning America's Global Leadership
Why Pakistan Can't Be Ignored ?
Love Seized
Tarifaço: Trump's Tariff Assault on Brazil and the Battle for Hemispheric Power
GAZA: The word 'ETHICS' is at stake
Kiss Cam Crisis
The Boomer Blockade: How an Aging Generation is Reshaping Global Power and Economics at Younger Generations' Expense
Fractured Faith: The Ken Paxton Divorce Scandal and the Crisis of Conservative Authenticity

The New American Empire In 2025
The Last Rock's Secret War: Okinotorishima and Japan's Fight for Tomorrow's Ocean
The Great Realignment
Trump's Siege on the Fed: Politics, Power, and the Fracturing of Global Finance
Nuclear Weapons in Space
Trump vs. Putin: The Secrets Of Alaska Summit 2025
Nuclear Orbits: From Soviet Satellites to Russian Space Power
Learn AI Fast: A Practical Guide for Busy Professionals
Rare Earth Metals in Pakistan: Geopolitics in the New Great Game
The Kulbhushan Affair: Espionage, Diplomacy, and Justice in the Shadow of South Asian Rivalry
Collision Over the Capital: The Untold Story of the 2025 Potomac River Mid-Air Disaster and the Fight for Safer Skies
The Holy Qur'an, Political Fire: The Extremism of Valentina Gomez
World War I of Climate Change: Geopolitical Parallels and Emerging Battles
International Relations: Theoretical Frameworks in the Pakistani Context
Equal and Orderly Multipolarization of the World: The Shanghai Cooperation Organization as a Catalyst
Selbstgehostete E-Mail-Server: Praxisanleitung für Datenschutz und Unabhängigkeit in Deutschland
From Gaza's Siege to Pakistan's Floods 2025: An Islamic Perspective on Collective Accountability and Calamities
Hero's Wings Over the 1965 War: Air Commodore Haider's Story
Zero-Knowledge Machine Learning (zkML): Revolutionizing Privacy in AI Applications
TikTok Bans: Navigating the Social and Political Labyrinth in a Digital Age
Nepal in Turmoil: The 2025 Gen Z Uprising Against Corruption and Censorship
Biography of a Politician
Youth Awakening in South Asia 2024-2025: Gen Z-Led Movements and the Struggle for Democracy in SAARC Countries
Stolen Fortunes: Unraveling Corruption, Economic Communalism, and the Hidden Wealth of Bangladesh's Hasina Era
International Relations in the Qur'anic Perspective
The History of Pakistan-Saudi Arabian Defence Treaties: From Friendship to Mutual Security
NATO-like Alliance Among Muslim Nations: Possibilities and Hurdles
Is Artificial Intelligence a Tool of Dajjal?
Nobels of 2025
The Solution of Gaza by Trump 2025

Storm in the Mountains
Quantum Ancestors
Ghosts in the Machine
The Echo Chamber Escape: Finding Empathy and Growth Through Conversations That Challenge Us
دل کی دھڑکنوں کا سرِ سپُردِگی
خاکسارِ محبت
Code and Cradle: AI's Silent War on Women's Economic Survival
Shadow Scores
India-US 10-Year Defence Pact: A Critical Global Perspective
Sudan in Flames
Are We The Last Generation On The Earth?
China as the Most Brutal Killer of the Muslims?
U.S.-Asia Relations: The Japan Pivot
Two Wars, Two Centuries: A Comparative History of the 1857 Rebellion and the 1971 Bangladesh War
Culture Wars in 2025
Global Conflicts in a Trump World
Civilizational Pragmatism Theory : A Comprehensive Framework for Understanding Chinese International Relations
The Fall Line: America and the Historical Pattern of Superpower Decline
Machiavelli in Practice: Modern Leaders and the Enduring Legacy of The Prince
Saddam's Execution to Trump's 20 Points
Will Palestine Go Extinct?
Evidence Architecture: Bridging Global Policy Gaps in a Post-Truth Multilateral System
Personalist Diplomacy
The Logic of Giants: Understanding the Mindsets of America, China, and Russia
U.S.-China Rivalry: From Trade Wars to Tech Cold War

Watch for more at https://www.naimtahirbaig.com.

About the Author

Dr. Naim Tahir Baig can be described as a Political Analyst, Geopolitical Strategist, Military and Security Studies Expert, Intelligence and Espionage Scholar, Social Commentator, Philosopher of Contemporary Issues, Digital Economy Specialist, Islamic Scholar and Interfaith Commentator, Poet and Literary Author, Regional Studies Expert, Multidisciplinary Intellectual, and Pakistan-Centric Analyst, reflecting his diverse expertise across politics, geopolitics, military strategy, intelligence, social commentary, business, religion, literature, and regional studies.

Published Books of Dr. Naim Tahir Baig

Learn AI Fast: A Practical Guide for Busy ProfessionalsNuclear Orbits: From Soviet Satellites to Russian Space PowerTrump vs. Putin: The Secrets Of Alaska Summit 2025Nuclear Weapons in SpaceTrump's Siege on the Fed: Politics, Power, and the Fracturing of Global FinanceThe Great RealignmentThe Last Rock's Secret War: OkinotorishimaThe New American Empire In 2025Fractured Faith: The Ken Paxton Divorce Scandal and the Crisis of Conservative AuthenticityThe Boomer Blockade: How an Aging Generation is Reshaping Global Power and Economics at Younger Generations' ExpenseKiss Cam CrisisGAZA: The word 'ETHICS' is at stakeTarifaço: Trump's Tariff Assault on Brazil and the Battle for Hemispheric PowerLove SeizedWhy Pakistan Can't Be Ignored ?Abandoning UNESCO, Abandoning America's Global LeadershipKnowledge at the Cost of Drinking WaterArtificial Intelligence Reshapes Nations' Strategic CulturesAmerica PartyGeopolitical Realignments And U.S. DeclineEchoes of Love After LifeAfter The Break-upMental Health and Digital Wellness: Navigating the Hyper-

Connected WorldShadow War 2025: Israel's Secret Army Inside IranOperation True Promise 32nd Edition: Operation Rising Lion: Israel's Strike Against Iran's Nuclear ProgramBehind The Veil Of Deception: Catherine Perez-ShakdamOperation Rising Lion 2025: Israel's Strike on Iran's Nuclear Program

Read more at https://www.naimtahirbaig.com.

www.ingramcontent.com/pod-product-compliance
Lightning Source LLC
LaVergne TN
LVHW082013200926
848481LV00010B/2851